M

PH.D.
editor

Searching for ADAM

Genesis &
the Truth
About
Man's Origin

Second printing: December 2016

Master Books®, P.O. Box 726, Green Forest, AR 72638
Master Books® is a division of the New Leaf Publishing Group, Inc.

ISBN: 978-0-89051-975-2`
Library of Congress Number: 2016916096

Cover by Diana Bogardus

Please consider requesting a copy of this volume be purchased by your local library system.

Printed in the United States of America

Please visit our website for other great titles:
www.masterbooks.com

For information regarding author interviews,
please contact the publicity department at (870) 438-5288.

I dedicate this book to Margie, my godly, loving wife of 40 years and wonderful mother and homeschool teacher of our 8 children and serving grandmother to our 11 grandchildren, and to our Lord Jesus Christ, who gave her to me as my helpmeet and best friend, knowing so well how badly I would need her.

Contents

Introduction

by Dr. Terry Mortenson

The cover story of *Christianity Today* in June 2011 read "The Search for the Historical Adam."[1] The subtitle was "Some scholars believe genome science casts doubt on the existence of the first man and woman. Others say the integrity of the faith requires it." Since then the debate about Adam has intensified with many books rolling off the press: Peter Enns, *The Evolution of Adam* (2012); Hans Madueme and Michael Reeves, eds., *Adam, The Fall and Original Sin* (2014); William VanDoodewaard, *The Quest for the Historical Adam* (2015); John Walton, *The Lost World of Adam and Eve* (2015); and Abner Chou, ed., *What Happened in the Garden* (2016), to name a few.

The Internet has been buzzing too. In 2010, Old Testament scholar Bruce Waltke caused quite a stir with a 3-minute video posted on the BioLogos website, in which he said that if evangelicals don't accept evolution, they will become a "cult."[2] Founded by Francis Collins (former director of the Human Genome Project), BioLogos is the leading promoter of theistic evolution in America (including the evolution of man). Many prominent scholars and leaders have joined the chorus by posting comments or articles at Biologos, including Trempor Longman III, Alister McGrath, N.T. Wright, Dennis Alexander, and Tim Keller. I will have more to say in the last chapter about the growing influence of BioLogos on the question of origins.

In 2013, editors Matthew Barrett and Ardel B. Caneday published the Zondervan debate book, *Four Views on The Historical Adam*. All six contributors are professing evangelicals who claim to believe in inerrancy.

1. R. Ostling, "The Search for the Historical Adam," *Christianity Today* 55:6 (June 2011): 23–27.
2. http://biologos.org/resources/videos/bruce-waltke-why-must-the-church-accept-evolution. Originally posted on March 24, 2010, it was withdrawn at Waltke's request nine days later on April 2, 2010. The short video was so controversial that Waltke resigned the same day from his position at Reformed Theological Seminary. He still believes what he said, and the video was on the BioLogos site again some time before I looked on April 12, 2016.

Denis Lamoureux believes Adam is a myth and Gregory Boyd is open to that possibility. John Walton, C. John Collins, and Philip Ryken hold to a historical Adam, but have different views about how many of the details of Genesis 1–3 are literally true. William Barrick argues for the literal truth of how Adam and Eve were created and fell and is the only young-earth creationist among the six.

In addition to the *Four Views* book, Lamoureux, Walton, Collins, and Barrick debated the issues at the annual meetings of the Evangelical Theological Society in 2013 and 2014. At the annual meeting in 2015, Darrell Falk (a theistic evolutionist) and Nathaniel Jeanson (an author in this volume) debated the genetic evidence related to Adam.

So, many Christians are asking lots of questions. Did Adam exist in history or is he a myth? Was he created supernaturally from literal dust or did he evolve from an ape-like creature? Was he the first human or did God select him out of a group of early *Homo sapiens*? Did he come into existence on the sixth literal day of history about 6,000 years ago (as a literal interpretation of Genesis 1–11 would indicate), or was that event tens or hundreds of thousands of years ago and 13.8 billion years after the big bang? If we believe the Bible, do we have to stick our head in the sand and deny science? And does it matter anyway as long as we believe in Jesus Christ as Savior and Lord? Are these just interesting questions that curious minds with too much free time think about? What is the truth about man's origin?

The books on Adam mentioned above and others primarily look at these questions from a biblical, theological, and historical perspective with minimal discussion of scientific issues. This book is different. First, all the authors are convinced young-earth creationists who believe in the inspiration, inerrancy, and supreme authority of Scripture and therefore believe that the Bible should be interpreted by comparing Scripture with Scripture and using the historical-grammatical hermeneutic. Second, we will be presenting biblical, theological, historical, paleontological, anatomical, genetic, anthropological, archeological, and social arguments in confirmation of the literal truth of all that Genesis and the rest of the Bible say about Adam and human origins.

It is our hope that this book will not only be a useful text for seminary students and professors, but also be understandable to college students, lay people, and teenagers who want to dig deeper. As such, we have transliterated and translated all Greek and Hebrew terms and sought to make the scientific arguments understandable to non-experts.

Before we plunge into the various topics covered in this volume, I want to comment on that often vaguely defined term "science."

In the introduction of their book on Adam, Madueme and Reeves briefly discuss their concern about the "epistemological status of natural science for theology." They say,

> Some argue that traditional beliefs simply have to change, one way or another, before what they see as the assured results of science. Other Christians have become militantly anti-science because they sense a growing threat from emerging scientific theories. On the one hand we need to recognize that the noetic effects of sin infect all strata of scientific investigation. Science should not usurp the authority of Scripture. Yet on the other hand there needs to be a due recognition that the empirical investigations of scientists can glorify God by helping us understand and relish his creation more deeply.[3]

Several remarks are needed in response. First, I don't know which Christians Madueme and Reeves have in mind when they refer to them as "militantly *anti*-science," because they don't cite any examples. I know of no Christian who fits that description. I suspect, however, that it is a veiled criticism of young-earth creationists. But young-earth creationists are not opposed to science at all. The Creation Research Society has about 700 voting members who have an MS or PhD in some field of hard science. Answers in Genesis, the Institute for Creation Research, Creation Ministries International, and many other creationist organizations in America and many other countries have MS or PhD scientists on their staff. In this book, five of the contributing authors have a PhD in science from one of several top secular universities in America, and they are presenting scientific evidence in confirmation of the truth of Genesis regarding Adam and human origins. Young-earth creationists love science, and we use the fruits of it all the time in our daily lives.

What young-earth creationists oppose are the naturalistic, uniformitarian, philosophical, worldview assumptions that are controlling science today and are disguised as objective science. Those atheistic assumptions are the source of the evolutionary interpretations of the scientific evidence from astronomy, geology, and biology. And it is that atheist worldview controlling science that required the academic paleontologist in Madueme and Reeves' book to discuss the fossil evidence related to the origin of man by using a pseudonym and being excluded from the list of contributors in the back of the book. This anonymity was needed because, as they say, "neither

3. Hans Madueme and Michael Reeves, eds., *Adam, The Fall and Original Sin* (Grand Rapids, MI: Baker Academic, 2014), p. x.

his guild nor his colleagues will look kindly on what he has written here." In other words, he could lose his job or have his scientific career demolished if it became known that he believed the Bible and doubted the evolution of man. Of course, if science were simply the unbiased, objective pursuit of truth, there would be no need for anonymity or fear of losing one's job for holding a view contrary to the majority. But that is not reality, as many have learned from evolutionary scientific persecution.[4]

Second, and related to the previous point, we certainly do need to take account of the noetic effects of sin on the mind of man. But old-earth creationists and theistic evolutionists need to take this into account far more than they do. Paul tells us that lost sinners are "suppressing the truth in unrighteousness" (Rom. 1:18–20) and their mind and heart are "darkened" resulting in foolish speculations (Rom. 1:21–22 and Eph. 4:17–18). Sin darkens the minds of scientists, no matter how many degrees they have, how brilliant they are, or how many books or scientific papers they have published. And the more that scientific questions pertain to questions of the existence of God, the truth of the Bible, and man's purpose and destiny, the more sin can and does distort the thinking of sinners.

Third, to think carefully about the question of origins we need to distinguish between two broad categories of science.

OPERATION Science vs ORIGIN Science

Operation science is what we all normally think of when we hear the word *science*. It uses what is often called the "scientific method," which can be defined this way:

> The use of *observable, repeatable* experiments in a controlled environment (e.g., a lab) to understand how things operate or function in the *present* physical universe in order to find cures for disease, produce new technology, or put a man on the moon, put a cell phone in everyone's pocket, etc.

This kind of science is also called "experimental science" or "observational science." Most of biology, chemistry, physics, engineering research, and medical research are in the realm of operation science. They enable us to manipulate nature to improve life for everyone. Just like everyone else, young-earth creationists love and benefit from this kind of science. However, this kind of science won't answer these kinds of questions:

4. This is well documented in the Ben Stein documentary, *Expelled*, and in Jerry Bergman, *Slaughter of the Dissidents* (Southworth, WA: Leafcutter Press, 2012, 2nd ed.).

- How and when did Saturn with its rings come into existence?
- How and when were the rock layers in the Grand Canyon deposited, and how was the canyon eroded through those layers and how long did it take?
- How and when did man come into existence?

Those are historical questions about the *unobservable, unrepeatable* past. We can't recreate Saturn or the Grand Canyon or the first man in the laboratory. For those kinds of questions we need origin science.

Origin science is concerned with looking at evidence that exists in the present to reconstruct a history of the past. It can be defined this way:

> The use of reliable, eyewitness testimony (if any is available) and observable evidence to determine the *past, unobservable, unrepeatable* event(s), which produced the observable evidence we see in the present.

Because origin science deals with the past, it is also called *historical* science. Examples of origin science would include historical geology, paleontology, archeology, cosmology (or cosmogony), and forensic science.

Now, a scientist's religious or philosophical worldview has very little, if any, influence on his research in the realm of operation science. This is because that influence is largely held in check by the fact that other scientists who may have a different worldview can repeat the experiments to see if they get the same results. So if an atheist scientist does an experiment that points to a cure for cancer, then an orthodox Jewish scientist, a Hindu scientist, and a Christian scientist can duplicate the experiments to see if they get the same results. Their various religious worldviews will likely have no effect on the results, since they are all highly motivated to find a cure for the disease, and finding such a cure will not threaten their worldview. It certainly has no bearing on the truth of the Bible, since Scripture says nothing about cancer and its physical cause.

In contrast, worldview has a tremendous influence in origin sciences that focus on reconstructing the past history of the creation and in particular the history and origin of man. This is so because the Bible very specifically speaks to these questions and relates them to the existence, character, and activities of the Creator. What a person believes about God, His Word, and His relation to the creation will have a significant effect on his interpretation of the physical evidence. A person's view of the origin of man will profoundly affect his view of the purpose and meaning of life, his moral values, his perspective on life after death, how he views other people, and almost every other aspect of life.

By way of illustration, if a white police officer is racist toward black people, he could very well misinterpret evidence in a homicide case and conclude that an innocent black man committed the crime. Assumptions and prejudices can and often do affect the gathering and interpretation of the evidence. A good detective in pursuit of the truth will not only seek to restrain his prejudices and be honest about his assumptions as he examines the evidence, he will also look for eyewitness testimony to solve the case. And demonstrably trustworthy eyewitness testimony will always trump the interpretations of the circumstantial evidence.

In the question of origins, both creation and evolution are in the realm of origin science, not operation science. Theistic evolution, progressive creation, young-earth creation, neo-Darwinian evolution, and evolution by punctuated equilibrium are all stories about the past trying to explain the evidence that we see in the present. The difference is that young-earth creationists fully trust the eyewitness testimony of the Creator in Genesis 1–11, whereas the others reject some or all of that testimony. As will be discussed more in the last chapter, this controversy is not between science and the Bible, but between the worldviews being used to interpret the scientific evidence and the Bible.

Most evolutionists deny any distinction between operation science and origin science because either they have not carefully considered the issue or they want to use the success of operation science from which we all benefit to defend the evolutionary story about the past. In other words, science is the path to truth because it produces technology and cures for disease. Therefore the sciences of astronomy, geology, and biology are leading us to the truth about origins as well. So they reason.

But some evolutionists do recognize the distinction between these two broad categories of science. For half a century, Ernst Mayr was professor of biology at Harvard University. An atheist until his death in 2005, he is considered by many to be one of the greatest evolutionists of the 20th century. He rightly said in a book defending evolution for a lay audience, "Evolution is a historical process that cannot be proven by the same arguments and methods by which purely physical or functional phenomena can be documented."[5] In a lecture for scientists he put it this way: "For example, Darwin introduced historicity into science. Evolutionary biology, in contrast with physics and chemistry, is a historical science — the evolutionist

5. Ernst Mayr, *What Evolution Is* (New York, NY: Basic Books, 2001), p. 13.

attempts to explain events and processes that have already taken place."[6] Here he was only partially correct; it was not Darwin who introduced historicity into science, but rather the geologists over 50 years before Darwin's famous book.[7]

So, thinking carefully about the nature of science and this origins debate is extremely important.[8]

Karl Giberson, formerly professor at Eastern Nazarene College and from 2008–2010 vice-president of the BioLogos Foundation, also falsely accuses young-earth creationists of "rejecting science." He writes,

> The challenge of taking "God's Two Books" (nature and the Bible) seriously has grown dramatically in recent years as genetic evidence has made it clear that Adam and Eve cannot have been historical figures, at least as described in the Bible. More scientifically informed evangelicals within conservative traditions are admitting that the evidence is undermining Creation-Fall-Redemption theology. . . . Christians have struggled to preserve this central Christian understanding in a way that is faithful to both the Bible and science; literalists have tried to preserve it by rejecting science or making increasingly strange claims about the world.[9]

However, as Jeanson and Tomkins have decisively shown in their chapter, the genetic evidence not only shows that Adam and Eve existed in history, but in fact that evidence powerfully confirms the literal truth in Genesis about Adam and Eve. It is not those who take Genesis 1–11 as literal history who are rejecting science, failing to take the Bible seriously, and making increasingly strange claims about the world. Rather, it is the secular evolutionists, old-earth creationists, and theistic evolutionists who are rejecting or misinterpreting scientific evidence and inventing absurd, just-so myths about how humans and the rest of creation came into existence, as they ignore or misinterpret the Bible's teaching (as other authors in this book show) and thereby undermining the gospel of redemption.

---

6. Ernst Mayr, "Darwin's Influence on Modern Thought," based on his lecture to the Royal Swedish Academy of Science, Sept. 23, 1999; published at ScientificAmerican.com, Nov. 24, 2009.
7. Terry Mortenson, *The Great Turning Point: the Church's Catastrophic Mistake on Geology — Before Darwin* (Green Forest, AR: Master Books, 2004), p. 25–33 and 228–233.
8. For more on operation science and origin science see Ken Ham and Terry Mortenson, "Science or the Bible?" https://answersingenesis.org/what-is-science/science-or-the-bible/.
9. Karl Giberson, "Creating Adam, Again and Again," http://www.patheos.com/blogs/peterenns/2015/06/creating-adam-again-and-again/, June 12, 2015.

Furthermore, like so many professing Christian theologians and scientists, Giberson has the erroneous view that nature is a book co-equal with Scripture and that by studying nature (while ignoring or denying Scripture) scientists can work out the origin and history of the creation.[10] Stated another way, *general* revelation and *special* revelation are co-equal revelations of God. But as Mayhue has demonstrated from all the relevant verses,[11] Scripture teaches that nature *infallibly* reveals nature's Creator, so atheists and agnostics and other idolaters are without excuse for their unbelief and lack of thankfulness to God. No Scripture teaches that nature is a "book." Nor does the Bible teach that by studying nature divorced from God's Word men can discover the truth about origins and history. As Psalm 19 reveals, nature does "speak" in non-verbal language, but that "speech" is inferior to the propositional verbal truth of Scripture. Furthermore, the creation is cursed and in bondage to corruption (Gen. 3:14–18, 5:29, 8:21; Rom. 8:19–23; and Rev. 22:3), whereas Scripture is perfect, sure, right, pure, clean, and true, without any defect or error (Ps. 19:7–9). Those who reject its truth are in darkness (Isa. 8:20). Therefore, special revelation must be used to interpret general revelation, not vice versa.

Theistic evolutionist and Bible scholar Kenton Sparks clearly lays down the challenge regarding Genesis 1–11, which has clear implications for our discussion about Adam.

> From where we stand now, at the dawn of the twenty-first century, in a time when we've sequenced the Neanderthal genome and traced out in the DNA our shared genetic heritage with primates and other mammals, it is no longer possible for informed readers to interpret the book of Genesis as straightforward history. There was no Edenic garden, nor trees of life and knowledge, nor a serpent that spoke, nor a worldwide flood in which all living things, save those on a giant boat, were killed by God. Whatever the first chapters of Genesis offer, there is one thing that they certainly do not offer, namely, a literal account of events that actually happened prior to and during the early history of humanity. If Genesis is the word of God, as I and other Christians believe, then

10. The misleading idea of the "two books of God" (Scripture and nature) became popular because of the writings of the famous English statesman, scientist, and philosopher Francis Bacon (1561–1626). See Mortenson, *The Great Turning Point*, p. 21–24.
11. Richard L. Mayhue, "Is Nature the 67th Book of the Bible?" in *Coming to Grips with Genesis*, eds. Terry Mortenson and Thane H. Ury (Green Forest, AR: Master Books, 2008), p. 105–130.

> we must try to understand how God speaks through a narrative that is no longer the literal history that our Christian forebears often assumed it to be.[12]

The authors of this book accept his challenge and will show that not only is belief in a literal Adam and Fall consistent with historic Christian orthodoxy and sound biblical exegesis, but it also is powerfully confirmed by many lines of solid scientific evidence. We will also show that this belief about Adam is foundational to the gospel and the integrity and authority of the whole Bible.

The search for the historical Adam begins and ends with Scripture. It is telling us the truth about the origin, history, and nature of man. People who are still searching for Adam won't find him in the shifting sands of evolutionary misinterpretations of fossils and DNA and the ever-changing paintings and sculptures of imaginative evolutionary artists.

It is the prayer of the authors of this book that our collective work will glorify our great Creator and encourage His people to believe all of His holy, inerrant Word, starting with the very first verse.

---

12. Kenton Sparks, "Ancient Historiography," in Charles Halton, ed., *Genesis: History, Fiction, or Neither? Three Views on The Bible's Earliest Chapters* (Grand Rapids, MI: Zondervan, 2015), p. 110.

Chapter 1

Old Testament Evidence for a Literal, Historical Adam and Eve

by Dr. William D. Barrick

Introduction: Why Trust the Old Testament on This Topic?

Trust in a written record depends heavily upon the reputation and qualifications of that record's author — and rightly so. The same principle applies to the books of the Old Testament and the Bible as a whole. Therefore, it is significant to observe that, as Tremper Longman maintains, "The coherence of the Bible is grounded in the ultimate divine authorship of the whole."[1] Since God is true and trustworthy, we must accept the fact that His words are true and trustworthy. Therefore, when we approach the matter of the historicity of Adam and Eve, we must accept the Bible's testimony on the matter as authoritative. Biblical inerrancy and infallibility result directly from God's own truthfulness. What Scripture says is true because God said it. It is not as is so often said, *"God said it; I believe it; that settles it."* Rather it should be, *"God said it; that settles it."*

Unfortunately, many who classify themselves as evangelicals intentionally subordinate the biblical text to extra-biblical ancient Near Eastern literature. The way that they do so results in the following paradigm: *The biblical writers said it; ancient Near Eastern literature confirms it; therefore, I can now accept it.* Gordon Wenham writes that it should not be so difficult for Bible readers to understand Genesis 1–11: "With careful attention to the ancient Near Eastern context in which the text originated, it is possible to define the genres used in Genesis 1–11 and thereby attune ourselves to the message that

1. Tremper Longman III, *How to Read Genesis* (Downers Grove, IL: IVP Academic, 2005), p. 31.

was intended to be conveyed."[2] Perhaps he assumes that the first task is to read the biblical text itself in its own literary context and to understand first what it itself says. Thankfully, he does get around to internal literary analysis, but only as a second step — and then, it is only literary without reference to grammatical exegesis. It is as though he refuses to accept the biblical record as *prima facie* evidence.[3] He assumes the human author and audience are primary, not the divine Author. Such a strategy far too often occurs among professing evangelicals — a strategy that demotes the Scriptures to a secondary role and makes it subservient to pagan literature and an unbelieving worldview that dominated Israel's ancient Near Eastern neighbors.

The debate over the origins of the universe, the earth, and humankind has subtly shifted in recent years. From the 1920s until the 1960s, the origins debate between biblicists and non-biblicists[4] focused on evolution vs. creation. From the 1960s until 2000, the origins debate focused on Noah's Flood, the length of the creation days, and the age of the creation. From 2000 until the present, the debate rages on whether the biblical Adam is the historical and genetic parent of all human beings. As we involve ourselves in the debate, we must understand that our views about the Bible and about God have a profound impact on what we believe about the historicity of Adam and Eve as the original parents of the entire human race.[5] If we elevate ancient worldviews and literature over Scripture, or insist upon limiting the biblical writers to such a worldview, we will go along one path in the debate. If we believe the Bible to be primarily revelation from God, rather than an independent product of fallen men, we will take a different path in the debate. The path we take will carry us to a distinct destination. One path ends with denying that Adam and Eve were the originating, historical, and genetic progenitors of the entire human race. The other ends with a full acceptance of their originating, historical, and genetic headship for all mankind.

Just as our views about the Bible and God significantly impact what we believe about the historicity of Adam and Eve, our conclusions regarding the historicity of Adam and Eve have a profound impact on a number of

2. Gordon J. Wenham, *Rethinking Genesis 1–11: Gateway to the Bible*, Didsbury Lecture Series (Eugene, OR: Cascade Books, 2015), p. 2.
3. See the discussion of "Biblical Inerrancy and Biblical Authority" later in this chapter.
4. By "biblicist" I mean someone who claims to believe what the Bible says and to accept it as having some degree of authority over what he or she believes. A "non-biblicist" gives no credence to the Bible, rejecting it as just another religious book.
5. See William VanDoodewaard, *The Quest for the Historical Adam: Genesis, Hermeneutics, and Human Origins* (Grand Rapids: Reformation Heritage Books, 2015) for an excellent historical treatise on the debate over the historicity of Adam and Eve throughout the history of the Christian church.

key biblical teachings. Kenneth Keathley and Mark Rooker make this point quite emphatically:

> We believe the historicity of Adam and Eve is so important that the matter should serve as a litmus test when evaluating the attempts to integrate a proper understanding of Genesis 1–3 with the latest findings of science. It must be realized that any position which denies that a real fall was experienced by a real couple will have adverse effects on other significant biblical doctrines. . . . we should recognize the consequences of trying to alter doctrines that have solid scriptural footing.[6]

In this chapter I will focus on the testimony of the Old Testament, especially Genesis 1–5 with regard to the debate over the historicity of Adam and Eve. A full treatment of the material in those five chapters of Scripture could fill an entire volume. One recent volume illustrates my point. C. John Collins's *Genesis 1–4: A Linguistic, Literary and Theological Commentary* (P&R, 2006) spends 278 pages of published text on just the first four chapters of Genesis — and, it is by no means exhaustive. Therefore, the current chapter must confine itself to a summary of the evidence and brief discussion of its implications.

Mankind: The Apex of the Creation Week (Gen. 1:1–2:3)

The orderly progression of six days in the creation account indicates a chronologically arranged historical narrative. In this narrative, a global focus dominates. It is not an account about Israel; it is an account that relates the history of the entire earth and all of its occupants. At the same time that the text focuses on the existence of life upon this planet,[7] it also reflects a theocentric theme — the text reveals much about God Himself, the Creator. The third word in the Hebrew text is "God" ("In-beginning created

---

6. Kenneth D. Keathley and Mark F. Rooker, *40 Questions about Creation and Evolution* (Grand Rapids: Kregel Academic, 2014), p. 237. Readers will also find that C. John Collins, *Did Adam and Eve Really Exist? Who They Were and Why You Should Care* (Wheaton, IL: Crossway, 2011), makes a similar point throughout his volume, as the subtitle implies.

7. The heavens, sun, moon, and stars are mentioned in the narrative, but only with reference to the earth — those entities are not the main point. This takes place as soon as the author employs the literary hinge with "earth" ending 1:1 and beginning 1:2. Genesis is not about the heavens, the universe, or space, or angels, or the abode of dead humans. It is about the earth and living mankind. That does not mean that there are no pertinent facts about the universe, the heavens, the sun, moon, or stars in the text. Those factual statements are not the focus, but not being the focus does not make statements about them untrue or insignificant.

God . . ."[8]). The creation account describes the divine preparation of earth for the sustaining of life, and not just life per se, but life as represented in the climax or pinnacle of all created life: human beings. The way in which God carefully and purposefully provides for the existence, blessing, environment, work, and companionship of the first couple highlights the significance of mankind.[9] According to John Murray, "The platform of life for man is prepared by successive steps and life itself appears to an appreciable extent in an ascending scale until it reaches its apex in man."[10] A straightforward reading of the creation narrative impresses upon its readers that mankind has been the goal of the Creator all along. The rest of Genesis begins to explain why mankind is so significant to God's program for His Kingdom and for redemption — the rest of the Bible carries that explanation forward detail by detail until the full scope of divine revelation appears in all its glory.

God's orderly and purposeful provision for life on planet Earth serves as strong evidence for understanding the six days of the creation account as a linear sequence, rather than some form of cross-over or framework type of structure. The best way to observe this structure is by means of a chart that starts at the conclusion, the sixth day, and works back to the first day.

Day	Text	Creation	Description	Provision
6	1:26–31 1:24–25	Mankind Land animals	Made in God's image to rule over all of the animals.	The animals over which mankind must rule. Plants for mankind's food. Plants for the animals' food.
5	1:20–23	Birds and water creatures	Flying in the atmosphere* and swarming in the waters.	Water creatures require water. **See Day 1.** Birds require atmosphere in which to fly. **See Day 2.**
4	1:14–19	Lights in the expanse	Ruling over and identifying daytime and nighttime, days, years, and seasons so man can tell time.	Seasons require vegetation. **See Day 3.** Placement "in the expanse" (v. 14) requires prior existence of the expanse.** **See Day 2.** Time requires light and darkness. **See Day 1.**

8. The translation represents a literal reading of the Hebrew text. The hyphen between the first two English words indicates that the Hebrew is but one word.
9. Gordon J. Wenham, *Genesis 1–15*, Word Biblical Commentary 1 (Waco, TX: Word, 1987), p. xlix.
10. John Murray, "The Origin of Man," in *Collected Writings of John Murray*, 3 vols. (Edinburgh: Banner of Truth, 1977), 2:3.

3	1:11–13	Vegetation	The dry land sprouts with vegetation	Vegetation requires soil, water, and light. **See Days 1–3.**
	1:9–10	Dry land	The appearance of the dry land out of the waters	Soil requires a raised land surface standing out of the water.
		Seas	The gathering of waters into seas	Seas require lowering the earth's crust to produce ocean basins.
2	1:6–8	Expanse	Separating the waters	A separation of waters requires the presence of water. An expanse requires a planet above which to exist and space beyond it to mark its boundary. **See Day 1.**
1	1:1–5	Light Darkness	Separating between light and darkness to produce day and night	Light requires a light source outside the darkness. Day and night require a rotating planet.
		Water	Covering the entire earth	Water requires a planet which it might cover.
		Earth	The focal point	The planet requires space in which to exist.
		Heavens	That which is beyond the earth, like the Creator Himself	Creation of space requires a Creator.

* This is one of several points of order that argue against the so-called framework hypothesis that equates days 1 and 4, days 2 and 5, and days 3 and 6; see Andrew S. Kulikovsky, *Creation, Fall, Restoration: A Biblical Theology of Creations*, Mentor (Fearn, Scotland: Christian Focus, 2009), p. 158–60. For a superb response to the framework hypothesis, see Robert V. McCabe, "A Critique of the Framework Interpretation of the Creation Week," in *Coming to Grips with Genesis: Biblical Authority and the Age of the Earth*, eds. Terry Mortenson and Thane H. Ury (Green Forest, AR: Master Books, 2008), p. 211–49.

** Kulikovsky, *Creation, Fall, Restoration*, p. 158–60.

The literary structure of 1:26–28 helps to understand what man is and what God intended for man to do. Eugene Merrill offers the following diagram of the structure:

A God's description of man's nature (26a)
  B God's description of man's purpose (26b)
A' God's creation of man (27)
  B' God's commission to man (28)[11]

11. Eugene H. Merrill, *Everlasting Dominion: A Theology of the Old Testament* (Nashville, TN: B & H, 2006), p. 169.

In this diagram, the **A** members express what man is, while the **B** members refer to what God wants man to do.

"Let Us make man in Our image" (1:26; NKJV[12]) uses the first person plural pronoun to identify the participation of multiple persons within the Godhead.[13] Making human beings in two genders (male and female) reveals the purpose of the Creator and establishes a permanent necessity for fulfilling His mandate to "be fruitful and multiply; fill the earth and subdue it" (1:28). The biblical statement regarding the "image" of God highlights the uniqueness of the creation narrative in the ancient world. In other words, mankind receives a much higher place in the created order as compared with ancient Near Eastern stories outside the Bible. In extra-biblical literature, human beings are merely creatures that exist as an afterthought.[14] One reason for understanding the biblical account as describing the origin of the first man relates to his being created in God's image. If Adam is not the first human being, the seminal head of the entire human race, then God only values Adam's descendants among all other humans who might be said to have existed before or contemporaneously with Adam, as well as any of their descendants until the time of the global Flood of Noah's day. Those who reject a global Flood hold a view that results in multitudes of humans existing outside the Adamic line. As such then, without the image of God, their earthly lives might be counted as unworthy of any retributive justice if they are murdered (see Gen. 9:5–6). Herman Bavinck argued that the image of God actually "constitutes our humanness."[15] In other words, apart from the image of

12. Unless otherwise noted, all quotations from the English Bible in this chapter are from the New King James Version (NKJV).
13. For a fuller discussion of the identification of "Us" and "Our" with the Trinity, see Derek Kidner, *Genesis: An Introduction and Commentary*, Tyndale Old Testament Commentaries (1967; reprint, Downers Grove, IL: InterVarsity Press, 1973), p. 51–52; L. Berkhof, *Systematic Theology*, 4th rev. ed. (Grand Rapids: Eerdmans, 1996), p. 182; Wayne Grudem, *Systematic Theology: An Introduction to Bible Doctrine* (Grand Rapids: Zondervan, 1994), p. 227. The Hebrew grammar involved does not support the concept of a plural of majesty here; see Paul Joüon, *A Grammar of Biblical Hebrew*, trans. and rev. by T. Muraoka, Subsidia Biblica 14/I–II (Rome: Pontifical Biblical Institute, 1993), 2:376 (§114e n. 1).
14. Wenham, *Genesis 1–15*, Word Biblical Commentary, p. xlix. See also John Oswalt, *The Bible Among the Myths: Unique Revelation or Just Ancient Literature?* (Grand Rapids: Zondervan, 2009), p. 59–60 and 69–90.
15. Herman Bavinck, *In the Beginning: Foundations of Creation Theology*, ed. by John Bolt, trans. by John Vriend (Grand Rapids: Baker, 1999), p. 194. Even Hugh Ross, *Navigating Genesis: A Scientist's Journey Through Genesis 1–11* (Covina, CA: RTB Press, 2014), p. 72, sees this point about the impossibility of humanity apart from the image of God. Ross states that the hominids known from fossil remains were only "human-resembling" but not human (p. 76).

God there is no humanity or human being — to speak of other humans existing either before Adam or contemporaneously with him becomes a contradiction of terms, as well as of biblical teaching.

According to Othmar Keel and Silvia Schroer, the literature of the ancient Near East hardly even mentions "the origin of humanity as man and woman, male and female."[16] Indeed, the overt discussion of the relationship between man and woman distinguishes the biblical account from the extant extra-biblical creation narratives.[17]

In our current day and age, scholars are preoccupied with what they consider to be unwarranted application of biblical teachings or statements to matters of science. By focusing on the issue of the Bible and science, they totally miss the real issue concerning a difference of worldviews. The worldview of the biblical authors does not reflect the worldview of the surrounding ancient Near Eastern cultures. Modern evangelicals, who denounce so-called "scientific creationism," spend far too much time and effort trying to immerse the biblical writers and their product in the ancient unbelieving cultures. To the contrary, the Bible presents a picture at odds with the prevailing opinions of the ancient Near Eastern peoples. The biblical writers do not take a stance in harmony with the rest of their contemporaries.[18]

Genesis 2:4–24 — A Detailed Explanation of Genesis 1:26–28

In the greater structure of the Book of Genesis, 2:4 presents the first occurrence of a *toledot* formula. In NKJV, *toledot* is translated as "history" (2:4; 37:2) and "genealogy" (5:1; 6:9; 10:1; 11:10, 27; 25:12, 19; 36:1, 9). Other common translations include "account" (2:4 NASU[19]) and "generations" (5:1 NASU). The following represents the structure adapted from Jason DeRouchie's excellent exegetical analysis:[20]

16. Othmar Keel and Silvia Schroer, *Creation: Biblical Theologies in the Context of the Ancient Near East*, trans. by Peter T. Daniels (Winona Lake, IN: Eisenbrauns, 2015), p. 109, 113. See also footnote 13, above.
17. Keel and Schroer, *Creation: Biblical Theologies in the Context of the Ancient Near East*, p. 117.
18. See Todd S. Beall, "Reading Genesis 1–2: A Literal Approach," in *Reading Genesis 1–2: An Evangelical Conversation*, ed. by J. Daryl Charles (Peabody, MA: Hendrickson, 2013), p. 52.
19. New American Standard, Updated
20. Jason S. DeRouchie, "The Blessing-Commission, the Promised Offspring, and the *Toledot* Structure of Genesis," *Journal of the Evangelical Theological Society* 56, no. 2 (2013), p. 219–47 (esp. p. 233).

Section	Topic	Reference
I.	Book Preface: Creation Narrative	1:1–2:3
II.	The Genealogy of the Heavens and the Earth	2:4–4:26
III.	The Book of the Genealogy of Adam	5:1–6:8
IV.	The Genealogy of Noah *And* the Genealogy of Noah's Sons	6:9–9:29 10:1–11:9
V.	The Genealogy of Shem *And* the Genealogy of Terah *And* the Genealogy of Ishmael *And* the Genealogy of Isaac *And* the Genealogy of Esau	11:10–26 11:27–25:11 25:12–18 25:19–35:29 36:1–8; 36:9–37:1
VI.	The Genealogy of Jacob	37:2–50:26

The writer of Genesis (Moses) sets the mission of God's chosen family into a global context by transitioning step by step from the heavens and the earth (2:4) to Adam (5:1) to Noah (6:9) to Shem (11:10) and to Jacob (37:2). In this way he draws the readers' attention from all creation to humanity in general, to all surviving humanity following the Flood, to a specific clan of the survivors (Shem and his descendants), and ultimately to Israel. The mission of God's chosen line is therefore placed within its global context.

Of what importance is all of this? Without a historical Adam, there is no father of global humanity, thereby jeopardizing the global emphasis of the resulting message of divine blessing. Further, if Adam is but a myth, legend, or symbolic figure, at what point can the readers be certain that they can start reading the text of Genesis as history?

Now that the context has been set within the structure of Genesis, let's look at 2:4–24. First, Moses does not present a second or alternate creation account in this text unit. It is but a detailed expansion of what was revealed in 1:26 regarding God creating mankind as "male and female."[21] This movement from general to specific characterizes Moses's narratives. In Genesis 10 and 11 he also presents a general overview (chap. 10) and then returns to a detail mentioned in the overview ("everyone according to his language"; 10:5) in order to develop it and to explain its significance more fully (chap. 11). The time statements at the start of the text unit in 2:4–24 identify things not yet existing ("before" in 2:5 — the wild plants or shrubs, the rain to provide water for them, and the man to cultivate them) when God

21. Murray, "The Origin of Man," 2:6, "We do not have divergent accounts of creation. Genesis 2 is supplementary, and obviously furnishing details that would not be in accord with the structure and design of Genesis 1."

provides the "mist" (2:6; or, "springs" NLT or "streams" NIV) to water the ground. The complex sentence in 2:5–6 reveals the time for God providing water for the ground by using four temporal adverbial clauses to modify the main verb ("rose" or "went up" NKJV):

> **Before** every wild bush was on the earth,
> **Before** every wild herb sprouted,
> **When** Yahweh God had not yet caused it to rain on the earth,
> **[When]** there was no man to till the ground,
> A mist/stream **rose** from the ground and it watered all the ground's surface.

Therefore, it is clear grammatically that the purpose is not to describe the time when God created mankind in relation to plants. It consists, instead, of a statement that God provided for His creation by making certain that the plants had water before He created them. He made the provision before He gave rain and before He appointed mankind to irrigate and till the soil. By introducing the concept of provision, the writer sets the stage for a detailed description of the creation of human beings — God's creative activity is purposeful and beneficial. Mankind has a role to fulfill in caring for the earth and is also a special recipient of God's provision of the plants, which the Creator has watered. The theme of provision is not a minor one in this text unit — it is a major one. Indeed, elsewhere in the Bible we learn that even before He created the earth, God had made preparation for His program to restore mankind spiritually in anticipation of mankind's disobedience and fall (see Eph. 1:4; 1 Pet. 1:20).

According to the text, God formed a single individual (Gen. 2:7a), not multiple individuals (as will be demonstrated later in this essay). This fact requires the reader to understand that Adam is not only an individual created by God, but the very first individual human being whom God made. Into the nostrils of that single individual God breathed "the breath of life" (v. 7b) and he became a "living being" (v. 7c). Then, God placed him in a garden, which He had prepared for him (v. 8).

The Hebrew at the end of 2:7 (*nephesh chayyah*) also occurs in 1:21, 24; 2:19; and 9:10 to refer to land animals, birds, and sea creatures. God made all of these as living beings/living creatures (though, of course, they are not made in the image of God, which distinguishes mankind from these other living creatures). Genesis 2:7 says that God made man, added the divine breath, and then man became a living being/creature. It does not say that God made a *living being*, **then** added the divine breath so that he became a man. Paul says something very similar in 1 Corinthians 15:45 — "the first man, Adam, became a living soul."[22] Therefore, the idea that God used an evolutionary process to create only the body of Adam finds no exegetical support in the Genesis account.

The following chart highlights the areas of Adam's distinctiveness as revealed in the creation account:[23]

Adam's Distinctiveness

Aspect	Text	Biblical Statement
Unique Product of God's Counsel	Gen. 1:26	"Let Us make man" — not like "Let there be light" (1:3) or "Let the earth bring forth" (1:11) or "Let the waters abound" (1:20)
Unique Pattern of God's Endowment	Gen. 1:26	"in Our image, according to Our likeness"
Unique Potential in God's Program	Gen. 1:26	"let them rule over" all the creatures and all the earth
Unique Procedure in God's Creative Act	Gen. 2:7	"the LORD God . . . breathed into his nostrils the breath of life"

The author of Genesis 2:10–14 places Eden within the geography of the ancient pre-Flood world, not in some mythological or imaginary world. Such details contribute to identifying the text unit as historical narrative. The first human being resided in Eden, a real geographical location. God did not, however, place the man in the garden to experience permanent bliss and an inactive existence. Instead, the Creator assigned work for the man (v. 15). Adam's job description included caring for the garden and guarding it ("to

22. Without paying careful attention to the context of Paul's argumentation and noting that he did not intend for his readers to understand that Adam was a man before he became a living soul, this passage might appear to support theistic evolution. Paul is only identifying about whom he speaks, not indicating the chronological process. The ancient Jewish commentator Philo (ca. 25 B.C.–A.D. 50) relied on an allegorical hermeneutic to reach his unbiblical conclusion. "Philo's exegesis of Gen. 2:7 (*Alleg. Interp.* 1.31) is sometimes proposed as relevant to Paul's interpretation. However, the differences outweigh the similarities. Philo takes Adam's becoming a living soul to mean that God breathed into his corruptible, earthlike mind the power of real life. Whereas for Paul the earthly man is Adam and the heavenly man is Christ, for Philo both of these can be found in Genesis (albeit allegorically)"; Roy E. Ciampa and Brian S. Rosner, "I Corinthians," in *Commentary on the New Testament Use of the Old Testament*, ed. by G.K. Beale and D.A. Carson (Grand Rapids: Baker Academic, 2007), p. 746.

23. Adapted from the outline of Murray, "The Origin of Man," 2:4–5.

tend and keep it").[24] Adam worked to cultivate the soil as a husbandman of crops and to protect the garden. Interestingly, the same verbs are used in describing the work of the priests in the Tabernacle (Num. 3:7–10; "attend" is the same verb as "keep" and "do the work" is the same verb as "tend"). Note that "attending to" (the same verb as "keep" in Gen. 2:15) occurs in Numbers 3:10 to explain that the priests were to protect the Tabernacle by keeping unqualified people out of the Tabernacle. Adam's assignment included protecting the garden of Eden, not just cultivating it — a point I will establish below in the section on Adam's Disobedience.

In addition, the garden did not provide the man with an unregulated existence. It is clear from God's prohibition with regard to eating from the tree of the knowledge of good and evil (v. 16–17) that the man was under his Creator's authority. This perfect, sinless human being was not a god himself — he was the servant of the Creator God. To emphasize the seriousness of the prohibition, God also announced the penalty for disobedience: "you shall surely die" (v. 17). Although the statement referred ultimately to physical death, the immediate reality consisted of spiritual death — separation from fellowship with God.[25] As Collins points out, the best understanding of the text is that the two kinds of death are but two aspects of one experience.[26]

Evidence that there were no other human beings in existence comes when God Himself declared that the man was "alone" (2:18a). The term "alone" does not mean "lonely." "Lonely" refers to a state of mind and emotions, rather than to a state of existence. Adam's lone existence was "not good," because it did not allow for God's mandate to be obeyed and fulfilled. In other words, God did not consider Adam's situation good, "not because Adam is lonely or has no lively intellectual conversation when he comes in from the garden at night but because he will have no chance at all of filling the earth so long as there is only one of him."[27] God then provided an appropriate counterpart or "helper comparable to him" (v. 18b). The man could not find any such counterpart among the animals (v. 19–20) — demonstrating that

24. See Keathley and Rooker, *40 Questions about Creation and Evolution*, p. 101–6 for a fuller discussion of the various views on these two activities assigned to the man.
25. Bruce K. Waltke with Cathi J. Fredricks, *Genesis: A Commentary* (Grand Rapids: Zondervan, 2001), p. 87.
26. C. John Collins, "Adam and Eve in the Old Testament," in *Adam, the Fall, and Original Sin: Theological, Biblical, and Scientific Perspectives*, ed. by Hans Madueme and Michael Reeves (Grand Rapids: Baker Academic, 2014), p. 18.
27. David J. A. Clines, *What Does Eve Do to Help? and Other Readerly Questions to the Old Testament*, Journal for the Study of the Old Testament Supplement Series 94 (Sheffield, UK: JSOT Press, 1990), p. 35.

he himself was not an animal like them. That distinction also applied to the woman, who did not come from the animals either directly or indirectly.

The biblical text does not contain anything consistent with the secular science hypothesis regarding the biological evolution of mankind. The biblical details in the account of God's creation of both Adam (from dust) and Eve (from Adam's rib) provide the most blatant inconsistency between the Bible and the theory of the biological evolution of human beings.[28] If the Bible is correct, the evolutionary viewpoint is wrong; if the evolutionary viewpoint is right, the Bible is wrong. It is that simple, since there is total disagreement between the two viewpoints concerning how mankind originated.

The name "Adam" first occurs in NKJV's translation at 2:19, but at 2:20 in NASU, ESV, and NIV. HCSB waits until 3:17. The translators' choices reflect some degree of subjectivity, but the NASU, ESV, and NIV consistently rely upon an objective indicator, together with the context. That indicator consists of the Hebrew noun *'adam* with the definite article (*ha'adam*). The name "Adam" most consistently occurs when the definite article is absent. This fits the practice throughout the Old Testament regarding personal names. For example, "Abraham" or "Jacob" or "David" never take a definite article. Significantly, the occurrence of the proper name "Adam" comes in the context of the man naming the animals (v. 20). That is a fitting context. The following chart (with shading explained in the footnote) displays the occurrences of the Hebrew *'adam* and *ha'adam* and its translation in selected English translations of Genesis 1:1–6:8.[29]

Reference	Hebrew	NKJV	NASU	ESV	NIV	HCSB
1:26	*'adam**	man	man	man	man	man
1:27	*ha'adam***	man	man	man	man	man
2:5	*'adam*	man	man	man	man	man
2:7a	*ha'adam*	man	man	the man	the man	the man
2:7b	*ha'adam*	man	man	the man	the man	the man
2:8	*ha'adam*	the man	the man	the man	the man	the man
2:15	*ha'adam*	the man	the man	the man	the man	the man

28. Keathley and Rooker, *40 Questions about Creation and Evolution*, p. 385.

29. The text unit comprises the entirety of the first two major sections of Genesis as indicated by the use of toledot ("history" 2:4; "genealogy" 5:1). The English versions are NKJV (New King James Version), NASU (New American Standard Updated), ESV (English Standard Version), NIV (New International Version), and HCSB (Holman Christian Standard Bible). Light grey shading indicates where the context supports a generic meaning referring to "mankind" or "humankind." Dark grey shading indicates where the context, in my opinion, best supports the name "Adam."

2:16	*ha'adam*	the man	the man	the man	the man	the man
2:18	*ha'adam*	man	the man	the man	the man	the man
2:19a	*ha'adam*	Adam	the man	the man	the man	the man
2:19b	*ha'adam*	Adam	the man	the man	the man	the man
2:20a	*ha'adam*	Adam	the man	the man	the man	the man
2:20b	*'adam*	Adam	Adam	Adam	Adam	the man
2:21	*ha'adam*	Adam	the man	the man	the man	the man
2:22a	*ha'adam*	man	the man	the man	the man	the man
2:22b	*ha'adam*	the man	the man	the man	the man	the man
2:23	*ha'adam*	Adam	the man	the man	the man	the man
2:25	*ha'adam*	the man	the man	the man	the man	the man
3:8	*ha'adam*	Adam	the man	the man	the man	the man
3:9	*ha'adam*	Adam	the man	the man	the man	the man
3:12	*ha'adam*	the man	the man	the man	the man	the man
3:17	*'adam*	Adam	Adam	Adam	Adam	Adam
3:20	*ha'adam*	Adam	the man	the man	Adam	Adam
3:21	*'adam*	Adam	Adam	Adam	Adam	Adam
3:22	*ha'adam*	the man	the man	the man	the man	man
3:24	*ha'adam*	the man	the man	the man	the man	man
4:1	*ha'adam*	Adam	the man	Adam	Adam	Adam
4:25	*'adam*	Adam	Adam	Adam	Adam	Adam
5:1a	*'adam*	Adam	Adam	Adam	Adam	Adam
5:1b	*'adam*	man	man	man	man	man
5:2	*'adam*	Mankind	Man	Man	man	man
5:3	*'adam*	Adam	Adam	Adam	Adam	Adam
5:4	*'adam*	Adam	Adam	Adam	Adam	Adam
5:5	*'adam*	Adam	Adam	Adam	Adam	Adam
6:1	*ha'adam*	men	men	man	men	mankind
6:2	*ha'adam*	men	men	man	men	mankind
6:3	*ha'adam*	man	man	man	man	mankind
6:4	*ha'adam*	men	men	man	men	mankind
6:5	*ha'adam*	man	man	man	man	man
6:6	*ha'adam*	man	man	man	man	man
6:7a	*ha'adam*	man	man	man	mankind	mankind
6:7b	*'adam*	man	man	man	men	—

* The Hebrew noun without the definite article (*ha-*).
** The Hebrew noun with the definite article (*ha-*, "the").

Throughout the narrative the name characteristically occurs without the definite article while the form of *'adam* with the definite article (*ha'adam*) refers either to "the man" or to "mankind/humankind."[30] The generic use of *'adam* without the definite article in 1:26 is followed by its use with the definite article in 1:27. This fits the normal pattern of the creation narrative in which the writer often refers to a created entity in its first mention without the definite article and then uses the definite article as previous reference in a subsequent mention of the same entity. For example, 1:2 does not have the definite article on the Hebrew word for "darkness" but verse 4 does, verse 3 does not have the definite article on the Hebrew word for "light" but verse 4 does, and verse 6 does not have the definite article on the Hebrew word for "firmament" (NKJV; a better translation would be "expanse") but verse 7 does. Therefore, since 2:5 and 5:1–2 are at the beginning of new text units, the generic uses of *'adam* without the definite article are not an unexpected phenomenon. The only anomaly in 1:1–6:8 occurs in 6:7b. It might be best to treat the use of *'adam* without the definite article here as an inclusio (envelope figure) closing the text unit (5:1–6:8) just as it began. The inclusio forms the center elements of a chiasm (inverted parallels):

A 5:1a — heading: "This is the book of the genealogy of Adam."
B 5:2b — "In the day that God created man [*'adam*]"
B' 6:7b — "I will destroy . . . man [*'adam*] and beast"
A' 6:8 — Transitional statement: "But Noah found grace in the eyes of the Lord."

Inclusio is one form of repetition, so it also brings out an emphasis. By being the center elements of the chiasm, the inclusio is emphasized in a second way. The implication is that all who died in the Flood were descendants of Adam.

When God created the female, He did so from *one* individual's side — Adam's own flesh and bone (v. 21). And, from that flesh and bone God made *one* woman (v. 22). God created Adam out of the dust of the ground and breathed life into his nostrils, but He created Eve out of Adam's living

30. Collins, *Genesis 1–4: A Linguistic, Literary and Theological Commentary*, p. 135–36. Cf. Richard S. Hess, "Splitting the Adam: The Usage of Genesis I–V," in *Studies in the Pentateuch*, ed. by J.A. Emerton, Vetus Testamentum Supplement 41 (Leiden, The Netherlands: E.J. Brill, 1990), p. 1–15 and Victor P. Hamilton, *The Book of Genesis: Chapters 1–17*, New International Commentary on the Old Testament (Grand Rapids: Eerdmans, 1990), p. 160.

flesh. She was living from the start — indeed, she "is from the beginning living and life-giving."[31] There were no other men and there were no other women. This couple was the beginning of the human race. Adam is the seminal (genetic) head of all mankind. Adam himself described the relationship he had to this one woman (v. 23). His statement stands out as articulate, sophisticated, and emphatic — God created Adam with the full capacity for using language to compose poetry. This individual did not gesture and grunt; he spoke clearly, purposefully, and dramatically (as a literal translation from the Hebrew indicates):

> "**This one!** — at last, is bone of my bones and flesh of my flesh!
> "**This one** shall be named 'Woman,'
> "because from 'Man' was taken **this one!**"

Adam's sophisticated poem exhibits the poetic features of parallelism, assonance, word play, chiasm, repetition, and a tricolon.[32] That Adam possessed such capabilities from the very start of his existence speaks to the fact that the biblical text does not present him as some sort of primitive being, prescientific and ignorant. He had already demonstrated that by naming the animals.

Most readers of Genesis 2 admit that the Creator purposefully established heterosexual and monogamous marriage as the primary human relationship. This is God's design: one man and one woman forming a union that is capable of fulfilling the divine mandate (v. 24–25). Throughout the following chapter (Gen. 3) the account continues to be about just these two people — no others existed on the planet (cp. 3:1, 4, 6, 7, etc.) until Adam and Eve produced their sons Cain and Abel.

The following table identifies some of the key elements of the narrative in Genesis 2:5–25 that indicate that Adam and Eve are the historical originating parents of the entire human race:

Adam and Eve: Humanity's Historical Heads

Reference	Element	Significance
Gen. 2:5–6	Divine provision for the earthly environment before Adam	All prior creative activity bears witness to a culmination of creation with the creation of Adam. This implies only one creation sequence preparing for the very first human being.

31. Keel and Schroer, *Creation: Biblical Theologies in the Context of the Ancient Near East,* p. 119.
32. Wenham, *Genesis 1–15*, Word Biblical Commentary, p. 70.

Gen. 2:7a	Divine formation of the man (*'adam*) out of the ground (*'adamah*)	The first man is out of the earth itself — he has an affinity to his environment in the same fashion as the animals that God created out of the ground. This origin is not repeated — after the first man, all others are procreated through the sexual relationship of man and woman.
Gen. 2:7b	Divine breath exhaled into the man's nostrils	This act of initial creation does not occur again — it is unique to the first man. The Creator thus initiates the entire human race through the one man.
Gen. 2:7c	The man becomes a living creature	God creates the man directly from the soil and gives him instant life and constitutes him as a living creature. This does not speak of divine selection of Adam out of a pool of previously existing human beings or hominids.
Gen. 2:8	Divine placement of the man in the divinely prepared garden	God places one man in the garden. The special, unique place speaks of a special, unique individual who inhabits the garden.
Gen. 2:9	Divinely provisioned garden including two special and unique trees	The special, unique provision implies a special, unique individual for whom the trees are provided.
Gen. 2:10–14	The garden as a specific geographical and historical location	Just as the garden is a geographical and historical reality, so the first human is a physical and historical reality — not a myth or a mere archetype.
Gen. 2:15	Divine purpose for the original man — to till the ground and to guard the garden	God assigns the first man tasks that demonstrate his vice-regency over the earth (see 1:28). The man's dominion over the earth begins with his rule over his God-given home.
Gen. 2:16–17	Divine command and test to prove the first man's obedience and worthiness to be vice-regent	God commands Adam to eat the fruit from the trees in the garden except for the tree of the knowledge of good and evil. The penalty of death makes the prohibition very serious and makes any disobedience a matter of high treason. This sets up a situation by which human death might commence.
Gen. 2:18a	Divine statement that it is "not good" for the man to be "alone"	Only the sole existence of Adam makes sense of this statement. If any other human being existed, God's declaration regarding Adam's aloneness would be a misrepresentation of reality.
Gen. 2:18b	Divine determination to provide the man with a counterpart as helper	If Adam were not truly the sole human being on the earth, God would not have to make a counterpart for him.

Gen. 2:19–20a	Divine arrangement for the animals to come before Adam so that the man might name them	God brings the animals to Adam so that he does not have to locate them as well as name them. Adam demonstrates his mental acuity and linguistic ability by naming the animals and, by so doing, he begins his rule over the animals.
Gen. 2:20b	Absence of any counterpart for Adam among the animals	The man is truly alone — the only one of his kind on the planet. He is the historical and genetic head of the human race. But without a counterpart, he cannot fulfill the divine mandate to reproduce and fill the earth.
Gen. 2:21–22	Divine provision of a counterpart by making a woman out of part of the flesh and bones of the man	This act of making the woman does not occur again — it is unique to the first woman. The Creator makes the one woman out of the one man. Therefore, the DNA of the first woman must have been basically the same as the DNA of the first man (though with genetic information to produce the variation we see among humans*). There are no others. The human race will be procreated by what these two produce.
Gen. 2:23	The man's poetic expression of joy	The man sees very clearly the distinct difference between the woman and the animals. He also understands the woman's close relationship to him — there is no other like her, literally. Adam's naming the woman implies his headship over her — this is not a result of the Fall.
Gen. 2:24–25	Divine design for fulfilling the mandate to be fruitful and multiply — marriage	The first man and the first woman become the first married couple. They propagate the human race. There is no other divine pattern for marriage.

* See the later chapter on genetics by Jeanson and Tomkins.

Genesis 3: Adam's Disobedience

The role Adam played in the Fall might not seem so clear at first blush. The focus in Genesis 3 seems to be on the serpent's tempting of Eve and her giving in to that temptation. However, it is possible that Eve's temptation took place in Adam's presence (see Gen. 3:6). If Adam was there, his silence condemns him. "He should have interrupted. He should have chased the serpent off."[33] According to 2:15, God had placed Adam in the garden of Eden "to tend and keep it" (NKJV). The first infinitive can be translated "to work" or "to cultivate." The second can be translated "to guard" or "to preserve." In other words, God commanded Adam to not only work the soil of the garden for producing food, but to guard it or protect it from anything harmful. Were Satan to come into the garden as an angel of light or as a powerful spirit being, Adam might quickly submit to such a show of supernatural power. However,

33. Longman, *How to Read Genesis*, p. 111.

as C.F. Keil suggested, "If, instead of approaching them in the form of a celestial being, in the likeness of God, he came in that of a creature, not only far inferior to God, but far below themselves, they could have no excuse for allowing a mere animal to persuade them to break the commandment of God."[34] By allowing the serpent to tempt Eve, Adam failed in this second aspect of God's command.[35] His disobedience had already begun even before Eve gave in to the temptation — no wonder Adam had no compunction at all in accepting the fruit and eating it himself.

When Adam sinned, he passed on a heritage of pain, toil, and death. As part of the punishment for disobedience, God expelled Adam (and Eve with him) from the garden. The creation no longer remained "very good" (1:31) — it had been defiled or polluted by the first man's disobedience. In place of blessing, the Creator imposed a curse upon the serpent and the other animals (3:14)[36] and upon the ground (3:17–18). By the repeated use of "you" (singular and masculine in the Hebrew text), Moses, through the Spirit's superintending work, emphasized Adam's responsibility for his disobedience and for the fallen condition of mankind and the world.

However, God had not completed His plan for mankind and for creation. Even as He was announcing the curse, He also proclaimed the first gospel, or good news (3:15). Theologically, this proclamation provides yet another piece of evidence supporting the historicity of the text. God purposed to restore His creation from the harmful effects of the Fall. If the account of the Fall is merely an allegory, a legend, a myth, or fiction, the history of salvation through a promised Messiah lacks a reason for existence. Indeed, without a historical Adam involved in a historical act of disobedience, there is no necessity for salvation, no necessity for a historical Redeemer. Thus, Richard Gaffin stresses that "What Scripture affirms about creation, especially the origin of humanity, is central to its teaching about salvation."[37] He brings the matter down to the person and historicity of

34. C.F. Keil, *The Pentateuch,* 3 vols., trans. by James Martin, *Biblical Commentary on the Old Testament,* C.F. Keil and F. Delitzsch (repr., Grand Rapids: Eerdmans, 1971), 1:93.

35. The divine command anticipated Adam's disobedience, which would not occur until after Satan's fall (sometime after the seventh day). Even the prohibition against eating the fruit of the tree of the knowledge of good and evil anticipated Adam's disobedience. God knew *before* He created the heavens and the earth that the Fall would occur and had already determined how He would accomplish redemption and restoration (see Matt. 25:34; Eph. 1:4; 1 Pet. 1:20; Rev. 13:8). In other words, God anticipated His promise in Genesis 3:15 even before He made it. God did not switch to "Plan B" when Adam disobeyed — God still operates according to His only plan.

36. The curse on the serpent was "more than" that which God placed on the other animals.

37. Richard B. Gaffin Jr., *No Adam, No Gospel: Adam and the History of Redemption* (Philadelphia: P&R, 2015), p. 5. See also James K. Hoffmeier, "Genesis 1–11 as History

Adam by saying, "If Adam is not the first, who subsequently fell into sin, then the work of Christ loses its meaning. Without the 'first' that Adam is, there is no place for Christ as either 'second' or 'last.' "[38]

Another point of significance appears when Moses states that Eve "was the mother of all living" (3:20). The declaration indicates that she is the historical first woman and co-progenitor with Adam of the entire human race.[39] James Hamilton understands that this description of Eve implies a reference back to the promise in verse 15:

> When Moses shows the man naming his wife Eve (3:20), we are to understand that the knowledge that she will have children and be "the mother of all living" has come from the announcement that her seed will bruise the head of the serpent (3:15). From Eve's remarkable statement, "I have gotten a man with the help of the LORD" (4:1), the audience sees that she is looking for her offspring who will vanquish the serpent (3:15), and (after Cain has shown himself seed of the serpent by killing Abel) at the birth of Seth, Eve announces that God has given her "another offspring" (4:25). All these indications show a strong interconnectedness between Genesis 3 and 4, and I have not even mentioned the similarities between the wording of the curse in Genesis 3:16 and the warning to Cain in 4:7.[40]

With that explanation of interconnectedness, let's move on to a consideration of the content and role of Genesis 4 in the study of the historicity of Adam and Eve.

Genesis 4: Mankind's Sinfulness and God's Grace

The account concerning Cain and Abel (Gen. 4) continues the history of the first couple and their family. The account displays some common characteristics for historical narrative: (1) specific individuals identified by name and relationship, (2) geographical locations, (3) descendants identified by name and relationship, and (4) descriptions of actual events — especially events that could be taken as indicating the wickedness of some of the participants.

---

and Theology," in *Genesis: History, Fiction, or Neither? Three Views on the Bible's Earliest Chapters,* ed. by Charles Halton, Counterpoints: Bible and Theology (Grand Rapids: Zondervan, 2001), p. 58.

38. Gaffin, *No Adam, No Gospel: Adam and the History of Redemption*, p. 10.
39. Collins, *Genesis 1–4: A Linguistic, Literary and Theological Commentary*, p. 188.
40. James M. Hamilton, "Original Sin in Biblical Theology," in *Adam, the Fall, and Original Sin: Theological, Biblical, and Scientific Perspectives*, ed. by Hans Madueme and Michael Reeves (Grand Rapids: Baker Academic, 2014), p. 193–94.

As Hamilton alluded above, there are a number of parallels between the account of the Fall in 3:13–24 and the account in 4:1–8. The following chart presents those parallels that I have identified in my own study of the text.

Element	Genesis 3	Genesis 4
New topic and section introduced by Hebrew "and" + non-verb.	v. 1 — "And the serpent was cleverer than. . . ."*	v. 1 — "And the man knew his wife Eve. . . ."
Main character: the woman	v. 2 — "and the woman said. . . ."	v. 1—"she conceived . . . and she said. . . ."
Produce as food	v. 2 — "from the fruit of the trees. . . ."	v. 3 — "from the fruit of the ground. . . ."
Produce as a test and means to bring the narrative to a climax	v. 3 — "but from the fruit of the tree which is in the midst of the garden God said. . . ."	v. 4–5 — "and God had regard for Abel and his offering, but for Cain and his offering He had not regard"
Revelation from God before the disobedience	v. 3 — "God said. . . ."	v. 7 — "And Yahweh said. . . ."
Acts of disobedience with two people present	v. 6 — "so she took of its fruit and ate it, then also gave it to her husband, who was with her"	v. 8 — "while they were in the field, Cain rose up against his brother and killed him"
Divine mercy by means of an animal's death	v. 21 — "Yahweh made garments of hide for Adam and his wife and clothed them."	v. 7 — "at the entrance a sin offering* is lying down"
God confronts the offender	v. 11 — "Who told you that you are naked? Did you eat from the tree that I commanded you not to eat?" v. 13 — "Yahweh God said to the woman, 'What have you done?' "	v. 9 — "Where is your brother Abel?"
Statement of submission and responsibility	v. 16 — "'your desire is for your husband, and he will govern you'" [Eve's God-given desire is for the one to whom she must submit, because he is the God-appointed leader in the relationship.]	v. 7 — "its desire is for you and you must govern it" [The God-given sin offering animal submits to the God-appointed individual who must offer the sacrifice.]
The curse on the ground	v. 17 — "the ground is cursed because of you"	v. 11 — "But now you are cursed more than the ground"
Challenging agricultural labor	v. 17 — "with painful labor you shall eat of it all the days of your life"	v. 12 — "When you cultivate the ground, it will no longer give its produce to you"

Expulsion from a place and from the divine presence	v. 23 — "Yahweh God sent him from the garden of Eden" v. 24 — "Thus He expelled the man"	v. 14 — "Today You have expelled me from the face of the ground and I am hidden from Your presence"
A pregnancy to commence a line of descendants	4:1 — "Adam knew his wife Eve, so she conceived and bore Cain"	v. 17 — "Cain knew his wife, so she conceived and bore Enoch"

- All English translations of the Hebrew text in this chart are my own.

** Readers will note that my suggested translation goes contrary to how most English translations read. Most translations have "sin," not "sin offering." This current essay is not the place for me to offer a detailed explanation. My interpretation of Genesis 4:7 will appear with extensive and detailed argumentation when my Genesis commentary in the Evangelical Exegetical Commentary (Logos/Lexham) has been finished and published. Also, one of my students at The Master's Seminary wrote a paper for me that I recommended for publication: Chris Burnett, "A Sin Offering Lying in the Doorway? A Minority Interpretation of Genesis 4:6-8." *Master's Seminary Journal* 27, no. 1 (Spring 2016), 45-55.

The parallels between chapters 3 and 4 provide readers with greater certainty that both accounts possess equal authenticity and historicity. If the account of the Fall in chapter 3 is merely legend or allegory, then the account of Cain and Abel must be categorized as the same. If the account of Cain and Abel is a historical reality preserved with integrity in chapter 4, then the account of the disobedience of Adam and Eve in chapter 3 must also be accepted as real history. Indeed, in Luke 11:50-51 Christ Himself accepted the historicity of the murder of Abel and mentioned it together with the murder of Zechariah (see 2 Chron. 24:20-21).

At the same time, Genesis 4 reveals a bit more about God's grace despite Adam's disobedience and Cain's violent act of fratricide. The key to that grace is obscured by the usual translation in 4:7 ("sin lies at the door"; NKJV). The word translated "sin" by many of the English versions is a Hebrew word occurring over 270 times in the Hebrew Bible and translated over one hundred times as "sin offering." Also, the verb "lies" occurs to speak of flocks of sheep and goats lying down to rest (Gen. 29:2, 49:14; Ps. 23:2), not of "lurking" or "crouching" in readiness to attack. Therefore, the picture presented here bears a resemblance to an event that will occur later when God will provide a sacrificial ram in place of Isaac (Gen. 22:13). God provides Cain with a compliant animal for a sin offering. Cain need only accept the gracious gift and sacrifice it in order to "do well" and to be forgiven and restored to fellowship with God.[41] Cain, however, refuses to do so and suffers the consequences.

41. An earlier commentator, F.P. Ramsay, *An Interpretation of Genesis* (New York: Neale Publishing, 1911), p. 87, noted that God instructed Cain on the proper steps to take in the case of sin: "If you do not do well, a sin-offering is available; present that, and be accepted." See also

A genealogy of Cain's line (4:17–24) and a transition back to the line of promise (4:25–26) close the chapter. Real historical events involving real people have served to advance the narrative and to reinforce the reality of Adam's physical headship over both lines of mankind. In one line Abel had offered acceptable sacrifices; in the other line Cain had refused to offer a God-provided sacrifice. The spiritual lines are drawn and the ugliness of sin has become terribly clear. The hope still rests with the "seed" ("offspring") of the woman.

Genesis 5: The Genealogy of Adam

Following the genealogy of Cain's line (4:17–24), the storyline returns to Adam and Eve to reveal how the line of promise (see 3:15) was restored. Thus, in 4:25–26 Moses introduces godly Abel's replacement: Seth. Then, as with the previous history of Cain, a genealogy of Seth's line (commencing with Adam) becomes the theme of chapter 5. These genealogies emphasize the historical nature of the biblical narrative involved in the primeval history (Gen. 1–11). Hoffmeier points out that, "Genealogical texts in the ancient Near East, by their very nature, are treated seriously by scholars and not cavalierly dismissed as made up or fictitious, even if such lists are truncated or selective."[42] Since the author of Genesis structured the entire book by means of "family history,"[43] readers must approach the text as historical narratives providing accounts of historical individuals[44] — beginning with a historical Adam and Eve as the progenitors of the human race.

According to Genesis 5:3, "And Adam lived one hundred and thirty years, and begot a son in his own likeness, after his image, and named him Seth." This demonstrates that Adam is the seminal (or, physical) head of the human race. Adam was created in God's image, but, even after the Fall, that image continues to be conveyed "seminally to each individual."[45] In fact, the purpose of the genealogy in Genesis 5 is to identify Noah as the legitimate descendant of Adam who both bears the divine image and receives the divine blessing.[46]

The detailed genealogy implies that God cares about each individual. The genealogy reveals that physical death has entered the world of humankind

---

Frederick W. Grant, *The Numerical Bible*, 7 vols., 4th ed. (New York: Loizeaux Brothers, 1903), 1:38, and Arthur W. Pink, *Gleanings in Genesis* (Chicago, IL: Moody, 1950), p. 59, "if thou doest not well — if the offering you brought has been rejected the remedy is simple — 'sin lieth at the door,' i.e., a suitable and meet offering, a sin offering is right to your hand."

42. Hoffmeier, "Genesis 1–11 as History and Theology," p. 30.
43. Wenham, *Genesis 1–15,* Word Biblical Commentary, p. 55, 119, 121.
44. Hoffmeier, "Genesis 1–11 as History and Theology," p. 32.
45. Waltke with Fredricks, *Genesis: A Commentary*, p. 70, 113–14.
46. R.R. Wilson, *Genealogy and History in the Biblical World* (New Haven, CT: Yale University Press, 1977), p. 164.

— only Enoch escaped this earth without dying physically (5:24). Enoch's grandson, Lamech, named his son "Noah" because he hoped that "This one will comfort us concerning our work and the toil of our hands, because of the ground which the Lord has cursed" (v. 29). The line of Seth continued to look for the hope as announced in 3:15; the line of Cain continued to ignore or outright reject the grace of God, who is always ready to forgive and restore. The authenticity and integrity of the genealogy in Genesis 5 equals that of the genealogy in 1 Chronicles 1, which likewise begins with Adam and concludes with Noah's three sons: "Adam, Seth, Enosh, Cainan, Mahalalel, Jared, Enoch, Methuselah, Lamech, Noah, Shem, Ham, and Japheth" (v. 1–4). The identical genealogy occurs yet again in the New Testament in the lineage of Jesus (Luke 3:36–38), but in reverse order to conclude with Adam as one produced by "God." Why did the divine Author of Scripture see fit to repeat the genealogy of Genesis 5 three different times? Its repetition provides evidence of its truth, its integrity, its significance, and its reality as trustworthy history. Adam was, indeed, the originating head of the human race, just as a straightforward reading of Genesis 1–5 indicates.

The Rest of Genesis (Gen. 6–50)

The narrative record continues with the history of original sin as it spread throughout the world and dominated the human scene, resulting in God's decision to bring a global judgment that would wipe out all life on the earth (6:1–7). One godly descendant of Adam, Noah, experienced the grace of God as a result of his faithful living and obedience to God (6:8–9). Divine judgment by the waters of the Flood destroyed all life except for that which God brought to Noah for preservation in the great boat that He instructed Noah to build (6:10–8:14). When Noah, his family, and the animals disembarked from the ark, God repeated His original mandate that He had given to Adam and Eve (8:17; 9:1; compare 1:28). The parallelism is unmistakable — Noah is like a second Adam. Just as Adam and Eve were the only people on the earth at the beginning, so Noah and his wife together with their sons and daughters-in-law were the only people on the planet (9:19). If someone denies the historicity of Adam as the originating physical head of the entire human race, they would, of necessity, be forced to deny the historicity of the Flood and the new beginning with Noah and his family alone.[47]

Noah proves not to be the promised offspring of the woman. Moses provides an account that reveals that Noah differs from the original Adam

47. See Keathley and Rooker, *40 Questions about Creation and Evolution*, p. 282–83, for a helpful set of charts depicting the parallels between the creation narrative and the Flood narrative.

in one very key point — Noah was born a sinner and never was sinless or perfect — nor were his sons (9:20–24). The genealogical entry at 9:28–29 returns the readers to 5:32 and wraps up Noah's life by a similar entry to those found in the genealogy of Adam. The report of Noah's death echoes 5:4–5 and its record of Adam's death. Once again, the use of genealogical forms and entries confirms the historical nature of the Genesis record and supports the historicity and centrality of Adam and Eve in the biblical narrative.

The narrative regarding the judgment of Babel and the division of human language into a variety of languages (Gen. 10–11) continues the early history of mankind. Collins observes that "The genealogies of Genesis 5 and 11 connect the primal pair to subsequent generations, particularly to Abraham."[48]

Abraham, as the vehicle for divine blessing upon all the peoples of the planet (12:1–3), brings the history of mankind back to the point of 3:15 — the solution to the Fall. The Abrahamic Covenant speaks of a future redemption through a descendant of Abraham. This theological topic of redemption must be founded upon a reason for the need of redemption. That foundation has been laid in chapters 1–11 (especially chapters 3–4). If there is a real historical need for redemption or salvation, then the condition requiring redemption must be equally historical and real. This fact alone ought to demonstrate the historicity and authenticity of the primeval history. As Gordon Wenham points out, "Genesis, so pessimistic about mankind without God, is fundamentally optimistic, precisely because God created men and women in his own image and disclosed his ideal for humanity at the beginning of time."[49]

The Rest of the Old Testament

Elsewhere in the Old Testament the writers make mention of the fact that God had created mankind on the planet (for example, Deut. 4:32 and Isa. 42:5). Isaiah's reference to God giving "breath to the people" on the earth clearly alludes back to Genesis 2:7. Like Malachi 2:10, Isaiah 42:5 identifies God as the Creator of all mankind. Malachi's text identifies God as the "Father":

> Have we not all one Father?
> Has not one God created us?
> Why do we deal treacherously with one another
> By profaning the covenant of the fathers?

48. Collins, "Adam and Eve in the Old Testament," p. 23.
49. Wenham, *Genesis 1–15*, Word Biblical Commentary, p. liii.

Malachi does not mean that God has specially created every individual from the dust or clay of the earth and breathed "the breath of life" into their nostrils, just as He did with Adam. Malachi's point is that all mankind possesses the same origin. Some translations choose not to capitalize "Father" (for example, NRSV) and appear to leave the reference open to Adam as mankind's "father." However, the parallel line makes the strongest point for "Father" being a title of God, not a reference to Adam. That does not, however, negate the association with Genesis 1:26–28. We might compare the association with the implied relationship indicated in the genealogy of Christ in Luke 3:38 — "the son of Enosh, *the son* of Seth, *the son* of Adam, *the son* of God."

One of the earliest mentions of Adam occurs in Job 31:33 ("If I have covered my transgressions as Adam"). Job alludes to Adam's disobedience in the Garden of Eden and speaks of how Adam sought to hide himself, and thus his transgression, from God (Gen. 3:10). Some apparent references to Adam prove, upon further exegesis, to be more generic references for which "man" or "mankind" would provide a better translation. One of these is Deuteronomy 32:8 which refers to the division into nations at the judgment of Babel (Gen. 11:8).

Hosea 6:7 has stirred a lot of debate over the centuries. At least seven different views are to be found in the writings of commentators and theologians: (1) "Adam" might refer to a town in the Jordan Valley.[50] Thus, Hosea 6:7 identifies the beginning of the rebellion of Pekah (736/735 B.C.) and understands the breach of treaty as an act of treachery against Yahweh. One problem facing this interpretation consists of the fact that there is only one other mention of this city in the Old Testament — at Joshua 3:16. Therefore, as even A.A. Macintosh admits, such an identification is speculative. (2) One of the most popular interpretations believes that "Adam" could refer to the original man in Genesis 1–3 (see ASV, RSV, NRSV, NASB, NASU, NIV, NET, ESV, HCSB, NLT). Adam, then, would be the model for Israel's unfaithfulness.[51] As Duane Garrett points out, however, " 'there'

50. A.A. Macintosh, *A Critical and Exegetical Commentary on Hosea*, International Critical Commentary (Edinburgh: T&T Clark, 1997), p. 237–38; Michael A. Eaton, *Hosea*, Focus on the Bible (Fearn, Scotland: Christian Focus, 1996), p. 108.

51. Leon J. Wood, "Hosea," in *The Expositor's Bible Commentary*, ed. Frank E. Gaebelein, 7:159–225 (Grand Rapids: Zondervan, 1985), p. 195, according to whom, "there" merely refers to Israel's land which God had covenanted to them. See also Thomas Edward McComiskey, "Hosea," in *The Minor Prophets*, 3 vols., ed. Thomas Edward McComiskey, 1:1–237 (Grand Rapids: Baker, 1992), p. 95, who prefers to take "there" in the same generic, nongeographical sense as its use in Psalm 14:5, pointing out the state of transgression; and Collins, *Genesis 1–4: A Linguistic, Literary and Theological Commentary*, p. 112–14, who does not regard the covenant as one of works or merit.

implies that 'Adam' is a place, as do the parallels 'Gilead' and "Shechem.' . . ."[52] In response, M. Daniel Carroll R. (Rodas) argues that elsewhere in the Old Testament "break the covenant" (*'abar berit*, "transgress a covenant") always speaks of a breach of a covenant between Yahweh and Israel (*parar berit*, "break/destroy a covenant," is used for violating human agreements or treaties), the text specifies that it is a betrayal before God, and verses 4–6 suggest that it refers to a lack of covenant loyalty (*hesed*, "loyal love" or "lovingkindness").[53] (3) Some commentators suggest that the name should be emended to read "Admah," the city that God destroyed along with Sodom and Gomorrah in Genesis 19:29. Hosea mentions Admah again in 11:8. But, this emendation has no real textual (or contextual) support and must be abandoned as overly speculative. (4) Those who suggest an emendation of "Adam" by changing it to "Aram" at least provide a familiar potential scribal error (the visual similarity of the letters *d* and *r* in the Hebrew alphabet). But there is no known reason for taking Syria as the violator of the covenant in this context.[54] (5) If the reader takes the Hebrew as "dirt" ("But look — they have walked on my covenant like it was dirt"[55]), another improbable viewpoint results, though unlikely since it also relies upon emending the Hebrew text. (6) Garrett concludes that Hosea uses a pun by juxtaposing the name of the town in the Jordan Valley with the name of the original man: "Like Adam (the man) they break covenants; they are faithless to me there (in the town of Adam)."[56] This view still allows a reference to the original human being. However, any view that results in a reference to Adam here leads to a greater difficulty — identifying a biblical covenant that God established with the historical Adam. If a covenant was established with Adam, it is very strange that it is not clearly stated anywhere else and no text anywhere contains any clear pronouncements associated with such a covenant or even refers to the existence of such a covenant. The earliest covenant consists of the one God made with Noah and it is clearly identified as such and its stipulations and provisions specified (Gen. 6:18, 9:8–17). A covenant with Adam would certainly have been so significant that it would have merited mention in the Genesis record — but such mention is absent. Some

52. Duane A. Garrett, *Hosea, Joel*, New American Commentary 19A (N.p.: Broadman & Holman, 1997), p. 162.
53. M. Daniel Carroll R. (Rodas), "Hosea," in *The Expositor's Bible Commentary*, rev. ed., eds. Tremper Longman III and David E. Garland, 8:213–305 (Grand Rapids: Zondervan, 2008), p. 260.
54. Garrett, *Hosea, Joel*, New American Commentary, p. 162, n185.
55. Douglas Stuart, *Hosea-Jonah*, Word Biblical Commentary 31 (Nashville, TN: Thomas Nelson, 1987), p. 98.
56. Garrett, *Hosea, Joel*, New American Commentary, p. 163.

well-known covenant theologians also take issue with taking Hosea 6:7 as evidence for any Adamic covenant.[57] (7) The final option consists of understanding the text ("like *'adam*") as a general reference to "mankind" (see KJV, NKJV, JPS, NJPS), rather than to the historical Adam himself. The Septuagint (LXX) supports such an understanding by its *hōs anthrōpos* ("as/like a man" or "as/like mankind").[58] The context of Hosea 6:7 indicates that this particular "covenant" involves the Mosaic Covenant, because Israel had violated the Mosaic Law and had incurred its curses (Hos. 4:1–2, 6; 8:12).[59]

Biblical Inerrancy and Biblical Authority

The spirit of the age consists of a hermeneutic of suspicion and doubt, which demeans the Bible, turns it into a purely human production, and tosses it out as a viable authority for how one thinks or lives. Consider David Clines' musings:

> Does not the very concept of "authority" come from a world we have (thankfully) left behind? To imagine that the Bible could be "authoritative" sounds as if we still are wanting to plunder it for prooftexts for theological warfare. As if one sentence from the immense unsystematic collection of literature that is the Bible could *prove* anything. As if truth in matters of religion could be arrived at by a process like that of the mediaeval academic disputation. As if texts mattered more than people.[60]

In direct contrast to Clines' reasoning, which demotes the testimony of the biblical text, the concept of *prima facie* (literally, "at first view") evidence stands at the forefront of American and British jurisprudence with regard to the role of evidence. *Prima facie* evidence consists of that evidence which is sufficient enough to raise a presumption of fact or to establish the fact in question, unless the rebuttal can counter with evidence of equal veracity. This evidential system presumes innocence until guilt has been proven. It also demands that witnesses present facts, not opinions. In biblical studies, such methodology contrasts significantly with the hermeneutics of doubt

---

57. Anthony A. Hoekema, *Created in God's Image* (Grand Rapids: Eerdmans, 1994), p. 119–21.
58. William Rainey Harper, *Hosea*, International Critical Commentary (Edinburgh: T&T Clark, 1905), p. 288. However, the LXX makes "a man" (or, "mankind") the subject of the verb "break" ("transgressing"), although the Hebrew verb is a plural.
59. Stuart, *Hosea-Jonah*, Word Biblical Commentary, p. 111.
60. Clines, *What Does Eve Do to Help? and Other Readerly Questions to the Old Testament,* p. 47–48 (emphasis is Clines').

(or, the Troelschian principle of skeptical criticism).[61] One of the world's premier Old Testament scholars, Robert Dick Wilson, wrote, "Our text of the Old Testament is presumptively correct . . . its meaning is on the whole clear and trustworthy."[62] Historically, evangelical scholars have approached the biblical text with a presumption of factuality. The new generation of evangelicals, however, have more in common with Clines than with Wilson. That bent shows up quite clearly in the debate over the historical Adam taking place *within* the camp of evangelicalism.

One example of some evangelicals' drift away from traditional evangelical views regarding biblical inerrancy and biblical authority shows up in the recent writings of John Walton regarding a historical Adam and Eve. Walton emphasizes that he accepts as fact that Adam and Eve were real people living in a real past.[63] However, he casts doubt on their being the first human beings or the ancestors of all other human beings.[64] In regard to accommodation to secular science's conclusions (which are quite obviously in conflict with the traditional evangelical view of Adam and Eve), Walton responds,

> This does not mean that such a person should accept the scientific consensus uncritically, but interpreters would not be in a position to say that specific biblical texts or theology in general demand the rejection of the scientific consensus. Any science must be weighed on its merits, but the Bible would not predetermine the outcome.[65]

How does Walton deal with accusations that he has cast aside biblical inerrancy? He responds by saying that his view

> adheres to inerrancy in that it is distinguishing between claims that the Bible makes, and more importantly, to claims it does not make. It accepts the existence of a historical Adam and Eve and honors the

61. See V. Philips Long, "Historiography of the Old Testament," in *The Face of Old Testament Studies: A Survey of Contemporary Approaches*, ed. by David W. Baker and Bill T. Arnold (Grand Rapids: Baker, 1999), p. 154, 169.
62. Robert Dick Wilson, *A Scientific Investigation of the Old Testament*, rev. by Edward J. Young (Chicago, IL: Moody, 1959), p. 9. For a more detailed examination of the implications of *prima facie* evidence for the exegesis of the biblical text, see William D. Barrick, "Exegetical Fallacies: Common Interpretative Mistakes Every Student Must Avoid," *Master's Seminary Journal* 19, no. 1 (Spring 2008), p. 16–18.
63. John H. Walton, "A Historical Adam: Archetypal Creation View," in *Four Views on the Historical Adam*, ed. by Matthew Barrett and Ardel B. Caneday, Counterpoints: Bible and Theology (Grand Rapids: Zondervan, 2013), p. 89.
64. Walton, "A Historical Adam: Archetypal Creation View," p. 93–94, 108, 112.
65. Ibid., p. 113.

> doctrine of original sin associated with a historical event, though it works with an alternate model of the transmission of original sin. It does not promote evolution nor accept evolution, though the view offers a biblical and theological interpretation that would allow us to accept evolution if we are so inclined.[66]

In other words, the early chapters of Genesis need not be read as presenting the material creation of man nor the genetic headship of Adam and Eve for the human race, because, according to Walton, the Bible makes no such claims. Even Denis Lamoureux, an evangelical evolutionist, questions Walton's attempt to excise the material origin of Adam from the biblical account.[67] Walton's view exceeds the boundaries of an objective, straightforward reading of the biblical text in an attempt to mute its clear witness.

One way by which some evangelicals have sought to reinterpret the Genesis account involves imposing a prescientific (or, Old World Science[68]) viewpoint upon the authors of the biblical text. After all, they reason, the ancients could not and did not possess our modern scientific acumen and knowledge. Didn't the ancients adhere to a three-tier cosmic geography with a flat earth set on pillars, a solid sky above, and waters above the solid sky?[69] Walton and Lamoureux,[70] along with many other evangelicals, include the biblical writers among the ancients who possessed an inaccurate view of the true cosmic geography. These evangelicals assert that the following illustration[71] reflects the worldview of both the Israelites and their neighbors.

But did the ancients themselves all accept that construct so readily imposed upon them by modern scholars? In recent years a growing number of scholars have presented evidence that the ancient people used metaphors

---

66. Ibid.
67. Denis O. Lamoureux, "Response from the Evolutionary View," in *Four Views on the Historical Adam*, ed. by Matthew Barrett and Ardel B. Caneday, Counterpoints: Bible and Theology (Grand Rapids: Zondervan, 2013), p. 120.
68. John H. Walton and D. Brent Sandy, *The Lost World of Scripture: Ancient Literary Culture and Biblical Authority* (Downers Grove, IL: IVP Academic, 2013), p. 56–59.
69. Walton, "A Historical Adam: Archetypal Creation View," p. 117, n. 47.
70. Denis O. Lamoureux, "No Historical Adam: Evolutionary Creation View," in *Four Views on the Historical Adam*, ed. by Matthew Barrett and Ardel B. Caneday, Counterpoints: Bible and Theology (Grand Rapids: Zondervan, 2013), p. 48. See also Denis O. Lamoureux, "Beyond Original Sin: Is a Theological Paradigm Shift Inevitable?" *Perspectives on Science and Christian Faith* 67, no. 1 (March 2015), p. 38–40.
71. The graphic is a Logos production, one of several that are available at logosres:fsbinfographics;art=ancienthebrewconceptionoftheuniverse.

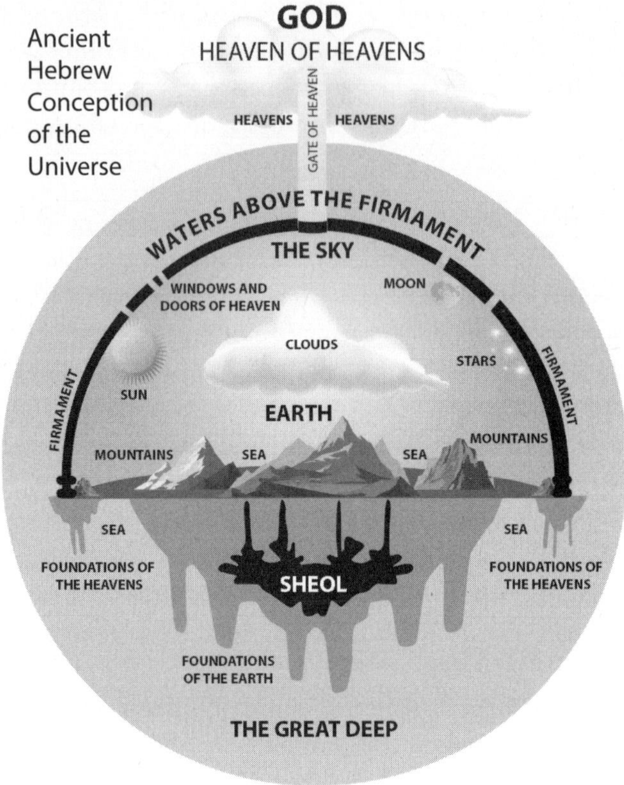

that they did not take as being the equivalent of reality.[72] Take the pillars of the earth, as one example. In the oldest book of the Bible, Job speaks of the "pillars" of the earth shaking (Job 9:6; see also "the pillars of heaven" in 26:11). Yet he also says that God "hangs the earth on nothing" (26:7). It would appear then that Job knows that he is using a metaphor when speaking of "pillars." Another such biblical example can be observed with references to "the windows of heaven" (Gen. 7:11, 8:2; Mal. 3:10). However, an officer in Samaria who was questioning Elisha's claim that God would supply an abundance of flour says, " 'Look, if the Lord would make windows in heaven, could this thing be?'" (2 Kings 7:2, 19). The officer clearly treats the picture as metaphorical rather than reality. Job, from the era of the patriarchs (21st to 18th centuries B.C.), and the Israeli officer in Samaria (ninth century B.C.) both use the figures of pillars and windows metaphorically.

72. For example, Jeffrey Burton Russell, *Inventing the Flat Earth: Columbus and Modern Historians* (1991; reprint, Westport, CT: Praeger, 1997); Noel K. Weeks, "Cosmology in Historical Context," *Westminster Theological Journal* 68, no. 2 (2006), p. 283–93; Jonathan F. Henry, "Uniformitarianism in Old Testament Studies: A Review of *Ancient Near Eastern Thought and the Old Testament* by John H. Walton," *Journal of Dispensational Theology* 13, no. 39 (2009), p. 19–36 (esp. p. 25–28); Ian Taylor and Paula Weston, "Who Invented the Flat Earth?" *Creation* 16, no. 2 (March, 1994), p. 48–49; Jonathan Sarfati, "The Flat Earth Myth," *Creation* 35, no. 3 (July 2013), p. 20–23; Gleason L. Archer, "The Metallic Sky: A Travesty of Modern Pseudo-Scholarship," *Journal of the American Scientific Affiliation* 31 (December 1979), p. 220–21; John Byl, "Genesis and Ancient Cosmology," blog posted February 19, 2010 at http://bylogos.blogspot.com/2010/02/genesis-and-ancient-cosmology.html (accessed January 2, 2016).

Why do many modern scholars continue to denigrate the scientific knowledge of ancient peoples and ignore their ability to utilize sophisticated metaphors? According to Jeffrey Russell, in the 15 centuries between Christ and Columbus, only five authors rejected the spherical shape of planet Earth. They included Lactantius (ca. A.D. 245–325), who was later condemned as a heretic. Imposing the flat earth myth upon the ancients became orthodoxy in the 19th century. At that time "it became widespread conventional wisdom from 1870 to 1920 as a result of 'the war between science and religion,' when for many intellectuals in Europe and the United States all religion became synonymous with superstition and science became the only legitimate source of truth."[73] Russell also placed the modern adherence to the myth of a flat earth among the ancients in the context of a larger picture about modern thinking. "Our determination to believe the Flat Error arises out of contempt for the past and our need to believe in the superiority of the present."[74] Russell also writes, "The assumption of the superiority of 'our' views to that of older cultures is the most stubborn remaining variety of ethnocentrism."[75] Such ethnocentrism raises its head in the American Association for the Advancement of Science (AAAS) and *Science* magazine collaboration to highlight the 96 most important scientific discoveries in history.[76] Dick Teresi exposed the prejudice of the time-line of the discoveries:

> Of those ninety-six achievements, only two were attributed to non-white, non-Western scientists: the invention of zero in India in the early centuries of the common era and the astronomical observations of Maya and Hindu "skywatchers" (the word *astronomer* was not used). According to the journal, those "skywatchers" used astronomy for "agricultural and religious purposes" only — not for anything like science.

---

73. David Noble, "Foreword," in Jeffrey Burton Russell, *Inventing the Flat Earth: Columbus and Modern Historians* (1991; reprint, Westport, CT: Praeger, 1997), p. x.
74. Noble, "Foreword," p. x. See also Russell, *Inventing the Flat Earth: Columbus and Modern Historians,* p. 76, "The hope that we are making progress toward a goal (which is not defined and about which there is no consensus) leads us to undervalue the past in order to convince ourselves of the superiority of the present."
75. Russell, *Inventing the Flat Earth: Columbus and Modern Historians*, p. 76.
76. Floyd E. Bloom, "The Endless Pathways of Discovery," *Science* 287, no. 5451 (January 14, 2000), p. 229–31, available online with the full two-page full-color chart titled "Pathways of Discovery" at http://www.ganino.com/games/Science/science%20magazine%20 1999-2000/root/data/Science%201999-2000/pdf/2000_v287_n5451/p5451_0229.pdf (accessed January 2, 2016).

> Most interesting is the first entry in the time-line: "Prior to 600 B.C., Prescientific Era." *Science* proclaimed that during this time, before sixth-century B.C. pre-Socratic philosophers, "Phenomena [were] explained within contexts of magic, religion, and experience." *Science* thus ignored more than two millennia of history, during which time the Babylonians invented the abacus and algebra, the Sumerians recorded the phases of Venus, the Indians proposed an atomic theory, the Chinese invented quantitative chemical analysis, and the Egyptians built pyramids. In addition, *Science* gave Johannes Gutenberg credit for the printing press in 1454, though it was invented at least two centuries earlier by the Chinese and Koreans. An essential precursor of the printing press is paper, which was invented in China and did not reach Europe until the 1300s. *Science* cited Francis Bacon's work as one of its ninety-six achievements, yet ignored his opinion that inventions from China created the modern world.[77]

In his review of Russell's volume, Steven Sargent identifies two lessons which Russell takes away from his study of the common wrong-headed view of the ancients, their worldview, science, and cosmic geography: (1) "historians (and others) pass on error as well as truth, especially when they consult their biases more than the evidence" and (2) "no intellectual paradigm, including scientific positivism, can claim privileged insight into the meaning of the past."[78] Adding to this summary in his own way and in an unrelated journal article, Noel Weeks concludes with a warning: "Of course, it also follows that if we falsely accommodate part of Scripture's unique view of reality to either the surrounding pagan views or to modern secular views, then we will be in danger of doing the same with other aspects of Scripture's views."[79]

Within the early chapters of Genesis, Moses describes the ability of the second generation of human beings (Adam > Cain) to build a city (Gen. 4:17) and the technological acumen of the eighth generation (Adam > Cain > Enoch > Irad > Mehujael > Methushael > Lamech > Jabal, Jubal, and Tubal-Cain) to engage in agriculture and animal husbandry (v. 20), in the

77. Dick Teresi, *Lost Discoveries: The Ancient Roots of Modern Science — from the Babylonians to the Maya* (New York: Simon & Schuster, 2002), p. 12–13. Studies such as Teresi's serve as an antidote to modern hubris by revealing how much true scientific knowledge and acumen ancient peoples actually possessed.

78. Steven D. Sargent, Review of Jeffrey Burton Russell, *Inventing the Flat Earth: Columbus and Modern Historians, JSTOR* 84, no. 2 (June 1993), p. 353.

79. Weeks, "Cosmology in Historical Context," p. 293.

production of musical instruments and composition of music (v. 21), and metallurgy (iron working, v. 22). Such evidence should suffice to eliminate the cultural, ethnic, and technological hubris of modern interpreters of the biblical text. Many scholars use "prescientific" as a label enabling them to conveniently dismiss what the Bible says — if the writers are prescientific in their knowledge and worldview, we need not accept what they say about the world as truth. That prejudicial treatment of the Bible becomes even more apparent when someone like Lamoureux accuses the Apostle Paul of "belief in ancient science"[80] when the Apostle lived in a time nearly seven centuries later than the era *Science* magazine labeled as "Prescientific."

Acceptance of the biblical record includes believing that the biblical writers held a totally different worldview from unbelieving Hebrews/Israelites and their pagan neighbors. Ignoring that distinction repeatedly pops to the surface in debates with evangelicals who stubbornly reject a straightforward reading of the biblical record and who insist upon subjecting the Bible to the unbelieving worldview of that time. By doing so they miss the primary point of the early chapters of Genesis: divine revelation presents the history of the universe, of the earth, and of mankind that was consistently at odds with unbelievers and ancient cultures from the earliest eras.

Conclusion

Genesis 1–5 offers a large amount of evidence to identify Adam and Eve as the originating heads of the human race. God created them in His own image (1:26–27), a unique characteristic that marks every human being (see 9:6). The very processes involved in creating the man (2:7) and the woman (2:21–22) were also never to be repeated in the formation or birth of any other man or woman — and, most clearly, quite distinct from any process of development claimed by adherents to secular science's evolutionary hypothesis for human beings. Adam recognizes that his wife Eve is "the mother of all living" — the mother of all mankind (3:20).

The biblical text describes Adam as possessing a full capacity for the sophisticated use of language (2:19–20, 23). His descendants give no indication of being prescientific, backwards, gesturing brute hominids.[81] They are city builders, agriculturalists engaged in crop production and animal husbandry, tent makers, craftsmen, artisans, musicians, and metal workers (4:2, 17, 20–22). It also required considerable knowledge of shipbuilding,

80. Lamoureux, "No Historical Adam: Evolutionary Creation View," p. 50.

81. For further evidence of ancient man's intelligence and creativity, see chapter 14 in this volume.

engineering, carpentry, and animal husbandry for Noah and his co-workers to build the ark to house the food and care for the animals on board that survived the yearlong, global, catastrophic Flood. At least one line descending from Adam worshiped the Lord with sacrifices (4:3–4, 8:20) and prayer (4:26), looking for the promise of the victorious offspring of the woman (3:15, 5:29). The relationship of Adam and Eve comprises the first marriage, an institution designed by God for the fulfillment of His mandate for mankind to populate the earth and to rule over it (1:26, 28, 2:24–25). Such details demonstrate that the biblical account is about real human beings with identifiable acumen, skills, social associations, and vocations. Nothing marks the text as conveying a legend, a myth, or an allegory.

The geography and genealogies in Genesis 1–11 also contribute to the historical nature of the biblical narrative. Real history involving real people takes place in real locations. The text includes the names and descriptions of geographical locations (2:8, 10–14; 3:24; 4:16–17; 8:4; 10:10–12, 19, 30; 11:2, 28, 31–32). Genealogies occur on a regular basis (4:16–22, 25–26; 5:1–32; 9:18–19, 28–29; 10:1–32; 11:10–32) and the Hebrew term for a genealogy (*toledot*) marks the structural divisions of the entire Book of Genesis (2:4; 5:1; 6:9; 10:1; 11:10, 27; 25:12, 19; 36:1, 9; 37:2). The genealogies not only provide a list of families and descendants by name, they also include time markers for their ages, and brief accounts of remarkable events. Such records require that the reader take all of the book as historical narrative, not just chapters 12–50. That, then, adds to the assurance of the history of Adam and Eve as the first human beings and progenitors of the entire human race.

Besides all of these evidences, we could also mention the Fall, when Adam disobeyed God, and its impact upon the spiritual condition of all mankind, and the subsequent entrance of both spiritual and physical death into the world (3:1–19). That event not only sets the tone for the ongoing issue mankind has with sin, it also sets the stage for God's program of redemption through the promised offspring of the woman (3:15). Without a historical Fall, there is no need for a historical Redeemer and a real historical redemption.

Also, the Genesis account of the Flood in Noah's day makes no sense apart from the concomitant reality of Adam and Eve being the first human beings. If the Flood truly wiped out all people on the earth except for the eight persons of Noah's family on the ark, then Noah is the new physical head of the human race. In that regard he is like Adam and likewise receives God's mandate to repopulate the entire earth (8:17, 9:1; compare 1:28).

Lastly, within the Tower of Babel narrative mention is made of the fact that the sons of Noah were the originating heads of all peoples and nations upon the post-Flood earth (10:32). This also accounts for the one human language prior to God's judgment on Babel (11:1). The narrative of Genesis is united in declaring that the entire history of the human race started with Adam and Eve.

Although there is little direct reference to Adam and Eve in the rest of the Old Testament, those passages that have a bearing upon them assume their historicity. In fact, the Bible is not the source of doubt concerning the reality of Adam and Eve as the originators of the human race. Rather, human commentators and theologians (even those who count themselves as evangelicals) have cast doubt and incredulity on the historicity of Adam and Eve. That approach, as we have seen, is actually an attack upon the inerrancy, integrity, and authority of the biblical text as the revealed Word of an all-knowing and all-wise God. In an age when the biblical foundations are under attack, believers must rally in defense of the stronghold of all biblical history and theology, Genesis 1–3. Those who defend the integrity of the first three chapters of Genesis must recognize the close ties those chapters have with the entire primeval history of mankind in Genesis 1–11 and the necessity of its accuracy and historicity as the foundation for Genesis 12 through to the conclusion of the New Testament.

In the battle about origins, the biblical record stands as strong opposition to the secular hypothesis of biological evolution. Some scholars, like Peter Enns, insist that "evolution requires us to revisit how the Bible thinks of human origins."[82] To the contrary, the biblical record demands that we revisit, counter, and correct what the majority of secular scientists think about human origins.

82. Peter Enns, *The Evolution of Adam: What the Bible Does and Doesn't Say about Human Origins* (Grand Rapids: Brazos Press, 2012), p. 82.

Chapter 2

The Question of a Historical Adam: A New Testament Perspective

by Dr. David A. Croteau and Dr. Michael P. Naylor

Introduction

For those approaching the question of a historical Adam, the opening chapters of Genesis are a natural and appropriate place to begin, and the interpretation of these chapters is crucial for this issue. Although written much later, the New Testament likewise plays an important role, especially for those who hold to the unity and authority of Scripture. In surveying the contents, there are more than just a few passing references to Adam in the New Testament. This chapter attempts to demonstrate that the New Testament authors believed that Adam was a historical figure in an environment in which not everyone agreed and the importance of this for the theology of the writers of the New Testament. First, before considering the references in the New Testament itself, the Jewish cultural context around that time period will be discussed to demonstrate that some, though not all, believed that Adam was a historical figure. Second, the two main passages in the New Testament that seem to require a literal, historical Adam will be examined in detail: 1 Corinthians 15 and Romans 5. Significant objections to this interpretation will be addressed. Finally, several other New Testament passages that mention Adam (and where relevant, Eve) in a historical way will be discussed.

Could the New Testament Authors Really Have Interpreted Genesis 3 as Historical?

The Cultural Context of the New Testament

Those who believe in a historical Adam have been accused of reading back into the New Testament authors certain convictions about Adam that are driven by our own view of Genesis rather than the biblical authors' view. This assertion can be helpfully addressed by considering the views of other Jewish authors around the time of the New Testament. An examination of several other Jewish writings of this day outside of Scripture indicates that this interpretation of Adam and the Fall was not unique to the Christian interpretation found in the New Testament.[1]

The book *4 Ezra*, written after A.D. 70, addresses the problem of Adam, transgression, and death:

> O sovereign Lord, did you not speak at the beginning when you formed the dust and it gave you Adam, a lifeless body? Yet he was the workmanship of your hands, and you breathed into him the breath of life, and he was made alive in your presence. And you led him into the garden which your right hand had planted before the earth appeared. And you laid upon him one commandment of yours; but he transgressed it, and immediately you appointed death for him and for his descendants (4 Ezra 3:4–7).[2]

A similar conviction, as will be explored later, is expressed in 1 Corinthians 15 and Romans 5 concerning the relationship between Adam's sin and the death that resulted. The author goes on to state,

> Yet you did not take away from them their evil heart, so that your Law might bring forth fruit in them. For the first Adam, burdened with an evil heart, transgressed and was overcome, as were also all who were descended from him. Thus the disease became permanent; the law was in the people's heart along with the evil root, but what was good departed, and the evil remained (4 Ezra 3:20–22).[3]

---

1. The following is a selection of Second Temple Jewish texts illustrating views of Adam present during the first century. Further examples could be noted. For a concise introduction to Adam and Eve, see John R. Levison, "Adam and Eve, Literature Concerning," in *Dictionary of New Testament Backgrounds*, eds. Craig A. Evans and Stanley E. Porter (Downers Grove: InterVarsity Press, 2000), p. 1–6.
2. James H. Charlesworth, ed., *The Old Testament Pseudepigrapha* (London, England: Darton, Longman & Todd, 1983–1985), 1:528.
3. Ibid., 1:529.

Finally, the author later laments,

> This is my first and last word: It would have been better if the earth had not produced Adam, or else, when it produced him, had restrained him from sinning. For what good is it to all that they live in sorrow now and expect punishment after death? O Adam, what have you done? For though it was you who sinned, the fall was not yours alone, but ours also who are your descendants (4 Ezra 7:116–119).[4]

The author of *4 Ezra* discusses Adam in a very similar way to Paul. He appears to view Adam as a historical figure and uses this conclusion as the basis for his argument and lament.

Another Jewish text, *2 Baruch*, written after the fall of Jerusalem in A.D. 70, likewise connects Adam's sin with the corruption of death:

> O Adam, what did you do to all who were born after you? And what will be said of the first Eve who obeyed the serpent, so that this whole multitude is going to corruption? And countless are those whom the fire devours. But again I shall speak before you. You, O Lord, my Lord, you know that which is in your creation, for you commanded the dust one day to produce Adam; and you knew the number of those who are born from him and how they sinned before you, those who existed and who did not recognize you as their Creator (2 Baruch 48:42–46).[5]

Finally, although not as extensive in their discussion of the connection of Adam, sin, and death, several other Jewish writings address particular details of the account in Genesis. Tobit 8:6 mentions Adam and Eve in a discussion of marriage. Although the main focus in the prayer of Tobias in 8:5–7 is upon marriage as reflected in Genesis 2, the statement in verse 6 notes the relationship between Adam and the rest of the human race: "You made Adam, and for him you made his wife Eve as a helper and support. From the two of them the human race has sprung" (NRSV). Sirach 33:10 affirms the creation of Adam from the earth.[6] Lastly, Josephus, in his discourse concerning nature, describes the creation of Adam from the dust of the earth.[7]

---

4. Ibid., 1:541.
5. Ibid., 1:637.
6. The NRSV uses "humankind," but the Greek word is the name "Adam." Sirach 49:16 could likewise be noted for its inclusion of Adam in a series of individuals from the Old Testament.
7. *Antiquities* 1.1.1–2; 1.2.3.

In *4 Ezra* and *2 Baruch*, the connection is made between Adam's actions and the sin and death and corruption that followed or the relationship between Adam and the human race. Examples from Tobit, Sirach, and Josephus likewise indicate an affirmation of Adam as a historical person. Paul's interpretation of Genesis 3, as will be seen, is in keeping with at least some of his Jewish contemporaries who wrote within the same time period of his writing.[8] The evaluation of the predicament of the human race as being a result of Adam's actions is a conviction held by others of his day.

Was this the only interpretation found at this time? Were there other options available other than seeing Genesis as depicting a historical Adam? The answer is, admittedly, yes. The Jewish author Philo of Alexandria provides a good example of this. Philo, in approaching the text in an allegorical fashion under the influence of the Platonic tradition, sees the narrative as representative of the subjugation of the reason to the senses, leading to a sort of slavery.[9] Given Philo's view, does this argue against a view of Adam as a historical person as seen in the New Testament?

Peter Enns contends that these different Jewish authors were free to handle the Genesis text in a way that fit their different arguments and that Paul (along with other New Testament authors) is simply doing the same thing. In Enns' view, this is a literary appeal rather than an appeal to history.[10] However, in looking at Paul's interpretation, in particular, in light of Jewish interpretation at the time, the lack of unanimity among Jewish authors actually strengthens the argument that Paul and the other New Testament authors understood Adam as a historical person. Paul's interpretation of Genesis 1–3 was *an* interpretation available in his day but was not *the only* interpretation of Genesis. In other words, given the choice of interpreting Adam as historical or as non-historical, Paul interprets Adam as a historical person (as will be shown below), responsible for the entrance of sin and death into the world.

---

8. See E. Earle Ellis, *Paul's Use of the Old Testament* (Eugene, OR: Wipf and Stock, 1981), p. 60.
9. See *Legum Allegoriae* 3.76; *De Opificio Mundi* 165; Jonathan Worthington, "Philo of Alexandria and Romans 5:12–21," in *Reading Romans in Context: Paul and Second Temple Judaism*, eds. Ben C. Blackwell, John K. Goodrich, and Jason Maston (Grand Rapids, MI: Zondervan, 2015), p. 82.
10. Enns says, ". . . Paul's handling of Adam is *hermeneutically* no different from what others were doing at the time: appropriating an ancient story to address pressing concerns of the moment." Peter Enns, *The Evolution of Adam: What the Bible Does and Doesn't Say about Human Origins* (Grand Rapids: Brazos, 2012), p. 102. Enns is selective in his data as well. His assertion that Adam simply "goes out" from the garden in *Jubilees*, for example, disregards the preceding material in that narrative. The narrative in *Jubilees* does omit verses 8–13, but it does not follow that the couple leave "rather innocently."

A Historical Adam: Major New Testament Passages

1 Corinthians 15

In terms of historical order of the books of the New Testament, 1 Corinthians contains the first reference by Paul to "Adam." Chapter 15 deals with the question of the nature of the resurrection from the dead. It appears that some in Corinth were denying the bodily resurrection of the dead.[11] In this lengthy passage, Paul challenges this assertion on a number of fronts. He refers twice to Adam in verse 22 and verse 45. In verses 20–22, Paul writes,

> But in fact Christ has been raised from the dead, the firstfruits of those who have fallen asleep. For as by a man came death, by a man has come also the resurrection of the dead. For as in Adam all die, so also in Christ shall all be made alive.[12]

As Paul asserts the surety of Christ's Resurrection from the dead, he draws the readers' attention to the implication for all Christians: Christ has been raised and is the firstfruits of the Resurrection. Paul supports this assertion by noting the correspondence between death coming by a man and the resurrection by a man. As the firstfruits, Christ's Resurrection anticipates the rest of the harvest, an implication that Paul makes explicit in verse 22.

Regarding the words "by a man" in verse 21, commentators are likely correct in noting the emphasis on the necessity of the incarnation — since death came about *by a man*, it was necessary for the resurrection to come *by a man* as well.[13] This initial clause could be translated as "by man came death," which communicates the human source. Verse 22 ("for as in Adam . . ."), however, makes the identification clear. In these two verses, Paul uses both the generic term for "man" (*anthrōpos*) as well as the personal name "Adam." It is through a human being that death has come, and it is specifically in Adam that all die. This identification of the "man" through whom death has come with "Adam" reflects the narrative in Genesis 2–3 and is consistent with the statement Paul will make later in 15:45. Although Paul's focus in 15:20–22 is upon the reality enacted through the coming and Resurrection of Christ, this new life is necessary due to the present state of humanity, which Paul connects here with Adam. Paul does not make explicit in verses 20–22 the relationship between Adam's transgression and the consequence

11. On the situation in Corinth, see Gordon D. Fee, *The First Epistle to the Corinthians*, NICNT, 2nd ed. (Grand Rapids, MI: Eerdmans, 2014), p. 793–796.
12. Unless otherwise noted, Scripture verses are from the English Standard Version.
13. See Fee, *First Epistle to the Corinthians*, p. 751. The author of Hebrews likewise appeals to the necessity of the incarnation (i.e., Hebrews 2:14–18).

of death, but this connection is made clear, as will be seen, in Paul's discussion in Romans 5. Here, however, Paul's point is that all humanity, in solidarity with Adam, is subject to death, and that those in solidarity with Christ by faith experience the effects of His Resurrection from the dead. Paul continues in 15:42–49:

> So is it with the resurrection of the dead. What is sown is perishable; what is raised is imperishable. It is sown in dishonor; it is raised in glory. It is sown in weakness; it is raised in power. It is sown a natural body; it is raised a spiritual body. If there is a natural body, there is also a spiritual body. Thus it is written, "The first man Adam became a living being"; the last Adam became a life-giving spirit. But it is not the spiritual that is first but the natural, and then the spiritual. The first man was from the earth, a man of dust; the second man is from heaven. As was the man of dust, so also are those who are of the dust, and as is the man of heaven, so also are those who are of heaven. Just as we have borne the image of the man of dust, we shall also bear the image of the man of heaven.

The purpose of this study does not permit an explanation upon the nature of this resurrected body, which is Paul's central focus in this section.[14] But note Paul's explicit mention of Adam. Paul refers to the creation of man in Genesis 2:7 and identifies the "first man Adam" by name in order to draw a contrast with the last Adam, Christ. A comparison of Paul's clear reference to Genesis 2:7 with the Hebrew and Greek texts of the Old Testament helps to clarify Paul's view on this matter.

In the Hebrew text, the term *adam* is used, a term that could be translated either as "man" (in a generic sense) or as "Adam" (as a personal name). In translating the Hebrew *adam* into Greek, generally speaking, the Septuagint employs two different terms, *anthrōpos* ("man") and *Adam* (the name "Adam"), depending on the context. In this case, the Septuagint of Genesis 2:7 uses *anthrōpos* ("man") to translate the Hebrew term *adam*. Paul's quotation of Genesis 2:7 is notable for two reasons. First, Paul includes the adjective "first" (*prōtos*). The inclusion of this adjective anticipates contrast with Christ, "the last Adam," in the second part of 1 Corinthians 15:45, and can also be understood as addressing the "first" man in the Genesis narrative. Second, Paul includes both the Greek noun "man" (*anthrōpos*) and the personal name Adam (*Adam*). The remainder of the quotation in 1

14. This discussion in 15:42–49 appears to be tied to a misunderstanding of the nature of the resurrected body.

Corinthians 15:45 from Genesis 2:7 follows the wording in the Septuagint. It appears that Paul has, unlike the Septuagint, translated the Hebrew term *adam* with *both* possible Greek translations. In doing so, Paul has removed potential ambiguity from the Hebrew text and has identified the first "man" with "Adam."[15]

As he continues in the passage, Paul draws attention to the contrast between Adam and Christ. The first Adam was "natural," of dust,[16] and became a "living being." The last Adam is "spiritual,"[17] "of heaven," and a "life-giving spirit."[18] In drawing this contrast, Paul demonstrates our participation in the Resurrection of Christ, as Christians will bear the image of the man of heaven. This Resurrection is characterized not by the limitation of natural man but by the full experience of the Spirit in a body raised in glory.

In 1 Corinthians 15, it is clear that Paul articulates the significance of Christ's work using the historical man Adam as the point of contrast. For Paul, Adam is not merely a "symbol" or "figure" to contrast with Christ but also the explanation for the predicament faced by all who follow Adam.[19] D.A. Carson argues here:

> . . . the point of the argument is not simply that Christ has introduced a new historical factor into the status quo of universal sin, but that just as all death can trace its roots back to one man, so all resurrection from the dead can trace its roots back to one man. Contextually, Paul's argument for the resurrection of Christ's people depends on the resurrection of Christ; and the structure of this resurrection argument depends on the parallel structure, viz: that all

---

15. Such an identification is in agreement with the narrative in Genesis and with the flow of thought in 1 Corinthians 15. See Robert W. Yarbrough, "Adam in the New Testament," in *Adam, the Fall, and Original Sin: Theological, Biblical, and Scientific Perspectives*, eds. Hans Madueme and Michael Reeves (Grand Rapids, MI: Baker Academic, 2014), p. 34–35.
16. Cf. Genesis 2:7.
17. This should not be read as "non-corporeal" but rather as affirming the relationship of the control of the Spirit with the resurrected body. See Fee, *First Epistle to the Corinthians*, p. 786; Anthony C. Thiselton, *The First Epistle to the Corinthians*, NIGTC (Grand Rapids, MI: Eerdmans, 2013), p. 1276–1281.
18. The view that Paul was utilizing some form of an Urmensch or "primal man" cannot be sustained, and Paul's description of Christ as the "last Adam" is sufficiently explained in its connection with the Genesis text. So Yarbrough, "Adam in the New Testament," p. 46–47; James D. G. Dunn, "1 Corinthians 15:45 — Last Adam, Life-giving Spirit," in *Christ and Spirit in the New Testament: Studies in Honor of Charles Frances Digby Moule*, eds. Barnabas Lindars and Stephen S. Smalley (Cambridge, England: Cambridge University Press, 1973), p. 136.
19. Contrast C.K. Barrett, *A Commentary on the First Epistle to the Corinthians*, Harper New Testament Commentaries (Peabody, MA: Hendrickson, 1987), p. 352.

participate in death because of the introduction by Adam of death as a kind of firstfruits.[20]

Looking at verses 21 and 22, in particular, the parallelism between the two statements affirms this conclusion. If Paul was simply comparing a general human source of sin and then the importance of Christ coming as a man to deal with this, verse 21 would have been sufficient. Verse 22 removes any ambiguity by tying "death," and therefore the reason for Christ's defeat of death, to Adam.[21]

Romans 5

As in 1 Corinthians 15, Paul contrasts Adam and Christ in Romans 5:12–21. Although Paul does not use the term "last Adam" here, it is clear that this passage demonstrates the same theological conviction as does 1 Corinthians 15. Christ comes as the one whose work addresses the problems associated with Adam. Paul writes in Romans 5:12–14,

> Therefore, just as sin came into the world through one man, and death through sin, and so death spread to all men because all sinned — for sin indeed was in the world before the law was given, but sin is not counted where there is no law. Yet death reigned from Adam to Moses, even over those whose sinning was not like the transgression of Adam, who was a type of the one who was to come.

Three key aspects of Paul's discussion here should be noted. First, as in 1 Corinthians 15, Paul is concerned in Romans 5 more broadly with the salvific effects of Christ's actions. While it contains an allusion to the Resurrection in Paul's references to "life" (5:17 and also in view in 6:5; 8:11, 23), Paul focuses on the "gift" bringing "justification" and being "made righteous" as well. Secondly, the Adam/Christ contrast reflects the wider concerns of Paul with the universal problem of sin (1:18–3:20) and the offer to all, regardless of ethnic background, of salvation on the basis of faith in Christ.[22] At this point in his argument, Paul appeals to Christ's work in undoing the effects of Adam's sin in providing the salvation and reconciliation that he has asserted in Romans 5:6–11. Finally, although the focus is on Christ, what Paul says about Adam plays a central role in his argument.

---

20. D.A. Carson, "Adam and the Epistles of Paul," in *In the Beginning . . . A Symposium on the Bible and Creation*, ed. N.M. de. S. Cameron (Glasgow, Scotland: The Biblical Creation Society, 1980), p. 31.
21. See ibid., 31; see also Fee, *First Epistle to the Corinthians*, p. 751.
22. This is reflected in the assertion that there is "no distinction" in the offer of the righteousness of God on the basis of faith (Romans 3:22–24).

Paul begins by stating in verse 12 that sin came into the world through one man, and death came about at as result of sin. In 1 Corinthians 15:21–22, Paul drew the connection between death and the man Adam; here the Apostle identifies the connection between sin and death. Verse 12 appears to be an allusion to Genesis 3, and this is confirmed in verse 14 as Paul refers to the transgression of Adam and to the experience of those living (and dying!) between Adam and Moses. The "one man" of verse 12 is Adam, and Paul continues to refer to Adam in the series of contrasts in verses 15 and following.[23] Paul uses several words to describe the actions of Adam — "sin" (*hamartia*), "transgression" (*parabasis*), and "trespass" (*paraptōma*). The act on Adam's part has resulted in death (v. 12, 15 and 17) and condemnation (v. 16 and 18) for all men. Paul is engaging the narrative in Genesis 3 as an explanation for the universal problem of sin and death in the human race.[24]

The argument in verses 12–14 can be potentially confusing, so it deserves a closer examination. Paul asserts in verse 12 that sin entered the world through one man, and death through sin. The second half of verse 12 ("and so death spread to all men because all sinned") has elicited some debate. A strong argument can be made that Paul is speaking of our solidarity with Adam, that is, with him functioning as our representative head.[25] In verses 13–14, Paul addresses the issue of the problem of sin and death prior to the giving of the law. Although sin was not identified as "transgression" or "law-breaking" prior to the law, with the exception of Adam who did transgress the command of God, sin's presence can nevertheless be identified by the continued presence of death. Paul's assertion that "death reigned from Adam to Moses" could in some ways be assumed, since the law was given later, but this could be seen as an allusion to Genesis 5 and the repetition of the phrase in the genealogy "and he died." This then serves

23. Yarbrough stresses the importance of Adam in these subsequent verses, despite not being identified by name. See Yarbrough, "Adam in the New Testament," p. 43. In view of Adam's pervasive role in this section, Yarbrough notes, "Paul's soteriology, Christology, theological anthropology, and hamartiology come together in these ten verses, none of which is intelligible without Adam in his historical existence and real after-effects, which Christ came to address and remedy."

24. Collins rightly notes that this argument gains its coherency from the sequence of events. See C. John Collins, "A Historical Adam: Old-Earth Creation View," in *Four Views on the Historical Adam*, Counterpoints: Bible & Theology, eds. Matthew Barrett and Ardel B. Caneday (Grand Rapids, MI: Zondervan, 2013), p. 163.

25. This seems to be the thrust of the argument concerning the relationship of Christ to the believer. See Thomas Schreiner, "Original Sin and Original Death," in *Adam, the Fall, and Original Sin: Theological, Biblical, and Scientific Perspectives*, eds. Hans Madueme and Michael Reeves (Grand Rapids: Baker Academic, 2014), p. 271–88.

to introduce the far-surpassing salvific work of Christ in the verses that follow.

Although Paul does address sin as the personal actions of an individual (which results in consequences), Paul speaks here not of the individual experience of sin and death but rather traces the problem of sin to its root cause. By tracing the storyline in this passage, the following can be seen:[26]

1. Sin (and death) has entered the world as a result of Adam's transgression/sin/trespass. The fact that sin "came into" the world indicates that sin was not present in the world prior to this act.

2. From this time on, sin (and death) continues, even though human beings are not breaking the law, as the law was not given until the time of Moses.

3. The law was given, which served to increase the trespass rather than deal fully and finally with the problem of sin.

4. Christ has entered the world, and, through His obedience and righteousness, He has provided righteousness and life to all who are in Him.

It can be deduced, then, that Paul presents Adam as a historical figure whose disobedience to God's command resulted in the entrance of sin and death into the world. All of humanity, as a result, continues to suffer from the effects of this transgression. Several challenges have been raised against this interpretation of Paul's theology that need to be addressed.

Major Objections to a Historical Adam in 1 Corinthians 15 and Romans 5

Objection 1: In Paul's theology, the starting point is Christ, not Adam. Has that not driven his theology, rather than the Old Testament text itself?[27]

---

26. Ellis offers the following logical argument: 1) "Death is the penalty of Sin," 2) "Sin is not counted if there is no law," 3) "Yet death came upon people before the law of Moses was given," 4) Death even came upon people who did not sin in the way Adam did, that is, upon infants who had not sinned against the law of conscience or of natural or special revelation," 5) "Hence, their death is the result of Adam's sin." *Paul's Use of the Old Testament*, p. 58–59.

27. Peter Enns, *Evolution of Adam*, p. 82, declares, "In making his case, Paul does not begin with Adam and move to Christ. Rather the reality of the risen Christ drives Paul to mine Scripture for ways of explicating the wholly unexpected in-breaking of the age to come in the crucifixion and resurrection of the Son of God. Adam, read as "the first human" supports Paul's argument about the universal plight and remedy of humanity, but it is not a necessary component for that argument."

This objection deals with several related issues concerning Paul's use of the Old Testament and the development of Paul's Christian theological convictions. Looking at Paul's own history, certain significant theological convictions were present prior to his encounter with the risen Christ on the road to Damascus. By his own confession and the testimony of Luke in the Book of Acts, Paul was a committed Jewish man who held to the worship of the one true God and to the writings comprising the Old Testament as authoritative Scripture. In his encounter with Christ, Paul's assessment of Jesus' divine identity radically changed. As can be seen from Paul's writings, he maintains these pre-existing theological convictions concerning the nature of the Old Testament. Rather than abandoning these Scriptures, Paul affirms throughout his epistles the abiding significance of these writings, a stance that can be seen throughout the New Testament as a whole. As Paul deals with the Old Testament, he approaches it not simply as a set of proof texts to be mined. Rather, he attempts to demonstrate that the gospel, God's work in Christ, provides the proper interpretation of the Old Testament. Paul's discussion of Abraham in Romans 4, for example, can be seen as demonstrating this very thing. The language of Genesis 15:6 provides not simply a helpful analogy or proof text for Paul; instead, it demonstrates the consistency between the Old Testament and the gospel concerning the relationship of faith, works, circumcision, promise, and law.

As discussed above, Paul is doing the same thing in Romans 5:12–21. The recognition of Jesus as Messiah and the effects of His death and Resurrection caused Paul to think more carefully about the problem addressed by Jesus' actions. This does not mean, however, that Paul cannot think critically about the nature of the account in Genesis 3. For Paul, there is coherence between the Old Testament and God's work in Christ. The actions taken by Christ address the very real problem of sin and death, which entered the world through the actions of Adam. Although Paul's focus in Romans 5 and 1 Corinthians 15 is upon the outcome of Christ's work, that work is addressing the continued problem of sin and death that entered the world through Adam's transgression.

Objection 2: Is not Paul merely accommodating the view of his day?

Some have argued that Paul's view of a historical Adam can be abandoned today because he was simply accommodating the cultural views of the day. Denis Lamoureux argues that even though Paul refers to a historical Adam, two reasons suggest that Christians do not have to take this at face value. First, every first-century Jew believed this, suggesting that Paul was simply reflecting the only view of his day.[28] Second, he says that if Christians accept Paul's view of Adam, they must accept Paul's view of a "3-tier universe" as depicted in Philippians 2:10.[29]

On the first of these concerns, Lamoureux cites Collins, saying he provides "solid evidence,"[30] but Collins doesn't give enough of a treatment of Philo as discussed in this chapter.[31] Jewish thought was more diverse than Collins asserts, and Paul's line of interpretation is in keeping with the dominant, though not exclusive, view of the day. On the second concern noted by Lamoureux, further consideration must be given to the argument of Philippians 2. Paul's description of "in heaven and on earth and under the earth" (Philippians 2:10) is really an elaboration of the word "every" (*pas*). The whole point is "universal homage"[32] being given to Christ. To take Paul's words in this (presumed) hymn in an overly literal way is unfair to Paul.

Objection 3: Does our own ongoing experience with sin really necessitate a historical Adam? Isn't Adam simply an analogy of the problem of individual sin? Doesn't Paul just provide a literary pattern illustrating the point that sin leads to consequences?

Everyone taking a realistic look at their own lives should be able to admit the reality of the presence of sin and its effects. Are individuals not culpable for their own sin? Paul has made the argument in the first three chapters of Romans that both Gentiles and Jews are under sin. In Romans 1:18–32, Paul points to a number of behaviors demonstrating the sinfulness of the Gentiles.[33] In Romans 2:1–3:8, Paul challenges the notion that the Jewish individual is exempt from God's judgment on the basis of the possession of the law or the practice of physical circumcision. He then demonstrates in Romans 3:9–20 that the Old Testament likewise affirms the assessment that

28. Denis O. Lamoureux, "No Historical Adam: Evolutionary Creation View," in *Four Views on the Historical Adam*, eds. Matthew Barrett and Ardel B. Caneday (Grand Rapids, MI: Zondervan, 2013), p. 61.
29. Ibid., p. 48–49, 61–62.
30. Ibid., p. 61.
31. C. John Collins, *Did Adam and Eve Really Exist? Who They Were and Why You Should Care* (Wheaton, IL: Crossway, 2011), p. 75. Although Philo does distinguish between a "heavenly man" and an "earthly man" in *Leg.* 1.31, the references in *Legum Allegoriae* 3.76 and *De Opificio Mundi* 165 reflect a non-literal interpretation by Philo.
32. Gordon D. Fee, *Paul's Letter to the Philippians. NICNT* (Grand Rapids, MI: Eerdmans), p. 224-225.
33. Paul's assessment in 1:18–32 is in keeping with the assessment of the author of *Wisdom of Solomon*, who likewise condemns the nations for the sinful acts stemming from idolatry (see *Wisdom of Solomon* 13–14).

both Jews and Gentiles are all under sin.[34] It appears evident in Paul's writings, and in Scripture as a whole, that individuals are responsible for their own sin before God. In individual human experience, the pattern of Adam can be seen — temptation, sin, and consequences. Some have suggested that in 1 John 2:16 the Apostle may be alluding to this pattern present in Genesis 3.[35] Although this pattern can be seen in this sense, this does not exclude a historical fall as depicted in Genesis 3. Rather, Genesis 3 provides the historical explanation for the universality of human sin. Those who continue to sin and continue to die do so as a result of Adam's sin.

The Testimony of the Rest of the New Testament

Outside of the two major passages that demonstrate the importance of viewing Adam as a historical individual, the first man, who sinned and corrupted all his posterity, the New Testament contains several direct and indirect references to Adam (and Eve) that can be used to show this as well. Standing alone, these are not equally convincing. The previous two passages provide the evidence for the most compelling arguments. However, the following passages are relevant and function to support the conclusions reached above.

Direct References

First Timothy 2:11–14 has been a key passage in the debate over the proper role of women ministering in the local church. The way in which this passage may or may not restrict the role of a woman is irrelevant to the purpose at hand. However, the premise Paul provides for his command is relevant. So regardless of how someone interprets and applies the restriction Paul gives about a woman teaching or having authority over a man, the underlying reason Paul provides for this command is very important for the topic of a historical Adam. Paul follows the restriction with a Greek conjunction (*gar*). This conjunction typically "introduces explanatory material that strengthens or supports what precedes."[36] Levinsohn expands on this understanding: "Background material introduced by γάρ provides explanations or expositions of the previous assertion. . . . The presence of γάρ constrains the material that it introduces to be interpreted as *strengthening* some aspect of the previous

34. The catena of Scripture in 3:10–18 asserts that what is said of the "fool" and the "wicked" in the Old Testament is true of "all."

35. Raymond E. Brown, *The Epistles of John*, Anchor Bible Commentary 30 (New York, NY: Doubleday, 1982), p. 310.

36. Steven E. Runge, *Discourse Grammar of the Greek New Testament: A Practical Introduction for Teaching and Exegesis* (Peabody, MA: Hendrikson, 2010), p. 54.

assertion, rather than as distinctive information."[37] Many times the connection is not just one sentence, but multiple sentences or the following paragraph. In 1 Timothy 2, verses 13–14 provide the material to strengthen Paul's previous assertion in verse 12: "For Adam was formed first, then Eve; and Adam was not deceived, but the woman was deceived and became a transgressor."

The first explanation provided by Paul to strengthen his assertion is that Adam was formed before Eve. Paul is appealing to the account in Genesis 2:20–23 where the creation of Eve is explained. Genesis makes it clear that man (Adam) was created before woman (Eve). Paul goes back to before the Fall and explains that the created order of humans is one reason behind his explanations for the prohibition given in verse 12. However one understands what Paul is trying to prove, it rests upon a false pretense if there was not a literal creation of Adam before Eve. His entire argument proves to be unconvincing. Schreiner's conclusion is prudent: "Paul maintains that the Genesis narrative gives a reason why women should not teach men: Adam was created first and then Eve."[38]

Connecting the second reason Paul gives in verse 14 for his prohibition is much more difficult. While several perspectives have been proposed, the logic provided by Barnett and Schreiner appears to be the most convincing. The verse emphasizes the deception of Eve by the serpent. This is a reference to Eve's own admission in Genesis 3:13. In fact, since "the woman" isn't given the name "Eve" until Genesis 3:20, Paul avoids it here.[39] Instead, Paul refers to her using the same word (*gunē*) as the Septuagint, but he slightly modifies the verb, prefixing it with the preposition *ek*.[40] It seems slightly more likely that he does this to emphatically stress the degree to which Eve was deceived by the serpent. So even though Paul says Eve was deceived (probably a reference to her being deceived *first*), that does not mean that Adam was not also deceived in some way. Romans 5 makes it clear that

37. Stephen H. Levinsohn, *Discourse Features of New Testament Greek: A Coursebook on the Information Structure of New Testament Greek*, 2nd ed. (Dallas, TX: SIL International, 2000), p. 91.

38. Thomas R. Schreiner, "An Interpretation of 1 Timothy 2:9–15: A Dialogue with Scholarship," in *Women in the Church: An Analysis and Application of 1 Timothy 2:9–15*, 2nd ed., eds. Andreas J. Köstenberger and Thomas R. Schreiner (Grand Rapids, MI: Baker, 2005), p. 105.

39. As will be explored in turn, 2 Corinthians 11:3 indicates that Paul identifies the "woman" in Genesis 3:13 as "Eve."

40. Paul had several words he could use to communicate the concept of deception. The nouns include *planos* (2x in NT), *planē* (4x in Paul), *phrenapatēs* (1x in NT [in the Pastoral Epistles]), and *apatē* (3x in Paul); the verbs include *planaō* (6x in Paul; 3x in Pastoral Epistles), *apoplanaō* (2x in NT; 1x in Pastoral Epistles), and *phrenapataō* (1x in Paul), *apataō* (2x in Paul; 1x in Pastoral Epistles), and *exapataō* (6x in Paul; 1x in Pastoral Epistles).

sin entered the world through Adam, not through Eve. So the serpent approached Eve to deceive her, and Paul uses this detail from Genesis 3 to advocate for male leadership in verse 12. Paul is explaining that the pattern of male leadership, which was before the Fall (as verse 13 explained), was subverted in Genesis 3.

Regardless how one applies the restriction in verse 12 today, whether it is explained as a permanent universal principle, a temporary restriction based upon the poor education of women, or temporary prohibition due to women being false teachers in first century Ephesus, the basis for Paul's restriction is his appeal to the historical account regarding Adam and Eve.[41] Carson concludes: "If there were no Adam and Eve at the head of the race, no fall, no creation narratives as recorded in Gen. 1–3, Paul's argument would simply not hold up: its basis would have been destroyed."[42]

In Luke 3:38, Adam is explicitly identified as an ancestor of Jesus in a genealogy. While Hendriksen's traditional explanation of this as the family line of Mary is a plausible explanation for the list of names,[43] it most likely refers to Joseph's line.[44] In introducing the genealogy, Luke 3:23 says, "being the son (as was supposed) of Joseph." Luke uses the Greek verb translated "supposed" (*nomizō*) more frequently than any other writer in the New Testament.[45] He uses it when the thing "supposed" or "assumed" is incorrect, as in Luke 2:44; Acts 7:25, 8:20, 14:19, 16:27, 17:29, 21:29.[46] In other words, this assumption that Jesus was the biological son of Joseph was not correct. This is a good example of how meticulous Luke was being as he introduced and constructed the genealogy. Joseph was not Jesus' biological father (hence, the virgin birth), but the genealogy that follows is based on Joseph's lineage. Bock adds: "In the first century, legal status depended on the father."[47]

Many of the names in the genealogy are previously unknown, though at points it converges with the genealogy in Matthew's Gospel. Luke includes this genealogy for a very specific reason, which merges with a

41. Note that Enns, *Evolution of Adam*, p. 150, n. 10, believes that this "brief comment adds nothing of importance to the topic that is the focus of this book."
42. Carson, "Adam in the Epistles of Paul," p. 38.
43. William Hendriksen, *Exposition of the Gospel according to Luke*, New Testament Commentary (Grand Rapids, MI: Baker, 1978), p. 222–25.
44. See Darrell L. Bock, *Luke*, Baker Exegetical Commentary on the New Testament (Grand Rapids, MI: Baker, 1994), p. 1:352; Mark L. Strauss, *Four Portraits, One Jesus: A Survey of Jesus and the Gospels* (Grand Rapids, MI: Zondervan, 2007), p. 412–415.
45. Of the 15 uses, Luke accounts for 9.
46. Only the use in Acts 16:13 is ambiguous.
47. Bock, *Luke*, p. 1:352.

major emphasis of his presentation of the life of Christ: "the Lucan concern for Gentiles."[48] Luke's emphasis is "a universal application of the gospel,"[49] and that is related to the fact that Jesus, the Savior of the world, has Adam as his ancestor.[50] Given that Luke begins his gospel by telling his readers that he investigated everything very carefully to give them accurate truth about Jesus (1:3–4), it is clear that he is presenting this list of ancestors as completely historical. Independent affirmations of Jesus as the descendent of David (e.g., Romans 1:3; Revelation 5:5, 22:16) or a member of the tribe of Judah (Hebrews 7:14; Revelation 5:5) in the New Testament argue against the view that this is a mere literary creation of Luke. Additionally, if Adam is merely a symbol rather than a historical individual, it is difficult to ascertain where the historical figures start and stop in this list. Was Abraham simply a literary figure? What about David? Indeed, if any man in the genealogy is not historical, including Adam, then Jesus is descended from a myth or a metaphor and therefore not truly man and therefore not our Redeemer.

Adam is referred to as "the son of God." While this finds no parallel in ancient genealogies, it probably has two important implications for this study. First, this phrase probably means that Luke is declaring that Adam was the result of the direct creation by God. Second, by bestowing this title on Adam, Luke invites a comparison between Adam as "son of God" and Jesus as "son of God."[51] Strauss concludes: "Whereas Adam, the first son of God, failed in his obedience to God, Jesus, the true Son of God, succeeds when tested."[52] What Luke is trying to accomplish with this genealogy, and by referring to Adam as the "son of God," fails, if Adam was not a real man in history.

In 2 Corinthians 11:3, Paul warns that the way the serpent deceived Eve (by getting her to doubt and then deny God's Word) is also how Satan (cf. 11:14) will attempt to deceive the Corinthians and all Paul's readers since then. The verb used to describe Eve being deceived (*exapataō*) is the same verb used in 1 Timothy 2:14 to describe Eve being deceived.[53] While this

48. Ibid., p. 1:360.
49. Mark Strauss, "Luke," in *Zondervan Illustrated Bible Background Commentary*, vol. 1, ed. Clinton E. Arnold (Grand Rapids, MI: Zondervan, 2002), p. 358.
50. See Bock, *Luke*, p. 1:348, 360; Yarbrough, "Adam in the New Testament," p. 40–41.
51. See Luke 1:35; 4:3, 9, 41; 22:70 for possible references to Jesus as "son of God" in Luke.
52. Strauss, "Luke," p. 358.
53. The word used to describe Adam being deceived is similar, without the prefixed preposition (*ek*). The form with the preposition (used of Eve) could be an emphatic reference to deception or it could simply be synonymous with the uncompounded form. See conclusion above. For a brief discussion, see George W. Knight III, *The Pastoral Epistles: A Commentary on the Greek Text*, NIGTC (Grand Rapids, MI: Eerdmans, 1992), p. 144.

text does not reference Adam, Paul refers to the narrative in Genesis 3 and Eve to warn the Corinthians. This verse fits comfortably within a framework that acknowledges a historical Adam.

In Jude 14, the author reflects on the Old Testament genealogies in Genesis 5 and 1 Chronicles 1 in identifying Enoch as the seventh from Adam. This is used to introduce a quote from 1 Enoch 1:9.[54] Jews counted inclusively, meaning that they included the first and last in a series. When the names are listed in order (Adam, Seth, Enosh, Kenan, Mahalalel, Jared, and Enoch), Enoch is the seventh. It was not uncommon for Jewish writers to focus on Enoch being the "seventh," since that number was the symbol for perfection.[55] The fact that Jude cites 1 Enoch does not mean that he believed that the Enoch of Genesis wrote the book.[56] However, Jude refers to the Exodus from Egypt (v. 5), the judgment of Sodom and Gomorrah (v. 7), the death of Moses (v. 9), and the sins of Cain, Balaam, and Korah (v. 11) as historical events. Because of this, it is very likely Jude did believe that Enoch was the seventh generation after Adam. There is nothing in Jude that would contradict the idea of a historical Adam.

Indirect References

While direct references are probably considered to be the most helpful in the debate regarding the historical Adam, indirect references are supportive of the conclusions reached above.[57] In Paul's speech to the Athenians in Acts 17, he states: "And he made from one man every nation of mankind to live on all the face of the earth, having determined allotted periods and the boundaries of their dwelling place" (Acts 17:26, ESV).[58] Although some have suggested that Paul is referring to the general Hellenistic notions of

54. For a helpful discussion on Jude's use of 1 Enoch, see Thomas R. Schreiner, *1, 2 Peter, Jude,* NAC (Nashville, TN: Broadman & Holman, 2003), p. 468–70.
55. See Douglas J. Moo, "Jude," in *Zondervan Illustrated Bible Backgrounds Commentary: Hebrews to Revelation*, vol. 4, ed. Clinton E. Arnold (Grand Rapid, MI: Zondervan, 2002), p. 240.
56. See Schreiner, *1, 2 Peter, Jude*, p. 470–71.
57. Dunn has suggested that Romans 7:7–25 and Philippians 2:5–11 should be considered allusions to Adam or to Christ as the second Adam (in the case of Philippians 2). In both cases, the identification is not convincing and will not be considered in this section. See James D.G. Dunn, *The Theology of Paul the Apostle* (Grand Rapids, MI: Eerdmans, 2006), p. 103–104, 114–121.
58. The earliest and best Greek manuscripts do not contain the word "blood," including ℵ (300s), B (300s), A (400s), and 𝔓76 (600s). Most English translations agree with these manuscripts, including the HCSB, ESV, NASB, NET, NLT, and NIV. Other translations (including the KJV and NKJV) side with the evidence for including "blood," which includes D (400s) and E (probably 500s). Either way, based upon the above analysis of Romans 5 and 1 Corinthians 15, we can be certain the reference is to Adam. Paul clearly believed that Adam was the father of the human race.

common ancestry, it is more likely that Paul is referring to Adam.[59] The Greek word for "one" is defined as "a single entity."[60] Paul is making a strong allusion back to Adam as the founding figure of the entire human race. Luke has already indicated that the human race descended from one man, Adam, in Luke 3:38. Also, Paul uses the same Greek word for "one man" in Romans 5:17a twice: "For if, because of one man's trespass, death reigned through that one man." The "one man" in Romans 5:17a is a reference to Adam and is contrasted with the "one man" of 5:17b: Jesus Christ (cf. Acts 17:31).

In Matthew 19:4–6, Jesus is asked a question about divorce. He answered the Pharisees' question by quoting from Genesis 1:27 and 2:24 to say that God created the first two humans as "male and female," and He created marriage as a covenantal, life-long union of one man and one woman. Jesus also mentioned "the beginning," which the Gospel of Mark clarifies as a reference to "the beginning of creation" (Mark 10:6). Jesus viewed the creations of Adam and Eve and the first marriage as historical accounts that could be used for theological argumentation. If the creation of Adam and Eve and marriage, as described in Genesis, were fictitious events, then Jesus' argument holds no weight.[61] If Jesus believed in the creation of Adam and Eve, Christians today should as well.

In Ephesians 5:28, Paul explains the obligation that husbands have to love their wives. He then constructs the following argument: 1) a husband loves his own body; 2) loving his wife is actually loving himself; 3) nobody hates his own flesh; 4) Genesis 2:24 demonstrates that husband and wife are one flesh.[62] Paul's basis for obligating a husband to love his wife[63] is that God

59. See Joseph Fitzmyer, *The Acts of the Apostles*, The Anchor Bible (New York, NY: Doubleday, 1998), p. 609; I. Howard Marshall, *Acts*, Tyndale New Testament Commentaries 5 (Grand Rapids, MI: Eerdmans, 1999), p. 287; Ben Witherington, *The Acts of the Apostles: A Socio-Rhetorical Commentary* (Grand Rapids, MI: Eerdmans, 1998), p. 526.

60. William Arndt, Frederick W. Danker, and Walter Bauer, *A Greek-English Lexicon of the New Testament and Other Early Christian Literature* (Chicago, IL: University of Chicago Press, 2000), p. 291–92.

61. Paul likewise appeals to Genesis 2:24 as providing instruction concerning sexual ethics in 1 Corinthians 6:16. Although he does not directly address Adam and Eve, his view of sexual intercourse is consistent with the view articulated in the accounts in Matthew and Mark. In his instructions concerning marriage and singleness in 1 Corinthians 7, Paul, in his statement in verse 10 ("not I, but the Lord"), appears to allude to this teaching of Jesus.

62. For a similar view on Paul's argumentation, see Stephen E. Fowl, *Ephesians: A Commentary*, The New Testament Library (Louisville, KY: Westminster John Knox Press, 2012), p. 191.

63. While Ephesians 5:25 contains an explicit command for a husband to love his wife, verse 5:28 contains an indicative verb with a complementary infinitive which has the pragmatic impact of a command, though technically there is no imperative verb form in the verse.

joined Adam and Eve in the first marriage. If they were not real, historical people, then Paul's argument becomes simply a literary expression, undermining the force of the command.

Finally, Paul's discussion of head coverings in 1 Corinthians 11:2–16 refers to the creation of man and woman in Genesis 2. This passage is a challenging text in many regards, but Paul's argument reflects a concern for the historical order of events in Genesis. Paul identifies man as the "image and glory of God" and woman as the "glory of man" (1 Cor. 11:7).[64] His description of woman as created from man and for man (1 Cor. 11:8–9) reflects the narrative of the creation of Eve in Genesis 2:18–25. The woman, according to Paul, was created from man (and not vice-versa), and this argument reflects the order of the events in Genesis 2, as the woman was formed after the creation of the man (Gen. 2:7–8, 18–29). The creation of the woman "for" man reflects God's assessment of the need for a "helper" for the man in Genesis 2:20. Lest this be misunderstood, though, Paul affirms the mutual interdependence of men and women in Christ. The process of procreation continues to bear this out, as men are now born from women (1 Cor. 11:11–12). At the very least, the rejection of this cultural symbol disregards the unique nature of men and women and the reality that both are the glory of another.[65] Although in Christ justification is now offered equally to both man and woman (see Galatians 3:23–29), the gospel does not lessen the distinctive glory that men and women possess. For the purpose of the present discussion, Paul's argument affirms the narrative order concerning the creation of man and woman as described in Genesis 2.

Conclusion

Is the historical nature of Adam an important question? By all means it is, since one's view of Adam has important implications for areas of theology and ethics. The New Testament authors appeal to the opening chapters of Genesis on issues related to our understanding of sin, the problem of death, the atoning work of Christ, the resurrection from the dead, sexuality and marriage, and issues of race. The gospel itself is impacted by one's view on Adam. If the historical Adam did not exist, then the historical Christ did not

64. The "image of God" in verse 7 is a reference to Genesis 1:26–27. The omission of "image" with regard to the woman isn't to deny that women are created in the image of God, a fact that Genesis 1:27 makes clear. Rather, Paul's focus is upon the "glory" present in each. See David E. Garland, *1 Corinthians*, Baker Exegetical Commentary on the New Testament (Grand Rapids, MI: Baker, 2003), p. 522–523.

65. See Garland, *1 Corinthians*, p. 524; Thiselton, *The First Epistle to the Corinthians*, p. 834.

need to come to redeem a human race that inherited Adam's sinful nature and guilt.

Several pieces of evidence from the New Testament indicate that Paul, Jesus, and other New Testament authors affirmed a historical Adam. In a brief fashion, some of the major objections to this have been answered. The importance of this can be seen in the many implications this topic has for several areas of theology. Most directly, according to 1 Corinthians 15 and Romans 5, Paul appeals to Adam's disobedience in explaining the need for Christ's redeeming actions on our behalf. Jesus, as the Last Adam, has initiated the age to come, defeating death and providing salvation for all who repent of their sins and trust in Him as Savior and Lord.

Chapter 3

Adam's Place in the History of the Church's Theology

by Dr. Tom Nettles

Debates over the nature of the church brought numerous divisions in Reformation Christianity in the 16th and 17th centuries. One of these groups, the English Separatists, described their differences with Anglicans and Puritans in 29 articles of their confession of faith. Before the differences, however, they emphasized points of agreement in 16 articles. Central to these common places was commitment to a literal Adam and Eve and their determinative place in the history of the world.

> 4. That in the beginning God made all things of nothing very good: and created man after his own image and likeness in righteousnes and holines of truth. That streight ways after by the subtiltie of the Serpent which Sathan used as his instrument himself with his Angells having sinned before and not kept their first estate, but left their own habitation; first Eva, then Adam by hir meanes, did wittingly & willingly fall into disobedience & transgression of the commandement of God. For the which death reigned over all: yea even over infants also, which have not sinned, after the lyke maner of the transgression of Adam, that is, actually: Yet are all since the fall of Adam begotten in his own likenes after his image, being conceyved and borne in iniquitie, and soo by nature the children of wrath and servants of sinne, and subiect to death, and all other calamities due unto sinne in this world and for ever.[1]

1. William L. Lumpkin, *Baptist Confessions of Faith* (Valley Forge, PA: Judson Press, 1969), 83. Original spelling maintained with the exception of the inconsistent exchanges of "u" and "v."

Affirmed in this brief article are *fiat ex nihilo creation*, the original holiness and righteousness of the first humans, Adam and Eve, the fall of Satan and his angels, his provocation of the Fall of humanity, and the natural and covenantal headship of Adam in relation to the moral standing of every individual human being. This basic view of Adam's place of priority both racially and theologically prevailed in Christian confession well into the 19th century except among those who were "nominal Christians . . . openly Socinian, deist, agnostic, or atheist, despite their church affiliations."[2] When expositors and theologians in historically orthodox denominations adopted the epistemological and philosophical views of naturalistic science, the theological implications created views unrecognizable as historic confessional Christianity. That is the thesis of this chapter. It will be illustrated through the views of selected Christian thinkers from the patristic era through the early 20th century.

Adam Before Augustine

Apostolic exegesis of Genesis brought into focus the importance of Adam and the depth of meaning deposited in his disobedience. Paul's arguments in Romans 5 and 1 Corinthians 15 in particular gave the historical narrative of Adam a peculiarly important place in the Old Testament preparation for the New. The sentence, "For as in Adam all die, even so in Christ shall all be made alive" (1 Corinthians 15:22; KJV), served as hermeneutical dynamite for giving determinative importance to those events surrounding the creation of Adam, his divinely established marriage to Eve, the stipulations that were to govern his treatment of the rest of creation, and the consequences of his disobedience. All Christian commentators, therefore, have necessarily been drawn to seek to understand the place of Adam in God's purpose for the world.

Patristic writers, working from an assumption of the theological connectedness of all Scripture, fill their comments on the creation, Adam, Eve,

2. William VanDoodewaard, *The Quest for the Historical Adam* (Grand Rapids, MI: Reformation Heritage Books, 2015), p. 131. This book is a massively documented historical discussion of "Genesis commentary on human origins from the patristic era to the present" (p. 8). Focusing mainly on hermeneutics and the acceptance or rejection of a literal, historical Adam, VanDoodewaard naturally and inevitably moves into the theological implications of hermeneutical changes. The philosophical and scientific milieu from which these changes developed constitutes the burden of the argument. His conclusion that "the literal tradition on Genesis and human origins coheres with the Genesis text and the Adam it reveals [and] maintains the beginning components of a revealed unity of truth: a holistic, historic Christian theology from the word of God" (p. 312) is consistent with my own study and the simple thesis of this skeletal presentation of a bulky, muscular issue.

and the Fall with spiritual discussions and typological relations. They interacted with the pagan philosophies of the day as well as latent heresies, and sought to establish the unique sovereignty of God over the creation, the unicity, and the triunity of God, and His calling all things into being out of nothing. The Genesis account is nothing less than a historical narrative, even though it is much more.[3]

Clement of Rome (ca A.D. 96) highlighted the noxious influence of jealousy that has "estranged wives from their husbands and annulled the saying of our father Adam, 'This is now bone of my bones and flesh of my flesh.' " From the story of Cain and Abel he concluded, "jealousy and envy brought about a brother's murder." In writing of God's particular grace given through Christ, Clement reminded his readers, "All the generations from Adam to this day have passed away but those who by God's grace were perfected in love have a place among the godly, who will be revealed when the kingdom of Christ visits us."[4]

Justin Martyr (100–165) gave an oblique reference to Adam and the Fall in contending that a prophecy of Christ was given 5,000 years before he appeared.[5] In his *Dialogue with Trypho the Jew*, Justin made the fall of Satan and Adam as vitally connected to the sin of the race and the coming of Christ:

> He [Christ] submitted to be born and to be crucified, not because He needed such things, but because of the human race, which from Adam had fallen under the power of death and the guile of the serpent, and each one of which had committed personal transgression.[6]

Irenaeus (ca. 140–202) established a strong connection between Adam and biblical theology. For the full truthfulness of Irenaeus' doctrinal rubric of recapitulation (that is, Christ became the head of the race for the purpose of restoring what Adam lost) nothing ahistorical about Adam could be tolerated. He was created from unspoiled virgin soil since it had not yet rained

---

3. *Ancient Christian Commentary on Scripture: Genesis 1-11*, ed. Andrew Louth, gen. ed. Thomas C. Oden (Downers Grove, IL: InterVarsity Press, 2001), p. 1–102.
4. Clement of Rome, "Letter to the Corinthians," in J.B. Lightfoot and J.R. Harmer, trans., Michael W. Holmes, ed. and rev. *The Apostolic Fathers*, second edition (Grand Rapids, MI: Baker Book House, 1989), p. 30–31, 56.
5. Justin Martyr, *The First and Second Apologies*, trans Leslie William Bernard (New York, NY: Paulist Press, 1997), p. 44.
6. http://www.earlychristianwritings.com/text/justinmartyr-dialoguetrypho.html, accessed on March 8, 2016.

and no man had tilled the ground, just as Christ, the second Adam, was born of Mary while she still was a virgin.[7] "The second Adam, Christ, came in the same flesh as that of the first Adam, and as ours."[8] It is not so much that Christ's incarnation reflected Adam's creation, but that Adam's creation was in the image of Christ, and was for the purpose of setting the stage for the appearance of the Son of God.

> And as the protoplast himself, Adam, had his substance from untilled and as yet virgin soil ("For God had not yet sent rain, and man had not tilled the ground") and was formed by the hand of God, that is, by the Word of God, for "all things were made by Him," and the Lord took dust from the earth and formed man; so did He who is the Word recapitulating Adam in Himself, rightly receive a birth, enabling Him to gather up Adam [into himself], from Mary, who was as yet a virgin. . . . if the former was taken from the dust, and God was his Maker, it was incumbent that the latter also, making a recapitulation in Himself, should be formed as man by God, to have an analogy with the former as respects His origin.[9]

Athanasius (296–373) also explained the incarnation by relating it to a "dilemma" created by Adam's Fall. God could allow neither His original purpose for humanity as established in the creation of Adam to fail, nor could he fail to execute His word, "You shall die." God's wisdom, justice, and mercy all cohered in the incarnation of the Son of God to effect both by taking the curse and glorifying humanity. "His [Christ's] part it was and His alone, both to bring again the corruption to incorruption and to maintain for the Father His consistency of character and all."[10]

Acceptance of the plain truth of the creation narrative appears clearly in comments of Ambrose (339–397) on the creation of Eve.

> Not without significance, too, is the fact that woman was made out of the rib of Adam. She was not made of the same earth

7. Irenaeus, *Adversus Haereses* III.21. 10 as cited in Latin in J.T. Nielsen, *Adam and Christ in the Theology of Irenaeus of Lyons* (Assen, The Netherlands: Koninklijke Van Gorcum & Comp., 1968), p. 12. This printed dissertation has pivotal selections from Irenaeus cited both in Greek and Latin.
8. Ibid., p. 23.
9. Irenaeus, *Adversus Haereses in The Ante-Nicene Fathers*, eds. Alexander Roberts and James Donaldson (New York, NY: Charles Scribner's Sons, 1908), 1:454 [III.xxi.4].
10. Athanasius, *On The Incarnation* (Crestwood, NY: St. Vladimir's Seminary Press, 1998), p. 7, 33.

> with which he was formed, in order that we might realize that the physical nature of both man and woman is identical and that there was one source for the propagation of the human race. For that reason, neither was man created together with a woman, nor were two men and two women created at the beginning, but first a man and after that a woman. God willed it that human nature be established as one.[11]

Commenting on the same verse, Chrysostom (ca. 344–407) noted that this was no simple "drowsiness that came upon him nor normal sleep; instead the wise and skillful creator of our nature was about to remove one of Adam's ribs." God did not want the experience to cause Adam to be "badly disposed toward the creature formed from his rib and through memory of the pain bear a grudge against this being at its formation."[12]

Augustine's Construction of Adam's Importance

Augustine of Hippo (354–430) worked to defend the city of God, the grace of God, and the revelation of God.[13] He challenged every intellectual and religious current within his sphere of acquaintance which exalted itself against the Christian faith. "The city of God we speak of," Augustine explained, "is the same to which testimony is borne by that Scripture, which excels all the writings of all nations by its divine authority, and has brought under its influence all kinds of minds, and this not by a casual intellectual movement, but obviously by an express providential arrangement."[14] He derived both his content and his confidence in his philosophical battles from a conviction "that the Spirit of God taught His prophets so much of His will as He thought fit to reveal." On the other hand, "the philosophers . . . were deceived by human conjecture."[15]

Though on some elements of his thought, including this one, Augustine saw the need for greater clarity and sometimes correction, as he admitted in his *Retractions* near the end of his life, he continually sought a more perfect congruence with Scripture in all his doctrine. This determination motivated him because the Son of God as Mediator infallibly secured divine revelation against all mistakes. He spoke "first by the prophets, then by His own lips,

11. *Ancient Christian Commentary on Scripture: Genesis 1-11*, p. 69.
12. Ibid., p. 67.
13. Augustine, *The City of God* Book XIII. chapter 16. I am using the translation in *Basic Writings of Augustine*, 2 vols., ed. Whitney J. Oakes (Grand Rapids, MI: Baker, 1980 reprint of 1948 printing by Random House).
14. Ibid., XI.1 [2:143].
15. Ibid., XIII.16 [2:224].

and afterwards by the apostles," and also secured the writing of the canonical Scripture "which has paramount authority, and to which we yield assent in all matters of which we ought not to be ignorant."[16]

These prophets and apostles who spoke and wrote affirmed, "In the beginning God created the heavens and the earth." Showing his knowledge of the philosophies and worldviews of the time, Augustine argued that the consecutive order of God's creative acts did no violence to His immutability. Creation necessarily involved what we call time, but "God, in making it, did not alter His eternal design."[17]

At the core, therefore, a worldview must engage the origin and purpose of the world and the nature of evil. Those core issues set the stage for the appearance of the Redeemer, which necessarily implies the triunity of God.[18] The distinguishing details "must be believed in without any doubt on the evidence of the witnesses by whom those writings that have already gained the name of sacred scripture were compiled."[19] Sacred Scripture teaches clearly that "the cause of created things, whether in heaven or on earth, visible or invisible, is nothing other than the goodness of the creator who is the one true God, and that there is nothing that is not either himself or from him, and that he is Trinity, that is, Father, the Son begotten from the Father and the Holy Spirit who proceeds from the same Father, and is one and the same Spirit of Father and Son."[20]

The stakes involved, therefore, in the narrative of the creation and Fall are insuperably important for understanding the nature and purpose of God and the nature and destiny of man. Every aspect of it is embedded with layers of theological importance and spiritual significance because the narrative still is literally true.[21] God created everything that is not Himself in six sequential days and rested on the seventh. He discussed various interpretations of "In the beginning" and "heavens and earth," to make way for

16. Ibid., XI.3 [2:145].
17. Ibid., XI.4 [2:147].
18. Ibid., XI.2 [2:144]
19. Augustine, *The Augustine Catechism: The Enchiridion on Faith, Hope, and Love*, trans. Bruce Harbert (New York, NY: New York City Press, 1999), p. 35.
20. Ibid., p. 40. Subsequent to this writing, Augustine himself brought more refined theological reflection and clear definition to the doctrine of the double procession of the Holy Spirit.
21. Augustine, *City of God*, XI.5-29 [2:147–172]. He discussed the nature of light and darkness, how Satan was a liar "from the beginning," the difference between fallen and elect angels, the Trinity and the love intrinsic to the three persons, the type of knowledge angels have of God, the difference between "begotten" and "made," how God is both simple and trinitarian, the identifiable traits of beauty, the origin of evil in the will and not in the nature, differentiation in ranks of creatures, the errors of Origen, the "drivel" of the Manichaeans, contemplations on love, existence, and happiness, and other subjects.

the creation and fall of the angels. Their presence is necessary in order to account for the distinction between the city of God and the earthly city, or the city of the proud. He tended, therefore, to see references to this in Genesis 1:1, which he accepted as a summary of the whole creation. The division of six days displayed the order in which God brought all things into being. He wrote, "First of all, the creation is presented in sum, and then its parts are enumerated according to the mystic number of the days."[22]

Augustine saw the six days, which in the citation above he calls "the mystic number of days," as a purposeful manifestation of the perfection of each day's creation, the perfection of the entire creation, and the immutability of God. Even the establishment of time and sequentiality arose from an eternal purpose intrinsically expressive of His own inner being. "These works are recorded to have been completed in six days . . . because six is a perfect number." God used six days for creation, "not because God required a protracted time, as if He could not at once create all things . . . but because the perfection of the works was signified by the number six." In a discussion of the relation between mathematical factors and sums, Augustine showed what he meant by the "perfection" of six and its mystic signification.[23] That the days were numbered as six was not a mere allegory or non-literal spiritualized figure, but was the actual number six, mystically signifying the original perfection of the entire created order and unvarying perfection of each day.[24]

22. Ibid., XI.33 [2:176].
23. Ibid., XI.30 [2:172–73].
24. Based on Augustine's *The Literal Meaning of Genesis*, trans. and annot. John Hammond Taylor, S.J. (New York, NY: Newman Press, 1982), Augustine's view of the six days may be viewed in more than one way. In one place he said, similarly to the statement from *City of God*, "Are we to understand that by the expression, 'heaven and earth' all that God made is to be included and brought to mind first in a general way, and that then the manner of creation is to be worked out in detail, as for each object the words 'God said' occur? For whatever God made He made through His Word." In chapter 15 of the same work he wrote, "Accordingly, the sacred writer was able to separate in the time of his narrative what God did not separate in time in His creative act" seeming to see the actual creation as one moment of creative energy by God. Luther interpreted Augustine accordingly to "perceive a world created suddenly and at the same time, not successively through six days" [This is from Luther's commentary on Genesis, to be quoted later in this text cited in John A. Maxfield, *Luther's Lectures on Genesis and the Formation of Evangelical Identity* (Kirksville, MO: Truman State University Press, 2008), p. 41]. Later, however, Augustine seems to assume sequentiality in creation when he noted, "There were as yet no living creatures for whose well-being such a succession of light and darkness *would be provided*, as we see it is provided now by the course of the sun for the *living beings later created*" (italics mine). And again sequence seems to be in mind when, after detailed reasoning about the meanings of darkness, light, day and night, he wrote, "But evening, during all these three days *before the creation of the heavenly bodies*, can perhaps be reasonably understood as the end of

Even more positively necessary to the order of the world, the nature of history, the revelation of God's perfections and immutable purpose are the historical Adam and Eve. After extensive investigation of angels and the nature of evil, we come to those that shall inhabit the City of God with these elect angels, namely mortal men. "For from one man, whom God created as the first," Augustine observed, "the whole human race descended . . . some of them to be associated with the good angels in their reward, others with the wicked in punishment."[25]

Adam, through his Fall, begot "corrupted and condemned children" weakened by sin, bound by death, and justly under divine wrath. From Adam's willful trespass

> there originated the whole train of evil, which, with its concatenation of miseries, convoys the human race from its depraved origin, as from a corrupt root, on to the destruction of the second death, which has no end, those only being excepted who are freed by the grace of God.[26]

So integrally involved in God's purpose in creation is Adam, that Augustine used his headship to explain the distinction between the original creation and the final state of the blessed in heaven. "For as the first immortality which Adam lost by sinning consisted in his being able not to die," Augustine explained, "while the last shall consist in his not being able to die; so the first free will," Augustine continued, "consisted in his being able not to sin, the last in his not being able to sin." This involves no loss of true freedom, for both happiness and piety, perfected in that state, conspire to give us a desire only for the presence and holy beauty of God. "Are we to say that God Himself is not free because He cannot sin?" No, for in that final city "there shall be free will, one in all the citizens, and indivisible in each, delivered

---

each work accomplished, morning as an indication of *a work to follow*" (italics mine). Augustine, *Literal Meaning*, p. 22, 36, 37, 40. It seems to me that Augustine settled on the interpretation of successive days, but every interpreter of Augustine must recall what he noted about the nature of Scripture interpretation when seeking to isolate him to one clearly identifiable position. "In matters that are obscure and far beyond our vision, even in such as we may find treated in Holy Scripture, different Interpretations are sometimes possible without prejudice to the faith we have received. In such a case, we should not rush in headlong and so firmly take our stand on one side that, if further progress in the search of truth justly undermines this position, we too fall with it. That would be to battle not for the teaching of Holy Scripture but for our own, wishing its teaching to conform to ours, whereas we ought to wish ours to conform to that of Sacred Scripture" (*Literal Meaning*, p. 41).

25. Ibid., XII.27 [2:209].
26. Ibid., XIII.14 [2:221].

from all ill, filled with all good, enjoying indefeasibly the delights of eternal joys."[27] For Augustine, the Bible's presentation of past, present, and future in relation to humanity rotated around the historical Adam, the first human created by God, the crown of the sixth day of creation.

Adam's Pivotal Importance to Martin Luther and John Calvin

Augustine's view of Adam, in varying degrees, dominated the entire stream of theological development through the Middle Ages. After the Council of Orange (529) condemned semi-Pelagianism, the theological position survived, nevertheless, under the development of a highly nuanced discussion of grace. None of these disagreements of the degree to which Adam's sin had affected his posterity, however, diminished the importance of Adam as the historically identifiable head of all of humanity. The preachers and theologians of the Reformation went back to a more concentrated and simple Augustinian perception of the results of Adam's Fall. With so much theological freight bound up in historical Adam, they also were careful to protect both the clarity of Scripture in its narrative and the historical truthfulness of that narrative concerning Adam.

Martin Luther (1483–1546) built virtually his entire doctrinal system of bondage of the will and justification by faith on the historical veracity of the Adam narrative in Genesis. He described the doctrine of the Trinity, the ideals and difficulties of domestic life, the perversions and errors of the papacy, the expectation of the incarnation, the purpose of justification, sanctification, and glorification, the necessity of atonement, and the bondage of the will from these opening narratives of the Bible.[28] For example, on the creation of man in God's image, Luther commented that "it is no doubt true that as God delighted in the creation of man, so also He delights in restoring this His work to perfection through His Son, Jesus Christ, our Lord." He continued, "It is most comforting for us to know that God should think so highly of us and have such pleasure in His counsel to restore us to spiritual life, when at last He will raise up all who have believed n Christ."[29]

In Luther's preface to the first chapter of Genesis, he stated clearly his acceptance of the chronological years listed in the genealogical structure and noted, "Now we know from Moses that about six thousand years ago the world was not yet in existence, though of this fact no philosopher can be

27. Augustine, *City of God*, XXII.30. [2:662].
28. Martin Luther, *Luther's Commentary on Genesis*, 2 vols, trans. J. Theodore Mueller (Grand Rapids: Zondervan Publishing House, 1958), 1:1–88.
29. Ibid., p. 34.

convinced."[30] As Luther discussed varieties of expression in the early verses of Genesis, he laid a foundation for his discussion with the words, "the Decalogue, as also the whole Bible, attests that God made heaven and earth and all other creatures within six days."[31] On Genesis 1:14, the phrase "to divide the day from the night," Luther explained, was "to indicate the difference between the natural day of twenty-four hours, including day and night, and the 'artificial' day without the night." When God denominated each day by the phrase "evening and morning" He "had in mind the natural day of twenty-four hours."[32] In distinguishing his view from those who speculated that God created all things in a moment, Luther responded that "we have proof that the six days of creation were six natural days, since the text states expressly that Adam and Eve were made on the sixth day." To make his point more strongly, Luther continued with a clear affirmation of more details in the text, with the warning, "That text permits no meddling." He pointed to the next chapter in which Moses showed, "in what order man was made. Eve was created a little later than Adam and not indeed out of the dust of the ground as Adam, but from a rib which God took from Adam's side while he slept."[33]

At the close of his consideration of the first three chapters of Genesis, Luther briefly reminded the reader of

> their story of the creation of all creatures, the Garden of Eden, which was to be a palace for man and a temple for him in which to worship God, the tree of knowledge of good and evil, which was to test man's obedience to God, and his terrible Fall by which he sinned against God and lost the glory of his innocence and immortality.

He then summarized his style and the reason for it. "I have explained all this in a simple way and in a historical sense which is reliable and correct." Clinging to his own observation in the preface that Moses is a "better teacher, whom we may follow more safely than the philosophers that dispute about things which they do not know without the Word of God," Luther emphasized that Christians "should seek above all to find the simple and certain meaning of Holy Scripture, especially since so many interpreters do not agree (*on the text*). They (*usually*) show little regard for its historical truth and (*in addition*) they obscure and falsify (*the Scriptures*)."[34]

30. Ibid., p. 3.
31. Ibid., p. 9.
32. Ibid., p. 22.
33. Ibid., p. 34, 35.
34. Ibid., p. 5, 88. The parentheses and italics were inserted by the translator.

Like Luther, John Calvin (1509–1564) tied his theology with unyielding precision to the historical reality of Adam and his natural and federal headship of the entire human race. So momentous and shaping was Adam's position as head and his eventual Fall, that should it appear that the history was untrue, the entire scheme of the Bible's theology would fail. If the consequences of Adam's Fall depend on revealed truth, so do his historical circumstances. We learn, therefore, by revelation that the world was created about 6,000 years ago. Many philosophers, "shallow and imaginative people," will always have their own answers and avoid what the Holy Spirit teaches us and thus it will be "incredible to them that the world was created six thousand years ago."[35] The world, "declining to its ultimate end, has not yet attained six thousand years," but, at the same time, "within six thousand years," he has "shown evidences enough on which to exercise our minds in earnest meditation!"[36]

The nature of the world is so rational, so purposeful in its parts, so beautiful in its conception that "We cannot open our eyes without God's showing himself to us, whether we like it or not."[37] So obviously did the world originate by the power and majesty of God, that all attempts to explain it otherwise Calvin labeled as "obtuse and absurd" and giving rise to his retort, "Could anyone think up a scenario more stupid than that?" We must pay close attention to the word "create" so as to resist all "diabolical illusions" and remain "steadfast in the knowledge that everything was made from nothing because there is no existence except in God alone, and that we have from him all that we have and are."[38] In his commentary he added, "Hence the folly of them is refuted who imagine that unformed matter existed from eternity."[39]

Calvin rejected the error of those "who maintain that the world was made in a moment." Those who pretend that the normal sense of "six days" is a mere literary device for "conveying instruction," commit "too violent a cavil." Instead we should conclude "that God himself took the space of six days, for the purpose of accommodating his works to the capacity of men."[40] His preaching reaffirmed that God "took six days to create the things we now see

35. John Calvin, *Sermons on Genesis*, trans Rob Roy McGregor (Edinburgh, Scotland: Banner of Truth Trust, 2009), p. 8.

36. John Calvin, *Institutes of the Christian Religion*, 2 vols. Ed. John T. McNeill, trans. Ford Lewis Battles (Louisville, KY: Westminster John Knox Press, 2006), 1:160f [I.xiv.1]. This refers to book, chapter, and paragraph numbers.

37. Calvin, *Sermons*, p. 5.

38. Ibid., p. 12–13.

39. John Calvin, *Commentaries on the First Book of Moses called Genesis* (Grand Rapids, MI: Baker Book House, 1996), p. 70.

40. Ibid., p. 78.

and laid them out and directed them in an orderly fashion" to give us a pattern for rest and order. These days, so Calvin argued, must be seen as regular natural days consisting of proportioned division of darkness and light. No matter how one figures the beginning and end of a day, "Moses wanted to indicate that one entire day was made up of two parts: from evening till morning, and from morning till the following evening."[41] Even beyond the original six days of creation, God continually manifests this same power and order in sustaining the world and us.[42] The sad fact is that "if we possessed a tracc of discrimination and reason, Moses would not have had to be God's witness, testifying that everything was created by him, for our capacity to reason and the order of nature show us that."[43] Given the purpose of God in His creation that it be a constant witness to His incomparable glory, "let us heed what David shows us, namely that because the day and the night, each following in its order, proclaim the glory of God, we are to receive Moses' teaching."[44]

All of theology, beginning with the Mosaic narrative, consists of knowledge of God and knowledge of ourselves. Knowledge of ourselves includes "what we were like when we were first created and what our condition became after the fall of Adam."[45] In unfallen Adam, human nature excelled in qualities of mind, reason, and conscience sufficient for "the direction of his earthly life," and to increase in the knowledge of God. He could have attained eternal life through an unbroken course of obedience. His disobedience destroyed himself and "corrupted his own blessings."[46]

Following our knowledge of "what we were like when we were first created," the second part consists of calling "to mind our miserable condition after Adam's fall."[47] From Adam's Fall the spiritual corruption of the entire race proceeded. "Adam so corrupted himself that infection spread from him to all his descendants." This is so because "Adam, when he lost the gifts received, lost them not only for himself but for us all." Rotten branches have come forth from a rotten root, for Adam's corruption was such "that it was conveyed in a perpetual stream from the ancestors into their descendants." Calvin stated specifically his agreement with Augustine that "whether a man is a guilty unbeliever or an innocent believer, he begets not innocent but guilty children, for he begets them from a corrupted nature."[48]

41. Calvin, *Sermons*, p. 29.
42. Ibid., p. 14, 17.
43. Ibid., p. 12.
44. Ibid., p. 34.
45. Calvin, *Institutes*, 2:183. [I.xv.1].
46. Ibid., 1:195 [I.xv.8].
47. Ibid., 1:242 [II.i.1].
48. Ibid., 1:249–150 [II.i.7].

Calvin also expressed this quite clearly in his sermon on Ephesians 2 when, in unleashing all his verbal power in describing human sinfulness, he reminded his readers [hearers] that the divine image "was utterly lost and defaced in us by Adam's sin."[49] He continued with startling imagery, "We are only wretched putrefying flesh. There is nothing but rottenness and infection in us. God loathes us. . . . We must always consider that man brings death with him even in his birth, not only because he is mortal, but because he is separated from God. . . . Our souls are altogether sinful. There is neither thought nor affection in us, which does not tend to evil. . . . No man may pretend . . . or think that anything is as grievous as the corruption of our nature."[50] Adam himself exchanged his original purity and "entangled and immersed his offspring" in the "most filthy plagues, blindness, impotence, impurity, vanity and injustice."[51] "It was not for nothing," reminded Calvin, "that the Lord Himself and also this apostle shut us out from life completely while we remain in Adam."[52] Our corruption remains a present phenomenon because we "are not now born such as Adam was at first created, but we are the adulterous seed of degenerate and sinful man."[53]

His commentary on Romans 5:12–21 sealed the historical interdependence of Christ and Adam for "the purpose of Christ's coming was to redeem us from the calamity into which Adam had fallen." Gratitude for "what we possess in Christ can come only when we have been shown what we have lost in Adam."[54] As Adam received grace for the race at his creation, so in his Fall "he corrupted, vitiated, depraved, and ruined our nature," determining that his only seed could be "that which bore resemblance to himself."[55] If the argument from Adam does not stand, then the argument from Christ falls equally as surely.[56]

He made this same point in a summary section of the Institutes as he plowed through the "nonsense" and "sacrilege" of the Pelagians.

---

49. John Calvin, *John Calvin's Commentary on Ephesians,* trans. Arthur Golding (Edinburgh, Scotland: Banner of Truth Trust, 1973), p. 129.
50. Ibid., p. 129–130.
51. Calvin, *Institutes,* 1:246 [II.i.5].
52. John Calvin, *Calvin's New Testament Commentaries; Galatians, Ephesians, Philippians and Colossians,* trans. T.H.L. Parker, ed. David W. Torrance, Thomas Torrance (Grand Rapids: Eerdmans, 1965), p. 139.
53. Ibid.,p. 141–142.
54. John Calvin, *New Testament Commentaries: The Epistles of Paul to the Romans and Thessalonians,* trans. R. Mackenzie, ed. David W. Torrance, Thomas Torrance (Grand Rapids: Eerdmans, 1965), p. 111.
55. Ibid., p. 111–112.
56. Ibid., p. 114–120. See many arguments on the parallel between Adam and Christ.

> But if it is beyond controversy that Christ's righteousness, and thereby life, are ours by communication, it immediately follows that both were lost in Adam, only to be recovered in Christ; and that sin and death crept in through Adam, only to be abolished through Christ. These are no obscure words: "Many are made righteous by Christ's obedience as by Adam's disobedience they had been made sinners." . . . Here, then, is the relationship between the two: Adam, implicating us in his ruin, destroyed us with himself; but Christ restores us to salvation by his grace."[57]

That all of theology and the entire biblical scheme of redemption depended on the monogenetic origin of the entire race of mankind, and that the sin of that one person, Adam, explains the origin and pervasive power of sin is unquestionably the conviction of John Calvin. If one dismisses Adam as a real historical person, Calvin would see no consistent biblical rationale for Christ as Redeemer.

Reformed Orthodoxy

The entire Reformed tradition followed in his train, or rather, saw in the Bible the same things so clearly developed by Calvin. Matthew Poole (1624–1679) served as a paradigmatic figure for biblical interpretation among Reformed thinkers. His work was "highly revered among the Protestant orthodox" and "received heavy use throughout the period as normative readings of the text for both laity and clergy."[58] A five-volume work entitled *Synopsis Criticorum* was called by C.A. Briggs "a monument of Biblical learning which has served many generations of students, and will maintain its value forever."[59] A two-volume work, originally entitled *Annotations on the Holy Bible*, served as a chastely and plainly written commentary for use by pastors, families, and other Bible students and teachers.[60]

The *Annotations* highly influenced other interpreters such as Matthew Henry, John Gill, and even John Wesley. Wesley used both Poole and Henry freely and, omitting their Calvinism, sought, like them, a very simple

57. Calvin, *Institutes*, 1:248 [II.i.6].
58. Donald K. McKim, ed., *Historical Handbook of Major Biblical Interpreters* (Downers Grove, IL: Intervarsity Press, 1998), p. 146.
59. *Schaff-Herzog Encyclopedia of Religious Knowledge*, 12 vols, plus index (Grand Rapids, MI: Baker Book House,1957), IX:125, s.v. Poole, Matthew.
60. Matthew Poole, *A Commentary on the Holy Bible*, 3 vols. (Edinburgh, Scotland: Banner of Truth Trust, 1962). Citations will be taken from volume 1 of this edition from commentary on the respective Scripture passages referenced. Banner of Truth expanded the two volumes to three.

straightforward exposition of the text. For example, on the creation of man, Wesley said simply, "He created him *male and female, Adam and Eve: Adam* first out of earth, and *Eve* out of his side. God made but *one male* and *one female*, that all the nations of men might know themselves to be *made of one blood*, descendants from one common stock, and might thereby be inspired to love one another."[61]

Commenting on Genesis 1:26, Poole demonstrated that the plural language "shows that there are more persons in the Godhead." This seeming difficulty is reconciled only "by acknowledging a plurality of persons in the unity of essence." On the words, "were the first day," Poole explained that the word *day* should be taken as the natural day "consisting of twenty-four hours." Since the repetition of the phrase "evening and morning" was consistent, "the like is to be understood of the succeeding days." As the text unequivocally indicates, God, "who could have made all things at once, was pleased to divide his work into six days." On the sixth day, God created man from dust, and in his initial form he was but a "dull lump of clay" until God breathed into him the breath of life, giving him "reason and understanding." When Poole described the creation of the woman on the sixth day from Adam's rib, he argued that this implied neither an initial superfluity nor a consequent deformity. His three-fold explanation sealed his commitment to the unvarnished historicity of the creation narrative of Adam and Eve. It carried too much doctrinal freight for it to be otherwise.

On the continent, Poole's Reformed contemporaries argued the same case. In Geneva, Francis Turretin (1623–1687), gave an expansive defense of the Reformed tradition in his *Institutio Theologiae Elencticae*.[62] Among the Dutch, Herman Witsius (1636–1708) emerged as a leader of Reformed Orthodoxy.

Turretin accepted the biblical narrative of creation in its simplest most obvious meaning. The days of creation were consecutive days of 24 hours. Each of the six days contained specific creative acts of God giving a describable origin and succession to all things.[63] "Although its distinct work is assigned to each day," Turretin explained, "it does not follow that a whole day was employed in finishing each work; or that God needed that interval of time to perform it. Rather God, on each of those distinct days, produced nothing besides."[64]

61. John Wesley, *Explanatory Notes Upon the Old Testament* (Bristol, England: Printed by William Pine, 1765), p. 8.
62. Francis Turretin, Institutes of Elenctic Theology, 3 vols., trans. George Musgrave Giger, ed. James T. Dennison, Jr. (Phillipsburg, NJ: P & R Publishing, 1992).
63. Ibid., 1: 444–452.
64. Ibid., p. 445.

On the sixth day, however, a necessary combination of instantaneous moments and connected events occurred. He explained, "Although various works are referred to the sixth day (which could not have been performed at the same time), this is not an objection against each having been finished in a moment." Obvious examples of this kind of combination are seen in God's creation of Adam from dust. The bodily form was created "in a moment, in another he breathed life into it, in another he sent a sleep upon him and took out one of his ribs, from which in another moment he formed Eve." Adam's naming the animals required both the momentary and the successive. "The beasts also in a moment received the impulse of coming to Adam (although from that impulse they went to him successively)."[65] He viewed the creation of Adam as "the most excellent work and the epitome of the whole." Not only was this creation reserved for the final place "but made in a peculiar method above the others and (as it were) after a consultation." This does not indicate deliberation, as if any uncertainty existed prior to its execution, or difficulty in its organization and completion, but "the dignity of the work itself."[66]

Turretin rejected clearly any attempt to establish a pre-adamite race of men as "absurd in itself and foreign to all reason (no less than to the Scripture revelation itself.)" He affirmed that Adam was the "first of mortals, before whom no man existed and from whom all have sprung." Both the male and the female, Adam and Eve, were created on the sixth day. Because Eve is the "mother of all living" and, according to Paul, "God hath made of one blood all nations of men," it is impossible that any race has another beginning than Adam and Eve, or that any line of humanity exists outside of Adam's headship. Adam is "deservedly reckoned to be the first man from whom sin and death passed upon all men," based on Romans 5:12 and 1 Corinthians 15:22. Holding to any humanity prior to Adam, or other than that which descended from Adam, gives no context for the definition of sin, the promise of redemption, the nature of marriage, or the equality of all people in one human race.[67]

In his eating of the forbidden tree, Adam transgressed not only the specific positive prohibition "but also the whole law of nature engraved upon his heart."[68] In sinning, Adam lost the principal part of the image of God "which consisted of holiness and wisdom (usually termed original righteousness)." While Adam lost the moral image, the natural elements from which moral responsibility arises remained, but the moral excellence

65. Ibid., p. 446.
66. Ibid., p. 451–452.
67. Ibid., p. 457–62.
68. Ibid., p. 604.

— holiness, righteousness, and loving knowledge of God — dissolved. Adam became subject upon his Fall to moral and physical evil. Morally, both guilt and pollution flooded his being incurring "the wrath of God with his descendants," and contracting "universal corruption and impurity for himself and his." The physical evil that came on him and his posterity were "miseries of all kinds . . . and death itself (both temporal and eternal) to which he became exposed."[69] Adam's posterity inherited the effects of his Fall by an imputation that is "immediate and antecedent." Following Augustine's understanding of the place of Adam in relation to his posterity, Turretin explained,

> The relation of the divine image and of original righteousness (which Adam received for himself and his, not as a personal good and peculiar to himself, but as a common good to be transmitted to his posterity, if he had stood in his integrity; but of which his posterity was also to be deprived as soon as he fell); so that Adam here was like a beneficiary who, receiving a gift from his master, receives it both for himself and his posterity on this condition — that if he rebels against his master, he loses the benefit not only for himself but also for his posterity.[70]

In 1681 Herman Witsius published his *Sacred Dissertations on what is Commonly Called the Apostles' Creed*. He defined creation as "that act of God, in which, by the all-powerful command of his will, He made out of nothing, and perfected, the whole universe, in the space of six days."[71] He stated his doctrinal understanding of *ex nihilo* creation in the clearest of terms. God needed "no assistance from any, as nothing exists or even can exist independently of him," but "by the mere act of his sovereign will," he "commanded all things that are, to rise out of nothing."[72] He used the terms *immediate* and *mediate*, while specifically resisting any form of evolutionary thought.[73] On the first day, all things came immediately from nothing by

69. Ibid., p. 611f.
70. Ibid., p. 616–617.
71. Herman Witsius, *Sacred Dissertations on what is Commonly Called the Apostles' Creed,* trans. Donald Fraser (Edinburgh, Scotland: Printed for A. Fullerton & Co., 1823; reprinted 1993 by the den Dulk Christian Foundation), p. 181.
72. Ibid., p. 182.
73. While Witsius did not use the modern word "evolution," he was aware of such an idea. Henry Morris showed in *The Long War Against God* (Grand Rapids, MI: Baker, 1989) that evolutionary ideas long pre-dated Christ's earthly ministry. The evolutionist Henry Fairfield Osborn also documented this in *From the Greeks to Darwin* (London, England: MacMillan, 1896).

the creative word of God. On subsequent days, things "indeed were made of matter; but of matter that in itself was ill adapted to the purpose, that bore no resemblance to the things produced from it, and from which no such creatures could have been produced by any natural energy."[74] Witsius gave no place to "*natural generation*, which proceeds gradually from suitable matter, according to the rules of motion." He utterly detested the theory of those who sought to explain creation as the "concurrence of God" with the spontaneous emergence into existence by laws of motion. This, he contended, was an "absurd hypothesis."[75]

Based on his acceptance of the Hebrew Bible's chronology, Witsius positioned himself with those who argued, "that the world has not yet reached the age of six thousand years."[76] Witsius looked upon the Mosaic account specifying six days as the period of creation as perfectly clear and consistent with our understanding of a natural day. Though, from the nature of the narrative, we cannot "assign the moments of the commencement and termination of the works of each day," interpreters reasonably contend, according to Scripture, "that *six days*, not *six moments*, were employed in the creation of the world." This does not mean, however, that God had restrictions, like a workman, given a task according to the limits of time, and thus "laboured in the work from morning to evening." God's wisdom and perfect sense of order assigned each day its purpose in creation, and, though fully capable of creating all things in a single moment, was pleased "to employ six days in this work; as the Mosaic history, which ought by no means to be abased by rash and unnecessary allegories, expressly states."[77]

In an intriguing discussion of the possibility of life on other spheres in the created order, Witsius concluded from the creation of Adam on the last day of creation that the affirmation of such extraterrestrial men is a mockery and ridicule of Christian theology. In his narrative "respecting the creation of man," Moses showed "that at that time no living creature similar to him existed in the universe." Only then did God create a being in his own image, indicating that none had been so created to that point. The special preparation of the earth that it be fit for habitation (Isaiah 45:18), Paul's affirmation that from one blood God made all the nations of men to dwell on the earth (Acts 17:26), the fact that fallen angels as well as elect angels are mentioned but not other fallen, elect, or redeemed men, the very character of redemption requiring an incarnation and death in our nature

74. Ibid., p. 193–94.
75. Ibid., p. 209.
76. Ibid., p. 207. The translator gave a lengthy note at this point (p. 453).
77. Ibid., p. 208.

all serve to make the existence of life on other spheres of the universe a "monstrous" opinion.[78]

The creation of Adam not only posed virtual impossibilities for any argument for life being present any other place than earth, but determined the purpose of life on earth. In his highly influential work on the Covenants, Witsius determined the direction of his discussion with this definition: "This covenant is an agreement between God and Adam, formed after the image of God, as the head and root, or representative of the whole human race; by which God promised eternal life and happiness to him, if he yielded obedience to all his commands; threatening him with death if he failed but in the least point: and Adam accepted this condition."[79] Absent a historical Adam, created by the triune God on the sixth day, the biblical view of redemption would not exist.

Puritanism as Distilled in Jonathan Edwards

Jonathan Edwards (1703–1758) gave a distilled view of Puritanism, a particular type of Reformed Orthodoxy, concerning the place of Adam in Christian theology. Having no doubt about the six days of creation and the special creation of Adam in the image of God, Edwards viewed this narrative as fundamental to the entirety of Christian theology. A sermon on *God's Excellencies* brought a comparison from Edwards in which he assumed the age of the world to be about six thousand years: "Neither the earth we stand upon, nor the heavens over our heads; the sun, moon, nor stars; nor the angels of God, can claim a duration of six thousand years, but what is this to the duration of the great [God] who is from everlasting?"[80] Contemplation of Adam and his connections to the whole of biblical theology occupied many entries into Edwards' *Miscellanies* and his "Notes on the Bible."[81] In 1753, Astruc's theory of multiple layers of authorship, based on the different words for God in the early chapters of Genesis, prompted Edwards to respond with more than 24,000 words in his "Notes" observing all the internal evidences of unity and single authorship of the Pentateuch, closing with these words:

78. Ibid., p. 213–221.

79. Herman Witsius, *The Economy of the Covenants between God and Man: A Complete Body of Divinity*, 2 vols. Trans. William Crookshank (London, England: Printed for R. Haynes, 1822), 1:50.

80. *The Works of Jonathan Edwards*, Harry Stout, gen. ed., *Sermons and Discourses, 1720–1723*, ed. Wilson Kimnach (New Haven and London: Yale University Press, 1992), p. 418.

81. *The Works of Jonathan Edwards*, Harry Stout, gen. ed., *The "Miscellanies,"* ed. Thomas A. Schafer (New Haven and London: Yale University Press, 1994), p. 323–25, 382–83, 484–87, et al. See also, Jonathan Edwards, *The Works of Jonathan Edwards*, 2 vols. (Edinburgh, Scotland: The Banner of Truth Trust, 1976 [first published 1834]), 2:676–692.

"Places in the New Testament, which suppose Moses to be the penman of the Pentateuch, John v. 46, 47. Mark xii. 26, compared with Exod. iii.6. Acts xv. 21. 2 Cor. iii. 14, 15. Heb. xii. 21." In one of several summaries of his evidence, Edwards stated, "History and law are everywhere so grafted one into another, so mutually inwrought, and do, as it were, so grow one out of and into another, and flow one from another in a continued current, that there is all appearance of their originally growing together, and not in the least of their being artificially patched and compacted together afterwards. It seems impossible impartially and carefully to view the manner of their connexion, and to judge otherwise."[82]

One element of his showing the dependency throughout Scripture on this coherent unit began, "In the fourth commandment, there is such a mention made of the creation of the heavens and the earth, and the sea, and all that in them is, and of God's resting the seventh day, as is a kind of epitome of the first chapter of Genesis, and the beginning of the second." He claimed that the commandment is "unintelligible without that history." In addition, Edwards pointed to Deuteronomy 4:32 as a reference to "God's creation of man, and there is mention in the prophetical song of Moses of the name of *Adam*, as the grand progenitor of mankind, Deut. xxxii. 8." Also, Edwards drew doctrinal observations from the first three chapters of Genesis that indicate that the doctrinal coherence of Scripture would be a mere charade if those chapters were anything less than historical. After concise observations made about the words of God to Adam and Eve in Genesis 1:27–30, Edwards summarized, "The blessings he pronounces are given him in the name of the whole race, and therefore the favour manifested in blessing them is implicitly given to him as the head of the race. . . . Hence the covenant must be made with Adam, not only for himself, but all his posterity."[83] This fact in itself explained virtually the whole of biblical theology.

The inextricable relation of Adam and the divine covenant initiated with him to the doctrine of original sin made it a cornerstone of the incarnation, atoning work of Christ, and the manner of God's making sinners right with himself. In 1757, Edwards explained his purpose in writing his book *Original Sin:*

> I look on the doctrine as of *great importance*; which everybody will doubtless own it is, if it be true. For, if the case be such indeed, that all mankind are by nature in a state of total ruin, both with

82. Edwards, *Works* (Banner of Truth), 2:681.
83. Ibid., 2:689f.

> respect to the moral evil, of which they are the subjects, and the afflictive evil to which they are exposed, the one as the consequence and punishment of the other; then, doubtless, the great salvation by Christ stands in direct relation to this ruin, as the remedy to the disease; and the whole gospel, or doctrine of salvation, must suppose it; and all real belief, or true notion of that gospel, must be built upon it.[84]

After he demonstrated human sinfulness from empirical evidence,[85] Edwards dealt with the evidence from biblical passages, beginning with "Observations relating to things contained in the three first chapters of Genesis, with reference to the doctrine of original sin."[86] Edwards affirmed that the original created state of Adam involved a disposition of holiness and that Adam, was "perfectly righteous, righteous from the first moment of his existence; and consequently, created or brought into existence righteous."[87] The history of the beginning of Genesis "leads us to suppose of the great favours and smiles of Heaven, which Adam enjoyed while he remained in innocency" and that "till Adam sinned, he was in happy circumstances, surrounded with testimonies and fruits of God's favour."[88] Edwards contended that a coherent biblical theology and a realistic view of the world rest squarely on a literal and fully historical understanding of these chapters. He wrote,

> I have now particularly considered the account which Moses gives us in the beginning of the Bible, of our first parents, and God's dealings with them, their transgression, and what followed. And on the whole, if we consider the manner in which God apparently speaks to Adam from time to time; and particularly, if we consider how plainly and undeniably his posterity are included in the sentence of death pronounced on Adam after his fall, founded on the foregoing threatening; and consider the curse denounced on the ground for his sake, and for his and his posterity's sorrow: and also consider what is evidently the occasion of his giving his wife the new name of Eve, and his meaning in it, and withal consider apparent fact in constant and universal events, with relation to the

84. Jonathan Edwards, *Original Sin*, volume 3 in *The Works of Jonathan Edwards*, ed. Clyde A. Holbrook, John E. Smith, General Editor (New Haven and London: Yale University Press, 1970), p. 103.
85. Ibid., p. 107–219.
86. Ibid., p. 223.
87. Ibid., p. 228.
88. Ibid., p. 231.

> state of our first parents, and their posterity from that time forward, through all ages of the world; I can't but think, it must appear to every impartial person, that Moses' account does, with sufficient evidence, lead all mankind, to whom his account is communicated, to understand that God, in his constitution with Adam, dealt with him as a public person, and as the head of the human species, and had respect to his posterity as included in him: and that this history is given by divine direction, in the beginning of the first-written revelation, to exhibit to our view the origin of the present sinful, miserable state of mankind, that we might see what that was, which first gave occasion for all those consequent wonderful dispensations of divine mercy and grace towards mankind, which are the great subject of the Scriptures, both of the Old and the New Testaments; and that these things are not obscurely and doubtfully pointed forth, but delivered in a plain account of things, which easily and naturally exhibits them to our understandings.[89]

He followed a discussion of other Old Testament passages by affirming, "and doubtless it was expected, by the great Author of the Bible, that the account in the three first chapters of Genesis should be taken as a plain account of the introduction of both natural and moral evil, into the world."[90]

Edwards also gave a lengthy consideration to Romans 5:12–21. He believed that any assertion of obscurity in this text was unwarranted and hiding those assertions in "artificial mists" betrayed a lack of candor in accepting its bright and clear meaning.

> 'Tis really no less than *abusing* the Scripture and its readers, to represent this paragraph as the most *obscure* of all the places of Scripture, that speak of the consequences of Adam's sin; and to treat it as if there was need first to consider other places as more plain. Whereas, 'tis most manifestly a place in which these things are declared, beyond all, the most plainly, particularly, precisely and of set purpose, by that great Apostle, who has most fully explained to us those doctrines, in general, which relate to the redemption by Christ, and the sin and misery we are redeemed from. And it must be now left to the reader's judgment, whether the Christian church has not proceeded reasonably, in looking on this as a place of Scripture most clearly and fully treating of these things, and in using its

89. Ibid., p. 260.
90. Ibid., p. 272.

determinate sense as a help to settle the meaning of many other passages of Sacred Writ.[91]

Two Nineteenth Century Evangelical Baptists: Andrew Fuller and Charles H. Spurgeon

Fuller

Andrew Fuller (1754–1815), a pastor and a major force behind the origin of the modern foreign missions movement, gave an exposition of the Book of Genesis to his church in Kettering and published it in 1805.[92] He accepted the entire book as historical narrative, including the account of the creation of the earth, all of its constituent parts, the prototypes of all plants and animals from which all subsequent flora and fauna proceeded, and Adam and Eve. Nothing indicates that this account was anything less than a plain narrative of events as they took place by the will and power of God.

At every point of his exposition, Fuller affirmed that Scripture is superior to all alternative views of origins. "The foundation of this vast fabric is laid in an adequate cause — *Elohim, The Almighty.* Nothing else would bear it," Fuller judged. "Man, if he attempt to find an adequate cause for what is, to the overlooking of God," Fuller observed with prophetic profundity, "shall but weary himself with very vanity."[93] As it was brought forth initially by the word of God, the earth was "a chaos, *without form, and void;* a confused mass of earth and water, covered with darkness, and void of those fruits which afterwards covered the face of it." After this general account, "the sacred writer proceeds to particulars." Fuller gave a brief description of each day of creation with observations about the wisdom of the creator at each step, culminating in the creation of man, an event to which special attention is given in Scripture. "It is described as though it were the result of a special counsel and as though there were a peculiar importance attached to it."[94]

Fuller drew on other parts of Scripture to fill out some of the importance attached to this moment of creation. "Under the Great Supreme, man was to be the lord of the lower world" and its most distinguished connection to the spiritual world. He possessed "that consciousness of right and wrong which should render him a proper subject of moral government." Fuller saw man as the image of God both in natural and moral substance. The natural image consisted in "*reason*, by which he was fitted for dominion over the

91. Ibid., p. 348.
92. Andrew Fuller, *The Complete Works of the Rev. Andrew Fuller*, 3 vol., ed. Joseph Belcher (Philadelphia, PA: American Baptist Publication Society, [1845]), 3:1200.
93. Ibid., p. 2.
94. Ibid., p. 6.

creatures, James iii.7." The moral image consisted in "*righteousness and true holiness*, by which he was fitted for communion with his Creator." Genesis 2 was a "review of the creation, with the addition of some particulars, such as the institution of the Sabbath, the place provided for man, the law given him, and the manner of the creation of woman." He discussed the Sabbath as a creation ordinance and gave examples of evidence that time was considered in terms of the Sabbath arrangement from creation forward. "After reviewing the whole in general," Fuller noted, "and noticing the day of rest, the sacred writer takes a special review of the vegetable creation, with an intent to mark the difference of its first production and ordinary propagation. Plants are now ordinarily produced by rain upon the earth and human tillage; but the first plants were made before there was any rain, or any human hand to till the ground."[95]

He continued his pursuit of the idea that Genesis 2 is a complementary and detailed review of selected events of chapter 1 by looking at the creation of woman. "We had a general one before," Fuller summarized, "but now we are led to see the reasons of it." "The woman," he noted, "was made for the man; not merely for the gratification of his appetites, but of his rational and social nature." Man was not to be alone, for that was not good, but a suitable helper was given him. "The place assigned to the woman in heathen and Mahomedan countries has been highly degrading," he noted, having received first-hand knowledge of this from his missionary friend William Carey (1761–1834). He added, "and the place assigned her by modern infidels is not much better. Christianity is the only religion that conforms to the original design, that confines a man to one wife, and that teaches him to treat her with propriety." He challenged his readers to "go among the enemies of the gospel, and you shall see the woman either reduced to abject slavery, or basely flattered for the vilest of purposes; but in Christian families you may see her treated with honour and respect; treated as a friend, as naturally an equal, a soother of man's cares, a softener of his griefs, and a partner of his joys."[96]

Fuller also knew of objections to the order of creation that came from enlightenment skeptics.[97] On the relation between light and the sun, Fuller stated with disarming plainness, "The light here mentioned was not that of the sun, which was created afterwards." After referring to the objections of "a late infidel writer" concerning this phenomenon, Fuller affirmed the biblical

95. Ibid., p. 7.

96. Ibid., p. 9.

97. Andrew Fuller, *The Gospel its Own Witness; or the Holy Nature and Divine Harmony of the Christian Religion contrasted with the Immorality and Absurdity of Deism*, in Fuller, *Complete Works*, 2:3-96.

presentation that "a flood of light was produced on the first day of creation, and on the fourth it was collected and formed into distinct bodies." Prior to this, day and night were "ruled by the Creator's so disposing of the light and darkness as to *divide* them," so that what was afterward done "ordinarily by the sun was now done extraordinarily by the division of darkness and light."[98]

Fuller's discussion of the prohibition given to Adam and the disobedience that followed showed that Adam's status as federal head of the race in relation to the person and work of Christ assumed the full historicity of the account. Invoking Romans 5:12–21 and Hebrews 9:27–28, Fuller argued that, "the original constitution of things provided for the existence of every individual that has since been born into the world, and that whether man should stand or fall." Adam was "the public head of all his posterity, so that his transgression involved their being transgressors from the womb, and alike exposed to death with himself." The history of the world proves that this scriptural representation of the original state of man is so, and that God's judgment according to its truth in the end will prove perfectly consistent with his impeccable credentials as a moral governor.

Adam's obedience also would have had beneficial results for all his posterity. Showing his Augustinian propensity, Fuller argued, "There is every reason to believe that if man had obeyed his Creator's will, he would, of his own boundless goodness, have crowned him with everlasting bliss." God delighted to impart his own "infinite blessedness as the reward for righteousness." Should Adam, therefore, "have continued in the truth, he and all his posterity would have enjoyed what was symbolically promised him by the tree of life." This would have been the same in substance "as that which believers now enjoy through a Mediator; for the Scriptures speak of that which the law could not do (in that it was weak *through the flesh*, that is, through the corruption of human nature) as being accomplished by Christ."[99]

Fuller's handling of the Fall and its results continued in the simple presentation of historical narrative. "We have hitherto seen man as God created him, upright and happy. But here we behold a sad reverse; the introduction of moral evil into our world, the source of all our misery."[100] Fuller isolated two major components of the historical narrative as pertinent to redemptive history.

First, the serpent's judgment must extinguish all hope of victory for him. He would be crushed by the seed of the woman. His ruin would come from the seed, not of the man, but of the woman, through whom Satan had tempted the human race. This victory would be enjoyed by many adherents

98. Fuller, *Complete Works,* 3:3.
99. Ibid., p. 9.
100. Ibid., p. 10.

to the woman's seed and, in the end, would be complete, an absolute vindication of divine wisdom.[101] Fuller, showing the seriousness of this historical moment, pointed to its pervasive implications throughout Scripture.

> Finally, Though [sic] it should be a long war, and the cause of the serpent would often be successful, yet in the end it should be utterly ruined. The *head* is the *seat of life,* which the *heel* is not: by this language, therefore, it is intimated that the life of Christ's cause should not be affected by any part of Satan's opposition; but that the life of Satan's cause should by that of Christ. For this purpose is he manifested in human nature, that he may *destroy* the works of the devil; and he will never desist till he have utterly crushed his power.[102]

Second, Fuller connected Adam's sin and guilt to the general condition of this present world. "Man himself is doomed to wretchedness upon it [the ground]; he should drag on the few years that he might live in sorrow and misery, of which the *thorns and thistles* which it should spontaneously produce were but emblems."[103] At the same time, the grace of justification made its first historical appearance. Fuller noted that Romans 5:18 summarizes the Fall and justification, vitally linking the two, in saying that one act led to condemnation and one act led to justification.

> By the coats of skins wherewith the Lord God clothed them, it seems to be implied that animals were slain. . . . Sacrifices therefore appear to have been ordained of God to teach man his desert, and the way in which he must be saved. It is remarkable that the clothing of Adam and Eve is ascribed to *the Lord God*, and that it appears to have succeeded the slender covering wherewith they had attempted to cover themselves. Is it not natural to conclude that God only can hide our moral nakedness, and that the way in which he does it is by covering us with the righteousness of our atoning sacrifice?[104]

Such profound and substantial hope cannot be founded on a fiction.

Spurgeon

The theology of the "Prince of Preachers" depended without reservation on the historical reality of Adam and his representative status as the first man

101. Ibid., p. 15–16.
102. Ibid., p. 16.
103. Ibid., p. 16–17.
104. Ibid., p. 17–18.

and federal head of the race. His sermons, filled with the theology of the covenants, could not exist in their preached form apart from his firm commitment to the historical truth of Adam's Fall.[105] The doctrinal underpinnings of his sermonic power are seen in his exposition of Romans 5. "It was by one man's sin that we all fell through the first Adam," Spurgeon observed. An objection to that would eliminate the sinner's only hope.

> If you and I had each one sinned for himself or herself, apart from Adam, our case would probably have been hopeless . . . but inasmuch as we fell representatively in Adam, it prepared the way for us to rise representatively in the second Adam, Christ Jesus our Lord and Saviour.[106]

We fell by another and can rise by another. Ruined in Adam, restoration comes from the second man, "the Lord from heaven." Spurgeon likened the effectuality of Adam's Fall upon humanity to the effectuality of Christ's death for His people: "for on behalf of all those for whom he died his atonement so prevails as to put their sins away for ever."[107] We see the same interdependence of Adam and Christ in his sermon "Christ the Maker of all things New," based on 2 Corinthians 5:17. "As Adam acted for the seed in him," Spurgeon again employed the biblical analogy, "so Christ hath acted for the seed in him." In his death, Christ came before the judgment seat "with our sins upon him, the representative of those of whom he is the

---

105. Spurgeon was not quite sure what to do with the apparently strong evidence from geology that death preceded the appearance of man on earth. Seeking to respond to this without surrendering the historical reality of Adam, Spurgeon said: "Geology tells us that there was death among the various forms of life from the first ages of the globe's history, even when as yet the world was not fitted up as the dwelling of man. This I can believe and still regard death as the result of sin. If it can be proved that there is such an organic unity between man and the lower animals that they would not have died if Adam had not sinned, then I see in those deaths before Adam the antecedent consequences of a sin, which was then uncommitted. If by the merits of Jesus there was salvation before he had offered his atoning sacrifice, I do not find it hard to conceive that the foreseen demerits of sin may have cast the shadow of death over the ages, which preceded man's transgression. Of that we do not know much, nor is it important that we should; but certain is it that as far as this present creation is concerned death is not God's invited guest, but an intruder whose presence mars the feast." Charles Spurgeon, *Christ's Glorious Achievements* (Fearn, Ross-shire, Scotland: Christian Focus Publications, nd), p. 106–107. Also, although he believed in creation in six 24-hour days, and consistently ridiculed the theory of evolution, he accepted the gap theory. See David Harding, *C.H. Spurgeon on Creation and Evolution* (Leominster, England: Day One Publications, 2006), p. 13, 120–24.

106. Charles Spurgeon, "Exposition on Romans V" in *Spurgeon's Expository Encyclopedia*, 15 vols. (Grand Rapids, MI: Baker Book House, 1977 reprint), 8:218.

107. Ibid.

head; and in him death, which was the penalty of sin, was fulfilled to the letter."[108]

The real history of Adam as vital to the entire scheme of redemption comes through clearly again in a sermon entitled "The Wondrous Covenant." God's purpose for the world, which necessarily included redemption, pivoted on the historic reality of Adam and the initial requirement of obedience to a command. "The human race in the order of history, as far as this world is concerned, first stood in subjection to God under the Covenant of Works," Spurgeon declared. Then, building on his covenantal understanding of theology, he continued, "Adam was the representative man. A certain Law was given him. If he kept it, he and all his posterity would be blessed as the result of obedience. If he broke it, he would incur the curse, himself, and entail it on all represented by him." Our first father failed the test of obedience and "in his fall he involved us all, for we were all in his loins and he represented us before God. Our ruin, then, was complete before we were born!" Having been ruined by him who was our first representative, salvation "by the works of the Law is impossible, for under that Covenant we are already lost." Should rescue from the curse be possible it must now come by divine mercy, "interposed and provided" in another covenant made with "Christ Jesus, the Son of God, who is fitly called by the Apostle, 'the Second Adam,' because He stood again as the Representative of man." Since the perfect righteousness of the first covenant was not merely arbitrary, this second covenant was for our new representative also a "Covenant of Works quite as much as the other!" He honored all commandments out of a heart of love; he suffered every required penalty. He did "what the first Adam could not accomplish" and He reclaimed what Adam "forfeited by his transgression."[109]

In the sermon "God's First Words to the First Sinner," Spurgeon explored the implications embedded in the question, "Where are you?" After a summary of the historical event and its immediate effect upon Adam, Spurgeon investigated how Adam's response to God modeled the response of Adam's posterity. The text reveals "the alienation of the human heart from God, so that man shuns his Maker and does not desire fellowship with Him." That incongruous fact in itself "reveals, also, the folly which sin has caused. Sin made man a fool!" Created in the image of God and endowed with wisdom, true wisdom but obviously mutable, "now, since the trail of the serpent has passed over his nature, he has become an arrogant fool, for is not he a fool who would cover the nakedness of sin with fig leaves? Is not he indeed mad,"

108. Spurgeon, *Christ's Glorious Achievements*, p. 72.

109. Charles Spurgeon, *Metropolitan Tabernacle Pulpit*, Vol. 58 (Pasadena, TX: Pilgrim Publications, 1969, reprint of 1912 edition), p. 517–528.

Spurgeon continued the narrative, "who would hide from the omniscient Jehovah beneath the spreading branches of trees?" What strange darkness invaded the soul and mind of this first man! "Did not Adam know that God fills all space, and dwells everywhere, that from the highest heaven to the deepest hell there is nothing that is hid from His understanding?" He certainly had known it in his position of purity and knowledge, but now "so ignorant and stupid is he, that he hopes to escape from God, and make the trees of the garden a covert from the fiery eyes of divine wrath!" This spiritual condition has been passed down, for apart from this event, the universal manifestation of ignorance and rebellion of man searches in vain for explanation. "Ah, how foolish we are! How we repeat the folly of our first parent every day when we seek to hide sin from conscience, and then think it is hidden from God."[110] God's first question is not a prop for a parable, but a real event that revealed the noetic and spiritual devastation wrought by the sin of Adam extending to all generations after him.

Goodbye to Adam and All That Goes with Him

William Newton Clarke (1841–1911) sought an amalgamation of evolution with Christian theology. He worked at this with conviction during the 20-year bridge from 1890, when he became professor of theology at Colgate University, until his death in 1911. His book *Sixty Years With the Bible* described his movement from traditional conservatism to an exuberant, optimistic liberalism. He said, "I began, as a child must begin, with viewing the Bible in the manner of my father's day, but am ending with a view that was never possible until the large work of the Nineteenth Century upon the Bible had been done."[111]

His view of Scripture began its fall when the apparent contradiction between the Bible and modern geology challenged him. He concluded that the world of facts and the world of religion operated on different planes. The doctrine of a six-thousand-year-old earth "was forever irreconcilable with Geology and impossible of belief."[112] His rejection of infallibility crystallized when the doctrinal doubts that emerged from his personal study seemed justified by the discipline of historical criticism. He concluded that verbal inspiration was impossible and was puzzled that "any one ever took it seriously at all."[113]

110. Charles Spurgeon, "God's First Words to the First Sinner," *MTP*, 7 (1861): 514
111. William Newton Clarke, *Sixty Years With the Bible* (New York: Charles Scribner's Sons, 1909). p. 3.
112. Ibid., p. 27.
113. Ibid., p. 47.

His work on a doctrine of the atonement led him to believe that Peter, John, and Paul had irreconcilable presentations of the doctrine. In fact the entire Bible was flat, external, and unsatisfying on the issue. Rather than adopt the Apostles' propositions, he adopted their spirit and entered the spiritual stream of personal reflection on this topic in pursuit of his own view. He described this freedom from the text as "an impulse that I knew to be from God" leading him to grapple "with the prime moral facts of existence"[114] in the way that the biblical writers had done before him.

His thorough capitulation to higher criticism solved for him all the biblical tensions on the character of God, level of ethics, and legalism vs. spirituality. He testified, "The higher criticism removes the cause of the deepest of those moral difficulties," for it frees Christians to follow the God of Christ without accepting the "inferior moral light" attributed to the God of Israel. Jesus corrected all the errors with which the Old Testament is so larded so that the "Old Testament law itself was redeemed from its evil name by the help of the higher criticism."[115]

When Clarke reached this point, he became Professor of Christian Theology. Clarke was ready with his new method of theological interaction. He felt no need for discussion of biblical inspiration, other than to dismiss it, for it wielded no authority in ethical or doctrinal enquiry. His classroom became the place where his students learned to grasp the powers of their own inspiration. None could limit another's freedom by an established version of truth, for "orthodoxy is a human invention, not a divine, and God has never set it up as a barrier in the way of thought concerning divine realities."[116]

Through "trained spiritual reasonableness," the proper function of a Christian man is to know Christian truth when he sees it. The only true objective standard of Christianity is that which conforms to the "powers that are given us for discernment of truth." The spirit of Jesus Christ is the "real standard of what Christianity is, not subjective, and perfectly intelligible." We have no need of a standard "so unequivocal that it can be understood in only one way." In fact, "there can be none.[117]

How does all of this relate to our theme of Adam? This method of doing theology requires both a deconstructive and a reconstructive element in

114. Ibid., p. 116.
115. Ibid., p. 190.
116. Ibid., p. 225. He began in 1890 at Madison University, which became Colgate Theological Seminary.
117. William Newton Clarke, *The Use of the Scriptures in Theology* (New York, NY: Charles Scribner's Son, 1906), p. 74.

order to recreate an ostensibly Christian theology. Everything non-Christian (according to spiritual reasonableness) must be left behind; those aspects of biblical narrative that treat factual material better addressed by modern science must be "remanded" to those disciplines. No more should we be bothered by problems of "six days," the age of the earth through genealogical study, or the existence of Adam, why he sinned, and how his sin affects us. Rejecting these as valid questions for theology is a "wise and happy course" and "sets Christian theology in its rightful place in harmony with all sound knowledge."

To remand these questions to contemporary science means that theology will "receive from them an evolutionary answer" for the body and for the development of the higher powers of spirit and intellect. The evolutionary process testifies to God's presence in this universal method of development. The Genesis account presents a "human tradition or conception of beginnings" and is not a "literal narrative of occurrences." So, foe need not hope and friend need not fear that "Christianity must retire if the evolutionary idea gains entrance."[118]

In a series of four lectures on how a Christian should use Scripture in theology, Clarke gave a sharp and emphatic rejection of any usefulness of Scripture for understanding the origin of the world, man, or sin.

> We used to suppose that the first chapters of Genesis were witnesses concerning the manner in which the world and man were created, and, through connection with the time-record of the book, concerning the age of the world and mankind. But we have learned to understand these writings better, and now we know that they are not historical records, and bear no testimony as to the age of the world and man, or the manner of creation. If this testimony be omitted, the Scriptures contain no testimony on these subjects, and hand nothing over to theology concerning them. Theology needs a right conception of the human race, but does not obtain from the Bible an account of its origin, or the origin of the world. The facts must be learned from other sources. This is a case in which the Scriptures, rightly read, withdraw their contribution.
>
> More reluctantly but under equal necessity, theology begins to see that Genesis withdraws its contribution concerning the origin of human sin. The impossibility of maintaining the historical character

118. William Newton Clarke, *An Outline of Christian Theology* (New York, NY: Charles Scribner's Sons, 1922 [originally 1898]), p. 222–226.

> of the narrative is enough, for we are under the vow of honesty to use the Scriptures for what they are. We have no historical narrative of the beginning of sin, and theology receives from the Scriptures no record of that beginning. It is not enough that we admit this as a fact, we must use it as a fact; and that means that theology must account for sin, if at all, without the aid of such a narrative.[119]

In Clarke's theology, Adam is gone; his disobedience never happened; he has no connection, either natural or covenantal, with humanity in its present state; he has no influence on the development of theological ideas. The ethically elevated Christian conscience, evolutionary science, and the Bible as rearranged and purged by historical criticism must combine, according to Clarke's theological method, for whatever task theology presently can pursue.

First, the loss of Adam and his Fall meant a complete reinterpretation of the doctrine of sin. For Clarke, the doctrine of sin had to be developed purely through observation of the present condition of humanity along with assumptions from evolutionary science, comparative religion, ethnology, and an exalted sense of ethics and the mind of Christ. Though the Bible does not explain the origin of sin, as Clarke read it, common observation shows sin as "utterly appalling."[120] This universal and pervasive sense of sin arises from an axiomatic "oughtness" in men, a witness that "Man is created in the likeness of God's moral nature and responsibility, as well as in the likeness of his thinking, feeling, and willing."[121]

We are not to understand *created*, however, in the biblical sense of special creation but as a gradual evolution through the immanency of God in the entire process, producing God-awareness. No matter what produced him, "man is what he is today," Clarke opined, "and theories of his origin do not change the facts concerning him."[122]

We are not surprised, therefore, to find that Clarke conceived of the aboriginal expression of sin to be bound up in that mysterious transition from brute to human. "It is true," he proposed, "that man as we find him is struggling up from animalism to the full life of a spiritual being, and much of his sin is accounted for by the survival of the animalism that he is outgrowing." Sin comes, therefore, at the points where, "the nature that is akin to God yields to the nature that is common to man and beasts."[123]

119. Clarke, *Use of Scriptures*, p. 88–90.
120. Clarke, *Outline*, p. 227-230.
121. Ibid., p. 203–204.
122. Ibid., p. 223.
123. Ibid., p. 232.

Other cultural and personal factors contribute, but this factor fundamentally introduced sin into the race of humanity.

According to Clarke, therefore, never in the history of mankind has a time existed when he was holy, righteous, in unclouded fellowship with God, and conscious of the promise of eternal life. Nor is there an act of disobedience establishing guilt before God. "So the race was born with passions of animalism and self-will that were not sinful until the higher life of the spirit had become developed." His capitulation to naturalistic science and historical criticism depleted his version of Christianity of any explanation of the unity of the race and of the pervasiveness of sin.[124] Clarke reluctantly and with disappointment admitted that the progress of evolution had not ruled sin out of the race.

> All thoughtful observers know how disappointing human progress is. Old evils wear away; but the new and better conditions that follow develop new evils of their own, which in turn must be slowly and painfully overcome. Despite all changes, that central alienation of man from God and from his brothers in which sin consists has not come to an end. Its forms change, and the passing generations vary in their expressions of it, but it has never yet been abolished. God has indeed imparted a curative power to experience, but its working is slow, and the stream of life still flows a tainted stream.[125]

The ideal for man, therefore, lies only in the future and is seen in the incarnation of Christ. In this way, "Christ is represented as the second Adam, the head of a new and true humanity, more genuine than the historic humanity itself." With the acceptance of evolution, some suggested that Christianity would drop "the idea of incarnation." Clarke, explained, "the doctrine of evolution represents the stream of existence as continuous, each stage being the outcome of what has gone before it." To the Christian, this only illustrates "the steadiness of God's purpose" and the depth of the meaning of the "fullness of time." In a "slowly rising race," there is no fall, only progress and upward stumbles as we work, however slowly and falteringly, toward likeness to Christ.[126]

---

124. See his juxtaposition of the historic view and his evolution-driven view, ibid., p. 240–45. It is quite informative to contemplate the number of inconsistencies to which he must adapt in this phenomenon and to conclude that he has utterly failed in giving a satisfactory appraisal of the relation between evolution and the doggedness of "race-connection" in the continuity of sin from one generation to another.
125. Ibid., p. 243.
126. Ibid., p. 241f; 304–310.

Second, in addition to the necessity of redefining sin, when Adam did not fall, the doctrine of atonement and justification did. Paul's argument in Romans 5 must be rejected as sub-Christian for its dependence on a literal Adam and the unethical ideas of imputation of both sin and righteousness in the account of Christ's saving work.[127] Clarke rejected "changing of places" and imputation of sin or righteousness.[128] These concepts depend too much on Old Testament legalism and sacrifice and acceptance of the creation/fall narrative as actual history. "Old Testament matter found in the New Testament," Clarke reminded his readers, "is to be judged as to its relation to the Christian element just as we judge it in the Old Testament." Neither quoting it nor using it illustratively alters its impertinence.[129] No matter how literally Paul may accept the historical narrative or how profoundly he relates the death of Christ to the idea of substitution and propitiation, his use is below the Christian ideal and is to be relegated to irrelevance in Christian theology.

Clarke referred to Christ as "truly a new Head for mankind."[130] From 1 Corinthians 15 and Romans 5, Clarke argued that, "there has been a natural humanity, but now there is a spiritual humanity." Christ is "the second man" and also the "last Adam," thus the new head of humanity to be the "founder of a new humanity." The natural humanity bears "in one aspect the likeness of its earthly head, and in another it bears the likeness of God in spiritual constitution." Christ had none of the remnants of animalism and embodied true humanity in its unimpeded connection with the intent and righteousness of the Heavenly Father. Only in union with Him, therefore, do we finally rise to the originally intended position of sharing His "love of holiness, his hatred of sin, his acquaintance with the Heavenly Father, and his willingness to sacrifice self for the saving of others." This transformed internal life is what "God had in view throughout his long process of creation."[131] So how does this come about?

Even with humanity's original parentage — single or multiple — hidden from observation, Clarke still finds himself driven to refer to "the first man," and "the founder of humanity," and "its earthly head." The continued flow

---

127. Clarke's brief dismissal of these connections begins with the admission, "Christian theology, taking the third chapter of Genesis as authoritative history, has always held that man was created and began his career with such mental and moral endowments that he could justly be subjected to a decisive test of his virtue." *Outline*, p. 240.
128. Ibid., p. 333.
129. Clarke, *The Use of the Scriptures*, p. 120.
130. Clarke, *Outline*, p. 358.
131. Ibid., p. 359.

of corruption to all generations and to all peoples throughout the world does not arise from any covenantal headship; so, rightness with God involves no covenantal transactions, but must be explained in terms of God's purpose in the "long process of creation."

One of the commonly received doctrines that must go by the wayside, therefore, is that forgiveness is procured by the death of Christ through His receiving, in our stead, the punishment due us on account of our sins. Clarke looked upon such a doctrine as impossible and utterly unnecessary, as well as contradictory to the way of salvation through divine mercy and grace. If salvation truly is by grace, then substitution that involves punishment is impossible, for "the same sin cannot be both punished and forgiven." These two actions, punishing for sin and forgiving that sin, "cannot coexist in the same person." Even more incongruous morally would be his determination for "punishment of sin to be visited upon any one else than the one who has committed it." Punishment is absolutely non-transferable.[132] Jesus died for our sins only in the sense that His "holy and righteous love" must exhibit infinite patience in the face of resistance and rejection, which, to have full display, must come to "nothing short of death."[133]

Since forgiveness comes apart from fulfillment of the law, so does justification. Free grace nullifies the necessity of a merit according to perfect legal performance. Standing before God on the basis of merit "is not the true righteousness." The gospel is not merely a "veiled legalism."[134] To be saved, therefore, "is to be delivered from sin — that is, from sinning and the spirit that will sin — and brought to righteousness — that is, to the spirit that is right and will do right." Reconciliation is accomplished when men "come to think and feel with Christ." For that reason, "no man is reconciled to God except as he does come to think and feel essentially with Christ, nor can any man be completely saved except by becoming like him."[135]

Clarke believed that in dismissing Adam he ridded Christianity of a fatal embarrassment. An Anglican contemporary of Clarke, noting this pernicious courtesy in all of modernism, wrote, "The attempt of modernism to save the supernatural in the second part of the Bible by mythicalizing the supernatural in the first part, is as unwise as it is fatal."[136] What

132. Ibid., p. 330.
133. Ibid., p. 341, 343, 353.
134. Ibid., p. 336f.; 348.
135. Ibid., p. 355.
136. Dyson Hague, "Doctrinal Value of the First Chapters of Genesis," in *The Fundamentals,* 4 vols., ed. R.A. Torrey (Grand Rapids, MI: Baker Book House, 1972, reprint from 1917 Bible Institute of Los Angeles), 1:287.

Clarke achieved was not a genuinely renewed spirituality and deepened repentance, but an explanation of sin that removed its moral foundation. Instead of more profound and expansive knowledge of ultimate issues, he got a Bible that has nothing to say about the origin of the world, mankind, or sin. Instead of an objective narrative that reveals truth open to the investigation of all who will read, he left the Christian world with no more authority than the "spiritually sensitive" Christian conscience. Sin is little more than an ontological difficulty with a persistent irrational animalism. The Cross is devoid of any saving efficacy. The law requires neither obedience nor punishment. Grace is nothing more than compromised works-righteousness.

A Present Challenge

William Newton Clarke was more optimistic than he had a right to be. In trying to salvage a Christianity purified of myth and legend, with evolutionary thought as the purgative, he demonstrated that the task is impossible — the reconstruction becomes something entirely distinct, losing all the defining features of historic Christianity. Since Darwin's theory of natural selection seemed to give evolutionary theory a demonstrable mechanism, Christians have sought to find a way to interact with the growing dominance of evolutionary thought in the scientific community, even with all its many, and sometimes rapid, permutations.

Benjamin Breckenridge Warfield (1851–1921) personified this serious engagement. A pure evolutionist before age 30, Warfield rejected it in about 1880 in the prevailing form in which it stood at that time. By 1888 he had established a position of "critical agnosticism,"[137] in which he saw nothing finally convincing in any form of evolutionary theory so far proposed. His biting and insightful critiques of several of the forms that appeared in his lifetime would seem fully to eliminate the model as a Christian option in any sense. Any attempt to propagate non-teleological views of the development of the natural order he rejected as outright atheism, as pure prejudicial philosophy, and as alien to the legitimate interests of true science.[138] He also knew that Calvin believed in a six-day

---

137. Fred G. Zaspel, *The Theology of B.B. Warfield* (Wheaton, IL: Crossway, 2010), p. 386. This is Zaspel's summarizing phrase of Warfield. Zaspel engages with the theses of David Livingstone and Mark Noll and provides a needed nuancing, if not strictly a corrective, of their thesis of Warfield as an "evolutionist."

138. Benjamin Breckenridge Warfield, *Review of Darwinism Today* by Vernon Kellogg in *The Princeton Theological Review*, vi. (1908), p. 640–650, in *The Works of Benjamin B. Warfield*, 10 vols. (Grand Rapids, MI: Baker Book House, 1981 [reprint]), 10:79–90.

creation that happened about six thousand years ago.[139] Most importantly, he accepted the reality of Adam as the fountain of all humanity and as essential for the development of true Christian doctrine. In summary he stated that "the three-fold doctrine of imputation — of Adam's sin to his posterity, of the sins of His people to the Redeemer, and of the righteousness of Christ to His people — at last came to its rights as the core of the three constitutive doctrines of Christianity — the sinfulness of the human race, the satisfaction of Jesus Christ, and justification by faith." Imputation, a doctrine that requires the real historical Adam as the monogenetic origin of the race, was the hinge of these doctrines and the "guardian of their purity."[140] He remained open, however, to evidence. This evidence must show evolution to be sympathetic, not with mere theism, but with clearly articulated Christianity. One hesitates, however, to join Warfield's openness, for no form of evolution can be made to consist with a six-day creation and the intrusion of death as a result of the Fall.

In 1917, in a series of four volumes entitled *The Fundamentals,* a number of conservative Christian scholars challenged the attempt of liberalism to restructure virtually every point of the historical confessions. The articles were written by a diverse group of scholars, scientists, laymen, pastors, and professionals. Reverend Henry Beach wrote, "Darwinism degrades God and man," and lamented, "The teaching of Darwinism, as an approved science, to the children and youth of the schools of the world is the most deplorable feature of the whole wretched propaganda."[141] An anonymous "occupant of the pew" was amazed that so many Christian ministers adopted the philosophy of evolution and "were so ready to give up large portions of Holy Scripture because they could not be reconciled with it." Accordingly, the "story of creation as given in Genesis was set aside, and the whole book discredited." Massive theological denials and innovations followed in an effort to make room for an ever-changing and chronically unverified philosophy. Pointing to absurdities in the language and lack of objectivity in both Charles Darwin and Herbert Spencer, this writer observed that "it becomes evident to every intelligent layman that such a system can have no possible points of contact with Christianity."[142]

George Frederick Wright of Oberlin College pointed to the lack of demonstrability, the wildly differing attempts at explaining phenomena incompatible with the system, and the impossibility of overcoming the necessity of design. He concluded, "The evidence for evolution, even in its

139. Warfield, *Works*, 5:290, 292, 295.

140. Warfield, *Works*, 9:305.

141. Henry H. Beach, "The Decadence of Darwinism," *The Fundamentals*, 4: 64, 71.

142. *The Fundamentals*, 4:88, 89, 92.

milder form, does not begin to be as strong as that for the revelation of God in the Bible."[143]

Professor Charles B. Williams, a teacher of New Testament at the Southwestern Baptist Theological Seminary, wrote, "Paul testifies that sin entered our race in and through the disobedience of Adam." He found this testimony as the scriptural account of sin convincing doctrinally, for Paul actually focused on grace with Adam as incidental, a fact that "does not depreciate his testimony," but "makes it all the more trustworthy and convincing." Williams believed that Romans 5 made it impossible to reduce Adam to anything less than purely historical in light of the biblical teaching on sin and death. The "natural scientists" who say that man would have died even if Adam had never sinned have no scientific base, for the only man we know is the man fallen in Adam.[144] Williams was unintimidated by the attack on Adam and set forth simply and candidly his exegetical and theological confidence in the biblical narrative.

J.J. Reeve, a colleague of Williams, taught Old Testament and wrote an article, "My Experience with Higher Criticism," for *The Fundamentals.* Having given himself to that method early in his academic career, he soon discovered its flaws as a system of thought and its intrinsic antagonism to revealed truth, specifically the Christian faith. Reeve examined the *presuppositions* of the higher criticism, its *methods*, its *spirit*, and its *result.* At every point, Reeve found the higher criticism indefensible, both from objective standards of research and from the hostile posture the discipline took toward the content of its subject matter. It was not the biblical record, Reeve discovered, that was invented and falsified, but "the critics who were the inventors and falsifiers." Not the biblical writers but the critics manufactured history "to suit their theories and were doing so fast and loose." The movement fundamentally was "anti-supernatural and anti-miraculous," having accepted "a naturalistic evolution which is fundamentally contradictory to the Biblical and Christian point of view." Most vulnerable, therefore, to their bias was the narrative of Genesis 1–11, for "no theory of naturalistic evolution can possibly admit the truth of these chapters."[145]

None of the 80 articles of *The Fundamentals* is more foundational to the entire project than the article entitled "The Doctrinal Value of the First Chapters of Genesis," by Dyson Hague, a professor of liturgics at Wycliffe College in Toronto. In these chapters we confront the naked fact of divine

143. George Frederick Wright, "The Passing of Evolution," *The Fundamentals*, 4:72–87.

144. Charles B. Williams, "Paul's Testimony to the Doctrine of Sin," in *The Fundamentals,* 3:30, 37.

145. J.J. Reeve, "My Personal Experience with the Higher Criticism," in *The Fundamentals,* 1:350, 353, 355,

revelation and our dependence on it, the being and power of God, the origin of the universe, the creation of man, the origin of the soul, the introduction of sin, the promise of salvation, the division of languages and of the human race, the reality and perverse intentions of Satan, the stream of electing mercy, and the cause of death and corruption. "In this inspired volume of beginnings," Hague pronounced, "we have the satisfactory explanation of all the sin and misery and contradiction now in this world, and the reason of the scheme of redemption." Inextricable from these doctrines is the reality that "Adam was not a myth, or an ethnic name," but "a veritable man, made by God." On the credibility of that historical narrative stands the entire veracity of the Christian faith. Hague explained with a cogency and rhetorical earnestness that will bring to summation the contention of this chapter.

> With regard to our redemption, the third chapter of Genesis is the basis of all Soteriology. If there was no fall, there was no condemnation, no separation and no need of reconciliation. If there was no need of reconciliation, there was no need of redemption; and if there was no need of redemption, the Incarnation was a superfluity, and the crucifixion folly (Gal. 3:21). So closely does the apostle link the fall of Adam and the death of Christ, that without Adam's fall the science of theology is evacuated of its most salient feature, the atonement. If the first Adam was not made a living soul and fell, there was no reason for the work of the Second Man, the Lord from heaven. The rejection of the Genesis story as a myth, tends to the rejection of the Gospel of salvation. One of the chief corner stones of the Christian doctrine is removed, if the historical reality of Adam and Eve is abandoned, for the fall will ever remain as the starting point of special revelation, of salvation by grace, and of the need of personal regeneration. In it lies the germ of the entire apostolic Gospel.[146]

146. Dyson Hague, "The Doctrinal Value of the First Chapters of Genesis," *The Fundamentals,* 1:272–273, 282, 285. Hague mentions that the Noahic prediction of the future traits of the descendants of his three sons "was foretold in Genesis four thousand years ago" (p. 286). He does not, however, say how long ago Adam was created or how old the rest of creation is.

Chapter 4

"Where Are You, Adam?" The Disappearance of Adam and the Death of Truth

by Dr. Eugene H. Merrill

First, an Illustration from Personal Experience

A few years ago, the author was invited to a Christian university to serve as an impartial outsider on an investigative committee to determine if a professor of Bible at the school had violated the institution's statement of faith in a recent work he had published. I read it carefully with statement in hand and determined at once that he was well outside the boundaries of the document he had signed declaring his commitment to its affirmations. In the course of the proceedings I asked him about his doubts as to the historicity of Genesis 1–11. He admitted that he did not view those chapters as historical texts in the "normal" sense of the term, whereupon I asked him about the historicity of Abraham and the following patriarchs. What line could he draw and where between the "historical" and the "a-historical"? Why should Genesis 11 be construed as doubtful, whereas chapters 12 and following could be confessed as historical? He then made clear that he had strong doubts even about the historicity of Abraham and the patriarchs and that, in fact, not much in Genesis should be considered as historiography because its purpose was "theological" and not "historical." Finally, I cut to the chase and inquired as to whether he accepted the historicity of the virgin birth, blood atonement, Resurrection, ascension, and Second Coming of Jesus Christ. He seemed taken aback by the question and replied that he, of course, believed all that and more. When pressed as to his change of stance regarding these New Testament affirmations as compared to those of the Old Testament, he said he had to believe the testimony of the Gospels about Jesus and the miracles associated with His person and work because "they are essential to the Christian faith." His point was that "necessary" parts of the Bible must be true, but the rest is up for grabs. This may seem naïve, but this kind of utilitarian skepticism is illustrative of what has become all too common in some quarters of contemporary evangelicalism, whether in lay or scholarly circles.

Introduction

The first interrogation in the Bible is the haunting question asked of man and woman by God in the garden of Eden, one expressed by a single word in the Hebrew Bible, אַיֶּכָּה, "Where are you?" (Gen. 3:9).[1] The utter simplicity of the query almost obscures the profundity of its full existential and theological implications. Obviously, this was not the frantic cry of a parent whose child has wandered off, for the Father here knows full well the answer to His own question. Rather, it was a question, the self-condemnatory answer to which the primeval pair must respond. They had not gone anywhere in a locative sense, a fact of which they knew the omniscient Creator God was well aware. He had something else in mind, then, and that could only be, "Where have you gone in relation to the fellowship we have hitherto enjoyed? Where are you in reference to the Great Commission I entrusted to you as fountainhead of the human race created as my image-bearer and where are you as regards the probationary test with which I challenged you, namely, the prohibition to eat of the forbidden tree?"

Adam's feeble response was that he hid from Yahweh because he saw for the first time that he was naked (Gen. 3:10), a condition that was purely physical here, but to Yahweh and even to Adam it was an admission of a terrible baring of the soul, a nudity that shamed and embarrassed him for it spoke of broken fellowship, of the opening of a great chasm between himself and God that could not be bridged because his nakedness stood in sharp contrast to and in conflict with the garments of holiness with which the Almighty Himself is appareled (2 Chron. 6:41; Ps. 93:1, 104:1; Isa. 6:1, 63:1).[2] He did well to be afraid, because he had committed grievous sin and, with his mate, had fallen into a pit of utter aloneness, despair, and helplessness. He had heard Yahweh walking

1. Unless otherwise noted, Scripture in this chapter is from the New International Version (NIV) of the Bible.
2. The Hebrew עֵירֹם ("naked, undressed") is often associated with guilty shame or wickedness in the OT (Gen. 9:23; Hos. 2:5; Isa. 47:3; Eccles. 1:8; Ezek. 16:7, passim; 23:10, 18, 29; Nah. 3:5; Hab. 2:15).

about in the garden, treading under foot as it were the whole creation over which He was sovereign and which He had designed for man to tread with Him as His vice-regent (Gen. 1:26–28).[3] That now could not be done; in fact, he must be evicted from the garden, consigned to a life of pain and back-breaking labor, enslaved, as it were, to the very soil he had been created to work and to oversee (Gen. 3:16–19), and now to which he would be consigned in death.

The narratives of Genesis 1–11 on their very surface are clear and plain. Their object is to explain in the simplest way possible for any reader to understand, regardless of race or culture or education level, how the human condition came to be and what measures God will take to ameliorate and at last overcome the awesome separation between God and His image that man's own sin has engendered. Through the more than 3,000 years since the composition of the stories and untold ages before that in which they may have existed orally, the narratives have been understood as reliable, historical accounts of beginnings, including the beginning of the fall and its aftermath. Only with the advent of the so-called Enlightenment of the 17th century and its continuing influence to the present day have the stories been dismissed as etiologies or myths.[4] Hence, any suggestion that it relates sober history in the finest form of historiography ensures that the proponent of that viewpoint

3. For the verb הָלַךְ as a term connoting sovereignty and submission in the Hithpael (הִתְהַלֵּךְ), see Eugene H. Merrill, "'Footnotes' in the Old Testament: A Study of the Verb 'To Walk,'" forthcoming, and the many examples given there.

4. "Etiology" refers to the explanation of or accounting for how and why present conditions or circumstances exist as they do. The term is commonly used in medicine to trace the history of a given presentation in the hope of offering appropriate treatment. In historical or sociological settings (as here), an etiology is a story about the past that best explains why things are as they are in the present. Often the etiological story is labeled "myth," not in the sense of a fairy tale or the like, but as a rational attempt to understand present realities. For a helpful survey of the development of studies on Israelite historiography in general since Gunkel and Gressmann and its inter-connection with the historical-critical method and the Old Testament, see John Van Seters, *In Search of History* (New Haven: Yale University Press, 1983), p. 209–248. Van Seters' own understanding of the Old Testament as history and any people's history in general is that "it arises out of a legend whose focus is upon the public figure, as in *Heldensagen*, but the political events themselves and not preformed *Märchen*-like episodes are seen as providing the story (p. 211)." One can see here a developmental scheme in which the Patriarchs (the *Helden*) are actors in a great drama around which mythical or legendary historical events occurred, including, of course, an Adam-figure. See also Julius Wellhausen, *Prolegomena to the History of Ancient Israel* (Cleveland: World, 1965 [1878]). He says of the Genesis history, "it [early history] could not have begun with the patriarchs and gone on to the kings, it must have begun with the kings and then gone up higher to the patriarchs; it must have begun at the lower end, where alone it had any firm ground to stand on" (p. 309). Thus spoke the shaper of the historical-critical method in whom modern skeptics find a "father-figure" in their cynical stance relative to Old Testament early history.

will be considered out of touch with the "assured results" of modern scholarship and, worse still, fundamentalist in his unstudied naiveté.[5]

Premise of This Essay

The premise of this essay is that the story of the creation of an original pair, whose purpose was to reign under the sovereignty of God over all creation but who lost that privilege because they yielded to temptation, meets all the criteria of reliable reportage and, more important, coincides with a holistic biblical theology of the entire revelation of God in both Old and New Testaments. The following sub-premises underlie the concerns of this study:

- The matter of sin and fallen-ness is so dominant a theme in the Bible, it is impossible to suppose that the Bible would supply no historically reliable account of how it came about; i.e., every observable effect must have a reliably documented cause.
- Attention to the societal, moral, and spiritual devastation of humankind demands that its causation be addressed in no uncertain terms so as to understand and justify the remedies to it, which the Bible outlines in both Testaments.
- The inordinate prevalence of biblical genealogies, and the extent to which their authors are careful to trace the biological and societal lines of nations, tribes, clans, families, and even individuals, constitutes strong evidence that they are to be taken as reliable witnesses to the past, even to the beginning. In some cases, the genealogies either begin or end with Adam, as though he were as much a literal, historical figure as were any other of the men and women listed subsequently.
- The role played by Adam as the father of both humankind and human failure is a major New Testament theme. The New Testament displays no evidence of doubt regarding the historicity of either Adam or the events surrounding him. Jesus and the Apostles clearly were of that mind.
- The plea that the primeval stories of Genesis cannot be read as history in the ordinary sense, but rather as sagas, legends, etiologies, myths, or anything else other than history is, in the final analysis, a special pleading designed to minimize the "surreal" aspects of persons and events for which there are no other historical analogues or parallels, but only those of ancient Near Eastern exemplars universally

5. See Herbert H. Klemment, "Modern Literary-Critical Methods and the Historicity of the Old Testament," *Israel's Past in Present Research*, SBST 7, ed. V. Philips Long (Winona Lake, IN: Eisenbrauns, 1999), p. 439–459.

construed as a-historical. The argument that human experience in the here and now is the touchstone by which events of the ancient past must be tested as to their historical veracity is unscientific and, worse still, dangerous to the notion of the historical integrity of Scripture and thus its character as the divinely inspired witness to the person and acts of God.

Current Trends vis-à-vis the Historicity of Adam

Evangelical scholars who at one time spoke and wrote confidently of the historicity of Adam are now questioning this viewpoint (for reasons known perhaps only to themselves) in favor of positions that range anywhere from a blunt, unqualified denial of Adam's reality to a hedging on the matter.[6] Their shift in understanding may be attributed to (1) new readings of the texts engendered by an almost faddish attention to literary genres that insist on reading these texts form-critically and rhetorically as a-historical and as myth or legend, and to do so in light of comparisons to similar themes and literatures of the ancient Near East — not as texts written indigenously in Israel;[7] and (2) new methods of rendering the past such as the so-called "Copenhagen" and "Annales" schools. The former subordinates the biblical text to archaeological data and the latter to the social sciences.[8] Evangelicals

6. See, among others, Denis O. Lamoureux, "No Historical Adam: Evolutionary Creation View," in *Four Views on The Historical Adam*, eds. Matthew Barrett and Ardel B. Caneday (Grand Rapids: Zondervan, 2013), p. 58 ("since ancient science does not align with physical reality, it follows that Adam never existed."); Gregory A. Boyd, "Whether or not There Was a Historical Adam Our Faith Is Secure," in *The Historical Adam*, p. 265 ("one could in principle affirm the message of what Jesus and Paul say about Adam while yet denying that he was the first actual human"); Kenton L. Sparks, "Genesis 1–11 as Ancient Historiography," in *Genesis: History, Fiction, or Neither?* ed. Charles Halton (Grand Rapids: Zondervan, 2015), p. 111 ("one thing that [the early chapters of Genesis] certainly do not offer [is] a literal account of events that actually happened prior to and during the early history of humanity."); Johnny V. Miller and John M. Soden, *In the Beginning . . . We Misunderstood* (Grand Rapids: Kregel, 2012), p. 40 ("[The Bible] is not revealing the science of creation. Instead, it is revealing the Creator of science, albeit in a pre-scientific way).")

7. Brettler attributes these shifts in attitude to three modern developments: (1) an emphasis on social rather than political history; (2) the rise of rhetoric in general (and biblical) history; and (3) the drive to study the Bible as literature rather than history. Mark Zvi Brettler, "The New Biblical Historiography," in *Israel's Past in Present Research: Essays on Ancient Israelite Historiography*, SBTS 7 ed. V. Philips Long (Winona Lake, IN: Eisenbrauns, 1999), p. 48–49. For examples of some who embrace this school of thought in evangelical scholarship, see *Faith, Tradition, and History*, eds. A.R. Millard, J.K. Hoffmeier, and D.W. Baker (Winona Lake, IN: Eisenbrauns, 1994).

8. For a brilliant assessment of these trends, see Jens Bruun Koefed, "Epistemology, Historiographical Method, and the 'Copenhagen School,' " in *Windows into Old Testament History*, eds. V. Philips Long, David W. Baker, and Gordon J. Wenham (Grand Rapids, MI: Eerdmans, 2002), p. 23–43.

who have bought into some or all of these new alleged avenues to Israel's past are, at the same time, quick to assert that the Scriptures are inerrant inasmuch as their authors and/or redactors were led by the Spirit to adopt and adapt such concepts as the creation traditions of Israel's neighbors, or to imagine that the biblical writers could and did employ some creative imagination (hopefully also Spirit-driven) to compose accounts quite at odds with reality as seen in the modern "scientific" evidence.[9] Thus, the vehicle of the great truths of creation, a first family, and the fall of humankind are preserved, but in a dressing of myth or legend that may or may not pass the test of historiography as normally defined. Richard E. Averbeck, representative of the "quasi-historical" school of thought, puts it this way: "From the perspective of Israelites in the process of forming their nation in Canaan, the account of the Conquest and Settlement is the contemporary history, the history of Israel in Egypt and the Exodus would be the previous history, the legendary history would be that of the patriarchs, and Genesis 1–11 would be the mythic history."[10] To the contrary and in the same volume, Alan Millard speaks of these records as unqualified "history": "Israelite history cannot be fully comprehended without knowledge of her faith nor can her faith be understood without a realistic portrayal of her history."[11] To this we heartily assent.

A number of preliminary objections can be raised against comparative methodologies that either deny altogether any similarities between ancient Israelite and ancient pagan notions of the nature of history and its recital or overstate them to the point that the whole definition of history vis-à-vis Israel must be changed to something short of objective factuality. These objections clearly apply to the topic at hand: Adam: history or legend?

1. As the earlier chapters by Barrick and Croteau and Naylor demonstrate, nowhere does the record of the Old or New Testaments suggest the slightest hint of disbelief in the reality of a historical Adam.[12]
2. To the contrary, Adam's historicity is affirmed many times as necessary to theological arguments, implicit and explicit, in sacred history and

---

9. Miller and Soden, *In the Beginning . . . We Misunderstood.* Speaking of Moses they write, "Genesis 1 in its original language and setting leads us to conclude that it is a broadly figurative presentation of literal truths" (p. 48) and "[Moses] leaves intact a completely different view of the universe that is scientifically incorrect" (p. 160).
10. Millard, et al., "The Sumerian Historiographic Tradition," p. 98–99.
11. Millard, et al., "Story, History, and Theology," p. 64.
12. Gerhard Maier observes that "ancient Jewish and New Testament exegesis knows no diastasis of truth and reality in the Old Testament texts." [Rather,] "it brooks no doubt that Old Testament history took place in the very sequence and form of the events that are portrayed for us in the Old Testament." Maier, "Truth and Reality in the Historical Understanding of the Old Testament," *Israel's Past in Present Research*, p. 201.

in particular to the problem of sin, the Fall, and redemption (Gen. 2:20; 1 Chron. 1:1; Hos. 6:7; Luke 3:38; Rom. 5:14; 1 Cor.15:22, 45; 1 Tim. 2:13, 14; Jude 14).

3. The denial of the historicity of Adam leads logically and naturally, if not necessarily, to a skeptical view of the integrity of subsequent narratives. What is to be made of the Flood narrative (Gen. 6–8), that of the assumption of Enoch to heaven (Gen. 5:21–24), of the story of the Tower of Babel (Gen. 11:1–9)? Can anything at all in Genesis be taken at face value?
4. Those kinds of questions are generally answered more in the affirmative when the magic line between Genesis 11 and Genesis 12 is crossed. Now, we're told, we're on the solid ground of historical reality attestable from Sumerian, Akkadian, and Egyptian written documentation. Now the supernatural has given way to the natural, and the miraculous to the scientifically credible. But on what grounds can the divide between chapters become the Maginot Line between two quite different, even opposing, worlds of thought?[13] Is it because the patriarchal stories have the "feel" of reality or the perception that what happened after 2000 B.C. is more like what we know about the world 4,000 years later? The subjectivity of such a way of evaluating matters of history has no place in solid scholarship.[14] One's uninformed emotional reaction to an account renders it neither believable nor unbelievable. Besides all this, the pesky problem of miracles in the Old Testament by the score as late as the time of Daniel (ca. 530 B.C.), followed by an explosion of the supernatural throughout the New Testament era, keeps plaguing the secularist whose credibility loses ground with every miracle explained away.[15]

---

13. "Maginot Line" refers to the defensive positions constructed by the French against looming German threats of invasion in World War II.
14. See the fine objection to this putative division by James K. Hoffmeier, "Genesis 1–11 as History and Theology," in *Genesis: History, Fiction, or Neither*, ed. Charles Halton (Grand Rapids: Zondervan, 2015), p. 24–25.
15. In his classic work on the subject, Herbert Lockyear counts at least 148 miracles in the Bible. See his *All the Miracles of the Bible* (Grand Rapids: Zondervan, 1961). Among other matters of note to begin with, (1) the Pentateuch and the Gospels have about the same number of recorded miracles, 45 and 48 respectively. Since the Gospels are ca.60% of the length of the Pentateuch, the density of miracles is greater in the Gospels. (2) The greatest concentration of miracles in the Bible occurs in Genesis (13) and Exodus (23), mostly in connection with the Exodus), the ministries of Elijah and Elisha (ca. 21), and the ministry of Jesus (ca. 38) and the Apostles (ca. 21) in the first century. Both the Pentateuch and the Gospels speak of Beginnings, the one of the age of Adam and other of the age of the Second Adam. Surely both are needed to complete the symmetry. The miracles of Exodus

5. The non-historical Adam is set in such juxtaposition to the historical Jesus in the New Testament that one can hardly believe in the historical reality of one without believing it of the other. It makes little literary, logical, and theological sense to say that "as in the (mythical) Adam all died, so in the (historical) Christ shall all be made alive." The same Bible that speaks of the reality of the man-God Jesus Christ speaks similarly of the God-image Adam (see Appendix to this chapter).

Assumptions as to the Reality of an Historical Adam and Evidence in Their Support

The Genesis (and following biblical) accounts concerning Adam are intended to be taken prima facie as historical in genre and purpose.

The question of what kind of recollections, reflections, and written discourses about the past constitute historiography in both form and intent is extremely complicated. What are the criteria to which it must conform in order to be judged history writing in the truest sense?[16] From a negative stance, the radical New Testament scholar D.R. Strauss offered two

---

herald the creation of a new people; those of Kings the preparation of a line of prophets to announce a new creation; those miracles of the Gospels a new and sovereign Adam; and those of the Acts a new manifestation of the people of the Kingdom.

The following lists of biblical miracles are not exhaustive, but they are extensive enough to demonstrate the utterly supernatural character of the Bible from cover to cover. The *Pentateuch*: creation, Enoch's translation, the Flood, confusion of tongues, Sarah's conception, destruction of Sodom and Gomorrah, the burning bush, the rod of Moses, the Plagues, crossing of the Red Sea, the manna, Miriam's leprosy, bronze serpent, Balaam's donkey; *Historical books*: crossing the Jordan, destruction of Jericho, sun "standing still," Elijah's being fed by ravens, the meal and oil, contest at Carmel, fire from heaven, Elijah's translation, the widow's oil, the poisoned pottage, Gehazi's leprosy, floating iron, Uzziah's leprosy, slaughter of Assyrian army, Hezekiah's healing; *Poetry*: no narrative of miracle; *Prophecy*: the fiery furnace, handwriting on the wall, lions' den, the great fish, the sheltering gourd; *Gospels*: virgin birth, water into wine, healing of nobleman's son, impotent man, great haul of fish, healing of demoniac, healing of Peter's mother-in-law, cleansing of the leper, healing of the paralytic, the centurion's servant, raising of the widow's son, stilling of the storm, healing of Jairus' daughter, feeding the 5,000, walking on the water, healing of the blind, the Transfiguration, the coin in the fish's mouth, man born blind, Lazarus' resuscitation, ten lepers, the fig tree, Jesus' resurrection; *The Book of Acts*: the ascension of Jesus, Pentecost, the lame man, Ananias and Sapphira, opened prison doors, Saul's conversion, raising of Dorcas, Peter's deliverance from prison, Eutychus' resuscitation, Publius' father; *The Epistles*: no narratives of miracles; *The Apocalypse*: countless miracles to come.

16. The comment of Ernst Breisach with respect to the difficulty of rightly construing the past is heuristic: "Once the link between history writing and the human condition is grasped in all its complexity, simple solutions vanish." *Historiography: Ancient, Medieval, and Modern*, 2nd Edition (Chicago: The University of Chicago Press, 1994), p. 4.

such standards: A composition is non-historical if it (1) claims authenticity for the supernatural and (2) fails the tests of internal self-consistency and external non-contradiction.[17] Alan Millard is helpful in his more positive observation that "the witness of the text itself should take pride of place until unassailable cases can be made against it." He continues by noting with regard to biblical texts that "modern scholarship has shown too critical and too skeptical a mind. If some refuse to accord to Genesis . . . the common privilege of the accused in British law, 'innocent until proven guilty,' the converse of that maxim should be vigorously opposed."[18] In another publication on this matter, I have denoted the following seven traits or attributes of historical narrative and likewise seven features that should not disqualify a document as history writing.[19]

The very nature of the Old (and New) Testament as a meta-narrative with a beginning, progression, climax, dénouement, and conclusion presupposes either that everything in it is historically reliable or nothing in it can make that claim with confidence.

Scholars who assert, for example, that they are stalwart Evangelicals who hold fast to the essentials of the Christian faith, such as the virginal conception and birth of Jesus, His sinless life, His miracles, His atoning death on a Cross, His triumphant Resurrection from the dead, and His bodily ascension to heaven (all of which originate in narratives), but deny the historicity of other events prior to and preparatory of these indispensable doctrines

---

17. Cited by V. Philips Long, *The Art of Biblical History* (Grand Rapids: Zondervan, 1994), p. 110–111.
18. A.R. Millard, "Methods of Studying the Patriarchal Narratives as Ancient Texts," *Essays on the Patriarchal Narratives*, eds. A.R. Millard and D.J. Wiseman (Winona Lake, IN: Eisenbrauns, 1983), p. 40–41. For an excellent analysis of the state of modern (or post-modern) scholarship in general and its stubborn resistance to the idea of a historically reliable Hebrew Bible, see Iain W. Provan, "In the Stable with the Dwarves: Testimony, Interpretation, Faith, and the History of Israel," *Windows into Old Testament History*, eds. V. Philips Long, David E. Baker, and Gordon J. Wenham (Grand Rapids: Eerdmans, 2002), p. 162–164.
19. Eugene H. Merrill, "Genesis 1—11 as Literal History," in *The Genesis Factor: Myths and Realities*, ed. Ron J. Bigalke, Jr. (Green Forest, AR: Master Books, 2008), p. 77–82. See also my "Old Testament History: A Theological Perspective," in *A Guide to Old Testament Theology and Exegesis*, ed. Willem A. VanGemeren (Grand Rapids, MI: Zondervan, 1997), p. 65–82. *Qualifying Criteria* are (a) usually narrative; (b) person and event centered; (c) purposeful, entelic; (d) coherent; (e) self-consistent, non-contradictory; (f) focused; (g) interpretive, not only "brute facts"; *non-disqualifying criteria* are (a) the supernatural, that is, manifestations of God in theophany or epiphany; (b) the miraculous, events or acts contrary to human experience and capability; (c) uniqueness of an event; (d) antiquity of the text recounting the event; (e) religious or theological content; (f) selectivity of content; (g) non-narratival texts such as genealogies.

are committing intellectual and spiritual suicide.[20] The dangerous illogic of positing that one can pick and choose this or that link in the chain of sacred history and reject those that seem to defy scientific rationality or that "just seem too hard to believe" is all too characteristic of those today who want to have their cake of evangelical identity but "eat it too" by disallowing the credibility of its foundational assertions such as the subject of our present concern, the historicity of Adam and of the Adam narratives.

The logical corollary to the previous point is that the story of Adam is a historical account of a historical individual inasmuch as it is embedded in a network or matrix of meta-narrative that is so tightly bound together that to unravel one thread is to unravel the whole eventually and to leave it absurd, powerless, and irrelevant.

With these preliminaries in mind, the task now is to examine the Scriptures to see "whether these things [about Adam] are so" (Acts 17:11).

Supporting Evidence for the Historicity of Adam

The following case will be made from two perspectives, the literary-exegetical and the theological, with the recognition that the two may sometimes overlap or become mutually supportive.

"Adam" in Literary-Exegetical Texts

The Hebrew term אָדָם (*adam*), apart from its meaning "man," "mankind," and the like, occurs 12 times in the Hebrew Bible (Gen. 2:20; 3:17, 20, 21; 4:1, 25; 5:1, 3, 4, 5; 1 Chron. 1:4; Hosea 6:7) and the Greek equivalent Ἀδάμ (*adam*) occurs nine times in the New Testament (Luke 3:38; Rom. 5:14 (2x); 1 Cor. 15:22, 45 (2x); 1 Tim. 2:13, 14; Jude 14). Of the 21 occurrences in the Bible, 8 are in genealogies, 8 in commentary or theologizing passages, and the remaining 5 in narratives. The procedure here is to consider first the literary perspective with the categories of narrative and genealogy. As to the former, it is limited in the Old Testament to the first five chapters of Genesis in which are found Adam's naming of the animal world (2:20), his sin (3:17, 20, 21), and his fathering of sons (4:1, 25). Genealogies with his name appear in only Genesis 5:1–4 (4x) and 1 Chronicles 1:4.

20. Thus, e.g., Kenton Sparks, who testifies, "While I am myself an evangelical, and understand this strong impulse [to deny the Bible has errors so that its inerrancy is thereby questioned], I don't believe that the Bible's status as the Word of God places any necessary limitation on the range of generic possibilities." in *Genesis: History, Fiction, or Neither?* p. 115–116. Finally, a moderate stance is assumed by Gordon J. Wenham, who prefers for Genesis 1–11 the label "proto-history" as opposed to "history," a subtlety not to be ignored, in *Genesis: History, Fiction, or Neither?* p. 85.

Not one New Testament passage can be construed as an Adam narrative. The name appears in one full genealogy (Luke 3:38) and once in what might be called a truncated genealogy (Jude 14). The remaining citations fall under the category of theological discourse.

"Adam" in Theological Texts

Just a single passage in Genesis "theologizes" Adam's behavior, one that is embedded in narrative, namely, Genesis 3:1–24. Likewise, only a single passage elsewhere in the Old Testament refers to Adam theologically, the disputatious in Hosea 6:7.[21]

As just noted above, Adam is mentioned in the New Testament almost exclusively in theological contexts, just the obverse of the evidence from the Old Testament. The ratios are instructive: The theological references to Adam in the Old Testament make up at best 33 percent of the total references to the patriarch; in the New Testament the Apostles allude to Adam theologically 89 percent of the time. As for the genealogies, two with reference to Adam are Old Testament and one is New Testament. An interpretation and application of these data follow presently.

For now it is sufficient to posit the following: the Old Testament provides the accounts of the human progenitor and his Fall; the New Testament draws from these narratives appropriate theological interpretations and conclusions. We will argue that an incongruity of enormous proportions results from attempting to erect the structure of the gospel message of redemption and reconciliation of the race on the quicksands of a non-existing man and an unhistorical narrative that, to the Apostles, necessitated the saving work of God in Christ in the first place.

---

21. The complication lies in the inseparable preposition כְּ of the Masoretic text ('like, as') instead of the expected בְּ ('in'). However, "like Adam" (rather than "in Adam") is the better reading since it (1) is the more difficult and therefore most likely original, (2) makes sense in the context of God's intention for man that he should have dominion in God's place (Gen. 1:28), and (3) is more likely given the probable lateness of the idea of sinning "in Adam." However, as many scholars have argued, the ב can also bear the meaning "as" as well as "in" (thus E. Kautzsh and A.E. Cowley, eds., *Gesenius' Hebrew Grammar*, 2nd English ed. (Oxford, England: Clarendon, 1957), §119i. On the other hand, "in Adam" could also be understood as a reference to the place name Adam, a site located in the upper Jordan Valley (Josh. 3:16), a rendering that has the support of the following adverb "there." Nevertheless, on balance "like Adam" seems best, especially if "Adam" is understood as *adam*, "man," or "a man." See Hans Walter Wolff, *Hosea, Hermeneia* (Philadelphia, PA: Fortress.1974), p. 105; for the view that the prophet is speaking of Adam and original sin, see Richard D. Patterson, *Hosea, An Exegetical Commentary* (Richardson, TX: Biblical Studies Press, 2008), p. 72.

The OT Narratives Surrounding Adam

The stories of Adam and Eve suffer from such a surfeit of familiarity to the average reader that they are seldom dissected and read critically as historical and theological episodes that need repetitive "deep" re-reading lest their very familiarity should breed contempt. The following is an attempt to offer a reading that is friendly (1) to the notion that they are, until proven otherwise, intentional attempts to recount "actual" history and (2) to the proposition that their narratives are invested with theological insights demonstrably at home in the New Testament and in pre-critical Jewish and Christian scholarly tradition.

First, the delimitations of the Adam narratives *per se* and their differentiation from contextual narratives in their support must be clarified. For example, virtually everything related in the first five chapters of Genesis could be said to constitute the context of the specifically Adam stories, as seen in the graph:

Table 1: Analysis of the Adam Narratives[22]

Textual Boundaries	Contextual Boundaries	Episodic Boundaries*	Epicentric Narrative**
Gen. 1:1–4:26	1:1–2:4a	1:26–28	
	2:4b–25	2:7–17; 18–25	2:20–25
	3:1–24	3:1–7; 8–21, 22–24	3:17–21
	4:1–24	4:1–15a, 15b–24	4:1–2
	4:25–26	4:25–26	4:25–26

* "Episodic" denotes the beginnings and endings of discrete literary units within longer narratives.

** "Epicentric" refers to the key or central idea in each of the episodes. In the first instance, the making of the man (2:7–17) and the function of the man (2:18–25) focus on the term "man." The same is true of the following three instances.

For the purpose of this paper, the accounts of creation in Genesis 1:1–2:3 and of 2:4–17 are of only marginal relevance since they do not speak of Adam by name and therefore have nothing to do with his historicity. However, "the man" (הָאָדָם) occurs 10 times in Genesis 1:1–2:20, at which point he is identified not generically but a proper name, that is, no longer as a mere *Homo sapiens* but a specific individual (אָדָם) mentioned 6 times in the

22. George W. Coats, *Genesis: With an Introduction to Narrative Literature*, FOTL I (Grand Rapids: Eerdmans, 1983), p. 41–69; for a more extended analysis of this kind, see Robert D. Bergen, "Word Distribution as an Indicator of Authorial Intention: A Study of Genesis 1:1–2:3," in *Do Historical Matters Matter to Faith?* eds. James K. Hoffmeier and Dennis R. Magary (Wheaton, IL: Crossway, 2012), p. 201–218.

narratives of 2:20–4:25. In addition, the generic הָאָדָם continues alongside אָדָם in 12 more instances where Adam is clearly the referent. Once more, it may be helpful to ponder a few points regarding the historicity of the record:

1. Since the Adam stories *prima facie* read as much like historical narrative as any other Old Testament (or New Testament) texts of the same genre, the burden of proof, as in any case of legal disputation, attaches to the skeptic who denies their historicity.
2. Genesis recounts things uncommon to contemporary human experience, such as divine creation of the heavens and the earth and everything in them, the quotation of the exact words of God, the inherent potency of the trees of the garden for ill or good, a talking serpent, and the guarding of the garden by cherubim. Although such things are not common to contemporary human experience, what law of logic or rationality do these episodes violate except the "laws" that (1) the present is the key to the past and (2) that miracles, by definition, cannot occur. Or put another way, the skeptic seems to reason, "What I have not seen or heard cannot be believed."
3. If God were to tell how he created the entire cosmos, what language of heaven would be adequately perspicuous to enable humankind to understand it? The Scriptures were not designed to obfuscate but to communicate to every generation and to every level of intelligence who God is and what He has done.
4. Are the narratives of creation and the existence of a historical Adam any more difficult to believe and understand than the incarnation of God himself through the fragile vessel of a Jewish peasant teenager, an incarnation known to the inspired Apostles as "Second Adam"?[23]
5. Can the concept of a "Last Adam" have meaning at any level apart from the concept of a First Adam, that one known in the Old Testament?

23. This remarkable statement of correspondence is structured by the Apostle as follows: ὁ πρῶτος ἄνθρωπος Ἀδαμ // ὁ ἔσχατος Ἀδαμ: "The first man Adam // the last Adam" (1 Cor. 15:45, cf. v. 47). Paul's intent clearly is to identify Adam as a real person ("man") who became a living being (ψυχὴν ζῶσαν) and Jesus as πνεῦμα ζῳοποιουν ("life-giving spirit"). As Taylor puts it, "The first Adam received life. The second Adam imparts life." Mark Taylor, *1 Corinthians,* NAC 28 (Nashville, TN: B&H, 2014), p. 408.

Evidence of Adam's Historicity in Old Testament Genealogies

Analysis of the Adam Genealogies[24]

Of late, genealogies have come to be understood as having much more to do with historical narrative than was hitherto thought to be the case. Like chronological texts, they provide a literary and historical framework and sometimes a precise *Sitz im Leben*[25] against which to understand narratives often intertwined with them. Westermann puts it this way: "The genealogies are an essential constitutive part of the primeval story and form the framework of everything that is narrated in Gen. 1–11."[26] Mark Chavalas underscores this special function of genealogies when he notes that "it can be shown that these texts [genealogical records] do have value, mainly as explanations of the milieu in which they were created."[27]

Two forms of genealogical listings appear in the Old Testament, the linear and the segmented. The former traces the lineage of given figures from generation to generation through one line, usually through the eldest son. The segmented contains branches, as it were, thereby establishing descent through brothers to certain stages, producing parallel lines until more segmentation occurs or to the end of the listing with linear forms in each of the branches. These will be noted in the following examples. Those in which Adam is included will receive detailed analysis. Moreover, the lifespans of the persons listed will not be taken into account since genealogy, not chronology, is the thrust of this study.[28]

---

24. For important literature on genealogy in general and on those of the Bible in particular, see Marshall D. Johnson, *The Purpose of the Biblical Genealogies* (Cambridge, UK: Cambridge University Press, 1988); Yigal Levin, "From Lists to History: Chronological Aspects of the Chronicler's Genealogies," *Journal of Biblical Literature* 123 (2004): 601–636; Yigal Levin, "Nimrod the Mighty, King of Kish, King of Sumer and Akkad," *Vetus Testamentum* 52 (2002): 350–366; Jeremy Northcote, "The Lifespans of the Patriarchs: Schematic Orderings in the Chrono-Genealogy," *Vetus Testamentum* 57 (2007): 243–257; James T. Sparks, *The Chronicler's Genealogies: Towards an Understanding of 1 Chronicles 1–9* (Atlanta: SBL, 2008); Robert R. Wilson, "Between 'Azel' and 'Azel': Interpreting the Biblical Genealogies," *Biblical Archaeologist* 42 (1979): 11–22; Robert R. Wilson, *Genealogy and History in the Biblical World* (New Haven: Yale University Press, 1977); Robert R. Wilson, "Old Testament Genealogies in Recent Research," *Journal of Biblical Literature* 94 (1975): 169–189. Also in process is Nancy S. Dawson, *Genealogies of the Bible* (pre-published at Grand Rapids: Zondervan, 2016).
25. This German phrase means "setting in life" and denotes the social context in which a narrative was written.
26. Claus Westermann, *Genesis 1–11: A Commentary*, trans. John J. Scullion (Minneapolis, MN: Augsburg, 1984), p. 6.
27. Mark Chavalas, "Genealogical History as 'Charter': A Study of Old Babylonian Period Historiography and the Old Testament," in *Faith, Tradition, & History*, eds. A.R. Millard, J.K. Hoffmeier, and D.W. Baker (Winona Lake, IN: Eisenbraun, 1994), p.108.
28. In general, see Wilson, *Genealogy and History*, p. 137–138.

Genealogy 1. "The Written Account of Adam from the Time of His Creation" (Gen. 5:1–32)

Relevant observations:

1. The term סֵפֶר תּוֹלְדֹת (*sepher toledoth*, "book of the generation") occurs not only here with a genealogy (as it does also in 10:1–32; 11:10–26, 27–32; 25:12–18; 36:9–30) but as a tag indicating narrative passages (cf. Gen. 2:4–25; 6:9–9:29; 25:19–49:33). With *sepher* ("book," only here in 5:1), the idea is that a written (not oral) text is in view. Its use exclusively with Adam's genealogy suggests that his genealogy is unique and formative, one that must be preserved as a historical record with utmost accuracy.
2. The verb form בְּרֹא (*bero*, "creating"), used in conjunction with *beyom*, is striking in that it is used nominally only here in the Genesis genealogies, perhaps with the idea of "from the time when." Again, the implication of Adam's creation as a historical benchmark can hardly be avoided.
3. The very fact that Adam is here, in a genealogy, distinguished from merely "man" is significant in that he is portrayed not just as a faceless supposition but as the first of a line of individuals whose historicity at some point or other can withstand any reasonable challenge. That might not be true in this genealogical text alone, but its tight and indisputable linkage with succeeding genealogies bears this fact out most amply. Now if Abraham's historicity was up for grabs, one might have to go still further down the line to make the Abraham-to-David connection, something easily done with later generations, such as the bridge connecting Abraham to Judah (1 Chron. 1:34, 2:1) and the more full genealogy commencing with Judah and ending with David (1 Chron. 2:3–15; cf. Ruth 4:18–22). Was there an actual King David? If so, how far back must he go in his lineage to prove his rights to the messianic throne? Where in the greater line from Adam to David does fancy end and reality begin?
4. The elaborate description of Adam as the eponym of humankind and as male and female is clearly intended to underscore his historicity as the "father" of the human race (v. 1–2). His immediate offspring is "in his likeness" בִּדְמוּתוֹ (*bidmuto*) and "according to his image" כְּצַלְמוֹ (*kitsalmo*; cf. 1:27), that is, like Adam and therefore with Adam's privileges and responsibilities. One presumes that all following descendants inherit that trait, including those whose actuality is questioned.

5. As a result of Abel's death and Cain's disqualification as an heir, Seth, the only other son mentioned, becomes sole inheritor and his descent is strictly linear for the next eight generations, ending with Noah, for a total of ten generations.[29]
6. Beginning with Noah, the genealogy becomes segmented, split among the three sons of Noah (Gen. 5:32; 6:9).

Genealogy 2. "These Are the Accounts of Noah's Sons, Shem, Ham, and Japheth" (Gen. 10:1)

Relevant Observations:

1. Adam is not mentioned directly here, but the mandate given to Noah is precisely the one given to Adam, thus cementing their historical and theological relationship (Gen. 9:1; cf. 1:28).
2. Though Shem was not the eldest son, his genealogy is most theologically important, leading as it does to Abraham, so it occupies the climactic place of being last in the narrative.
3. All three genealogies are segmented, with Japheth siring 7 sons, Ham 4, and Shem 5. Only 2 of Japheth's sons' genealogies are included in the text, those of Gomer and Javan (Gen. 10:2–5). Of Ham's 4 sons, 3 are attested as fathers of their lines: Cush, Mizraim, and Canaan. Cush is distinguished as having been ancestor of the Assyrians and Babylonians (10:6–12). Mizraim's (Egypt's) line was most famous as the one that included among others the notorious Philistines, who proved to be one of Israel's most obstinate foes. Shem's 6 sons originated segmented lines as well as sub-segmented in the case of the most noteworthy, namely, Eber (10:24–25; cf. v. 21). His 2 sons were

29. The fact that this genealogy lists ten patriarchs prior to the Great Flood and ten afterward does not by any means make the case, often proposed, for a "borrowing" by the biblical author of a similar scheme in the "Sumerian King List" (SKL) in which ten kings are commonly said to have preceded and succeeded the Deluge in Sumerian legend. This matching is done, however, by selectively joining various lists to make the number 10 jibe with the number in Genesis. For the principal and authoritative rendition, see Thorkild Jacobsen, *The Sumerian King List*, Assyriological Studies 11 (Chicago, IL: University of Chicago Press), 1966. However, in the Weld-Blundell edition of the text, the most complete, only 8 royal names occur before the Flood — simultaneously in some cases in five different cities; and after the Flood, 14 reign at Kish, 1 at Eanna, 12 at Uruk, 4 at Ur, 3 at Awan, 8 again at Kish, 1 at Hamazi, 3 again at Uruk, 4 again at Ur, 6 at Adab, 1 again at Kish, 1 at Akshak, 7 at Kish, 1 at Uruk, and finally on the solid ground of history with the Aggadian (Akkadian) Dynasty under Sargon the Great (2360–2305 B.C.). That totals some 66 post-diluvian kings who occupy the same period of time as the 10 patriarchs between Noah and Abraham (2100 B.C.). For a devastating case against the Genesis=Sumerian/Babylonian traditions, see Westermann, *Genesis 1–11: A Commentary*, p. 348–352.

Peleg and Joktan, the further line of the former ending here with him, not resuming until its completion in Genesis 11:32 with Abraham.

Genealogy 3: "These Are the Accounts of Shem" (Gen. 11:10–32)

Relevant Observations:

1. The genealogy of Shem related here differs from that of Genesis in that (1) it provides the ages of the patriarchs and (2) it is in a strictly linear form. This is because the line of salvific history is increasingly narrowing from Adam to Noah to Abraham.
2. The data in v. 10–16 are essentially identical to those of 10:21–25. However, Joktan is by-passed and full attention is on Eber,[30] great-grandson of Shem, the son of Noah. Counting both Shem and Abra(ha)m, there are ten generations between Noah and Abraham, the channel of covenant hope of redemption (cf. 1 Chron. 1:1–4).

Genealogy 4: The Genealogy of 1 Chronicles 1:1–27, 34; 2:1–15

Relevant Observations:

1. The genealogy begins with a mere listing of the pre-Noah patriarchs, commencing, of course, with Adam (v. 1–4). Clearly, the historian — writing ca. 400 B.C. — is familiar with the Genesis renditions and therefore needs not provide details for the earliest era.
2. However, far from supposing that the Chronicler is disinterested in history, he names Adam along with all the rest as though each is to be taken as historical.[31]
3. The Chronicler attests 9 "sons" of Shem (whereas Gen. 10:22–23 lists only 6),[32] only 1, Arpachshad (as in Gen. 10:24), whose line is singled out as the one carrying with it the salvific hope of the world.

---

30. "Eber" (עֵבֶר) is the patronym of the later people called "Hebrews" (עִבְרִים), the first of whom named in Scripture is Abraham (אַבְרָהָם).
31. It is of interest to note that the Chronicler makes reference to written sources no doubt available to him (1 Chron. 4:33, 41; 5:1, 7, 17; 7:2, 4–5, 7, 9, 40; 8:28; 9:1, 9, 22, 34). This shows his care as a historian for the accuracy best assured in authentic texts. Again, at what point does the historian betray his shift from pure myth and legend to what he no doubt considered to be the firm ground of historical reality? He seems to consider all he has composed as a record of true events containing the names of historical persons. The skeptic's burden is to prove otherwise.
32. The difference is easily accounted for: Three sons of Shem in Chronicles are considered grandsons in Genesis, the three being sons of Aram. For a discussion of literary and theological aspects of the Chronicler's work, see Eugene H. Merrill, *1 and 2 Chronicles* (Grand Rapids: Kregel, 2015), p. 47–68. The uses of the terms "one," "one man," "the one," "the one man" are striking in their evidential value attesting to the historicity of "the man" in question, either Adam or Jesus, a point also to note in the creation accounts of Genesis 1 and 2.

Despite minor differences here and there occasioned by idiosyncratic concerns of the Chronicler, it is clear he has made use of the Genesis genealogies as the historical bases for his own work which, all agree, is solid and scientific historiography.

4. Going beyond the tables of the Genesis author for obvious chronological reasons, the Chronicler extends the genealogies of Genesis 10 and 11 beyond Abraham to David (2:1–15) and thence, through Solomon, to the time of the Babylonian exile (586 B.C.; cf. 3:1–16), and even beyond, after the return from exile (3:17–18), perhaps as late as 400 B.C. (v. 19–24).

Evidence for the Historicity of Adam in the New Testament Genealogies

Genealogy 5: The Genealogy of Matthew 1:1–17

General Observations:

Though the major purpose of this genealogy is to trace the ancestry of Jesus back to David through his foster father Joseph, its beginning is helpful in establishing the Apostle's view that not only is the record from David historically accurate, but by implication so is that from Abraham to David (Matt. 1:1–6). One might assume also that he likely would have labeled the prior historical records of Genesis "history" as well. However, since our interest here is to examine genealogies that commence at the very beginning with Adam, this one of Matthew is only secondarily of relevance at most.

Genealogy 6: The Genealogy of Luke 3:23–38

General Observations:

Scholars have long noted that Luke's genealogical structure is anomalous in that it begins with the latest generation and works backward to the first.[33] Since Luke's consuming interest is the Incarnation of Jesus Christ, his Gospel rendition of Jesus' birth and ancestry begins there and then retrogressively seeks to establish the audacious claims of Jesus that he is the Son of God and yet the son of man, a claim, it seems, that must find its authenticity in evidence of his descent from both God and man.[34] That best explains Luke's startling conclusion to the genealogical list when he speaks of Jesus as "the son of Enos, the son of Seth, the son of Adam, the son of God!" If God exists, and he does, then surely Adam also existed — this seems to be the

33. Numerous questions could be raised with regard to the genealogy, such as Luke's source for the names in v. 23–27, otherwise unattested, but this is not the place to deal with that and other issues. It has no bearing on the matter of Adam's historicity.

34. Thus I. Howard Marshall, *The Gospel of Luke: A Commentary on the Greek Text*, NIGTC (Grand Rapids: Eerdmans, 1978), p. 161.

message of the inspired Apostle. Could Jesus, the literal and historical son of God-man, have descended from any ancestors except literal and historical persons, including Adam?

In terms of substance, Luke's presentation is virtually identical to those in Genealogies 2 and 3. The differences are accounted for, first of all, by the Greek transliterations of Hebrew names; adding or subtracting bits of information (Enoch's translation in Genesis 5:24 mentioned only here); and differing formulae of introduction and linkage: (1) Genealogies 2 and 3 read, "A lived x years and sired B, C, and D; A lived more years, had more children, and died at z years." (2) Genealogy 4 states: "The sons of A were *a1, a2*, and *a3*; the sons of B were *b1, b2,* and *b3*; the sons of C were *c1, c2,* and *c3*." Luke 3, like 1 Chronicles 1:24–27, merely lists the principal names of each generation—Joseph, Heli, Matthat, Levi, Melchi, etc., but, as noted above, in reverse order of names to the genealogies of the Old Testament.[35]

Evidences for Adam's Historicity in New Testament Exegesis and Theology

The name "Adam" occurs ten times in the New Testament, once in the Gospels (Luke 3:38), and eight times in the Epistles (Rom. 5:14 [2x]; 1 Cor. 15:22, 45 [2x]; 1 Tim. 2:13–14; Jude14). Thus, the New Testament case for Adam's historicity is made almost exclusively by Paul, but not with the tools of historical research or literary maneuvering — he does it on the basis of theological necessity. He must explain the origin of sin and the Fall and what God has done through Christ to make all things new and right.

In his two discourses devoted specifically to "original" sin, Paul argues in terms of an oscillation between Adam and Jesus in a logical structure stated formulaically "just as . . . so is."[36] In this kind of asseveration, a protasis/apodosis relationship, the second clause of the analogy depends for

35. For a full discussion of the complexities of the Luke genealogy, vis-à-vis that of Matthew and both against the backdrop of the OT genealogies, see Darrell L Bock, *Luke Volume 1:1–9:50*, BECNT 3A (Grand Rapids: Baker, 1994), p. 348–362.

36. The clause structure is called a "protasis/apodosis" in which the first clause is introduced by a term such as "if," "since," "as," and the like, and the following clause will read "so," "then," "thus," or the like. In this kind of construction, a comparison is made between two persons, things, or concepts that necessarily depend on the nature or reality of each other for the comparison to have the intended meaning. Most Greek grammars label such structures as comparative clauses. See A.T. Robertson, *A Grammar of the Greek New Testament in the Light of Historical Research* (Nashville, TN: Broadman, 1980), p. 966–969. Common protases in Greek are εἰ, ὥσπερ, followed by οὖν, οὕτω, and the like. For the terms and structures of Hebrew comparative clauses, which are very much similar to the Greek, see Bruce K. Waltke and M. O'Connor, *An Introduction to Biblical Hebrew Syntax* (Winona Lake, IN: Eisenbrauns), 1990, 38.4; Bill T. Arnold and John H. Choi, *A Guide to Biblical Hebrew Syntax* (Cambridge, England: Cambridge University Press, 2003), 5.2.6.

its meaning or certitude upon the meaning or certitude of the first clause. For example, "Just as the Spartans defeated the Athenians at Thermopylae, so Harvard will defeat Yale at New Haven." If the former proposition is false, the certitude of the second is questionable by logical sequence. There is little comfort to the Harvardian if the prediction of the Crimson's win over the Yalies is based on a false premise. Paul's great affirmation of the power of Christ's Resurrection to save sinners is couched in precisely the same analogical pattern: "As in Adam all died, so in Christ shall all be made alive" (1 Cor. 15:22).

Table 2: Greek Protases and Apodoses in Romans 5 and 1 Corinthians 15

References	Passages	Particles (re: italicized English words)
Rom. 5:12	"*just* as sin entered the world through one man, and death through sin. . . ."	ὥσπερ . . . no comparative (anacoluthon)
5:15	"*if* the many died by the trespass of the one man, how *much more* did God's gift that came by the grace of the one man, Jesus Christ, overflow to the many."	εἰ . . . πολλῷ μᾶλλον
5:17	"*if*, by the trespass of the one man, death reigned through the one man, how *much more* will those who receive . . . the gift of righteousness reign in life through the one man, Jesus Christ."	εἰ . . . πολλῷ μᾶλλον
5:19	"*just as* through the disobedience of the one man the many were made sinners, *so also* through the obedience of the one man the many will be made righteous."	ὥσπερ . . . οὕτως
5:21	"*just as* sin reigned in death, *so also* grace might reign . . . through Jesus Christ our Lord."	ὥσπερ . . . οὕτως
1 Cor. 15:22	"For *as* in Adam all die, *so* in Christ will all be made alive."	ὥσπερ . . . οὕτως
15:45	"The first man Adam became a living being; the last Adam a life-giving spirit."	comparison without comparative terms

Table 3: Occurrences of Various Forms of "Man" in the Creation Accounts and the NT

Reference	"Adam"	"Mankind"	"The Man"	"One Man"	"A Man"
Gen. 1:26		X			
1:27		X			
2:5					X
2:7			X (2x)		
2:8			X		
2:15			X		
2:16			X		
2:18			X		

2:19	X (2x)				
2:20	X		X		
2:21			X		
2:22			X (2x)		
2:23	X				
2:25			X		
3:8	X		X		
3:9	X		X		
3:12			X		
3:17	X				
3:20	X				
3:21	X				
3:22			X		
3:24			X		
4:1	X				X
4:25	X				
5:1–5	X (4x)	X			
Rom. 5:12					
5:14*	X (2x)				
5:15				X Adam & Jesus	
5:16				X Adam	
5:17				X Adam (2x) & Jesus	
5:19				X Adam & Jesus	
1 Cor. 15:21					X (2x)
15:22	X				
15:45–49	X (2x)		X (2x)	X Adam (2x) & Jesus	X (2x)
1 Tim. 2:13	X				
2:14	X				
Jude 14	X				

* Paul notes here that Adam was a "type [Gr. τύπος] of the one who was to come," obviously Jesus. This clearly suggests a one-to-one comparison and connection. Moo asserts (correctly) that "Paul read Gen. 2–3 as a historical account of real people, and no reason at all for us to think we must 'demythologize' what Paul took to be real." Douglas J. Moo, *The Epistle to the Romans*, NICNT (Grand Rapids: Eerdmans, 1996), p. 324–325, n. 53.

Observations concerning Table 3

- Of a total of 59 occurrences of "Adam," "mankind," "the man," "one man," and "a man," in Genesis 1–5 and the New Testament, 36 are found in Genesis and 23 in the New Testament.

- In the New Testament, 5 are in Paul's treatise on original sin in Romans 5 and 11 are in 1 Corinthians 15.
- The name "Adam" occurs 10 times in Genesis 1–5 and 5 times in Romans and 1 Corinthians.
- The theologically important "the man" occurs 16 times in the Old Testament and only 2 times in the New Testament.
- The equally important "one man" never occurs in the Old Testament but does occur 9 times in Romans and 1 Corinthians.

The major conclusions to be drawn from these data are that (1) Adam and pronouns referring to him are significant cross-testament evidences of his existence and role in the matter of original sin; and (2) implicit references to Adam as "one man" in conjunction with the same descriptor as of Jesus Christ (7 times in Rom. 5:15–19 and twice in 1 Cor. 15:45–49) puts beyond any reasonable doubt that the inspired Apostle considered Adam to be as historical a figure as Jesus Christ Himself. Surely the burden of proof lies with the one who supposes that an imaginary or mythical Adam is a fit counterpart to the historical Jesus. "As was . . . so is" should be enough.

The Converging Lines of Evidence for a Historical Adam

Having looked at all the data in both the Old Testament and the New, we now offer the following synthesis of what has been argued from the various angles of approach. The presentation takes the following form and order: (1) The nature of the Bible; (2) Genre and the Bible; (3) History and Historiography; (4) Exegesis and Hermeneutics; and (5) Theology and Relevance of the OT and the NT to the Church.

The Nature of the Bible

Until the onset of the Enlightenment in Europe in the 17th century, a near universal consensus regarded the Bible as the very Word of God, inspired, revealed, inerrant, and authoritative.[37] All that changed, at least in the academy, with the encroachment of Enlightenment skepticism vis-à-vis history, science, and the Bible until the present day. By the mid-19th century the Bible had become subjected to the historical-critical method which, among other things, denied its historical and scientific veracity and, as a logical

37. For a brief but comprehensive history of the movement, see Mark S. Gignilliat, *A Brief History of Old Testament Criticism* (Grand Rapids: Zondervan, 2012). A much lengthier, detailed account is Eugene H. Merrill, Mark F. Rooker, and Michael A. Grisanti, *The World and the Word: An Introduction to the Old Testament* (Nashville, TN: B & H, 2011).

corollary, its authority as the Word of God written and regulative of faith and life. The evangelical response to this, waged valiantly over many years by godly scholars, oftentimes at the expense of ridicule and disbarment from the academic establishment, now finds itself engaged in intra-mural disagreement as to the very nature of the Old Testament and its accounts of the past and an assessment as to the reliability of those accounts. This is especially true when it comes to the matter of beginnings, the central idea of the Book of Genesis without which all subsequent biblical claims to revelation, sin, and redemption lose their force. As Jesus said to the critics of his day, "If they do not listen to Moses and the Prophets, they will not be convinced even if someone rises from the dead" (Luke 16:31).

Literary Genres and Categories

The dispute concerning the historicity of Old Testament Adam tends to lean heavily upon genre questions: If the accounts about Adam are not intended to be historical in nature but, rather, allegories, parables, tales, legends, or even myths created to account for present realities like sin and death, then efforts to defend them as historical are doomed to fail and are nothing but colossal wastes of time. If, however, the narratives are taken to be intentional historical narratives of actual persons and events, those who read them otherwise stand in grave danger of undermining the very basis of the Christian faith. More is said on this below.

As we have noted above, though not generally considered to be historiographical texts in the strict sense, the genealogies which speak of persons known in narrative accounts help to place them in their historical and cultural contexts. If, however, these persons in fact never lived, the "endless genealogies" that meticulously set them in order are, indeed, of little value and need not be the subject of honest inquiry. The same denigration is in order for any other mention of these characters except as means of teaching morality and other virtues. However, they are of no worth whatsoever as bases upon which to build sound theological structures.

Historicity and Biblical Theology

This last sentence reinforces our contention that sound theology cannot be based on false premises, no matter what they are. To be more specific and more applicable to our argument for the historicity of Adam, is the logical extension of the last point made: sound theology cannot be derived from or be erected upon the shifting sands of historical relativism that permits one to cherry-pick this or that nugget from the Old Testament, arbitrarily declare it to be either historically credible or not, and then integrate into a biblical theology of his own making.[38] There is, after all, such a thing as "whole-cloth" truth or error. Jesus and the Apostles understood this and rested their case for the miserable state of the world on the Fall of the first man, Adam, and its glorious redemption and eschatological return to perfection on the basis of the work of another man, even the God-man Jesus, the Second Adam.

In another place we have expressed concern about the current mood in evangelical circles that dismisses historicity as fundamental to a proper biblical theology:

> . . . the reason for an insistence on the historical integrity of the Old Testament is that a large part of the content of its theology is its interpretation of the meaning of historical events. Events did not occur and are not included in the record merely as random acts. They are part and parcel of the out-workings of a sovereign God who does all things ultimately as part of a grand design. . . . Though some theologians propose that sacred history need not be based on authentic historical events but only on ancient Israel's perceptions of historical reality, it is epistemologically and rationally absurd to suppose that interpretation of nonexistent acts can have theological power and vitality.[39]

The Crossway publication *Do Historical Matters Matter to Faith?* contains a number of essays that support the previous contention. In it, for example, James K. Hoffmeier asks, "If orthodox Christian faith based on the Bible does not require its foundational events to be real and historical, one must ask, Why have anti-Christian polemicists . . . been so obsessed with undermining the Bible's historicity and accuracy, along with ridiculing the supernatural?"[40] In the same volume, Graham A. Cole presses the matter home by asserting that "History — what happened — is vital for any systematic theology that has a high view of Scripture's value."[41]

---

38. For the indispensable connection between a truly *biblical* theology and a fully authentic biblical history, see my *Kingdom of Priests: A History of Old Testament Israel*, 2nd ed. (Grand Rapids: Baker, 2008), p. 19–36; and my "Old Testament History: A Theological Perspective," in *A Guide to Old Testament Theology and Exegesis*, ed. Willem A. VanGemeren (Grand Rapids: Zondervan, 1997), p. 65–82.
39. Eugene H. Merrill, *Everlasting Dominion: A Theology of the Old Testament* (Nashville, TN: B & H, 2006), p. 26–27.
40. "Why a Historical Exodus Is Essential for Theology," in *Do Historical Matters Matter to Faith?* p. 133.
41. "The Peril of a 'Historyless' Systematic Theology," in *Do Historical Matters Matter to Faith?* p. 66.

Conclusion

Finally, we return to the title of this essay: " 'Where Are You, [Adam]?' The Disappearance of Adam and the Death of Truth." The interrogative here is first of all addressed to Adam by the Lord God in the garden (Gen. 3:9). It is not that the omniscient One could not determine the spatial location of the man; he was searching rather for the spiritual whereabouts of Adam the sinner whose disobedience had alienated him from his Creator and thus rendered him fallen and "lost." Until Adam could own up to where he now stood with reference to God there was no hope of his being pardoned and drawn back into "foundness" and fellowship.

Sadly, Adam has been lost again, but not by his having made a fatal choice. He has become lost as a historical figure to the minds of modern critics and by their choice. Wooed as they have been by the alluring spell of academic recognition and post-modern humanism, many have dismissed him from their presence as an outmoded and unnecessary relic of a former time when historical reality and biblical theology were thought to be joined at the hip, codependent, as it were, at least in the thinking of intellectually shallow "fundamentalists." But just as the whole creation died with Adam, so truth has died along with the death of biblical orthodoxy, "collateral damage" of the worst imaginable kind. Rebuttals to this enterprise notwithstanding, its defenders continue to buttress its claims in any number of ways, including the following typical attempts at self-justification by the segment of evangelical scholarship addressed in this paper:

- History has to do with "real" events that can be documented; theology concerns itself with attempts to categorize, formulize, and dogmatize logically constructed (or revealed) concepts concerning God, man, and the cosmos.
- These two independent worlds can co-exist, even if they cannot be harmonized. Neither needs the other. History is what is; theology, in some circles, is what can be philosophically and epistemologically derived from history, science, and creative imagination. To some current evangelical thinkers, theology must acknowledge the mystery of divine revelation, but it can be the kind of revelation at the same time that is quite capable of embracing a history devoid of factuality with regard to persons and events. Things need not have happened as written in order to serve as paradigmatic examples of what to believe and how to act.

- New hermeneutical advances focusing on new linguistic discourse analyses, new insights into certain types of genre criticism, and new, post-modern reader-centered ways of looking at texts have made possible new ways of integrating a-historical biblical events with soundly orthodox, God-honoring theological truth.[42] What seems to be a contradiction between history and theology to the uninitiated is, to the practitioners of the new hermeneutics, a healthy tension that leads to better exegesis and better understanding of the mysteries of God in the Scriptures.

However, the implicit affirmation that one can have his cake of theological truth, conviction, and power and, at the same time, relish the crumbs of a fractured historicism as though both were baked by the same heavenly Baker, have no good thing to offer to the Church of Jesus Christ. If the Adam of history is irrecoverably lost, the truth of a biblical theology founded on the eschatological Christ, the Last Adam, must ultimately perish.

---

42. Typical of these are essay collections in Charles E. Carter and Carol L. Meyers, eds., *Community, Identity, and Ideology: Social Science Approaches to the Hebrew Bible* (Winona Lake, IN: Eisenbrauns, 1996); Paul R. House, ed., *Beyond Form Criticism: Essays in Old Testament Literary Criticism* (Winona Lake, IN: Eisenbrauns, 1992); Douglas A. Knight and Gene M. Tucker, eds., *The Hebrew Bible and Its Modern Interpreters* (Philadelphia: Fortress, 1985); Steven L. McKenzie and Stephen R. Haynes, eds., *To Each Its Own Meaning* (Louisville, KY: Westminster John Knox, 1999).

Chapter 5

When Was Adam Created?

by Dr. Terry Mortenson

Introduction

When did Adam come into existence? Evolutionists say *Homo sapiens* came into existence 200,000 to 400,000 years ago (depending on which evolutionist you consult, because they do not all agree on what a *Homo sapiens* is). Can we harmonize that with the teaching of God's Word? Today, many Christians, including many leaders and scholars, think they can.

From my reading and interaction with old-earth creationists of all varieties in 25 countries over the last 35 years, I think one reason many of them think they can harmonize the two is that they have not paid very careful attention to the relevant biblical texts. They have just assumed that the scientists have proven the age of the creation to be billions of years and the age of mankind to be many tens or hundreds of thousands of years. They often recite the mantra that "the Bible is not a science textbook" (thereby confusing the vital difference between *origin* science and *operation* science, as discussed in this book's introduction). Therefore, it is claimed, the Bible does not deal with the issue of the age of mankind or even how man came into existence.

Another reason that a great many Christians think that the age of man and the universe does not matter and that the scientific establishment's view does not conflict with Scripture is because they or their teachers have been influenced by William Henry Green.[1] The famous Old Testament professor at Princeton Theological Seminary wrote an article in 1890 in which he

1. William Henry Green, "Primeval Chronology," *Bibliotheca Sacra* 47 (1890): 285–303.

argued that "the genealogies in Genesis 5 and 11 were not intended to be used, and cannot properly be used, for the construction of a chronology."[2] He concluded that "the Scriptures furnish no data for a chronological computation prior to the life of Abraham; and that the Mosaic records do not fix and were not intended to fix the precise date either of the Flood or of the creation of the world."[3] In other words, Green contended, the Bible is silent about the age of man and also the age of the earth and universe, so scientists are free to determine these ages according to the scientific evidence, and Christians need not reject or fear any date so determined.

Of course, Green was not the first to reject the biblical chronology prior to Abraham. Most of the Church had accepted the millions of years at the beginning of the 19th century. Christian leaders proposed the gap theory[4] or the day-age view[5] of Genesis 1 to accommodate all those years. Other reinterpretations were developed in the 20th century, such as the revelatory day view,[6] the framework view,[7] the Promised Land view,[8] the analogical day view,[9] the day-gap-day-gap-day view,[10] and the cosmic temple/functionality view,[11] to name a few. Most advocates of these views have also reinterpreted the account of Noah's Flood to be a large but localized flood in the Mesopotamian Valley (modern-day Iraq) or a myth, which in either

2. Ibid., 286.
3. Ibid., 303.
4. Popularized by Thomas Chalmers, C.I. Scofield and others, it puts the millions of years somewhere between Genesis 1:1 and 1:3, before six literal days of re-creation.
5. One of the early advocates was the Anglican theologian, George Stanley Faber, in his book in 1823. Today one of the most well-known promoters is Hugh Ross and Reasons to Believe. This view says that each of the days of Genesis 1 are long ages of hundreds of millions or billions of years each.
6. Advocated by P.J. Wiseman, it says that the days of Genesis 1 are days of revelation, not creation, when on six literal days God revealed what He had created over who knows how long a time.
7. Popularized by Bruce Waltke, Meredith Kline, and others, it says that Genesis 1 is not historical narrative, but a literary framework to teach theology.
8. Developed by John Sailhamer in *Genesis Unbound*, it says everything but man was created in Genesis 1:1 and then from verse two onward the text is referring to the preparation of the Promised Land, which he equates with the Garden of Eden.
9. Advocated by C. John Collins in *Science and Faith: Friends or Foes?* this is similar to the day-age view but says that God's creation days are like our days but not exactly like them.
10. The view of John Lennox (in his *Seven Days that Divide the World*) inserts an indeterminate (but long) amount of time between each of the six literal days. But Lennox also believes day 1 starts at Genesis 1:3 with an indeterminate amount of time before that.
11. John Walton is the leading proponent and insists in *Lost World of Genesis 1* that God did not create anything in Genesis 1 but only gave function to pre-existing things so as to change a disordered creation into a cosmic temple for the Lord. He insists that the Bible says nothing about when or how God created things, including Adam. So whatever the scientific majority says is true is acceptable for Christians.

case has no bearing on the geological record, which supposedly reveals the millions of years.

Nevertheless, Green had a significant influence on a great many scholars who have taught Christians that we all need to simply "agree to disagree" about the time before Abraham. They insist that the age question is an unimportant and divisive side issue that we can leave to the scientists to determine. These influential evangelical scholars who followed Green, directly or indirectly, include B.B. Warfield (who in turn many recent evangelical theologians and others cite in support of their old-earth views being consistent with Scripture),[12] Francis Schaeffer,[13] Wayne Grudem,[14] Millard Erickson,[15] Walter Kaiser,[16] Robert Newman,[17] C. John Collins,[18] Norman Geisler,[19] and Ronald Youngblood.[20] In this chapter I will present some of the reasons for concluding that these great scholars were wrong on this important point and have thereby misled many pastors and lay people.

---

12. Mark A. Noll and David N. Livingstone, eds., *Evolution, Science and Scripture: Selected Writings* (Grand Rapids, MI: Baker, 2000), p. 217–222. Warfield was heavily influenced by Green and concluded, "It is precarious in the extreme to draw chronological inferences from these genealogies" (217) . . . because they are "so elastic that they may be commodiously stretched to fit any reasonable demand on time." He thought "the period from the creation of Adam to Abraham may have been nearer two hundred thousand years than two thousand years" (222).
13. Francis Schaeffer, *No Final conflict* (1975), p. 37-43, and *Genesis in Space and Time* (Downers Grove, IL: IVP, 1972), p. 122, 155.
14. Grudem did not cite Green, but cited Schaeffer who cited Green. Wayne Grudem, *Systematic Theology* (Grand Rapids, MI: Zondervan, 1994), p. 290–292.
15. Erickson does not cite Green, but cites Warfield who relies on Green. Millard Erickson, *Christian Theology* (Grand Rapids, MI: Baker, 1983), p. 484. His second edition (1998) and third edition (2013) say the same.
16. Walter C. Kaiser Jr., Peter H. Davids, F.F. Bruce, and Manfred T. Brauch, *Hard Sayings of the Bible* (Downers Grove, IL: InterVarsity Press, 1996), p. 101–103, and Walter C. Kaiser Jr., *The Old Testament Documents: Are They Reliable and Relevant?* (Downers Grove, IL: InterVarsity Press, 2001), p. 69–75. Kaiser republished Green's whole 1890 article in *Classical Evangelical Essays in Old Testament Interpretation*, ed. Walter Kaiser, Jr. (Grand Rapids, MI: Baker, 1972). On p. 7 Kaiser describes it as one of "the finest moments in Old Testament scholarship."
17. Robert C. Newman and Herman J. Eckelmann Jr., *Genesis One and the Origin of the Earth* (Hatfield, PA: IBRI, 1977), also reprinted Green's essay.
18. C. John Collins, *Science and Faith: Friends or Foes?* (Wheaton, IL: Crossway, 2003), p. 107–109.
19. Norman L. Geisler, *Baker Encyclopedia of Christian Apologetics* (Grand Rapids, MI: Baker, 1999), p. 267–270. Geisler cites Green, Warfield, Schaeffer, and Newman as sources for his view that Genesis 5 and 11 do not contribute anything to "satisfy our curiosity about the date of human creation."
20. Ronald Youngblood, *The Book of Genesis*, 2nd ed. (Grand Rapids, MI: Baker, 1991), p. 75–76.

Genesis 1–11 Is History.

Before attempting to determine the date of Adam's creation, I want to make a few more comments about the historicity of Genesis to supplement and complement the arguments in previous chapters. The early chapters of Genesis are not poetry,[21] a series of parables or prophetic visions, or mythology. The chapters recount God's acts in time-space history: acts of creation, providence, and redemption. When we insist that Genesis 1–11 is history, we are not saying that this section of the Bible is *only* history, i.e., that it was only inspired to satisfy some of our curiosity about origins. It is far more than history for it teaches theology, morality, and redemption, and those truths are vitally important. But Genesis 1–11 is not less than history, and what it teaches on the latter themes is rooted in that history. If the history is not true, then the theology, morality, and gospel based on that history is seriously called into question if not rejected.

Several lines of evidence demonstrate that this introductory section of Scripture is to be understood as history. First, the Hebrew *waw*-consecutive verb forms used in Genesis 1 (and continuing through the rest of the book) are characteristic of Hebrew narrative, but not of Hebrew poetry.[22]

Second, Genesis 1 does not have the dominant characteristic of Hebrew poetry, namely parallelism, where the truth in the first part of a verse is repeated in different ways in the second part (e.g., Ps. 19:1, 30:10, 32:1, 37:1, 103:1). But those who hold to the Framework view claim there is a different kind of parallelism in Genesis 1 that should lead us to conclude that Genesis 1 is not straightforward history. They say that days 1–3 describe the created space and days 4–6 discuss the creatures that fill those spaces, where day 1 is linked to day 4, day 2 to day 5, and day 3 to day 6. But this claimed parallelism only works if one overlooks the details of the text. The heavenly bodies made on day 4 were placed in the expanse, which was made on day 2 (not day 1). The sea creatures made on day 5 filled the water (which was made

21. The fact that Genesis records Adam's poetic and romantic statement in Genesis 2:23 and the words of Jacob's poetic prophecy given to his sons in Genesis 49:2–27 does not negate the fact that Genesis is history. It accurately records what those men poetically said on those occasions.

22. See the in-depth analysis of Steven Boyd, "The Genre of Genesis 1:1–2:3: What Means This Text?" in *Coming to Grips with Genesis*, eds. Terry Mortenson and Thane H. Ury (Green Forest, AR: Master Books, 2008), p. 163–192. A layman's summary of Boyd's research is in Donald DeYoung, *Thousands, Not Billions: Challenging an Icon of Evolution* (Green Forest, AR: Master Books, 2005), p. 157–172. A fuller technical discussion is Steven Boyd, "Statistical Determination of Genre in Biblical Hebrew: Evidence for a Historical Reading of Genesis 1:1–2:3," in *Radioisotopes and the Age of the Earth*, Vol. 2, eds. Larry Vardiman, et al. (El Cajon, CA: ICR, 2005), p. 631–734, http://www.icr.org/i/pdf/technical/Statistical-Determination-of-Genre-in-Biblical-Hebrew.pdf.

on day 1) of the seas, which was formed on day 3 (not day 2). And nothing was made on day 6 to fill the seas, which were made on day 3. There are many more serious exegetical problems with the framework view.[23]

Third, Genesis 1–11 has the same characteristics of historical narrative as Genesis 12–50, most of Exodus, much of Numbers, Joshua, 1 and 2 Kings, etc. Genesis 1–11 describes real people by name, real events in their lives, real places and geographical areas by name,[24] real times (days, months, years[25]), etc.

Fourth, the eleven *toledoths* ("these are the generations of") sprinkled through Genesis tie the whole book together as a unit, and no truly evangelical Bible scholar doubts that Genesis 12–50 is history.

Fifth, in every case that Jesus, New Testament authors, and Old Testament authors referred to the events in Genesis 1–11, they always treated the text as straightforward, literal history. And they all knew the difference between truth and myth.[26] Jesus referred to Genesis more than any other book, and the Gospels record Him saying "it is written" 30 times and "have you not read?" 11 times in reference to all three divisions of the OT: the Law (Pentateuch), Prophets, and Psalms (e.g., Luke 24:44). This shows that Jesus' default hermeneutic was: just read it, it means what it says.[27] Even most old-earth proponents recognize that Genesis 1–11 is history.[28] And virtually all Christians prior to the 19th century read it that way.

So there are many good biblical and historical reasons for taking Genesis 1–11 as literal history in which all the details matter and are inerrant. Given that fact, we need to look carefully at those details.

---

23. For a thorough refutation of the Framework view see Robert McCabe, "A Critique of the Framework Interpretation of the Creation Week," in *Coming to Grips with Genesis*, eds. Mortenson and Ury, p. 211–250.
24. The reason old-earth Bible scholars can't find the Garden of Eden and the location of Cain's city in our present Middle East geography is because those places no longer exist, having been destroyed in the global Flood that radically rearranged the surface of the earth and buried the pre-Flood land under thousands of feet of sediments.
25. The account of Noah's Flood reads almost like a very simplified ship's log or diary.
26. See, for example, Mark 10:6–9; Luke 3:23–38, 11:50–51; Matt. 24:37–39; Rom. 5:12; 1 Cor. 15:21–22; 1 Pet. 3:20; 2 Pet. 2:4–9; Ezek. 14:12–20; and Isa. 54:9. Jesus, since He is the truth, knew the difference between truth and myth and would never use myth as a basis for teaching truth. Likewise, the Apostles clearly knew the difference between truth and myth (1 Tim. 1:4, 4:7; 2 Tim. 4:4; 2 Pet. 1:16.)
27. Of course, Jesus Himself used figurative language ("I am the light of the world," or "I am the door") and would not have "taken everything literally" in a woodenly literal manner. But He clearly implied that we should assume a literal interpretation, unless of course there are clear contextual reasons for not taking the text literally.
28. See, for example, the arguments by Walter Kaiser, *The Old Testament Documents: Are They Reliable and Relevant?* (Downers Grove, IL: IVP, 2001), p. 53–83, and Edward J. Young, *Studies in Genesis One* (Phillipsburg, NJ: P&R Publ., 1964), p. 82–83.

From the Beginning of Creation to Adam: How Long?

How long was it from the first moment of creation to the creation of Adam? According to evolutionists, the big bang (when, they say, nothing suddenly became something) was about 13.8 billion years ago, and the first true man appeared 13.7998 billion years after the beginning (or about 200,000 years ago).

In contrast to the evolutionary view, young-earth creationists believe the whole creation is only a few thousand years old. But it should be noted that while they do all agree that there were only five literal days of history before Adam, they do not all agree about the age of the earth and therefore about how long ago Adam was created. Some argue that there may be missing names in the genealogies of Genesis 5 and 11 and therefore up to a few thousand years could be added between Adam and Abraham (so that the first day of creation was perhaps 10,000 to 12,000 years ago).[29] On the other hand, three of the world's leading young-earth creationist organizations (Answers in Genesis, Institute for Creation Research, and Creation Ministries International) argue that there are no gaps and that therefore the beginning (Gen. 1:1) was a little more than 6,000 years ago.[30] Though open to gaps in the 1960s, by 1976 Henry Morris, the most influential young-earth proponent of the 20th century, also took Genesis 5 and 11 as strict chronologies.[31]

The evidence that the evolutionary dates are utterly false and that there were only five literal days before Adam was created is discussed briefly as follows (for more depth, consult the footnoted sources).

The Meaning of "Day" (Hebrew: Yom) in Genesis 1

The very dominant meaning of *yom* in the Old Testament is a literal day, and the context of Genesis 1 confirms that meaning there. *Yom* is defined

29. For example, Whitcomb concluded that the two genealogies "have nothing to do with the actual length of the overall period" and therefore "it is unnecessary to press them into a rigid chronological system." See John C. Whitcomb Jr. and Henry M. Morris, *The Genesis Flood* (Grand Rapids, MI: Baker, 1977 reprint of 1961), p. 474–489, quotes on p. 477. Also arguing for possible missing names and gaps of time is Mark Snoeberger, "Why a Commitment to Inerrancy Does Not Demand a Strictly 6000-Year-Old Earth: One Young-earther's Plea for Realism," *Detroit Baptist Seminary Journal* 18 (2013): 3–17, https://www.dbts.edu/journals/2013/Snoeberger.pdf.
30. See for example, Larry Pierce and Ken Ham, "Are There Gaps in the Genesis Genealogies?" https://answersingenesis.org/bible-timeline/genealogy/gaps-in-the-genesis-genealogies/; James J.S. Johnson, "How Young Is the Earth? Applying Simple Math to Data Provided in Genesis," http://www.icr.org/article/how-young-earth-applying-simple-math-data-provided/; Jonathan Sarfati, "Biblical Chronogenealogies," http://creation.com/biblical-chronogenealogies.
31. Henry Morris, *The Genesis Record* (Grand Rapids, MI: Baker, 1976), p. 152–155.

in its two literal or normal senses in verse 5 (the light portion of the dark/light cycle and the whole dark/light cycle).[32] It is repeatedly modified by a number (one day, second day, etc.), which elsewhere in the Old Testament always means a literal, normal, 24-hour day. Each of the six days ends with the refrain "evening was and morning was," and everywhere in the OT where *'ereb* ("evening"), *boqer* ("morning"), and *layalah* ("night") are used, they always mean a literal part of a literal day. *Yom* is defined again literally in verse 14 in relation to the movement of the heavenly bodies, and the sun, moon, and stars do enable us to measure literal days, literal years, and literal seasons.

The numbering of the days and the repeated refrain along with the repetition of "and it was so," (6x), "God saw" (7x), and "it was good" (6x) coupled with Exodus 20:8–11 (see below) emphatically indicate that these creation days were sequential and non-overlapping. The creative acts of one day were complete before the next day began.

We also should note that if God indeed created over long ages of time, there are various ways in Hebrew that He could have said that. He could have used *dor* (translated as time, period or generation in Genesis 7:1; Exodus 3:15, 31:13; Deuteronomy 32.7).[33] Or He could have used a phrase such as "after many days" (Josh 23:1), or "thousands of ten thousands" of years (cf. Gen. 24:60), or "myriad thousands" of years (cf. Num. 10:36), or "years of many generations" (Joel 2:2). He could have borrowed a word from a neighboring language, as many languages do today and as God did with the Aramaic time words *zeman* or *iddan* in the books of Nehemiah and Daniel.[34] Instead, God chose to use the only Hebrew word (*yom*) that means a literal 24-hour day.

The Order in Which God Created

Not only does the time period of creation in Genesis 1 contradict the time claimed for the evolution of all these things, but the order of creation in Genesis 1 also contradicts the order of events in the evolutionary story in

32. For an in-depth analysis of the meaning of *yom* in Genesis 1 see Gerhard F. Hasel, "The 'Days' of Creation in Genesis 1: Literal 'Days' or Figurative 'Periods/Epochs' of Time?" *Origins* 21:1 (1994): 5–38; Andrew E. Steinmann, "אֶחָד as an Ordinal Number and the Meaning of Genesis 1:5," *JETS* 45:4 (2002): 577–84; Jim Stambaugh, "The Days of Creation: A Semantic Approach," https://answersingenesis.org/days-of-creation/the-days-of-creation-a-semantic-approach/, 1 April 1991; Robert McCabe, "A Defense of Literal Days in the Creation Week," DBSJ 5 (2000): 97–123; and Trevor Craigen, "Can Deep Time Be Embedded in Genesis?" in *Coming to Grips with Genesis*, p. 193–210.
33. Unless otherwise noted, Scripture in this chapter is from the New American Standard Bible (NASB).
34. He used *zeman* in Nehemiah 2:6 and Daniel 2:16, 2:21, 4:36, and 7:25, and *iddan* in Daniel 4:16, 23, 25, and 32.

at least 30 points. For example, the Bible says the earth was created before light and before the sun and stars, just the opposite of the big-bang theory. The Bible says that fruit trees were created before any sea creatures and that birds were created before dinosaurs (which were made on day 6, since they are land animals), exactly the opposite of the evolutionary story. Evolution says that initially the earth was a hot molten ball that cooled to develop a hard crust, and then evolved an atmosphere that produced rain, and then with the help of melted asteroids produced oceans. But Genesis says the earth was completely covered with water for two days and then dry land appeared. According to evolution, the earth has never been covered with a global ocean. But according to the Bible the earth has been completely covered with water twice: the first two days of creation and Noah's Flood. It is impossible to harmonize Genesis 1 with big-bang cosmology or the evolutionary story of earth's development.[35]

In addition to these contradictions, another obstacle to adding millions of years to the days or between the days relates to the order. If the "days" are figurative of long ages, then so are the "evenings" and the "mornings." But how could plants survive millions of years of darkness? Or how could they reproduce if they had to wait hundreds of millions of years before insects and animals were created that would pollinate the plants?

How Did God Create?

Many old-earth advocates say, "Genesis 1 tells us *that* and *why* God created, not *how* and *when* He created." Actually, the chapter does not tell us why God created but certainly does tell us when and how. He created the first animate and inanimate things supernaturally and virtually instantly. On the day that they were created they were fully formed and fully functioning.[36] For example, plants, animals, and people were created as mature adult forms (not as seeds or fertilized eggs or infants). These statements are very clearly contrasted with how all the subsequent plants, animals, and people would come into existence: reproduction by natural procreation "after their kinds." When God said, "let there be . . ." He did not need to wait millions of years for things to come into existence. He spoke, and creatures came into existence immediately, as Psalm 33:6–9 emphasizes. To postulate millions of

35. See Craigen, ibid., p. 195–197; and Terry Mortenson, "Evolution vs Creation: the Order of Events Matters!" https://answersingenesis.org/why-does-creation-matter/evolution-vs-creation-the-order-of-events-matters/, April 4, 2006.
36. When God said, "Let the earth sprout vegetation," it could have been a supernatural growth to maturity, just as occurred when God made a plant to grow large enough in a few hours to provide shade for Jonah (Jonah 4:6).

years between these supernatural acts of creation is an insult to the wisdom of God. Why would God create the earth and leave it covered with water for millions of years, when He says He created it to be inhabited (Isa. 45:18)? Why would He create plants and then wait millions of years before creating animals and people who would eat plants for food? Why would He create sea creatures and birds and wait millions of years before creating land animals and people?

Objections to Literal Days

Many objections have been raised against the literal, 24-hour days interpretation, such as: (1) 24 hours would be insufficient to accomplish all the events attributed to the sixth day, (2) Genesis 2:4 uses *yom* in a non-literal sense, showing that the days of Genesis 1 were not literal, (3) the seventh day does not conclude with the refrain of the other days implying that it was not literal, (4) days 1–3 cannot be literal if the sun was not created until day 4, and (5) Hebrews 4:1–11 says that the seventh day continues and therefore is at least 6,000 years long. All of these and other objections have been refuted for years in creationist literature,[37] but I conclude from their published writings that old-earth advocates seem to pay little or no attention to creationist literature, and so they keep raising the same objections without responding to young-earth refutations.

God's Commentary on Genesis 1: Exodus 20:8–11

Exodus 20:8–11 stands as an insurmountable stone wall against any attempts to add extra time (months, years, millennia, or millions of years) anywhere in Genesis 1 or before Genesis 1:1. The fourth commandment says that God created everything in six days, just as the Israelites were to work six days and rest on the seventh.

Verse 20:11 rules out the day-age view and the day-gap-day-gap-day view because it says "for in six days"[38] God made everything and He used the plural *yamim* just as He did in the first part of the commandment. So the days of the Jewish workweek are the same length as the days of Creation

37. Ken Ham, ed., *The New Answers Book* (Green Forest, AR: Master Books, 2006), p. 88–112; Terry Mortenson, "Biblical Creation: Strengthening Your Defenses" DVD; Tim Chaffey and Jason Lisle, *Old-Earth Creationism on Trial* (Green Forest, AR: Master Books, 2007), p. 23–79; Andrew Kulikovski, *Creation, Fall, Restoration* (Fearn, Ross-shire, Scotland: Christian Focus Publ., 2009), passim; Jonathan Sarfati, *Refuting Compromise*, 2nd rev. ed. (Powder Springs, GA: Creation Book Publ., 2011), p. 67–104; Jonathan Sarfati, *The Genesis Account* (Powder Springs, GA: Creation Book Publ., 2015), passim.

38. There is no Hebrew word for "in" here, but if it is taken out of the English "For in six days God created," the verse still means the same: "For six days God created."

Week. As noted above, God could have used several other words or phrases here or in Genesis 1, if He meant to say "work six days because I created over six long, indefinite periods."[39] But He didn't.

These verses also rule out the gap theory or any attempt to add millions of years before Genesis 1:1, because God says He created the heavens, the earth, the sea, and *all that is in them* during the six days described in Genesis 1. Exodus 20:11 also proves that the first day of creation begins in Genesis 1:1 (when the earth was created), not 1:3 (when God made light). He made nothing before those six days. It should be noted that the fourth commandment is one of only four of the Ten Commandments that contains a reason for the commandment. If God created over millions of years, He could have commanded Sabbath-keeping without giving a reason, or He could have given a theological or redemptive reason, as He did elsewhere.[40]

Most old-earth proponents ignore this vital passage. A few have tried to reinterpret the verse to open the door for accepting millions of years. For example, Grudem says that in the very next verse (Exod. 20:12) " 'day' means 'a period of time,' " implying a non-literal meaning.[41] Of course, a literal day is a period of time, though obviously by this statement Grudem wants to make room for millions of years. More importantly however, the verse does not use the singular *yom* (day), as Grudem's statement implies, but rather the plural *yamim* (days). The non-literal word in the verse is "prolonged," not "days." In other words, God is saying that if the Jews honor Him by faithfully keeping the Sabbath, the total number of days that they dwell in the land will be long (i.e., many), not that their days will be lengthened to be more than 24 hours. Exodus 20:12 does *not* show that the days in 20:8-11 are not literal.

Collins and Lennox assert that Exodus 20:11 teaches the difference between man's *work* and *rest* and God's *work* and *rest* (i.e., that man's work and rest are "like," but not identical to, God's creation work and rest).[42] But the fourth commandment is not *contrasting* the *work* of man and the *work* of God at all. Rather, it is *equating* the human *week* with God's creation *week*.

To these previous considerations we can add the following biblical arguments against the billions of years of cosmic and geologic history before Adam.

---

39. See also James Stambaugh, "The Days of Genesis: A Semantic Approach," *TJ* 5:1 (1991): 70–78. www.answersingenesis.org/tj/v5/i1/semantic.asp.
40. Exodus 31:13 and Deuteronomy 5:13–15.
41. Wayne Grudem, *Systematic Theology* (Grand Rapids, MI: Zondervan, 1994), p. 296.
42. C. John Collins, *Science and Faith: Friends or Foes?* (Wheaton, IL: Crossway, 2003), p., 65, 85–86, 97–99; John Lennox, *Seven Days That Divide the World* (Grand Rapids, MI: Zondervan, 2011), p. 57.

Purpose of the Heavenly Bodies (Genesis 1:14)

God tells us why He created the sun, moon, and stars: so man could tell time. This is a ridiculous purpose if the evolutionary story of 13.8 billion years is true. In that case, for most of the years of existence of those heavenly bodies they did not accomplish the purpose for which they were made.

Adam and Eve Were to Rule Over the Animals (Genesis 1:26–28)

If millions of years of history really happened before Adam and Eve, most of the creatures that ever lived also died and many kinds of creatures became extinct before Adam and Eve could ever rule over them. What kind of a God would make such a ridiculous assignment?

Jesus and the Biblical Authors

Several passages show that Jesus believed that man was created at the beginning of creation, not billions of years after the beginning (as all old-earth views imply), which confirms the young-earth creationist view (Mark 10:6, 13:19; Luke 11:50–51).[43] His miracles also confirm the young-earth view. From His first miracle (in His earthly ministry) of turning water into wine (which revealed His glory as the Creator, cf. John 2:11 and 1:1–5) to all His other miracles (e.g., Matthew 8:23–27, Mark 1:40–42), His spoken word brought an immediate, instantaneous result, just as His word did in Creation Week.[44]

Paul also made it clear that he was a young-earth creationist. In Romans 1:20 he says that God's existence and at least some of His attributes have been clearly understood by people "since the creation of the world"[45] so that they are without excuse for not honoring Him as God. Surely this great student of Scripture would have had in mind what David said 1,000 years

---

43. I am not saying that the age of the earth was the focus of these verses. Rather, they reflect the young-earth creationist worldview of Jesus. For a thorough discussion of Jesus' words and old-earth attempts to reinterpret them, see Terry Mortenson, "Jesus, Evangelical Scholars and the Age of the Earth," *Coming to Grips with Genesis*, p. 315–346. A short layman's discussion is Terry Mortenson, "But from the beginning of . . . the institution of marriage?" www.answersingenesis.org/docs2004/1101ankerberg_response.asp, which is a response to a web article by John Ankerberg and Norman Geisler on Mark 10:6.
44. This is true even of the two-stage healing of the blind man (Mark 8:22–25). Each stage of the healing was instantaneous. Jesus apparently did this miracle in stages for a pedagogical purpose.
45. So read the NASB, ESV, NKJV, NIV, NLT, and NRSV. The KJV, KJ21, and HCSB render *apo ktiseos kosmou* as "from the creation of the world." But *apo* ("from") here surely means "since." For reasons behind this conclusion, see Ron Minton, "Apostolic Witness to Genesis Creation and the Flood," in *Coming to Grips with Genesis*, p. 351–354.

earlier (Ps. 19:1, cf. Ps. 97:6) and what Job said 1,000 years before that (Job 12:7–10). The creation has always revealed the Creator to man from the beginning. Paul's language, like Jesus' language, is inaccurate and misleading if man was created billions of years after the creation of the world.

Similarly, Isaiah 40:21 shows that the prophet was a young-earth creationist. The parallelism of the verse shows that "from the beginning" and "from the foundations of the earth" refer to the same point in time. What the people of Isaiah's day knew about God is what people (Adam and Eve, and Cain and Abel, etc.) knew right at the foundation of the earth (the beginning of creation), which is also what all idolaters in Paul's day knew and what atheists throughout history and today have known. He is a fool who says there is no Creator for His glory is seen in His creation (Ps. 14:1, 19:1).

If the evolutionary view of 13.8 billion years is true, then Jesus, Paul, and Isaiah were badly mistaken and cannot be completely trusted in other things they teach.

No Death before the Fall

A critically important theological reason that we cannot add long ages of time before Adam is because that would mean millions of years of animal death, disease, carnivorous behavior, and extinction as well as thorns and thistles, earthquakes, tsunamis, asteroid impacts, etc. in God's "very good" vegetarian creation (Gen. 1:29–31).

The fossil record in the sedimentary rock layers of the earth is where the evolutionary geologists and paleontologists supposedly got their evidence for millions of years of history before man. Radiometric dating was not invented until the early 20th century, almost 100 years after millions of years was locked into the minds of most geologists (and other scientists).[46] But in that fossil record we find evidence of carnivores eating other animals; cancer, arthritis and brain tumors in dinosaurs; diseases and cannibalism in supposedly pre-human hominids; thorns and thistles; and at least five mass extinction events when anywhere from 60 to 90 percent of the species living at the time went extinct due to some kind of natural evil (such as the supposed asteroid that wiped out all the dinosaurs and most other life "65 million years ago").

Not only does this evolutionary reconstruction of history contradict the picture of a "very good" creation in Genesis 1, it destroys the Bible's teaching in Genesis 3:14–19, 5:29, and Romans 8:19–23 about the cosmic impact of

46. Terry Mortenson, "The Historical Development of the Old-Earth Geological Time-Scale," https://answersingenesis.org/age-of-the-earth/the-historical-development-of-the-old-earth-geological-time-scale/, August 8, 2007.

the Fall. Furthermore, it undermines what the Bible teaches about the final redemptive work of Christ in the whole cosmos (Acts 3:21; Col. 1:15–20; Rev. 21:3–5, 22:3). It also assaults the character of God as revealed in Scripture. What kind of God would create over millions of years using all that natural evil and call it all "very good"?

Belief in the impact of the Fall on the whole creation, not just man, was Christian orthodoxy until the early 19th century.[47] Today, however, from my experience and reading, it is clear that most old-earth proponents have never even thought about these issues. Many theologians believe that the Fall affected the whole creation, just as they believe that after the Second Coming of Jesus Christ in the new heavens and new earth there will be no more human death and suffering for the redeemed but also no more natural evils (animal predation, death, disease, extinctions, earthquakes, tornadoes, etc.). But these theologians fail to see the inconsistency between these biblically and historically orthodox beliefs and their acceptance of millions of years.[48] Elsewhere I have given a thorough, documented discussion of the Fall and millions of years and responded to old-earth objections, and I urge readers to carefully consider this vital point.[49]

Christians who accept the evolutionary date for the first *Homo sapiens* (200,000–400,000 years ago) and for the age of the cosmos do not impress

---

47. See for example, Thane H. Ury, "Luther, Calvin, and Wesley on the Genesis of Natural Evil: Recovering Lost Rubrics for Defending a Very Good Creation," in *Coming to Grips with Genesis*, p. 399–424.
48. See examples of this inconsistency in my critique of three leading systematic theology texts which make this error: Terry Mortenson, "Systematic Theology Texts and the Age of the Earth: a Response to the Views of Erickson, Grudem, and Lewis and Demarest," https://answersingenesis.org/age-of-the-earth/systematic-theology-texts-and-the-age-of-the-earth/, December 16, 2009.
49. See Terry Mortenson, "The Fall and the Problem of Millions of Years of Natural Evil," https://answersingenesis.org/theory-of-evolution/millions-of-years/the-fall-and-the-problem-of-millions-of-years-of-natural-evil/, July 18, 2012. See also James Stambaugh, "Whence Cometh Death? A Biblical Theology of Physical Death and Natural Evil," *Coming to Grips with Genesis*, eds. Mortenson and Ury, p. 373–398.

    William Dembski has made a valiant attempt to wed an orthodox understanding of natural evil being a result of the Fall with the evolutionist claim that the natural evil happened for millions of years before the Fall. Even though his book, *The End of Christianity: Finding a Good God in an Evil World* (Nashville, TN: Broadman and Holman, 2009), has been endorsed by a host of evangelical leaders (including Josh and Sean McDowell, Frank Turek, Gary Habermas, Norman Geisler, Hank Hanegraaf, Chuck Colson, J.P. Moreland, C. John Collins, and many others) I argue that Dembski's proposal is fatally flawed. See Terry Mortenson, "Christian Theodicy in the Light of Genesis and Modern Science," https://answersingenesis.org/reviews/christian-theodicy-in-light-of-genesis-and-modern-science/, 11 November 2009. This article links to an excellent critique of Dembski's book by Dr. Tom Nettles.

non-Christians or motivate them to believe the Bible and the gospel. The late atheist Christopher Hitchens remarked about such old-earth thinking,

> Let's say that the consensus is that our species, being the higher primates, *Homo sapiens*, has been on the planet for at least 100,000 years, maybe more. . . . In order to be a Christian, you have to believe that for 98,000 years, our species suffered and died, most of its children dying in childbirth, most other people having a life expectancy of about 25 years. . . . Famine, struggle, bitterness, war, suffering, misery, all of that for 98,000 years. Heaven watches this with complete indifference. And then 2,000 years ago, thinks, "That's enough of that. It's time to intervene," and the best way to do this would be by condemning someone to a human sacrifice somewhere in the less literate parts of the Middle East. . . . This is nonsense. It can't be believed by a thinking person.[50]

Without a literal Adam and a literal Fall, the gospel is nonsense. But you cannot with any exegetical consistency believe in a literal Fall and simultaneously deny the literal six-day creation of a "very good" world devoid of death and suffering and natural evil. The evolutionary view of death and other natural evils is diametrically opposed to the biblical view.

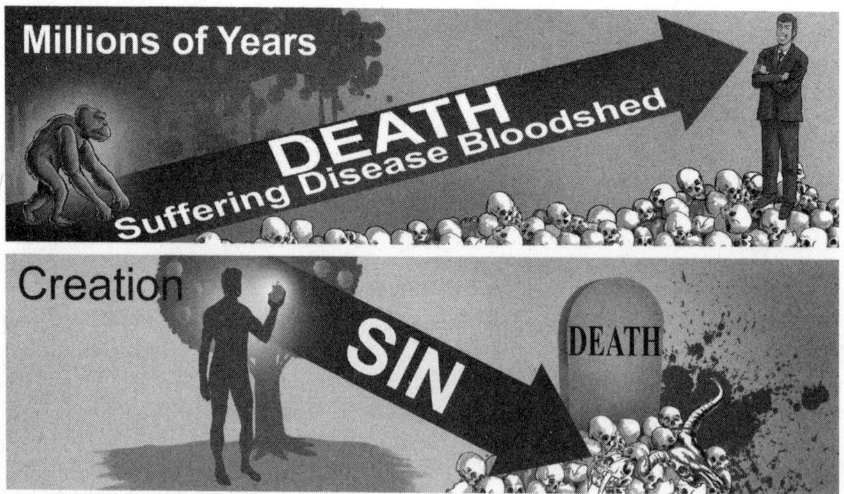

For all these reasons, the only biblically possible view is that Adam and Eve were created on the sixth, literal, normal, 24-hour day after the beginning of time. So now we turn to the time between Adam and us.

---

50. Christopher Hitchens, https://ashleyfmiller.wordpress.com/2010/09/24/hitchens-briefly-on-the-immorality-of-christianity/. The video of Hitchens saying this is on this page.

From Adam to Us Today: How Long?

As noted earlier, due in part to the influence of William Henry Green, the majority of evangelical scholars and leaders today say or think that Genesis 5 and 11 provide no chronological information about the time from the beginning of creation to Abraham. But every sincere Bible reader before the 19th century strongly believed that Genesis was telling us *when* God created the world. Even non-Christians had chronologies presenting an age of the world very similar to what is derived from a literal interpretation of Genesis.[51] Furthermore, conservative Jews take the text that way for their calendars today.[52]

But this is no great wonder. Genesis sure looks like God wants to convey a chronology. He gives the age of each patriarch when he dies and when the next man in the genealogy was born, when instead He could have just listed names, as He did in 1 Chronicles 1:1–27, Matthew 1:1–16, and Luke 3:23–38. He also numbers the days of Creation Week, gives time markers for events during the Flood, tells us how old Abraham, Isaac, and Jacob were at key events in their lives, and tells the Jews to pay attention to the calendar for religious festivals. He tells us how long the Israelites were in Egypt, how long they wandered in the wilderness, and how long it was from the Exodus to the building of Solomon's temple. He gives us chronological information about the reigns of the pre-kingdom judges, and the kings of Israel and Judah, and some neighboring kingdoms. He tells us how long the Babylonian captivity would last, and gives us plenty of chronological information in the Gospels and Acts to follow the ministry of Jesus and the Apostles. God has given a history in Scripture, and He evidently wants us to know when things happened.

If God doesn't want us to glean chronological information from Genesis 5 and 11, then why did He put it there? Does that mean that none of the dates in Genesis 6–8 has chronological information either, in which case we have no idea how long it rained and how long the Flood lasted? Without even looking at the biblical details, to think that Genesis 5 and 11 give no chronological information relevant to determining the age of mankind or of the universe seems extremely doubtful.

As I explained earlier, among young-earth creationists who do think the Genesis genealogies give us some chronological information there are two views. Some say that there very likely are missing names and therefore gaps

51. Bodie Hodge, "How Old Is the Earth?" in *The New Answers Book 2*, ed. Ken Ham (Green Forest, AR: Master Books, 2008), https://answersingenesis.org/age-of-the-earth/how-old-is-the-earth/.

52. So, May 31, 2016, is 23 Iyyar 5776 in the Jewish calendar. See https://www.hebcal.com/ and http://www.haaretz.com/jewish/this-day-in-jewish-history/1.679000.

of time, in which case Adam was created perhaps 8,000–12,000 years ago. Others, clearly the majority of leading creationists today, think there are good reasons to conclude that Genesis 5 and 11 are strict chronologies with no missing names or years. Hence, Adam and Eve (along with the whole universe) were created a little over 6,000 years ago. I will present some of the reasons for concluding the latter and encourage the reader to dig deeper in the resources in the footnotes.

Arguments for Gapless Genealogies and No Missing Years in Genesis 5 and 11

Unlike other genealogies in the Bible that simply list names (e.g., 1 Chron. 1–8; Ruth 4:18–22; Matt. 1:1–17; Luke 3:23–38), in Genesis 5 and 11 we are given the age of each "father" when the "son" was born and how many years the father lived after that birth. Genesis 5 and 11 are in fact the only genealogies in the Bible and in ancient Near Eastern literature that do this,[53] which draws our attention to this information even more. Furthermore, we know there are missing names in Matthew 1, not only because we might suspect it from the arrangement of three groups of 14 names, but also because we can check the genealogy against other texts in the Old Testament to find the omitted people. But we have no texts that would fill in the supposed missing names in Genesis 5 and 11. The extra Cainan in Luke 3:36 is almost certainly due to scribal error in copying manuscripts, for that Cainan is not in the oldest manuscripts of Luke and the Septuagint.[54]

Another evidence that Matthew has omitted some names is that if his list was complete, the average generation time between David and Jesus would be 35 years, which seems too long. But Luke's genealogy from Jesus all the way to Adam has 41 generations between David and Jesus, averaging a very reasonable 24 years for each. Luke also expressly states that in writing his Gospel he "investigated everything carefully" to present the "exact truth" concerning Jesus (Luke 1:3–4), giving us reason to think that Luke was giving us a complete genealogy from Jesus back to Adam.

---

53. Jeremy Sexton, "Who Was Born When Enosh Was 90? A Semantic Reevaluation of William Henry Green's Chronological Gaps," *Westminster Theological Journal* 77 (2015): 194, http://pastorsexton.com/articles/. Sexton cites the thorough work of Old Testament scholar, Gerhard Hasel on this point.

54. That was the conclusion of the great Baptist Hebraist of the 18th century, John Gill, in his commentary on Luke 3:36 in John Gill, *An Exposition of the Old and New Testament; The Whole Illustrated with Notes, Taken from the Most Ancient Jewish Writings* (1746–1763), quoted in https://answersingenesis.org/bible-timeline/genealogy/gaps-in-the-genesis-genealogies/. See also J. Paul Tanner, "Old Testament Chronology and Its Implications for the Creation and Flood Accounts," *Bibliotheca Sacra* 172 (January–March 2015): 33–34; and Jonathan Sarfati, *The Genesis Account*, p. 679–683.

But what about the highly influential article by Green in 1890 mentioned earlier? Sexton has carefully examined Green's argument and exposes his logical fallacies.[55] Sexton affirms that Green was correct in the two examples he cited[56] to show that the Hebrew verb יֹולֵד (*yoled*, the hiphil form of *yalad*, "beget"), which is used in Genesis 5 and 11, does not always mean a literal parent-child relationship in Scripture, a fact which corrects what I have written elsewhere.[57] But Tanner notes that *yoled* is used 170 times in Genesis, and in all other cases outside of chapters 5 and 11 the context makes clear that a literal parent-child relationship is in view.[58] Additionally, because of non-chronological details given about six of these relationships, we know they are literal father-son links.[59] But since in both chapters it says that each of these six patriarchs had "many [other] sons and daughters," which surely is referring to immediate family members, this is strong evidence that all the links in Genesis 5 and 11 are literally father-son.[60]

Sexton also shows from various Scriptures and comments by modern Hebrew scholars that Green was right that *yoled* describes the birthing process or actual delivery of the child. But Green's argument collapses when he assumes that since *yoled* indeed *may* refer to a distant relative, there *must* be genealogical gaps in Genesis 5 and 11. More importantly, as Sexton demonstrates, Green erred in assuming (without explicit argument) that *genealogical* gaps necessarily imply *chronological* gaps. In other words, even if names (i.e., generations) are missing, that does not mean that there must be missing time too. It does not matter, for example, if Kenan was the son or grandson or great grandson, etc., of Enosh. In any case, Kenan was born when

55. Sexton, "Who was born when Enosh was 90?" p. 193–218.
56. The two examples were Deuteronomy 4:25 (referring to both children and grandchildren) and 2 Kings 20:18 (in a prophecy that was fulfilled in the lives of Hezekiah's descendants living 4–5 generations after him: 2 Kings 24:12–17, 25:1–7).
57. Terry Mortenson, "Systematic Theology Texts and the Age of the Earth," https://answersingenesis.org/age-of-the-earth/systematic-theology-texts-and-the-age-of-the-earth/, just before endnote 51.
58. Tanner, "Old Testament Chronology," p. 31.
59. They are Adam-Seth, Seth-Enosh, Lamech-Noah, Noah-Shem, Shem-Arpachshad and Terah-Abraham. Adam named Seth because, as Eve said, he replaced Abel who was murdered (Gen. 4:25). Seth named his son Enosh (Gen. 4:26). Lamech named his son Noah and prophesied about him (Gen. 5:29). Shem was on the ark with Noah. Arpachshad was born two years after the Flood (Gen. 11:10). Abraham traveled with his father Terah to Haran where Terah died at age 225 when Abraham was 75 (Gen. 11:27–12:4).
60. While "son of" doesn't always mean a literal son but can refer to a distant descendant (e.g., Jesus, son of David), in the cases of Genesis 5 and 11 it surely refers to literal sons and daughters in 6 cases and it therefore seems inexplicable why it would mean anything different in the other 13 cases. What would be the point of conveying by this phrase the obvious fact that these 13 patriarchs had other distant descendants?

Enosh was 90 years old. So, again, while theoretically the Hebrew verb *yoled* could allow for missing names, there is no basis for imagining missing years. Genesis 5 and 11 provide us with a strict chronology from Abraham back to Adam (and thereby back to the very beginning of creation). Sexton, Tanner, and Freeman (cited in the notes) present other strong arguments to show that Green was mistaken and thereby has misled many other good scholars and that the position taken in this chapter is strong. But I will discuss a few more arguments here.

Many have argued that Genesis 5 and 11 each contain two lists of 10 names.[61] But this is simply not correct. In Genesis 5 if we count from Adam to Shem in the segmented genealogy of Noah, we have 11 names. In Genesis 11, if we start with Shem and count to Abraham in the segmented genealogy of Terah, we have 10 names. If we leave off the three sons of Noah, then we have 10 names in Genesis 5. But then to make a fair comparison we must leave off the three sons of Terah, giving us 9 names. We can count Noah in Genesis 11 to get 10 names to Terah, but Noah is not listed in the genealogy of Genesis 11.[62] Even if both genealogies did contain 10 names, this would not nullify the conclusion that we have here a strict chronology.

Some have denied that Genesis 5 and 11 have chronological value because these chapters do not total up the years, as other Scriptures give total years between two events. In support of this argument Youngblood cites Exodus 12:40 (giving the years the Jews were in Egypt) and 1 Kings 6:1 (giving the time from the Exodus to the building of Solomon's temple).[63] But surely Moses and God would expect the Jews to do the simple addition of the obvious numbers in Genesis 5 and 11. By contrast, it would take considerable effort and detective work to arrive at the total years in the two cases Youngblood cites.

Some have argued that the drop in ages after the Flood is evidence of missing names and missing time in Genesis 11. In particular, there is a 162-year drop in lifespan between Shem and Arpachshad and a 225-year drop in lifespan between Eber and Peleg. But there is a difference of 350

61. For example, Ronald Youngblood, *The Book of Genesis*, 2nd ed. (Grand Rapids, MI: Baker, 1991), p. 74.
62. See further, Travis R. Freeman, "Do the Genesis 5 and 11 Genealogies Contain Gaps," in *Coming to Grips with Genesis*, p. 283–314; and Tanner, "Old Testament Chronology," p. 26.
63. Youngblood, *Genesis*, p. 76. Citing the same two verses, Kaiser et al., *Hard Sayings*, p. 103, actually give "one final warning": "do not add up the years of these patriarchs and expect to come up with the Bible's date for the birth of the human race."

years between the lifespans of Noah and Shem. So this indicates missing names and years, it is argued. However, when the ages in Genesis 11 are analyzed mathematically, the drop in ages nicely fits an exponential decay curve, just as we would expect in the aftermath of the world-changing Flood.[64]

Formerly, some creationists attributed the drop in lifespans in Genesis 11 to significant environmental changes resulting from the collapse of a vapor canopy during the Flood. Not only is the idea of vapor canopy in the pre-Flood world no longer widely accepted by leading creationists,[65] but also today creationist experts think that genetics is the primary factor influencing lifespan, which will be addressed in the later chapter by Jeanson and Tomkins.[66]

Some have suggested that the ages of the pre-Flood patriarchs are inflated ten-fold, but in that case, Enoch and Mahalalel had kids at the unbelievable age of 6.5 years old, Kenan at age 7, and Enosh at age 9. Christensen has argued that these ages cannot be literal because each age is the product of 5s and 7s.[67] He correctly observed that the age of each patriarch in Genesis 5 is the product either of 5s, or of 5s plus one 7, or in the case of Methuselah, 5s plus two 7s. However, he never stated what the theological significance of these multiples of 5s and 7s is, and the pattern is different in Genesis 11, where the ages are made up of the multiples of 5 and either four or seven 7s. Besides this, we should note that every number above 18 (except for 23, 33, 43, 53, 73, 83, and 93) is a multiple of 5s, 7s, or a combination thereof. So this numerical analysis reveals nothing.

Furthermore, even if Genesis 5 and 11 are open genealogies with gaps, we cannot add enough years to harmonize Genesis with the evolutionary timescale for *Homo sapiens* without making the genealogies absurd. Since, as noted, 6 of the genealogical links are clearly literal, father-son relationships,

---

64. Philip M. Holladay, "An Exponential Decay Curve in Old Testament Genealogies," *Answers Research Journal*, vol. 9 (Oct. 2016), at https://answersingenesis.org/answers/research-journal. See also Sarfati, *The Genesis Account*, p. 685–688.
65. See Bodie Hodge "The Collapse of the Canopy Model," https://answersingenesis.org/environmental-science/the-collapse-of-the-canopy-model/, September 25, 2009; and Andrew Snelling, *Earth's Catastrophic Past*, 2 Vol. (Dallas, TX: ICR, 2009), I:471–473 and II:662–670.
66. David Menton and Georgia Purdom, "Did People like Adam and Noah Really Live Over 900 Years of Age?" in *The New Answers Book 2*, ed. Ken Ham (Green Forest, AR: Master Books, 2008), p. 129–137, https://answersingenesis.org/bible-timeline/genealogy/did-adam-and-noah-really-live-over-900-years/. See also Snelling, *Earth's Catastrophic Past*, I:65.
67. Duane L. Christensen, "Did People Live to Be Hundreds of years Old Before the Flood? NO," in *The Genesis Debate*, ed. Ronald F. Youngblood (Grand Rapids, MI: Baker, 1986), p. 166–183. See also Youngblood, *Genesis*, p. 76.

that leaves 13 links where there could *possibly* be missing time. However, if we add 1,000 years between each of those men, which would be equivalent to the time gap implied by the genealogical link, "Jesus, the son of David," this still would not harmonize with the evolutionary dating of man. But adding even this much time between these patriarchs (most of whom we know nothing about) seems unreasonable in the extreme and would call into question why any genealogy was given. To match the evolutionary timescale, we would need to add tens or hundreds of thousands of years to Genesis 5 and 11, which creates even more problems, as illustrated next.

In 2005 in *Who Was Adam?* Rana and Ross said that God created Adam and Eve "50,000–70,000 years ago."[68] But ten years later in their 2015 updated and expanded second edition they said, "In 2005, we predicted that God created human beings between 10,000 and 100,000 years ago."[69] If the evolutionist dating methods are so reliable, as Rana and Ross believe, why this difference in ages? The 2015 statement had no footnote to the page in the 2005 book, so without searching in the 2005 book readers would never know (1) that Rana and Ross did not accurately report what their own 2005 book said and (2) that they backed off from their 2005 relatively close range of ages to a less precise and wider range of dates. But Rana and Ross continued in the very next sentence of their 2015 book:

> The latest results from molecular anthropology place humanity's origin between 100,000 and 150,000 years ago. We were wrong [in 2005]. However the new dates line up with estimates of humanities' origin from the fossil record (between 100,000 and 200,000 years ago). Though these dates are older than those reported in the first [2005] edition of *Who Was Adam?* we argue that they still harmonize with Scripture.[70]

How can any thoughtful Christian accept this? Adam was 50,000–70,000 years ago, then 10,000–100,000 years ago or 100,000–150,000 years ago or even 150,000–200,000 years ago, and this all harmonizes with Scripture? Really? In the very next sentence in 2015 they continue,

> After carefully reconsidering our interpretation of the genealogies in Genesis 5 and 11, we now take the position that the biblical

68. Fazale Rana and Hugh Ross, *Who Was Adam?* 1st ed. (Colorado Springs, CO: NavPress, 2005), p. 248.
69. Fazale Rana and Hugh Ross, *Who Was Adam?* 2nd rev. ed. (Covina, CA: Reasons to Believe, 2015), p. 376. It should be noted that Rana and Ross follow William Henry Green in arguing for gaps in Genesis 5 and 11 to allow for all this extra time. (p. 50).
70. Ibid.

> text implies that Adam and Eve were created while an ice age, probably the most recent one, was in effect.[71]

But when was that last ice age according to Rana and Ross? They don't tell the reader. Instead they have an endnote after this sentence, pointing the reader to several pages in Ross's 2014 book *Navigating Genesis.* Of course, unless the reader has that 2014 book, he cannot check and see that Ross says there (p. 97–98) that the last ice age (when Adam was supposedly created) was 15,000–50,000 years ago. And the reader won't know that in the same book (p. 75) Ross says that "Noah would have been alive roughly 40,000 years ago and Adam and Eve anywhere from 60,000 to 100,000 years ago." This, says Ross in 2014 on the same page, shows that "the biblical account of creation retains its credibility in light of advancing [scientific] research."[72] But this statement about biblical credibility will seem reassuring to readers, *only* if they think that Genesis 5 and 11 have no chronological value *and* if they don't examine the conflicting numbers Rana and Ross are presenting in several books or on even different pages of the same book. To make matters worse, in *Who Was Adam?* (2015), Rana and Ross said (p. 51) that the Flood was "roughly 20,000 to 30,000 years ago." But going off the dates in Ross's 2014 book, that puts the Flood 10,000–20,000 years *after* Noah existed!

The vast majority of Rana and Ross's readers will never see this confusing and contradictory collection of dates. Sadly, their books have been warmly endorsed by many leading theologians and apologists[73] who apparently never bothered to do some simple math. So, let's do some.

Given that (as all agree) Abraham was born about 2000 B.C., the timeframe of Adam being 10,000–100,000 years ago (Rana and Ross's 2005 range) would put 6,000–96,000 years between Adam and Abraham. After taking out the 1,149 years covered by the 6 demonstrably literal father-son links,[74] Rana and Ross would need to account for another 4,851–94,851 years. This means that they would need to add an average of 373 to 7,296 years between *each* pair of names in the 13 *supposedly* non-literal links. If we consider that, apart from Noah's age of 502 when Shem was born, all

71. Ibid.
72. Ross, *Navigating Genesis*, p. 75.
73. *Who Was Adam?* (2015) is endorsed by Walter Kaiser, Ted Cabal, Ken Keathley, Norman Geisler, John Bloom, Jack Hayford, C. John Collins, and John Ankerberg.
74. Adam was 130 when Seth was born, Seth was 105 when Enosh was born, Lamech was 182 when Noah was born, Noah was 502 when Shem was born (Japheth was the first born: cf. Gen. 5:32 and 10:21), Shem was 100 when Arpachshad was born, and Terah was 130 when Abraham was born.

the other begetting ages were less than 188 years (and most were below 100 years), then even 373 years for the ages of all the other patriarchs when the next man was born is ridiculous. Using Rana and Ross's 2015 range of 100,000 to 200,000 years would put Adam 96,000–196,000 years before Abraham, or an average of 7,296 to 14,988 years between *each* pair of names in the supposedly non-literal links from Adam to Abraham! As Sarfati has shown and documented, these errors and "harmonizations" of Scripture and "science" made by Ross and Rana are just the tip of the iceberg of the biblical and scientific errors that they and Reasons to Believe have been presenting to the Christian public for several decades (with strong endorsements by some very prominent evangelical theologians, apologists, and other Christian leaders).[75]

This cavalier dating of Adam (following the constantly changing claims of evolutionists) certainly raises serious questions about Ross and Rana's claims to believe in the inspiration and inerrancy of Scripture.

Where Are All the Human Bones and All the Living People?

Where are all the fossilized and unfossilized bones, if mankind is 50,000 or 100,000 or even more years old? The earth should be overflowing with skeletal remains and human artifacts, but we find very little. And why isn't the human population today much larger and written records and other evidences of civilization much older than about 6,000–10,000 years (by secular dating of civilizations), if *Homo sapiens* came into existence 100,000 to 400,000 years ago? From the eight people coming off the ark about 4,500 years ago, the present world's population can be easily explained.[76] But if mankind is as old as the evolutionists claim, the world's population today is far, far too small. Reality confirms the Bible, not evolutionary dates.

What About the Scientific Dating Methods?

All scientific dating methods are based on naturalistic uniformitarian assumptions (see chapter 16 for discussion of these critically important assumptions). Many physical processes could theoretically be used to date

---

75. Jonathan Sarfati, *Refuting Compromise: A Biblical and Scientific Refutation of "Progressive Creationism" (Billions of Years), as Popularized by Astronomer Hugh Ross,* 2nd rev. ed. (Powder Springs, GA: Creation Book Publ., 2011). This revised second edition refutes the rebuttals that Ross made in response to Sarfati's first edition.
76. For a layman's discussion see Brian Thomas, "Population Study Standoff," http://www.icr.org/article/9132, January 18, 2016. For the technical arguments, see Robert Carter and Chris Hardy, "Modelling biblical human population growth," *Journal of Creation* 29, no. 1 (2015): 72-79, http://creation.com/images/pdfs/tj/j29_1/j29_1_72-79.pdf.

the earth or any object in the earth (e.g., radioactive decay, or the erosion of the continents, or the increase in the salinity of the oceans, or the buildup of helium in the atmosphere). But every such dating method involves making assumptions about the initial conditions when the process started, the rate of change since then, and whether the physical process was changed in any other way prior to human observations. Because scientists have no way to verify the accuracy of their assumptions about the unobserved and unrepeatable past, no scientific method can confidently determine the age of the earth, the universe, or a fossil.

With respect to human history, archeological dates based on carbon-14 are most untrustworthy.[77] The research that the BBC summarized and reported in 2001 is still true:

> A complete rewrite of the history of modern humans could be needed after a breakthrough in archaeological dating techniques. British and American scientists have found radiocarbon dating, used to give a rough guide to the age of an object, can be wrong by thousands of years. . . . They found that the carbon dates were wrong by thousands of years and that the further back in time they went, the more out-of-date they were.[78]

Creation scientists contend that the Flood is very important in explaining why prior to about the time of Christ, the C-14 dates become less and less reliable.[79]

Archeology is dominated by the same naturalistic philosophical presuppositions that control biology, geology, and astronomy, and most archeologists judge the Bible's history based on the standard of Egyptian chronology. But in addition to the fact that the Bible is God's inspired inerrant Word and Egyptian writings are not, there are strong reasons to reject this reverence for Egypt's historians.[80] The anti-biblical assumptions controlling archeology

77. To understand this dating method see Andrew Snelling, "Carbon-14 Dating, Understanding the Basics," https://answersingenesis.org/geology/carbon-14/carbon-14-dating/, October 1, 2010, as well as parts 2 and 3 linked in the article. A recent example of why C-14 dating doesn't work is discussed in Elizabeth Mitchell, "The Bible Wins the Debate with Carbon-Dated Camel Bones," https://answersingenesis.org/is-the-bible-true/the-bible-wins-the-debate-with-carbon-dated-camel-bones/, February 10, 2014.

78. Anon., "Dating Study 'Means Human History Rethink,'" http://news.bbc.co.uk/2/hi/science/nature/1413326.stm, June 29, 2001.

79. Andrew Snelling, "The Creationist Puzzle: 50,000-year-old Fossils," *Answers Magazine,* https://answersingenesis.org/geology/carbon-14/a-creationist-puzzle/, April 1, 2011.

80. The problems with Egyptian chronology are discussed in Elizabeth Mitchell, "Doesn't Egyptian Chronology Prove That the Bible Is Unreliable?" in *The New Answers Book 2*, ed. Ken Ham (Green Forest, AR: Master Books, 2008), p. 245–264, https://answersingenesis.org/archaeology/ancient-egypt/doesnt-egyptian-chronology-prove-bible-unreliable/.

and thereby discrediting the history of the Bible, especially in Genesis and Exodus, are clearly revealed in the recent excellent documentary film, *Patterns of Evidence*.[81]

The only way we can know with certainty the age of the creation or the age of mankind is if there was an absolutely trustworthy eyewitness of those creation events. We have one, the only one, in God Himself. He observed everything described in Genesis 1–11, which is His inspired, inerrant eyewitness testimony about those people and events.

Conclusion

It is simply impossible to apply sound hermeneutical principles to the biblical text and harmonize Genesis 1–11 with the evolutionary claims about the antiquity of man (or the earth and universe). It is exegetically impossible to put more than six days between Adam and the first moment of creation. Even if names are missing in Genesis 5 and 11 (I think this is highly unlikely), there are no missing years because the age of the patriarch is given when the next man is born. William H. Green, like Charles Hodge, A.A. Hodge, B.B. Warfield, and likely the rest of the faculty at Princeton at the time, were wrong about the age of the earth and man and unintentionally misled many others.

But we cannot be dogmatic about the precise date of Adam's creation. Johnson helpfully suggests that it is highly unlikely that each son was born on the birthday of his father. This requires a "fudge factor" of a partial year for the time between the father's birthday and the son's birth.[82] Nevertheless, given the ages in Genesis 5 and 11 in the Masoretic Hebrew Bible (and reflected in our modern translations), Adam (along with the rest of the universe) was created a little before 4000 B.C., and Noah's Flood was a little before 2400 B.C.[83] Even if the Septuagint were shown to be more correct on all the begetting ages of the patriarchs,[84] that would push the date of the

81. http://store.patternsofevidence.com/.

82. See James J.S. Johnson, "How Young Is the Earth? Applying Simple Math to Data Provided in Genesis," www.icr.org/article/4124. Johnson also assumes that the begetting refers to conception, not birth, but Sexton's article above (p. 195–196) gives strong biblical evidence to the contrary. Johnson also mistakenly counted Abraham as being born when Terah was 70. However, Haran was Terah's first-born and Abraham was not born till Terah was 130 (Abraham was 75 when Terah died at 205: cf Gen.11:32 and 12:4). So these points invalidate Johnson's calculations just a little.

83. Readers who are not convinced are urged to consider the articles by Tanner and Sexton and the chapter by Freeman cited above.

84. It appears that young-earth creationists need to investigate this question more deeply. Sarfati argues (*The Genesis Account*, p. 460–462) that the Septuagint (LXX) obviously has inflated ages because it has Methuselah living 14 years after the Flood, that the LXX also

Flood back only 750 years and the date of Adam's creation back another 586, making the age of the creation only around 7,350 years.[85]

The approximate date of Adam's creation (and therefore the creation of the universe) must be determined from the inerrant Word of God, not on the basis of fallible ancient pagan chronologies or equally fallible modern scientific dating methods that are controlled by equally pagan, naturalistic, philosophical assumptions.

But does it matter? Yes, it matters because God has given us many chronological details in His inerrant Word. He could have easily inspired Moses and the other biblical writers to speak in vague terms of "thousands of years" or "long ago." The details matter because every Word of God matters. It also matters because Jesus and the Apostles all clearly took Genesis as literal history. There is no reason to suppose that they thought any differently about the genealogies of Genesis 5 and 11. If their word cannot be trusted on this matter, then their truthfulness and authority are undermined on all other matters. Furthermore, it bears repeating that if we accept the evolutionary dates and view of history, then we must insert death, disease, and other natural evils long before the Fall, which contradicts the Bible's teaching on that subject and thereby undermines the truth of the gospel.

So the only real question regarding the dating of Adam's creation is whether or not we will believe God's Word. Or will we instead make secular archeology, paleontology, geology, and astronomy and their dating methods as well as ancient pagan chronologies our final authority on this matter? Put more simply, whose word do we supremely trust: God's or man's?

---

shows evidence of having been altered to fit with Egyptian chronology, and that the Dead Sea Scrolls strongly confirm the Hebrew Masoretic text as the faithful copy of the original. On the other hand, Sexton presents a more in-depth argument in favor of the ages in the LXX in the appendix of his "Who Was Born When Enosh Was 90?" p. 210–218. See also Jeremy Sexton and Henry B. Smith Jr., "Primeval Chronology Restored: Revisiting the Genealogies of Genesis 5 and 11," *Bible and Spade* 29.2 (2016): 42-49. Regardless, both Sarfati and Sexton take the genealogies of Genesis 5 and 11 as tight chronologies.

85. In the Masoretic Text (MT) the time from the creation of Adam to the beginning of the Flood is 1,656 years; in the LXX it is 2,242 years, an increase of 586 years. The time from the beginning of the Flood to the birth of Abraham is 353 years in the MT and 1,103 years in the LXX (if we omit the extra Cainan in later copies of the LXX), adding 750 years to the chronology. So if all the ages in the LXX were correct, we would add a maximum of 1,336 years between the creation of Adam (and the whole universe) and the birth of Abraham.

Chapter 6

What's Lost in John Walton's *The Lost World of Adam and Eve*?

by Steve Ham

The Lost World of Adam and Eve, the latest of John Walton's *Lost World* trilogy,[1] discusses the nature of biblical anthropology in the light of his perception of the true context of ancient Israel. Walton has attempted to construct this context through his understanding of the ancient Near East (ANE) as the setting in which Israel received the Scriptures. In doing so, he discusses the nature of the first three chapters of Genesis and proposes that the text is giving an account not of material origins (i.e., of how and when the creation came into existence), but of the inauguration of creation as God's cosmic temple in which we find the role of humanity. Within this framework, Walton presents his case for uncovering the history of human origins.

This essay contends that Walton has given a magisterial authority to the ancient Near East mythic texts in order to interpret the Genesis accounts. In doing so, he has eliminated Genesis as an account of material origins and inevitably redefined key biblical doctrines to such a degree that infringes on the very nature of orthodoxy. Further to this, his attempt to accommodate modern evolutionary philosophy is unwarranted and unsubstantiated.

The Importance of Old Testament Backgrounds

The study of Old Testament backgrounds has gained increasing prominence in biblical scholarship. The excavations of the libraries from the ancient Near East and the decryption of ancient languages have produced many

1. *The Lost World of Scripture* (2009), *The Lost World of Adam and Eve* (2015), and the forthcoming *The Lost World of Noah*.

examples of literature revealing notable similarities to the biblical accounts of creation, the Fall, the Flood, the patriarchs, and the Tower of Babel. In addition to this literature, archeological dig sites have uncovered buildings, communities, water systems, and city layouts. They have uncovered artifacts including jewelry, pottery, weaponry, and a host of other helpful keys to constructing a picture of life in ANE cultures. Victor Matthews, specialist in the ANE social world, has summarized this idea:

> The gulf of thousands of years that separates us from them can be bridged, at least in part, by insights into their everyday life. Such insights can be garnered through close examination of biblical data with written and physical remains from other ancient civilizations.[2]

While this statement would find general agreement in biblical scholarship, there is a wide-ranging application of the archeological data as it is applied to biblical hermeneutics. The evidence produced from the mounds of Nineveh and Nippur and other ANE locations is common to all. Even so, major differences in biblical scholarship appear on the basis of one's interpretation of the common evidence and the level of priority given to Scripture in the process.

Archeology and studies in ANE languages and culture are fields that pose much promise to strengthen the Church through an enhanced understanding of biblical backgrounds and use in biblical apologetics. However, an increased level of discernment is required from people in the pews who read the works of some scholars who vocally proclaim commitment to biblical authority and inerrancy while positing vastly different views of key biblical texts.

The work of John Walton has been produced as a trilogy for lay readers. The series of three books, written to be accessible to the wider church, share *The Lost World* as a common element in their titles. The first book, *The Lost World of Scripture*, was a discussion about ANE culture and biblical authority. It is Walton's contention that it is only after recent discoveries and study of ANE literature that scholars have been able to reconstruct a true understanding of the context of the Old Testament Scriptures. This context, he proposes, vastly changes the way that the church has traditionally understood Genesis as an account of material origins (its physical origins).[3] In light of the ANE literature, Walton now contends that the "author of Genesis" nowhere

2. Victor H. Matthews, *Manners and Customs in the Bible: An Illustrated Guide to Daily Life in Bible Times*. 3rd ed. (Grand Rapids, MI: Baker Academic, 2006), p. 11.
3. John H. Walton, *The Lost World of Genesis One: Ancient Cosmology and the Origins Debate* (Downers Grove, IL: IVP Academic, 2009), p. 21–35.

suggests that the creation week is an account of material origins. Walton's theory is that because ancient Israel's neighbors described the cosmos in terms of the temple of the gods and creation in terms of making that temple function, so too Israel understood the creation account in Genesis 1 as describing God giving function to His cosmic temple and not as an account of how things came into existence. As this essay will show, this has major implications for central Christian doctrines that have coherency only if the early chapters of Genesis present us with trustworthy history.

Chapter Summaries of *The Lost World of Adam and Eve*

In *The Lost World of Adam and Eve*, Walton presents his case through a series of 21 propositions. Each proposition is a chapter heading. I will briefly summarize each chapter before I analyze the argument.

Proposition 1: Genesis is an ancient document

Walton sets the scene for the book with a discussion on context. A careful differentiation is made between high and low context settings. In a high context setting for communication, terms and descriptors do not need to be carefully defined because all communicants (i.e., author and his contemporary readers) are aware of their meaning.[4] Walton asserts that modern readers of Genesis are in a low context setting of communication because we are separated by vast amounts of time, as well as differences in culture, language, and — usually — geography, all of which significantly hinders our ability to understand the biblical text.

Proposition 2: In the ancient world and the Old Testament, creating focuses on establishing order by assigning roles and functions

Walton presents the Genesis 1 account of creation as an account of bringing order to an unordered preexisting creation rather than a history of how and when God made the creation. Genesis 1:1 is seen as the summary statement and the pre-ordered creation is described in Genesis 1:2. Genesis 1:2 also marks the beginning of the creation week as the process of bringing order to a non-ordered world that has already existed materially. This means that the traditional understanding of the Hebrew words for "create" (ברא, *bara*), "formless" (תהו, *tohu*), "void" (בהו, *bohu*), and "make" (עשׂה, *'asah*) must be redefined and removed from their material context to a functional one.[5]

4. John H. Walton and N.T. Wright, *The Lost World of Adam and Eve: Genesis 2–3 and the Human Origins Debate* (Downers Grove, IL: IVP Academic, 2015), p. 16–17.
5. Ibid., p. 28–31.

Walton attempts to do this through a study of the semantic range of these words found in other biblical and extra-biblical texts. In light of the ANE texts, to create means to bring order. The description of formlessness is to lack purpose or worth, and combined with being void describes the earth as lacking order and function. He states,

> It now becomes clear that the starting condition in Genesis 1:2, the pre-creation situation that describes nonexistence, is a condition that is not lacking material. Rather, it is a situation that is lacking order and purpose. "Formless" is not a good choice because it still implies that material shape is the focus. It is not. This leads us to the conclusion that for Israel, creation resolves the absence of order and not the absence of material.[6]

The pre-creation condition is stated as "negative cosmology" or "denial of existence." Evidence of such a condition of non-order in a pre-creation context is derived from the *Enuma Elish*, the Babylonian creation story. In line with the view that the rest of Genesis 1 is not an account of material origins, Walton also notes that the image of God in human beings is not a description of the unique creation of the first two humans but of the function of their being God's representatives for all humanity.

Proposition 3: Genesis 1 is an account of functional origins, not material origins

How this functionality is explained in the terms of each day of creation is found in chapter three. Various similarities are proposed between Scripture and ANE literature. The Assyrian king placed his image in conquered territories to proclaim his presence. This is related to humans bearing God's image. Other ANE sources describe animals coming out of the earth, and this is related to God's creation of land animals (Gen. 1:24).[7] Walton therefore argues that Genesis 1 should be understood in terms of functionality: bringing order from non-order.

Proposition 4: In Genesis 1, God orders the cosmos as sacred space

The concept of functionality comes to light here in terms of God making Himself a "home." As the ANE creation texts are often associated with the creation of sacred space (as in a temple), so in Genesis 1 the cosmos is being ordered as God's sacred space. This then requires some consideration of the

6. Ibid.
7. Ibid., p. 41–42.

concept of rest. While the traditional understanding of God's rest described in Genesis 2:1–3 is that God had completed His work of creating the material world in the previous six days, Walton rejects this and understands this rest as God taking up residence in an ordered, sacred space.

Proposition 5: When God establishes functional order, it is "good"

Chapter five describes how the functional order of creation is "good." It would seem that as each stage of ordering in creation is completed, the function is considered to be good. Walton describes it like the process of making a house into a home. The house is not functioning as a home until everything is moved in and functioning well. This does not mean that the creation is completed in perfect order when God says that it is "very good." The example is used of Joshua and Israel coming into the Promised Land.

> For example, the same description is given to the Promised Land (Num. 14:7), though it is filled with enemies and wicked inhabitants, not to mention wild animals who are predators.[8]

Walton is content to allow for non-order to be a part of the sacred space that God calls "very good." This non-order includes death (both human and animal), disease, suffering, bloodshed, and natural disasters. Furthermore, it seems that the difference between non-order and disorder (which results from sin) is not death, suffering, and natural disasters. These things were already present in the "very good," yet not quite very good order of the sacred space. It is a confusing dialogue that leads one to conclude that for God, even on the sole basis of order, "very good" means "good enough," and "good enough" includes death and suffering.

Proposition 6: Adam is used in Genesis 1–5 in a variety of ways

With the foundational context laid, the remainder of the book focuses attention on anthropology. Walton does not identify Adam as a "representative head (in which one is serving as an elect delegate on behalf of the rest)." Instead, he describes Adam as an "archetype (all are embodied in the one and counted as having participated in the acts of that one)."[9] Where a representative head determines that which proceeds for all, an archetype is an original that is simply typical of all. It is because of this distinction that both Walton and his writing companion, N.T. Wright, spend considerable time discussing how the archetypal view of Adam affects Romans 5 and 1 Corinthians 15.

8. Ibid., p. 57.
9. Ibid., p. 61.

Proposition 7: The second creation account (Genesis 2:4–24) can be viewed as a sequel rather than as a recapitulation of Day Six in the first account (Genesis 1:1–23)

The profundity of depicting Adam as an archetype rather than a representative head is brought to light in this proposition. For Walton, this removes the requirement of viewing Adam and Eve as the very first human beings. While he does accept that Genesis 2 is discussing an historical Adam and Eve, he also suggests that humanity mentioned in Genesis 1:26–28 is a whole group of people that may or may not include Adam and Eve.[10] He describes Genesis 1 as the inchoate condition of the cosmos and Genesis 2 as the terrestrial inchoate condition. Where formless and void are descriptors of an inchoate cosmos, Walton suggests that the plants "not yet cultivated" in Genesis 2:5 are descriptors of an inchoate terrestrial setting. Walton proposes that this is similar to the way ANE cosmologies describe functionality being brought to the cosmos.[11]

Proposition 8: "Forming from dust" and "building from rib" are archetypal claims and not claims of material origins

The formation of Adam from dust and Eve from Adam's side is also described archetypally. In the consistency of not yielding to Genesis being a description of material origins, Walton again attempts to show that a Hebrew word typically understood as "formed" (יצר) is not required to have a material object, although he admits that in many cases it does. The Genesis 2:7 description of Adam formed of dust is explained as an archetypal depiction of human mortality. Ancient Israelites knew what it was like to see ancestor's bones decaying to dust, thus seeing the evidence of mortality. Likewise, Walton believes Adam's sleep depicts a visionary experience of Eve as one of his whole sides and thus archetypal of an important one-flesh union in his life.[12] It is not seen as an account of the actual creation of Eve. What the Church has typically understood as creation events, Walton has explained as archetypal examples of life, death, and relationship between men and women.

Proposition 9: Forming of humans in ancient Near Eastern accounts is archetypal, so it would not be unusual for Israelites to think in those terms

In solidifying his view that Genesis 2 is describing archetypal functionality in humanity, Walton discusses archetypal functionality in the ANE texts.

10. Ibid., p. 64.
11. Ibid., p. 76.
12. Ibid., p. 80.

He identifies three main examples of how ANE literature describes human functionality. This also impacts his interpretation of what it means to be in the image of God. Man being "in the image of God" means:

1. Functioning in place of the gods (doing menial labor so the gods need not do it)
2. Functioning in service to the gods (performance of religious ritual, providing for the temple)
3. Functioning on behalf of the gods (rule either over the non-human creation or over other people)[13]

Proposition 10: The New Testament is more interested in Adam and Eve as archetypes than as biological progenitors

Here Walton explains how the creation/temple functionality view and archetypal humanity impact the interpretation of key New Testament passages. He gives particular attention to Romans 5 and 1 Corinthians 15. Most significantly, he interprets Paul as using both Adam (the first Adam) and Jesus (the second/final Adam) in an archetypal manner. All humans sin because Adam as an archetype displays the human condition.

> We can see that Paul uses Adam on a number of levels in Romans 5, but one of them is as an archetype. Nevertheless, here the archetypal use is connected to the fall, not to his forming. First Corinthians 15 is the other most extensive treatment of Adam by Paul. In 1 Corinthians 15:21 Paul observes that death came through a man, in so doing, addresses Adam as an individual who is acting. But in 1 Corinthians 15:22 he expands his vision to the archetypal level: as in Adam all die, so in Christ will all be made alive.[14]

A question that is never answered in this chapter, or any following, is how one can associate with Jesus (the perfect God-man) as an archetype. Walton does mention that not all humanity is "in Christ," but he does not explain how being "in" Christ relates to Christ being archetypal rather than our new representative head.

Proposition 11: Though some of the biblical interest in Adam and Eve is archetypal, they are real people who existed in a real past

Walton presents Adam and Eve as historical figures in space and time, and sin as a historical event. To understand how this can be in light of Walton's

13. Ibid., p. 90.
14. Ibid., p. 93.

previous points, one has to see the example of Melchizedek and Abram. He argues that just as Abram gave a real tithe to a real person and serves as an example for all of Israel in tithing, so too Adam and Eve must be real persons who really sinned in history and serve in a similar archetypical fashion. However,

> At the same time, it must be observed that for them to play these historical roles does not necessarily require them to be the first human beings, the only human beings or the universal ancestors of all human beings (biologically/genetically). In other words, the question of the historical Adam has more to do with sin's origins than with material human origins.[15]

Proposition 12: Adam is assigned as priest in sacred space, with Eve to help

Walton describes Adam and Eve as priests serving in sacred space. He cites two main evidences for this view. One relates to the words "work" and "keep" (עבד and שׁמר, respectively). These same Hebrew words elsewhere are translated as "serve" and "guard" and associated with priestly duties around the Tabernacle and Temple in later passages (Num. 3:7–8, 8:25–26; Ezek. 44:14). The second evidence is from ANE literature (particularly the Babylonian *Gilgamesh Epic*) where priests had the duties of ordering sacred space. Again, the priestly duties of Adam are seen as an archetype for how humanity functions.

Proposition 13: The Garden is an ancient Near Eastern motif for sacred space, and the trees are related to God as the source of life and wisdom

Walton cites various ANE myths correlating to Edenic garden imagery around sacred space. Various biblical temple passages are also cited to show a connection of the Temple to Eden.

Proposition 14: The serpent would have been viewed as a chaos creature from the non-ordered realm, promoting disorder

Walton contends that the serpent in the Garden is not a representation of Satan in physical form but as a representation of what would be known in the ANE as a creature of disorder. The associated physical aspects concerning the serpent (such as crawling in the dust) are explained in the sense that the creature of cosmic disorder would be tamed. Israel would apparently understand this on the basis of its own experience of this cosmic battle.

15. Ibid., p. 103.

Proposition 15: Adam and Eve chose to make themselves the center of order and source of wisdom, thereby admitting disorder into the cosmos

Here Walton suggests that sin is better explained by what it does rather than what it is. This is because Walton believes that the semantic range for "sin" (חַטָּאת) is difficult to pin down to one major definition. He seems, however, to fall on a definition that explains sin as "missing the mark" and leans on biblical theologian Mark E. Biddle for further explanation:

> The biblical model sees sin as the disequilibrium pervasive in a system in disarray. . . . Authentic human existence . . . aspires to realize its full potential of godlikeness while consistently acknowledging its creatureliness and limitations. Sin is disequilibrium in this aspiration: humanity failing to reflect its divine calling, humanity forgetting its limitations.[16]

In the context of Walton's "Lost World" ideology, sin in Genesis 3 is seen as Adam and Eve failing to achieve a solution to bring order to non-order in God's way thereby bringing about disorder by their own wisdom. Walton does not position sin as the breaking of a divine command but he provides no discussion of the reality of the nature or seriousness of God's spoken command to Adam in Genesis 2. As a result, for Walton, sin prohibited access to the tree of life and thus now the mortality of Adam and Eve becomes an unsolvable reality. Also the point is not that Adam and Eve were expelled from the garden but that they were forbidden entry into it and access to the life-giving tree.

Proposition 16: We currently live in a world with non-order, order, and disorder

Disorder is ultimately positioned against both order and non-order. Humans bring disorder by being their own source and center of wisdom.[17] This sets the stage for discussing how living in a non-ordered world affected the first human beings.

Proposition 17: All people are subject to sin and death because of the disorder in the world, not because of genetics

In the continuation of the discussion on human sin, Walton explains categories of evil and suggests that not all evil is associated with sin. He describes

16. Ibid., p. 142.
17. Ibid., p. 150–151.

sin as a ritual or moral impropriety that damages man's relationship with God.[18]

If sin is not counted where this is no law (Rom. 5:13), Walton suggests, then prior to any law in the garden, humans were not counted responsible for their actions even though created in the image of God. He states,

> . . . this human population would have been in a state of innocence (not sinlessness) since they were not yet being held accountable, even though they were in the image of God. In this scenario we would expect to find predation, animal death, human death and violent behavior. Endowment with the image of God and the initiation of sacred space would provide the foundation for accountability through law and revelation.[19]

He also discusses the transmission of sin to all humanity. If Adam is archetypal, then people typically sin because we live in a state of disorder. Sin is not imputed from a representative head to all mankind. Walton's view of archetypal sinning also bears on the need for the virgin birth. Walton submits that Jesus' divine nature is what immunizes him from the effect of disorder and the Fall. While Walton discusses Jesus' divine nature, there is no further discussion on why Jesus needed to be born in a human line, and if He was immunized to disorder, why He needed to be born of a virgin. The consequences of seeing Jesus as archetypal rather than a representative head seem extensive and very problematic.

Proposition 18: Jesus is the keystone of God's plan to resolve disorder and perfect order

Walton discusses the "resolve" of disorder in the new creation. While man had once attempted to regain sacred space according to his own merits (Genesis 11 and the Tower of Babel), a full "resolve" will be made in Christ in the coming age. Walton does not see the Tower of Babel event as a judgment on human pride because ANE texts indicate that making a name for oneself is simply a way of carrying on memory in successive generations. Humanity at Babel attempted to make sacred space for the improvement of their situation rather than to serve and worship God. God gives hope for a resolve in setting apart His people Israel in whom He will "write the law on their hearts." Walton suggests that writing on man's heart would be meaningful to the ancient world because they were

18. Ibid., p. 154.
19. Ibid., p. 159.

aware of reading animal entrails in divination (somewhat like modern palm readers do).[20]

Proposition 19: Paul's use of Adam is more interested in the effect of sin on the cosmos than in the effect of sin on humanity and has nothing to say about human origins (N.T. Wright)

In this chapter, N.T. Wright proposes that the Pauline doctrine of salvation (particularly in Romans 5) is not what he calls the traditional Christian view of simply being saved from a state of sin and death under the judgment of God by the atoning sacrifice of Christ, but that Paul views salvation as putting God's plan for the ordering of creation back on track.

> Here is the problem to which Romans is the answer: not simply that we are sinful and need saving but that our sinfulness has meant that God's project for the whole creation (that it should be run by obedient humans) was aborted, put on hold. And when we are saved, as Paul spells out, that is in order that the whole-creation project can at last get back on track. When humans are redeemed, creation groans a sigh of relief and says, "Thank goodness! About time you humans got sorted out! Now we can be put to rights at last."[21]

Wright maintains that when Paul is talking about Adam in Genesis, he is focusing on the vocation of Adam and not the position of Adam. The vocation is put right in Christ to put the ordering of creation back on track. Wright does not discuss the imputation of sin or righteousness that Paul discusses in Romans 5:12–21.

Proposition 20: It is not essential that all people descended from Adam and Eve

In the final two chapters, Walton discusses the impact of this position as it relates to modern "science." But he restricts his discussion to the realm of evolutionary ideas. If Genesis does not require Adam and Eve to be the very first parents of the human race created in the image of God, then modern biological evolution can easily find compatibility with Walton's creation functionality position. If Genesis is not talking about material origins, then the whole realm of origins science is up for grabs.

20. Ibid., p. 166.
21. Ibid., p. 173–174.

Proposition 21: Humans could be viewed as distinct creatures and a special creation of God even if there was material continuity

Finally, Walton proclaims that humans are distinct, but not on the basis that they are created this way in the image of God. Rather, real human beings living as material creatures were at one point given God's image through how they functioned. That distinct function was to bring order to a non-ordered creation in the terrestrial setting. Even so, bearing God's image is not a matter of being distinguished ontologically from other creatures, but solely a matter of having a different function.[22]

Critical Evaluation of Walton's View

ANE Hermeneutical Priority: Undermining Biblical Authority and Inspiration

To what extent should a responsible theologian engage with the ANE literature? Perhaps a better question to ask is, should the ANE literature attain a level of priority in which it is given magisterial authority over the text of Scripture? The varying degrees of usage of ANE texts are often determined by the theologian's commitment to the doctrines of biblical authority, inerrancy, infallibility, sufficiency, and perspicuity. Walton has spoken of his own view in *The Lost World of Scripture*.

> At the fountainhead (of biblical authority) is either an authority figure who, empowered by the Holy Spirit, generated the information (e.g., Moses, Jeremiah) or, more abstractly, the tradition itself (passed on by various tradents[23]) whose origins are untraceable (e.g., narratives whether in Genesis or Judges).[24]

The point being conveyed is that biblical authority comes by the way of authors and traditions in which the text was assembled (whether oral or written and/or compilations of scribes). There will be no argument that God has used different methods to write His inspired Word. Luke obviously researched materials for the writing of Luke/Acts (Luke 1:1). The question is where we lay the weight of authority and what we consider to epitomize inspiration and authority. Paul makes it clear that all Scripture is breathed out by God (2 Tim. 3:16). The Bible attributes the weight of authority and

22. Ibid., p. 194–195.
23. One who is responsible for preserving and handing on the oral tradition, such as a teacher, preacher, or missionary.
24. Walton and Sandy, *Lost World of Scripture*, p. 63.

inspiration to the words of Scripture (Matt. 5:17–18), not to the process or to the culture in which the process took place. There is no argument that certain humans are involved in the process and that they use different methods, but it is also evident in Scripture that these individuals knew that they were writing and speaking the very inspired words of God. We see this wherever the prophets say, "Thus says the Lord." We see it in the way Peter attributes inspiration to the letters of Paul (2 Peter 3:14–16). This also means that an understanding of ANE materials and the transmission traditions within ANE cultures must only have a ministerial place (possibly enhancing but never determining meaning) in our understanding of Scripture. Despite Walton's protestations to the contrary, the weight that he seems to place upon ANE traditions and backgrounds puts them more in the realm of magisterial authority (i.e., governing the interpretation of the biblical text).

Peter Enns has more explicitly stated a similar concept to that revealed in Walton's thinking above.

> First, a contemporary evangelical doctrine of Scripture must account for the Old Testament as an ancient Near Eastern phenomenon by going beyond the mere observation of that fact to allowing that fact to affect how we think about Scripture.[25]

While Walton and Enns come to varied conclusions about Genesis and associated doctrines, they have both, to different degrees, attributed hermeneutical weight to ANE texts in regard to their doctrines of inspiration and authority.

In contrast, Eugene Merrill has maintained that Scripture alone holds the magisterial authority by stating:

> A history of Israel must depend for its documentary sources almost entirely upon the Old Testament, a collection of writings confessed by both Judaism and Christianity to be Holy Scripture, the Word of God. The degree to which historians are willing to submit to this claim will inevitably affect the way they think about their task.[26]

One would not expect Walton to admit or even believe that he has placed a magisterial authority upon the ANE sources. The claim of this reviewer

---

25. Peter Enns, *Inspiration and Incarnation: Evangelicals and the Problem of the Old Testament*, annotated edition (Grand Rapids, MI: Baker Academic, 2005), p. 67.

26. Eugene H. Merrill, *Kingdom of Priests: A History of Old Testament Israel*, 2nd ed. (Grand Rapids, MI: Baker Academic, 2008), p. 20.

(and others) is that the ANE magisterial weight is derived from the display of the critical influence of these sources in his work. This serves as a solemn reminder to us all that a Christian can attribute authority to Scripture in words but display the contrary in practice (cf. James 2:14, 18–20).

ANE Hermeneutical Priority: Undermining the Perspicuity of Scripture

In the very first proposition, Walton makes a case for upholding biblical perspicuity. He states, "Such study is not a violation of the clarity ("perspicuity") of Scripture propagated by the Reformers. They were not arguing that every part of Scripture was transparent to any casual reader."[27] Of course, no student of Scripture today would disagree. But one has to take his statement in connection with his later disclaimer that reads,

> However, since the beginning of the massive archeological undertakings in Iraq in the middle of the nineteenth century, more than one million cuneiform texts have been excavated that expose the ancient literature by which we can gain important new insight into the ancient world. This is what provides the basis for our interpretation of the early chapters of Genesis as an ancient document.[28]

From the 1st century to the early 19th century the church had uniform agreement that Genesis was a material account of creation (i.e., a historical account of the creation of the physical cosmos). There may have been differing opinions in the detail but the predominant view was that God materially created everything in the six literal (essentially 24-hour) days (most widely held to be normal, consecutive days of a first week) and rested (ceased from His work) on the seventh. Walton is vastly underestimating the difference that his view of a non-material functional creation has had on perspicuity. In a full and careful reading of his book, one finds translation alterations, word definitions, and reshaping of major doctrines that reveal his position to be completely foreign to 1,800 years of biblical coherency in the Church. It is one thing to state a commitment to perspicuity, but it is entirely another to practice it.

Furthermore, Walton quotes Martin Luther's comment about not finding anyone in the church with adequate skill to explain everything in the Genesis account.[29] Statements about human inability to explain every action of God do not mean that the truth of history is unclear. There is no doubt

27. Walton and Wright, *Lost World of Adam*, p. 22.
28. Ibid., p. 23.
29. Ibid.

that Luther understood that Genesis 1 describes God's creation of the material world that happened over six days. His commentary on Genesis clearly shows this. Elsewhere he succinctly stated,

> When Moses writes that God created heaven and earth and whatever is in them in six days, then let this period continue to have been six days, and do not venture to devise any comment according to which six days were one day. But, if you cannot understand how this could have been done in six days, then grant the Holy Spirit the honor of being more learned than you are.[30]

Luther maintains that the truth is clear and evident even if we cannot understand how God did it. He is willing to grant the Holy Spirit precedent in authority over the scholars of his day.

Hermeneutical Authority

Walton's stated position, as quoted above, is that the ANE literature "provides the basis for our interpretation of the early chapters of Genesis." Other scholars are opposed to such methodology and reject the ANE texts as an interpretative grid for determining biblical meaning. They are not a "basis" but they enhance our understanding of the historical background applicable to the truth that is already evident in the text. Furthermore, while Walton does acknowledge that both similarities and dissimilarities should be noted between the biblical text and ANE literature, the major impact on meaning of the texts of Scripture have come from his focus on the similarities. This exegetical approach should be rejected given the profundity of the differences.

Currid has made careful enquiry into the significance of these differences. He has summarized them by stating that "dissimilarities are not superfluous but are of great magnitude and import."[31] Currid has identified the genre of ANE texts as mainly "mythic narrative" in contrast to the biblical "historical narrative."[32] While the Bible is consistently purposed to glorify the "one" Creator God, ANE texts are polytheistic.[33] Magic is the ultimate power in the universe in ANE texts and is a power above the gods. In the biblical account, there is nothing with power over the all-powerful

30. Martin Luther and Ewald M. Plass, *What Luther Says: An Anthology* (Saint Louis, MO: Concordia Publishing House, 1986), p. 1523.
31. John D. Currid, *Against the Gods: The Polemical Theology of the Old Testament* (Wheaton, Illinois: Crossway, 2013), p. 40.
32. Ibid., p. 60.
33. Ibid., p. 46.

and sovereign God.[34] Oswalt comes to the same conclusions in his helpful analysis.[35] Currid therefore states,

> The uniqueness of the biblical account is a good argument for its independence from rather than its dependence on the pagan mythic texts. They are perhaps two separate traditions that stem from a historical flood. If biblical stories are true, one would be surprised not to find some references to these truths in extra-biblical literature.[36]

This makes sense on many levels. First, there are creation, Flood, and Tower of Babel legends found in cultures all over the world, as Chaffey discusses in a later chapter. A shared history shown in Genesis 9–11 would indicate that similarities in cultural legend have a common point of reference. This also testifies to the internal biblical testimony that it alone is the Word of God and the authentic inerrant history. Those legends of idolatrous peoples were corruptions of the true history, as recorded in Genesis. The legendary elements are a result of human ignorance and depravity but also very likely the influence of demons, for Moses, one of the Psalmists, and Paul tell us that when the pagans worshiped idols they unknowingly worshiped demons (Lev. 17:7; Psa. 106:34–36; 1 Cor. 10:20).

Second, one must consider that Genesis is part of "The Law," written by Moses (as attested throughout Scripture: Exod. 17:14; Josh. 1:7–8; 1 Chron. 22:13; Dan. 9:11; Matt. 8:4; Luke 24:44; 1 Cor. 9:9). It was written in the time of the wilderness wandering of Israel. Prior to this, the Israelite generation of the exodus was enslaved in Egypt. They were working tirelessly to make Pharaoh his mud bricks. One has to wonder whether there really was a truly "high context" in communication between Israelite slaves and nomads and the rest of the ancient world when they received the Scriptures, such that they would be very conversant with the pagan creation, Fall, Flood, and Babel myths. It seems doubtful.

Third, as Israel traveled to the Promised Land, God gave them a warning not to be ensnared by or to integrate with the nations that would be dispossessed. They were to be holy/separate in their worship of Yahweh (Deut. 12:29–31). So why would God lead Moses to write Genesis based on the pagan myths or in a way that would require the Israelites to be well acquainted with those myths?

34. Ibid., p. 41.

35. John N. Oswalt, *The Bible Among the Myths: Unique Revelation or Just Ancient Literature?* (Grand Rapids, MI: Zondervan, 2009).

36. Currid, *Against the Gods*, p. 61.

These considerations would, at the very least, prompt the theologian to take extreme care to ensure that any ANE literature serves to enhance biblical background knowledge and not to determine the meaning of the biblical text.

Functional vs. Material

Many responses to Walton's first book, *The Lost World of Scripture*, have addressed Walton's claim that the creation accounts in Genesis 1 and 2 are not speaking of material origins but only to assigning functionality associated with the inauguration of sacred space. On this matter there is little that has changed in his latest contribution except for how this view impacts humanity. The main objections already voiced are that Walton is overstating his view that ANE literature describes origins according to functionality, and that his excessive use of word studies are inconclusive for making the functionality view work. One of the major ANE texts cited by Walton is the Babylonian *Enuma Elish*, but other Old Testament scholars are not convinced that this text solely describes a functional cosmogony. Ashmon remarks,

> Walton's view of Genesis 1 and the ANE goes too far. ANE cosmogony was concerned with material and functional (and nominal) origins. *Enuma Elish* does not just read "When destinies were undetermined"; rather, it binds separated matter (no gods), name (no name), and function (no destinies) together in its ontological description of the pre-creation cosmic state. Marduk's creation of the cosmos in the *Enuma Elish* reflects this ontological mixture. Marduk made the firmament from half of Tiamat's corpse to cover the deep waters below and hold back the heavenly waters above; he made the earth out of the other half to uphold heaven.[37]

Walton's creation-functionality view also relies on a heavy use of word studies and very particular selections within a semantic range. When the entire case is pieced together, it is clear that if even one of Walton's selections is not correct, the entire system crashes as the door is cracked open to the consideration of a material origin. The material connections made with the words "create" (ברא), "make" (עשׂה), and "form" (יצר) must all be disallowed wherever there is a reference to creation in Genesis (and in the Old Testament), if there is to be any case at all for a functional-only view. It should also be noted that each verb depends on the nature of its direct object, which

37. Scott A. Ashmon, "Review: The Lost World of Genesis One," *Concordia Theological Quarterly* 77:1–2 (January–April 2013): 187.

in Genesis happens to be material.[38] Walton's particular translations also require one to understand that God's rest on the seventh day had nothing to do with the finality of an original material creation. Furthermore, God's description of "good" and "very good" can have no material significance. Every term describing God's action in creation and descriptions of creation must be specific solely to function and bringing about order. This includes the creation of mankind in God's image (Gen. 1:26–28). While many of these word studies are spread throughout the book, placing them together and admitting their interconnectedness requires a stretch that has been beyond the Church for over 1,800 years.

The text itself depicts both material origin and function. As an example (and only one is required to make the functionality position untenable), on day 4 of creation week, Genesis describes not only the function of the lights in the sky to rule day and night and give light on the earth and to be a sign for seasons, days, and years, but God also explicitly says, "Let there be lights in the expanse of the heavens" (Gen. 1:14–19). The function is not possible without its material origin. By the word of His mouth, God brings forth the material origin of the celestial lights and then says what they are for. Psalm 33:6–9 and 148:5 are equally clear that when God spoke, things came into existence immediately and we should worship Him for His supernatural power. Apart from this, Walton would also need to explain why New Testament texts that are clearly alluding to Genesis 1 also depict it in terms of material origins (John 1:1–3; Hebrews 11:1–3). In answering the Jews about matters of divorce, Jesus sets the scene by telling them that "from the beginning of creation God made them male and female therefore a man shall . . ." (Mark 10:6–7). Because mankind was materially created as male and female from the beginning of creation, this is the way they are meant to function in a life-long covenantal marriage.

Archetypal vs. Representative Head

Walton's refusal to consider Adam as a representative head most significantly impacts commonly held evangelical Christian doctrines and eradicates any sense of immediate imputation of sin. Walton himself offers no discussion of imputed righteousness in Christ. Instead he gave N.T. Wright the task of writing on Romans 5 and the Pauline view of Adam. Wright and other advocates of the "New Perspective on Paul" are in direct conflict with the concept of imputed righteousness in justification.

38. Brian Webster, "Review: The Lost World of Genesis One," *Bibliotheca Sacra* 168, no. 3 (September 2011): 358.

A discerning reader of Walton's work should carefully note the differences between "representative head" and "archetype" and the implications. As noted above (proposition 6), Walton has already defined archetype as "all are embodied in the one and participating in the actions of the one." So "archetype" is a typological term basically meaning that Adam is an example of the original "type" of human. This is significantly different than saying that Adam actually was the original man and represents all mankind. It is in the representative head, not just a typical human in a shared paradigm, where we obtain (and have traditionally understood) human corporate solidarity.

In his rejection of the representative head concept, Walton has incorrectly perceived that those who hold it also hold to a view that sin is passed from Adam to all humanity through a genetic process. This is not a necessity in the representative view in which immediate imputation can be maintained without even discussing genetics. At the same time, Christians believe that all human beings have a soul/spirit, but all do not insist that a soul is genetically transmitted. Whether there is a genetic component or not, the biblical transmission of the human sin problem commences at our very conception and is an inherent problem (e.g., Ps. 51:5).

In effect, the archetypal view seems to lead to something more consistent with a "mediate imputation" view. Reymond describes the mediate imputation view as follows: "In other words, men are not born corrupt because God imputed Adam's sin to them; rather, God imputed Adam's sin to them because they are corrupt. In sum, their condition is not based on their legal status, but their legal status on their condition."[39]

Even further to this, Walton believes people obtain their sinful condition by living in a disordered world (see summary on proposition 17). This is because his definition of sin revolves around man claiming his own wisdom to bring order out of non-order but actually producing disorder. Humanity lives in and contributes to a world of disorder. This view of sin causes further problems in the consideration of justification. If someone is considered a sinner because he has contributed to a disorderly world just as man's archetype once did, then a believer is considered righteous because he has brought order in the same way as his second/final archetype (Jesus) did. Just as Walton and N.T. Wright believe Adam is an archetypal rather than a representative head, they believe Jesus has the same archetypal relationship with those "in" Him. This is the basis of their treatment of Romans 5 and 1 Corinthians 15.

39. Robert L. Reymond, *A New Systematic Theology of the Christian Faith*, 2nd revised ed. (Nashville, TN: Thomas Nelson, 2010), p. 438.

Both Walton and Wright downplay the idea that salvation includes being saved from sin and death and coming eternal judgment through the atoning sacrifice and Resurrection of Jesus Christ reconciling us with God. They downplay the idea of justification, regeneration, and imputed righteousness. While they do not openly deny this, it would seem that these traditionally and biblically central aspects of salvation are all but placed aside by the overpowering concentration upon "getting the creational project back on track."[40] The emphasis is not on a positional restoration to righteous standing before God but on a vocational one of bringing creation order to the kingdom. Their concentration takes us away from personal regeneration, justification, and positional sanctification. Most Christians would not deny that Christ's work is greater than an individual's salvation and spiritual regeneration: it also will bring about the reconciliation of the whole creation (Col. 1:20; Eph. 1:10, Rom. 8:21–25). However, the Scripture (and specifically Paul) often describes our spiritual, positional standing as being given new life (personal regeneration) (Phil. 3:9; Gal. 1:3–5, 2:20–21; John 15:6, 15:18–19; Eph. 1:3–6). Walton and Wright would seem to emphasize the purpose of the Cross as obtaining a corporate vocation rather than an individual's salvation. This emphasis would greatly conflict with the message of the gospels, and especially John's, who states that his Gospel was written "that you may believe that Jesus is the Christ, the Son of God, and that by believing you may have life in His name" (John 20:31; ESV).

The archetypal view also contributes to Walton's view that mankind described in Genesis 1:26 refers to a whole group of humans (perhaps thousands), not one man and one woman, that bear the image of God. He does allow for the possibility that Adam and Eve may be a part of the Genesis 1 group of humans, but makes a clear distinction between humanity described in Genesis 1 and the description of Adam and Eve in Genesis 2. This means that the description in Genesis 2:7 of God creating Adam out of dust cannot be a historical event but is only archetypical of human mortality. Likewise, Eve is only the archetype (original type) of human living. Walton believes that prior to any commands being given in Genesis 2, humanity was not held accountable for sin but was no less created in the image of God. This means that prior to the Fall, Walton allows for image bearers of God to live, die, and sin without accountability. The case for such lack of accountability is made from Romans 5. Walton posits that Romans 5:12–14 means that without the law yet given in Genesis 2, the humans described in Genesis 1 were not accountable because "sin is not charged where there is no law."

40. Walton and Wright, *Lost World of Adam*, p. 177.

He also points out that the word "because" makes a huge difference when Paul writes that death came to all because all sinned (Rom. 5:12). The very same text undermines Walton's position, however. If one word is important as an emphasis, then why didn't Walton choose the word "from" (ἀπό) in Romans 5:14? When talking about the absence of the Mosaic Law here, Paul also very specifically refers to the relevant time period. It is from Adam to Moses when death still reigned. Death (the consequence of sin) did not reign before Adam and not before the first command was given to Adam. In this very text Paul is assuming Adam as the first man from which death spread to all humanity because of his sin.

Walton also places great emphasis on what it means for mankind to be in the image of God. Consistent with his position, he cannot allow any ontological meaning for God's image but only functional meaning. Therefore, the image of God is associated with having dominion and bringing order. Casas and Fuller have noted that the prepositions and word constructions point to an ontological view of image bearing in Genesis 1 (see also Casas' chapter in this book).[41] God created mankind "in" (בְּ) His image, and after having done so He says, "Let them have dominion" (וְיִרְדּוּ). Ontology precedes functionality. The function is what they are commanded to do as humans who already bear the image of God.

Resolving vs. Reconciling

Walton's view also has great consequence for our understanding of the eschatological consummation of all things. He does comment on Romans 8:17–26 and Colossians 1:20 as referring to the work of Christ and His impact on the hope for a fully ordered new heavens and earth with no presence of disorder. But one noticeable omission in Walton's excessive word studies is the term "reconciliation" (ἀποκαταλλάσσω) in Colossians 1:20. There is a significant discussion about Colossians 1:15–23 in his book and instead of using the biblical term "reconcile," Walton opts instead to use the word, "resolve." The discerning reader will note that reconciliation (or restoration [ἀποκατάστασις], as in Acts 3:21) has to do with actions to rectify something to a previous condition. There is no sense of this in the word "resolve." One can resolve a situation that has always required it. For example, we do not reconcile a bug in a piece of computer software. Often software companies have to recognize bugs that have always been present and bring a resolution for their users. This is how Walton discusses Colossians 1. While recognizing

41. David Casas and Russell Fuller, "The Difference Maker: What Makes Us Special?" *Answers* 9:4 (2014): 80.

that the word "reconciled" is used in the text, he uses the word "resolve" in all of his explanations of it. One example of such suffices: "Through him all things are reconciled to God. (As Christ resolves the disorder of sin and the disorder brought by sin, he also provides for the eventual resolution of non-order in new creation.)"[42]

Renowned Greek scholar A.T. Robertson made a careful analysis of the word "apokatallasso" (ἀποκαταλλάσσω) translated as reconciliation. He stated:

> This double compound (ἀπο, κατα with ἀλλασσω) occurs only here, verse 22, and Eph. 2:16, and nowhere else so far as known. Paul's usual word for "reconcile" is καταλλασσω (2 Cor. 5:18–20; Rom. 5:10), though διαλλασσω (Matt. 5:24) is more common in Attic [Greek]. The addition of ἀπο here is clearly for the idea of complete reconciliation.[43]

Even if Walton does not claim intentionality in his word choice of "resolve," a consistent application of the meaning of reconciliation exposes the impossible nature of his claims about the physical condition of a pre-Fall world. Regardless, the text only allows for a word that, in its meaning, looks forward to a future restoration of a past condition. If Walton were to accept the words "reconciliation" or "restoration" and apply them to his own view he would also have to accept that the new heavens and earth are going to be non-ordered. In his view, non-ordered also includes death, suffering, disease, bloodshed, sin (without consequence), and natural disasters. It would seem that Walton desires a materially perfect eternity. Walton therefore ignores the very obvious context in Colossians 1:20 to maintain that the non-order will be resolved rather than that the sin-cursed creation will be reconciled. There is a vast difference in the specificity of the text in comparison to Walton's obvious bias that ignores such specificity. Even so, Scripture only describes such an eternity on the basis of reconciliation of the presently cursed creation to return it to the materially perfect state of the original creation that God called "very good."

Evolutionary Views

Walton insists that he is not espousing an evolutionary view, but the evidence from his writings contradicts the claim. He is on the advisory council

42. Walton and Wright, *Lost World of Adam*, p. 163, emphasis added.
43. A.T. Robertson, *Word Pictures in the New Testament*, 6 Vol. (Nashville, TN: Broadman & Holman Publishers, 1960), IV: 480–481.

of the most influential promoter of theistic evolution in America.[44] Walton strongly contends that Genesis is not a scientific text, implying that others with material views of creation suggest that it is. This is also a misconception. Biblical creationists argue that the text is historical narrative that relates to the real world that we study scientifically, but is not a scientific text itself. In other words, the history has scientific ramifications. Even so, Walton has suggested that his view can easily correlate with the scientific consensus view of human origins. In doing so, he has both made allusions and given significant space to the discussion of evolution and genetics. He suggests that the archetypal interpretation of Adam allows for one to believe that the first two humans were not created de novo. This can then be held without contestation from Scripture.[45] He removes the conflict with "modern science" (a term, in context, implying evolutionary belief) by saying that Genesis 1 does not describe material origins.[46] His discussion of "hominids" implies acceptance of evolutionary human development.[47] He affirms "common descent"[48] and suggests that the theory of evolution is not inherently atheistic or deistic.[49] Walton seems to imply and discuss a lot about human evolution for one who confidently asserts that the Genesis text is not talking about science or material origins.

In the final chapters, Walton affirms that Adam and Eve could have been among an initially small human/hominid population, possibly around 150,000 years ago. The theory is built on genetic studies tracing Mitochondrial Eve and Y-chromosomal Adam. Walton states that these studies, tracing differences in DNA back to a common sequence, suggest an original pool of around 5,000 to 10,000 humans around 150,000 years ago.[50] But this argument is fallacious, as Jeanson and Tomkin's chapter in this book demonstrates. And as the other chapters here show, it is impossible to harmonize this evolutionary view with the biblical truth about Adam.

Creation and the Temple

Many orthodox scholars have seen the connecting imagery between the Garden of Eden, the new heaven and earth, and the temple. This can be seen within the text of Scripture alone. If the connection between the temple and

44. http://biologos.org/about-us/advisory-council/.
45. Walton and Wright, *The Lost World of Adam and Eve*, p. 81.
46. Ibid., p. 103.
47. Ibid., p. 177.
48. Ibid., p. 190.
49. Ibid., p. 191.
50. Ibid., p. 184–185.

the Garden of Eden is to be made, it should be on the basis of the purpose of the temple. This purpose was to be a place of religious animal sacrifice which would point to the once-and-for-all sacrifice of the Lamb of God, Jesus Christ, who by His death and Resurrection would reconcile to God not only all those who will repent and believe in Jesus Christ as Savior and Lord, but also will one day reconcile the entire material creation to Himself in the coming consummation (Col. 1:13–20; Acts 3:21).

The Garden of Eden was certainly a part of the creation with very special significance, and yet the whole creation that included the Garden is described in Genesis 1 as very good. It would contradict Genesis 1 to describe the creation outside of the garden as anything substandard. So the significance of the Garden of Eden compared to the rest of creation must be related to mankind as the central focus. The waters are flowing from it as a central source, Adam is put into the Garden and Eve was created there. They were commanded there to subdue, dominate, and multiply and fill the earth in worshipful obedience to their Creator. As Beale has argued, obedience to these commands is part of our worship of God.[51]

Genesis 3 gives us the account of Adam and Eve's rebellion against God. The serpent distorts and questions the Word of God while Adam and Eve reject God's wisdom as they trust the serpent and eat the forbidden fruit. Their rebellious pursuit of wisdom immediately produced shame in their nakedness. Rather than having dominion over the animals, Adam and Eve succumb to the temptation of the serpent. They rejected their kingship under God and neither Adam nor Eve admitted responsibility for their sin.

In response, God revealed His holy character in both judgment and salvation. The consequences of judgment for humanity included pain in childbearing, struggle in relationship between the man and woman, and a physically cursed ground (including thorns and thistles) bringing forth hardships in producing food from the ground. Made from the dust, mankind will now in death return to the dust in which we toil and will be deprived of the original intimacy with God. It is important to note that these consequences came upon the whole creation as a result of sin. Moses does not indicate forbidden access to the Garden from a non-ordered world. Nothing in the text implies that only the special Garden was very good. Because Adam listened to Eve instead of guarding her against the attack of Satan, God actually cursed the very ground outside the Garden to which Adam and Eve were expelled and in which they would toil. It was not the

51. G.K. Beale, *The Temple and the Church's Mission: A Biblical Theology of the Dwelling Place of God* (Downers Grove, IL: InterVarsity Press, 2004), p. 83.

Garden of Eden that was cursed, for God banished Adam and Eve from the Garden and then stationed angels to guard the entrance to it. The sphere of the consequence of sin is clearly shown not only as a spiritual reality for mankind but a physical reality for all of creation.

God's character of grace and mercy is revealed in Genesis 3:14–15. While there will be an ongoing conflict between the seed of the woman and the seed of the serpent, there will also be a defeat of the serpent enemy of God and salvation to repentant, believing sinners by the seed of the woman, which later Scriptures would reveal to be the Messiah of Israel, the Savior of the world.

The Tabernacle and the Garden of Eden

Beale, Walton, and other scholars, note that there are many similarities in wording and function between the tabernacle (and the later temple) and Eden.[52] They suggest there is strong textual evidence that Moses saw the Garden of Eden as a distinct model of God dwelling with mankind, and it seems that this Garden is represented in the tabernacle that God instructed Moses to build. It is profitable, therefore, to at least see the claims that are made directly from the analysis of the biblical text without reference to any ANE literature. This does not, however, justify Walton's restrictive definition of "rest" in Genesis 2:2–3 as only meaning that God took up residence in sacred space. One only needs to turn to Isaiah 66:1 to see that God's residence is greater than an earthly temple.

Obviously, Moses was aware that the tabernacle was the place where God's presence was uniquely among the Israelites. And he was to make the tabernacle as well as its furniture according to what God had shown him (Exod. 25:8–9, 40). It is in the tabernacle that God would meet with Moses in the Holy of Holies to give His instructions to Israel (Exod. 25:22). Genesis 3 seems to imply God's special presence in Eden by the description of God "walking" in the Garden. With the tabernacle at the center of the camp of Israel, God is also walking among them and identifies them as His people (Lev. 26:12, note the need for cleanliness).

Man is given the task to work and keep the Garden. Beale argues that the Hebrew words for "work" (or "cultivate") and "keep" in Genesis 2:15 are translated as "serve" and "guard" in connection to the priestly service in the tabernacle and later temple (Num. 3:7–8; 8:25–26; 18:5–6; 1 Chron.

52. Ibid, p. 66–75; cf. Stephen G. Dempster, *Dominion and Dynasty: A Biblical Theology of the Hebrew Bible* (Downers Grove, IL: InterVarsity Press, 2003), p. 100–104; and James M. Hamilton, *God's Glory in Salvation through Judgment: A Biblical Theology* (Wheaton, IL: Crossway, 2010), p. 74.

23:32; Ezek. 44:14).[53] Therefore, it is argued, Adam's duties were not only kingly duties of dominion given to him in the Garden but were also priestly ones of keeping and guarding the Garden (Gen. 3:8). Adam's role was to guard the temple as was the priests of Israel, but when Adam failed, God placed cherubim to guard the way to the Garden (Gen. 3:24). In the tabernacle there are guarding cherubim sewn on the curtain to the Holy of Holies and statues of cherubim over the mercy seat (Exod. 25:18–22, 36:35–38).

There is a lampstand with seven lamps in the tabernacle that is made like a tree with cups shaped like almond blossoms (Exod. 25:31–36). The Hebrew word for the lamps in the tabernacle is the same word for the description of the lights (sun, moon, and stars) created on the fourth day (Gen. 1:14–20; Lev. 24:2; Exod. 25:6). The tabernacle had an eastern entrance, which was guarded to prevent unworthy people from entering (Exod. 38:13; Num. 3:38). So also the cherubim guarded the eastern entrance to the Garden, preventing a now unclean humanity from entering it (Gen. 2:24). God's wisdom associated with the tree of the knowledge of good and evil in the middle of the garden is emphasized as God gives Adam the one and only command that if Adam disobeyed would result in death (Gen. 2:16–17). In the tabernacle is the law that leads to wisdom and touching the ark in which it resides would also result in death.

While this is not all that Beale suggests in the tabernacle as a representation of Eden, these similarities should at least be noted in the consideration of how Moses *may* have been looking at the tabernacle. But none of these textual similarities negate the clear teaching of Genesis 1–3 that before sin, the whole material creation was very good (clearly meaning without corruption or curse or death or sin). Walton's view that Genesis 1 is not describing a material creation but merely God giving functionality to an already existing creation relies not on the biblical text but on his interpretation of ANE texts and his acceptance of evolutionary presuppositions (though he denies this influence) and interpretations regarding the origin and history of the creation.

The fact that the tabernacle (and later the temple) may be a type of the Garden of Eden strengthens the notion that wherever the tabernacle (and later the temple) is, Israel will live in the abundant blessing of God as they live in obedience and worship of Him. The blessings of the Promised Land are connected to a people dwelling in obedience to their God who dwells among them. Even the pagan prophet, Balaam, recognized the beauty of God dwelling in the midst of His people and pronounces it with Edenic

53. Beale, *The Temple*, p. 67.

vocabulary.[54] The suggestion here is that the Scripture seems to use Eden and Edenic imagery as a general reference for the beautiful condition of God dwelling with His people. Apart from the account of Balaam in Numbers 24, Isaiah similarly speaks of the hope of the return of exiles (51:3). While typology is not meant to be an exact correspondence or precise repeat of history, the biblical authors seem to be referencing the reality of Eden (and perhaps even representing the entire creation) as a typological quality to give hope in the reconciliation of all that is to be fulfilled in Christ. In this way we can say that heaven is Edenic, the Promised Land is Edenic, the return from exile is Edenic, and it is all accomplished in the Cross. Jesus brings the true new Eden.

Clowney suggests that "an Old Testament event or institution may be typical only of the truth which it symbolizes. The only difference is the prospective reference of typology to that truth in its New Testament realization."[55] If the tabernacle and temple are symbolizing a future hope for a new Eden, they typify something with future material significance. Through sacrifice, the temple typifies a restoration of the entire creation as a shadow of the One to come. This significance is fulfilled in Jesus Christ whose spiritual body, the Church, is the new temple (1 Pet. 2:5; Eph. 2:17–22; 1 Cor. 3:16, 6:18) and in Christ we have access to a new Eden (in which we can walk with God in loving relationship) both now in Christ and yet to come in the new heavens and earth of the final consummation. In Revelation 21 we read of this Edenic city where all of the curses upon man's sin (including death) will be forever conquered and reversed (21:2–21). The city needs no temple because the Lord God Almighty and the Lamb are its temple (21:22–27). The reliability of this hope is founded in the credibility of the One who promises. Every Christian can have perfect confidence in Christ who originally created this material world (as the events in Genesis 1 describe) to be the perfect historical reference point by which the Edenic temple types prefigure the restoration of an "Edenic" quality of perfection in the new heavens and earth (Col. 1:20; Eph. 1:7–10). Only if the original reference point depicts the same original pristine physical condition does the typology of the temple give hope for a future physical reality.

54. Dempster (*Dominion and Dynasty*, p. 115) states in reference to Numbers 24:5–9, "The passage draws from Eden and exodus imagery. Israel is compared to rivers and gardens, trees that the Lord has planted; the Israelite tents are like the trees planted by Yahweh. This was the divine intention when Israel was brought out from Egypt. It was to be planted in God's mountain (Exod. 15:16); that is, it was to be returned to Eden."

55. Edmund P. Clowney, *Preaching and Biblical Theology* (Phillipsburg, NJ: P&R Publishing, 1961), p. 111.

But regardless of how strong the typological connection of the tabernacle/temple to the Garden of Eden may be, that connection is dependent for its significance on the historical reliability of the original reference point. It may be that a good biblical theology will see a thread in Scripture that runs from creation to the tabernacle and temple, to Christ and the Cross, and finding final consummation in the new heavens and earth. If there is credibility in the creation/temple correlation, it should be seen in the purpose and reconciliation of creation being shadowed in the temple and fulfilled in the new temple that is Christ and His Bride. If there is a connection in historical context between Israel and other ANE nations, we should not be surprised to see these nations depicting their creation myths in terms of worshiping their deities, and explanations that depict temple imagery.

Even though there is dispute with Walton's position that ANE literature primarily describes creation in terms of pure functionality, Walton's commitment to the functionality view only serves to reveal evidence of magisterial use of his own interpretation of the ANE literature. Whatever temple/creation connections are in the text do not deny, but rather enhance, the strength of Genesis as a literal historical account of the creation of a very good material universe. To reject Genesis 1 as the description of the creation of the material world and embrace Walton's view of a functional ordering of a pre-existing creation is an eisegetical imposition upon Scripture and should be rejected by the Church. Such an action ultimately determines the meaning in the biblical text by relying on a particular interpretation of non-biblical pagan mythical sources that are not even the same genre as the historical narrative of Genesis.

Conclusion

Walton has provided an example of what happens when one gives extra-biblical texts magisterial authority over the text in the process of interpreting Scripture. His basis for interpreting the text of Genesis comes from ancient people who were polytheistic, believed in the ultimate source of the power of magic, and wrote much of their history in the form of mythic narrative. While these ANE views are glaringly dissimilar to Scripture, the similarities between Genesis and ANE creation and flood myths do point to a common shared history among humanity, as Chaffey's chapter later shows, and to a picture of the ancient world that surrounded the people of Israel. The application of Walton's use of the ANE texts has resulted in extensive redefinition of the commonly understood biblical words, a rejection of any material significance in the history of the early chapters of Genesis, and a serious distortion of key Christian doctrines. Walton's view essentially means that the Church has been without access to the real meaning of Genesis 1–11 (and related Scriptures) for over 1,800 years.

The history in Genesis is necessary for biblical coherency. Every major doctrine in the Bible has its historical foundation for coherency in Genesis. The degree to which Walton has altered this foundational understanding has resulted in seriously distorted views of sin, salvation, and consummation. If the Church is to maintain biblical orthodoxy, the ideas in Walton's *Lost World* trilogy must be rejected.

Chapter 7

ADAM AND THE IMAGE OF GOD

By David Casas

On April 15, 1970, the astronauts of Apollo XIII traveled the farthest distance from earth ever by humans.[1] In 2011, Joe Hill created an anamorphic sidewalk artwork measuring 12,500 feet,[2] while 12-year-old Sergey Karjakin qualified as an international chess grandmaster nine years earlier.[3] Humankind's scientific, technological, artistic, and intellectual capacities are complemented by an impressive list of physical achievements; nevertheless, it is the remarkable inner abilities, such as those listed above, that testify to the human being as God's crowning creation.

Secularists and atheists view humans as simply material beings like all other animals. In many ways, this is the predominant view of popular culture. According to this view, the human being may have evolutionary advantages over the animals in his reason, in his communication, and in some physical abilities. But humans are not spiritual or sacred beings, with a purpose and destiny higher than that of the animals. In the end, humanity lives and dies like the beast. Thus, concentration camps, gulags, killing fields, and abortion clinics are all monuments to secularism and atheism. Such degraded views of humanity — particularly in denying that the human being is made in the image of God — inevitably institutionalizes human misery.

1. *Guinness World Records 2013* (Guinness World Records, 2012), p. 20.
2. Ibid., p. 105.
3. Ibid., p. 106.

God's Word stands in contrast to this view, "Yet you have made him a little lower than the heavenly beings and crowned him with glory and honor" (Ps. 8:5).[4] It also testifies of unique human abilities, "And nothing that they propose to do will now be impossible for them" (Gen. 11:6). It is humanity whom God gave dominion over the rest of creation, "You have given him dominion over the works of your hands; you have put all things under his feet" (Ps. 8:6). If we return to the garden, we find that Adam and Eve are the pinnacle of God's handiwork. On the sixth day of creation, as his final work, God created Adam as a physical and spiritual being. His physical aspect was formed from the ground (Gen. 2:7) and his spiritual aspect[5] came from God (Eccles. 12:7). The animals, created on day 5, resemble Adam in that they were also formed from the ground (Gen. 2:19) and have the breath of life (Gen. 1:30; 6:17; 7:15, 22; Eccles. 3:19). But although the animals resemble the first man in certain aspects, Adam surpasses them by God's breathing directly into him and by making him in His own image.

But what exactly is the image of God in Adam? The answers and applications of such a question are essential to the Christian because they dictate human happiness or wretchedness — and often life and death. The image of God consists of the spiritual part of humankind that reflects the character of God and is the only firm basis for advocating human dignity, the sanctity of life, and the gracious redemption of sinners.

The image of God is further explained in Genesis 1:26 by the complementary prepositional phrase, "according to our likeness." *Likeness* means "resemblance" or "similitude."[6] Often used in comparisons (something is like something else), *likeness* usually describes appearances (something resembles something else in appearance). Ezekiel, for example, compares the likeness (appearance) of the faces of heavenly beings to the face of man (Ezek. 1:10). The preposition in the phrase "*according to* his likeness" means *the like of*, *like*, or *as*, so God created Adam in His image *as the like of* His likeness. Simply put, God's image reflects similarities between God and Adam.

But how was Adam similar to God? Certainly, the resemblance excludes the physical body because God is a spirit (John 4:24) and invisible (Col.

---

4 Unless otherwise noted, all Bible references in this chapter are taken from *The Holy Bible, English Standard Version* (Wheaton, IL: Crossway, 2008).

5 Throughout this chapter, "spiritual aspect" is defined as man's soul/spirit.

6 Francis Brown, Samuel Rolles Driver, and Charles Augustus Briggs, *Enhanced Brown-Driver-Briggs Hebrew and English Lexicon*, electronic (Oak Harbor, WA: Logos, 2000), 198a.

1:15; 1 Tim. 1:17, 6:16).[7] Moreover, it excludes creaturely limitations because God is infinite, eternal, and unchangeable in all His attributes (Ps. 90:2; Mal. 3:6; Jer. 23:24). Adam resembled God in having a free, rational, personal spirit, including a conscience with God's law written upon his heart (Rom. 2:14–16); therefore, he could rule over nature in a way similar to how God reigns. The Targums (the ancient Aramaic interpretation of the Hebrew Bible) explain Adam's rational, personal spirit in Genesis 2:7, "and it (the breath of life) became in man as a spirit that speaks." Adam, in contrast with the animals, could reason, converse, and fellowship with like human beings. But most important, because Adam resembled God spiritually, he could fellowship with God.

The single most distinctive aspect of Adam's creation is that he was created in the image of God and his nature bears that image.[8] There is, however, a definitive divide among theologians as to the meaning of *image of God*. Whatever position taken as to the meaning of image, scholars agree that the essential meaning is plain: "it is that man is in some way and in some degree like God."[9] What is determined to be that image in Adam is true of all humanity, and thus is the question explored in this chapter.

Historical Understanding of God's Image in Adam

Jewish Rabbis

In order to have a proper understanding of Adam and the image of God, it is necessary to briefly review the history of interpretation, and we begin with the rabbinic writers. The rabbis understood the deliberate creation of Adam as the beginning of God's spiritual work in a material universe. Rabbi Zlotowitz, elaborating on rabbinic thought on this matter, observed Adam's role as a spiritual endeavor:

---

7 Note that this interpretation does not devalue the human body, because together with the spirit that bears the image of God, man is a living being. And as a physical being, he rules over physical nature. Although I reject the recent views that the body is part of the image of God, the traditional understanding of the image of God does not devalue the body. Indeed, because man's spirit bears God's image, man's body becomes a type of temple housing God's image, just as the Holy Spirit residing with our spirit makes the body of a Christian the temple of the Holy Spirit (1 Cor. 6:19). Accordingly, the Scriptures often speak of our bodies as instruments of righteousness (Rom. 6:12–13), as putting to death the deeds of the body as dominated by sin (Rom. 8:13), and as presenting our bodies living and holy sacrifices (Rom. 12:1). The image of God elevates the body above all earthly creation.

8 Anthony A. Hoekema, *Created in God's Image* (Grand Rapids, MI: Eerdmans Publishing Company, 1986), p. 11.

9 David J A Clines, "The Image of God in Man," *Tyndale Bulletin* 19 (1968): 53.

> Thus, God satisfied the motive of creation: He would be able to confer good upon man. . . . Man could attain it only by elevating the spiritual in himself and by uniting it with the spiritual in creation. . . . By uniting his intellect with that of God through the study of Torah and by perfecting his deeds through the performance of the commandments, man earns the degree of perfection that it is possible for him to attain, and the degree of reward that God seeks to give.[10]

Rabbi Abarbanel (1437–1508) claimed that the divine deliberation in Adam's creation was evidence that God did not associate humanity with the earth, but instead served as "the deepest involvement of Divine Providence and wisdom."[11] The rabbis noted that concerning the beasts, God commanded, "Let the earth bring forth," but in the case of Adam, God said, "Let us make man," in order to clearly distinguish his spirituality. Ramban (1194–1270) called the verb "make" (*na'ăśeh*) a special utterance in which the earth produced "the body [of Adam] from its elements as it did with cattle and beasts . . . and He, blessed be He, to give the spirit from His mouth."[12] Rabbi Kimhi (Radak) (1160–1235) related Adam's name to the word "ground" (ʾăḏāmāh) in order to highlight his constitution, now endowed with a spiritual element. He wrote,

> When God created man from the upper and lower elements He called him Adam, as if to say, although his spirit is from the heavens, he is nevertheless *adam*, for his body was formed from the *adamah*.[13]

Interestingly, Rabbi Naftali Zvi Yehuda Berlin (Netziv) (1816–1893) suggested that the name Adam was derived from *dmh*, meaning "liken," as in Isaiah 14:14, "I will make myself like the Most High." He noted, "Because man is in the likeness of God."[14] In the rabbinic mind, God's intimate involvement in Adam's creation was to emphasize the endowment of his unique spiritual qualities.

The rabbinic spiritual emphasis on humanity's creation is directly linked to the fact that Adam was created in God's image. Rabbi Abarbanel associated

10. Meir Zlotowitz and Nosson Scherman, *Bereishis = Genesis: A New Translation with a Commentary Anthologized from Talmudic, Midrashic and Rabbinic Sources* (New York, NY: Mesorah, 1977), p. 8.
11. Ibid., p. 67.
12. Charles B. Chavel, trans., *Ramban (Nachmanides): Commentary on The Torah: (Bereshis) Genesis* (New York, NY: Shilo Publishing House, 1971), p. 52.
13. Zlotowitz and Scherman, *Bereishis = Genesis*, p. 69.
14. Ibid.

image (*ṣelem*) with the word for shadow (*ṣēl*) in order to illustrate how man is related to his Creator. He wrote that man must follow God's every way, "as a shadow which faithfully follows the movements of its illuminated form."[15] Speaking in more plain terms, Rabbi Elijah ben Shlomo Zalman (the Vilna Gaon) (1720–1797) explained that "image" refers to spiritual image and content, thus "Man was also granted a degree of divine holiness so that he might properly serve God."[16] In another place, he explained that "in his image" refers to "an image commensurate with his lofty soul."[17] In his commentary on the adjoining prepositional phrase "after our likeness" (Gen 1:26), Rabbi Shlomo ben Yitzchak (Rashi) (1040–1105) associated "after our likeness" (*kidᵉmûṯênû*) with the ability "to understand and to gain wisdom."[18] He noted that man was made "with a stamp like a coin," and yet he observed that all men are physically different, unlike a coin.[19] Ramban concluded that both *ṣelem* (image) and *dᵉmûṯ* (likeness) speak to man's similarity to both his physical and spiritual origins, but the reason for the spiritual similarity is due to the "living creature" being immortal.[20] Rabbi Moshe ben Maimon (Rambam) (1135–1204) elaborated further and included human volition:

> Man alone among the living creatures is endowed — like his Creator — with moral freedom and will. He is capable of knowing and loving God and of holding spiritual communion with Him; and man alone can guide his actions in accordance with reason. He is therefore said to have been made in the form and likeness of the Almighty.[21]

There is no question that the rabbis understood the image of God as the spiritual qualities of humanity, men and women alike.[22] Zlotowitz summarized the rabbinic position best by affirming that *created in the image*

15. Ibid., p. 70.
16. Ibid.
17. Rabbi Malbim elaborated on Vilna Gaon's rendering and wrote that the verb "created" is used because it refers to the creation — *ex nihilo* — of man's living soul, something unprecedented in creation, ibid., p. 72.
18. Rabbi Yisrael Isser Zvi Herczeg et al., eds., *Sapirstein Edition Rashi: The Torah with Rashi's Commentary Translated, Annotated and Elucidated*, vol. 1 (Artscroll, 1999), p. 16.
19. Ibid., 1:17.
20. Chavel, *Ramban (Nachmanides)*, p. 53.
21. Zlotowitz and Scherman, *Bereishis = Genesis*, p. 70.
22. Rabbi Samson Hirsch noted that although all living creatures were created in both sexes, this is noted specifically only in the case of human beings to stress that both sexes were created directly by God in equal likeness to Him, ibid., p. 73.

of God describes Adam's spiritual resemblance to God.[23] God's image was spiritually interpreted in the rabbinic mind and thus they understood Adam, and all humanity, to be a unique creation of God.

Early Church Fathers

The church fathers, in line with rabbinic thinking, connected the image of God to Adam's spirituality. Berkhof suggested, "The early church fathers were quite agreed that the image of God in man consisted primarily in man's rational and moral characteristics, and in his capacity for holiness."[24] Irenæus elaborated further and believed that the image and likeness were corrupted at the Fall, and were restored at salvation,[25] which would serve as a foundational premise for all the church fathers that followed.

First generation theologians possessed the advantage of direct teaching by the 12 Apostles, and interpreted God's image as the possession of divine understanding or the demonstration of divinely inspired action — good works.[26] Every one remained in harmony with Pauline anthropology, which Gregg Allison succinctly summarized:

> The first Christians were deeply influenced by their Jewish roots, especially the Hebrew Bible's teaching about God's creation of

23. Zlotowitz writes, "Taken in sum total, then, the two parallel terms 'image' and 'likeness' describe man in his spiritual resemblance to his Creator: his endowment with the intellectual perception that gives him preeminence over the animals, that guides him consciously in the exercise of his free-choice, his moral sense of right and wrong, and finally that gives man his fundamental distinction of approximating some spiritual resemblance to his Creator," ibid., p. 71.
24. Louis Berkhof, *Systematic Theology*, new ed. (Grand Rapids, MI: Eerdmans, 1996), p. 202.
25. R Larry Overstreet, "Man in the Image of God: A Reappraisal," *Criswell Theological Review* 3, no. 1 (Fall 2005): 44.
26. Clement, (ca. 96) in his letter to the Corinthian church, related man's creaturely superiority to his ability to understand, which he attributed to the image of God. In his only mention of Genesis 1:26, he wrote, "Above all, with His holy and undefiled hands He formed man, the most excellent [of His creatures], and truly great through the understanding given him — the express likeness of His own image," Clement of Rome, "The First Epistle of Clement to the Corinthians," in *The Apostolic Fathers with Justin Martyr and Irenaeus*, ed. Alexander Roberts, James Donaldson, and A. Cleveland Coxe, vol. 1, ANF (Buffalo, NY: Christian Literature, 1885), p. 13. Ignatius (ca. 35–110) in his Philippian letter associated the image of God to the demonstration of Christian charity: "Love one another in the Lord, as being the images of God," Ignatius of Antioch, "The Epistle of Ignatius to the Philippians," in *The Apostolic Fathers with Justin Martyr and Irenaeus*, p. 119. A statement by John of Damascus preserved from fragments of the writings of Justin Martyr (ca. 100–165) stated, "As the good of the body is health, so the good of the soul is knowledge, which is indeed a kind of health of soul, by which a likeness to God is attained," Justin Martyr, "Other Fragments from the Lost Writings of Justin Martyr," in *ANF*, ed. Alexander Roberts, James Donaldson, and A. Cleveland Coxe, trans. Alexander Roberts, Vol. 1 (Buffalo, NY: Christian Literature, 1885), p. 302.

> human beings in his image (Gen. 1:26–31). Paul picked up this idea in addressing God's work in sanctification of "the new self, which is being renewed in knowledge in the image of its Creator" (Col. 3:9–10; cf. Eph. 4:22–24). Indeed, the apostle described the entire process of Christian growth as being progressively conformed to the image of Jesus Christ (Rom. 8:29; 2 Cor. 3:18). This insistence on renewal of the divine image can only mean that the image, prior to salvation and this sanctification process, is tragically marred and dreadfully corrupted by sin. Thus, the early Christians affirmed both human dignity, because people are created in the image of God, and human depravity, because the image of God in people is warped and perverted by sin.[27]

Human dignity and human depravity provided the framework for a complex anthropology in the early church. Nevertheless both served foundationally for connecting the image of God to spirituality, specifically the perverting of the image through sin and its restoration through salvation.

Irenæus (ca. 130–202) would be the first voice to contribute significantly to biblical anthropology in his polemic against gnostic heretics, and elaborate on how the image of God was disfigured at the Fall and restored through salvation. In his defense of Christ's humanity, he explained that it was the incarnate Christ that would restore the image that Adam corrupted:

> For I have shown that the Son of God did not then begin to exist, being with the Father from the beginning; but when He became incarnate, and was made man, He commenced afresh the long line of human beings, and furnished us, in a brief, comprehensive manner, with salvation; so that what we had lost in Adam — namely, to be according to the image and likeness of God — that we might recover in Christ Jesus.[28]

In his attempt to explain how the image was corrupted by sin, Irenæus ascribed image to what remains of the original creation, the earthly part, and argued that without a restoration of the likeness through God's Spirit, human beings remain imperfect.[29] He reasoned that by "receiving the Word

27. Gregg R. Allison, *Historical Theology: An Introduction to Christian Doctrine* (Grand Rapids, MI: Zondervan, 2011), p. 322.
28. Irenæus of Lyons, "Against Heresies," in *ANF*, ed. Alexander Roberts, James Donaldson, and A. Cleveland Coxe, Vol. I (Buffalo, NY: Christian Literature, 1885), p. 446.
29. Irenæus explained, "But if the Spirit be wanting to the soul, he who is such is indeed of an animal nature, and being left carnal, shall be an imperfect being, possessing indeed the image [of God] in his formation (in plasmate), but not receiving the similitude through the Spirit; and thus is this being imperfect," ibid., p. 532.

of God as graft,"[30] a person would participate in works of righteousness — those things that pertain to a spiritual man — and "arrive at the pristine nature of man — that which was created after the image and likeness of God."[31] It seems as though Irenæus understood image and likeness to refer to Christ's image that restores a human being to a point that he may relate to an invisible God:

> For in times long past, it was *said* that man was created after the image of God, but it was not [actually] *shown* for the Word was as yet invisible, after whose image man was created. Wherefore also he did easily lose the similitude. When, however, the Word of God became flesh, He confirmed both these: for He both showed forth the image truly, since He became Himself what was His image; and He re-established the similitude after a sure manner, by assimilating man to the invisible Father through means of the visible Word.[32]

The restitution of the likeness, as Irenæus understood it, occurred through a proper knowledge of God. He concluded, "For the knowledge of God renews man. And when he says, 'after the image of the Creator,' he sets forth the recapitulation of the same man, who was at the beginning made after the likeness of God."[33]

Augustine

Many in the Patristic period contributed to the understanding of the image of God, but it was Augustine (354–430) who significantly advanced the understanding of image bearing by insisting that the immortal image of God can only be found in the immortal aspect of a person, which is his soul and in particular, the rational part of his soul.[34] He reaches further than his predecessors, however, and identifies the locus of God's image in the "noblest part of the human mind."[35] The noblest part is the rational

30. Irenæus refers here to James 1:21, the "implanted word."
31. Irenæus of Lyons, "Against Heresies," p. 536.
32. Ibid., p. 544.
33. Ibid., p. 538.
34. Augustine of Hippo, "The City of God," in *St. Augustin's City of God and Christian Doctrine*, ed. Philip Schaff, trans. Marcus Dods, vol. 2, NPNF (Buffalo, NY: Christian Literature, 1887), p. 241. Augustine would also advance the idea of the image in man as being reflective of the Trinity; an idea abandoned by later scholars (Augustine, *On the Trinity*, p. 197).
35. Augustine of Hippo, "On the Trinity," ed. Phillip Schaff, trans. Arthur West Haddan, *A Select Library of the Nicene and Post-Nicene Fathers of the Christian Church* (Buffalo, NY: Christian Literature, 1887), p. 189.

mind,[36] which he pinpoints as the place where renewing, due to salvation, begins:

> If, then, we are renewed in the spirit of our mind, and he is the new man who is renewed to the knowledge of God after the image of Him that created him; no one can doubt, that man was made after the image of Him that created him, not according to the body, nor indiscriminately according to any part of the mind, but according to the rational mind, wherein the knowledge of God can exist.[37]

Furthermore, Augustine points to the rational mind as the definition of the image of God. He stated in *The Confessions* that the rational mind according to the image of God is what set Adam as ruler over creation.[38] He reasoned that the only immortal aspect of Adam that can relate to God's immortality is his rational mind: "We must find in the soul of man, i.e., the rational or intellectual soul, that image of the Creator which is immortally implanted in its immortality."[39] Augustine did not douse his reasoning with complexities, but very clearly associated the image of God to Adam's unique rational spirituality.

Augustine also believed the image of God was distorted by sin, but not "wholly blotted out" by it.[40] It seems that his beginning point was the natural good in humanity because of the Creator's goodness.[41] That goodness was preserved in the rational mind in the form of God's image after the Fall, and thus provided a point where Adam, and all humanity after him, could partake of God's salvation:

---

36. Augustine's use of "mind" and "rational mind" requires clarification. When Augustine refers to mind, what he means is the human soul. Yet, the human soul (the mind) encompasses much more than the seat of human emotions and volition. The mind includes the center of thinking and logic processes, which Augustine identifies as the rational mind: the place where the knowledge of God can exist.
37. Ibid., p. 159.
38. Augustine explained: "We behold the face of the earth furnished with terrestrial creatures, and man, created after Thy image and likeness, in that very image and likeness of Thee (that is, the power of reason and understanding) on account of which he was set over all irrational creatures," Augustine of Hippo, "The Confessions of St. Augustin," in *The Confessions and Letters of St. Augustin with a Sketch of His Life and Work*, ed. Philip Schaff, vol. 1, NPNF (Buffalo, NY: Christian Literature, 1886), p. 206.
39. Augustine of Hippo, "On the Trinity," p. 185–186.
40. Augustine of Hippo, "A Treatise on the Spirit and the Letter," in *Saint Augustin: Anti-Pelagian Writings*, ed. Phillip Schaff, trans. Peter Holmes, vol. 5, NPNF (Buffalo, NY: Christian Literature, 1887), p. 103–104.
41. Augustine of Hippo, "On Marriage and Concupiscence," in *Saint Augustin: Anti-Pelagian Writings*, ed. Phillip Schaff, trans. Peter Holmes, vol. 5, NPNF (Buffalo, NY: Christian Literature, 1887), p. 298.

> But we have come now to that argument in which we have undertaken to consider the noblest part of the human mind, by which it knows or can know God, in order that we may find in it the image of God. For although the human mind is not of the same nature with God, yet the image of that nature than which none is better, is to be sought and found in us, in that than which our nature also has nothing better. But the mind must first be considered as it is in itself, before it becomes partaker of God; and His image must be found in it. For, as we have said, although worn out and defaced by losing the participation of God, yet the image of God still remains. For it is His image in this very point, that it is capable of Him, and can be partaker of Him; which so great good is only made possible by its being His image. Well, then, the mind remembers, understands, loves itself; if we discern this, we discern a trinity, not yet indeed God, but now at last an image of God.[42]

Augustine therefore believed that the original image would be restored fully through salvation, "For it is the Spirit of grace that does it, in order to restore in us the image of God, in which we were naturally created."[43] Augustine shifted the focus back to the human soul as the aspect of the human being that can reason and relate to his Creator. Although the lost human being was deprived of God's glory, through the image of God — the noblest part of the human person — he could regain the lost relationship. His conclusions, except for connecting the image to the Trinity within us, would remain unchallenged until the modern age.

The Reformers

The Reform theologians did not do much to either advance or refute the traditional Christian position of God's image in Adam's spiritual aspect. Martin Luther (1483–1546) maintained that although Adam's nature before the Fall "remained perfect and uncorrupted by sin," the image of God was far different from any physical attribute; Adam was created for a life that was far more excellent than the earthly.[44] Nevertheless, he narrowly rejected Augustinian speculations (those pertaining to the image as reflecting the Trinity) and was very reserved in advancing any explanation of God's image on account that sin had blinded any human after Adam to its definition. He

42. Augustine of Hippo, "On the Trinity," p. 189.
43. Augustine of Hippo, "A Treatise on the Spirit and the Letter," p. 103.
44. Martin Luther, *Commentary on Genesis*, ed. John Nicholas Lenker, vol. 1 (Minneapolis, MN: The Luther Press, 1910), p. 108.

urged caution, because any natural qualities interpreted as the image, even those possessed by the soul, are corrupted by sin:

> I fear however that since this "image of God" has been lost by sin, we can never fully attain to the knowledge of what it was. Memory, mind and will we do most certainly possess, but wholly corrupted, most miserably weakened; nay, that I may speak with greater plainness, utterly leprous and unclean. If these natural endowments therefore constitute the image of God it will inevitably follow that Satan also was created in the image of God; for he possesses all these natural qualities, and to an extent and strength far beyond our own.[45]

Although he believed the image was "marred and obscured" by the Fall, Luther argued that Adam possessed it as a spiritual quality, "Adam possessed it in its moral substance or nature; that he not only knew God and believed him to be good, but that he lived also a life truly divine."[46] Like Calvin after him, Luther believed that God's image would be restored by the gospel, and once again would restore a spiritual, not physical, quality to humanity:

> Now the very intent of the gospel is to restore this image of God. Man's intellect and will have indeed remained, but wholly corrupted. The divine object of the gospel is that we might be restored to that original and indeed better and higher image; an image, in which we are born again unto eternal life, or rather unto the hope of eternal life by faith, in order that we might live in God and with God and might be "one" with him. . . . That is, he shall be a spiritual man, in which state he shall return to the image of God; for he shall be like unto God in life, righteousness, holiness, wisdom, etc.[47]

Luther kept himself from plainly explaining the substance and locus of the image of God, but nevertheless saw the image of God as relating to Adam's spiritual aspect as the most faithful to the text.

John Calvin (1509–1564) insisted that the image of God was in Adam's soul, "For though the divine glory is displayed in man's outward appearance, it cannot be doubted that the proper seat of the image is in the

45. Ibid., 1:115. Although Luther uses the word "lost," he clarifies what he means by lost when he says "wholly corrupted." For Luther, whatever remains of the image of God in man after the Fall, and however it is identified in man, is so distant from what it was before the Fall that it is unrecognizable in sinful man.

46. Ibid., 1:116.

47. Ibid., 1:118–120.

soul."[48] Moreover, even the "glory" that is manifested in Adam's physical body is in the form of spiritual qualities: "Only let it be understood that the image of God which is beheld or made conspicuous by these external marks, is spiritual."[49] Calvin specifically addressed distinguishing the terms *image* and *likeness* and rightly concluded that the terms do not stand for two different things, but that humanity is an image that is like God:

> Hence there is an obvious absurdity in those who indulge in philosophical speculation as to these names, placing the Zelem, that is the image, in the substance of the soul, and the Demuth, that is the likeness, in its qualities, and so forth. God having determined to create man in his own image, to remove the obscurity which was in this term, adds, by way of explanation, "in his likeness," as if he had said, that he would make man, in whom he would, as it were, image himself by means of the marks of resemblance impressed upon him.[50]

Consistent with Luther, and seemingly relying on Augustine, Calvin concluded that the image was corrupted by sin. He defined the original image as Adam's ability to be "united with God" in the "true and highest perfection of dignity," which would be impossible for Adam if he "were not like to him."[51] The image of God was not completely lost at the Fall, but it was severely damaged to the point of utter deformity. "Wherefore, although we grant that the image of God was not utterly effaced and destroyed in him, it was, however, so corrupted, that any thing which remains is fearful deformity."[52] But how did Calvin define such deformity? He argued that man

---

48. John Calvin, *Institutes of the Christian Religion*, trans. Henry Beveridge (West Roxbury, MA: B&R Samizdat, 2015), 1.15.3, Kindle.
49. Ibid. Calvin elaborated on this point elsewhere: "Thus the chief seat of the divine image was in his [Adam's] mind and heart; yet there was no part of him in which some scintillations of it did not shine out. In the mind perfect intelligence flourished and reigned, uprightness attended as its companion, and all the senses were prepared and molded for due obedience to reason; and in the body there was a suitable correspondence with this internal order," John Calvin, *Genesis*, Alister McGrath and J.I. Packer, eds. (Wheaton, IL: Crossway, 2001), p. 26.
50. Ibid. Rejecting Augustine's speculations "to fabricate a trinity in man," Calvin elaborated that a definition of the image of God "ought to rest on a firmer basis than such subtleties. As for myself, before I define the image of God, I would deny that it differs from his likeness. For when Moses afterwards repeats the same things (verse 27) he passes over the likeness and contents himself with only mentioning the image. We also know that it was customary for the Hebrews to repeat the same thing in different words," *Genesis*, p. 26.
51. Ibid., 1.15.6.
52. Ibid., 1.15.4.

lost the spiritual qualities of knowledge, righteousness, and holiness according to Paul's teachings in Colossians 3:19 and Ephesians 4:24, "after Paul, I make the image of God to consist in righteousness and true holiness."[53] Those spiritual qualities mentioned must be renewed when we come to salvation in Christ; "We now see how Christ is the most perfect image of God, into which we are so renewed as to bear the image of God in knowledge, purity, righteousness, and true holiness."[54] Therefore, Calvin concludes that the more a human being resembles God spiritually, the more he is the image of God:

> Therefore, as the image of God constitutes the entire excellence of human nature, as it shone in Adam before his fall, but was afterwards vitiated and almost destroyed, nothing remaining but a ruin, confused, mutilated, and tainted with impurity, so it is now partly seen in the elect, in so far as they are regenerated by the Spirit. Its full lustre, however, will be displayed in heaven. But in order to know the particular properties in which it consists, it will be proper to treat of the faculties of the soul.[55]

There is no ambiguity to the Reformer's position; instead it resulted in a reaffirmation that God's image and likeness is connected to Adam's unique spirituality.

More Recent Times

One of the most important questions in the history of interpretation of the image of God since the Reformation is to what extent God's image has been corrupted by sin.[56] Although the spiritual interpretation of the image dominated Old Testament scholarship for centuries, the lack of proper treatment and convincing answers to the above question in the post-Reformation period left the proverbial door open to a question that for some represented a crucial point of departure in understanding image-bearing. The theories and conditions that emerged in the late 19th century would set the stage for new approaches to Genesis 1:26–27, and new perspectives as to the connection between Adam and the image of God.

By the 1880s, the image of God, and Old Testament interpretation as a whole, had faced a paradigmatic shift as a result of three major developments.

53. Ibid., 1.15.9.
54. Ibid., 1.15.4.
55. Ibid.
56. A. Jónsson Gunnlaugur, *The Image of God: Genesis 1:26–28 in a Century of Old Testament Research*, trans. Svendsen, Coniectanea Biblica 26 (Stockholm, Sweden: Almqvist & Wiksell, 1988), p. 12.

First, Darwin's theory of evolution claimed no fundamental differences between humanity and higher mammals,[57] which forced modern biblical scholarship to revive efforts in identifying those things in Adam that would differentiate him from the animal world. Secondly, extra-biblical ancient Near-Eastern (ANE) documents discovered in Mesopotamia, particularly *Enuma Elish*,[58] caused many scholars to suppose the Bible's dependence on those ANE sources and therefore cast doubts on the origin of the biblical accounts of creation.[59] Finally, the influential contributions of modern critical scholars, such as Julius Wellhausen, to Israel's religious history and Old Testament scholarship as a whole, through the distinction of Old Testament sources, replaced salvation history with a history of religions approach.[60] During the 20th century, many new ideas regarding a historical Adam and the image of God would be introduced, complicating the landscape and making consensus on the topic almost impossible.

Hermann Gunkel (1862–1932) made the first major departure from the historic consensus of God's image as the spiritual aspect of Adam.[61] Gunkel, in some manner, accepted the Wellhausen documentary hypothesis,[62] but rejected the idea that Genesis 1 was a free composition by the author, a position held by Wellhausen. Instead, the account was a product of careful arrangement of oral history that pre-dates Moses.[63] In fact, he determined that the simpler narrative of the first chapters of Genesis were myth derived

---

57. Charles Darwin, *The Descent of Man and Selection in Relation to Sex*, rev. ed (Detroit, MI: Gale Research, 1974), p. 35.
58. Dating from at least the early first millennium B.C., the *Enuma Elish* tablets were written on seven tablets in Akkadian cuneiform. The saga is an ancient cosmology and theogony story about the god Marduk that parallels the Genesis creation account in several places. John Anthony Dunne, "Enuma Elish," ed. John D. Barry et al., *The Lexham Bible Dictionary* (Bellingham, WA: Lexham Press, 2014).
59. K.A. Matthews, *Genesis 1–11:26*, Vol. 1A, The New American Commentary (Nashville, TN: B&H Publishing Group, 1996), p. 91–92.
60. Bruce K. Waltke, *An Old Testament Theology: An Exegetical, Canonical, and Thematic Approach*, 1st ed. (Grand Rapids, MI: Zondervan, 2007), p. 65.
61. According to Claus Westermann, "Gunkel's study marked a decisive turning point in the exegesis of Gen. 1 beyond which there can be no return," Claus Westermann, *Genesis 1–11: A Commentary* (Minneapolis, MN: Augsburg Publishing, 1984), p. 30.
62. Relying on Wellhausen, Gunkel ascribed the image of God texts to the P source. Hermann Gunkel, *Creation and Chaos in the Primeval Era and the Eschaton: A Religio-Historical Study of Genesis 1 and Revelation 12*, trans. Heinrich Zimmern (Grand Rapids, MI: Eerdmans, 2006), p. 25. Gunnlaugur elaborated the point and vehemently argued, "Gunkel accepts the Wellhausenian documentary hypothesis without reservation, and assigns the *image of God* passages to the P source. In fact Gunkel's Genesis commentary presupposes the distinction of sources to such a high degree that it is entirely built up according to the sources." Gunnlaugur, *The Image of God*, p. 52.
63. Ibid.

from the simpler pagan roots of oral tradition. He insists that the simpler the narrative, the more pure, "The more independent a story is, the more sure we may be that it is preserved in its original form."[64] This forms the basis of Gunkel's religio-historical approach, not to mention his rejection of the historicity of Adam and Eve.

On the image of God, Gunkel blames the historical interpretation on Christian dogmatism and argues instead for a physical meaning alone. First of all, he based his conclusions on parallels drawn between biblical and Babylonian accounts, arguing for Babylonian origins to Genesis. Nevertheless, he believed that the adopted myths were transformed by Israel, thus rejecting direct dependence.[65] It cannot be ignored, however, that Gunkel's reliance on extra-biblical material was of prime importance, "The theologian will do well to treat the Marduk myth with respect. One does no honour to his parents by thinking poorly of his ancestors."[66] Secondly, Gunkel concluded that *selem* (image) was a Babylonian loan word, and using Genesis 5:1–3 and 9:6, the word had the natural meaning of deity that resembled a human body.[67] He argued that the physical is the simplest reading and would have fit the context of earlier, more primitive meanings:

> It is the common fate of older narratives preserved in younger form that certain features, which once had a clear meaning in their earlier context, have been so transmitted in their newer setting as to have lost their meaningful context. Such ancient features, fragments of an earlier whole, are thus left without context in their newer setting and so appear hardly intelligible in the thought-world of the narrator. Such features betray to the investigator the existence of an earlier narrative, and they even suggest something of its particular traits.[68]

Therefore, Gunkel regarded God's image as an external attribute and relied on Genesis 5:3 as the key text for a physical explanation.[69] Gunkel's influence would not be immediate; however, his reliance on ANE texts and his argument for the physical resemblance would form the foundation for modern understanding of Adam and image-bearing.

64. Hermann Gunkel, *The Legends of Genesis, the Biblical Saga and History*, trans. William Herbert Carruth (New York, NY: Schocken, 1964), p. 45.
65. Gunkel, *Creation and Chaos*, p. 25.
66. Ibid., p. 46.
67. Ibid., p. 29.
68. Ibid., p. 26.
69. This will be the position of Gerhard von Rad (1901–1971), Paul Humbert (1885–1972), Theodore Vriezen (1899–1981), and in some aspects Ludwig Köhler's "upright posture of man" position, Gunnlaugur, *The Image of God*, p. 92–125.

In his *Church Dogmatics*, Karl Barth (1886–1968) refused to accept an ontological interpretation of the image of God, and would argue for a relational representation instead. Although his finger may have been on the text, he rejected the historicity of Genesis.[70] Relying on the philosophical ideas of his day,[71] Barth argued that the only thing that we know apart from God creating Adam in His image is that He created them male and female.[72] Therefore, there exists an I-Thou relationship between God and Adam, as there is between the male and female:

> It is not palpable that we have to do with a clear and simple correspondence, an *analogia relationis*, between this mark of the divine being, namely that it includes an I and a Thou, and the being of man, male and female. The relationship between the summoning I in God's being and the summoned divine Thou is reflected both in the relationship of God to the man whom He has created, and also in the relationship between the I and the Thou, between male and female, in human existence itself. There can be no question of anything more than an analogy.[73]

The analogy therefore is what makes Adam human, according to Barth. The point of contact, or the existence of the point of confrontation, as he describes it, is what defines a human being, indeed human existence itself. "Thus the *teritum comparationis*, the analogy between God and man, is simply the existence of the I and the Thou in confrontation. . . . To remove it is tantamount to removing the divine from God as well as the human from man."[74] Therefore, Barth argues that the I-Thou confrontation is what defines the image of God, and not some ontological aspect:

> It is not a quality of man. Hence there is no point in asking in which of man's peculiar attributes and attitudes it consists. It does not consist in anything that man is or does. It consists as man

70. Barth rejected the historicity of Adam and Eve and of the Fall. Karl Barth, *Church Dogmatics. III.1*, ed. Geoffrey William Bromiley and Thomas F Torrance, Vol. III.1 (New York, NY: T. & T. Clark International, 2004), p. 200.
71. Perhaps Martin Buber's *I and Thou*, 1958, influenced Barth's I-Thou philosophy. Cairns claims that Barth's conclusions on the image of God and many other subjects would have "taken a different shape had not Martin Buber written *I and Thou*," David Cairns, *The Image of God in Man* (London, England: SCM Press, 1953), p. 187.
72. Barth, *Church Dogmatics. III.1*, III.1:186.
73. Ibid., III.1:196.
74. Ibid., III.1:185.

> himself consists as the creature of God. He would not be man if he were not the image of God. He is the image of God in the fact that he is man.[75]

Barth's contribution to the discussion places image-bearing outside the realm of any particular human quality, and thus eventually became the consensus view among modern liberal and neo-orthodox theologians and Old Testament scholars who would prefer to distance themselves from ontological explanations for the image of God.

Together with the archeological discovery of *Tell Fekheriyeh*,[76] and the presumed more concrete meaning of *selem*,[77] the functional, as opposed to the ontological, interpretation of the image of God quickly became the modern consensus. Gunnlaugur summarized this modern approach:

> It is remarkable, that the functional interpretation, which had until the 1960s only a minute support among OT scholars, has become the absolutely dominant interpretation in this intervening time. . . . The functional interpretation is a logical result of the dominant understanding that it is conceptually inappropriate to view man in the OT as divided into physical and spiritual components and then apply this dichotomy to one's interpretation of the image of God in man. Once this dichotomy is no longer acceptable the field of choices for the explanation is significantly narrowed and a holistic view becomes the most attractive. An emphasis on the importance of the contextual principle of course favours the functional interpretation, since the immediate context does, in fact, deal with man's mandate to rule over creation.[78]

75. Ibid., III.1:184.
76. The *Tell Fakhariyeh* inscription was a bilingual inscription found in 1979 on a large statute of King Hadduyithi of Gozan, an ancient city in modern-day Syria, written in tenth or ninth century (B.C.) Akkadian and Aramaic, which contained terms equivalent to the Hebrew for "image" and "likeness." It was not until 1982 that the inscription was published. Many scholars have relied on this discovery for added meanings to the two terms in Gen. 1:26. Gentry provides a good summary of the inscription's impact and how the cognates of the terms are applied to the study of the image of God. Peter John Gentry and Stephen J Wellum, *Kingdom Through Covenant: A Biblical-Theological Understanding of the Covenants* (Wheaton, IL: Crossway, 2012), p. 193. Gunnlaugur provides a good summary of the discovery's impact on OT studies, Gunnlaugur, *The Image of God*, p. 206–207.
77. Matthews, *Genesis 1–11:26: TNAC*, 1A:166–167.
78. Gunnlaugur, *The Image of God*, p. 221–222.

Gerhard von Rad (1901–1971), in particular, unequivocally relied on Mesopotamian meanings to understand Genesis 1:26, and interpreted the image of God as His physical viceroy on earth.[79] Claus Westermann seems to reject functionality for a more Barthian-like explanation;[80] nevertheless, he affirmed that God's image had no connection to Adam's nature and more to do with an action. "There can be no question that the text is describing an action, and not the nature of human beings."[81] Following von Rad, Anthony Hoekema maintains that man was created in the image of God in order to represent Him, much like an ambassador.[82] Bruce Waltke boldly states that *selem* "always" refers to a physical body.[83] Thus, also relying on ANE literature, he likewise settles on functionality as the best explanation for the image of God. "The definition of 'image of God' including notions of being physical and ruling as God's vice-regents coheres with God's intention for humanity to master/rule all creatures in the earth's three cosmic spheres of heaven, land, and sea (Gen. 1:26, 28)."[84] In his provocative work, John Walton also heavily relies on ANE literature to interpret Genesis 1:26, and while he will not include Adam and Eve in the image of God account,[85] he will advocate for functionality that is laced with Barthian influence as well:

> The image of God as an Old Testament concept can be understood in four categories. It pertains to the role and function that

79. Gerhard von Rad, *Genesis: A Commentary*, trans. John H. Marks (Philadelphia, PA: Westminster Press, 1972), p. 392.
80. Relying on Barth, Westermann couched the image of God as the process of human existence: "The creation of human beings in the image of God is not saying that something has been added to the created person, but is explaining what the person is." Indeed, Westermann argued that God's image is human existence: "The relationship to God is not something which is added to human existence; humans are created in such a way that their very existence is intended to be their relationship to God." Westermann, *Genesis 1–11*, p. 156–158.
81. Ibid., p. 155.
82. Hoekema, *Created in God's Image*, 67. Hoekema popularized the eclectic approach to the image of God, which in essence combines the concepts of man's nature, which he called structure, and man's functionality. This approach also has a Christological component that sees Jesus as the ultimate image-bearer and through His saving work restores the image of God so that man can do good works. Claus Westermann insisted that H. Holzinger, J. Hempel, and H. Gross popularized the functional view and that G. Söhngen and E. Schlink popularized the Christological view (Westermann, *Genesis: A Commentary,* [1974], p. 155).
83. Waltke, *An Old Testament Theology*, p. 215.
84. Ibid., p. 219.
85. John H Walton, *The Lost World of Adam and Eve: Genesis 2–3 and the Human Origins Debate* (Downers Grove, IL: IVP Academic, 2015), p. 63, Kindle.

> God has given humanity (found, for example, in "subdue" and "rule," Gen 1: 28), to the identity that he has bequeathed on us (i.e., it is, by definition, who we are as human beings), and to the way that we serve as his substitute by representing his presence in the world. When Assyrian kings made images of themselves to be placed in conquered cities or at important borders, they were communicating that they were, in effect, continually present in that place. Finally, it is indicative of the relationship that God intends to have with us.[86]

The Darwinian influence upon 20th-century scholars coupled with greater reliance on ANE discoveries eventually marginalized the historical interpretation of Adam and the image of God for a more physical or functional approach.

Ancient Near Eastern Texts, the Bible and the Image of God

The over-reliance on ancient Near Eastern sources and methods on the part of modern Old Testament scholars produces a flawed point of departure for understanding Adam and the image of God. John Currid's provocative work[87] thoroughly outlines major faults with ANE over-dependence, as well as problems that arise with ANE parallels to the Old Testament. Currid correctly outlines the problem on two fronts: the unhelpful symptom of relegating biblical narrative to myth in modern scholarship and the accepted theories of source criticism. He surmises,

> The reality is that modern scholarship commonly views biblical history as invention and propaganda. In other words, it was written by post-exilic authors who had limited access to true historical resources. And, obviously, a majority believe that the antediluvian accounts of Genesis 1– 11 are mere myth and legend, just like similar stories throughout the ancient Near East.[88]

---

86. Ibid., p. 40.
87. Although I quote Currid extensively here, both he and John Oswalt have been voices against the modern majority tendency to emphasize the similarities and parallels between ancient Near Eastern literature and the Bible, as well as to oppose the departure from the position that holds to an original, singular, and unique worldview on the part of the Hebrew writers. John D. Currid, *Ancient Egypt and the Old Testament* (Grand Rapids, MI.: Baker Books, 1997); John D. Currid, *Against the Gods: The Polemical Theology of the Old Testament* (Wheaton, IL: Crossway, 2013); John N. Oswalt *The Bible among the Myths: Unique Revelation or Just Ancient Literature?* (Grand Rapids, MI: Zondervan, 2009).
88. Currid, *Against the Gods*, p. 22–23.

The latter problem (source criticism) is alluded to obscurely, and to outline its deficiencies is beyond the scope of this chapter.[89] More to the point, Currid recognizes those aspects of Semitic writings that are similar due to the cultural vicinity; nevertheless, he "emphatically and graphically" demonstrates the "distinctions between the worldview of the Hebrews and the beliefs and practices of the rest of the ancient Near East."[90] He argues that while emphasizing the parallels, scholars ignore the "foundational differences."[91] And when it comes to the Genesis text, Currid strongly stresses the differences in

89. I believe that a reliance on source criticism (a.k.a. Documentary Hypothesis) has negatively affected the interpretation of the image of God. Richard Hess observed that some scholars have insisted that source criticism is the fundamental starting point for the study of the Bible and that those who do not accept this model are not competent to work as Bible scholars, Richard S. Hess, *Israelite Religions: An Archaeological and Biblical Survey* (Grand Rapids, MI: Baker Academic, 2007), p. 833–834, Kindle. I am aware of the criticisms that will arise for my efforts to deemphasize the documentary theories that have so framed Old Testament scholarship for the past century. However, I am also aware that I am not alone as an evangelical scholar, whereas others have opposed the theory, see e.g. Edward Young, *An Introduction to the Old Testament* (Grand Rapids, MI: Eerdmans, 1989), Gleason Archer, *A Survey of Old Testament Introduction* (Chicago, IL: Moody Press, 2007), and R.K. Harrison, *Introduction to the Old Testament* (Grand Rapids, MI: Eerdmans, 1969). Hess provides a very helpful excursus on source criticism and its development, and therefore I will not outline it in this chapter, Hess, *Israelite Religions*, p. 877–980, Kindle. Nevertheless, Hess makes an important point regarding multiple sources, which I wish to point out: "Thus the presence of multiple documents existing over many generations and being written as a single text at a date far removed from the earliest composition is neither proven nor necessary," Richard Hess, *Israelite Religions*, p. 856–859, Kindle. I also believe a fundamental flaw exists on the part of those who rely on source criticism, particularly assumptions made alleging post-exilic writers sanitized the mythical elements of Gen. 1. As Gerald Bray succinctly surmised, "It is hard to believe that a monotheistic writer of the exilic period would have left the plural for God unaltered and unexplained; hard too, to believe that his main purpose was to demythologize pagan beliefs," Gerald L Bray, "The Significance of God's Image in Man," *Tyndale Bulletin* 42, no. 2 (November 1991): 202. Eugene Merrill provided the best assessment of this methodological approach in his review of Gunkel, stating that his theory is fundamentally flawed due to the fallacies of documentary theory: "The emerging consensus in modern times as to the fallacy of such document distinctions vitiates the exegetical and theological conclusions of Gunkel to the extent that he allowed the hypothesis to provide the framework of his discussion," Eugene H Merrill, "Review of Hermann Gunkel's Genesis," *Bibliotheca Sacra* 155, no. 618 (April 1998): 241–42. This would also be true of any of his successors that hold to his conclusions. I do not deny that I too approach the study of Gen. 1 with certain presuppositions. One, in particular, is that Old Testament and New Testament witnesses ascribe authorship of Genesis to Moses — one single author. Of supreme importance is Jesus Christ. Evangelicals would be hard-pressed to assume that He would ascribe authorship to Moses knowing that other authors had compiled the book. Although the arguments advanced by Hess, Archer, Bray, Merrill, and myself would not satisfy source critics, the unity of Genesis cannot be denied and for the most part the arguments of source critics remain speculative.

90. Currid, *Against the Gods*, p. 25.

91. Ibid., p. 23.

the biblical and ANE cosmogonies as a premise to avoid pushing any similarity too far. Modern scholars have skewed the biblical cosmogony, as a whole, and of Genesis 1:26–27 in particular, by unreservedly ascribing to these theories. The objections to appealing to cultic legends are outlined as follows.

First, similarities abound among Near Eastern cosmogonies, including the Genesis account, and because of the multiple accounts, dependence on one source or another becomes questionable. Quoting Wilfred Lambert, Currid states that parallels to Genesis have been found among the Canaanites, Egyptians, Hurrians, Hittites, and early Greeks in addition to Mesopotamia, and therefore, "The question of dependence, if any, has to be approached with an open mind."[92] In fact, if parallels to the biblical creation account do exist, they are more likely Egyptian, rather than Mesopotamian.[93] But as Chaffey's later chapter in this volume shows, similar accounts of creation, the Fall, the Flood and the Tower of Babel appear in cultures all over the world, pointing not to the dependence of Genesis on those myths but to the reality of the literal history recorded in Genesis, which the pagan legends preserve in corrupted form.

Second, of greater magnitude and import, is that the God of the Bible is alone the Creator of the universe. As Currid observes, of all the ancient Near Eastern societies, Israel alone is monotheistic.[94] In fact, unlike ANE sources, the biblical account has no interest in theogony (the birth of the gods). Ancient sources ascribed powers of nature to their deities and, as a result, the gods were restricted to natural elements. Additionally, other creator-gods created the pantheon of gods. This is seen in all cosmogonies, except the Hebrew one. As Currid argues, the God of the Genesis account is "radically monotheistic," and contrary to all ancient Near Eastern sources, "the God of the Hebrews is presented as transcendent, that is, set apart from the cosmos."[95] In other words, while the pantheon struggles with one another, magic is presented as the ultimate power in the universe, and creation is a consequence of a power struggle among the gods, Genesis presents God as "all-powerful, incomparable, and sovereign."[96] He is God alone and fashions the universe "*ex nihilo* by means of verbal fiat."[97] The contrasts are so sharp, that a simple reading of the creation account would have left no doubt in the Hebrew reader's mind of its uniqueness.

92. Ibid., p. 36.
93. See Currid, *Ancient Egypt and the Old Testament*, p. 53–73.
94. Currid, *Against the Gods*, p. 40.
95. Ibid.
96. Ibid., p. 41.
97. Ibid., p. 43.

Third, the mythical nature of ancient Near Eastern cosmogonies stands in sharp contrast to the historical nature of the Genesis account. The writing style of ANE sources is that of legendary stories, or what Currid calls "mythic narrative." They are, as he observes, "without determinable basis in fact or history."[98] Indeed, the majority of the primordial tales are principally in the realm of the gods, and not on the physical earth. Genesis, on the other hand, is historical narrative, and as Sailhamer observes, the aim of the biblical writer "is to record what actually happened in human history."[99] Currid agrees that Genesis 1–2 "bears all the markings of Hebrew historical narrative."[100] There is an elevated style that contains all the aspects of the narrative type, whether it is chronology, well-developed characters, and literal historical sequence. For the Hebrew reader, Genesis 1–11 was as sequential and historical as the patriarchal narratives in the rest of Genesis.

Finally, and bearing most on the topic at hand, the Bible alone declares that God created Adam according to His image, barring obscure interpretations of certain Mesopotamian texts. According to Genesis 1:26–27, God confers upon Adam His image and as a result bestows upon him dignity, glory, dominion, and blessing. By contrast, Mesopotamian gods created humanity "simply to do the labor assigned by the deities."[101] Currid points out that in Egyptian cosmogony there is no separate, let alone detailed, account of human creation, because the origin of humanity "was not as important as it was in the Hebrew account."[102] Once again, the details conveyed in Genesis 1:26–27 would have left the reader in awe of its originality.

In sum, although similarities may be observed among all ancient Near Eastern cosmogonies, the biblical account stands uniquely apart. It is the distinctions rather than the similarities that provide the stark reminder. Currid provides the key point: "The differences are monumental and are so striking that they cannot be explained by a simple Hebrew cleansing of myth."[103]

---

98. Ibid.
99. John Sailhamer, *The Pentateuch as Narrative: A Biblical-Theological Commentary* (Grand Rapids, MI.: Zondervan, 1992), p. 16. Relying on Frei, he added that it was not enough to say that biblical narratives are only "history-like" and to relegate them to the level of "realistic narrative." Instead, "one can say with reasonable certainty that the authors of the biblical narratives give every indication of intending their works to be taken as history rather than fiction."
100. Currid, *Against the Gods*, p. 43.
101. Ibid., p. 42.
102. Ibid.
103. Ibid., p. 44.

Genesis 1 is unique and stands in stark contrast to the darkness of mythical legends and polytheism. We have very good reasons for trusting what it tells us about the origin and nature of man made in the image of God.

The Image of God in the Biblical Texts

Genesis references the image of God three times (Genesis 1:26–27; 9:6). In Genesis 1:26–27, God makes Adam and Eve in His image — a phrase repeated in verse 27 for emphasis — and commands them to reproduce and rule over nature. The word "image" often describes physical objects that are "cut out," such as the physical images of false gods (2 Kings 11:18) or the golden images (replicas) of the mice and tumors of God's plagues upon the Philistines (1 Sam 6:5).[104] Adam and Eve were created *in* His image. The preposition "in" depicts the state or condition in which God created: God created Adam and Eve *in* (the condition or state of) His image. In Genesis 9:6, the image of God is mentioned as the reason for capital punishment because humanity is made in the image of God. God's image sets Adam and Eve apart from the rest of creation as a reflection of God, equips them to rule over nature, and gives value to human life.

Let us take a closer look at the biblical texts that specifically address Adam and Eve and the image of God. Genesis 1:26–27 declares,

> Then God said, "Let us make man in our image, after our likeness. And let them have dominion over the fish of the sea and over the birds of the heavens and over the livestock and over all the earth and over every creeping thing that creeps on the earth." So God created man in his own image, in the image of God he created him; male and female he created them.

Genesis 5:1–3 closely resembles 1:26–27, but now includes Adam's offspring:

> This is the book of the generations of Adam. When God created man, he made him in the likeness of God. Male and female he created them, and he blessed them and named them Man when they were created. When Adam had lived 130 years, he fathered a son in his own likeness, after his image, and named him Seth.

Scholars that depart from the historical interpretation of the image of God in Adam see the terms *selem* and *d^e^mût* having two very different definitions, and thus functioning differently in the phrase "in our image, after

104. F. Brown, S.R. Driver, and C.A. Briggs, *Hebrew and English Lexicon of the Old Testament* (Oxford, England: Clarendon, 1906), p. 853b 1.

our likeness."[105] These modern approaches argue that Adam was a physical representation of God on the earth, and thus the image of God is a physical one. Peter Gentry admits that there is a large "possible range of meaning" of the words "image" and "likeness" because of "careful and exhaustive" lexical studies done on these words.[106] He, therefore, relies on word usage, particularly the ancient Near Eastern use of "image" and "likeness" as inscribed on a large statute of King Hadduyith of Gozan, better known as the *Tell Fakhariyeh* Inscription.[107] Presupposing the possibility that the Hebrew word carries the same meaning as the Aramaic words in the inscription, he concludes that *dᵉmût* "may refer to a physical entity" or "to express resemblance or relative similarity."[108] The term *selem* frequently refers to "an object in the real world," such as in the *Tell Fakhariyah* Inscription that makes the statute, as it were, the physical authority of the image it bears.[109] Differentiating the two terms and arguing for the interchangeability of the prepositions "in" and "according to,"[110] Gentry concludes that man is not made *in the image of God*, but made *as the image of God*; therefore, "Man *is* the divine image . . . both physical and yet goes far beyond being merely physical . . . but results in an emphasis such that the character of humans in ruling the world is what represents God."[111] In summary, if image and likeness denote different things, then a case can be made for Adam as a physical representation of God.

By contrast, other scholars hold to the position that grammatically *selem* and *dᵉmût* are only different ways of saying the same thing. Berkhof, in particular, points out that the prepositions reverse in Genesis 5.3; thus, he disregards the argument that the phrases are different.[112] In the

105. Peter John Gentry, "Kingdom Through Covenant: Humanity as the Divine Image," *Southern Baptist Journal of Theology* 12, no. 1 (Spr 2008): p. 16–42; Eugene H. Merrill, *Everlasting Dominion: A Theology of the Old Testament* (Nashville, TN: Broadman & Holman, 2006); Waltke, *An Old Testament Theology*; Tikva Kensky-Frymer et al., eds., *Christianity in Jewish Terms* (Oxford, England: Westview Press, 2000), p. 322, states Assyrian texts describe the king himself as *tsalam ili*, "image of the god" the representative of God on earth. In the same way, Genesis states that humans are to act for God on this earth, administering and performing other acts of dominion.
106. Gentry, "Kingdom Through Covenant," p. 27.
107. For a complete description of the linguistic analysis see ibid., p. 27ff.
108. Gentry, "Kingdom Through Covenant," p. 27.
109. Ibid., p. 28–29, Although ascribing to the meaning of the words through their usage, Gentry departs here from the functional model, as noted earlier, and states, "In this sense the divine image entails a covenant relationship between God and humans on the one hand, and between humans and the world on the other . . . exactly the character of relationships specified by covenants after the fall."
110. Ibid., p. 30–32.
111. Ibid., p. 32.
112. Berkhof, *Systematic Theology*, p. 204.

words of John Murray, ". . . we should take them [image and likeness] as explanatory or definitive rather than supplementary."[113] Müller found no exegetical grounds for interpreting the words differently and ascribed the duplication only to "render the meaning more definite or intense."[114] Hoekema observes that in Genesis 1:26 both *selem* and *d^e^mût* are used; in 1:27 only *selem* is used; in 5:1 only *d^e^mût* is used; and in 5:3 both are used, but in different order. Therefore, if they were intended to describe different things or different aspects of Adam, they would not have been used "almost interchangeably."[115] Hodge defines it in this manner: "Image and likeness means an image which is like."[116] Garrett claims that the synonymous view is held by a great majority of present-day Hebrew and Old Testament scholars, and phrases are simply an "instance of synonymous Hebrew parallelism."[117]

The latter exegetical interpretation of *selem* and *d^e^mût* seems the more reasonable for understanding Adam and the image of God. First, Adam was not a "statute" of God serving as a cultic figure; he is a reflection of the divine, and that reflection is best seen in his nature. Claudia Welz correctly assesses,

> For if the human being were indeed *die lebendige Statue Gottes*, as Bernd Janowski and Erich Zenger seem to suggest, this would imply that the human being, as God's living cult statue, embodies God. Then the human being would be God's epiphany. Yet, *d^e^mût* does not indicate an identity between God and man, but rather similarity, likeness, semblance, imitation. This word never denotes a cult image.[118]

At its root, *d^e^mût* cannot be used to denote a cult or representative statute of God, but the question remains regarding the meaning of *selem*. Gentry concedes that the lexical use of the word in Psalm 39:6–7 "can also be abstract and nonconcrete."[119] Garrett surmises that to relate the image of God to an

113. John Murray, *Collected Writings of John Murray*, vol. 2: Systematic Theology (Carlisle, PA: Banner of Truth Trust, 1976), p. 34.
114. Edward Robie, "Müller's Christian Doctrine of Sin," *Bibliotheca Sacra and Theological Review* 6, no. 22 (1849): 263–264.
115. Hoekema, *Created in God's Image*, p. 13.
116. Charles Hodge, *Systematic Theology* (New York, NY: Scribner, 1906), p. 97.
117. James Leo Garrett, *Systematic Theology: Biblical, Historical, and Evangelical*, 2nd ed, vol. 1 (North Richland Hills, TX: BIBAL Press, 2000), p. 393.
118. Claudia Welz, "Imago Dei," *Studia Theologica - Nordic Journal of Theology* 65, no. 1 (2011): 76.
119. Gentry, "Kingdom through Covenant," p. 28.

erect bodily form or statute would be difficult to apply to New Testament texts that pertain to the image.[120] Chafer, quoting Laidlaw, prefers a different argument: "Thus, by 'the divine image,' the Bible does not mean those elements in man from which an idea of God may be framed, but conversely those features in the Divine Being of which man is a copy."[121] The meaning of the words, under these definitions, simply cannot provide for a non-ontological (i.e., functional or relational only) interpretation of image.

Second, the issue of God's incorporeality arises. As previously discussed, rabbinic literature considered the image of God to be in the human soul, because to ascribe it to any physical aspect would necessitate God having a physical form. Similarly, Ross argues that the image of God in Adam cannot "signify a physical representation of corporeality, for God is spirit. The term must therefore figuratively describe human life as a reflection of God's spiritual nature."[122] Interestingly, Waltke holds that *selem* "always refers to a physical image, having a formed body," yet concurs with David Clines that one "should not infer with Gerhard von Rad that God has a corporeal form."[123] However, is holding to a physical image and ascribing to God's incorporeality possible? As discussed, the Rabbis and the vast majority of Christian scholars certainly did not think so.

Third, *selem* and *d^emût* in Genesis 1:26–28 are better understood as referring to the spirituality of Adam in light of Genesis 5:1–3. Grudem maintains,

> Seth was not identical to Adam, but he was like him in many ways, as a son is like his father. The text simply means that Seth was like Adam. It does not specify any specific number of ways that Seth was like Adam, and it would be overly restrictive for us to assert that one or another characteristic determined the way in which Seth was in Adam's image and likeness. . . . Similarly, every way in which man is like God is part of his being in the image and likeness of God.[124]

Thus, *selem* and *d^emût* cannot include physical form, since God is spirit; therefore, Mays adds, "The meaning is not, however, that Seth looked like Adam, but that that which in Adam made him an image/likeness of God

120. Garrett, *Systematic Theology*, 1:395.
121. Lewis Sperry Chafer, *Systematic Theology* (Dallas, TX: Dallas Seminary Press, 1947), p. 170.
122. Allen P. Ross, *Creation and Blessing: A Guide to the Study and Exposition of the Book of Genesis* (Grand Rapids, MI: Baker Book House, 1988), p. 112.
123. Waltke, *An Old Testament Theology*, p. 215–216.
124. Wayne A. Grudem, *Systematic Theology: An Introduction to Biblical Doctrine* (Grand Rapids: Zondervan, 1994), p. 444.

is passed on in the generational process."[125] Hodge offers this assessment: "God is a spirit, the human soul is a spirit. The essential attributes of a spirit are reason, conscience and will . . . in making man after his own image, therefore, God endowed him with those attributes which belong to his own nature as a spirit."[126] God's spiritual nature is the pattern, and the *selem* and *d^emût* of God in Adam is therefore spiritual in nature.

The command to exercise dominion and subdue the earth is a result of the image of God in humankind, as is the creation of Adam and Eve as male and female respectively and the mandate to reproduce. The waw-consecutive discourse indicators in the narrative indicate "logical sequel of actions, events or states mentioned immediately before."[127] The narrative structure of verse 27, "So God created man . . ." is sequential to verse 26, "Then God said, Let us make man . . ." and therefore followed sequentially by verse 28, "And God blessed them. And God said to them. . . ." Müeller holds that Adam and Eve were able to rule and subdue the earth as a result of being made in the image of God, but that is not what constitutes the image in man.[128] The dominion aspect is closely related to the divine image, but it is a result of Adam and Eve being made in His image. Because the image cannot be confined to dominion or relation, and because Adam and Eve were made in the image of God before they were given instructions to rule and to procreate, the image reflects a work that God did when He formed Adam and Eve with a spiritual aspect that reflected their Creator.

The Nature of the Image of God in Adam

The image of God in Adam and Eve has an ontological meaning, even when God's immanence is juxtaposed against man's finiteness. Human nature is not holistically irreducible; rather, it is dualistic in nature and capable of fellowship with God.

First of all, human nature is dualistic, principally composed of a spiritual aspect. In order to avoid over-generalizations on studies that span two millennia addressing the biblical view of anthropology, the explanation that

125. James Luther Mays, *The Self in the Psalms and the Image of God*, ed. R. Kendall Soulen and Linda Woodhead, God and Human Dignity (Grand Rapids, MI: William B. Eerdmans, 2006), p. 35–36.
126. Hodge, *Systematic Theology*, p. 97.
127. Wilhelm Gesenius, *Gesenius' Hebrew Grammar*, 2nd English ed., rev. in accordance with the 28th German ed. (1909) (Oxford, England: The Clarendon Press, 1910), p. 326.
128. Robie, "Müller's Christian Doctrine of Sin," 264, Mueller stated that "That this dominion is closely related to the Divine image, is clear, but the relation is one, not of identity, but of cause and effect."

best describes the scriptural view as a whole is dualistic holism.[129] Cooper explains,

> *Holism* means that humans are created and redeemed by God as integral personal-spiritual-physical wholes — single beings consisting of different parts, aspects, dimensions, and abilities that are not naturally independent or separable. *Dualism* means that our core personalities — whether we label them *souls, spirits, persons, selves,* or *egos* — are distinct and, by God's supernatural providence, can exist apart from our physical bodies after death.[130]

Cooper bases his findings on three observations. First, although the biblical worldview distinguishes God from creation, it views creation as having both a natural and spiritual dimension and God as an incorporeal Being intimately involved in the creation and operation of a physical universe, not apart from it. Adam was likewise dust and spirit; made of earth and also forming part of the spiritual realm.[131] Second, Genesis 2:7 recounts Adam's formation from material and immaterial substances to constitute an irreducible living being. The Old Testament will not often make "systematic division between the physical and spiritual parts" during this earthly life that would imply that body and soul are "distinct substances;" however, as Cooper correctly insists, "refined versions of substance dualism are not necessarily ruled out by the Old Testament."[132] Third, the Old Testament affirms an eternal existence of the soul that continues to survive in a disembodied state after physical death. The biblical text has in view a bodily resurrection, and as Cooper points out, to maintain a holistic earthly existence with a "dualistic view of death" is neither contradictory nor "synthesizing Hebrew and Platonic views of the soul."[133] In sum, God created Adam as a holistic, "single person-bodily being" for earthly existence and at death sustains him

129. So for Cooper, Christian intellectuals have done a disservice to the Church by challenging long-held positions on human nature. He asks, has the Church been wrong? To challenge historically orthodox conclusions is to invite doctrinal postmodernism. It is not that men are infallible, but certainly if the best Christian minds in Church history got theological anthropology incorrect, and if other "core doctrines are merely possible readings of Scripture," then we ought to acknowledge, as Cooper calls it, "doctrinal pluralism." The bottom line is that dualistic holism has been a doctrinal consensus affirmed by orthodox Christianity over two millennia and modern challenges hold philosophy and science as an authority above Scripture. John W. Cooper, "The Current Body-Soul Debate: A Case for Dualistic Holism," *The Southern Baptist Journal of Theology* 13, no. 2 (2009): 45–46.
130. Ibid., p. 34.
131. Ibid., p. 36–37.
132. Ibid., p. 37.
133. Ibid., p. 38.

as a whole person without a body, "but still possessing consciousness, bodily shape, and location."[134] Therefore Adam's constitution is irreducible by natural observation, but in reality he is a dual being, composed of body and soul, of which the latter relates to God, who is a Spirit.

Second, God created the person of Adam (like Eve) for the purpose of relating to an invisible God. Gerald Bray correctly concludes that God's image in Adam consists of the fact that Adam is a person,[135] yet personhood is so complex that the image only forms one component part of many biblical concepts, including name, heart, soul, and spirit, to name a few.[136] An individual is the same person throughout his existence, whether an embryo, a fully developed adult, or a resurrected body in the eschaton. Cooper explains,

> Each human remains the very same being throughout his or her existence even though we constantly change from the moment we are conceived, and even though our awareness of self-identity may change or be lost. Individual identity is metaphysical and logical, not just a matter of fact or of self-consciousness. It is absolutely impossible for me to be another person or for there to be two of me. . . . The soul, spirit, or core person that exists during this life endures after death until bodily resurrection and beyond. One and the same being continues from the beginning of existence forever, whether or not there is continuity between the earthly body and resurrection body.[137]

134. Ibid., p. 40.

135. According to Bruce Ware, there are two competing broad categories for personhood: the functionalist model and the essentialist model. The functionalist determines personhood when the individual manifests "certain minimal expressions of the relevant functions." Those not manifesting those functions are judged to be "non-persons." Contrariwise, the essentialist determines that an individual is a human person because he/she "possesses a natural capacity" for the full range of human expression. I concur with Ware that the essentialist model is the correct one. Take an embryo for example: it must be considered ontologically a human being because it has a precise organic wholeness. In other words, the embryo is "organically complete," and nothing can be added to it, even though a fully developed adult body is not present. So as Ware so succinctly summarizes, "an individual's personhood attaches not to variable functional capabilities but to the kind of essence one is, whose nature is rational, volitional, spiritual, etc., and hence, personal." Therefore, personhood is not defined by the qualities that must find expression, rather it is the nature whose natural kind is personal that the individual possesses. Bruce A. Ware, "Human Personhood: An Analysis and Definition," *The Southern Baptist Journal of Theology* 13, no. 2 (2009): 18–31.

136. Gerald L. Bray, "The Significance of God's Image in Man," *Tyndale Bulletin* 42, no. 2 (November 1991): 222–223.

137. Cooper, "The Current Body-Soul Debate," p. 41.

Therefore, those who would include the body in the image, as Bray surmises, have attempted to do so "largely on the ground that the body is essential to the person."[138] Those who claim that the image is only realized in community relationship fail to see that an incomplete image was not what God had in mind when he assessed man's need for companionship. Bray maintains, "When God decided that it was not good for the man to be alone, He did not indicate that one reason for this was that His image in man was imperfect on that account."[139]

One more point needs to be made regarding gender and the image of God. If God's image consists of a human physical form then it would have to be a bisexual form since both male and female are made in the image of God.[140] Or at a minimum, God's image would need to have female characteristics.[141] This point makes it inconceivably difficult to interpret *selem* and *d^emût* as referring to physical form. Yet, relationship is a consequence of it and thus part of the human experience. Therefore, as principally a person, Adam and Eve are made in the image of God with those ontological qualities that resemble and relate to God.

Third, it is generally agreed, as noted in the exegesis above, that dominion is a consequence of Adam being made in the image of God; as a person who resembles God, and thus exercises rule as a result of that personal likeness. As Bray suggests, ". . . the concept of dominion, however important in itself, is merely an attribute of the *tselem* and does not constitute part of its essence."[142] To elevate dominion and the exercise of rule to constitute the essence of God's image is actually a reductive interpretation, as Bayer points out.[143] Furthermore, the language of Genesis 1:26–28 clearly establishes dominion as arising out of the fact that the human person is made in God's image. Bayer concurs, "It is accurate to say that the *dominium terrae* immediately rises from being in the image of God."[144] Therefore, the text clearly shows that dominion is not a constituent part of the human person, and thus not a constituent part of the image of God, although certainly a consequence of such.

138. Bray, "The Significance of God's Image in Man," p. 223.
139. Ibid.
140. Ibid., p. 59.
141. Some may agree with Gösta Ahlström that man was created in the "same forms" as the pantheon of gods, which included female goddesses. This would provide the "female principle" in God's image, Gösta W Ahlström, *Aspects of Syncretism in Israelite Religion* (Lund: C.W.K. Gleerup, 1963), p. 50.
142. Ibid., p. 197; See also Horst, "Face to Face," p. 262.
143. Oswald Bayer, "Being in the Image of God," *Lutheran Quarterly* 27, no. 1 (2013): 83.
144. Ibid.

Finally, to fellowship with God, the image of God in Adam and Eve must reflect God's holy character, especially in knowledge, righteousness, and holiness of the truth. In Colossians 3:10, Paul speaks of God's image, "And have put on the new man, which is renewed in knowledge after the image of him who created him" (KJV). In regeneration, God is renewing His image within us in the knowledge of God. Such knowledge of God is eternal life, the spiritual life of the soul. In the parallel passage, Ephesians 4:24, Paul writes, "and to put on the new self, created after the likeness of God in true righteousness and holiness." This time God renews His image in righteousness and holiness of the truth. Paul reveals that God's image includes more than a free, rational, personal spirit, but that God's image possesses an original knowledge (of God), righteousness, and holiness in the truth. The righteousness and holiness of the truth reflects God's moral excellence. Again, humanity's resemblance to God is spiritual. Adam's sin destroyed this original knowledge, righteousness, and holiness of the truth, but regeneration begins the renewal process, which continues until death.

But even at death, when body and soul are separated, God's image in humanity continues. John, for instance, speaks of the souls under the altar (Rev. 6:9–11), the disembodied souls in the intermediate state awaiting the resurrection. Although without a physical brain, they remember their martyrdom, have a sense of justice, express emotions, and even desire vengeance. Although without a physical mouth, they cry out and communicate. Although without a physical body, they were given (spiritual) robes, as they wait for justice. As disembodied spirits, God's image suffers no loss or harm. In fact, at death, in the disembodied state, our spirits will be made perfect in resembling God (1 Cor. 13:12). At the resurrection, when all that God has purposed is consummated, our resemblance to Him will be complete.

The Implications of the Image of God

Because of God's image, Adam and his descendants resemble and reflect God. This has profound implications for Christian belief and practice.

First, the image of God establishes human dignity. By denying God's image, atheism diminishes human dignity by reducing humanity to a random product of matter. Pantheism, at the other extreme, also denies the image of God and diminishes human dignity by exalting all nature as a manifestation or action of God. The Scriptures, by contrast, testify to humanity's dignity. "Yet you have made him a little lower than the heavenly beings and crowned him with glory and honor" (Ps. 8:5). Being created in the image and after the likeness of God sets Adam and all his descendants above all nature.

According to Christ, one human soul is more valuable than the rest of nature (Matt. 6:26; Mark 8:36). In fact, God indicated His value of the soul by sending His Son to redeem it. This does not, to be sure, devalue the rest of nature, because God created it as well. Humanity in God's image should rule nature benevolently as good stewards of God's creation. Nevertheless, as Kohler wrote, "That which distinguishes man from the animal as well as from the rest of creation . . . is his self-conscious personality, his ego, through which he feels himself akin with God."[145] No human condition mitigates this truth, whether it is physical limitation, deformity, or cognitive capacity. Sin alone has a debilitating effect (Rom. 1:21–25, 3:9–18, 5:12), but it can only damage the image of God, not remove it. Not even naked lunatics living in tombs or paralytics on the side of the road were beyond the compassion of Christ (Matt. 4:24, 17:15; Mark 5:1–13).

Second, the image of God establishes the sanctity of life. Atheistic cultures reject the sanctity of life by devaluing the life of the born and unborn as state policy. The Word of God, however, protects the sanctity of life in its laws. In Genesis 9:5–6, God decrees that if anyone commits murder, the murderer must forfeit his life, because people are made in the image of God. The crime, therefore, is a direct assault against God. The personal tone and the three-fold repetition of the verb in Genesis 9:5 emphasizes the gravity of this crime against God, "And surely your lifeblood I will require, from the hand of every living being I will certainly require it. From the hand of man, from the hand of each man I will require the life of man." God *will* personally seek out the murderer and hold him accountable. God's retribution is sure. John Calvin observed that because the human being is God's image-bearer, God deems himself "violated in their person" and one cannot injure another human being without wounding God Himself.[146] Rabbinic literature also speaks of "impairing" the divine likeness through homicide.[147] God created human life sacred — to destroy this life invites divine judgment.

Third, the image of God establishes the need for God's redemption. Without God's image in the human person, the plan of redemption would not exist. This does not imply that possessing the image of God entitles

145. Kohler, Kaufmann (2003–07–12). *Jewish Theology: Systematically and Historically Considered* (Kindle Locations 3281–3282). BookMasters. Kindle Edition.

146. *The New Interpreter's Bible: General Articles & Introduction, Commentary, & Reflections for Each Book of the Bible, Including the Apocryphal/Deuterocanonical Books*, vol. 1 (Nashville, TN: Abingdon Press, 1994), p. 294.

147. *Bereishis = Genesis: a New Translation with a Commentary Anthologized from Talmudic, Midrashic and Rabbinic Sources*, Vol. 1, 1st ed., ArtScroll Tanach Series (New York, NY: Mesorah Publications, 1977), p. 291.

redemption to sinners, but redemption requires that sinners be made in His image. God's purpose for sending His Son in the likeness of Adam was to renew God's image in humankind through the Gospel (Eph. 4:24; Col. 3:10). Indeed, Christians have been foreknown and predestined to be conformed to the image of His Son (Rom. 8:29). As image-bearers, we are uniquely set apart from creation, including angels (1 Peter 1:12), to be restored to fellowship with God the Father and His Son (1 John 1:3). The Gospel, once believed, renews the image that was marred by both Adam's sin and our own sin so that the believer may "bear the image of the heavenly" (1 Cor. 15:49). Because God created us in His image, being crowned with glory and honor, and because of His infinite grace toward undeserving sinners, God sent His Son to redeem us.

Conclusion

Adam and his descendants bear the image of their Creator and as a result relate to God and one another, create magnificent things, and accomplish amazing feats. As image-bearers we all have value no matter our abilities or status in this life. As image-bearers each one of our lives is sacred. As image-bearers marred by the Fall, we each need a Savior. And as image-bearers, we are called by the redeeming love of our Creator to be renewed and conformed into the image of Him who is the perfect, beautiful, image of God.

Chapter 8

Did Humans Really Evolve from Ape-like Creatures?

by Dr. David Menton

Of all of the claims of biological evolution perhaps none is more repugnant to conservative Christians than the bestial origin of man. Even when much of the Church had come to accommodate evolution in the late 1800s, there continued to be widespread resistance to the idea of the evolution of man from animals. For this reason, when Darwin wrote his *Origin of Species* in 1859 he chose not to include his views on human evolution. In a letter to the evolutionist Alfred Russel Wallace, Darwin explained that while he considered the evolution of man to be "the highest and most interesting problem for the naturalist" he would not discuss it in his book because the whole subject is "so surrounded by prejudices."[1] Darwin waited 12 years for the leaven of his *Origin of Species* to do its work before he published *The Descent of Man* (1871) in which he finally made public his own prejudices about human origins. Darwin confidently claimed that all the evidence pointed to man sharing common ancestry with the apes.

Darwin's Lack of Fossil Evidence for Human Evolution

Darwin's "evidence" in *The Descent of Man* for the common ancestry of man and apes consisted primarily of comparative anatomical, embryological, and behavioral arguments, rather than fossil evidence. Fossilized human skulls were found in Belgium in 1829 and Gibralter in 1848 and later associated with the first recognized Neanderthal man fossils (discussed in the next chapter) found in Germany in 1856. But up until the

1. Charles Darwin, https://www.darwinproject.ac.uk/letter/DCP-LETT-2192.xml.

time of Darwin's death in 1882, no fossil evidence had been found for the supposed non-human or pre-human ancestors of man. Indeed, Darwin was puzzled by the lack of transitional fossils in general that might show how any two kinds of creatures could have evolved one into another. Darwin lamented: "Why, if species have descended from other species by fine gradations, do we not everywhere see innumerable transitional forms?"[2] Darwin assumed that this lack of fossil evidence was a result of the incompleteness of the fossil record in his day and predicted that as more fossils were discovered, the "missing links" supporting his theory would eventually be found.

The Nature of the Fossil Record

The fossil record favors the preservation of marine invertebrates. It is estimated that today over 250 million fossils have been found and cataloged, comprising about 250,000 species. Approximately 95% of all these fossils are marine invertebrates and of the remaining 5%, most (95%) are algae and plants. Out of the less than 1% of all remaining fossils, 95% are other invertebrates (including insects). The vertebrates (animals with bones) comprise less than 0.25% of all fossils, and the vast majority of these are fish! Finally, primates (humans, apes, monkeys, and lemurs) comprise less than 0.001% of all vertebrate fossils.[3] How then does one account for a fossil record where the vast majority of all invertebrates and vertebrates are aquatic? Clearly, something about the fossilization process strongly favored the preservation of aquatic creatures, particularly bottom dwelling immobile organisms with hard shells.

The Process of Fossilization

The fossilization of plants and animals requires special conditions that generally include rapid burial in sediment providing protection from predation and decay. These conditions are rarely met in a terrestrial environment. The vast majority of fossils were formed in layers of water-borne sediment. Where the sediment was sufficiently cementitious, the layers, with their imbedded fossils, become sedimentary rock. Stratified layers of fossil-bearing sedimentary rock cover about 75% of the earth's land area with many layers extending from continent to continent.

The global Flood of Noah's day would have provided optimal conditions for depositing cementitious sediment and promoting fossilization on a

2. Charles Darwin, *The Origin of Species by Means of Natural Selection* (London, England: Penguin Books, 1985, reprint of 1859 1st ed.), p. 205.
3. Andrew Snelling, "Where Are All the Human Fossils?" *Creation Ex Nihilo* 14:1 (1991): 28–33.

global scale. While this explanation has long satisfied many Bible-believing Christians, evolutionists are loath to consider fossils being a result of a global flood. Nevertheless, even the vast majority of fossilized land-dwelling creatures were clearly in a water environment at the time of their burial in sediment. Evolutionists insist that these creatures were either the victims of local floods or that they wandered too close to an inland sea or lake and fell in. But animals caught in local floods or that fall into seas and lakes today rarely become fossils.

How Complete Is the Fossil Record of Land-dwelling Creatures?

Creationists and evolutionists have very different expectations regarding the completeness of the fossil record. Evolutionists believe that a vast number of species evolved in the past 600 million years to produce the relatively fewer living species we have today. Using evolutionary assumptions, it has been estimated that less than 2% of all species that have existed on earth are preserved in the fossil record.[4] Yet despite the assumed paucity of the fossil record, evolutionists expect to find fossils showing transitional stages in the progressive evolution of one kind of animal into a different kind.

Most creationists believe that essentially all of the fossils we see today were formed during and shortly after the global Flood that happened about 4,000 years ago. They believe that animals and plants have changed only to a limited degree within their created kinds since the Flood, though many have become extinct. Therefore, creationists would expect that fossils can be found that are recognizably similar to a majority of today's living families, genera, and species. They would further expect that there would be no unambiguous fossil evidence of one kind of animal (such as a family or genus) progressively transforming into a different kind.

One way to estimate the relative completeness of the fossil record is to determine what percentages of the various kinds of animals living today have been found as fossils. If the fossil record were very incomplete one would expect that relatively few representatives of today's land-dwelling animals would be found as fossils. But this is not the case. Of the 43 orders of terrestrial vertebrates living today, one or more fossilized representatives have been found for 42 of the orders (97%). Of the 329 families of terrestrial vertebrates living today, fossilized representatives have been found for 261 families (79%).[5]

---

4. Kurt Wise, "Completeness of the Fossil Record," https://answersingenesis.org/fossils/fossil-record/completeness-of-the-fossil-record/, November 23, 2009.
5. Michael Denton, *Evolution: A Theory in Crisis* (London, England: Burnett Books, 1985), p. 190.

In a study focusing only on mammals, Bjorn Kurten reported that 88% of the living species of European mammals have been found in the fossil record of Europe, and 99% have been found in the worldwide fossil record. [6]We may conclude that the fossil record appears to be remarkably rich and clearly sufficient to reveal if any creature has slowly evolved by intermediate stages into a distinctly different kind of creature.

Human and Primate Fossils Are Rare

Given the nature of the fossil record it's not surprising that human fossils are exceedingly rare. So rare indeed that most anthropologists teaching in our colleges and universities have never had opportunity to work with original primate fossils. Most are confined to examining published data, and casts and reproductions of the actual fossils. Still, counting single teeth and bones, human fossils have been found representing more than 6,000 individuals.[7] Apes and monkeys are also rare in the fossil record though they are more numerous than human fossils. It should be noted that evolutionists generally refer to apes in the fossil record as "ape-like" creatures rather than apes. This avoids the embarrassment of saying apes evolved into apes.

Starting Assumptions about the Origin of Man

We often hear comments like "the fossils tell us," but in and of themselves fossils don't speak or tell us anything, including their age. Fossils exist in the present and it is people who speak and give their interpretation of the past history of fossils based on their starting assumptions. The prevailing starting assumptions for understanding the fossil record are special creation and evolution.

Christian Assumptions about the Origin of Man

Most Bible-believing Christians in America believe that God created man and all other kinds of animals and plants in essentially their present form (generally represented by the *family*, not the *species*, taxonomic classification) by the power of His Word and Spirit. They observe and recognize the ongoing processes of extinction and limited variation within each kind, but point out that this has never been shown to produce fundamentally new kinds of creatures. Thus, they believe God created apes and God created men, but God did not create "ape-men" and apes didn't change into man (with or without God's providence). There are, however, a substantial number of professing Christians who believe God used evolution to "create." But rarely do

6. Bjorn Kurten, *Pleistocene Mammals of Europe* (Chicago, IL: Aldine, 1968).
7. http://humanorigins.si.edu/evidence/human-fossils.

they specify what actual role God plays in evolution, or even if His existence is necessary for the evolution of the material cosmos.

Those Christians who attempt to accommodate evolution should reflect on the fact that professional evolutionists believe that religion itself is a product of evolution. Out of 14 billion years of purely materialistic cosmic evolution, religion is claimed to have evolved in the imagination of man's ancestors only a few hundred thousand years ago. As the evolutionist Julian Huxley once put it, "Evolution is the whole of reality, a single process of self-transformation."[8] Theologians and Christian laymen should be aware that evolution is a jealous "god" that will have no other gods before it.

Evolutionist Assumptions about the Origin of Man

The foundational assumption of evolutionism is that evolution is a purely scientific and materialistic (naturalistic) explanation for the origin of everything that is real (i.e., the material universe). Divine intervention and intelligent design are anathema to nearly all evolutionary scientists. Nothing is considered to be above or outside of evolution, including the origin of man and his mental faculties. Even religion is considered to be a product of evolution. For example, an evolutionist from Humboldt University in Berlin observed chimps throwing rocks at trees for no apparent reason and concluded that this was a "worship ritual" telling us something about the evolution of religion. This was widely and enthusiastically reported in the popular media under the banner "Chimps believe in God!"[9]

Evolutionists assume that amoeba-to-man evolution is an absolute fact, though they concede that the details regarding the actual mechanism of biological evolution and what creature evolved into what are theoretical or even speculative. In the case of human evolution, it is considered an unassailable fact that humans have evolved from nonhuman ancestors. Thus, paleoanthropologists never ask the question, "Did man evolve from ape-like creatures?" Indeed, such a question would likely be career-ending. Paleoanthropologists need only concern themselves with which of the ape-like creatures that have been found in the fossil record are our ancestors. They are certain that at least some of these fossil apes must be our ancestors or else we wouldn't have any ape-like ancestors, and that's unthinkable to an evolutionist.

Another primary assumption of evolutionism is that the degree of anatomical, functional, and genetic similarity between two creatures is considered

8. Julien Huxley, "Evolution and Genetics," in *What Is Science*, ed. J.R. Newman (New York, NY: Simon and Schuster, 1955), p. 278.
9. Antony Bushfield, "Chimps Believe in God, Research Claims," https://www.premier.org.uk/News/World/Chimps-believe-in-God-researcher-claims, March 4, 2016.

evidence of their degree of evolutionary relatedness. For example, humans are obviously more similar to apes than they are to fish, so our presumed evolutionary relationship to apes is considered to be much closer than it is to fish. But even fish are considered to be our distant relatives, because we both have vertebrae and other similarities common to vertebrates.

But there are countless examples of striking structural and functional similarities between unrelated organisms that make no sense in terms of evolutionary relatedness. For example,

- Opossums and primates have an opposable thumb.
- Australian koalas have fingerprints almost indistinguishable from humans.
- Bats, whales, and shrews have similar sonar-like echolocation.
- Among vertebrates, only mammals and certain salamanders and fish have non-nucleated red blood cells.
- There are many strikingly similar pairs of marsupial and placental mammals, yet evolutionists believe the two separated 160 million years ago.
- A single cell dinoflagellate (protozoan) has been found with a vertebrate-like camera eye consisting essentially of a cornea, lens, and retina derived from subcellular organelles including mitochondria and plastids.[10]

All of these similarities are "explained" by evolutionists with a rescuing hypothesis called "convergent evolution." Convergent evolution is when two distantly related or unrelated creatures are claimed to have independently evolved by chance the same trait or traits. It would seem that evolutionists consider anything possible, even probable, except intelligent design of biological systems by our Creator.

Comparative Anatomy of Apes and Humans

Most of the fossil evidence for human evolution is based on the comparative anatomy of primates and humans. This requires a knowledge of the anatomy of both living and fossil primates. The hard tissues (teeth and bones) are particularly important since primate fossils are generally partially preserved, disarticulated skeletons that rarely show evidence of soft tissues like the organs of the body.

---

10. Canadian Institute for Advanced Research, "Human-like 'Eye' in Single-celled Plankton: Mitochondria, Plastids Evolved Together," *ScienceDaily*, www.sciencedaily.com/releases/2015/07/150701133348.htm, July 1, 2015.

The layman considering the fossil evidence for human evolution will be overwhelmed with unfamiliar anatomical terms. But there are some basic differences in the hard tissue anatomy of apes and humans that can be easily understood and that clearly distinguish apes from humans. This knowledge can be insightful when one visits a human evolution display at a natural history museum or examines illustrations and descriptions of presumed ape-men in the popular media. Indeed, the whole purpose of this chapter is to help the non-specialist critically evaluate the current and future fossil evidence for the presumed "missing links" of human evolution.

Differences between Ape and Human Skulls

Small Brain vs. Big Brain

Skulls are perhaps the most interesting primate fossils because they house the brain and give us an opportunity, with the help of imaginative artists, to look our presumed ancestors in the face. The normal human skull is easily distinguished from all living apes, though there are of course similarities.

The cranial capacity of the skull is large in humans because of their relatively large brain compared to that of apes. The average brain size of an adult human is about 1,400 cm^3, but can vary among individuals over a nearly threefold range from about 700 cm^3 to 2000 cm^3. It should be noted that the size range of the normal human brain does not correlate with intelligence. Rather, brain size generally correlates with body size. As a result, adult human males have a brain volume that averages about 100 cm^3 larger than the brain of adult human females, reflecting the relative difference in their average body size.

Adult apes have brains that are generally about one-third the size of normal adult human brains. As in humans, the brain size of apes varies with body size and is generally in the range of 300–500 cm^3. But the profound difference in intelligence between apes and humans is not a simple matter of the human brain being three times larger. The difference in the complexity of the interconnections between individual brain cells, for example, is far more important in cognitive ability than mere brain size. This important difference is not perceivable in fossils.

Position of the Foramen Magnum

The position of the *foramen magnum* of the skull is often used as an indicator of bipedality (habitually walking on two legs), since it usually indicates the orientation of the head to the trunk of the body. The *foramen magnum* is a large oval opening in the occipital bone on the base of the skull where the spinal cord exits the cranial cavity. This opening is generally located farther forward in upright walking bipeds and farther back on the skull in quadrupeds. This difference is obvious when comparing non-primate quadrupeds like a dog to a human. But the situation is more complicated in primates.[11]

There are two common methods for quantifying the relative position of the *foramen magnum* in primates: the basion-biporion distance and the basion-bicarotid chord distance. These measurements can give conflicting results.[12] The basion-bicarotid method, for example, distinguished between apes and humans, but the basion-biporion method is less successful. In the case of chimpanzees, the basion-bicarotid method shows a sexual difference in the relative position of the *foramen magnum* being more anterior in males than females.

Sloped vs. Vertical Face

Perhaps the easiest way to distinguish an ape skull from a human skull is to examine it from a side view (Figures 1 and 2). From this perspective, the face of the human is nearly vertical while that of the ape slopes forward from below the eye sockets to the tip of its upper jaw. The easiest way to evaluate the slope of the face in a skull is to compare the angle of the face to the zygomatic arch (cheek bone). The human face is nearly perpendicular to the zygomatic arch while the ape face is sloped at an obviously oblique angle. By this criterion alone, one can easily distinguish the skulls of living apes from humans.

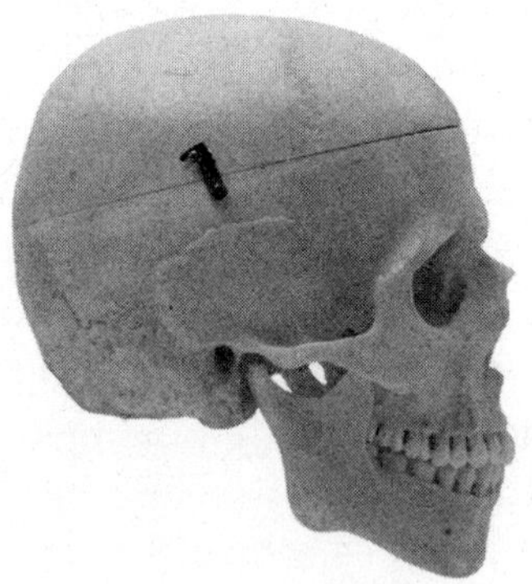

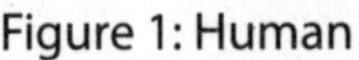

Figure 1: Human

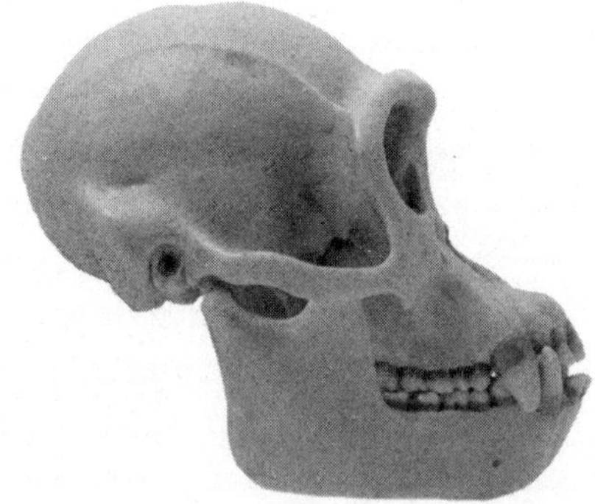

Figure 2: Chimp

11. Anon., "The Foramen Magnum: How Do We Know?" https://afarensis99.wordpress.com/2006/04/22/the_foramen_magnum_how_do_we_k/, April 22, 2006.
12. J.C. Ahern, "Foramen Magnum Position Variation in Pan troglodytes, Plio-Pleistocene Hominids, and Recent Homo sapiens: Implications for Recognizing the Earliest Hominids," *American Journal of Physical Anthropology* 127(3): 267–276.

Flat vs. Curved Forehead

The skull above the base of the orbits (eye sockets) is flat in apes and curved in humans. From a side view of the skull, the bony socket of the ape's orbit is obscured by its broad, flat, upper face. Humans, on the other hand, have a horizontally curved upper face and forehead, clearly revealing the orbit of the eye from a side view (figures 1 and 2). Also, when viewed from the front, the orbit of the human eye is slightly wider than it is tall, while the orbit of apes is usually slightly taller than wide, making them look goggle-eyed.

Flat vs. Protruding Nasal Bones

The nasal bones are a pair of bones meeting in the midline covering the upper part of the nasal cavity. Human nasal bones are distinctive in that they protrude from the face (the nose bones that eyeglasses rest on). Apes, by comparison, have flat nasal bones. As a result, the slight protrusion of the ape's nose is made up entirely of soft tissue and cannot be fractured like the human nose. Another difference is that humans have a protruding nasal bone, which anchors the nasal septum, while apes lack a protruding nasal bone [Figures 3 and 4]. The human nasal bone can be felt by placing your finger across your upper lip under your nose and then attempting to raise the finger.

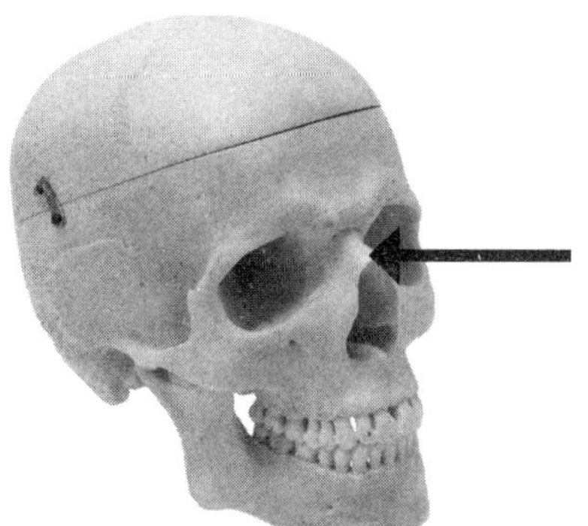

Figure 3: Human nasal bone (see arrow)

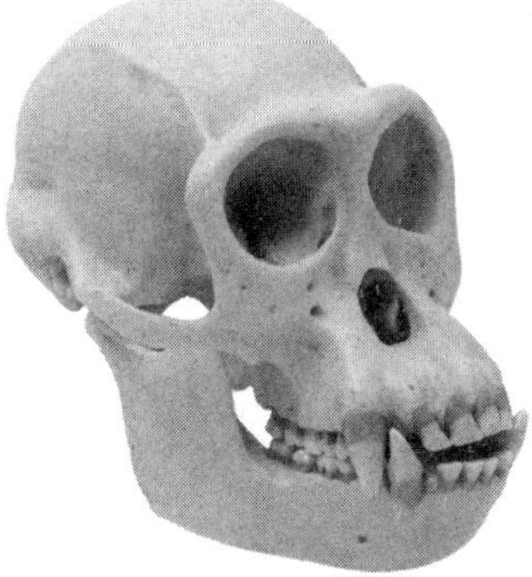

Figure 4: Chimpanzee (with flattened nasal bone)

Jaws and Teeth

Because of their relative hardness, teeth and jaw fragments are the most frequently found primate fossils. Tooth enamel is the hardest biological substance known. Essentially, all of the living cells and organic tissue that produce the enamel in the developing tooth are replaced by mineral crystals of hydroxyapatite. One might say that the enamel of our teeth is one part of our body that is fossilized while we are still alive. Thus, much of the evidence for the ape ancestry of man is based on similarities of teeth and jaws.

In contrast to man, apes tend to have incisor and canine teeth that are relatively larger than their molars. Ape teeth usually have thin enamel, while humans generally have thicker enamel. Finally, the jaws tend to be more U-shaped in apes and more parabolic in man, though there can be considerable variation among individuals of a species.

The problem in declaring a fossil ape to be a human ancestor (i.e., a hominin) on the basis of certain human-like features of the teeth is that some living apes have similar features and no living ape is considered to be an ancestor of man. Some species of modern baboons, for example, have relatively small canines and incisors. While most apes do have thin enamel, some apes such as the orangutans have relatively thick enamel. Teeth are likely to tell us more about an animal's diet and feeding habits than its supposed evolution. Nonetheless, relatively thick enamel is a commonly sighted criterion for declaring an ape fossil to be a hominin.

Pelvis and Legs

Humans are the only living primates that habitually walk on two legs. Thus, the most eagerly sought-after evidence in fossil hominins is any anatomical feature that might suggest *bipedality* (the ability to walk on two legs). Any hint, real or imagined, of bipedal locomotion in fossil apes is considered by evolutionists to be compelling evidence for their status as human ancestors.

Nonhuman primates generally walk in an essentially quadrupedal fashion, using both their feet and hands. Only the bonobo (pygmy chimpanzee) is capable of extended (25% of the time) bipedal locomotion. While nonhuman primates do occasionally walk briefly on two legs, their manner of walking is entirely different from that of humans. The distinctive human gait requires the complex integration of many skeletal and muscular features in our hips, legs, and feet. Thus, evolutionists closely examine the hipbones (*pelvis*), thighbones (*femur*), leg bones (*tibia* and *fibula*), and foot bones of fossil apes in an effort to detect any anatomical features that might even remotely suggest bipedality.

Pelvis

The pelvis (hip bones) plays a critically important role in walking, and the distinctive human gait requires a pelvis that is anatomically and functionally different from that of the apes. Indeed, one has only to examine the pelvis to determine if any hominin was likely to have had the ability to walk like a human.

The part of the hip bone that we can feel just under our belt is called the ilium or the iliac blade. Viewed from above, human ilia are curved forward like the handlebars of a tricycle. The iliac blades of the ape, in contrast, project straight out to the side like the handlebars of a scooter (figures 5 and 6). This is important because the shape of the iliac blades of the hipbones determine the function of an important pair of muscles called the gluteus medius and clearly reveal if a creature is capable of human-like bipedal walking.

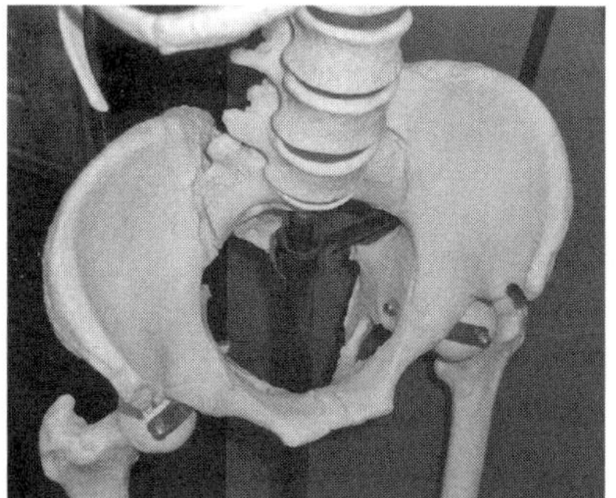

Figure 5: Human iliac blades

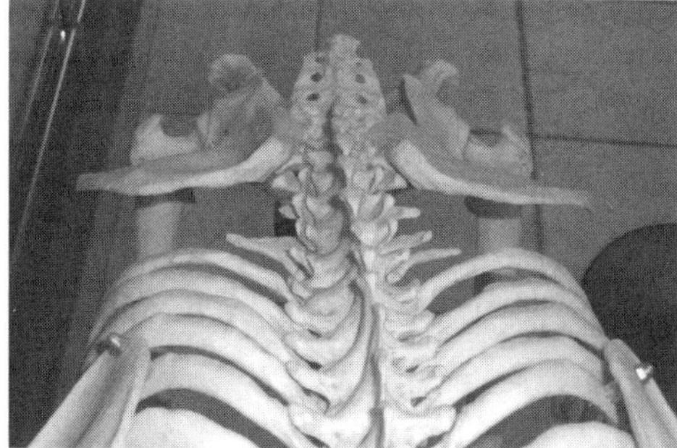

Figure 6: Chimpanzee iliac blades

In both apes and humans, the gluteus medius has its origin on the superficial surface of the iliac blade and inserts into the greater trochanter of the femur. Because of the anteriorly curved iliac blade of humans, the gluteus medius muscle runs down the side of the hip (like a holster) to where it inserts on the greater trochanter of the femur. In the case of the ape with its straight iliac blade, the gluteus medius runs dorsally down the back from its origin in the iliac blade to its insertion on the greater trochanter of the femur. This results in two distinctly different actions of the human vs. the ape gluteus medius. The human gluteus medius serves as an abductor of the leg (swings the leg out to the side). The ape gluteus medius serves as an extensor of the hip which brings the upper body of the forward-leaning ape to a more vertical position.

In the human, the gluteus medius stabilizes the hip when walking. This is important because the articulation of the head of the femur with the pelvis is a ball-socket type joint with a wide range of mobility. When we lift our left foot off the ground to make a step, our hip would fall on the left side, were it not for the contraction of the gluteus medius on the side of our planted foot.

Because of the shape of the pelvis and orientation of the gluteus medius muscles, humans are able to walk while keeping the left and right hips essentially parallel to the ground. When apes walk on two legs, however, they must swing their upper body from side to side in the familiar "ape walk" fashion, to keep their weight over the planted foot. The reason for this difference in gait is largely a matter of pelvic anatomy resulting in a difference in the orientation of the gluteus medius muscles.

Carrying Angle of the Knee

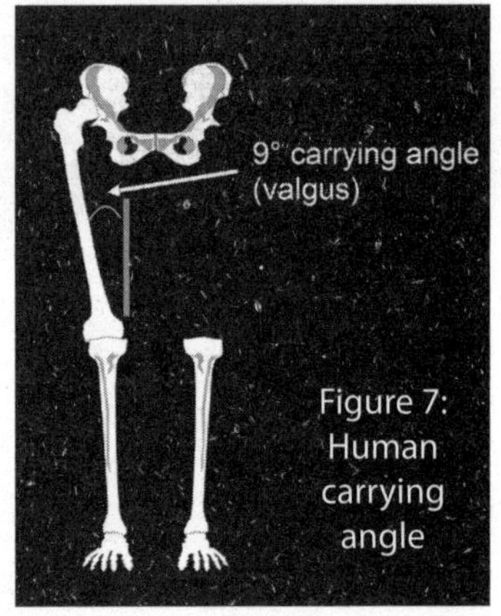

Figure 7: Human carrying angle

Evolutionists are particularly interested in the angle at which the femur and the tibia meet at the knee (called the *valgus* or *carrying angle*). Humans are able to keep their weight over their feet while walking because our femurs converge toward the knees, forming a carrying angle of approximately nine degrees with the tibia, making us sort of knock-kneed (figure 7). In contrast, chimps and gorillas have widely separated straight legs with a carrying angle of essentially zero degrees.

Evolutionists assume that fossil apes with a high (human-like) carrying angle were bipedal and thus evolving into man. For example, certain australopithecines (an ape-like creature) are considered to have walked like us and thus to be our ancestors largely because they had a high carrying angle. But high carrying angles are not confined to humans. They are also found in some modern apes and monkeys that walk gracefully on tree limbs and only clumsily on the ground.

Living apes and monkeys with a high carrying angle (values comparable to man) include apes such as the orangutan and monkeys such as the spider monkey — both adept tree climbers and capable of only an ape-like bipedal gait on the ground. The high carrying angle in these creatures allows them to keep their feet close together when walking on limbs of trees. The point is that there are *living* tree-dwelling apes and monkeys with some of the same anatomical features that evolutionists consider to be definitive evidence for bipedality, yet none of these animals walks like man and no one suggests they are our ancestors or descendants.

Locking Knee

Another distinctive difference between the legs of humans and apes is that the human knee locks when the leg is straightened and unlocks when the knee is bent. The lock is achieved by the tibia rotating about five degrees outward in relationship to the femur when the leg is straightened at the knee. This explains why our footprints point outward at the toes. Apes lack this locking mechanism and must walk with slightly bent knees. Humans have only to walk a few minutes with slightly bent knees to appreciate the value of locking knees. It requires considerably more energy to support walking on two legs when the legs are even slightly bent at the knee.

The locking knee is also of value when standing for a long period of time. When standing at attention, for example, our toes point forward but our femurs rotate inward relative to the tibia and the lock is set. Thus when a prankster clips a standing person behind the knee, it can cause them to fall before they can reset the lock.

Foot Bones

The human foot is unique compared to any other primate because it is designed specifically for walking, while the feet of other primates are used for grasping as well as walking. The big toe of the human foot is inline with the foot, not jutting out to the side like an ape foot. Human toe bones are relatively straight rather than curved and grasping like ape toes. The human big toe points forward and is in alignment with the other toes. The big toe of the apes, by contrast, angles inward from the rest of its toes and is a grasping toe used almost like a thumb in climbing trees.

Another distinctive feature of the human foot is its complex arches. Our foot has three distinct arches, the longitudinal medial and longitudinal lateral arches running from the heel to the base of the toes on each side of the foot, and one transverse arch running across the mid foot from medial to lateral sides. These arches are made up of bones, ligaments, and tendons, and are essential for bearing weight and forward propulsion in bipedal locomotion. To serve these functions the foot must be highly stable yet flexible. All living apes by comparison are flat-footed and lack the longitudinal and transverse arches.

When a human walks, the heel of the foot hits the ground first, then the weight distribution spreads forward from the heel along the outer margin of the foot up to the base of the little toe. From the little toe the weight bearing spreads inward across the base of the toes and finally pushes off with the big toe. No ape has a foot or push-off like that of a human and thus no ape is capable of walking with the distinctive human stride or capable of making human-like footprints. As a result, a series of fossilized footprints can provide compelling evidence for both foot anatomy and stride. But as we will see, when evolutionists encounter footprints that appear to be human in both anatomy and stride, but are considered too old to be human, they attribute them to ape-like hominins, not humans.

Hand Bones

The human hand is easily distinguished from that of nonhuman primates. While the human hand is designed to serve exclusively for grasping and manipulating, the hand of other primates is designed to serve both as a hand and a foot. Nonhuman primates use their hands to either fist walk (bonobos and orangutans) or knuckle walk (chimpanzees and gorillas).

The thumb is perhaps the most distinctive feature of the human hand. Our thumb is longer than that of any other primate, extending well beyond the knuckle of our forefinger. All other primates have a shorter thumb that barely reaches the knuckles. Most primates have opposable thumbs, but none have the range of motion of the human thumb. The human thumb is more muscular and mobile, and unlike apes, can touch all four of our fingers.

Human finger bones are relatively shorter, straighter, and flatter than the fingers of nonhuman primates, which have longer and more curved fingers. Finger curvature is very pronounced in knuckle-walkers and in the suspensory adapted hand of tree climbers. In addition, the wrist (carpel) bones of knuckle-walkers can move into a configuration that locks the wrist.

Scapula (Shoulder Blade)

In all primates (and limbed vertebrates in general), the only bony attachment of the arm to the rest of skeleton is by way of the scapula (shoulder blade) and clavicle (collar bone). The humerus (upper arm bone) articulates with the scapula at a shallow ball-socket joint called the glenoid cavity. The scapula articulates with the clavicle, which in turn articulates with the manubrium of the sternum (upper end of the breast bone). This arrangement gives a much greater range of motion to the upper limbs than is possible with the deep ball-socket joint of the lower limbs.

In the case of humans, the joint between the humerus and the scapula only allows us to raise our arm to a position approximately parallel to the ground. Any further elevation of the arm requires the scapula to be rotated by means of muscles on our shoulder and back. Thus it requires more effort to use our arms over our head than to use them below shoulder level.

Arboreal apes and monkeys have suspensory adapted forelimbs that are often used in a highly elevated position when grasping limbs of trees. This is facilitated in primates by an up tilted glenoid cavity that permits the forelimbs to be elevated over the head with little or no rotation of the scapula. Thus the anatomy of the scapula can reveal if a primate is a tree-dweller.

Other Variables That Must Be Considered

Sexual Dimorphism

The anatomical differences between the human male and female skeleton are subtle though apparent to the trained eye, but the differences between male and female ape skeletons are usually much more obvious. These skeletal differences are called sexual dimorphism. Sex-related differences in non-human primate anatomy are particularly common and particularly evident in the skull.

If one compares a male gorilla skull with that of a female gorilla, the male skull is much bigger (after taking account of differences in body size) and more robust in appearance. Another major difference is that the male gorilla skull has a much larger sagittal crest than the female does. The sagittal crest is a bony ridge or plate that runs lengthwise along the midline on the crest of the skull. This bony ridge serves to anchor jaw (chewing) muscles called the temporalis muscle. Humans, by contrast, have nothing resembling a sagittal crest because their much smaller and thinner temporalis muscle attaches to the side of the skull (temporal region). A noticeable sagittal crest is found on the males of the more robust apes such as the gorilla and orangutan but occurs only rarely among the males of smaller apes such as the chimpanzee.

Age Differences

Bones are very dynamic structures that change in shape and density both with age and use. The primate skeleton in particular shows substantial developmental change with age. The skull of juvenile primates, for example, is relatively large for its body size compared to adults, due to the relatively rapid early development of the nervous system. Thus a juvenile ape might appear to have a relatively large brain for its body size and be interpreted as human-like, if age and development is ignored.

Pathology

Pathological conditions can profoundly change the anatomy of bones. Failure to consider pathological change can lead to a gross misinterpretation of fossil primates. For example, an early Neanderthal fossil known as La Chapelle-aux-Saints showed obvious osteo-degenerative disease including loss of teeth, advanced resorption of mandibular bone, and advanced arthritis. A reconstruction of this specimen by Marcellin Boule in 1911 failed to take pathology into account, which led to portraying Neanderthals as having a stooped posture, a thrust-forward skull, bent knees, and divergent big toe. As a result of this misinterpretation and evolutionary bias, Neanderthals were not considered to be direct ancestors of humans until the fossil was properly re-examined by Straus and Cave in 1957 and shown to be human.

Fragmentation of Fossils

Primate fossils are often highly fragmented and rarely articulated. The famous KNM-ER 1470 skull, for example, was assembled from more than 150 fragments. Accurate assembly requires a thorough knowledge of primate anatomy, a good eye, and a freedom from observer bias. The skull of 1470 is classified as *Homo habilis* (or *Homo rudolfensis*) but some evolutionists believe it is an australopithecine. The confusion arises in part from the fact that the cranial capacity of skull 1470 is quite large (800 cm^3) for the size of the skull, but the skull has been reconstructed with a sloping face giving it an ape-like appearance. However, in this specimen the only attachment of the face below the orbits of the eyes to the rest of the skull is a slender bone fragment that allows the lower face to be reconstructed as either sloped like an ape or vertical like a human.

Three Ways to Make an Ape Man

Both apes and humans are found in the fossil record, but is there really compelling evidence for fossilized ape-men? Evolutionists use three ways to construct ape-men from ape and human fossils.

1. Combine ape and human fossils declaring them to be one individual
2. Upgrade fossil apes to ape-men
3. Downgrade fossil humans to ape-men

Combining Fossil Bones of Apes and Humans to Make Ape-men

One way to make an "ape-man" is to combine fossilized ape bones with fossilized human bones and then declare the mixture to represent one individual. This could be either intentional deception or an unintentional mistake.

The most famous example of an ape-man proven to be a combination of ape and human bones is "Piltdown Man." In 1912, it was announced at the Geological Society of London that Charles Dawson, a medical doctor and an amateur paleontologist, had discovered a mandible (lower jaw) and part of a skull in a gravel pit near Piltdown, England. A canine tooth was found later and added to the collection. The jawbone was ape-like but the teeth were described as showing wear similar to the human pattern. The skull fragments, on the other hand, were very human-like indicating a very large brain. These three specimens were combined to form what was also called "Dawn man," and was confidently dated to be 500,000–1,000,000 years old, which "afford us a link with our remote ancestor, the apes."[13] The fossils went into the Natural History Museum (NHM) in London and only plaster casts of the evidence were shown to scientists or the public.

Finally, in 1953, after scientists outside the NHM examined the actual fossils, the whole thing was exposed as an elaborate hoax perpetrated by someone who knew what evolutionists were looking for. The skull was indeed human (dated to be about 500 years old), while the jaw was that of a modern female orangutan whose teeth had been obviously filed to crudely resemble the human size and wear pattern, and the canine tooth came from a chimpanzee. The long chimp canine tooth was filed down so far that it exposed the pulp chamber, which was then filled in by the hoaxer in an apparent effort to hide the mischief. It would seem that any competent scientist examining this tooth would have concluded that it was either a hoax or the world's first root canal. But the deliberate hoax apparently involved some of the leading scientists in Britain.[14] The success of this hoax for over 50 years in spite of 500 research papers written on the find[15] and the apparently careful scrutiny of some of the best authorities in the world led the prominent evolutionist Lord Solly Zuckerman to declare, "Students of fossil primates have not been distinguished for caution when working within the logical constraints of their subject. The record is so astonishing that it is legitimate to ask whether much science is yet to be found in this field at all. The story of the Piltdown Man hoax provides a pretty good answer."[16]

The fossil bones of apes and humans are rarely found in an articulated condition. Fossilized primate bones are often widely scattered. Where several bones are found in one location it can be difficult to determine if they are parts of one individual creature or several. Fossil bones believed to be

---

13. "A Discovery of Supreme Importance to All Interested in the History of the Human Race," *Illustrated London News*, Dec. 28, 1912, p. 4–5.
14. Glen Levy, "Piltdown Man," *TIME*, http://content.time.com/time/specials/packages/article/0,28804,1931133_1931132_1931125,00.html), March 16, 2010. Levy says that no culprits other than Dawson have ever been implicated. But actually, evidence points to the involvement of some of the leading British scientists at the time. See Robin McKie, "Piltdown Man: British Archeaology's Greatest Hoax," https://www.theguardian.com/science/2012/feb/05/piltdown-man-archaeologys-greatest-hoax, February 5, 2012.
15. Levy, ibid.
16. Solly Zuckerman, *Beyond the Ivory Tower* (New York, NY: Taplinger Publishing Co., 1970), p. 65.

from one individual may be widely scattered and discovered over a period of months and years.

Upgrade Fossil Apes to Ape-men

Another way to make an "ape-man" is to find something about the apes in the fossil record that can be used in an effort to promote them to a more human-like status. Since even living apes and humans share many skeletal similarities, it is quite easy to make a list of similarities between fossil apes and humans. But these similarities do not prove an evolutionary relationship. There are also distinctive features of the human skeleton that make it quite easy to distinguish today's humans from today's apes. The two-part question is simply this: are fossil ape-like creatures really significantly different from modern apes, and are they really more similar to humans?

Of the four genera of hominins that evolutionists believe to be ancestral to humans, three are clearly very ape-like. The ardipithecines, australopithecines, and paranthropithecines are apes and would doubtless be recognized as such if they were living today. Not only is their anatomy very ape-like, but their fossils are never directly associated with human artifacts such as tools, art, hunting weapons, ritual burials, lodgings, or use of fire. The jump from these ape-like creatures to members of the genus *Homo* is dramatic and consistent with the fact that God created apes and men but not "ape-men."

Downgrade Fossil Humans to Ape-men

There are clearly fossil humans in the fossil record, though they are rare. But if there is to be evidence for evolution of humans from nonhumans, fossils of "primitive" humans must be found with differences in anatomy that are ape-like and clearly fall outside the normal range of human variability.

When these human fossils are considered to be too old to be human they become ape-men regardless of their anatomy. Thus, the obviously human-like footprints found by Mary Leakey at the Laetoli site in Tanzania are considered to be made by the very ape-like *Australopithecus afarensis* because they have been "dated" at 3.66 million years old and thus are too old to be human, in spite of the fact that they look so human in both anatomy and stride (see below).

The Role of the Artist in Promoting Human Evolution

Several things should be noted about the artistic reconstructions of ape-men that we find in museum displays, textbooks, and news articles.

The "March of Progress"

Nowhere is the key roll of the artist in promoting belief in evolution more evident than in an illustration published in 1965 in the Time-Life Book *Early Man,* featuring a foldout illustration of 13 presumed ancestors of man over 25 million years of evolution.[17] As one progresses from left to right the "ancestors" stand a little taller and more erect and assume a progressively more human-like posture and gait (Figure 8). Such a linear and progressive ancestor-descendant parade was known to be untrue even at the time it was drawn, but has nonetheless become an enduring icon of evolution known as the "March of Progress."

Figure 8: "The Road to *Homo Sapiens*"

Many consider the "March of Progress" to be the most famous and influential image in the history of scientific illustration. It has been copied in a shorter form on countless t-shirts, buttons, book covers, record albums, commercial advertisements, programs for scientific meetings, and is even used as the emblem of the Leakey Foundation. As a result of this wide exposure, many laymen base their belief in the evolution of man more on this easy-to-understand image of linear "progress" than on any actual scientific evidence. But evolutionary anthropologist Bernard Wood informs us:

> There is a popular image of human evolution that you'll find all over the place. . . . On the left of the picture there's an ape . . . On the right, a man . . . Between the two is a succession of figures that become ever more like humans. . . . Our progress from ape to human looks so smooth, so tidy. It's such a beguiling image that even the experts are loath to let it go. But it is an illusion.[18]

The Whites of Their Eyes

Artistic renderings of fleshed-out fossils of presumed ancestors of man often show the face of a very ape-like creature with very human-like eyes. This is accomplished by merely putting a white sclera in the eyes (the whites of the

17. F. Clark Howell, *Early Man* (New York, NY: Time-Life Books, 1965), p. 41–45.
18. Bernard Wood, "Who are we?" *New Scientist*, 2366 (Oct. 26, 2002): 44.

eye). All apes and monkeys have a brown sclera that is nearly as dark as their brown iris, while all humans with normal, healthy eyes have an essentially white sclera. Obviously, the fossil record for scleral color is nonexistent so this is simply artistic license used to influence the viewer.

Artistic Extrapolation

In his book *Life on the Mississippi,* Mark Twain wryly commented, "There is something fascinating about science. One gets such wholesale returns of conjecture out of such a trifling investment of fact." Nowhere is this more evident than in the field of evolution. Where data are missing, evolutionists often employ artists to fill in all the desired missing evidence. Artistic imagination has been used to illustrate entire "ape-men" from nothing more than a single tooth. In 1922, Henry Fairfield Osborne, director of the American Museum of Natural History, reported on a molar tooth from the Pliocene strata of Nebraska that he claimed had characteristics of both man and ape. The tooth was given the scientific name *Hesperopithecus* but became commonly known as "Nebraska man." The *London Illustrated News* (*LIN*) even showed a fleshed-out, double-page illustration of Nebraska man and his wife in their natural habitat!

"Nebraska man" along with "Piltdown man" (now known to be a hoax) were the prevailing evidence for human evolution during the time of the famous Scopes "monkey trial" in 1925. It is said that even many theologians of the time accepted the evolutionary claim for the bestial origin of man on the evidence of these imaginary ape-men. In 1927, parts of the skeleton of *Hesperopithecus* were discovered together with more teeth, and Nebraska man was found to actually be an extinct peccary (wild pig)! Making an ape-man out of a pig tooth is an example of the extreme observer bias often found in paleoanthropology. One might sum up this bias as, "I wouldn't have seen it if I hadn't believed it." The reinterpretation of the fossil evidence was announced in a technical journal, the popular picture from the *LIN* was quickly removed from literature, and the general public was never the wiser.[19]

The Fossil Hominins (Man and His Ape-like "Ancestors")

The reader should now have sufficient background to critically examine specific examples of the current crop of presumed ape-like ancestors of humans. There will no doubt be many more proffered examples of "missing links"

19. For creationist historical analysis of this discovery with the LIN picture, see Ian Taylor, *In the Minds of Men* 6th ed. (Foley, MN: TFE Publishing, 2008), p. 227–229. The five-year process of reinterpreting the fossil evidence is described by William K. Gregory, "*Hesperopithecus* Apparently Not An Ape Nor A Man," *Science*, 66:1720 (Dec. 16, 1927): 579–581.

between apes and humans in the future. The popular media will be eager to present each new "ape-man" to you with the assurance that this is finally the true missing link that all evolutionists have been waiting for. But you must learn to be critical, think for yourself, and dare to question scientific (or theological) authority. The hominin fossils discussed in this chapter follow the organization and nomenclature of an exhibit from the Smithsonian National Museum of Natural History (entitled "What does it mean to be human?") that is traveling to public libraries across America.[20]

The Classification of Hominins

The taxonomic classification of living plants and animals has become chaotic in recent years. In the past, classification was largely based on anatomical similarities. But now embryological, genetic, and molecular similarities, as well as presumed evolutionary relationships are considered in classification. But these different approaches frequently lead to very different classification schemes. When such differences arise, assumptions about evolutionary relatedness generally trump everything else.

The classification of man's presumed fossil ancestors is chaotic at best. One problem is that the nomenclature is constantly changing. Currently, the term "hominid" refers to modern humans as well as all modern and extinct Great Apes and their immediate ancestors. A newer term "hominin" refers to modern humans and all of our presumed ancestors, which include the genera *Homo, Paranthropus, Australopithecus*, and *Ardipithecus*. Note that humans are the only living hominins; all other hominins are speculations from the fossil evidence. This classification is obviously based on evolutionary starting assumptions.

The Common Ancestor of Apes and Humans

While evolutionists are certain that modern apes (like the chimpanzee) and modern humans shared a common ancestor six to seven million years ago, this ancestor has never been specifically identified. Several fossilized ape-like creatures have been proposed as being ancestral to humans, but rarely are fossil ape-like creatures identified as being only ancestral to modern apes. It would appear that when paleoanthropologists are lucky enough to find a rare fossil ape-like creature it will not be wasted on simply being an ancestor of apes, when with a little more effort it can be declared to be an ancestor of humans. There is obviously more fame and fortune to be had in finding a supposed ape ancestor of humans than an ape ancestor of apes.

20. http://humanorigins.si.edu/evidence/human-family-tree.

In a 2015 study published in the *Proceedings of the National Academy of Sciences,*[21] evolutionists suggest the common ancestor of apes and humans looked a lot like a chimpanzee or a gorilla — they're just not sure which. Is there any other field of empirical science where something this tenuous and trivial would be accepted for publication in the prestigious *PNAS*?

Ardipithecus Group

The Ardipithecus group is considered by evolutionists to be the very earliest ape-like human ancestors, which evolved in Africa four to six million years ago. The genus name *Ardipithecus* is derived from an Afar Ethiopian word, *ardi*, which means "ground" or "floor," and a Greek word *pithekos*, which means "ape." Thus the name *Ardipithecus* or "ground ape" reflects the evolutionists' belief that these were the first ape-like creatures to begin to habitually walk upright on the ground. All the adult members of this group are very ape-like and are about the size of chimpanzees.

Ardipithecus Ramidus

The first fossils named *Ardipithecus* were found in 1994 by paleoanthropologist Tim White in the Middle Awash region of Ethiopia. Initially, the fossil was attributed to the *Australopithecus* genus, but was later declared to be a new genus *Ardipithecus*. The species name *ramidus* is derived from "ramid," which in the Afar language of Ethiopia means "root," referring to the belief that this ape is at the very root of humanity. White and his co-workers have found about 100 partial fossil specimens that are attributed to *Ar. ramidus*.

Evolutionists claim that *Ar. Ramidus* is 4.4 million years old, making it over a million years older than the famous australopithecine fossil called "Lucy" which had long been believed to be the oldest hominin to walk on two legs. But the evidence for anything resembling human-like bipedality in "Ardi" is hardly compelling. First, the foot bones of this creature reveal a very ape-like, divergent, grasping big toe and rigid foot. The pelvis was reconstructed from crushed fragments and, according to some evolutionists, retained considerable arboreal capabilities and is at most only suggestive of bipedalism.

Ardipithecus kadabba

The fossil known as *Ar. Kadabba* was found in the Middle Awash region of Ethiopia by paleoanthropologist Yohannes Haile-Selassie in 1997. It was

21. The abstract to the *PNAS* technical article is linked in Sergio Prostak, Natali Anderson, and Enrico de Lazaro, "Study: Last Common Ancestor of Humans and Apes Looked Like Gorilla or Chimpanzee," http://www.sci-news.com/othersciences/anthropology/science-homo-pan-last-common-ancestor-03220.html, September 9, 2015.

originally considered to be a subspecies of *Ar. ramidus*, but was later declared to be a separate species on the basis of perceived differences in its teeth. The first specimen found was a lower jaw, but eventually 11 specimens, including partial bones from the hand, foot, arm, and clavicle were found representing at least five individuals. Like *Ar. ramidus*, this creature was similar in body and brain size to a chimpanzee, but was claimed to be over a million years older than *Ar. ramidus* (5–6 million years old).

It comes as no surprise that *Ar. ramidus* was claimed to be capable of bipedal walking. But the evidence for this is based on a single bone from the big toe found ten miles away from the other fossil specimens! It is claimed that this toe has a broad, robust appearance used for the push-off that is distinctive of the bipedal human gait. This sort of evidence is only convincing to those who begin with the premise that humans have evolved from ape-like animals.

Australopithecus Group

Like the *Ardipithecus* group, the australopithecines are another group of ape-like hominins found in eastern Africa, with most found in Hadar in the Afar region of the Great Rift Valley in Ethiopia. These Hadar australopithecines are claimed to range in age from 2 to 4 million years old. Although evolutionists concede that they were clearly adept as tree climbers, the *Australopithecus* group are claimed to have walked upright on a regular basis. The scientific name *Australopithecus* means "southern ape," suggesting whatever else might be said about these creatures, they are apes. The distinguished paleoanthropologist Lord Solly Zuckerman rejected the notion that australopithecines have anything to do with human evolution, and is reported to have said, "They are just bloody apes."[22]

Australopithecus Anamensis

At a claimed age of 3.9 to 4.2 million years old, *Au. anamensis* is believed to be the oldest of the australopithecines, even older than Lucy which *Au. anamensis* resembles. The first fossil of this type was found in Kanapoi in northern Kenya in 1995 by a team led by Meave Leakey and coworkers. The fossil consisted of several teeth and bone fragments.

But 30 years earlier, in 1965, a single arm bone (distal end of the humerus) known as KNM-KP 271 was discovered at the same site and was dated at 4.5 million years old, making it the oldest human ancestor that had been

---

22. Quoted in Roger Lewin, *Bones of Contention* (New York, NY: Touchstone Books, 1988), p. 165.

found at that time. The problem is that studies using computer discriminate analysis have shown that the Kanapoi humerus is strikingly similar to that of modern *Homo sapiens.* For example, the evolutionist Henry M. McHenry concluded, "The results show that the Kanapoi specimen, which is 4 to 4.5 million years old, is indistinguishable from modern *Homo sapiens*."[23] The only reason that evolutionists dismiss this humerus as being human is that they consider it to be far too old to be human. If it had been found in strata considered to be less than 200 thousand years old, it would be considered to be unquestionably human. As a result, this apparently human humerus is now considered to be *Au. afarensis.*

Australopithecus Africanus

Raymond Dart acquired this very ape-like fossilized skull in 1924, and after 20 years of debate it was the first fossil to convince evolutionists that humans had their origin in Africa. Called the "Taung child," dates proposed for it have ranged between 3.3 and 0.87 million years. Still, it is generally considered the earliest ancestor of humans found in southern Africa. The "Taung child" is a juvenile estimated to be 3 to 4 years of age. Though Dart was convinced of its direct ancestry to man, he published no detailed study of the skull.

Much has been made of the supposed human-like brain development of this creature based on cranial sutures. In humans, the continued rapid growth of the brain after birth is made possible by the skull bones being separated by fibrous connective tissue called the fontanelles. These skull sutures generally close between 12–14 months of age, but may not completely close until about five years old. In apes, with their much smaller brain development, the cranial sutures are closed or nearly closed at the time of birth. Evolutionists have argued that the Taung skull has signs of human-like delayed cranial suture closure. But this has been called into question by a more recent study.[24]

Australopithecus Afarensis

Australopithecus afarensis derives its species name from the Afar region of Ethiopia where most of the apes of this type have been found. Bones and

23. Henry M. McHenry, "Fossils and the Mosaic Nature of Human Evolution," *Science* 190:4213 (1975): 425–431.
24. R.L. Holloway et al, "New High-resolution Computed Tomography Data of the Taung Partial Cranium and Endocast and Their Bearing on Metopism and Hominin Brain Evolution," *Proceedings of the National Academy of Sciences USA* 111:36 (2014): 13022–13027.

teeth from over 300 individuals of this species have been found and "dated" from 3.85 to 2.95 million years old. The most famous and most complete specimen, popularly known as "Lucy," has become a commonly used synonym for the whole species *Au. afarensis*. Lucy has been considered the "gold standard" by which other ape-like ancestors of man are judged and is certainly the best known among laymen. For this reason, we will go into greater detail in critically evaluating this fossil.

Lucy was discovered in the Afar region of Ethiopia in 1974 by a team led by the American paleoanthropologist Donald Johanson. Lucy's fossilized skeleton consists of 47 bones (comprising about 20% of the whole skeleton), including parts of both upper and lower limbs, vertebrae, ribs, and pelvis. While most of the hand and foot bones are missing, as well as most of the skull (except for the mandible and cranial fragments), these have been partially filled in by the discovery of other presumed specimens of *Au. afarensis*. Lucy appears to have been a fully grown female primate that would have stood about 3.5 feet tall.

Lucy has been widely portrayed in the media and in museums all over the world as the supreme example of a "missing link" between apes and humans, though she is not considered to be directly related to humans. Still, Lucy has been touted as the "mother of all human kind" and her fossil bones were displayed on a tour of major museums in America under the banner "Lucy's Legacy — Her Story Is Your Story." Most creationists consider Lucy and all the other australopithecines to be nothing more than extinct apes with similarities to both chimpanzees and gorillas.

Skull

Even a layman would be unlikely to confuse the skull of *Au. afarensis* with a human skull. The cranial capacity is small even by ape standards. The sloping face, flat nasal bones, and robust gorilla-like jaw are all typical of ape skulls. But evolutionists claim the teeth of *Au. afarensis* were human-like with relatively thick enamel and relatively small canine teeth. But as noted earlier, some living apes have these characteristics, so this is not decisive.

Pelvis

A great deal of attention has been given to the pelvic bones of Lucy in an effort to support the possibility of bipedal locomotion. The orientation of the pelvic iliac blades is a key requirement for bipedality. The orientation of the iliac blades on the human pelvis allows the human to use gluteal muscles to counterbalance the lifting of the opposite leg during bipedal walking. This stabilizes the hips and prevents the collapse of the hip on the side of the lifted leg. The orientation of the straight iliac blades of the ape pelvis, in contrast, provides no stability to the hip, forcing the ape to swing the upper body from side to side to keep from falling over sideways with each step.

Evolutionists Stern and Susman[25] as well as Tuttle[26] believed that Lucy's pelvis was well-adapted for arboreal (tree-dwelling) life. Like many others, they noted that the orientation of the pelvic iliac blades was similar to that of chimpanzees, not humans. But Owen Lovejoy, who worked with Johanson analyzing the Lucy fossils, believed that the first reconstruction of Lucy's pelvis was in error and, in a much-publicized video shown on public television, Lovejoy demonstrated how casts of Lucy's pelvis could be cut apart and rearranged to produce the desired more human-like pelvis that might be capable of human-like bipedal locomotion.[27]

Other analyses of the pelvis by evolutionist Christine Berge, who has taken advantage of modern technology, offer a different reconstruction.[28] Berge writes, "The results clearly indicate that australopithecine bipedalism differs from that of humans." She pointed out that the extended limb of australopithecines would have lacked stabilization during walking, suggesting a retention of a partly arboreal behavior.

Feet and footprints

Much of the presumed evidence for Lucy walking upright in a human-like bipedal fashion, comes from the evidence of footprints found by Mary Leakey in the Laetoli site in Tanzania. Leaky discovered a 73-foot long trail of fossilized footprints consisting of 20 prints of an individual the size and shape of a modern ten-year-old human and 27 prints of a smaller person. The paleoanthropologist Timothy White who was working with Leakey at the time said,

> Make no mistake about it, they are like modern human footprints. If one were left in the sand of a California beach today, and a four-year-old were asked what it was, he would instantly say that

25. J.T. Stern and R.L. Susman, "The Locomotor Anatomy of *Australopithecus afarensis*," *American Journal of Physical Anthropology* 60 (1983): 279–217.
26. R.H. Tuttle, "Knuckle-walking and the Problem of Human Origins," *Science* 166:3908 (1969): 953–961.
27. Donald Johanson, "In Search of Human Origins (Part 1)," *Nova*, PBS Airdate: June 3, 1997. Transcript at http://www.pbs.org/wgbh/nova/transcripts/2106hum1.html.
28. Christine Berge and Dionysis Goularas, "A New Reconstruction of Sts 14 Pelvis (*Australopithecus africanus*) from Computed Tomography and Three-dimensional Modeling Techniques," *Journal of Human Evolution* 58 (2010): 262–272.

> somebody had walked there. He wouldn't be able to tell it from a hundred other prints on the beach, nor would you. The external morphology is the same. There is a well-shaped modern heel with a strong arch and good ball of the foot in front of it. The big toe is straight in line. It doesn't stick out to the side like an ape toe.[29]

Louis Robins of the University of North Carolina, who also analyzed the footprints, said, "The arch is raised, the smaller individual had a higher arch than I do — the toes grip the ground like human toes. You do not see this in other animal forms."[30]

In a lecture I attended at Washington University in St. Louis in 1982, Mary Leaky pointed out one additional feature of her Laetoli footprints rarely mentioned in the literature — all of the larger footprints of the trail have a smaller footprint superimposed on them! This could be interpreted as a child increasing its stride to step in an elder's footprints, as children often do. In addition, she reported that there were tracks of a wide variety of animals that are similar or identical to animals living in the area today, including antelopes, hares, giraffes, rhinoceroses, horses, pigs, and two kinds of elephants. Even several bird eggs were found, and many of these could be easily correlated with eggs of living species.

Mary Leaky assumed that the footprints were made by some hominid, but not by *Homo sapiens*, because the stratum in which the prints are found is estimated to be 3.66 million years old. Since that falls roughly near the presumed age of *Au. afarensis,* Johanson has steadfastly insisted that they must have been made by *Au. afarensis*. This conclusion is made despite the fact that the Laetoli footprints are located about 1,000 miles away from the location of the Hadar australopithecines such as Lucy.

Mary Leaky disagreed with Johanson's claims for *Au. afarensis* as the maker of her footprints. Also, two groups of scientists working independently have challenged the claim that Lucy had completely abandoned the trees and walked fully upright on the ground.[31] Anthropologist Russel Tuttle from the University of Chicago said that the Laetoli footprints that Leaky discovered in Tanzania were made by another more human species of ape-man that coexisted with *Au. afarensis* about 3.6 million years ago and that it was this unknown hominid that is the direct ancestor to man. After

29. Donald Johanson and Maitland Edey, *Lucy, The Beginnings of Humankind* (New York, NY: Simon and Schuster, 1981), p. 250.
30. Louis Robins, quoted in Anon, "The Leaky Footprints: An Uncertain Path," *Science News* 115:13 (March 31, 1979): 196.
31. Anon., "Was Lucy a Climber?" *Science News* 122:8 (1982), p. 116.

a careful examination of the Laetoli prints and foot bones of the Hadar *Au. afarensis* Tuttle concluded that the Hadar foot is ape-like with curved toes, whereas the footprints left in Laetoli are virtually human.[32]

Australopithecus Sediba

In 2008, the young son of paleoanthropologist Lee Berger found the first specimen named *Australopithecus sediba* in the Malapa cave north of Johannesburg. The elder Berger, who is well known for self-promotion, reported the discovery to mixed reviews in the April 9, 2010, issue of *Science*. The species name *sediba* means "wellspring," and is commonly known as "Malapa boy." The problem is that with a claimed age of 1.78–1.95 million years old *Au. sediba* is considered by most evolutionists to be too young to be an ancestor of *Homo*.

There are many nontrivial differences between *Au. sediba* and humans. *Au. sediba* has a brain measuring about one-third the size of that of a typical human but well within the range of apes. A comparison of the skull of *Au. sediba* with that of humans reveals that the lower face of *Au. sediba* is sloped like that of apes. And, like apes, the forehead of *Au. sediba* is flat, making the orbits of the eyes barely visible when viewed from the side. The mandible of *Au. sediba* bears no close resemblance to that of man (or even a chimpanzee) but rather is more similar to that of a gorilla.

The postcranial skeleton of *Au. sediba* is also very ape-like. It has a small body with ape-like large-jointed upper and lower limbs. The arms and hands of *Au. sediba* extend down to the knees, typical of long-armed knuckle walkers. The up-tilted glenoid fossa (shoulder joint) of *Au. Sediba,* together with its long, curved fingers are typical of the suspensory adapted upper limbs of tree-dwelling apes. The feet are described as primitive and similar to other Australopiths. But are these striking differences between *Au. sediba* and humans outweighed by the similarities?

Paleoanthropologist Tim White said, "The characteristics shared by *A. sediba* and *Homo* are few and could be due to normal variation among australopithecines."[33] The claimed "*Homo*-like" features of the *Au. sediba* pelvis are based on a composite reconstruction of the juvenile MH1 specimen. Any claim of human-like bipedality based on this pelvis is necessarily speculative and subject to the bias of the observer. *Au. sediba* is claimed to have protruding nasal bones like that of humans (and unlike the flat nasal bones

32. R.H. Tuttle, D.M. Webb, and M. Baksh, "Laetoli Toes and Australopithcus Aferensis," *Human Evolution* 6:3 (1991): 193–200.

33. M. Balter, "Candidate Human Ancestor From South Africa Sparks Praise and Debate," *Science* 328:5975 (2010): 154–155.

of living apes). But this "similarity" is based on a slight bony raphe between otherwise flat nasal bones typical of australopithecines in general.

Paranthropus Group

The members of this group were formerly considered to be a more robust type of australopithecine, but now have been given the genus name *Paranthropus.* All are very ape-like with large teeth, massive jaws, and large chewing muscles. These apes are claimed to have lived 1.2 to 2.7 million years ago, making them broadly overlap in time with the australopithecine group. There is no compelling reason to think that any of these apes had anything to do with humans. But evolutionists consider the members of this group to be bipedal based on perceived similarities in the hip joint and big toe to that of humans.

Paranthropus Robustus

In 1938, Robert Broom discovered a very ape-like fossil jaw fragment and molar in Kromdraai, South Africa. Other teeth and bones were found later and attributed to the genus *Paranthropus,* which fancifully means "beside man." This ape had a highly sloped face and a large gorilla-like sagittal crest on its skull for the attachment of massive chewing muscles. About the only thing that can be said to be human-like about this ape is relatively thick tooth enamel.

Paranthropus Boisei

In 1959, Mary Leakey discovered the most famous fossil specimen of this species, commonly known as "Zinj" (short for *Zinjanthropus*), in the Olduvai Gorge of northern Tanzania. It is very similar to the other members of the *Paranthropus* group in being very ape-like with a broad sloping face, gorilla-like sagittal crest, massive chewing muscles, and small brain. The cheek teeth were even larger than those of *P. robustus* and about four times the size of human molars. Once again, the relative thickness of the tooth enamel is sighted as being "human-like," but that again is not a uniquely human quality.

Paranthropus Aethiopicus

Evolutionists debate whether or not this is really a different species from the other robust australopithecine, paranthropithecine, and zinjanthropithecine apes. One problem is the scanty fossil evidence for this species, which consisted only of a toothless partial mandible until Alan Walker and Richard

Leakey found a skull (known as the "Black Skull") west of Lake Turkana in eastern Africa that they believed to be of the same species. Like the other *Paranthropus* fossils, *P. aethiopicus* is very ape-like with the usual sagittal crest, massive jaws and teeth, huge chewing muscles, and sloping face.

Homo Group

With the Homo group, excepting *Homo habilis*, we suddenly encounter humans. Not only are they large brained and anatomically human with unambiguous evidence of human-like bipedality, but we also find evidence of tools and other artifacts unique to humans. It should be noted that evolutionists believe that the Homo group dates from the present back to 2.4 million years ago, making them broadly overlap with *Paranthropus* group, which in turn broadly overlap with the *Australopithecus* group. This means that when we find evidence for tools, butchery, and use of fire, we cannot reflexively attribute them to the nonhuman genera of hominins. If a modern land-filled garbage dump were excavated, we might find chicken bones in close association with plastic spoons and forks, but this is hardly evidence that the chicken was the "tool maker."

Homo Habilis

Homo habilis is considered to be one of the earliest members of the genus *Homo* that are presumed to have lived between 1.4 and 2.4 million years ago. But even many evolutionists consider *H. habilis* to be an empty taxon consisting of a collection of several dozen controversial and confusing fossil specimens.

It all began in 1964 when Louis Leaky, Phillip Tobias, and John Napier reported in *Nature* the discovery of fossil skull fragments as well as hand and foot bones from four juvenile specimens. The foot and hand bones were reported to be human-like and capable of human-like functionality, but the skull was more ape-like. But the skull bone fragments were not found next to the foot and hand bones, leading some scientists to conclude that the *H. habilis* fossils were actually a mixture of *H. erectus* and australopithecine fossils.

Some years earlier, Louis Leaky found stone tools at the same site and attributed them to a fossil he called *Zinjanthropus*, now considered to be an ape. With the discovery of the new fossils, Leakey declared them to be the toolmaker, thus the name *Homo habilis,* which means "handy man."

To add to the confusion, in 1986, Tim White and Donald Johanson discovered fossil bones in Olduvai Gorge which were "dated" to be 1.8 million years old, and also claimed to be *H. habilis* on the basis of similarities of the skull and teeth. But this fossil known as Olduvai Hominid 62, had an ape-like body that was even smaller than the australopithecine Lucy, which was only a little over three feet tall. Indeed, some evolutionists regard *H. habilis* to be australopithecine.

Homo Rudolfensis

The first, and some would say the only, specimen of *Homo rudolfensis* is a skull discovered in 1986 by Richard Leaky in Koobi Fora in the Lake Turkana basin of Kenya. It is perhaps best known by Leakey's original designation, KNM-ER 1470. First "dated" at three million years old, it is now dated at 1.9 million years (based on pig fossils found nearby[34]) in an effort to make it more consistent with its human-like appearance.

Skull 1470 serves as a good example of the problems encountered in interpreting the reconstruction of highly fragmented fossils. The nearly 300 fragments required two months to reconstruct into a remarkably complete skull. The cranial capacity was estimated to be nearly 800 cm^3. Considering the relatively small size of the skull, this is well within the range of modern human variability. But the relatively long sloping face below the orbits gives 1470 an ape-like appearance. The problem is the maxilla (upper jaw) of this specimen is attached to the cranium by only a narrow shaft of bone, allowing the face to look sloped like an ape or vertical like a human. Alan Walker, who worked with Leaky in interpreting 1470, said: "You could hold the maxilla forward and give it a long face, or you could tuck it in making the face short. How you held it really depended on your preconceptions."[35] All commercially available replicas of the 1470 skull show the maxilla swung forward giving an ape-like appearance.

If one ignores the presumed "date" of 1470 and examines the skull with maxilla swung in, it has the distinct appearance of a human skull. The orbits are slightly wider than tall, and are visible when viewed from the side, much like a human skull. There is no trace of a brow ridge or sagittal crest. The forehead is tall and nearly vertical as in humans. If this skull had been found in strata believed to be less than 200,000 years old, it would have been declared to be a human.

Homo Erectus

Homo erectus includes the early fossil skull "Java man" discovered by the Dutch anatomist Eugene Dubois in 1891, and "Peking man" found in

---

34. The fascinating account of the ten-year dating controversy is reported in Marvin Lubenow, *Bones of Contention* (Grand Rapids, MI: Baker, 1992), p. 247–266.
35. Quoted in Roger Lewin, *Bones of Contention* (New York, NY: Touchstone Books, 1988), p. 160.

Zhoukoudian, China, which comprised 200 human fossils from more than 40 individuals, nearly all of which were lost during World War II. Evolutionists believe *H. erectus* lived between 1.9 million and 144,000 years ago, overlapping with the *Paranthropus* group and modern *Homo sapiens.*

The most complete fossil considered to be *H. erectus* is known as "Turkana Boy," discovered by Richard Leaky in 1984 near Lake Turkana in Kenya. This nearly complete skeleton consisting of 108 bones has been estimated to be about 11–12 years old. The pelvic anatomy indicates that this individual would have been fully bipedal. The brain size was estimated to be about 800 cm^3. Unlike apes, Turkana Boy shows clear evidence of protruding nasal bones.

In general, *H. erectus* had human-like body proportions with relatively short arms and long legs compared to the size of the torso. These fossils are often found in association with tools such as hand axes and cleavers, as well as evidence of fire hearths for cooking.

Homo Heidelbergensis

The first fossil specimen of this type was found in 1908 near Heidelberg, Germany. The specimen was a complete mandible missing the premolars and first two left molars. Most of the fossil specimens claimed to be of this type have been found since 1997 in northern Spain, Ethiopia, Namibia, and South Africa. It is claimed *H. heidelbergensis* lived between 700,000 and 200,000 years ago.

There is an absence of any clear dividing lines between *H. erectus, H. heidelbergensis,* and Neanderthals. As a result, some evolutionists classify *H. heidelbergensis* as *H. erectus.* The problem is that there are no obvious transitions among this group and no unique characteristics that clearly distinguish *H. heidelbergensis* from *H. erectus* and *Neanderthalensis.* This chaos in classification serves to emphasize that evolutionists are not even in agreement on what exactly constitutes the genus *Homo.*

Fossil evidence indicates that the male *H. heidelbergensis* averaged about 5'9" tall with a cranial volume of 1100–1400 cm^3, well within the range of normal modern human variability. There is evidence *H. heidelbergensis* built shelters, buried their dead, and made hand axes and stone-tipped spears for hunting and various other wooden tools.

Homo Neanderthalensis

As Lubenow will discuss more fully in the next chapter, the fossilized bones of nearly 500 Neanderthals have been found since the first recognized

Neanderthal fossils were discovered in the Neander Valley near Dusseldorf, Germany, in 1856. Neanderthal fossils have been found throughout most of central and western Europe, the Carpathians, Balkans, Ukraine, western Russia, and northern Asia. So far, none have been found in Africa. Evolutionists claim that Neanderthals lived between 400,000 and 40,000 years ago, making them broadly overlap with modern *Homo sapiens.*

Neanderthals are clearly human in every respect, having no physical traits that fall outside the range of normal human variability. But the cultural evidence makes their fully human nature even more compelling. Neanderthal fossils have been found in association with numerous artifacts such as tools, musical instruments, jewelry, cooking hearths, fabricated shelters, and evidence that they buried their dead. For many years, Neanderthals have been classified as *Homo sapiens* with a subspecies name *neanderthalensis.* More recently, the name has been changed to *Homo neanderthalensis*, in an effort to distinguish the Neanderthals from modern man.

Homo Floresiensis

The fossils designated *Homo floresiensis* were first found in 2003 on the Island of Flores in Indonesia, and thus far they have been found nowhere else. These fossils are commonly referred to as "Hobbits" because they are estimated to have been only about 3 feet 6 inches tall! To make matters even more enigmatic, bones throughout their skeletons were deformed in places. Evolutionists have been in considerable disagreement about the correct interpretation of the fossil evidence, but the evidence indicates that they were most likely true humans who remained small and deformed because of disease (such as microcephaly or Down syndrome) or malnutrition. They certainly present no evidence for human evolution from apes.[36]

Homo Sapiens

Evolutionists believe that *Homo sapiens* (anatomically modern humans) evolved in Africa about 200,000 years ago. The main difference between *H. sapiens* and most other members of the *Homo* group is that *H. sapiens* is less robustly built. Differences in cranial capacity, pronounced brow ridges, and jaw anatomy are inconsistent.

Fossils of several anatomically modern humans have been found including the following:

---

36. Elizabeth Mitchell, "Is *Homo floresiensis* a Legitimate Human 'Hobbit' Species?" https://answersingenesis.org/human-evolution/homo-floresiensis/homo-floresiensis-legitimate-human-hobbit-species/, 1August 19, 2014.

- Cro-Magnon man — Europe
- Neanderthals — western Europe and Asia
- Grimaldi man — Italy
- Chancelade man — France
- Predmosti — Czech Republic
- Denisovan — southwestern Siberia

There is no agreement among evolutionists regarding which if any of the other claimed species of *Homo* is our direct ancestor. Indeed, not a single hominin can be shown to be the direct ancestor of any other; all is conjecture. But evolutionists generally maintain that *Homo* evolved from some australopithecine.

Conclusion

As we have seen in this survey of the "evidence" presented in the traveling exhibit of the Smithsonian Museum (in a public library near you some day), the classification of man's presumed ancestors (hominins) is constantly in flux and is a subject of often testy disagreements among paleoanthropologists themselves. In contrast, the modern classification of living humans is very straightforward, leaving no room for confusion. Thanks to the success in sequencing the human genome, there is now a consensus among scientists that there is only one living genus of humans (*Homo*), one species (*sapiens*), one subspecies (*sapiens*) and one race (human). This is certainly consistent with all humans sharing ancestry with one pair of human parents, Adam and Eve. There is no scientific reason to doubt the literal truth of Genesis 1–5 about their origin (or the origin of anything else in those chapters).

Chapter 9

Neanderthals: Our Worthy Ancestors

by Marvin Lubenow

There are three lines of evidence demonstrating that the Neanderthals were fully human ancestors of modern humans in spite of their undeserved sordid reputation. First is the most recent: the nuclear DNA evidence. Second, there is strong fossil evidence that Neanderthals lived in close association and integration with modern humans. Third, the cultural evidence demonstrates that Neanderthal behavior and thought was fully human. The evidence in all these areas is extensive.

The DNA Evidence

The turning point in DNA research was the discovery of techniques to identify and manipulate genetic material by using the polymerase chain reaction, affectionately known as PCR. This discovery was such a remarkable breakthrough in modern biotechnology that Kary B. Mullis shared the 1993 Nobel Prize in chemistry for inventing it.

Before PCR, there was a shortage of genetic material for experiments. This material was extremely difficult to obtain because it was always embedded in a living cell. It was hard to get an intact molecule of natural DNA from any organism except from extremely simple viruses. The PCR technique enables researchers to make unlimited copies of any specific DNA sequence independent of the organism from which it came.

Since DNA is such an incredibly complex molecule, when an organism dies its DNA breaks down rather rapidly. Eventually the strands of the molecule are so short that no information can be obtained from them. PCR, with its ability to replicate short strands of DNA, opened the door to the possibility of obtaining genetic information from fossil material, even though that material was degraded. Hence we've seen the successful recovery of mitochondrial DNA (mtDNA) from the discovery of the first recognized Neanderthal bones from the Neander Valley in Germany in 1856. This dramatic recovery was announced in the journal *Cell* on July 11, 1997.

The Swedish Expert on Neanderthals

The man who stands at the forefront of efforts to determine the relationship of modern humans to the Neanderthals is the Swedish biologist Svante Pääbo, Director of the Department of Genetics at the Max Planck Institute of Evolutionary Anthropology in Leipzig, Germany. Pääbo led a team of more than 50 scientists who on May 7, 2010, published in *Science*,[1] one of the most significant papers ever to be published in the history of anthropology. It was the genome sequenced from an extinct form of humans — a Neanderthal.

Geneticist and creationist, Dr. John C. Sanford (Cornell University), has the clearest definition of the term, *genome.*

> An organism's genome is the sum total of all its genetic parts, including all its chromosomes, genes, and nucleotides. A genome is an instruction manual that specifies a particular form of life. The human genome is a manual that instructs human cells to be human cells and the human body to be the human body. There is no information system designed by man that can even begin to compare to the simplest genome in complexity.[2]

It was through the sequencing of the Neanderthal genome that Pääbo discovered that humans and Neanderthals had interbred. Pääbo has had a lifelong interest in ancient DNA, but museums were hesitant to let him use specimens from their collections. Only in 1996 did he receive his first Neanderthal specimen, and in 2005 he began to sequence the Neanderthal genome, publishing it in 2010. In 2014 he published his most refined version, finding that Neanderthal DNA makes up 1% to 2% of the genome of many modern humans. In his recent book, *The Neanderthals*, Pääbo writes,

> The finding most likely to create controversy was that Neanderthals had contributed parts of their genome to present-day people

1. R.E. Green et al., "A Draft Sequence of the Neanderthal Genome," *Science* 328 (May 7, 2010): 710–722, plus Supplement.
2. John C. Sanford, *Genetic Entropy & the Mystery of the Genome*, third edition (Waterloo, NY: FMS Publications, 2008), p. 1, emphasis in the original.

> of Eurasia. But since we had come to this conclusion three times using three different approaches, I felt that we had definitively laid this question to rest. Future work would surely clarify the details of when, where, and how it happened, but we had definitively shown that it *had* happened.[3]

Also in 2014, teams led by David Reich (Harvard Medical School) and Josh Akey (University of Washington, Seattle) "pieced together a substantial portion — about 20% and 40% respectively — of the Neanderthal genome from bits lurking in the genomes of hundreds of living humans."[4] Henry Gee, a senior editor of *Nature*, tells of a humorous incident at a Royal Society meeting in London in 2013. David Reich spoke on the close relationship between Neanderthals and *Homo sapiens*. This irked a member of the audience. "Are you telling me," he asked in cut-glass tones, "that these different species copulated with one another?" Gee said he was seized by an impulse to stand up and reply, "Not only did they copulate, but their union was blessed with issue!"[5] The fact that unions of the Neanderthals with *Homo sapiens* were "blessed with issue," according to the DNA evidence, demonstrates that the Neanderthals were not a "different species" but were "human-kind," according to God's Word.

Pääbo then makes the most amazing statement about the Neanderthals that I have read by an evolutionist in my 30 years of studying the subject. He states,

> . . . we had by now shown . . . that there had been mixing between Neanderthals and modern humans, I knew that taxonomic wars over Neanderthal classification would continue, since there is no definition of a species perfectly describing the case. Many would say that a species is a group of organisms that can produce fertile offspring with each other and cannot do so with members of other groups. From that perspective *we had shown that Neanderthals and modern humans were the same species.*[6]

Initially working with mitochondrial DNA (mtDNA), Pääbo had determined, in 1997, that humans had not mixed with Neanderthals. However, when working with nuclear DNA, his computers began to spew out some

3. Svante Pääbo, *Neanderthal Man: In Search of Lost Genomes* (New York: Basic Books, 2014), p. 215. Italics are in the original.
4. Ewin Callaway, "The Neanderthal in the Family," *Nature* 507 (March 27, 2014): 416.
5. Henry Gee, "The Human Puzzle," *Nature*, 506 (February 6, 2014): 30.
6. Pääbo, *Neanderthal Man*, p. 237, emphasis is mine.

surprising results. Modern humans clearly had mixed with Neanderthals. David Reich, also working in this area, found that Neanderthal DNA seemed to be more similar to the DNA of Europeans and Asians than it was to African DNA. It is reported,

> "We were suspicious of the result," Reich says. "We found signals of mixture and then worked very hard to make them go away." He tried for a year, but to no avail. Finally, Reich and his colleagues had no choice but to conclude that Neanderthals had mated with humans. They estimated that the DNA of living Asians and Europeans was (on average) 2.5 percent Neanderthal. They had to reject a pure version of the out-of-Africa model. Instead, their model was closer to out-of-Africa-and-get-to-know-some-Neanderthals-very-well.[7]

Pääbo was most surprised at the reception of his work by young-earth creationists in the United States. He writes,

> First, there are "young-earth creationists," who believe that the earth, the heavens, and all life were created by direct acts of God sometime between 5,700 and 10,000 years ago. They tend to consider Neanderthals as "fully human," sometimes saying they were another, now extinct "race" that was scattered after the fall of the Tower of Babel. As a consequence, young-earth creationists had no problem with our finding that Neanderthals and modern humans had mixed.[8]

Just as Pääbo was surprised at the reception of young-earth creationists, he was shocked at the response of old-earth creationists:

> One major old-earth ministry is "Reasons to Believe," headed by a Hugh Ross. He believes that modern humans were specially created around 50,000 years ago and that Neanderthals weren't humans, but animals. Ross and other old-earth creationists didn't like the finding that Neanderthals and modern humans had mixed. Nick [Matzke, UC Berkeley] sent me a transcript from a radio show in which he [Ross] commented on our work, saying interbreeding was predictable "because the story of Genesis is early humanity getting into exceptionally wicked behavior practices," and that God

---

7. Carl Zimmer, "Interbreeding with Neanderthals," *Discover* (March 2013), p. 42.
8. Pääbo, *Neanderthal Man*, p. 221.

> may have had to "forcibly scatter humanity over the face of the earth" to stop this kind of interbreeding, which he compared to "animal bestiality."[9]

Questions arise in dealing with human fossil categories. The biblical word *kind* and the scientific word *species* are not equal and should never be equated. The scientific concept, *species*, is itself very complex and has not yet been defined with finality. Using the Neanderthals as an illustration, if we refer to the Neanderthals as *Homo sapiens neanderthalensis*, we are calling the Neanderthals a sub-species of modern humans, separate from but equal to *Homo sapiens sapiens.* The sub-species classification allows for reproduction among its members. This seems to be the better classification for the Neanderthals because the DNA evidence is quite strong that Neanderthals and modern humans have reproduced together in the past. However, the plot thickens. If we introduce the *time* element, the *species* concept becomes even more complex. Some authorities feel that because the Neanderthals are extinct, they cannot be compared to a living species such as we are. However, DNA studies show that about one to four percent of our genes as living humans come from the Neanderthals, and geneticists are attempting to reassemble the genome of the Neanderthals from those bits and pieces inside us modern humans. Does that mean that the Neanderthals are not extinct after all? This issue will not be settled here, or perhaps ever. Stay tuned.

The Fossil Evidence

Regarding the Neanderthals and their alleged setting in human evolution, my extensive research on this subject has convinced me that human evolution, not Genesis 1, is the real myth. Although I do not accept the evolutionary time scale, I use it for the sake of illustration. When I began my research on the fossil evidence for human evolution, I was curious to know how many human and alleged pre-human fossils had been discovered. My search took me to the back stacks of graduate school libraries, but I could find nothing up to date. There was the 3-volume *Catalogue of Fossil Hominids* published

9. Ibid., p. 221. I added bracketed material for clarity. Hugh Ross's Reasons to Believe website (http://www.reasons.org/rtb-101/hominids, accessed May 25, 2016) states, "RTB's biblical creation model identifies 'hominids,' Neanderthals, Homo erectus and others, as animals created by God. These extraordinary creatures walked erect and possessed enough intelligence to assemble crude tools and even adopt some level of 'culture.' The RTB model maintains that the hominids were not spiritual beings made in God's image. RTB's model reserves this status exclusively for Adam and Eve and their descendants (modern humans)."

by the British Museum, which I obtained, but that ended in the mid-1970s, and the hay-day of human fossil discovery came later. My search resulted in the most complete list of human fossils assembled — at least available to the public.[10] This virtually complete list of human fossils as of 2004 gives the lie to human evolution.

Evolutionists have divided the human fossil assemblage into categories as follows: Anatomically modern *Homo sapiens*, Neanderthals, Early African/Asian *Homo sapiens, Homo erectus*, and *Homo habilis*. When the fossils in these categories are all put on a time chart, according to the evolutionists' dating and descriptions, the result is nothing less than shocking.[11] Fossils that lie morphologically within the range of modern *Homo sapiens* go all the way back to 3.75 million years ago (Mya) without any evolution taking place beyond normal genetic variation. These include fossil footprints that indicate that bipedal locomotion is as old as humans are. Neanderthal fossils go back to 800 thousand years ago (Kya) without showing any evolution beyond normal genetic variation, and no indication of their evolving into modern *Homo sapiens*. The Early African/Asian *Homo sapiens* fossils go back to 600 Kya without showing any evolution beyond normal genetic variation, and no indication of their evolving into *Homo sapiens*. The *Homo erectus* fossils go back to 1.95 Mya without showing any evolution beyond normal genetic variation, and no indication of their evolving into *Homo sapiens*. The *Homo habilis* category is, in my opinion, invalid. It allegedly goes from 1.5 Mya to 2.0 Mya. However, *Homo habilis* did not do what it was "invented" to do — provide the needed transition between the australopithecines and the genus *Homo*. Milford Wolpoff (University of Michigan) stated it well: "The phylogenetic outlook suggests that if there weren't a *Homo habilis* we would have to invent one."[12] More than 40 years after his father, Louis Leakey, "invented" *Homo habilis*, Richard Leakey describes the problem:

> Of the several dozen specimens that have been said at one time or another to belong to this species [*Homo habilis*], at least half probably don't. But there is no consensus as to which 50 percent

10. See the extensive fossil charts in Marvin L. Lubenow, *Bones of Contention: A Creationist Assessment of Human Fossils* (Grand Rapids, MI: Baker Books, 1992; revised & enlarged, 2004). In the 1992 edition, see pages 54–55, 67, 79, 121–123, 128, 170–171, 180; in the 2004 revised edition, pages 336–353.
11. See Lubenow, *Bones of Contention*, revised edition, 2004.
12. Milford H. Wolpoff, review of *Olduvai Gorge, Volume 4: The Skulls, Endocasts, and Teeth of Homo habilis*, by Phillip V. Tobias, *American Journal of Physical Anthropology* 89, no. 3 (November 1992): 402.

> should be excluded. No one anthropologist's 50 percent is quite the same as another's.[13]

The human fossil record has failed its evolutionist practitioners. The average person is not aware of this failure because the evolutionist community has said virtually nothing about it. Many evolutionists *themselves* may not realize it. One of the few public statements about it was an item in *Nature* in the year 2000, by J.J. Hublin (also from the Max Planck Institute of Evolutionary Anthropology). He stated: "The once-popular fresco showing a single file of marching hominids becoming ever more vertical, tall, and hairless now appears to be a fiction."[14]

Now the evolutionist community has turned to the molecules, DNA, to try to demonstrate what it could not demonstrate with the fossils. These various fossil categories all show morphological consistency throughout their long history. The fossil record does not show them evolving from something into something else. Furthermore, anatomically modern *Homo sapiens,* Neanderthals, archaic *Homo sapiens*, and *Homo erectus* all lived as contemporaries at one time or another. Having believed a lie, evolutionists are not able to see the truth. What the human fossil record shows is not evolution, but the vast genetic variety within the human family. Because of vastly smaller population sizes in the past, as well as much greater isolation of populations, the human genome allowed much greater variation within humankind in the past than it allows today.

A New Kid on the Block

It was the skimpiest bit of evidence: just a tiny piece of a finger bone and two outsized teeth. Michael Shunkov (Russian Academy of Science) found them in Denisova Cave in the Altai mountains of Southern Siberia, where Russia, Kazakhstan, Mongolia, and China meet. The cave is named after a hermit called Denis who lived there in the 1700s. Suspicious that the bones might have a story to tell, Shunkov bagged them, labeled them, and sent them off for analysis — expecting that Svante Pääbo would find that they belonged to a Neanderthal. However, when Pääbo's equipment started to crank out the results, it didn't exactly match the DNA of the Neanderthals, nor did it match the DNA of modern humans. She was a little girl, but she turned out to be something quite big. Pääbo writes,

---

13. Richard Leakey and Roger Lewin, *Origins Reconsidered* (New York: Doubleday, 1992), p. 112. I added bracketed material for clarity.
14. *Nature* 403 (January 27, 2000): 363.

> . . . the nuclear genome of the Denisova finger bone was more closely related to the Neanderthal genome than to the genomes of people living today. In fact, it seemed to be only slightly more different from the Neanderthal genome than the deepest differences one could find among humans living today.[15]

In other words, the Neanderthals had a secret relative.

> Knowing that Neanderthals and humans had interbred, [David] Reich and his colleagues looked carefully for Denisovan DNA in the genomes of living humans. They found it in genomes from two populations, one from New Guinea and another from the nearby island of Bougainville. As much as 5 percent of their DNA came from the vanished Denisovans.[16]

Since the New Guinea Papuans also carried the Neanderthal genes, this meant that about seven percent of the genome of the Papuans came from earlier forms of humans — a remarkable finding. Vestiges of the Denisovan genome were also found in the Australian Aborigines and in the Mamanwa people of the Philippines. Does this mean that neither Neanderthals nor Denisovans are totally extinct? No traces were found in Mongolia, China, Cambodia, or anywhere else on mainland Asia, or in South America. Pääbo believes that there are other human relatives lurking in the human genome waiting to be discovered.[17]

A Cave in Spain Makes It Plain

"Denisovans are a genome in search of a fossil," said David Reich.[18] A site in Spain has put (fossil) bones on those Denisovan DNA molecules. In 2013, Pääbo received DNA from a fossil called *Homo Heidelbergensis*, found in a cave in northern Spain. At "430,000 years old," it is claimed to be the oldest human genome ever sequenced, and it revealed similarities to that of Denisovans. A unique assemblage of 28 ancient fossil individuals was found in the Sierra de Atapuerca limestone hills of northern Spain at a cave site known as Sima de los Huesos (Pit of the Bones). But Sima de los Huesos is no ordinary cave. It is a very deep, narrow, vertical cave with the bottom not visible from the top. The individuals who lived nearby at that time used this cave for burial purposes — as a mortuary. When a member of their group

15. Pääbo, *Neanderthal Man*, p. 242.
16. Carl Zimmer, "Interbreeding with Neanderthals," *Discover*, March 2013, p. 44.
17. Pääbo, *Neanderthal Man*, p. 249.
18. Michael Marshall, "Mystery relations," *New Scientist* (April 5, 2014): 38.

died, the body was carried to this hidden niche and deposited in the cave where it fell to the bottom and decayed beyond the reach of predators. For many years the site had been disturbed by amateurs. In 1992, a team led by Juan Luis Arsuaga (Universidad Complutense de Madrid) finally reached undisturbed fossil deposits.[19] What is remarkable about this site is that it gives us a whole population from the same age and place for study and comparison.

These fossils from Sima de los Huesos are fascinating because they show the folly of attempting to place humans in an evolutionary sequence either through fossils or through DNA. A 2014 *Nature* article, based on an mtDNA sample from one individual, showed that the Sima de los Huesos fossils were more closely related to the Denisovans than to the Neanderthals. A 2016 *Nature* article, authored by 14 DNA specialists, including Juan Luis Arsuaga and Svante Pääbo, states: "Here we recover nuclear DNA sequences from two specimens, which show that the Sima de los Huesos hominins were related to Neanderthals rather than to Denisovans."[20] This contradiction between *mtDNA* and *nuclear DNA* is also revealed in Svante Pääbo's book *The Neanderthals*. He tells in his book of an article in 1997, written with two others, in which they said: "The Neanderthal *mtDNA* sequence thus supports a scenario in which modern humans arose recently in Africa as a distinct species and replaced Neanderthals with little or no interbreeding."[21] That finding strongly supported the "Out of Africa" model of human evolution. In 2010, Pääbo published his *Magnum opus*, the complete Neanderthal genome, based upon *nuclear DNA*. He writes: ". . . we had shown that Neanderthals and modern humans were the same species."[22] That finding contradicts the "Out of Africa" model.

The entire fossil collection at Sima de los Huesos is nothing short of stunning. These fossils show so much variation within a single contemporaneous population that it gives the lie to the concept of human evolution. The "muddle in the middle" that paleoanthropologists have spoken of regarding the European fossils was the belief that all five grades of evolution within the Genus *Homo* had been represented in Europe. These five grades are now shown to be a fiction. These fossils all belong to one variable population. For instance, one of the Sima de los Huesos adult skulls is one of the smallest

19. Juan Luis Arsuaga, *The Neanderthal's Necklace*, trans. Andy Klatt (New York: Four Walls Eight Windows, 2002), p. 224, 271–272.
20. Matthias Meyer et al., "Nuclear DNA Sequences from the Middle Pleistocene Sima de los Huesos Hominins," *Nature* 531 (March 24, 2016): 504.
21. Pääbo, *Neanderthal Man*, p. 19.
22. Ibid., p. 237.

ever recovered from that time period while another adult skull is one of the largest. The physical variation found within this one fossil assemblage embraces all of the variation found within the entire European human fossil collection and denies human evolution one of its most striking showcases.

Chris Stringer, an "Out of Africa" supporter, believed that there were many species among the European fossils. After studying the wide variation within the Sima de los Huesos fossils, he recognized, "In spite of all the variation they display, they get sucked in with the Neanderthals. Once that happens, it becomes very difficult to prevent the rest of the European material from getting sucked in as well."[23] Stringer developed a list of 15 cranial characteristics. He concluded that the Sima de los Huesos fossils have seven similarities with *Homo erectus* fossils, seven similarities with *Homo sapiens* fossils, and ten similarities with Neanderthal fossils. He now chooses to call them all Neanderthals.[24]

The only legitimate species criterion is the fertility test. Obviously, that test cannot be applied to human fossils. However, by implication, it can be applied to the Sima de los Huesos fossils. They represent one local community. We have every reason to believe that these humans were all inter-fertile and represent the same species. Hence, when we see this amazing genetic variety elsewhere among human fossils, we can extrapolate and explain it within a biblical creationist context.

The Search for the Real Neanderthals

One hundred and sixty years have passed since the first recognized Neanderthal fossil individual was discovered in 1856 in the Neander Valley in Germany. Fossil remains of approximately 500 individual Neanderthals, ranging from almost complete skeletons to just a few tiny fragments, have been recovered. They have been found in various places in Europe and the Middle East. We should know them quite well. Not only do we have more fossils of them and more of their artifacts than of any other fossil group, but they also lived in recent times before modern humans. Yet, to evolutionists they are still mysterious with many questions about them just now being answered.

When the Neanderthals were first discovered, they were considered to be a separate species, *Homo neanderthalensis*. Since reproductive capability is normally on the species level, the significance of the original designation was that the Neanderthals were considered different enough from modern humans so as to not be able to reproduce with us.

23. James Shreeve, "Infants, Cannibals, and the Pit of Bones," *Discover* (January 1994): 40.
24. Ibid.

To young-earth creationists, the Neanderthals are not mysterious but incredibly intriguing. Based upon the Genesis testimony, we have always viewed the Neanderthals as the fully human ancestors of some modern humans — probably Europeans and western Asians, Hence, creationists have referred to them as *Homo sapiens sapiens*, or as a sub-species of modern humans: *Homo sapiens neanderthalensis*. Or, using biblical terminology, *human-kind*. Either way, we believed that they would be fully capable of reproducing with modern humans if they were living today. That has just been confirmed scientifically. From a biblical perspective, they were a post-Flood, Ice Age people, specializing in hunting the large, grazing animals that were abundant toward the end of the Ice Age and afterward.

In the 1960s, new studies on the Neanderthals revealed that their skeletal distinctions were not that significant, and even evolutionists gave them sub-species status with modern humans, *Homo sapiens neanderthalensis*. That situation persisted until it became possible to study DNA in fossil bones. Thanks to sequencing of *nuclear DNA*, it is now clear that Neanderthals did share genes with modern humans — not surprising if they were fully human. Genesis 11:1–9, the Tower of Babel and the confounding of human languages, conveys tremendous explanatory information. Every human scattered possessed the full human genome. However, every human scattered also carried some unique characteristics — the potential variety that God built into the human genome. The scattering and the resulting isolation of populations guaranteed that minor variations would be expressed in the human family. This certainly explains today's various "races" (a word impossible to accurately define) as well as the extinct peoples, the Neanderthals and the Denisovans of the past. The vast world population of today and its homogenizing effect upon the genome makes it far less likely that such unique groups would arise now.

The Fossil Evidence

Neanderthals and Modern Humans Were an Integrated Population

The "classic" Neanderthal differs somewhat from the typical modern human — the Neanderthal skull is a bit flatter and elongated, the chin is rounder, and the skeleton is more robust. However, there is much overlap. In fact, there should never have been a question about Neanderthal's status in the human family. When the first Neanderthal was discovered in 1856, even "Darwin's bulldog," Thomas Huxley, recognized that it was fully human and not an evolutionary ancestor. Donald Johanson, who discovered the famous fossil, Lucy, writes,

Neanderthal museum exhibit pre-2010

"From his bestial 19th-century persona to just another guy in a suit, Neanderthals have been pigeonholed according to the times."*

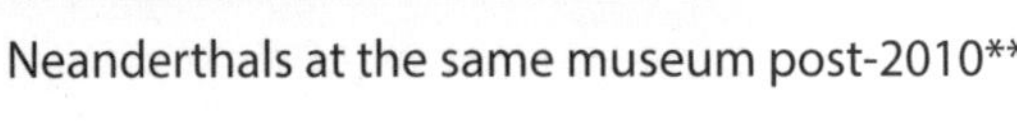

Neanderthals at the same museum post-2010**

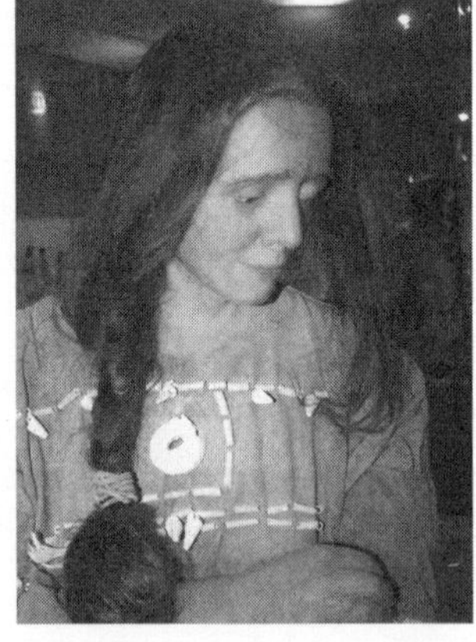

* Rick Gore, "The Dawn of Humans: Neandertals," *National Geographic*, vol. 189:1 (January 1996), p. 32–33. The quote is Gore's words in his caption for the picture. In the article, Gore uses both spellings for this man. A 1983 version and a 1909 version of the Neanderthals are pictured.

** Photo of old man: Uniesert, Creative Commons, Wikipedia. Photo of young man: Wikipedia. Photo of woman: Wikipedia.

> From a collection of modern human skulls Huxley was able to select a series with features leading "by insensible gradations" from an average modern specimen to the Neanderthal skull. In other words, it wasn't qualitatively different from present-day *Homo sapiens*.[25]

What Huxley discovered 150 years ago — gradations from Neanderthals to modern humans — is also clearly seen in the fossil record today. We are not referring to an evolutionary transition from earlier Neanderthals to later modern humans. We are referring to morphological gradations between Neanderthals and modern humans both living at the same time as contemporaries and representing a single human population.

Whereas evolutionists have chosen to divide these Europeans into two categories — Neanderthals and anatomically modern *Homo sapiens* — the individual fossils do not fit into those categories. There is a wide range of variation among modern humans, and there is also much variation within the Neanderthal category. A number of fossils in each group are very close to a subjective line that divides the two groups. The placement of that line is dependent upon the individual paleoanthropologist making the assessment. Since these fossil individuals could be categorized either way, they constitute a seamless gradation between Neanderthals and modern humans. They demonstrate that the distinction made by evolutionists is an artificial one.

Among fossils usually classified as Neanderthal are at least 26 individuals from six different sites who are clearly close to that subjective line which divides Neanderthals from anatomically modern *Homo sapiens*. These fossils constitute part of that continuum or gradation. Evolutionists recognize these fossils as departing from the classic Neanderthal morphology and describe them as "progressive" or "advanced" Neanderthals. Their shape is sometimes explained as the result of gene flow (hybridization) with more modern populations. This supports the interpretation of nuclear DNA that the Neanderthals and modern humans are the same species — since reproduction is on the species level.

Completing that continuum or gradation from Neanderthals to modern humans are at least 107 individuals from five sites who are usually grouped with fossils categorized as anatomically modern humans. However, since they are close to that subjective line which divides them from the Neanderthals, they are often described as "archaic moderns" or stated to have "Neanderthal affinities" or "Neanderthal features."

---

25. D. Johanson and J. Shreeve, *Lucy's Child* (New York: William Morrow and Company, 1989), p. 49.

Creationists maintain that the differences found in the fossil material between Neanderthals and modern humans are the result of geography, not evolution. Of the 133 fossil individuals that are "close to the line" between Neanderthal and modern European morphology, all but four of them are from Eastern or Central Europe. If the differences between the Neanderthals and modern Europeans were ones reflecting a degree of geographic isolation, perhaps Eastern Europe is where the hybridization or the homogenization began.

If the fossils mentioned above could constitute a gradation within a single, genetically diverse population, an obvious question is, "Why do evolutionists place them in two separate species?" The answer is that the theory of human evolution demands such separation. Humans are alleged to have evolved from the australopithecines — a group of extinct primates. In other words, we evolved from beings who were not only outside of our species, but were also outside of our genus. Hence, the evolutionist must create categories, species, or intermediate steps between the australopithecines and modern humans in an attempt to create an alleged evolutionary sequence. Fossils that are very similar are placed in one species. Fossils with some differences from the first group are placed in another species.

Evolutionists must create species, whether they are legitimate or not, in an attempt to show the stages or steps that they believe we passed through in our evolution from lower primates. Hence, many evolutionists today place the Neanderthals in a species separate from modern humans. Some evolutionists believe that the Neanderthals evolved into (some) modern humans. Others believe that the Neanderthals were a failed evolutionary experiment that did not quite make it to full humanity and became extinct. In either case, many evolutionists do not believe that the Neanderthals themselves were fully human, at least in a behavioral sense. The fossil evidence suggests otherwise. The full range of genetic and behavioral variation within the human family encompasses the Neanderthals.

Neanderthal Burial Practice

Approximately 500 Neanderthal fossil individuals have been discovered so far at about 124 sites in Europe, the Near East, and western Asia. This number includes those European archaic *Homo sapiens* fossils that are now called Neanderthal or pre-Neanderthal. Of these 500 Neanderthal individuals, at least 258 of them represent burials — all of them burials in caves or rock shelters. Further, it is obvious that caves were used as family burial grounds or cemeteries, as numerous sites show. The reason we have so many

Neanderthal fossils is because they did bury their dead. The bodies were thus protected from carnivore activity. Most anthropologists recognize burial as a very human and a very religious act. Richard Klein (Stanford University) writes: "Neanderthal graves present the best case for Neanderthal spirituality or religion."[26] Only humans bury their dead.

Neanderthals and Modern Humans Were Buried Together

Perhaps the strongest evidence that Neanderthals were fully human and part of our biblical "kind" is that at four sites people of Neanderthal morphology and people of modern human morphology were buried together. In all of life, few desires are stronger than the desire to be buried with one's own people. Skhul Cave, Mount Carmel, Israel, is considered to be a burial site of anatomically modern *Homo sapiens* individuals. Yet, Skhul IV and Skhul IX fossil skulls are closer to the Neanderthal configuration than they are to modern humans.[27] Qafzeh, Galilee, Israel, is also considered to be an anatomically modern burial site. However, Qafzeh skull 6 is clearly Neanderthal in its morphology.[28] Tabun Cave, Mount Carmel, Israel, is one of the classic Neanderthal burial sites. But the Tabun C2 mandible is more closely aligned with modern mandibles found elsewhere.[29] The Krapina Rock Shelter, Croatia, is one of the most studied Neanderthal burial sites. At least 75 individuals are buried there. The remains are fragmentary, making diagnosis difficult. However, the addition of several newly identified fragments to the Krapina A skull (now known as Krapina 1) reveals it to be much more modern than was previously thought, indicating that it is intermediate in morphology between Neanderthals and modern humans.[30]

That Neanderthals and anatomically modern humans were buried together constitutes strong evidence that they lived together, worked together, intermarried, and were accepted as members of the same family, clan, and community. The false distinction made by evolutionists today was not made by the ancients. To call the Neanderthals "Cave Men" is to give a false picture of who they were and why caves were significant in their lives.

26. Richard G. Klein, *The Human Career: Human Biological and Cultural Origins* (Chicago: The University of Chicago Press, 1989), p. 236–237.
27. Robert S. Corruccini, "Metrical Reconsideration of the Skhul IV and IX and Border Cave 1 Crania in the Context of Modern Human Origins," *American Journal of Physical Anthropology* 87:4 (April 1992): 433–445.
28. Ibid., p. 440–442.
29. R. M. Quam and F. H. Smith, "Reconsideration of the Tabun C2 'Neanderthal,'" *American Journal of Physical Anthropology* Supplement 22 (1996): 192.
30. N. Minugh-Purvis and J. Radovcic, "Krapina A: Neanderthal or Not?" *American Journal of Physical Anthropology* Supplement 12 (1991) 132.

The human family is a unified family. "From one man He [God] made every nation of men, that they should inhabit the whole earth" (Acts 17:26).[31]

Neanderthal Burial Practice and the Burial Practice in Genesis

In comparing the Neanderthal burial practice with Genesis, I do not wish to imply that Abraham or his ancestors or his descendants were Neanderthals. What the relationship was — if any — between the people of Genesis and the Neanderthals we do not know. Young-earth creationists tend to believe that the Neanderthals were a post-Flood people. What is striking is that the burial practice of the Neanderthals seems to be identical with that of the post-Flood people of Genesis. Genesis 23:17–20 records a business transaction between Abraham and the Hittite, Ephron. Abraham wanted to purchase property in order to bury Sarah. We read,

> Afterward Abraham buried his wife Sarah in the cave in the field of Machpelah near Mamre (which is at Hebron) in the land of Canaan. So the field and the cave in it were deeded to Abraham by the Hittites as a burial site (Gen. 23:19–20).

Upon his death (Gen. 25:7–11), Abraham was buried in that same cave. In Genesis 49:29–32, Jacob instructs his sons that he, too, is to be buried in that cave where Abraham and Sarah were buried. We then learn that Jacob buried his wife Leah there and that Isaac and Rebekah were buried there also. Abraham and Sarah, Isaac and Rebekah, and Jacob and Leah were all buried in the cave in the field of Machpelah which Genesis 23:20 states Abraham purchased "as a burial site." Only Sarah died in the geographic area of the cave. All of the others had to be transported some distance to be buried there, and Jacob's body had to be brought up from Egypt. It was important then, as it is today, to be buried with family and loved ones. Certainly, if the Neanderthal burial practice was similar to that of the people of Genesis, it suggests that the Neanderthals were very much like us. It is not without significance that both Lazarus and Jesus were buried in caves (Matt. 27:60; John 11:38), and that this practice has continued in many cultures up to modern times.

The Archaeological and Cultural Evidence

The claim that the Neanderthals were culture-thin is surprising considering the evidence now available. The Neanderthals are alleged to be less than fully human because, it has been claimed, they had no glue or adhesives for

31. Quoted Bible verses in this chapter are from the New International Version (1978).

hafting tools, no unequivocal art objects, no boats, canoes, or ships, no bows and arrows, no cave paintings, no domesticated animals or plants, no hooks, nets, or spears for fishing, no lamps, no metallurgy, no mortars and pestles, no musical instruments, no needles or awls for sewing, no ropes for carrying things, no sculpture, and no long distance overland trade.

The Indians of Tierra del Fuego, at the extreme southern tip of South America, were hunter-gatherers. They were considered to be among the most primitive people on earth. Ashley Montagu (Princeton University) writes about these Indians,

> [They] . . . live in perhaps the worst climate in the world, a climate of bitter cold, snow, and sleet, and heavy rains a great deal of the time, yet they usually remain entirely naked. During extremely cold weather they may wear a loose cape of fur and rub their bodies with grease.[32]

When Charles Darwin went on his famous around-the-world voyage, he visited the Fuegians. In his fascinating work, *The Voyage of the Beagle*, Darwin describes Fuegian life and culture.[33] It is difficult to compare people living in historic times with people we know only from fossils and cultural remains. Nevertheless, a strong case could be made that the cultural inventory of the Fuegians was less complex and extensive than was the cultural inventory of the Neanderthals. Yet, no one considered the Fuegians to be less than fully human, except Darwin, who believed that they were too primitive (sub-human) to be evangelized. Darwin was proven wrong by missionaries who did evangelize them. In fairness to Darwin, he later admitted his mistake regarding the spiritual potential of the Fuegians.[34]

One of the most brutal episodes in human history was the genocide of the full-blooded Tasmanians about a century ago. The genocide was allowed because evolutionists claimed that the Tasmanians were not fully human. The reason their full humanity was doubted was because evolutionists applied the false test of culture. Jared Diamond (UCLA) states that any anthropologist would describe the Tasmanians as "the most primitive people still alive in recent centuries."[35] Of all of the people in the world, they were considered

32. Ashley Montagu, *Man: His First Two Million Years* (New York, NY: Dell Publishing Co. 1969), p. 143–144.
33. Charles Darwin, *Voyage of the Beagle*, in the Everyman's Library series (London, England: J.M. Dent & Sons, 1959, reprint of 1836 original), p. 194–219.
34. Francis Darwin, ed., *Life and Letters of Charles Darwin* (London, England: John Murray, 1888, rev. 7th ed.), III:127–128.
35. Jared Diamond, "Ten Thousand Years of Solitude," *Discover* (March 1993): 51.

among the least technologically advanced. Hence, they were considered less evolved than other people. Like the Indians of Tierra del Fuego, the cultural inventory of the Tasmanians, as described by Diamond, was less complex and extensive than was the cultural inventory of the Neanderthals. Yet the Tasmanians proved that they were fully human. How did they prove it? They passed the fertility test. Although all full-blooded Tasmanians are now gone, there are many Tasmanians of mixed blood today because in those early days many Caucasian men married Tasmanian women.

Neanderthals as Occupational Hunters

The lifestyle of the Neanderthals can be summed up in just one word — hunting. To study the Neanderthal sites with their collections of the largest game animals gives the overwhelming impression that they were occupational hunters. Fossils of large animals are found in association with Neanderthal fossils at over half of the Neanderthal sites. The evidence is summarized:

1. The largest kinds of animals found at Neanderthal sites are the very same types of animals used by humans for food today. These animals are usually very large grazers, unlikely to be carried to the sites by carnivores.
2. Many show cut marks made by stone tools indicating that they were butchered.
3. The Neanderthals had the thrusting spears, hand axes, and other weapons to effectively hunt these animals.
4. The Neanderthal fossils show the injuries typical of those who handle large animals such as ranchers and cowboys.

Thus, it seems impossible to deny the Neanderthals the reputation they so richly deserve — stunning big game hunters. Especially stunning is that about half of the Neanderthal sites that have fossil animal remains have fossils of elephants and woolly mammoths. Paleontologist Juan Luis Arsuaga writes,

> The elephant is the largest possible game animal on the face of the earth. . . . Beyond the physical capacity of prehistoric humans to hunt elephants, the crux of the polemic is in their mental capacity to develop and execute complex hunting strategies based on seasonally predictable conditions. Planning is powerful evidence for [human] consciousness.[36]

36. Juan Luis Arsuaga, *The Neanderthal's Necklace* (New York, NY: Four Walls Eight Windows, 2002), p. 273. Bracketed material added for clarity.

At Schöningen, Germany, were found three fir spears, fashioned like modern javelins, cleft at one end to accommodate stone points. They are the world's oldest throwing spears, dated by evolutionists at about 400,000 years old. They are six to seven and one-half feet long, and required powerful people to use them. It proves that there were big-game hunters at that time, and suggests a long tradition of hunting with such tools. It is presumed that the Neanderthals used them.[37] "If they are what they seem to be, these would be the first known weapons to incorporate two materials, in this case stone and wood. The Neanderthals almost surely used the many stone points found in Mousterian sites for the same purpose."[38] At the same site was found on a bed of black peat a fossilized horse pelvis with a wooden lance sticking out of it.[39]

Neanderthals and Art

There is a problem in the recognition of evidence for "art" among the Neanderthals. The presence of art is considered a major indication of full humanity when dealing with fossil humans. Not only is other evidence regarding the full humanity of the Neanderthals not given proper weight, but the evidence for art among the Neanderthals has been seriously under-reported because of a subjective bias. The reason for this bias is an attempt to protect the field of paleoanthropology from the charge of racism.[40] It should also be noted that many modern people, including highly educated ones, have no artistic skills.

Prehistorian Paul Bahn, who writes regarding the attempts to make the Neanderthals a separate species, confirms this under-reporting of art among the Neanderthals:

> . . . in essence this boils down to stating that the Neanderthals were so different from ourselves that a firm line can be drawn between them and us, a view that is by no means universally held. To shore up this approach, all the growing body of evidence for "art" before 40,000 years ago is simply dismissed and ignored.[41]

---

37. Hartmut Thieme, "Lower Palaeolithic Hunting Spears from Germany," *Nature* 385 (February 27, 1987): 807–810.
38. Arsuaga, *The Neanderthal's Necklace*, p. 273.
39. Ibid., p. 182.
40. The details of this very real problem are beyond the scope of this chapter, but are fully explained in Section III of my book, *Bones of Contention* (Grand Rapids, MI: Baker Books, 2004, rev. ed.).
41. Paul Bahn, "Better Late Than Never," a review of *Timewalkers: The Prehistory of Global Colonization* by Clive Gamble, *Nature* 369 (June 16, 1994): 531.

Tools are found at most Neanderthal sites. Since they are not the artistic, delicate tools that are found in the Upper Stone Age, it has been assumed that the Neanderthals had not evolved mentally to the stage where they could make such tools. This criticism is absurd. The Neanderthal tools are what one would expect for a hunting people. Their tools are the utensils of the butcher shop, not the sterling silver utensils of a fancy French restaurant. Many archaeologists miss the point. It is not just a fancy tool that is a work of art; any tool is a work of artistic conceptualization.

Juan Luis Arsuaga states that making a stone tool is actually a work of art or sculpture. He writes: "Purposeful chipping at a stone is like sculpture in that it requires carefully chosen target points, very accurately aimed blows, a correctly calculated angle of impact, and well-regulated force."[42]

The story is told of a child who watched a sculptor take a large block of granite and over many weeks produced the statue of a man. Overcome with awe, the child asked the sculptor: "How did you know that man was in the rock?" The sculptor "knew" that the man was in the rock in the same way that the Neanderthals "knew" that the tool was in the stone. Both works are the product of a mind with conceptual ability. Evidence shows that the Neanderthals had such ability.

The Neanderthals also had other works of art. A few of them include jewelry ornaments (bone, teeth, and ivory) with Neanderthal fossils[43] and iron pyrites with engraving. One site had a 15-inch-long piece of an elephant tibia with what appears to be engraving with 7 lines going in one direction and 21 lines going in another direction. Two other pieces of bone have cut lines that seem to be too regular to be accidental. Archaeologist Dietrich Mania (University of Jena) says, "They are graphic symbols. To us it's evidence of abstract thinking and human language."[44]

In La Roche-Cotard, France, a stunning discovery of Neanderthal rock art is described as a human "face-mask" of palm-sized flint that has been reworked and altered. It was found in ice-age deposits. Its identification with the Neanderthals is based on its being "side by side with Mousterian tools"[45] in an undisturbed layer eight feet under the surface. The rock was hand-trimmed to enhance its human appearance by percussion flaking, the same way stone tools were made. Its human appearance

42. Arsuaga, *The Neanderthal's Necklace*, p. 32.
43. Jean-Jacques Hublin, et al., "A Late Neanderthal Associated with Upper Palaeolithic Artifacts," *Nature* 381 (May 16, 1996): 224–226. See also Paul G. Bahn, "Neanderthals emancipated," *Nature* 394 (August 20, 1998): 719–721.
44. Rick Gore, "The First Europeans," *National Geographic* (July 1997): 110–111.
45. Avis Lang, "French School, 300th Century B.C." *Natural History* (March 2004): 23.

was further enhanced "by a shard of animal bone pushed through a hole behind the bridge of the nose creating the appearance of eyes or eyelids." The report adds, "It is clearly not accidental since the bone is fixed firmly in place by two tiny flint wedges."[46]

In addition, a flute made from the thighbone of a cave bear using the same seven-note system as is found in western music was discovered in a cave in Slovenia. It is associated with Mousterian tools.[47] Mousterian tools are normally the type made by Neanderthals.

Neanderthals and Bone Tools

Evolutionists consider bone tools to be more sophisticated than stone tools. It is not unusual to read anthropologists who claim that the Neanderthals were too primitive to have made bone tools. These anthropologists have not done their homework. Besides the mention of bone jewelry above, the scientific literature records bone tools at the following sites:

1. Bilzingsleben, Germany. This Neanderthal site has many hearths and has produced the world's largest collection of bone artifacts, with workshops for working bone, stone, and wood.[48]
2. Castel di Guido, Italy. At this Neanderthal site, 5,800 bone and Acheulean stone artifacts were discovered.[49] Some bone implements were rather simple. "Other bone implements show a higher degree of secondary flaking and are comparable to the classic forms of stone tools; especially remarkable are several bone bifaces made with bold, large flake removals. The presence and abundance of undeniable, deliberately shaped bone tools make Castel di Guido a truly exceptional site."[50]
3. Fontana Ranuccio, Italy. This Neanderthal site contains some of the earliest artifacts found in Europe — Acheulean tools, including well-made hand axes, bone tools that were flaked, like stone, by percussion, and bifaces (hand axes) made of elephant bone.[51]

---

46. Douglas Palmer, "Neanderthal Art Alters the Face of Archaeology," *New Scientist* (December 6, 2003): 11.
47. Kate Wong, "Neanderthal Notes," *Scientific American* (September 1997): 28–30. Anon, "Early Music," *Science* 276 (April 11, 1997): 205.
48. Rick Gore, "The First Europeans," *National Geographic*, July 1997, p. 110–111.
49. Acheulean tools are those which are associated with the main, so-called, Lower Paleolithic culture in Europe, represented by hand-ax industries, and dated by evolutionists to be about 1,500,000–150,000 years ago.
50. F. Mallegni and A.M. Radmilli, "Human Temporal Bone from the Lower Paleolithic Site of Castel di Guido, Near Rome, Italy," *American Journal of Physical Anthropology* 76:2 (June 1988): 177.
51. Klein, *The Human Career*, p. 344 and 584.

4. La Ferrassie Rock Shelter, France. This Neanderthal site contains tools that are of the Charentian Mousterian culture,[52] together with an engraved bone found with the La Ferrassie 1 fossil individual.
5. La Quina Rock Shelter, France. This Neanderthal site contains bone tools such as antler digging picks and highly modified lower ends of wild horse humeri.[53]
6. Petralona Cave, Greece. Evidence of the controlled use of fire is seen by blackened fire-stones and ashes. It would be impossible for fire in the cave to be of non-human origin. Artifacts at this Neanderthal site include stone tools of the early Mousterian culture and bone awls and scrapers.[54]
7. Régourdou Cave, France. This Neanderthal site contains bone tools, such as an antler digging pick and an awl.[55]

Neanderthals and Space Allocation

The ability to allocate specific areas for living, working, trash, and other purposes is considered to be a characteristic of a fully developed human mind. For some reason, this mental and conceptual ability by the Neanderthals has been questioned. The scientific literature shows that the Neanderthals clearly had this ability.

1. Arago Cave (Tautavel), France. Excavations show the presence of structured and walled living areas, indicating cognitive and social capacity in Neanderthal populations.[56]
2. Arcy-sur-Cure caves, France. At this Neanderthal site there is evidence of a separation between ground that was littered with debris and clear ground, which suggests an original wall that separated the living area from the damp part of the cave, indicating the socially structured use of space.[57]
3. Bilzingsleben, Germany. The Neanderthal people here made structures similar to those made by Bushmen of southern Africa today. Three circular foundations of bone and stone have been uncovered, 9 to 13 feet across, with a long elephant tusk possibly used as a

52. Michael H. Day, *Guide to Fossil Man*, Fourth edition (Chicago: The University of Chicago Press, 1986), p. 39.
53. Brian Hayden, "The Cultural Capacities of Neanderthals: a Review and Re-evaluation," *Journal of Human Evolution* 24:2 (February 1993): 117.
54. Day, *Guide to Fossil Man*, p. 92.
55. Ibid., p. 120.
56. Hayden, "The Cultural Capacities of Neanderthals," p. 136.
57. Ibid., p. 123, 133.

center post. A 27-foot-wide circle of pavement made of stone and bone may have been an area used for cultural activities with an anvil of quartzite set between the horns of a huge bison.[58]

4. La Chaise Caves, France. This Neanderthal site contains the presence of structured and walled living areas indicating cognitive and social capacity.[59]
5. La Ferrassie Rock Shelter, France. This Neanderthal site contains a rectangle of calcareous stones, 3 x 5 meters, carefully laid one beside the other to construct a flat surface for "clearly intentional work."[60]
6. Le Lazaret Cave, France. Richard Klein states that this Neanderthal site contains "clusters of artifacts, bones, and other debris that could mark hut bases or specialized activity areas." Klein adds, "The presence of a structure is suggested by an 11 x 3.5 meter concentration of artifacts and fragmented animal bones bounded by a series of large rocks on one side and by the cave wall on the other. The area also contains two hearths. . . . The rocks could have supported poles over which skins were draped to pitch a tent against the wall of the cave."[61]

Neanderthals and Technology

The Neanderthal site at Umm el Tlel, Syria, is dated at about 42,500 years of age.[62] The site contains Mousterian tools hafted with bitumen at very high temperatures. Prior to this, the earliest hafted tools were dated at about 10,000 years of age. The *Nature* report continues: "These new data suggest that Palaeolithic people had greater technical ability than previously thought, as they were able to use different materials to produce tools."[63] Simon Holdaway (La Trobe University, Australia) states: ". . . evidence for hafting in the Middle Palaeolithic may indicate that more complex multi-component forms existed earlier, so *changing our perceptions of the relationships between the two periods*."[64] That is a remarkable statement. Just a few years ago, we were repeatedly told that the Neanderthals had no adhesives.

58. Gore, "The First Europeans," p. 110–111.
59. Hayden, "The Cultural Capacities of Neandertals," p. 136.
60. Ibid., p. 117, 133.
61. Klein, *The Human Career*, p. 349–350.
62. Tim Folger and Shanti Menon, ". . . Or Much Like Us?" *Discover* (January 1997): 33.
63. Eric Boëda, et al, "Bitumen as a Hafting Material on Middle Palaeolithic Artifacts," *Nature* 380 (March 28, 1996): 336–338.
64. Simon Holdaway, "Tool Hafting with a Mastic," *Nature* 380 (March 28, 1996): 288. Emphasis is mine.

Conclusion

The evidence strongly indicates that those who do not believe the literal history in Genesis need to rethink their attitude toward the Neanderthals. All that we could reasonably expect from DNA sequencing, the fossils, and the archaeological record supports the full humanity of the Neanderthals, our worthy ancestors.

Chapter 10

Genetics Confirms the Recent, Supernatural Creation of Adam and Eve

by Dr. Nathaniel Jeanson and Dr. Jeffrey Tomkins

Abstract

The advent of modern genetics has seen the evolutionary community redouble its efforts to argue *for* human-primate common ancestry and *against* the traditional Christian understanding of the origin of the human race. As has been argued in previous chapters, a careful reading of Genesis 1–11 indicates that God created Adam and Eve supernaturally and without prior ancestry, and that all of humanity traces their ancestry back to this original couple — and not to a group of primates or proto-humans. Combined with a careful reading of the rest of Scripture, this narrative places the creation date of Adam and Eve approximately 6,000 years ago and places another population bottleneck about 4,500 years ago at the time of the Flood. This scriptural framework leads to very specific expectations about the genetic differences among humans and other species, expectations that can be scientifically tested against modern genetic data. In this chapter, we contend that genetics confirms the recent, supernatural creation of Adam and Eve and refutes the evolutionary narrative on human origins.

Overview

Since most of the data that we're going to discuss is already present within the technical scientific literature, the purpose of this chapter is to take this relatively unknown and obscure knowledge and present it in what we hope is an understandable and accessible manner for non-geneticists. To expound the details of the genetics of human origins in great depth would require a book-length treatment. Conversely, since most of the contents of this book chapter have already been argued, defended, and published as separate technical papers, we will provide here a summary of these papers with references for the more technically minded reader to explore later.

Because the genetics of human origins is a scientifically complex issue that becomes technical very quickly, we have simplified this chapter by organizing it around four major questions:

1. *From whom* did humans originate: ape-like primates or fully human people?
2. *How many* individuals spawned the human race: a population or a pair?
3. *When* did humans originate: hundreds of thousands of years ago or about 6,000 years ago (i.e., ancient or recent)?
4. *Where* did modern human populations originate: Africa or Ararat?

Though specific elements that will be covered under each of these questions are probably more familiar to the average reader (e.g., claims like "humans are 99% genetically identical to the apes," "human chromosome 2 is the result of a fusion," etc.), we have chosen to take a more comprehensive view rather than an apologetic medley approach. Our intention is to demonstrate that the biblical creation model accounts, not just for a handful of select genetic observations, but for *the entire body of genetic evidence available today.*

Introduction: A Critical Scientific Point

To recognize the strength of our conclusions in genetics, the reader needs to understand only one major technical scientific point. Surprisingly, this point is not any singular genetic observation. It is rather a careful understanding of how science works.

What follows should be uncontroversial. Since creationists and evolutionists were both taught their understanding of science from a common source — the scholarly educational community of the Western world — both agree on the specifics of how science should operate. For example, evolutionists didn't learn their trade from creationist institutions, and we didn't learn science in the back closet of a cloistered creationist enclave, either.[1]

1. Nathaniel Jeanson received a B.S. in Molecular Biology and Bioinformatics from the University of Wisconsin-Parkside and Ph.D. in Cell and Developmental Biology from Harvard University. Jeff Tomkins received his B.S. in Agricultural Education from Washington State Univ., an M.S. in Plant Science from Univ. Idaho, and a Ph.D. in Genetics from Clemson University.

Like many scientists, we learned our most memorable lessons on the nature and operation of science via trial and error. For example, while in a graduate course on developmental biology, my fellow students and I (Jeanson) were required to prepare short, mock grant proposals in lieu of tests. Specifically, this assignment involved writing up the proposal and then presenting it orally before a small group of students and professors.

After completing my ten-minute presentation in which I described a battery of experiments to test the scientific question in which I was interested, the professor leaned back in his chair and gave his frank assessment of my ideas. He said (paraphrased),

> There are three types of experiments in the world. The first type distinguishes between two competing hypotheses, regardless of which way the experiment turns out. For example, if you hypothesize *A*, but the experiment demonstrates *B*, you've still learned something. This is the best and rarest type of experiment. The second type is valuable only if the experiment turns out one of the two possible ways. For example, if you hypothesize *A*, but the experiment does not support *A* and instead supports a whole host of alternative hypotheses, you've learned very little. If, instead, the experiment had confirmed hypothesis *A*, it would have been valuable.

He then said that I had proposed the third type of experiment — one in which nothing is learned regardless of the experimental outcome. Essentially, a type-3 experiment tests none of the hypotheses in question, including the one that the investigator has proposed. I had made a major — but memorable — error.

What my professor *didn't* say is also critically important. Implicit in the professor's description of my proposal was an assumption that experiments were actually going to be performed. If, instead of proposing a battery of experiments, I had simply asserted that my hypotheses were true, I would have been failed rather quickly. Stating hypotheses as fact is the cardinal sin of science, so much so that it doesn't even receive a *type* designation. In fact, it's not even in the domain of science. It's pseudoscience.

For example, consider the question of what molecule is the substance of heredity, the instruction manual for building our physical features during the process of development. If we claim that "vital forces and biorhythms from Jupiter" are the real substance, and if we perform zero experiments to test or reject our claim, we're simply spouting pseudoscience (and we would probably be laughed at by most intelligent human beings).

Instead, if we hypothesize that a chemical molecule called *DNA* is the substance, we have a hypothesis we can test. Another investigator might hypothesize that *protein*, not DNA, is the substance of heredity. If we try to test these hypotheses by analyzing the biochemical composition of sperm and egg, we would discover that we performed a type-3 experiment — sperm and egg possess both DNA and protein, which reveals nothing about which substance carries the hereditary information.

However, if we had discovered that sperm and egg *lacked* one of the two substances, we would have performed a type-2 experiment — the result would have eliminated one of the hypotheses, but it would not have positively confirmed the other (after all, there might be many hypotheses on what substances control heredity, and these hypotheses would need to be eliminated as well). To perform a type-1 experiment, we would have had to show that only DNA — and *not* protein — was the substance of heredity.

These sorts of experiments were done in the early part of the last century. In these experiments, investigators used organisms that were easy to work with, such as bacteria and viruses. Since some viruses infect bacteria by injecting certain chemical substances into their hosts that allow the virus to propagate itself, investigators found themselves with an elegant experimental system. In other words, if scientists could figure out what exactly the virus injected, they would know what the substance of heredity was in these organisms.

Since proteins contain certain chemicals (e.g., sulfur) that DNA lacks, and since DNA contains certain substances that proteins lack (e.g., phosphorus), chemically labeling sulfur in one experiment and phosphorus in the other would distinguish between these two hypotheses. When the viruses grown in the presence of chemically labeled sulfur were allowed to infect bacteria, the sulfur (e.g., protein) stayed on the outside of the bacteria. By contrast, when the viruses grown in the presence of chemically labeled phosphorus were allowed to infect bacteria, phosphorus (e.g., DNA) was found inside the bacterial cells. Furthermore, when the investigators analyzed the offspring of the viruses, these offspring contained chemically modified phosphorus — but not chemically modified sulfur. Clearly, the substance of heredity was DNA — and *not* protein.

Hence, to evaluate origins claims, we first have to determine if a claim is in the realm of science. In other words, we have to ask if the claim is simply a bold assertion of fact or if it is actually based on a scientific test. If it is based on the latter, we can proceed with determining which category of experiment the claim represents. Claims that represent type-3 experiments have no further relevance to the origins debate. In contrast, type-2 and type-1 tests have the potential to uncover something new about the competing origins hypotheses, but only type-1 experiments rigorously test young-earth creation (YEC) and evolution head-to-head (Table 1).

Table 1. Only One Type of Experiment Tests Creation and Evolution Head-to-Head

Experiment Type	Models Compared	Ramifications	Frequency in Origins Debate
1	Creation vs. Evolution	The only head-to-head test in the origins debate	Rare
2	Evolution vs. itself (or Creation vs. itself)	Useful in refuting one of the models; useless in confirming a model	Occasional
3	No models compared	Completely useless in the origins debate	Very frequent

Evolutionists agree with the essence of what we've just described.[2] This agreement is borne out both historically and presently. Historically, one of the most common criticisms of the creation model is that it falls in the realm of pseudoscience — that it doesn't make experimentally testable predictions but, instead, makes bald assertions of fact. Presently, in its promotion of theistic evolution (or as they say, evolutionary creation) the BioLogos community continues to repeat this accusation:

> The reason Christian anti-evolutionary approaches are absent from the mainstream scientific literature is not because scientists are theologically or philosophically biased against them, but rather because *they offer little in the way of useful tools for making accurate predictions about the natural world.*[3] [emphasis added]

Thus, all origins positions can agree that testable, accurate predictions are critical to science, and the ability of creationists and evolutionists to make them will be the major focus of this chapter.

However, while evolutionists agree with the nature of science as we described above, we intend to illustrate how evolutionists of all stripes fail to practice it — on each of the four major arenas of scientific investigation on

2. Michael Buratovich, "Biological Evolution: What Makes it Good Science? Part 1," https://BioLogos.org/blogs/archive/biological-evolution-what-makes-it-good-science-part-1. See also chapter 23 of Douglas J. Futuyma, *Evolution* (Sunderland, MA: Sinauer Associates, Inc., 2013). *"The most important feature of scientific hypotheses is that they are testable"* (emphasis his, p. 635).
3. Dennis Venema, "Theory, Prediction and Converging Lines of Evidence, Part 3." https://BioLogos.org/blogs/dennis-venema-letters-to-the-duchess/theory-prediction-and-converging-lines-of-evidence-part-3.

the question of human origins (from whom, how many, when, and where humans originated) — and that, in contrast to the assertion above, creationists *do* make accurate predictions about the natural world and about human origins in particular. We also intend to demonstrate that creationist predictions are scientifically superior to those of evolutionists.

I. From Whom: Ape-like Primates or Fully Human People?

When considering human origins, the most natural place to start is on the question of whether humans have an ape-like ancestry. Before we can discuss the minutiae of the genetics of the human race, we need to ask whether our race is indeed human or whether we are simply highly evolved primates. Ever since Darwin, evolutionists have claimed that apes represent our closest living biological relatives.[4] Evolutionary creationists (a.k.a. theistic evolutionists) agree and expect to find unequivocal genetic evidence of a common genealogical heritage between mankind and the orangutans, gorillas, and chimpanzees. Current evolutionary literature identifies the chimpanzee as the closest living relative of humans, and evolutionists place the split between these two lineages (from a common ape-like ancestor, not a chimpanzee) about 3 million to 13 million years ago.[5]

In contrast, a plain reading of Scripture reveals a starkly different narrative on human ancestry. As has been argued in an earlier chapter, Genesis 1–2 teaches that God created man in His own image, categorically distinct from any animals, and that He did so supernaturally by forming Adam from the dust and Eve from Adam's side. Human evolution from pre-existing ape-like creatures is not compatible with the Genesis narrative.

Furthermore, the rest of Scripture identifies Adam and Eve as the sole progenitors of the entire human race, and Noah, his wife, his three sons, and their wives as the most immediate ancestors of modern humans.[6] Shortly after the global Flood of Noah's day, the human ancestors of the modern "races"[7] or ethnic groups formed as a result of the confusion of languages at

4. The Chimpanzee Sequencing and Analysis Consortium, "Initial Sequence of the Chimpanzee Genome and Comparison with the Human Genome," *Nature* 437 (2005): 69–87, http://www.nature.com/nature/journal/v437/n7055/full/nature04072.html.
5. Kevin E. Langergraber et al., "Generation Times in Wild Chimpanzees and Gorillas Suggest Earlier Divergence Times in Great Ape and Human Evolution," *Proceedings of the National Academy of Sciences USA* 109 no. 39 (2012): 15716–15721, http://www.pnas.org/content/109/39/15716.full; Oliver Venn et al., "Strong Male Bias Drives Germline Mutation in Chimpanzees," *Science* 344 (2014): 1272–1275.
6. Eve was "the mother of all living" (Gen. 3:20) and from the eight people on the ark "the whole earth was populated" (Gen. 9:19; NKJV).
7. As is shown in the later chapter by Bergman, biblically speaking there is only one race, Adam's race.

Babel (Gen 11:8–9).[8] Apes as precursors to humans do not enter the picture under the creation view.

Because of the nature of the genetic discussion that follows, the time element of creation is also critical to the ancestry question. Under the young-earth creation (YEC) view, Adam and Eve were created approximately 6,000 years ago, and the global Flood of Noah and the population bottleneck that followed occurred about 4,500 years ago. The Tower of Babel incident followed shortly (i.e., a couple centuries) after the Flood.[9]

These two strikingly different accounts — evolution and YEC — for the origin of humans lead to very different expectations about the genetics of modern humans and apes. In some cases, however, the expectations are obviously the same. For instance, from an anatomical perspective, great apes are the most similar creatures to humans, and both sides can make a general prediction that, from a genetic perspective, apes should be the most similar to humans. While humans share different levels and traits of morphological similarity with gorillas, orangutans, and chimpanzees that don't seem to indicate any clear evolutionary pattern, the current evolutionary consensus is that humans should be most similar to chimpanzees genetically — although this widely accepted paradigm has recently been disputed based on analyses of morphological traits by several evolutionists who claim that orangutans are the closest human relative.[10]

As another example, both models accept the science of empirical genetic discovery. Hence, to claim that the existence of the basic science of genetics somehow validates one model over the other would be erroneous — a type-3 experiment that fails to distinguish among the competing ideas in question. Therefore, it is essential to clearly identify the specific predictions of each model in order to distinguish which genetic data actually constitute a type-1 experiment (e.g., one that differentiates YEC from evolution) and which constitute lesser types of experiments.

---

8. Note that the genealogies of Shem, Ham, and Japheth in Genesis 10 abruptly end after a few generations — consistent with the writer of Genesis 10 being unable to communicate with the members of additional generations due to a language barrier brought about by the Tower of Babel incident.
9. Chris Hardy and Robert Carter, "The Biblical Minimum and Maximum Age of the Earth," *Journal of Creation* 28 no. 2 (2014): 89–96, http://creation.com/images/pdfs/tj/j28_2/j28_2_89-96.pdf; Robert Carter and Chris Hardy, "Modelling Biblical Human Population Growth," *Journal of Creation* 29, no. 1 (2015): 72–79. Since Peleg was born 101 years after the flood and lived 209 years, and we are told that the division of humanity at the Tower of Babel was some unspecified date "in the days of" Peleg, we cannot be precise on the dating of the division.
10. John R. Grehan and Jeffrey H. Schwartz, "Evolution of the Second Orangutan: Phylogeny and Biogeography of Hominid Origins," *Journal of Biogeography* 36 (2009): 1823–1844.

Are Humans 99% Genetically Identical to Chimpanzees?

One common example of a type-2 experiment is predicting the genetic difference between humans and chimpanzees. The evolutionary model has very specific expectations about this figure, and a discrepancy between predictions and facts should result in the rejection of the evolutionary hypothesis. However, since the YEC model does not make specific predictions about human-ape genetic differences, a match between evolutionary expectations and scientific fact would not inform the origins debate (i.e., would not be decisive in evolution's favor).

But the silence of the YEC model on human-chimp genetic differences is not a weakness of the model. We could just as well challenge the evolutionists to predict the number of animals that were taken on board Noah's ark. This request would be fruitless and irrelevant to the debate since a global Flood and an ark are not part of the evolutionary model. However, if the YEC model failed to predict the numbers on board the ark accurately, then we would need to reevaluate aspects of the YEC model. Conversely, since human-ape ancestry is not part of the YEC model, the actual number of genetic differences between humans and chimpanzees is, at best, a type-2 experiment for testing the claim that humans descended from ape-like creatures — successful evolutionary predictions would not vindicate evolution in the origins debate, while evolutionary predictive failures could be grounds to reject the evolutionary view.

With these experimental parameters in mind, we can now investigate the actual human-chimp genetic comparison in depth. If we think of genetic inheritance as analogous to copying the text of a book, the process of passing on genetic information from one generation to the next is similar to the process of transcribing the text of a book. To make the analogy tighter, inheritance is like copying the text of a book without having a perfect spell checker,[11] and then using the corrupted copy as the template for the next round of copying.

Biologically, the text of the genetic book is contained in a chemical substance called *DNA*. The DNA in our cells is, in essence, a chemical instruction manual for building and maintaining our anatomy and physiology from conception to death. The actual instructions are encoded in a 4-letter chemical alphabet, and the combination of these letters into chemical "words" and "sentences" carries biological meaning. In total, the DNA in our cells is billions of letters long — a very large biological "book."

---

11. DNA repair machinery exists in the cell, but some copying mistakes still apparently slip through each generation.

When DNA is copied in sperm and egg cells prior to conception, the copying process is imperfect. The rate of copying mistakes (called *mutations*) has been measured in both humans and chimpanzees, and the rates are fairly similar. About 60 mutations happen each generation.[12]

Using rounded numbers, if the human and chimpanzee lineages split 3–13 million years ago, and if the years from one generation to the next are about 20 years, then 150,000–650,000 generations have passed since the two species last shared a common ancestor.[13] In each lineage, about 60 DNA mutations happen in each of those hundreds of thousands of generations leading to an expectation that the DNA of humans and the DNA of chimpanzees should differ by about 18–80 million DNA letters.[14]

Thinking of DNA again like a book, we can measure book sizes by their word count, and if we wanted to be very technical, we could measure it by the total letter count. Since the total letter count in humans and chimpanzees is around 3 *billion* DNA letters,[15] evolutionists expect about a 1–3% genetic (DNA) difference between these two species today.[16]

The actual difference is about 12% — a number that is about ten times higher than the predicted value.[17] Though the scientist responsible

12. For the chimpanzee reference, see Oliver Venn et al., "Strong Male Bias Drives Germline Mutation in Chimpanzees," *Science* 344 (2014): 1272–1275. The human rate has been measured on multiple occasions; for an example, see Donald F. Conrad et al., "Variation in Genome-wide Mutation Rates Within and Between Human Families," *Nature Genetics* 43 no. 7 (2011): 712–714, http://www.ncbi.nlm.nih.gov/pmc/articles/PMC3322360/.
13. An example of the math: 3,000,000 years / 20 years per generation = 150,000 generations.
14. An example of the math used to derive the figure of "80 million DNA letters apart" is as follows. In 13,000,000 years, about 650,000 generations pass [13,000,000 years / 20 years per generation = 650,000 generations]. Using this number, 60 DNA changes per human generation x 650,000 generations = 39,000,000 DNA changes total. Since the identical process would occur in chimpanzees, the total would need to be multiplied by two [39,000,000 x 2 = 78,000,000 DNA changes total in both the human lineage and the chimpanzee lineage]. Rounding numbers, the total is ~80,000,000 DNA changes in 13,000,000 years.
15. Technically, since our DNA comes in two versions (in technical terms, we are a *dipoid* species — versus a *haploid* species), humans have 6 billion total DNA letters (as do chimps). But 3 billion is a useful simplification for our purposes in this section.
16. An example of the math used: 78,000,000 predicted DNA differences between humans and chimpanzees / 3,000,000,000 total DNA letters in humans = 0.026 = 2.6%, or about 3% difference.
17. Jeffrey P. Tomkins, "Genome-Wide DNA Alignment Similarity (Identity) for 40,000 Chimpanzee DNA Sequences Queried against the Human Genome is 86–89%," *Answers Research Journal* 4 (2011): 233–241, https://answersingenesis.org/genetics/dna-similarities/genome-wide-dna-alignment-similarity-identity-for-40000-chimpanzees/; Jeffrey P. Tomkins, "Documented Anomaly in Recent Versions of the BLASTN Algorithm and a Complete Reanalysis of Chimpanzee and Human Genome-Wide DNA Similarity Using Nucmer and LASTZ," *Answers Research Journal* 8 (2015): 379–390, https://answersingenesis.org/genetics/dna-similarities/blastn-algorithm-anomaly/.

for identifying this fact is a young-earth creationist, this discovery is not the result of creationist manipulation of data to fit a pre-determined conclusion. If you read the fine print in the original evolutionary publication that announced the determination of the chimpanzee DNA sequence, you can reach a similar conclusion.[18] Humans and chimpanzees are not 99% identical. They are only 88% identical, which means that the two species differ by nearly *400 million* (400,000,000) DNA letters![19]

Thus, the question of human-chimpanzee DNA differences offers no assistance to the evolutionary model on at least three counts. First, whatever the difference is, it cannot falsify the YEC model, making it a type-2 experiment at best. Second, current evolutionary predictions for the human-chimp genetic difference fail to account for the gigantic genetic gap between these two species.

Third, the evolutionary prediction of a 1% difference isn't really a prediction at all. The evolutionary time at which the human and chimpanzee lineages split has been revised *to fit the genetic data.* Earlier predictions for the time of divergence for these species were originally in the 3 to 6 million year range,[20] and the measurement of the DNA copying error rate in chimpanzees caused some investigators to (controversially) bump the time back further to ~13 million years.[21] Thus, the absolute difference between

18. In the 2005 *Nature* paper describing the elucidation of the chimpanzee DNA sequence (accessable at http://www.nature.com/nature/journal/v437/n7055/full/nature04072.html), the authors stated, "Best reciprocal nucleotide-level alignments of the chimpanzee and human genomes cover ~2.4 gigabases (Gb) [2,400,000,000 DNA letters] of high-quality sequence, including 89 Mb [89,000,000 DNA letters] from chromosome X and 7.5 Mb [7,500,000 DNA letters] from chromosome Y" (p.71). Only these 2,400,000,000 DNA letters were used to calculate the published 1.23% DNA difference between humans and chimpanzees. In table 1 of the same paper, it is clear that 2.7 gigabases (GB) — 2,700,000,000 DNA letters — in total were sequenced, leaving 0.3 GB — 300,000,000 DNA letters (about 10% of 3 billion) — unaccounted for, consistent with Jeff Tomkins' independent findings. Furthermore, by last count (http://www.ncbi.nlm.nih.gov/genome/, accessed 09/28/15), the total number of DNA letters in chimpanzees is 3,309,000,000, and in humans it is 3,259,520,000 DNA letters, leaving even more potential DNA differences unaddressed. Clearly, a DNA difference between humans and chimpanzees of 1.23% represents a careful selection of a subset of the facts.
19. Assuming that humans possess 3,259,520,000 total DNA letters, a 12% DNA difference from apes (the result of only 88% identity — see previous footnotes) entails the following: 0.12 x 3,259,520,000 total DNA letters = 391,142,400 DNA letters difference, which is about 400 million DNA differences between chimps and humans.
20. Kevin E. Langergraber et al., "Generation Times in Wild Chimpanzees and Gorillas Suggest Earlier Divergence Times in Great Ape and Human Evolution," *Proceedings of the National Academy of Sciences USA* 109 no. 39 (2012): 15716–15721, http://www.pnas.org/content/109/39/15716.full.
21. Oliver Venn et al., "Strong Male Bias Drives Germline Mutation in Chimpanzees," *Science* 344 (2014): 1272–1275. We give special thanks to Rob Carter for bringing this evolutionary discrepancy to our attention.

humans and chimpanzees isn't a confirmed prediction as much as it is a *post hoc* retrofitting of predictions to facts.

These evolutionary problems aside, we are still left with the question of how to evaluate the YEC model on the human ancestry question. If human-ape genetic differences do not test validity of the YEC model of human origins, what experiment can? What genetic expectations follow from the specific YEC narrative?

In short, the answer is that, if YEC is correct, then YE creationists should be able to explain *human-human* DNA differences and *ape-ape* DNA differences [as opposed to *human-ape* DNA differences] without any need to reference or invoke common ancestry. In other words, YE creationists make predictions for genetic differences among individuals that share a common ancestor under the YEC view (i.e., all humans), not for individuals that were created separately (i.e., humans and apes), and these predictions can be compared to the genetic facts.

If genetic data matched these YEC expectations, would this result require rejection of the evolutionary model? Since evolutionists have spent years refining their own ideas about human-human and ape-ape genetic differences (and also believe that special creation as an alternative is unacceptable), this result would probably do nothing to settle the debate about human origins. In essence, it would be another example of a type-2 experiment — if the results are inconsistent with the YEC expectations, then perhaps the scientific elements of the YEC model should be reevaluated. But if the results confirm the YEC expectations, this discovery would probably do little to change the evolutionary claims about human-ape common ancestry.

Since subsequent sections will explore this question further, the major remaining question in this section is whether the claimed evolutionary evidences for human-ape ancestry are valid type-1 experiments. The evidences listed on the BioLogos website are presented as such — as being unequivocal proof of common ancestry and as very inconsistent with the YEC view. The evidences in the mainstream scientific literature assume the same. But is the claim true?

Relative Genetic Patterns/Nested Hierarchies

Nearly every single one of the evidences presented by BioLogos and mainstream geneticists represents a type-3 experiment or, at best, type-2. For example, one of the most common evidences cited in favor of an ape ancestry in the human lineage is the *relative pattern* of genetic differences between humans and apes, and between humans and other species. In short, evolutionists expect natural selection to produce a branching, tree-like pattern of genealogical relationships among the living species on this planet.[22] They further expect that, if humans arose via the process of natural selection from an ape-like ancestor, then genetic comparisons among humans, apes, and other species should reveal a branching, tree-like pattern as well.

This expectation contrasts to the expectation about the percent DNA differences between humans and chimpanzees that we discussed earlier. The earlier expectation was a *quantitative* prediction; the current expectation is a *qualitative* prediction. That is, qualitatively, if humans have ancestry prior to the first *Homo sapiens*, then evolutionists expect humans to be relatively close genetically to the great apes, then slightly less close genetically to the rest of the primates, then even less similar genetically to other mammals, and quite different genetically from invertebrates and plants. To be clear, the absolute number of differences is not so critical as long as the same relative pattern (in this case, a *nested hierarchical* pattern) holds true.

For this argument to carry any scientific weight as a type-1 experiment in support of evolution, the YEC model would need to predict a different pattern. Otherwise, this argument would represent another type-3 experiment — useless to the overall origins debate.

However, it doesn't take much reflection to see that YEC and evolution make the *same* prediction about the relative genetic hierarchies found in nature. Under the YEC model, God designed the entire universe, including the various kinds of biological life that exist in it, and we would expect to find that life fits a design pattern. Since humans are made in God's image, we can get a sense for what kinds of design patterns God might have used by examining the patterns that result from human designs. Examples of *nested hierarchies* abound among the designed things in our world.

For example, designed means of transportation easily fit a relative hierarchical pattern. This fact is unequivocal. Sedans resemble SUVs more than they resemble tractor trailers, and all three vehicles have more in common than do sedans and amphibious assault vehicles. The latter two vehicles have more in common with one another than with submarines, and this simple pattern matches the type of hierarchy that we see in biology.[23]

22. For example, see Michael Buratovich, "Biological Evolution: What Makes it Good Science? Part 1," https://BioLogos.org/blogs/archive/biological-evolution-what-makes-it-good-science-part-1; for a non-BioLogos reference see Douglas J. Futuyma, *Evolution* (Sunderland, MA: Sinauer Associates, Inc., 2013).

23. Nathaniel T. Jeanson, "Darwin vs. Genetics: Surprises and Snags in the Science of Common Ancestry," *Acts & Facts* 43 no. 9 (2014): 8–11, http://www.icr.org/article/darwin-vs-genetics-surprises-snags.

Therefore, nested hierarchical patterns are as much the expectation of the YEC view as they are of the evolutionary view. The relative hierarchy of genetic differences among humans, great apes, mammals, and invertebrates fits the YEC model at least as well as the evolutionary one. So, to claim nested hierarchical patterns in the biological world as exclusive evidence of evolution would be analogous to claiming that the existence of people proves YEC. Neither claim constitutes a legitimate scientific experiment. Both are type-3 experiments and, therefore, reveal nothing about the validity of either view, despite the confident claims of evolutionists to the contrary.[24]

While these two examples (absolute and relative genetic differences between humans and the apes) do not constitute an exhaustive review of all the claimed genetic evidences for human-ape ancestry, they represent some of the most prominent, and they illustrate the Achilles' heels of the remaining ones — failure to satisfy the requirements of a type-1 experiment.

Human Chromosome 2 Fusion?

Consider another example. If we return to our book analogy, just as the text of a book is broken up into chapters, so also the billions of letters in the DNA code for humans and chimpanzees are broken up into major divisions called *chromosomes*. However, because DNA comes from each parent, these chromosomes come in pairs.

Evolutionists have claimed for years that the human chromosome pair number 2 is actually an accidental fusion of two pairs of ancestral chromosomes inherited from ape-like creatures.[25] In short, they claim that the human-chimp ancestor had 48 chromosomes. Today, humans have 46. Since chromosomes come in two copies — e.g., the ape-like ancestor would have had 2 *pairs* of 24 chromosomes, and humans today have 23 *pairs* of chromosomes — and since humans have fewer total chromosomes than apes, evolutionists claim that one of the ancestral pairs of chromosomes fused to another ancestral pair of chromosomes. This would reduce the total chromosomes count from 48 to 46.[26]

24. For example, "Humans share more DNA with chimpanzees than with any other animal, suggesting that humans and chimps share a relatively recent common ancestor." See Anon., "What Is the Genetic Evidence for Human Evolution?" https://BioLogos.org/common-questions/human-origins/what-scientific-evidence-do-we-have-about-the-first-humans/.

25. See Anon., "Genetics," http://biologos.org/resources/audio-visual/genetics, and Dennis Venema, "Theory, Prediction and Converging Lines of Evidence, Part 3," http://biologos.org/blogs/dennis-venema-letters-to-the-duchess/theory-prediction-and-converging-lines-of-evidence-part-3.

26. Diagrams for this supposed evolutionary event typically show the fusion of only one member of each pair.

Since the YEC view makes no overt predictions about the differences between humans and chimpanzees in DNA organization or in the structure of DNA, the existence of a chromosome fusion would not have said anything relevant to the human origins debate. However, in this case evolutionists also made their claim prematurely, before all the evidence was acquired. Effectively, the evolutionary claims about the structure of human chromosome 2 represented a *prediction* rather than an observation.

Recent reanalysis of human chromosome 2 has contradicted this evolutionary prediction. No evidence for a fusion exists. In fact, the alleged site where the fusion supposedly took place actually represents a highly organized, functional *gene* (in our analogy, think of genes as words or sentences).[27] Thus, starting from the assumption of human-ape common ancestry, evolutionists have actually made a *failed* prediction about the structure and function of DNA within our cells.

The failed evolutionary prediction on chromosome function extends beyond the purported fusion site. The BioLogos community has claimed that overall arrangement of DNA along chromosomes among humans and the great apes is inexplicable apart from common ancestry: "There is no good biological reason to find the same genes in the same order in unrelated organisms, and every good reason to expect very different gene orders."[28]

Do evolutionists actually have a large body of experimental results demonstrating "no good biological reason to find the same genes in the same order in unrelated organisms"? In the few cases where functional analyses have been performed, the results contradict this evolutionary assertion. The chromosomal context in which genes find themselves appears to play a significant role in how the genes function.[29] In fact, human-designed computer

27. Jerry Bergman and Jeffrey Tomkins, "The Chromosome 2 Fusion Model of Human Evolution — Part 1: Re-evaluating the Evidence," *Journal of Creation* 25, no. 2 (2011): 106–110, http://creation.com/chromosome-2-fusion-1; Jeffrey Tomkins and Jerry Bergman, "The Chromosome 2 Fusion Model of Human Evolution — Part 2: Re-analysis of the Genomic Data," *Journal of Creation* 25, no. 2 (2011): 111–117, http://creation.com/chromosome-2-fusion-2; Jeffrey Tomkins, "Alleged Human Chromosome 2 'Fusion Site' Encodes an Active DNA Binding Domain Inside a Complex and Highly Expressed Gene — Negating Fusion," *Answers Research Journal* 6 (2013): 367–375, https://answersingenesis.org/genetics/dna-similarities/alleged-human-chromosome-2-fusion-site-encodes-an-active-dna-binding-domain-inside-a-complex-and-hig/.

28. Dennis Venema, "Signature in the Synteny," https://BioLogos.org/blogs/dennis-venema-letters-to-the-duchess/signature-in-the-synteny.

29. Michael D. Wilson et al., "Species-specific Transcription in Mice Carrying Human Chromosome 21," *Science* 322 no. 5900 (2008): 434–438, http://www.ncbi.nlm.nih.gov/pmc/articles/PMC3717767/; Nathaniel T. Jeanson, "An Update on Chromosome 2 'Fusion,' " *Acts & Facts* 42 no. 9 (2013): 13, http://www.icr.org/article/update-chromosome-2-fusion.

code must also follow specific formats and contextual guidelines as well. So our previous analogy of human-designed systems as we applied to the idea of hierarchy holds true here as well. Thus, whether applied to predicted DNA differences or DNA function, the evolutionary model of common ancestry has not been vindicated.

Conversely, the prediction of function is actually one of the few arenas in the question of human ancestry in which a type-1 experiment could be conducted. Evolutionists and creationists make very different predictions about the function of the billions of DNA letters in the human sequence, and experiments testing function would clearly distinguish which model makes better predictions, as we demonstrate below.

Shared Genetic "Mistakes"?

To make the point from a different angle, the members of BioLogos have made a host of claims on their website about shared "pseudogenes" and other types of purported shared biological "mistakes" in apes and humans. In fact, two of the three main "facts" that the website lists as genetic evidence for human evolution involve an implicit statement about function.[30] In reality, hardly any actual *experiments* have been performed on the billions of DNA letters in humans and chimpanzees. "Pseudogene" actually represents a premature label for a particular segment of DNA that resembles a broken gene but which had never been experimentally tested for function. Thus, virtually all claims that BioLogos and other evolutionists have made about genetic "mistakes" are not arguments for evolution but bald assertions without a basis in experimental fact. Technically, this would make these arguments *pseudoscience*. However, for the sake of discussion, we're willing to entertain these claims as *predictions* stemming from the *assumption* that evolution is true.

Conversely, from the assumptions about human ancestry inherent to the YEC model, creationists have published a testable, predictive model of genetic function[31] (see references for details). For the particular DNA

30. Anon., "What Is the Genetic Evidence for Human Evolution?" https://BioLogos.org/common-questions/human-origins/what-scientific-evidence-do-we-have-about-the-first-humans/. Evidence #2 references "genetic scars" and implicitly assumes that these sorts of genetic differences (the "scars") represent mutated and non-functional or functionally neutral sequences. For the "genetic synonyms" argument to work in Evidence #3, the argument must assume that these "synonyms" represent functionally neutral sequences.
31. Nathaniel T. Jeanson, "Recent, Functionally Diverse Origin for Mitochondrial Genes from ~2700 Metazoan Species," *Answers Research Journal* 6 (2013): 467–501, https://answersingenesis.org/genetics/mitochondrial-dna/recent-functionally-diverse-origin-for-mitochondrial-genes-from--2700-metazoan-species/.

differences that we examined, we expect them to function in each organism's respective biology, whereas the evolutionary model claims that these particular DNA sequences are functionally neutral and are a reflection, therefore, of ancestry alone. Since precious few experiments have actually been done on genetic function, we now have a basis for doing a type-1 experiment in the future. By experimentally changing these sequences, we can evaluate whether or not these differences are functional — and confirm or reject the predictions of each origins model.

For other DNA sequences, a few experiments have been performed, and the trajectory is not looking good for evolution. For example, after the human DNA sequence was elucidated in 2001, it was widely proclaimed that the vast majority of our billions of DNA letters were useless, non-functional leftovers of our evolutionary heritage and therefore called "junk" DNA.[32] However, scientists didn't actually do any *experimental* tests on the billions of letters until the Encyclopedia of DNA Elements (ENCODE) project was initiated in 2003. The first tier of ENCODE only examined about 1% of the human genome as an initial test, and they found preliminary evidence for pervasive function for the vast majority of those billions of letters.[33] Then after extending this type of research to the entire human genome, using mostly human cell lines (not fresh tissues from living humans) they reported in 2012 that at least 80% of the genome had significant levels of biochemical function.[34] It wasn't useless junk after all.

Many new discoveries in recent years are now pushing this level of functionality even higher. The leader of the ENCODE project, Ewan Birney, is predicting that the human genome will soon prove to be 100% functional.[35] Needless to say, the traditional neo-Darwinian evolutionists outside the practical biomedical genetics community of ENCODE

---

32. BioLogos Editorial Team. "On Reading the Cell's Signature," https://BioLogos.org/blogs/archive/on-reading-the-cells-signature; Dennis Venema, "Understanding Evolution: Is There 'Junk' in Your Genome? Part 1," https://BioLogos.org/blogs/dennis-venema-letters-to-the-duchess/understanding-evolution-is-there-junk-in-your-genome-part-1; Dennis Venema, "Is There 'Junk' in Your Genome? Part 2," https://BioLogos.org/blogs/dennis-venema-letters-to-the-duchess/is-there-junk-in-your-genome-part-2.
33. ENCODE Project Consortium, "Identification and Analysis of Functional Elements in 1% of the Human Genome by the ENCODE Pilot Project," *Nature* 447 (2007): 799–816.
34. ENCODE Project Consortium, "An Integrated Encyclopedia of DNA Elements in the Human Genome," *Nature* 489 (2012): 57–74, http://www.nature.com/nature/journal/v489/n7414/full/nature11247.html).
35. Ed Yong, "ENCODE: the Rough Guide to the Human Genome," http://blogs.discovermagazine.com/notrocketscience/2012/09/05/encode-the-rough-guide-to-the-human-genome/#.V_AxDtx4yoI.

are outraged that the data is not supporting their dogmatic evolutionary claims.[36]

In addition to these genome-wide results, other studies focusing on specific examples of "poster child" evolutionary pseudogenes regularly damage the credibility of the evolutionary claims. For example, the *beta-globin* pseudogene has obvious evidence for function,[37] and one of the favorite pseudogene examples (e.g., vitellogenin) of the BioLogos geneticist, Dennis Venema, can also no longer be labeled a non-functional relic.

Specifically, Venema claimed, "Humans have the remains of a gene devoted to egg yolk production in our DNA in exactly the place that evolution would predict."[38] But recent research has exposed this as nearly impossible to reconcile with the facts.[39] The supposed evidence for this "egg yolk" gene is so pitiful that it's hard to imagine how anyone could have seriously entertained this hypothesis in the first place. It's like identifying the letter "e" in the Bible, finding the same letter in Darwin's *On the Origin of Species*, and then claiming that the books were modified from a common ancestor — you really have to stretch your imagination to accept this claim. Conversely, there is so little DNA remnant of the supposed egg yolk gene that it requires a real strain of the imagination to see why some evolutionists pursued this line of reasoning in the first place. Current data suggest that they mistook a functional DNA sequence (enhancer element) inside a genomic address messenger gene involved with brain tissue function, for a non-functional egg yolk gene "remnant."[40]

Not surprisingly, the BioLogos community has downplayed the significance of these accumulating discoveries and tried to turn the tables on creationists with clever rhetorical games. Rather than admit the obvious damaging

36. For example, see Dan Graur et al., "On the Immortality of Television Sets: 'Function' in the Human Genome According to the Evolution-free Gospel of ENCODE," *Genome Biology and Evolution* 5 no. 3 (2013): 578–590, http://gbe.oxfordjournals.org/content/5/3/578; for a response to Graur et al., see: Nathaniel Jeanson and Brian Thomas, "The Resurrection of 'Junk DNA'?" http://www.icr.org/article/resurrection-junk-dna.
37. Jeffrey P. Tomkins, "The Human Beta-Globin Pseudogene Is Non-Variable and Functional," *Answers Research Journal* 6 (2013): 293–301, https://answersingenesis.org/genetics/human-genome/the-human-beta-globin-pseudogene-is-non-variable-and-functional/.
38. Rachel Held Evans and Dennis Venema, "Ask an Evolutionary Creationist: A Q&A with Dennis Venema," https://BioLogos.org/blogs/dennis-venema-letters-to-the-duchess/ask-an-evolutionary-creationist-a-qa-with-dennis-venema.
39. Jeffrey P. Tomkins, "Challenging the BioLogos Claim that a Vitellogenin (Egg-Laying) Pseudogene Exists in the Human Genome," *Answers Research Journal* 8 (2015): 403–411, https://answersingenesis.org/genetics/dna-similarities/challenging-BioLogos-claim-vitellogenin-pseudogene-exists-in-human-genome/.
40. Ibid.

implications for evolution,[41] the BioLogos staff has turned the argument around and challenged creationists to explain the remaining data that BioLogos claimed demonstrated non-function.[42] In fact, Dennis Venema recently went so far as to claim, "Having the complete genome sequences for a variety of great apes makes looking for additional shared mutations a trivial exercise, and it is no exaggeration to say that there are thousands of examples that could be used."[43]

But the BioLogos rejoinder misses the big picture and the point. First, preliminary biochemical evidence for function does not exist merely for the two examples of pseudogenes that we discussed. *It exists for at least ~80% of all the pseudogenes in humans.*[44] And the other 20% may still yet be found to be functional in some human tissue or under some physiological condition yet to be studied . . . and there are many. That's the catch: many noncoding RNA genes (like pseudogenes) are only expressed under certain conditions.

---

41. In his multi-part response (http://biologos.org/blogs/dennis-venema-letters-to-the-duchess/series/vitellogenin-and-common-ancestry) to Tomkins' rebuttal of the egg yolk gene claim, Venema tried to skirt Tomkins' main point — that the *actual molecular (e.g., DNA letter by DNA letter) evidence* supporting the existence of an egg yolk gene remnant in humans is nonexistent. Tomkins noted that "Sequence identity [between human DNA and chicken DNA] dropped as the fragment size increased, eventually leveling off to about 39% identity." In other words, when comparing the chicken egg yolk gene DNA sequence to human "egg yolk gene" DNA sequence, the match between the two is barely different from a random DNA match (25% identity represents a random DNA match). Even if we focus only on the few parts of the DNA where DNA sequence identity is higher, Tomkins' noted that "Even in an evolutionary sense, to say that a pseudogene can be identified by only 0.35% of the original sequence is quite a stretch of the Darwinian paradigm." In response to these data, Venema *never provided any numbers* to rebut Tomkins. Instead, Venema republished the diagrams from the original egg yolk gene paper, devoid of any percent identity labels. In other words, Tomkins reanalyzed the raw data and reported a serious criticism of the facts. In response, rather than deal with the facts, Venema created diagrams to make the similarity between chicken and human appear high — without actually constraining his depictions with numbers. At best, this is a tacit concession of defeat; at worst, it's deliberately deceptive. In addition to diagrams devoid of numbers, Venema attempted to corral other lines of evidence to support his contention, but these "evidences" were simply reassertions of *why* he expected a broken egg yolk gene to exist in humans — an expectation that has been falsified by the evidence.
42. Dennis Venema, "ENCODE and 'Junk DNA,' Part 1: All Good Concepts are Fuzzy," https://BioLogos.org/blogs/dennis-venema-letters-to-the-duchess/encode-and-junk-dna-part-1-all-good-concepts-are-fuzzy; Dennis Venema, "ENCODE and 'Junk DNA,' Part 2: Function: What's in a Word?" https://BioLogos.org/blogs/dennis-venema-letters-to-the-duchess/encode-and-junk-dna-part-2-function-whats-in-a-word.
43. Dennis Venema, "Common Ancestry, Nested Hierarchies, and Parsimony," https://BioLogos.org/blogs/dennis-venema-letters-to-the-duchess/adam-eve-and-human-population-genetics-part-6-common-ancestry-nested-hierarchies-and-parsimony.
44. See Figure 4A of Cristina Sisu et al., "Comparative Analysis of Pseudogenes Across Three Phyla," *PNAS* 111 (2014): 13361–13366, http://www.pnas.org/content/111/37/13361.long.

Second, challenging creationists to explain the remaining examples of "non-function" assumes that *actual experiments have been performed that demonstrate non-function.* They have not. The reality is that we have only just begun to uncover the functionality of the human genome.

Consider just how many experiments would need to be performed to conclude with any sort of confidence that a particular set of DNA sequences has zero function. The number of possible scenarios in which a DNA sequence might plausibly function is now proving to be enormous. For example, in the short nine-month window of time that represents human embryonic development, a single cell turns into a fully formed baby that contains hundreds of cell types that must execute an unimaginable number of cellular tasks. Surely the developing baby calls upon enormous swaths of DNA code to execute this developmental program — and then silences or repurposes them for the remainder of its life via another type of code (a code which is being studied by investigators in a scientific field termed "epigenetics").[45] The dynamic use of DNA sequence during development is very different than the vast majority of DNA sequence use in the adult.

Experimentally testing a DNA sequence during each of these unique windows of time in which sections of DNA are used and then silenced would be an enormous (and morally questionable) experiment. However, expressed RNA sequences have been analyzed in organ donors, aborted fetal tissue, and embryonic stem cells, with the latter two involving the murder of innocent babies. Nevertheless, these morbid data have only served to increase the known functionality and complexity of the human genome. In addition, until experiments are performed in living humans, which is also unethical, it is both inappropriate and scientifically uninformed to claim "non-function" for human DNA.

In short, the recent decade of experimental results on human DNA sequences that demonstrate biochemical evidence for function are just the beginning of our understanding as to the complexity and function of the genome. Perhaps the most important point that can be taken from all this is the trajectory of these results — we watched the scientific community go from claiming high levels of non-function in the early 2000s to claiming evidence for nearly pervasive function just a decade later. This suggests that more experiments will only increase the percentage of human DNA sequence that performs a biological function just as the current leader of the ENCODE project is predicting. This upward trajectory does not bode well for evolution, a fact that the BioLogos community is very reticent to admit.

---

45. Epigenetics is the study of heritable changes that do not involve changes in DNA sequence.

Neanderthal Ancestry?

On a side note, related to the question of human-ape ancestry is the question of the relationships between Neanderthals and modern humans. Interestingly, most people would be surprised to know that evolutionists consider Neanderthals to be fully human, hence they are given the technical name "archaic humans" as opposed to modern contemporary humans. An increasing number of publications claim to have recovered DNA from ancient human or human-like samples, and the comparison of these DNA samples with those of modern humans could inform the ancestry question.

Though YEC advocates and evolutionists both agree that modern humans and Neanderthals had a common ancestor (YE creationists would say that Neanderthals are post-Flood descendants of Adam and Eve), these two positions disagree on when the Neanderthals lived — tens to hundreds of thousands of years ago (evolutionary model) versus about 4,500 years or less (YEC model). Evidence for a prehistoric[46] human population could add credence to the evolutionary claim that human ancestry stretches far back in time — so far back that it touches on the boundaries of an alleged divergence from an ape lineage. Time is the magical key to the evolutionary equation, despite the fact that no viable human-ape transitional forms exist in the fossil record, as discussed in a separate chapter.

Without going into great technical detail, the short answer to the question of what Neanderthal DNA implies regarding the origins issue is that Neanderthal and ancient DNA samples appear to be too degraded and often untrustworthy for use in rigorous genetic analyses. In addition, analyses are perpetually plagued with DNA contamination from microorganisms and modern human DNA from lab workers.[47] Finally, no one knows the rate at which Neanderthal DNA changes from generation to generation — and it might change at a rate much faster than that reported for modern human individuals.[48]

As things stand now, the most credible research comparing Neanderthals to modern humans merely shows that their DNA is human. The dating of

46. E.g., a population living at the time that the evolutionists propose — hundreds of thousands of years ago.
47. Brian Thomas and Jeffrey Tomkins, "How Reliable are Genomes from Ancient DNA?" *Journal of Creation* 28 no. 3 (2014): 92–98.
48. Nathaniel T. Jeanson, "Mitochondrial DNA Clocks Imply Linear Speciation Rates Within 'Kinds,' " *Answers Research Journal* 8 (2015): 273–304, https://answersingenesis.org/natural-selection/speciation/clocks-imply-linear-speciation-rates-within-kinds/.

the bones from the sites in which Neanderthals are found are not based on DNA, but other types of spurious data, and the evolutionists are constantly changing the dates of the material found in these locations — a fact in and of itself that shows how subjective the whole process really is.

Summary

To summarize, on the question of human-ape common ancestry, all of the claimed evolutionary evidences are type-2 or type-3 experiments that fail to eliminate the main competing hypothesis, YEC (Table 2). Instead of being a minor side issue in the bigger human ancestry debate, this very poor scientific track record for evolution represents a systematic failure across the board. In nearly every type of genetic comparison that can be performed between humans and chimpanzees, the evolutionary model has made erroneous predictions (Table 3).

In an attempt to move the discussion forward and into the realm of type-1 experiments, creationists have published a testable, predictive model of DNA function from a YEC perspective on one of the few remaining areas of DNA function that has not yet been thoroughly investigated[49] (see reference for technical details). If the evolutionists are as confident in their ideas as they claim, then we invite them to publish similar predictions of genetic function, and then to do a head-to-head experiment to test both of the ideas in the laboratory. If evolutionists are unwilling to engage in the experiment that we have proposed, at a minimum, they need to propose a different type-1 experiment.

In short, on the question of human ancestry, evolutionists have a history of making erroneous scientific predictions; they have yet to articulate a genuine genetic test by which to eliminate YEC from the discussion; and their model does not look promising in light of the trajectory of experimental results in areas where evolution and YEC could theoretically be compared head-to-head.

II. How Many: A Population or a Pair?

For many years, the discussion of the number of individuals that spawned the modern human race was not accessible to science. Fossils don't record population sizes, and the antiquity and geography of our ancestors offer little in the way of direct data on the number of individuals alive on the

49. Nathaniel T. Jeanson, "Recent, Functionally Diverse Origin for Mitochondrial Genes from ~2700 Metazoan Species," *Answers Research Journal* 6 (2013): 467–501, https://answersingenesis.org/genetics/mitochondrial-dna/recent-functionally-diverse-origin-for-mitochondrial-genes-from--2700-metazoan-species/.

Table 2. Factually erroneous evolutionary claims about human-primate ancesty

Evolutionary Claim	Actual Data	Type of experiment
Human-chimpanzee genetic identity is 98-99%	Actual genetic identity is only 88% (i.e., 400,000,000 DNA differences exist between the two species)	2
Humans are genetically closer to apes than to other animal species, unequivocally demonstrating common ancestry	Relative hierarchies are characteristics of design	3
Human chromosome #2 arose via fusion of two ape-like chromosomes	The purported "fusion" site is actually a functional DNA element in a human gene	2
Gene order along chromosomes has no function, therefore shared gene order demonstrates common ancestry	Gene order along chromosomes does indeed perform a function	2
Humans and chimpanzees shared genetic mistakes (e.g., pseudogenes)	Pseudogenes appear to be functional DNA elements, not mistakes	2
Humans possess the broken remnants of an ancient chicken gene (vitellogenin)	No such remnant exists; instead the "fragment" appears to be a functional DNA element	2

Table 3. Grand Summary of Human-Chimpanzee Genetic Comparisons

Type of Genetic Comparison/Analysis	Evolutionary Success or Failure?
Total DNA differences between humans and chimpanzees	Failure to predict total genetic differences (a big genetic gap separates the two species)
Relative genetic differences between humans and chimpanzees	Irrelevant to debate (evolutionary comparison fails to refute the YEC model, thereby making it scientifically invalid)
Chromosome differences between humans and chimpanzees	Failure to predict chromosome differences (no evidence for claimed fusion event)
Total genetic function in humans	Current scientific trajectory points toward much more function than predicted by evolution
Specific examples of genetic function in humans	Failure to predict functional DNA sequences (pseudogenes and chromosomal gene order were mislabeled as "non-functional")

planet at the dawn of *Homo sapiens*. Only with the advent of modern genetics have scientists been able to more directly explore this question.

However, the raw genetic data say nothing about ancestral population sizes. The evolutionary conclusion that humanity arose from a large population[50] rather than a pair of individuals is a consequence of the arbitrary constraints that evolutionists bring to bear on the question. Implicit in the evolutionary claims is the assumption that DNA differences can arise only via the process of copying errors (mutations) that we discussed in the previous section. In other words, under the evolutionary model, the immediate reason why you are genetically different from your parents is that you inherited DNA from *each* parent. However, according to evolutionary reasoning, the ultimate reason why genetic differences exist at all in the human population is mutations in the distant past.

If you insist on this evolutionary assumption and forbid the consideration of any other hypotheses on the origin of genetic differences, then you are almost forced to conclude that humanity could *not* have arisen from two people in the last few thousand years. Millions of DNA letter differences exist among humans (about 3–5 million per person on average, which is about 0.1% of the total human DNA sequence),[51] and the measured 60 mutations per generation can't produce this much diversity among humans in just 6,000 years, assuming that mutation rates have always been constant.

However, it doesn't take much reflection to see that this assumption is shortsighted. Let's apply it to the YEC model and see how well it works. If we assume, for sake of argument, that mankind did indeed arise from two supernaturally created people (regardless of how long ago it was), and if we further stipulate that genetic differences can arise only via mutations, then we would be forced to conclude that Adam and Eve did not have any genetic differences between them (aside from the X and Y chromosomes, since these are involved in specifying gender).

But this hypothetical scenario leads to some bizarre conclusions. If Adam and Eve decided to fulfill God's command to be fruitful and multiply, they would have passed on two identical DNA sequences to their offspring. Aside from the few mutations that may have arisen (representing 0.00000001% of the billions of DNA[52] letters in our cells — a negligible fraction), Adam and Eve would have basically produced copies of themselves — not slightly modified versions of themselves as we are used to observing in our own

50. Dennis Venema and Darrel Falk, "Does Genetics Point to a Single Primal Couple?" https://BioLogos.org/blogs/dennis-venema-letters-to-the-duchess/does-genetics-point-to-a-single-primal-couple.

51. The 1000 Genomes Project Consortium, "A Global Reference for Human Genetic Variation," *Nature* 526 (2015): 68-74, http://www.nature.com/nature/journal/v526/n7571/full/nature15393.html.

52. Their offspring would have received 60 new mutations. So, 60 / 6,000,000,000 = 0.00000001%.

children, but *identical* copies of themselves. Offspring that are completely identical to parents receive a particular label in genetics: clones. Cloning as a means to fulfill the dominion mandate is a strange position to maintain. With all the debate that currently exists over the ethics of human cloning, it is somewhat disturbing to think that God instructed the first man and woman to fill the earth by this process.

A very simple alternative hypothesis resolves the conundrum and also makes straightforward scientific sense: God could have created Adam and Eve with genetic differences from the start (Figure 1). In fact, all of us possess not just 3 billion letters of DNA in our cells. With few exceptions such as red blood cells, the cells of our body possess *two versions* of our 3 billion letters, which means that each of our cells has 6 billion letters. Each parent passes on only 3 billion in sperm or egg, keeping the total of 6 billion letters constant across generations. Going back in time, Adam would likely have had the same cellular arrangement — two versions of his 3 billion letters — and the same would have been true of Eve.

This arrangement makes sense of the DNA differences that exist in the world today. Before the Fall and after the Fall, the two different copies of Adam and Eve's DNA would have been reshuffled via at least two processes termed *recombination* and *gene conversion*, making each offspring unique and leading to diversity within the human race. After the Fall, mutations (perhaps at a rate of 60 mutations per generation) would have occurred and added to the genetic diversity in their children,[53] and leading to the production of diverse offspring (in contrast to cloning). Calculations within the parameters of this model match the worldwide DNA diversity that we observe today.[54] Thus, to claim that the millions of DNA differences that separate each person from another somehow invalidates the clear teaching of Scripture about the origin of mankind from two people about 6,000 years ago is scientifically unsupportable. In fact, this type of creation model is considerably more supportive of the genetic paradigm of human diversity than the evolutionary model, as we will show.

53. Under the YEC model, there is no scientific reason to exclude mutations from happening after the entrance of sin into the world at the Fall. Instead, mutations likely played a minor role in generating the genetic diversity observable today — minor because of the sheer number of differences with which Adam and Eve were likely created.

54. Robert W. Carter, "The Non-Mythical Adam and Eve! Refuting errors by Francis Collins and BioLogos," http://creation.com/historical-adam-BioLogos; Nathaniel T. Jeanson and Jason Lisle, "On the Origin of Eukaryotic Species' Genotypic and Phenotypic Diversity," *Answers Research Journal* 9 (2016): 81–122, https://answersingenesis.org/natural-selection/speciation/on-the-origin-of-eukaryotic-species-genotypic-and-phenotypic-diversity/.

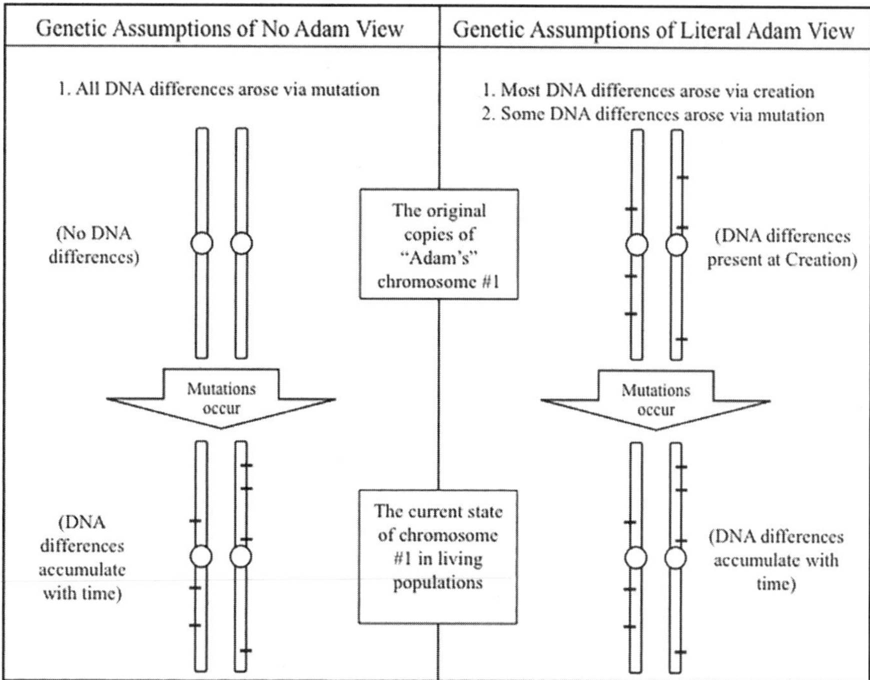

Figure 1. Fundamental assumptions about the nature of genetic change lead to very different conclusions on the original genetic state in Adam, and, therefore, on whether or not he existed in the recent past. The scenario on the left requires long periods of time to explain modern genetic diversity; the scenario on the right requires just a few thousand years to explain modern genetic diversity.

The BioLogos website lists at least two other lines of evidence[55] in support of their population-not-pair contention, but each of these falls prey to poor logic or unsound science, just like the argument above. One of the claims deals with a subsection of DNA that is repetitive in nature.[56] But in attempting to explain the origin and arrangement of these sequences, the BioLogos writers assume human-ape common ancestry. Thus, as an argument against the biblical position that humans were created as a pair and distinct from the apes, it is nothing more than circular reasoning.

The second claim[57] deals with the rate at which sections of DNA are swapped during sperm and egg cell production (the technical terms of two swapping processes are genetic *recombination* and *gene conversion*), but the

55. Dennis Venema and Darrel Falk, "Does Genetics Point to a Single Primal Couple?" https://BioLogos.org/blogs/dennis-venema-letters-to-the-duchess/does-genetics-point-to-a-single-primal-couple.

56. Specifically, the DNA sequences are called *Alu* sequences.

57. The second claim addresses the arrangement and groupings of DNA differences along chromosome (technically termed *linkage disequilibrium*).

conclusions that the BioLogos writers reach is based on erroneous assumptions and outdated science. With respect to the latter, in making their claim, the evolutionists assume only a single process of reshuffling DNA sequences (e.g., recombination) when, in fact, there are at least two (the second and, apparently, much faster process of reshuffling is gene conversion).[58] Had they included this faster process in their calculations, they would have discovered that mankind's genetic history is much shorter than they claimed.[59]

In summary, just like the evolutionary arguments for human-ape common ancestry, the evolutionary arguments for mankind's origin from a large population (rather than an original pair) are nothing more than type-3 experiments, which are useless in adjudicating between creation and evolution. There is no scientific evidence that we arose from a group of individuals rather than from Adam and Eve. If evolutionists wish to continue making their claims and be taken seriously, they need to propose a type-1 experiment.

Conversely, by starting with the assumption that God created Adam and Eve with genetic diversity from the start, the YEC model can easily explain the existing genetic diversity among living humans. In fact, the explanatory power of these human DNA findings is so strong that they have led to testable predictions for other species.[60]

III. When: Ancient or Recent?

As we've observed in the preceding section, using DNA sequences to function as a clock is not straightforward. In theory, just like the ticks of a clock mark off the passage of time, the transmission of another 60 DNA mutations from parent to offspring should be able to mark the passage of another generation. However, knowing how much time has passed requires knowing when the clock — whether mechanical or biological — actually started ticking. As we observed above, some (probably most) DNA differences may not represent mutations at all; they may have been supernaturally created

58. Jianbin Wang et al., "Genome-wide Single-Cell Analysis of Recombination Activity and De Novo Mutation Rates in Human Sperm," *Cell* 150 (2012): 402–412, http://www.cell.com/cell/abstract/S0092-8674%2812%2900789-1?_returnURL=http%3A%2F%2Flinkinghub.elsevier.com%2Fretrieve%2Fpii%2FS0092867412007891%3Fshowall%3Dtrue; Amy L. Williams et al., "Non-crossover Gene Conversions Show Strong GC Bias and Unexpected Clustering in Humans," *eLife* 4 (2015): e04637, http://elifesciences.org/content/4/e04637; Pier Francesco Palamara et al., "Leveraging Distant Relatedness to Quantify Human Mutation and Gene-Conversion Rates," *Am. J. Hum. Genet.* 97 (2015): 775–789.

59. Jeanson and Lisle, "On the Origin of Eukaryotic Species' Genotypic and Phenotypic Diversity," p. 81–122.

60. Ibid.

in Adam and Eve from the start — e.g., Adam and Eve would have been created with genetic differences. Thus, when we're evaluating the billions of DNA letters in our cells and trying to determine when the differences began arising, it's as if we were asked how long a clock has been ticking — but then were told that the clock has at least four hands instead of two.[61]

Therefore, to use DNA as a clock to measure when humanity began requires a very careful accounting of all potential means of genetic change and all potential genetic starting points. In other words, the only relevant DNA clock to the human origins debate is one in which evolutionists and creationists agree on the mechanism by which DNA differences arise as well as on the number of starting points from which DNA differences can arise.

Only one candidate DNA clock currently fulfills these criteria. Again, the vast majority of the billions of DNA letters in our cells do not lend themselves to a head-to-head comparison. Both sides may claim that the data fits their view, but claiming that the data support a view *to the exclusion of the other* is very challenging (as illustrated in the previous section).

Conversely, creationists and evolutionists agree on the origin of DNA differences in a tiny subsection of DNA (~16,559 DNA letters long) contained in the energy factories of our cells, called the *mitochondria*. Mitochondria and mitochondrial DNA ("mtDNA") are found in both males and females, but only females appear to pass on mtDNA to their offspring. In other words, we each received our mtDNA from our mother, and our spouses received theirs from their mothers. Each of our children in turn did not inherit their father's mtDNA; they inherited their mother's.

Evolutionists agree that the current mtDNA differences among modern humans are traceable to a single woman in the past, whom they label "Eve."[62] However, they insist that this woman was part of a population of humans, not a single pair. This conclusion arises, not because of anything inherent to the mtDNA data, but because of the data from the billions of letters in the rest of the DNA sequence and the evolutionary presuppositions that we discussed in the previous section.

From a biblical perspective, all humans trace their ancestry back to Adam and Eve. However, because mtDNA is maternally inherited, YE creationists would agree with evolutionists that mtDNA differences today are

61. Since Adam and Eve each would have been created with *two versions* of their 3 billion letter DNA sequence, and since Eve's versions may have been slightly different than Adam's, humanity may trace its genetic origins to 4 different starting points.

62. Dennis Venema, "Mitochondrial Eve, Y-Chromosome Adam, and Reasons to Believe," https://BioLogos.org/blogs/dennis-venema-letters-to-the-duchess/mitochondrial-eve-y-chromosome-adam-and-reasons-to-believe.

traceable to a single woman in the past — Eve (both creation and evolution refer to her with the same name). Furthermore, both evolutionists and creationists would agree that modern mtDNA differences are the result of copying errors (i.e., mutations). Unlike the 3 billion DNA letters of DNA in the cell's nucleus that come in *two versions*, mtDNA comes in only one version — effectively, the mother's version. Hence, mtDNA differences arise via copying errors and were not created in Eve.

Thus, on the question of the origin of mtDNA differences, evolutionists and creationists are in complete agreement, except for one point — when this maternal ancestor lived. (Again, the evolutionary claims about this woman being part of a population have nothing to do with the mtDNA data itself; the population claim is imposed from the outside on top of the mtDNA data.)

To summarize up to this point, when we're discussing mtDNA, both origins views hold to a single starting point. Because mtDNA comes in one version, not in two versions like the 3 billion letters of nuclear DNA sequence, both origins views also hold to copying errors (mutations) as the sole source of DNA variety (i.e., YE creationists do not believe that God created different mtDNA versions in Eve). Thus, mtDNA comparisons are one of the few type-1 experiments that can actually be performed to answer the question of *when* humanity began, and since the rate at which mutations occur in mtDNA has already been measured, this experiment can be performed right now.

To use mtDNA as a clock, we simply use this measured mutation rate to make testable predictions based on either the evolutionary timescale or on the YEC timescale and then compare the predictions with the scientific, observed facts. In other words, rather than starting with mtDNA differences in the present and then dialing the clock backward to see how long it would take to get to Eve, we're going to go backward in time to the beginning under each model and predict what would have happened if the clock were allowed to run forward to the present. Specifically, we will assume for sake of argument that humans originated a long time ago (180,000 years ago under the evolutionary model[63]) or recently (4,500 years ago under the YEC model,[64] representing the end of the Flood — see technical references for technical genetic reasons why the Flood date rather than the creation date

63. See references in Nathaniel T. Jeanson, "A Young-Earth Creation Human Mitochondrial DNA 'Clock': Whole Mitochondrial Genome Mutation Rate Confirms D-loop Results," *Answers Research Journal* 8 (2015): 375–378, https://answersingenesis.org/genetics/mitochondrial-genome-mutation-rate-/.

64. Ibid.

was chosen).[65] Then we will predict how many mtDNA differences should have accumulated in the timeframe specific to each model, after which we'll compare these predictions to the actual number of differences in the current human population.

Thus, by multiplying the measured mutation rate of mtDNA[66] by 180,000 years or by 4,500 years, we can make testable predictions about the timescale of human origins. Comparing these predictions to actual mtDNA differences at the global scale reveals a result that strongly contradicts the evolutionary timescale and confirms the YEC timescale (Figure 2).[67]

After 180,000 years, humans would have accumulated over 2,000 DNA differences (range = 1,220 to ~4,700)[68] via the process of mutation to mtDNA. In just 4,364 years,[69] humans would have accumulated only 30 to 114 mutations.[70] Currently, about 78 differences exist on average in African populations

---

65. Nathaniel T. Jeanson, "Mitochondrial DNA Clocks Imply Linear Speciation Rates Within 'Kinds,' " *Answers Research Journal* 8 (2015): 273–304, https://answersingenesis.org/natural-selection/speciation/clocks-imply-linear-speciation-rates-within-kinds/.
66. About 1 mtDNA letter is mutated every ~6 generations, on average. See Nathaniel T. Jeanson, "A Young-Earth Creation Human Mitochondrial DNA 'Clock': Whole Mitochondrial Genome Mutation Rate Confirms D-loop Results," *Answers Research Journal* 8 (2015): 375–378, https://answersingenesis.org/genetics/mitochondrial-genome-mutation-rate-/.
67. Nathaniel T. Jeanson, "Recent, Functionally Diverse Origin for Mitochondrial Genes from ~2700 Metazoan Species," *Answers Research Journal* 6 (2013): 467–501, https://answersingenesis.org/genetics/mitochondrial-dna/recent-functionally-diverse-origin-for-mitochondrial-genes-from--2700-metazoan-species/; Nathaniel T. Jeanson, "Mitochondrial DNA Clocks Imply Linear Speciation Rates within 'Kinds,' " *Answers Research Journal* 8 (2015): 273-304, https://answersingenesis.org/natural-selection/speciation/clocks-imply-linear-speciation-rates-within-kinds/; Nathaniel T. Jeanson, "A Young-Earth Creation Human Mitochondrial DNA 'Clock': Whole Mitochondrial Genome Mutation Rate Confirms D-loop Results," *Answers Research Journal* 8 (2015): 375–378, https://answersingenesis.org/genetics/mitochondrial-genome-mutation-rate-/; Nathaniel T. Jeanson, "On the Origin of Human Mitochondrial DNA Differences, New Generation Time Data Suggest a Unified Young-Earth Creation Model and Challenge the Evolutionary Out-of-Africa Model," *Answers Research Journal* 9 (2016): 123-130, https://answersingenesis.org/genetics/mitochondrial-dna/origin-human-mitochondrial-dna-differences-new-generation-time-data-both-suggest-unified-young-earth/.
68. The range of numbers is due to the fact that the measured mutation rate has (like all biological data) a range of statistical uncertainty. Combined with the fact that there's a range of generation times for humans (e.g., some women marry and bear children at age 15, others at age 35), we report a statistically reliable range of predictions for both creation and evolution.
69. We used one of the shortest estimated time frames from the Flood to the present. Arguments could be made for longer time frames, but since our calculations with the shorter time frame already show agreement with current data, longer time frames would simply underscore the veracity of our results.
70. Ibid.

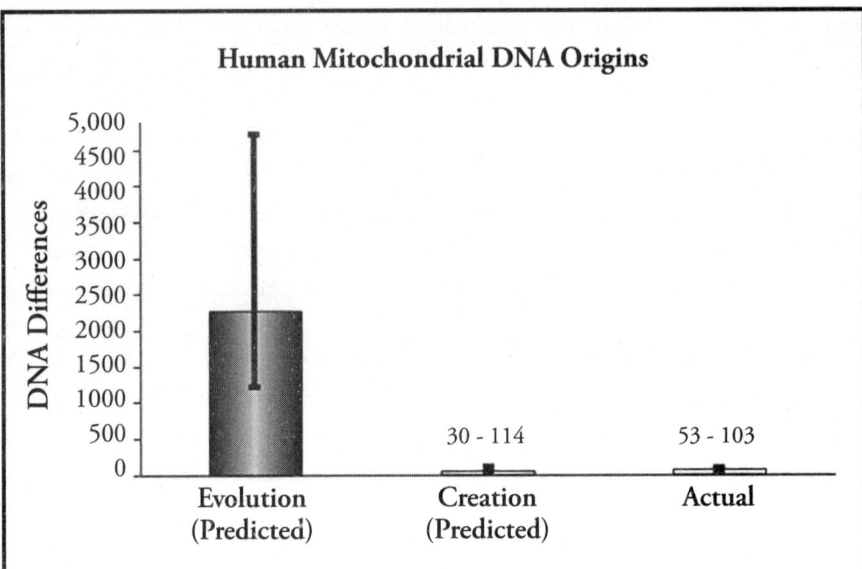

Figure 2. Comparison of origins predictions to actual human mitochondrial DNA differences. Differences were predicted by multiplying the measured mitochondrial DNA mutation rate by 2 and by the model-specific time of origin (e.g., for evolution, 180,000 years was used; for creation, 4,364 years was used as the (post-Flood) time of origin). The height of each column represents the average number of differences that would have accumulated under the model-specific time of origin ("Evolution" and "Creation"), and the black lines spanning the top of each column represent the full statistical range of each prediction, not the standard deviation (e.g., the lines represent the maximum best possible guesses under the evolutionary or creation timeframes). The height of the "Actual" column represents the average DNA differences in Africans today, and the black line spanning it represents the standard deviation. African DNA differences were used instead of non-African differences because Africans are the most genetically diverse group alive today and because evolutionists posit that Africans evolved first.

(i.e., the most genetically diverse of all the human ethnic groups), with a maximum difference of ~120. Clearly, the YEC timescale accurately predicts the number of DNA differences that we observe today, while the evolutionary timescale predicts numbers an order of magnitude higher. Similar results hold true in animal species, as illustrated in Figure 3.

These findings represent much more than an isolated, irrelevant data point in the bigger creation/evolution debate. As we observed above, mtDNA is one of the only arenas in which a straightforward type-1 experiment can be performed — one of the only arenas in which we can judge the scientific validity of the creation model versus the evolution model. Furthermore, performing this mtDNA experiment in a wide variety of animal species leads to the same conclusion: the biblical view of earth history is

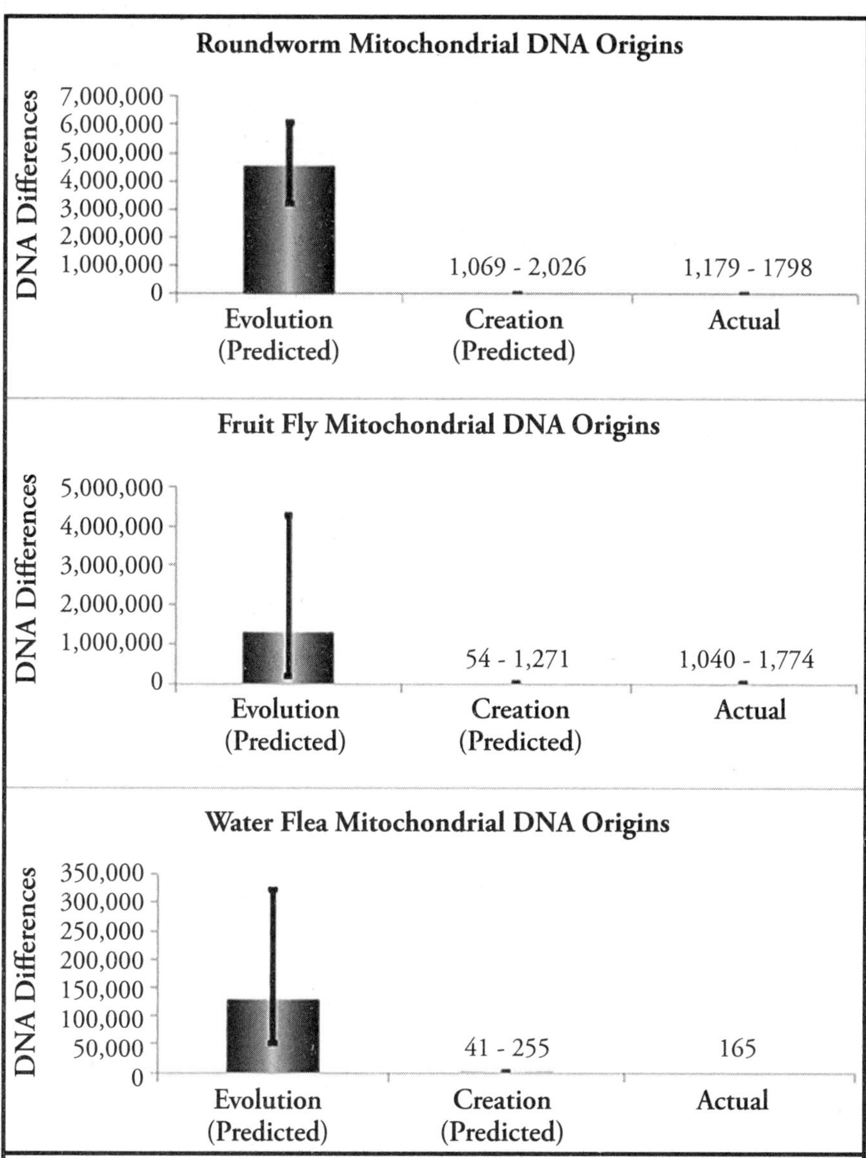

Figure 3. Comparison of origins predictions to actual animal mitochondrial DNA differences. Differences were predicted by multiplying the measured mitochondrial DNA mutation rate by 2 (roundworms, fruit flies) or by 1 (water fleas), and by the model-specific time of origin (e.g., for evolution, the time appropriate to each organism was used; for creation, 6,000 years was used as the time of origin). The height of each column represents the average number of differences that would have accumulated under the model-specific time of origin ("Evolution" and "Creation"), and the black lines spanning the top of each column represent the full statistical range of each prediction, not the standard deviation (e.g., the lines represent the maximum best possible guesses under the evolutionary or creation timeframes). The height of the "Actual" column represents the average DNA differences today, and the black line spanning it represents the range of differences (where appropriate).

correct.[71] Thus, the evolutionary timescale runs into trouble not only on the question of human origins but across a much wider swath of biological life.

Implicit in these calculations was the assumption that the mtDNA mutation rate has been constant with time. We made this assumption since it forms the basis for the entire millions-of-years paradigm in the evolutionary model. When evolutionists claim that the earth or the universe are ancient, their methods assume that the geologic or astronomical processes that they observe today have occurred at a constant rate throughout the history of the earth or universe.[72]

For decades, YE creationists have pointed out the arbitrary nature of this assumption,[73] especially in light of the global Flood element of the YEC model of geology.[74] Essentially, YE creationists have correctly identified the entire millions-of-years paradigm as nothing more than a type-3 experiment. In short, the evolutionary argument about the age of the earth and of the universe work only if the assumption about constant rates of change is true. Change that assumption and the entire paradigm collapses.

Thus, by assuming constant rates of genetic change in our calculations, we made the calculations overly generous to the evolutionary view. The fact that the evolutionary predictions could not be reconciled with reality even under generous assumptions makes the explanatory dilemma for evolutionists all the greater. If they claim that rates of genetic change were different in the past, they've just undermined the foundational assumption of their entire ancient universe/ancient earth view. If they do nothing, they are left with a glaring contradiction between predictions and facts. Hence, these mtDNA results have implications for the evolutionary view far beyond biology, and

71. Nathaniel T. Jeanson, "Recent, Functionally Diverse Origin for Mitochondrial Genes from ~2700 Metazoan Species," *Answers Research Journal* 6 (2013): 467–501, https://answersingenesis.org/genetics/mitochondrial-dna/recent-functionally-diverse-origin-for-mitochondrial-genes-from--2700-metazoan-species/; Nathaniel T. Jeanson, "Mitochondrial DNA Clocks Imply Linear Speciation Rates within 'Kinds,' " *Answers Research Journal* 8 (2015): 273–304, https://answersingenesis.org/natural-selection/speciation/clocks-imply-linear-speciation-rates-within-kinds/.

72. Anon., "How Are the Ages of the Earth and Universe Calculated?" https://BioLogos.org/common-questions/scientific-evidence/ages-of-the-earth-and-universe/.

73. For a recent discussion of the constant rate assumptions in astronomy, see: Jason Lisle, "Anisotropic Synchrony Convention — A Solution to the Distant Starlight Problem," *Answers Research Journal* 3 (2010): 191–207, https://answersingenesis.org/astronomy/starlight/anisotropic-synchrony-convention-distant-starlight-problem/.

74. The YEC community has even performed full-scale laboratory research projects to support this conclusion. For example, see Larry Vardiman, Andrew Snelling, and Eugene Chaffin, eds., *Radioisotopes and the Age of the Earth*, Vol. 2 (El Cajon, California: Institute for Creation Research; Chino Valley, Arizona: Creation Research Society, 2005).

Table 4. Summary of Human Genetic Differences under YEC View

Cellular compartment	Letters in DNA sequence	Inheritance	Origin of human-human differences under YEC view
Nucleus	3,000,000,000	Paternal and Maternal	Majority of DNA differences due to Creation, minority due to mutation
Mitochondria	16,559	Maternal	All DNA differences due to mutation

they make the evolutionary paradigm even harder to maintain in a scientifically consistent and coherent way.

Perhaps the evolutionists will invoke natural selection to explain why their predictions do not match up with facts. In other words, perhaps humans have fewer genetic differences than predicted under the evolutionary model because natural selection eliminated a number of copying errors that arose in the past. This hypothesis would be worth exploring — but only if it leads to testable, falsifiable predictions.

Summary

In summary, there is no genetic evidence to support an ancient origin for mankind. The DNA differences in the billions of DNA letters in the cellular compartment termed the *nucleus* are easily explicable from two people in the last 6,000 years (see previous section), and the mtDNA differences observable today are all the more explicable (Table 4; Figure 2). The mtDNA arena of comparison also happens to be one arena in which a type-1 experiment can be performed, and the evidence strongly contradicts the evolutionary timescale while confirming the YEC timescale. Since these results assumed constant rates of genetic change, and since evolutionary geology and astronomy also depend on the assumption of constant rates of change for their millions- and billions-of-years conclusions, these genetic findings throw into confusion these two fields of physical science as well. Genetically speaking, mankind appears to have originated only a few thousand years ago.

Again, the success of these initial genetic results gives us confidence that we can predict mtDNA mutation rates for other species, and we are willing to test these predictions in the lab. In fact, we invite our evolutionary colleagues to join us so that we can perform a type-1 experiment as accurately as possible. If our evolutionary colleagues are unwilling or unable to make and test a falsifiable prediction, why should we view their claims as scientific rather than pseudoscientific?

IV. Where: Africa or Ararat?

The mtDNA results discussed above hinted at the one element of human origins that we have not explored in detail — the timing and geography of the origin of African people groups. On the question of geography, creation and evolution are largely in agreement — except for the origin of African people groups. Evolutionists posit that Africans evolved first and then gave rise to the non-African groups.[75] In contrast, YE creationists posit the simultaneous origin of the major ethnic groups very soon after the dispersion at the Tower of Babel.

The genetic aspects of the evolutionary claim rests on a technical aspect of mtDNA comparisons. Both evolutionists and creationists use software to visualize the number of DNA differences among various individuals or ethnic groups, and one of the most common visualization tools is the creation of phylogenetic or family trees. Naturally, this implies a genealogical relationship among those connected on the tree, but, in the software employed, ancestry assumptions are not necessary. The tree simply depicts the number of DNA differences in a visually striking way.

When the evolutionists draw trees, they of course assume common ancestry regardless of the species compared, since one of the foundational tenets of evolution is universal common ancestry of all species on earth (i.e., all plants, animals, and humans are descended from a single common and microscopic ancestor). Not surprisingly, when evolutionists draw family trees of the human ethnic groups using mtDNA comparisons, they include chimpanzee DNA.[76] This resultant tree — which evolutionists interpret as genealogical relationships — shows some of the African branches splitting off first (about 120,000–180,000 years ago, as we alluded to in section III) followed by non-African groups later (about 50,000 years ago).

Even if you omit the chimpanzee DNA from the comparison and draw the tree using only modern human ethnic groups, it is still obvious that African ethnic groups have about twice as many mtDNA differences among them as do non-African ethnic groups. If you assume that the rate of mtDNA mutations is constant with time, the fact of greater mtDNA diversity in Africans implies that Africans have been around longer than non-Africans.

---

75. Dennis Venema, "Mitochondrial Eve, Y-Chromosome Adam, and Reasons to Believe," https://BioLogos.org/blogs/dennis-venema-letters-to-the-duchess/mitochondrial-eve-y-chromosome-adam-and-reasons-to-believe.
76. For example, see Max Ingman, et al., "Mitochondrial Genome Variation and the Origin of Modern Humans," *Nature* 408 (2000): 708–713.

Table 5. Age of First Marriage by People Group and Age (UN data from 1976)

	Age Bracket										
	15-19	20-24	25-29	30-34	35-39	40-44	45-49	50-54	55-59	60-64	65+
Africa: % of women married	32.0	67.4	81.3	83.3	83.6	79.2	74.4	64.7	56.8	44.4	28.2
non-Africa: % of women married	11.8	47.2	69.8	77.0	78.2	77.0	73.8	67.7	61.6	51.0	32.2
Fold-difference	2.7	1.4	1.2	1.1	1.1	1.0	1.0	1.0	0.9	0.9	0.9

However, implicit in this conclusion is a technical assumption about the mtDNA mutation rates. To measure these rates empirically, scientists must use pedigrees,[77] which means that the units are reported in terms of *mutations per generation*. To convert these units to absolute time (i.e., *mutations per year*), scientists must make an assumption about how many years pass per generation. Evolutionists implicitly assume that the generation times (time from birth of parent to birth of child) across all ethnic groups are the same.

However, marriage data from the United Nations suggests that this assumption is not valid (Table 5).[78] On average, African females marry earlier in life than non-African females. About 32% of African women are married by ages 15–19 whereas only 12% of non-African women are married by the same age. This roughly three-fold difference disappears at later ages (e.g., about the same number of African and non-African women are married by their 30's and 40's), suggesting that the generation time in Africans might be

77. E.g., they sequence the DNA from a parent-offspring pair (or perhaps even a grandparent-grandchild pair), and then count the number of differences that have arisen from ancestor to descendant. This represents one or more generational events; hence, units are reported in terms of *mutations per generation*.
78. United Nations, Department of Economic and Social Affairs: Population Division, Fertility and Family Planning Section, "World Marriage Data 2012," http://www.un.org/esa/population/publications/WMD2012/MainFrame.html; see also Nathaniel T. Jeanson, "On the Origin of Human Mitochondrial DNA Differences, New Generation Time Data Both Suggest a Unified Young-Earth Creation Model and Challenge the Evolutionary Out-of-Africa Model," *Answers Research Journal* 9 (2016): 123–130, https://answersingenesis.org/genetics/mitochondrial-dna/origin-human-mitochondrial-dna-differences-new-generation-time-data-both-suggest-unified-young-earth/.

about twice as fast as the generation time in non-Africans. Since mtDNA is passed on maternally, these data imply that some African ethnic groups have twice as many mtDNA differences because twice as many generations have passed in their lineages as compared to non-African lineages.

The data we presented in figure 2 made predictions for a variety of generation times (e.g., 15 years to 35 years). Under none of these generation times could the evolutionary model correctly predict the amount of DNA differences observable today. In contrast, the YEC predictions correctly predicted the African mtDNA differences under the assumption of a higher generation time (e.g., assuming a generation time of 15 years, the YEC model predicts 69 to 114 DNA differences in 4,364 years, which captures the average mtDNA differences — 78 — present today among Africans). The mtDNA differences among non-Africans (about 49, not displayed in figure 2) were predictable under the YEC model by assuming a generation time of 25 years (predicted range of differences = 41 to 69). Thus, the fact of higher mtDNA diversity in Africans does indeed appear to be due to their earlier age of marriage (and, presumably, of child-bearing), not to their supposed ancient evolutionary origin.

These data notwithstanding, evolutionists have also tried to buttress their out-of-Africa claims with data from the 3 billion DNA letters in the genome of the cell nucleus that we discussed previously — the main engine of heritability and diversity among humans. Specifically, Africans have more DNA differences among these 3 billion letters than non-Africans (only about 1.25-fold more), and they have more combinations of these differences (in technical genetic terms, *linkage disequilibrium* is lower in Africans).[79] To the evolutionist, these facts are consistent with an ancient origin of humans in Africa, and a more recent population bottleneck in their descendants who left Africa to found the modern non-African ethnic groups.

Again, these claims rest on assumptions of identical generation times among African and non-African ethnic groups, an assumption that is not borne out by current data. In addition, it appears that Africans reshuffle (e.g., in technical terms, *recombine*) their DNA at higher rates and/or in different places than non-Africans, which would explain their extra combinations (e.g., lower *linkage disequilibrium*) of DNA — a conclusion that even the evolutionary community concedes.[80]

79. The 1000 Genomes Project Consortium, "A Global Reference for Human Genetic Variation," *Nature* 526 (2015): 68–74, http://www.nature.com/nature/journal/v526/n7571/full/nature15393.html.

80. Anjali G. Hinch et al., "The Landscape of Recombination in African Americans," *Nature* 476 (2011): 170–175, http://www.ncbi.nlm.nih.gov/pmc/articles/PMC3154982/.

Table 6. Summary of YEC model on the origin of human ethnic groups

Cellular compartment	Inheritance	Genetic differences between Africans and non-Africans	Facts demonstrating contemporaneous origin of African and non-African people groups	Prediction
Nucleus	Paternal and Maternal	1.25-fold	Africans reshuffle their DNA faster (promotes retention of DNA differences)	
Mitochondria	Almost exclusively Maternal	1.5- to 2-fold	As compared to non-African women, twice as many African women marry early (more generations have passed in Africans, leading to more DNA differences)	
Y chromosome	Paternal	2-fold		Y chromosomes in Africans mutate/undergo gene conversion faster than in non-Africans

About the only genetic arena in which evolutionists can still hope to find evidence for an early origin of mankind out of Africa is in the Y chromosome — the chromosome unique to males, which is passed from fathers to sons. Current data indicate that African men have about twice as many Y chromosome differences as non-African men.[81] However, the rate at which the Y chromosome changes — either by mutation or by a process termed *gene conversion* — has not been published for Africans. We predict that African Y chromosomes will change twice as fast as non-African Y chromosomes. Conversely, if evolutionists are confident in their out-of-Africa model of human origins, we invite them to make a counter-prediction — and then test their ideas with us in the lab.

In summary, there is no straightforward genetic evidence for the origin of mankind first in Africa. Evolutionists reach this conclusion genetically by assuming human-ape common ancestry and by assuming that the generation times of all ethnic groups are identical. In the context of the origins debate, the first assumption represents circular reasoning, and the second

81. G. David Poznik et al., "Sequencing Y Chromosomes Resolves Discrepancy in Time to Common Ancestor of Males Versus Females," *Science* 341 no. 6145 (2013): 562–565, http://www.ncbi.nlm.nih.gov/pmc/articles/PMC4032117/.

assumption does not match published data. Africans reproduce earlier than non-Africans and reshuffle their DNA faster/in more places than non-Africans, and both of these facts appear sufficient to explain the data that we observe without invoking separate times of origin for the various people groups in existence today (Table 6).

Why Don't More Scientists Accept These Conclusions?

The conclusions that we've presented in this chapter are obviously at odds with the dominant scientific paradigm in the Western world today. How can our claims possibly be true? Evolutionists have an explanation that they've advanced for decades: YEC conclusions are *not* true. The justification that evolutionists cite for this claim is the absence of YEC conclusions from the mainstream peer-reviewed scientific literature. And why are creationist conclusions absent from this literature? The quote from BioLogos that we cited above is worth repeating here:

> The reason Christian anti-evolutionary approaches are absent from the mainstream scientific literature is not because scientists are theologically or philosophically biased against them, but rather because *they offer little in the way of useful tools for making accurate predictions about the natural world.*[82] [emphasis added]

As we've observed, this is factually untrue. In the realm of science that we've briefly examined in this chapter, YE creationists make *many* testable, accurate predictions about the natural world, and it's the *evolutionists* who historically have had trouble getting their predictions to match facts.

Furthermore, YE creation scientists do not publish un-reviewed technical papers. The major scientific players in the YEC field all earned their degrees from reputable secular universities with many also having many secular publications prior to making a career shift into origins research,[83] and we submit our findings to one another for peer-review prior to publication. Just like the secular peer-review system, some of our initial conclusions must be significantly refined or rejected before they have a chance of being published.

Naturally, evolutionists might criticize YEC scientists relying on like-minded individuals (e.g., fellow YEC scientists) for the peer-review process. Evolutionists might claim that this represents a self-reinforcing process that

---

82. Dennis Venema, "Theory, Prediction and Converging Lines of Evidence, Part 3," https://BioLogos.org/blogs/dennis-venema-letters-to-the-duchess/theory-prediction-and-converging-lines-of-evidence-part-3.
83. Anon., "Creation Scientists and Other Specialists of Interest," http://creation.com/creation-scientists.

is ultimately flawed and useless to scientific progress. But YEC scientists could say the same about evolutionists. The latter do not consult with YEC scientists before publishing their evolutionary conclusions. Instead, they solicit the assistance and review of the fellow, like-minded evolutionists!

Thus, on two counts, the common evolutionary reason for the absence of creationist ideas from mainstream scientific literature is wrong. First, creationists do indeed submit their research to peer review. Second, as we have demonstrated, they make testable scientific predictions that, in many cases, are more accurate than the predictions of the evolutionists (e.g., see preceding sections).

The latter fact raises an important question: *Why don't evolutionists submit their ideas to creationist peer-review before publication?* Why not solicit YEC PhD scientists for help and criticism before publishing a paper? Why not consult with the YEC community (at least informally) before taking evolutionary ideas public? Doing so might save the evolutionary model from further erroneous predictions.

To answer the question that heads this section, the BioLogos claim that we cited above would suggest that we are left with only one option: The vast majority of professional scientists are theologically or philosophically biased against creationist ideas. At first pass, this would seem conspiratorial and, therefore, difficult to accept.

Yet upon further reflection, this wooden interpretation of our options becomes much more nuanced in light of a few key facts. First, surveys show that the vast majority of scientists are unbelievers. Nearly 70% of scientific professionals cannot positively say that they believe in God.[84] Since belief in God is a necessary (but insufficient) profession for one to be a Christian, the number of non-Christian scientists is likely even higher than 70%.

Second, Scripture tells us that unbelievers do indeed have a bias. "For the wrath of God is revealed from heaven against all ungodliness and unrighteousness of men, who suppress the truth in unrighteousness, because what may be known of God is manifest in them, for God has shown it to them. For since the creation of the world His invisible attributes are clearly seen, being understood by the things that are made, even His eternal power and Godhead, so that they are without excuse" (Rom 1:18–20; NKJV). Not only do unbelievers suppress the truth about God, they suppress the truth about God that is revealed in nature. Thus, the creation/evolution debate is at the heart of the unbeliever's dealings with God.

84. Anon., "Scientists and Belief," http://www.pewforum.org/2009/11/05/scientists-and-belief/.

However, this passage in Romans does not suggest that all unbelievers go on the warpath against creationist ideas. Instead, Scripture says that unbelievers *suppress* the truth; they don't all violently try to destroy it. Conversely, suppressing the truth can take many forms — from passively ignoring contrary ideas, to never attempting to learn or understand uncomfortable contrary claims, to occasionally expressing strong dislike for an idea. In other words, non-Christian scientists are much like the unbelievers that we encounter every day. Most are passively disinterested in and ignorant of the things of God and of the scientific ramifications of the creation account. Only a few are visibly and adamantly opposed.

Sadly, as the above discussion demonstrates, evolutionists who are professing Christians appear to practice the same behavior.[85] For example, they seem to never have considered alternative hypotheses on the question of ancestral population size, and they regularly and prematurely turn highly speculative hypotheses into fact (e.g., Table 2).

The latter error should technically be termed pseudoscience. However, since the evolutionary creationists we cited are well trained and practiced scientists, we don't think this error stems from any lack of quality training. Instead, it is more likely to stem from an ignorance of the opposition. In other words, when a scientist is completely unaware of a contrary view, his hypothesis may seem like fact since nothing else seems able to explain the data he's observing.

In support of this conjecture, mainstream evolutionary literature demonstrates ignorance of creationist ideas.[86] For example, evolutionists regularly contend that accepting YEC requires throwing out science entirely:

> If someone challenges the current paradigm of [*sic*] by asserting that the Earth is not 4.5 billion years old, but rather was created by divine intervention 6000 years ago . . . the correct response is: "Well, maybe. But if that is what happened, then much else of what we think we know must also be wrong. We will need a new explanation for how the Sun gets its energy, as our laws about nuclear physics must be wrong. As this is the physics that has manifestly empowered engineers to build nuclear power plants, we need to explain how they are doing so well even though they are operating with the incorrect laws. The same would go for the empowerment

85. Note that most of our references to evolutionary ideas come from the BioLogos website.
86. For example, see chapter 23 of Douglas J. Futuyma, *Evolution* (Sunderland, MA: Sinauer Associates, Inc., 2013).

> provided by science for the use of radioisotopes in medicine X-rays in dentistry.[87]

The former president of BioLogos repeats this claim:

> The conclusion that creation is ancient does not come from interpretations at the periphery of these disciplines; it is at the core of all that nuclear physicists, geologists and astronomers do every day. For you or I to say that they are wrong is to say that these entire disciplines — geology, nuclear physics and astronomy — have got almost everything wrong.[88]

But it is nearly impossible to read and understand the YEC scientific literature and arrive at the conclusions above. These claims — that accepting YEC requires throwing out physics, geology, etc. — are as far from the truth as any stereotype of YEC science can be. Since we are confident that both of the men responsible for the quotes above are scholarly and logical scientists, we are left with one option: they haven't read and/or understood the YEC scientific literature.

Even more disappointing, the few evolutionary creation scientists with whom the authors of this chapter have personally communicated seem to have no interest in the YEC scientific literature. When we've presented them with the opportunity to engage the scientific data (e.g., by pleading with them to rigorously peer-review creationist findings before publication), they have declined. One theistic evolutionist has even admitted a past bias toward opponents, confessing that he viewed them as dumb and uninformed. If this is how professing Christians behave when confronted with contrary evidence, how much more so the unbelieving scientists!

In sum, the vast majority of the scientific world is at odds with the conclusions that we have presented here about human genetic origins because they appear to never have educated themselves on their opponents' scientific positions. More troubling is that, in some cases, evolutionists appear to have even deliberately avoided the opposition, and in the most extreme cases, intentionally suppressed it.[89] While this phenomenon could be labeled "bias," it does not appear to involve a deliberate and planned conspiracy

---

87. Steven Benner, "Challenge or Preserve the Paradigm?" https://BioLogos.org/blogs/archive/challenge-or-preserve-the-paradigm.
88. Darrel R. Falk, *Coming to Peace with Science: Bridging the Worlds Between Faith and Biology* (Downers Grove, IL: InterVarsity Press, 2004), p. 80–81.
89. Michael Behe, "Correspondence w/ Science Journals: Response to Critics Concerning Peer-Review," http://www.trueorigin.org/behe07.php.

among scientists in the Western world. Instead, for unbelievers, it appears to flow from their deeply rooted spiritual state. Since unbelievers are too proud to acknowledge God in their thinking,[90] and since all believers, ourselves included, are in the process of sanctification and can fall prey to some of the same sins that unbelievers practice, such as spiritual and/or intellectual pride, [91] the fear of man, and the desire for academic respect from the secular world,[92] "pride" rather than "bias" may be the better answer to the question that heads this section.

Summary and Ramifications

From the brief overview of the technical scientific literature that we've sketched, three facts emerge. First, the evolutionary model of human origins has a long history of scientific failure (Tables 2–3). It has repeatedly made public pronouncements of fact only to discover new data that contradict these claims. Hence, before we can even explore the question of whether evolution works as a scientific model today, we are struck with the dismal track record of evolution in times past.

Second, the evolutionary model does a poor job of explaining data in the present (Figure 2). When pressed to explain human-human genetic differences observable today, evolutionary predictions are an order of magnitude off the actual value. In essence, the evolutionary model cannot predict the rate of mtDNA mutation in humans. Since mutations are supposed to be the engine of evolution and the driver of all evolutionary change, this mismatch between predictions and facts is all the more profound.

Third, the YEC conclusions that we've highlighted in this chapter represent a comprehensive answer to the question of human genetic origins. Our claims and observations encompass virtually every genetic compartment present in human cells (Table 7), and they account for the millions of DNA differences across ethnic groups present in the world today. Furthermore, they robustly answer the questions of from whom humans originated (people, not apes), how many humans began our species (two — Adam and Eve), when humans originated (about 6,000 years ago), and where major human ethnic groups originated (near Ararat). In short, they explain all

90. "The wicked in his proud countenance does not seek God; God is in none of his thoughts" (Ps. 10:4; NKJV).
91. Note that pride need not pervade every area of a person's life. A Christian may be one of the most humble people you have ever met — in all areas but one, which happens to be the area in which he or she is currently undergoing sanctification.
92. All Christians, including the authors of this book, are susceptible to giving in to these two vices, as Scripture makes clear (e.g., Prov. 29:25 and John 12:42–43).

Table 7. Grand Summary of YEC Model on Human Genetic Origins

Type of Genetic Comparison	YEC Status
Human vs. human nuclear DNA	Successful prediction of mutation, genetic reshuffling rate (e.g., recombination & gene conversion) for entire sequence
Human vs. human mitochondrial DNA	Successful prediction of mutation rate
Human vs. human Y chromosome	Pending prediction for Y chromosome mutation/genetic reshuffling (e.g., gene conversion) rate

the data for which we have experimental results. For those areas in which experiments are forthcoming, we presented testable predictions that can be falsified in the lab (e.g., Table 5).

In light of these facts, it is all the more remarkable that evolutionists can continue to accuse creationists of being ignorant of the "big picture" of evolution. While this chapter covers only the question of human genetic origins, the accompanying chapters demonstrate the veracity of the biblical account of human origins from a variety of fields. To say that creationists are only capable of finding minor holes in evolutionary arguments while missing the larger body of evidence is unjustifiable.

Furthermore, the claim that "multiple independent lines of genetic evidence" support human evolution is false. Again, evolutionists are fond of appealing to the "big picture" when confronted with a contradiction between one of their predictions and fact. Logically, if every one of their claimed evidences fails, then the sum of these broken evidences cannot possibly add up to a successful model. As we have observed, all the claimed evolutionary evidences represent type-3 experiments, or they represent type-2 experiments that could falsify or have already falsified evolutionary predictions (rather than YEC predictions) (e.g., Tables 2–4, 6). Multiple independent lines of evidence demonstrate that evolutionary claims are unscientific.

As described at the beginning of this chapter, the gold standard of science is the ability of a model to make testable accurate predictions. From the assumptions of the YEC model, creationists have made testable predictions about the future that can be tested in the laboratory. If evolutionists have a problem with what we've concluded, we've given them a ready means by which to falsify our position. In other words, the YEC model of genetics has matured into a full-fledged scientific alternative to the evolutionary model, with much stronger predictive power.

Furthermore, the conclusions in this chapter represent only a fraction of the mature YEC model. We're in the process of publishing testable genetic predictions for a great assortment of animal species alive today for which genetic data is available.[93] The "big picture" of evolution can now be compared head-to-head with the "big picture" of YEC — if evolutionists are able to come up with some falsifiable predictions of their own.

In light of these advances, we would be fully justified in taking the evolutionists' criticisms of creation right back to them. If evolutionists want to be taken seriously in the origins debate, then they need to do more than make an isolated claim about an obscure species here and there that shows nothing but shifts in existing genetic variation or an isolated benefit due to the loss of genetic information. Instead, they need to give us a comprehensive model, a falsifiable explanation that accounts for the genetics of all species alive today. Science demands no less.

93. Jeanson and Lisle, "On the Origin of Eukaryotic Species' Genotypic and Phenotypic Diversity," p. 81–122.

Chapter 11

Human Anatomy: Unique Upright Design

by Dr. Stuart Burgess

Evolutionists claim that humans and modern apes have evolved over millions of years from a common ancestor. That supposed common ancestor is assumed to be a primitive ape-like creature that walked on all four limbs. The diagram below shows a typical monkey-to-man chart that often appears in biology books and popular literature. The picture gives the impression that it is a fact that humans evolved from an ape-like creature. However, the diagram is based entirely on speculation and not any scientific evidence. As one evolutionary anthropologist put it,

> There is a popular image of human evolution that you'll find all over the place. . . . On the left of the picture there's an ape. . . . On the right, a man. . . . Between the two is a succession of figures that become ever more like humans. . . . Our progress from ape to human looks so smooth, so tidy. It's such a beguiling image that even the experts are loath to let it go. But it is an illusion.[1]

The diagram (Figure 1) also gives the impression that it is not difficult for an ape-like creature to gradually evolve into a human being. However, the diagram is deceptive because there are vast differences in design between an ape-like creature and a human being, which make gradual evolution impossible.

This chapter and the next present a sample of some of the key anatomical differences between humans and apes to show that gradual evolution

1. Bernard Wood, Professor of Human Origins, George Washington University, "Who Are We?" *New Scientist*, 2366 (Oct. 26, 2002): 44.

Figure 1: Typical supposed monkey-to-man chart

from apes to humans is impossible. Even though the chapters will generally refer to the anatomy of modern apes, the arguments are nevertheless also relevant to extinct types of apes such as *Australopithecus*, which is a supposed common ancestor.

One of the biggest differences between apes and humans is that apes are designed to walk primarily on four limbs whereas humans are designed to walk on two legs. In addition, apes are not capable of running on two legs, whereas humans are very well designed for running on two legs.

Even though some apes walk upright along branches and sometimes on the ground, this is significantly different from the way humans walk on the ground. This is because when apes walk on branches, their feet grip the branches and such grips are not possible on the ground. When they do walk on the ground, they must shift their weight from side to side, unlike humans. Therefore, evolution has a major problem in attempting to explain the origin of bipedalism (two-legged standing and walking). This chapter will show why it is impossible for a four-legged creature (quadruped or knuckle-walker) to gradually evolve into a habitual biped. There are ten particular design features that are required for upright walking, as shown in Figure 2.[2] The following sections give a brief overview of each of these design features to show that upright walking and running cannot evolve step by step.

(1) Strong Big Toes

To walk and run properly on two legs it is necessary to have strength and stiffness at the front of the feet so that the feet can roll forward without collapsing. Only humans have feet that have the stiffness necessary for proper two-legged motion. The layouts of ape and human feet are shown in Figure 3 to illustrate how they are significantly different. Humans have a very stiff big toe that is orientated straight ahead so that it enables the foot to roll

2. Stuart Burgess, *In God's image* (Leominster, UK: Day One Publications, 2008), p. 6.

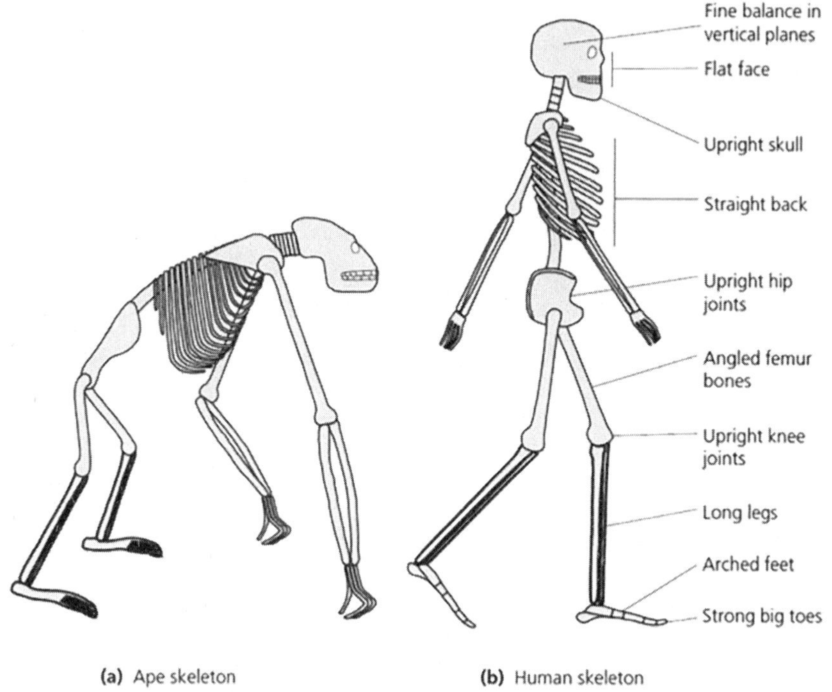

Figure 2: Ten design features required for bipedalism

forward in walking. In contrast, the big toe of apes is not stiff and does not point forward.

The big toe of apes is like a flexible thumb, which is good for gripping branches. Apes effectively have four hands to enable them to grip up to four branches at a time when climbing. When apes try to walk on two legs, they tend to lift up their big toe and walk on four fingers. As a result, apes can only walk on two legs for short distances and in a clumsy manner.

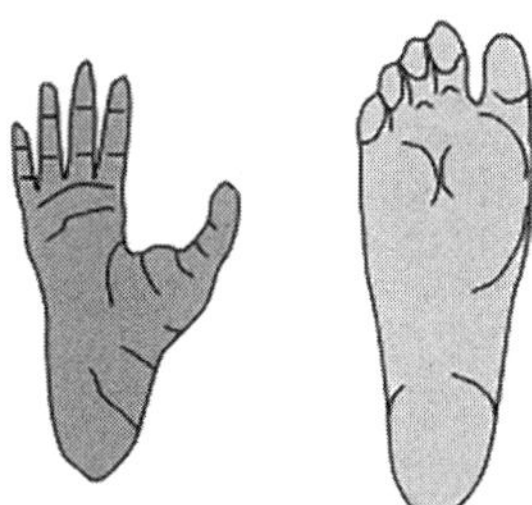

Figure 3: Ape foot and human foot

(2) Arched Feet

Arched feet are important for two-legged standing, walking, and running because they allow fine control of the position of the body over the feet. When standing upright, a person can maintain forward balance by adjusting the relative pressures on the heels and balls of the feet. If anything disturbs the balance in the forward direction while standing, corrective action can be carried out by leaning more on either the front or the back of the feet to keep the center of mass between the heel and the ball of the feet. When walking and running, arched feet enable a person to push off the feet without the feet collapsing.

Only humans have the necessary intricate arched structure in their feet for proper bipedal motion. This structure is not found in the feet of modern apes or extinct apes. Evolutionists have claimed that the famous supposed ape-woman, "Lucy," and her kind (*Australopithecus afarensis*) had arched feet, but this is not based on direct fossil evidence. Instead, it is based on the fact that fossils of Lucy-type creatures are found in the same rock layer as the human-like Laetoli footprints. However, as noted in chapter 5, the fossils are not attached to the footprints, so it is simply an evolutionist *assumption* that the fossilized creatures made the footprints.[3] As creationists have pointed out, the obvious explanation to the Laetoli footprints is that they are what they appear to be — human footprints in the same rock layer as the fossils of an extinct type of ape. Anatomist Dr. David Menton has pointed out that if Lucy's feet were accurately shown in evolutionist pictures and museum displays, it would be obvious to the public that her kind could never have made the Laetoli footprints.[4]

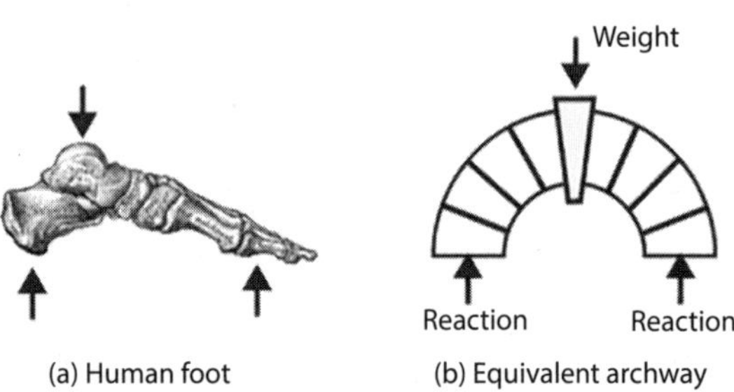

Figure 4: The arch in the human foot

The human arch in the foot is between the heel and the ball of the foot, as shown in Figure 4(a). The equivalent engineering arch is shown in Figure 4(b). The human foot has 26 precisely shaped bones, together with many ligaments, tendons, and muscles. Several of the bones are wedge-shaped so that a strong arch is formed.

In contrast to humans, apes do not have arched feet and instead have flexible feet that are designed to be like hands for gripping branches. In

3. Mary Leakey, who discovered the Laetoli prints, said, "I can only *assume* that the prints were left by the hominids whose fossils we also found in the beds." See Mary Leakey, "Footprints in the Ashes of Time," *National Geographic* 155, no 4 (April 1979): 456.
4. " 'Ape-woman' Statue Misleads Public: Anatomy Professor," *Creation* 19, no. 1 (Dec. 1996): 52, https://answersingenesis.org/human-evolution/lucy/ape-woman-statue-misleads-public-anatomy-professor/.

consequence, apes have little ability to shift pressure between the front and back of their feet when walking on two legs. This means that they have very limited abilities for standing and walking and have no ability to run on two legs.

Human feet actually have three points of contact with the ground as shown in Figure 5.[5] One point of contact is in the center of the heel, a second point of contact is the root (knuckle) of the big toe and a third point of contact is the root (knuckle) of the little toe. The arched foot has such a clear interface with the ground that it is possible for humans to stand on one leg. When balancing on one leg, the center of gravity of the body can be placed within the three points of contact of the foot to give a steady balance.

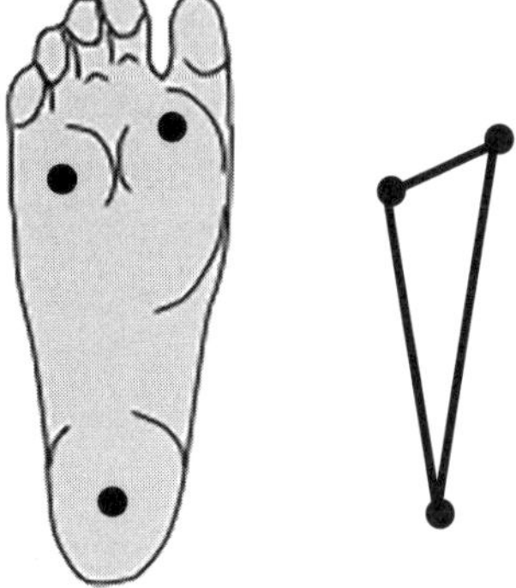

Figure 5: Three-point contact on the ground

It is well known in engineering that the most precise way of supporting a freestanding structure is to have three points of contact (like a three-legged stool). In contrast, apes have flat feet and it is therefore extremely difficult for them to stand on one leg. Apes also have no ability to run on two legs because their feet and toes do not have the required stiffness and strength.

Another unique feature of the human foot is that it has the ability to be both very stiff and yet flexible. The ligaments hold the bones together with enough stiffness to make arches which can hold the weight of the body, yet have enough flexibility to allow the foot to be flexed for walking and running. The flexibility of the foot helps it to absorb shock loads, which is particularly important during running. The foot can be flexed with precision because muscles can move the bones via a network of tendons.

The arched structure of the foot is an example of intricate design, because many separate bones have to fit together precisely to make an arch.[6] It is well known in engineering that an arched structure requires very careful planning and design. The main reason for this is that an arch consists of wedge-shaped blocks that must all fit together precisely. Even the construction of an arch requires intricate planning because it is necessary to support the blocks with some kind of scaffolding until the whole arch is in place. Only when the final block — called the keystone — is in place can the

5. I. Kapandji, "The Physiology of the Joints," *Lower Limb Volume 2* (London: Churchill, Livingstone, 5th edition, 1995), p. 218–223.
6. Stuart Burgess, *The Design and Origin of Man* (Leominster, UK: Day One Publications, 2013), p. 27.

scaffolding be removed. The reason the final block is called the keystone is that it is the "key" to making the arch a functional structure.

Since the human foot has parts equivalent to a keystone and wedge-shaped blocks, the human foot must be the product of intelligent design. Only an intelligent designer has the ability to think ahead and plan all the features needed to make an arch such as we find in the human foot.

Evolutionists have claimed that the little toe of humans is functionless and therefore an example of a vestigial organ. However, there are actually clear reasons why humans have a little toe. First, the root (knuckle) of the little toe is essential for the tripod balance as described above. Second, all of the toes help the push-off phase of running. Even though most people would not notice a difference in running if they lost their little toe, a top athlete would certainly notice a slight drop in performance. Even if there was not a physical function for the little toe, there would still be an aesthetic function, because having five toes creates symmetry with the hands.

When parts of the human foot are missing or damaged, the loss in functionality can be severe. For example, some people are "flat-footed" because their arch does not function properly due to damage in the foot. Such flat-footed people have much less agility and strength in their feet and are sometimes barred from certain jobs like military jobs because they cannot stand and run very well. The fact that functionality is lost quickly when there are defects is a sign of complex design. On the other hand, the fact that human feet can still function to some extent when parts are missing or damaged shows that they are robustly designed.

One of the reasons why creationists are confident that the fossil record supports biblical creation is that no so-called "ape-man" has ever been found that has any kind of intermediate type of foot between an ape foot and human foot. This is why the human foot is one of the "Achilles heels" of evolution!

(3) Long Legs

The length of human legs is about half the total length of the body. Whereas humans have long legs and relatively short arms, apes have short legs and long arms. The arms of apes must be longer than their legs because their hands must reach the ground to allow comfortable quadruped movement on land. The long legs of humans make it possible for them to walk and run long distances with relative ease. The world record for the maximum distance run in a 24-hour time period for humans is over 180 miles, which is vastly beyond what apes could do with two-legged walking. The fact that humans have long legs emphasises that there is a clear distinction between the design of a quadruped and biped.

It is important to note that ape-to-man charts do not show a gradual progression from quadruped to bipedal motion. Figure 6 shows the famous ape-to-man chart originally painted by Rudolph Zallinger from the Time-Life book *Early Man* (1965)[7] that supposedly shows 14 stages of human evolution over 25 million years. Notice how the second creature from the left is standing upright as if evolving bipedalism was a minor step in evolution. Also notice that an arched foot does not appear until the eighth creature from the left. This implies that for millions of years ape-men were walking clumsily on two legs without arched feet. However such a scenario is completely ridiculous because such creatures would be struggling to walk properly on two legs for millions of years while supposedly being habitually bipedal and fit for survival! This is a key example of how ape-to-man charts are misleading and false.

Figure 6: "Ape-to-man" chart has no intermediate forms of bipeds

(4) Upright Knee Joints

Effective upright standing and walking requires upright knee joints, because this greatly reduces loads in the muscles around the knee joint. The human knee joint extends to a fully upright position so that the leg can be made straight and the body upright. In fact, the human knee joint also *locks* in the upright position. This feature makes standing easy because the muscles do not need to be kept in tension. In contrast, the knee joint of apes is not fully extendable and apes cannot stand straight. When apes stand on two legs, they have to put significant effort into tensing their permanently bent knees.

The femur and tibia bones of the human knee joint are shown in Figure 7 in the squatting and upright position respectively. This diagram was developed by my own research group and published in an international journal to show the precision with which the knee joint rotates. The knee joint moves smoothly partly because of the rolling motion of the bones but also because ligaments guide the bones.

7. F. Clark Howell, *Early Man* (New York, NY: Time Life Books, 1965), p. 41-45.

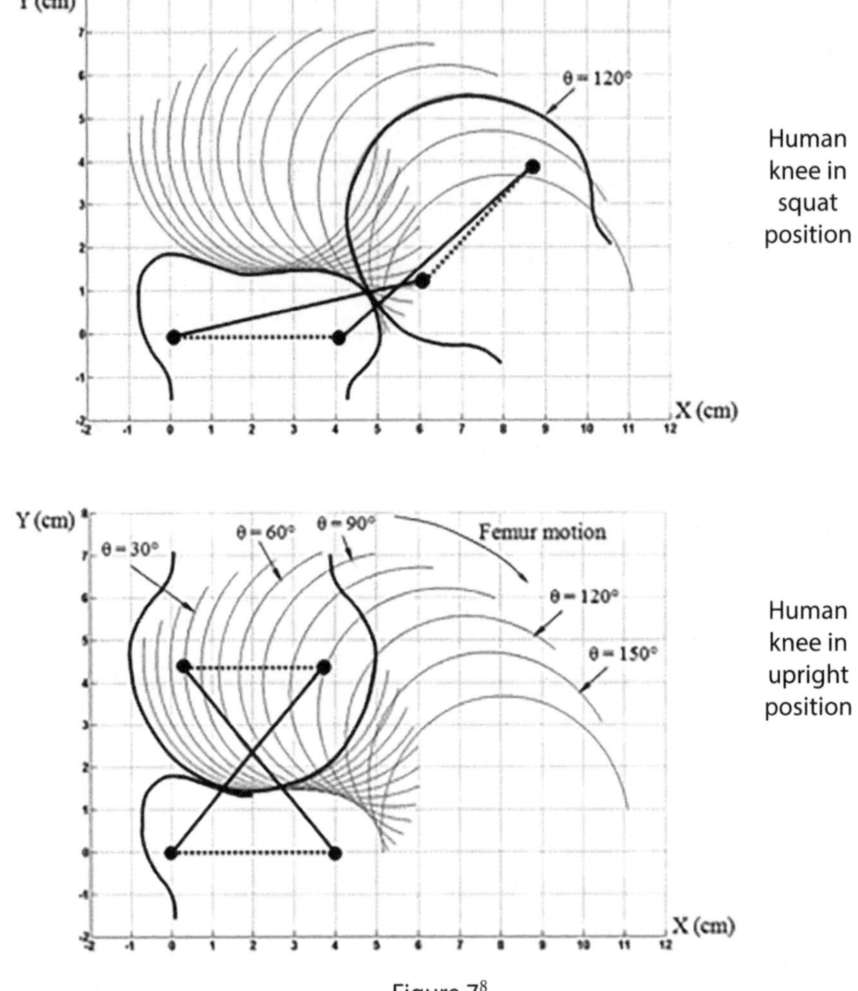

Figure 7[8]

The mammalian knee is a sophisticated joint because it incorporates two mechanisms: a cam mechanism and a linkage mechanism.[9] The cam system operates as the condyle (rounded end) of the femur rolls over the tibia. The linkage system within the knee joint is comprised of four "bars": two ligaments (often referred to as "cruciate ligaments" because of the way they cross one another) and two bones (the femur and tibia). These four bars create what engineers call a four-bar mechanism and this is shown in Figure 7.

8. Appolinaire Etoundi, Stuart Burgess, and Ravi Vaidyanathan, "A Bio-Inspired Condylar Hinge for Robotic Limbs," *ASME Journal of Mechanisms and Robotics*, 5, no. 3 (2013): 031011.
9. Stuart Burgess and Appolinaire Etoundi, "Performance Maps for a Bio-Inspired Robotic Condylar Hinge Joint," *ASME Journal of Mechanical Design*, 136, no. 11 (2014): 115002.

In order for the joint to operate, the motion generated by the four-bar mechanism must closely match the cam motion of the bones. This is achieved by careful placement of the ligament attachment points and by having a compatible profile on the condyles. It is a brilliant design because the four-bar system controls the movement of the joint without taking any load. Instead, the weight is carried entirely by the bones, bypassing the delicate linkage mechanism. The bones give a strong and stiff joint because the curved surfaces on the femur and tibia are closely matched.

(5) Angled Femur Bones

To walk and run effectively, it is necessary for the feet to be close to the centerline of the body. During walking and running, the body is supported by only one leg at any instant in time and so the body can easily topple over if the feet are not right under the body. This design feature is exactly what humans have, as shown in Figures 8 and 9. When looking at the human body face-on, the femur bones are angled inward as they come down from the hip joints to the knees. The angled femur bones have the effect of making the knees close together and the feet close together.

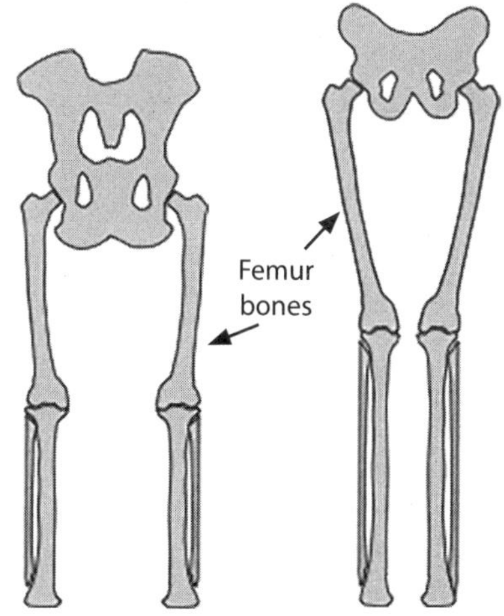

Figure 8: Ape and human femur bones, respectively

In contrast to humans, the femur bones of apes drop down vertically, making the knees relatively far apart and the feet far apart. As a consequence, when apes try to walk on two legs, they sway from side to side to maintain balance. Apes must have feet spaced wide apart because this gives stability in quadruped motion. The angled femur bone of humans also helps to explain why humans are able to stand on one leg.

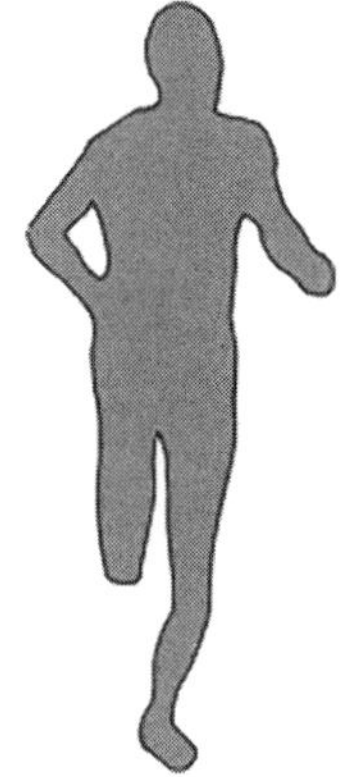
Figure 9: Human running showing the landing foot under the body

(6) Upright Hip Joints

Effective walking and running requires upright hip joints so that the back is upright and not bent forward. Humans have unique hip joints that give a fully upright stature. In particular, humans have a pelvis that allows a completely natural walking motion. In technical terms, the human hip joint is fully extendable. In contrast, the hip joints of apes cannot fully extend to the upright position and apes must always have bent legs, even if they stand on two legs.

Another important feature of an upright hip joint is that it is only useful if there is also an upright knee joint. If an ape had upright hips without upright knees, it would be in danger of falling backward when straightening its legs. On the other hand, if an ape had upright knees without upright hips, it would be in danger of falling over forward when straightening its legs. Therefore, evolution again is unable to explain a gradual transition from quadruped to bipedal locomotion.

(7) Upright Back

Effective bipedal motion also requires an upright back so that the head is directly above the hips. If the head was not above the hips, then there would be imbalance and large muscle forces would be required to stay upright. An upright back is exactly what humans have.

In contrast, the curved back of apes makes their torso project out in front of the hips. This means that apes must use their arms and hands to support their weight, as shown in Figure 2. This is why apes are sometimes referred to as "knuckle-walkers." When an ape tries to walk on two legs, its back bends forward which is very tiring.

In fact, humans have a slightly S-shaped back, as shown in Figure 10. That slightly undulating shape is a brilliant design feature because it helps prevent the spine from being shocked when there is a vertical load such as that experienced when jumping on hard ground. When a human jumps on the ground, the S-shape acts a little like a spring and deforms lengthwise (see Figure 10) to prevent high loads going through the spine.

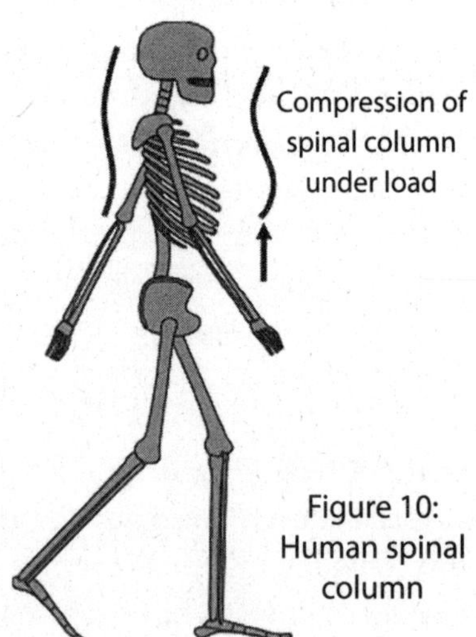

Figure 10: Human spinal column

The intricate human spine consists of 24 bones (called vertebrae), cartilage discs, spinal cord, nerves, and blood supply. The whole structure is an amazing integrated design where all the parts fit together in a complex assembly, as shown in Figure 11.

The vertebral bones are stacked vertically with a soft cartilage disc between each vertebra to reduce wear and tear and provide cushioning. The vertebrae are kept securely in place because they have protrusions (facet joints and transverse processes) that stack on top of each other in a similar way that drinking glasses stack. There are spaces in the vertebrae for nerves to enter and exit the spinal column and the vertebrae also have places where tendons can connect to muscles. These muscles help keep the spinal column in an upright position. It is well known in engineering that such complex integrated systems require immense foresight and planning. In the same way, the human spinal column must have been planned and designed.

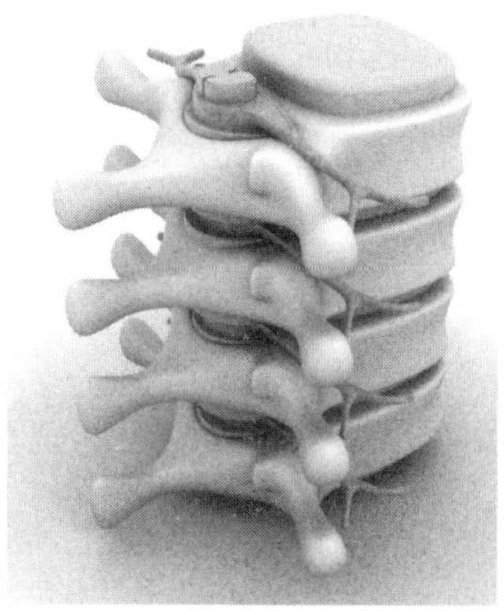

Figure 11: Portion of the human spinal column

(8) Upright Skull

The point at which the spinal cord enters the skull is called the *foramen magnum*. In the case of humans, the foramen magnum is located at the bottom of the skull, as shown in Figure 2. This means that the most natural position for the human head is looking forward in the upright position. If humans attempt to walk on all four limbs, the head has to be awkwardly forced up in order to look ahead. When babies crawl on four limbs, it can be observed that they have to lift up their head to look ahead.

In contrast to humans, apes have a foramen magnum located more to the back of the skull so that the most natural position for the head is looking forward in the horizontal position. Even though an ape can look forward when sitting upright, this is only possible when the head is bent downward. According to evolution, the skull of an ape-like creature changed so that the foramen magnum moved from the back to the bottom of the skull. But there is no fossil evidence that this happened.

(9) Flat Face

Humans have a uniquely flat face that gives them a large field of view that is required for effective bipedal movement. The flat face of humans means that when they are in an upright position and looking straight ahead, they can turn their eyes downward and look at the ground in front of their feet, as shown in Figure 12(b). In contrast, apes have a large protruding jaw and their field of view is much more restricted, as shown in Figure 12(a).

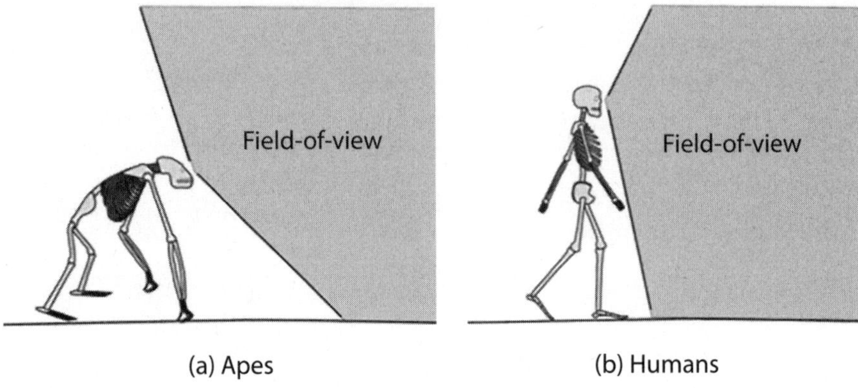

Figure 12: Field-of-view of apes and humans

The ability to see the ground just in front of the feet is very important for bipedal locomotion because of the high position of the body above the ground and the inherent instability of two-legged locomotion. When a human loses footing while walking or running, it can be very difficult to regain balance because the center of gravity of the body must be kept above two feet. In contrast, it is relatively easy for apes to regain balance because they are closer to the ground and have four points of contact with the ground.

An interesting feature of the human face is that it is well designed for wearing glasses, no doubt in part because the Creator foresaw the consequences of the Fall and the resulting need of humans. The human nose has an ideal ridge for glasses to sit on and the ears are placed just in the right position for anchoring the glasses.

(10) Upright Balance

Standing and moving on two legs requires a much finer sense of balance than moving on four legs. In order to balance on four legs it is only necessary to keep the center of gravity of the body within the four points of contact on the ground, which is a relatively large area. However, when standing on two legs, it is necessary to keep the center of gravity between the two feet and this represents a relatively small area. Another reason why it is difficult to balance on two legs is that the center of gravity is higher above the ground than for a four-legged posture.

Humans and apes achieve balance mainly through sensors in the inner ear. The inner ear has three semi-circular fluid-filled canals that are sensitive to movement and gravity. The semi-circular canals in the human ear are shown in Figure 13. The canals contain sensors that consist of fine hairs that send out signals to indicate the direction and speed of head movements. The canals are arranged in three planes that are at right angles to each other, as shown in Figure 13. This arrangement gives three-dimensional sensing.

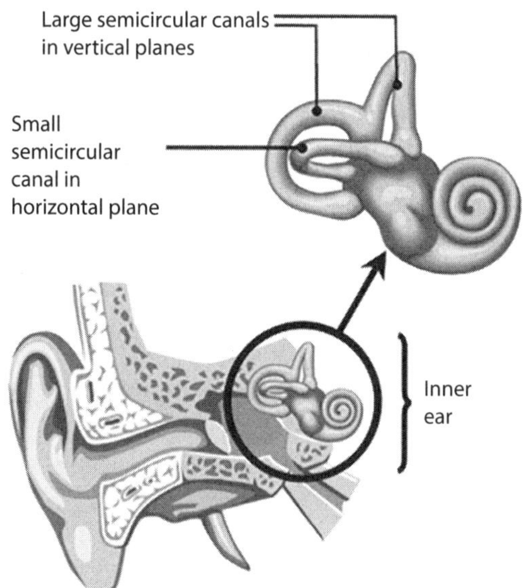

Figure 13: Human ear showing large semi-circular canals in the vertical plane

Humans have a relatively small semi-circular canal in the horizontal plane and two large semi-circular canals (anterior and posterior) in the vertical plane. This shows that humans have balance sensors specifically designed for walking upright. It also shows that walking upright requires a fine sense of balance.

In contrast, apes have three relatively small semi-circular canals and each is a similar size. The similar size of the semi-circular canals in apes shows that apes are designed for climbing in all different directions in trees. Such movement is called "arboreal" movement. Apes do not need any large semi-circular canals because they are not designed to walk upright.

(11) Unique Abilities

Humans have the unique ability to move on two legs with great agility. One of the key requirements for agile upright movement is the ability to stand on the front of the feet by balancing on the balls and toes of the feet. This is why sports coaches sometimes encourage their athletes to stay "on their toes." When balancing on the ball and toes of the feet, it is possible to move quickly in different directions.

As well as being able to stand on the front of the feet, humans have an amazing sense of upright balance. Interestingly, when athletes like football players lean to one side in order to run around a tight curve, even though their center of gravity is no longer between their feet, the overall reaction force of the body is still between the feet. The overall reaction force is a combination (in technical terms a "resultant") of the center of gravity plus the centripetal force due to circular motion. Human balance is so fine that athletes can sense exactly what angle they need to maintain in order to keep the overall reaction force between their feet.

The supreme ability of humans to move on two legs is demonstrated in many different sports. Top athletes can run, twist, and turn with breath-taking speed and precision. It is not only sports people who are capable of amazing upright balance. Everyday activities like walking up and down stairs, gardening, and housework often involve fine balance on two legs.

In contrast to the potential of the human body, apes have no ability to move on two legs with agility and speed. Apes cannot run on two legs and cannot stand on their toes. There have been attempts to train apes to perform some of the two-legged movements of humans. However, these have always served to prove that apes are incapable of matching human upright movement.

A film has been produced called *Most Vertical Primate* in which an ape supposedly becomes a competent skateboarder. However, even though a very well-trained chimpanzee was chosen for the part, it was incapable of performing even the most basic skateboarding maneuvers. It was found that the ape could not stay on the skateboard for more than a few seconds without falling off. Therefore, film sequences had to be produced by joining together tiny clips of film in which the ape managed to stay upright on the skateboard for a few seconds. Despite the title of the film, the film actually demonstrated that apes are not designed to be vertical!

(12) Purposeful Design

One of God's purposes for humans is to have dominion over all the creatures of the earth (Genesis 1:28 and Psalm 8:5–8). God has deliberately given humans an upright stature that makes it easy for them to subdue all the creatures on the earth. To secular scientists it is a puzzle that out of around 4,000 mammals only humans are bipedal. However, this unique design feature makes complete sense from a biblical perspective.

The upright stature of man also has the purpose of enabling him to enjoy physical activities like walking, running, and sports. The upright stature of man also encourages him to look up into the heavens to see the glorious splendor of the stars and to consider the reality of heaven. In commenting on Psalm 19:1, the famous Bible scholar Matthew Henry (1662–1714) said the following about the stature of human beings:

> Man has this advantage above the beasts, in the structure of his body, that whereas they are made to look downwards, as their spirits

> must go, he is made erect, to look upwards, because upwards his spirit must shortly go and his thoughts should now rise.[10]

The ape-to-man chart that is often used to popularize evolution is deceptive and false because it gives the impression that a four-legged ape-like creature can walk upright with hardly any anatomical changes. In reality, there is such a vast difference between a habitually bipedal human and a quadruped creature that gradual evolution is impossible. The principle of natural selection would prevent ape-like creatures from beginning to evolve into upright-walking creatures because those creatures that tried to walk upright would be so clumsy they would be quickly de-selected.[11]

Conclusion

The human frame is wonderfully made for upright locomotion. The joints are so well designed that they are inspiring the design of high performance robots. The body has all the necessary muscles and balance sensors for supremely agile bipedal locomotion. Leonardo da Vinci, one of the most brilliant scientists in history, said that "the human foot is a masterpiece of engineering and a work of art."[12] From head to toe there is abundant anatomical evidence that humans have been created by a Master Designer and are not the product of a blind, directionless, purposeless process of evolution.

---

10. Matthew Henry, *Matthew Henry's Commentary on the Whole Bible* (St. Louis, MO: MacDonald Publishing, 1985 reprint), Vol. 3, p. 301.
11. For a good summary of other reasons why humans have not evolved from apes, see David Menton (retired professor of human anatomy at Washington University Medical School), "Did Humans Really Evolve from Apelike Creatures?" in Ken Ham, ed., *New Answers Book 2* (Green Forest, AR: Master Books, 2008), p. 83-94.
12. http://discoveringdavinci.tumblr.com/post/32222942704/the-human-foot-is-a-masterpiece-of-engineering.

Chapter 12

Human Anatomy: Unique Skills and Beauty

By Dr. Stuart Burgess

Evolutionists claim that similarities between humans and apes are evidence proving common ancestry. One problem with this claim is that even though there are some similarities, there are also major differences between humans and apes.[1] The previous chapter showed how humans are two-legged (bipeds), whereas apes are four-legged (quadrupeds). This chapter will present six other major areas of anatomy where humans are very different from apes. These differences show that humans and apes do not share a common ancestor.

Another problem with the claim to common ancestry is that the similarities between humans and apes can be fully explained in terms of a biblical creation worldview because common design features can be seen as evidence for a common Designer. For example, if a heart or lung is a good design for a human, it will often be a good design for other mammals, including apes. Therefore, it is wrong to assume that similarities are evidence for evolution rather than creation.

In engineering it is well known that two artifacts can have similar components, but have very different overall designs. For example, a car and a train contain similar components such as bolts, nuts, wheels, and brakes. Yet cars and trains are completely different designs with very different functions. In a similar way, even though humans and apes have some similar components, they are actually two completely different creatures.

1. Stuart Burgess, *In God's Image* (Leominster, UK: Day One Publications, 2008); David Menton, "The Uniqueness of Man, *Answers Magazine* (April–June 2010), p. 54.

If similarity is measured in terms of similarities in materials and components, then humans and apes might be assessed as having 95% similarity. Evolutionists often quote this figure in order to claim that it supports evolution. However, this is a poor way of assessing similarity because it is focusing on individual components and not the *assembly* of those components. A true measure of similarity can only be made by considering the whole system and its functionality. When this is done it is found that humans and apes are very different, as this chapter will show.

The Purposeful Overdesign of Man

As well as a unique design, humans also have a design beyond what is needed for survival. For example, humans are designed to perform tasks in areas such as writing, music, artwork, textiles, and engineering. The term "purposeful overdesign" is used to describe how humans do much more than just survive.[2] Purposeful overdesign describes how something is designed with a high degree of functionality.

The purposeful overdesign of man is a concept seen in the Bible. When the Bible says that humans are made "a little lower than the angels" and are crowned "with glory and honor" (Ps. 8:5),[3] it clearly implies that humans are designed for more than surviving in the wild. When the Bible says that humans are made to "have dominion over the works" of God (Ps. 8:6), we should expect to see evidence that humans are purposefully overdesigned to be able to handle every situation they will face in that task.

The purposeful overdesign of humans is a major problem for evolution because evolution by definition cannot evolve something beyond what is needed for survival. Secular scientists admit that it should be possible to explain the entire human anatomy in terms of survival advantages in the wild. They admit that the anatomy of the human brain and hands should be totally explainable in terms of the need to perform survival functions such as throwing spears and making fires. The leading evolutionist Professor Stephen Jones from University College London has said, "Evolution does its job as well as it needs to and no more."[4] This is a crucial admission that evolution would never produce a feature that was beyond what is needed for survival.

The degree of overdesign present in humans is truly astonishing and should surely cause any evolutionist to reconsider their position. This chapter will show how humans are overdesigned in *six* major areas. For each area,

2. Stuart Burgess, *The Design and Origin of Man* (Leominster, UK: Day One Publications, 2004).
3. Scripture in this chapter is from the New King James Version (NKJV) of the Bible.
4. Stephen Jones, *Darwin's Ghost* (Random House, New York, 2000), p. 98.

the chapter will describe the purpose of man's design as it relates to his being made in the image of God.

(1) Unique Skillful Hands

One of the most significant anatomical differences between humans and apes is that humans have skillful hands designed for carrying out sophisticated tasks. In contrast, apes have crude hands designed mainly for gripping branches and knuckle-walking.

Human fingers have a full range of movement from a completely straight finger to a tightly curled finger. The ability to make a full range of finger movements is important for carrying out skillful tasks. In contrast to humans, apes' fingers are naturally curved and therefore have limited finger movement. The reason why apes have curved fingers is that this is ideal for gripping branches.

Another unique design feature of the human hand is that it has a fully opposable thumb that can make face-to-face contact with the end of each finger. Figure 2b shows how each finger can make a circular pinch grip with the thumb. Human thumbs are opposable for two main reasons. First, the human thumb is relatively long. Second, the palm of the hand is very flexible so that the thumb can be bent around to meet the tips of any of the four fingers. In contrast, apes have both relatively short thumbs and inflexible palms so they cannot make a pinch grip between the thumb and the fingers.

Figure 1: The human hand

The human hand contains muscles and nerves that allow very fine movement of the fingers and thumb (figure 1). One of the reasons for this fine control is the presence of small muscle units. A muscle consists of many individual bundles of muscle fibers called muscle units or motor units. Each of the individual units has a motor nerve for stimulation and the precision of movement is high when the individual units are small. For example, thigh muscles lack fine control and precision, as there are typically over 100 fibers in each motor unit. In contrast, the fingers typically have around 10 fibers within each motor unit and this small number of fibers allows very fine finger control.

The part of the brain responsible for muscular movements in the body is called the motor cortex. About a quarter of the entire human motor cortex is devoted to controlling the muscles of the hands, showing that humans have the software as well as the hardware necessary for skillful hand movements. The large part of the motor cortex dedicated to the hands is remarkable because the hands are a relatively small part of the body and contain only about 10% (by number) of the muscles of the body. Evolutionists acknowledge that apes do not have such a relatively large section of the motor cortex dedicated to controlling the hands.[5]

The unique design of human hands results in several unique abilities such as gesturing, pinch grips, and keyboard skills. Human hand gesturing is so precise and agile that it is possible to communicate solely using hand gestures. Of course, sign language also uses hand movements, facial expressions, and other body movements, but sign language is largely dependent on the very high dexterity of the human hand. While apes can make some crude hand gestures to communicate a very simple idea, they could never communicate meaningful thoughts through sign language because they do not have fine dexterity or fine control of the hands.

Pinch grips are very important for daily tasks such as tying shoelaces and doing up buttons and zippers. We take such tasks for granted, but they actually require skill and precision. Keyboard skills may seem ordinary, but they require precision and sometimes speed. A top pianist can play many different notes per second with precision and feeling. Apes could never be taught to play musical instruments because their hands do not have the required dexterity. Moreover, the ability to play any musical instrument at all has no evolutionary advantage.

Engineers (including myself) have tried to build robots that can produce a precision grip like a human hand. However, these robotic hands are vastly inferior to human hands and it is clear that there will never be a robotic hand that can come close to having the agility and control of the human hand because of the physical limitations of man-made components. Apes cannot make a precision grip with their hands because they do not have fine motor control or fully opposable thumbs. If the human mind has enough difficulty designing a precision grip, how can mindless evolution be a better explanation?

Evidence of Purposeful Overdesign

Evolutionists propose that the apparent design of human hands is a result

5. David Begun, *The Real Planet of the Apes: A New Story of Human Origins* (Princeton, NJ: Princeton University Press, 2016), p. 49.

of survival needs, such as holding crude tools for farming and throwing spears for hunting. Some evolutionists have claimed that one of the main drivers behind the evolution of human hands is bare-knuckle fist fighting.[6] However, tasks like farming, hunting, and fighting do not require the extreme level of skill that actually exists in human hands.

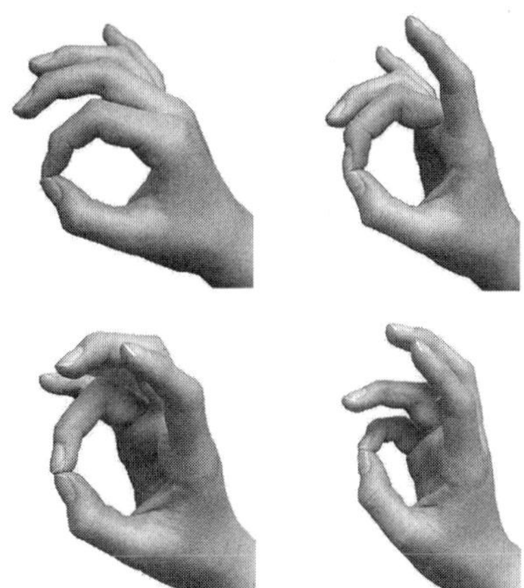

Figure 2A: The tripod grip is an example of purposeful overdesign

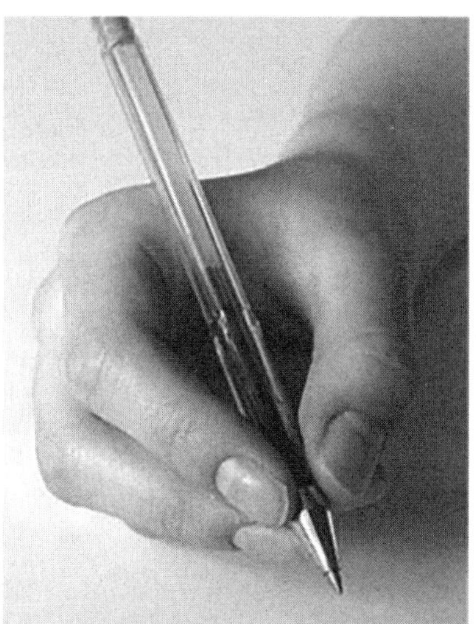

Figure 2B: Pinch grips in the human hand

Evolution cannot explain why humans can perform amazing feats in activities such as writing, surgery, carpentry, art, sports, and the playing of musical instruments. The great skill of human hands can only be explained by intelligent design and purpose.

The purposeful overdesign of human hands is alluded to in Scripture where the Psalmist refers to the skill of his right hand (Ps. 137:5). The skill of human hands is referred to in the very early history of mankind with respect to musical abilities (Gen. 4:21) and metalworking abilities (Gen. 4:22). Skills such as metalwork contribute to man's ability to have dominion over creation as God has commanded (Gen. 1:28), as for example in constructing and operating devices that subdue or train other creatures such as horses or lions.

The ability of humans to hold a pen with a tripod grip represents an interesting example of purposeful overdesign, which is very hard to explain by evolution. The tripod grip involves use of the thumb, index finger, and middle finger, as shown in Figures 2a and b. These three digits are perfectly designed to meet at a point to hold a pen with precision. Such a precision grip is what would be expected since God created man to communicate through writing,

6. Michael Morgan and David Carrier, "Protective Buttressing of the Human Fist and the Evolution of Hominin Hands," *The Journal of Experimental Biology*, 216:2 (January 2014): 236–244.

including the writing of God's inspired and inerrant Word by men working under the superintending influence of the Holy Spirit. But the tripod grip is not what would be expected if we had evolved from an ape-like creature, because writing has no survival function.

(2) Unique Fine Skin in Humans

Another major anatomical difference between humans and apes is that humans have fine skin with many unique properties. Fine skin plays an important role in enhancing skill and giving pleasure. In contrast, apes have much less sensitive skin and a body covered with fur. Of course, humans have hair covering most of their bodies, but most of these body hairs are tiny compared to fur and do not provide any appreciable amount of warmth. Many evolutionists see the fine hair covering the human body as a useless vestigial remnant of a shared evolutionary history with apes. However, this fine, or *vellus*, hair is not useless at all. The follicles housing these hairs provide an exit route for the oil that comes from oil glands, which keep the skin smooth, protecting it from cracking. And each hair follicle is a reservoir of cells that can help to re-epithelialize wounds, speeding the healing process. Also, body hair enhances fine touch sensory information about certain kinds of contact such as insects walking on the surface of the skin.

Figure 3 shows a simplified diagram of human skin in cross-section. This diagram gives a glimpse of the incredible complexity of human skin. Human skin consists of three main layers: epidermis, dermis, and a subcutaneous layer as shown in this figure. The epidermis contains skin cells that give a durable outer layer to the skin. The dermis is thicker than the epidermis and contains protein fibers for toughness. The dermis also contains most of the intricate structures of the skin such as sweat glands, oil glands, sensors, blood vessels, and nerves. There are four main types of sensors in the skin: heat sensors, cold sensors, pain sensors, and touch sensors.

The subcutaneous tissue is a layer at the base of the skin that contains fat cells. This subcutaneous layer provides a thin layer of insulation for the body and also provides some cushioning against impact forces. While apes have an epidermis and dermis, they do not have a significant subcutaneous layer as humans do.

The human epidermis is very thin. It varies in thickness from 0.05 mm on eyelids to 1.5 mm on palms and soles). However, the epidermis itself is a complex structure with multiple layers. The outer cells of the epidermis are constantly being shed and replaced by new layers. The epidermis is replaced about every four weeks. This renewal process allows human skin to stay healthy and

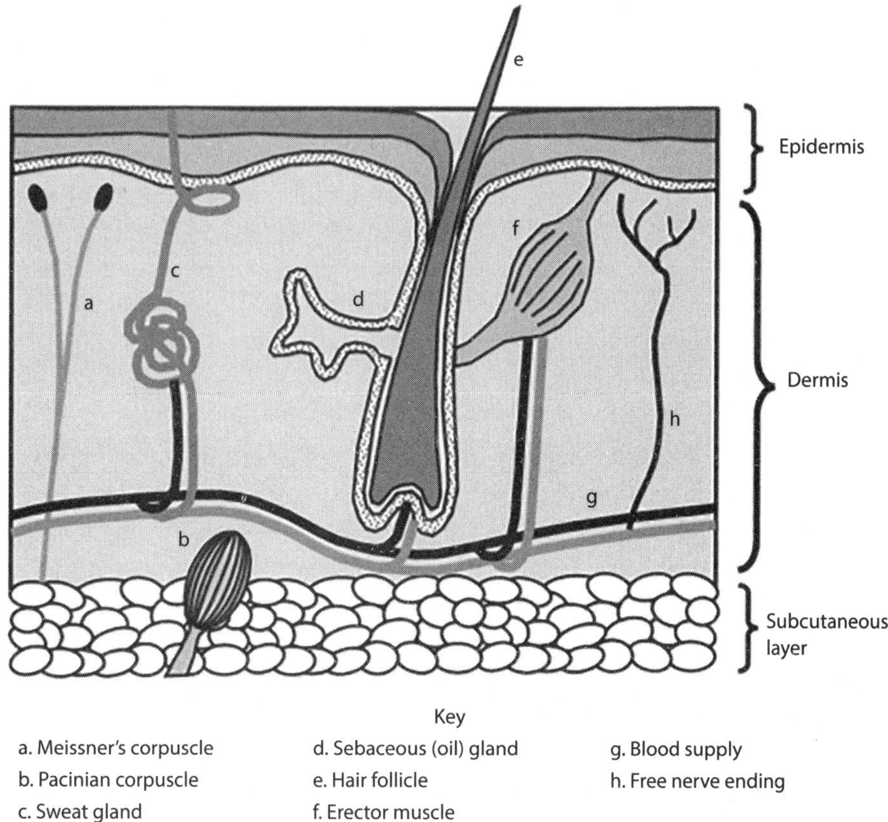

Figure 3. Cross-section of human skin

heal quickly after injury. In contrast, apes have a less complicated epidermis. In particular, apes have fewer layers in the epidermis and the epidermis is replaced less frequently.[7]

Humans have a very large and unique number of sweat glands to keep cool and remove waste products from the body quickly. An adult human has around 750 sweat glands per square inch,[8] which cover almost the entire body. This adds up to over a million sweat glands for the whole human body. The sweat glands of an adult can secrete up to 12 liters of water per day[9]

7. William Gregory, ed., *The Anatomy of the Gorilla; The Studies of Henry Cushier Raven, and Contributions by William B. Atkinson [and others] A Collaborative Work of the American Museum of Natural History and Columbia University* (New York, NY: Columbia University Press, 1950), p. 217.
8. Ashley Montagu, *Growing Young*, 2nd ed. (Greenwood, NY: Praeger, 1989), p. 41.
9. Graham Bates and Veronica Miller, "Sweat Rate and Sodium Loss During Work in the Heat," *J Occup Med Toxicol*, vol. 3 (2008): 4.

depending on the temperature and activity of the person. Apes only have a significant number of sweat glands around their armpits and can release far less water per day.[10]

One of the most remarkable features of human skin is that it has a high density of fine touch sensors, especially in areas like the hands and face. The human hand has over 2,000 touch sensors per square centimeter. In one human finger there are several thousand sensors and these result in an extremely sensitive sense of touch. In contrast to humans, apes have a far inferior sense of touch due to fewer touch sensors, a covering of fur, and the existence of tough skin (sometimes called friction skin) on their fingers.[11]

Touch sensors consist of delicate structures like membranes and capsules that are sensitive to tiny deformations. When the structures are deformed, nerve signals are sent to the brain to indicate that something has been touched. The fingertips can feel a ridge of just 10 microns in width (one hundredth of 1 mm). In addition, the fingertips have a two-point threshold of around 2 mm which means that the fingers can differentiate between two ridges that are only 2 mm apart. The human sense of touch is often used to determine the quality of many common objects like clothing and food in a way that is better than what our sense of sight can determine.

Another unique ability of human skin is that it enables a person to maintain a comfortable body temperature. Many animals have a permanent coat of thick fur, and overheat after exercise or when the environment is hot. To restore a normal temperature, animals must rest in order to cool down. In contrast, humans regulate temperature much better because skin quickly loses heat. The human body cools down quickly because the skin is thin and can release significant amounts of heat through vaporization. Vaporization occurs continually as water from the body escapes through sweat glands and evaporates. Water can carry a high amount of heat, so evaporation is an excellent design for lowering temperature within acceptable limits.

Another important reason why humans can regulate temperature so quickly is that they can quickly adjust their clothing. In the vast majority of climates, humans need to wear clothing to keep warm when at rest. This means that when humans get hot through vigorous activity, they can take off clothes to allow heat to escape from the body. In addition, when the weather

---

10. Gregory, *The Anatomy of the Gorilla*, p. 217.
11. Friderun Ankel-Simons, *Primate Anatomy: An Introduction*, 3rd ed. (Amsterdam: Academic Press, Elsevier, 2007), p. 349.

is very cold, humans can put on large amounts of additional clothing. In contrast, animals can get uncomfortably cold because when the temperature is very low they cannot put on extra insulation. But it is important to realize that humans started wearing clothes not because the climate changed but because man changed morally and spiritually when Adam and Eve sinned against God (Gen. 3:7, 21).

Evidence of Purposeful Overdesign

According to evolution, humans were adapted for hunting and farming only very recently. However, the sophisticated design of human skin means humans can perform highly sensitive tasks far beyond hunting and farming, such as in music, painting, and craftwork. Such activities are not needed for survival but are carried out for enjoyment and the appreciation of beauty.

The sense of touch in humans is so purposefully overdesigned that blind people can gather information about their environment through touch alone. In addition, blind people can learn to read by using braille. It is amazing how the sense of touch and the intelligence of the brain can convert groups of tiny bumps into words so quickly that reading can be carried out at virtually talking pace. In contrast, a blind ape would struggle to understand its surroundings by the sense of touch.

As well as being designed for skill, human skin has the purpose of giving the pleasure of touch. The touch of soft surfaces like petals, fur, wool, and cotton can enhance the pleasure of studying creation. A mother and baby or husband and wife can enjoy skin contact. Such sources of pleasure are exactly what would be expected through creation, because God's plan is for man to experience pleasure (1 Tim. 6:17).

(3) Unique Facial Expressions

Human facial expressions are another area of design where humans are remarkably different from apes. Humans have unique facial muscles and these give humans the unique ability to make on the order of 10,000 different facial expressions.[12] In contrast, apes can make only a handful of facial expressions.

There are about 50 separate muscles in the human face.[13] Facial muscles are present all over the face, including the eyelids, lips, nose, and

12. Paul Ekman, *The Mechanism of Human Facial Expression* (Cambridge, England: Cambridge University Press, 1990), p. 282.
13. www.meddean.luc.edu/lumen/MedEd/GrossAnatomy/dissector/muscles/master.html.

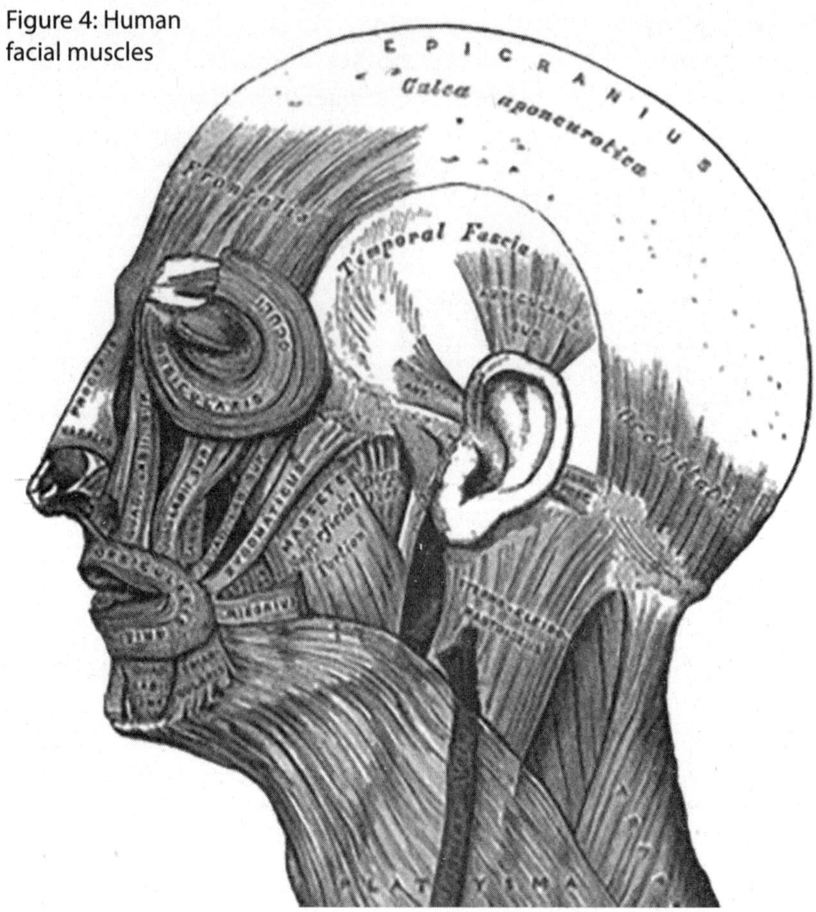

Figure 4: Human facial muscles

ears, and also within the cheek and scalp as shown in Figure 4. About half of the muscles of the face are needed for tasks like eating, speaking, and closing the eyes. However, about 24 muscles are dedicated to making facial expressions. This is remarkable because we normally think of muscles providing power, but the muscles for facial expressions are there simply to express emotions.

In contrast, the gorilla's facial muscles are significantly fewer and coarser than in humans (Figure 5). In studies of the gorilla, fewer than 30 facial muscles have been identified and none of them are dedicated to making facial expressions.[14]

There is a particularly sharp contrast between the cheek muscles of the human and the ape. In the case of the human face, there are several delicate

14. Gregory, *The Anatomy of the Gorilla*, p. 17.

Figure 5: Facial muscles in an ape

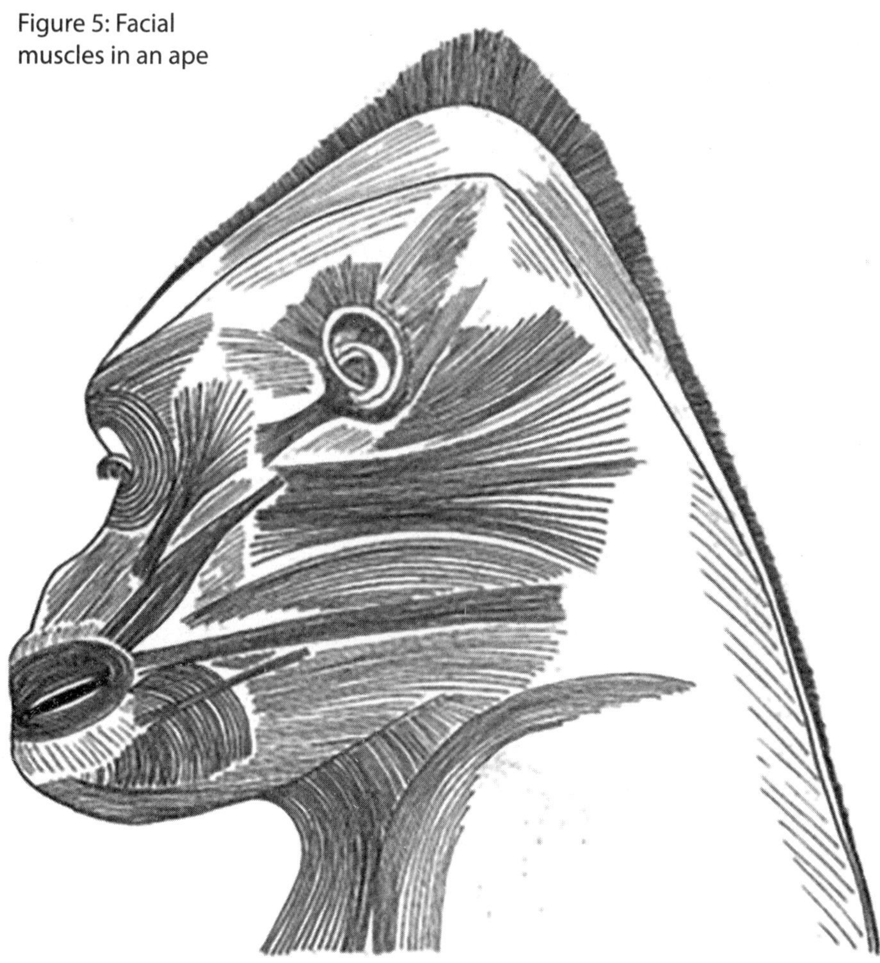

cheek muscles. In contrast, the ape has just one enormous cheek muscle for producing strong eating movements with the mouth. The delicate cheek muscles of humans are very important because they are used for making a variety of smiles. On the other hand, the cheek muscles of apes cannot produce even one smile.

To make facial expressions, a person must learn specific combinations of muscle movements. The ability to move the right combination of muscles is learned mostly during early childhood years when the whole muscular and nervous system is developing. Some expressions, like smiling, need only around four to six muscles to be activated. Other expressions, like frowning, can involve the use of up to 20 muscles.

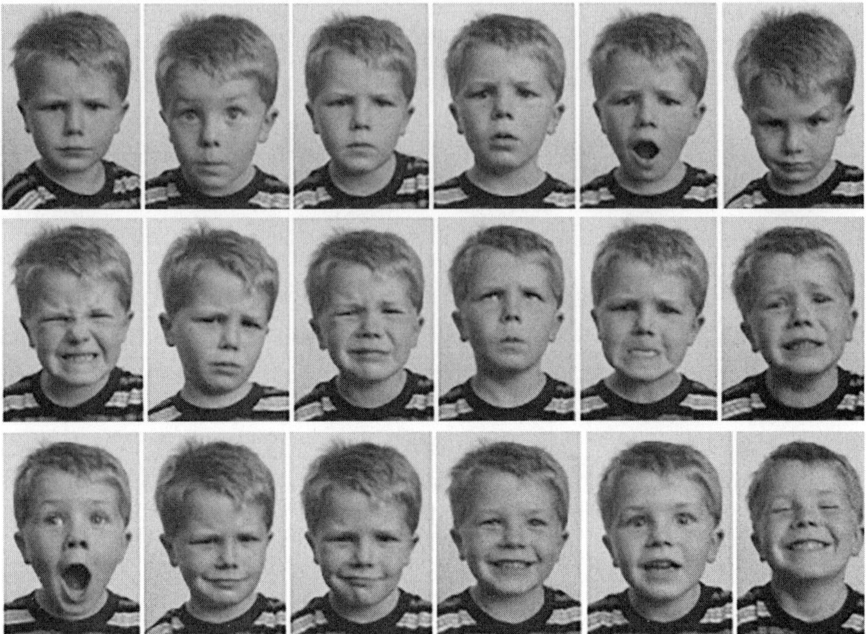

Figure 6: Examples of facial expressions in a five-year-old boy

There are many different types of expressions that can be made, such as smiling, disapproval, confusion, grief, anger, pain, surprise, and boredom. For each type of expression there are many variations and degrees of intensity. For example, there are many different types of smile and for each type there are many possible levels of intensity. In contrast, apes make only a few crude facial expressions.

Figure 6 shows some examples of different facial expressions by a five-year-old child. Even at this young age the child is capable of making sophisticated facial expressions!

Another reason why humans can make facial expressions is that the whites (sclera) of the eyes are seen clearly when the eyes are open. In contrast, the whites of the eyes of apes are not normally visible. Humans can use the whites of their eyes to emphasize certain facial expressions. For example, we can open our eyes wide to reveal larger white areas during a startled expression. Or we can slightly close our eyes, reducing the white areas, to reflect thoughtful concentration. The whites of the eyes also make it possible for others to see when we move or roll our eyes as an expression of annoyance or disrespect.

Having visible whites of the eyes also makes it possible to see if someone is looking in your direction when he is some distance away. In contrast, it can be very difficult to see if an ape is looking in your direction even when it is quite close. In communication, it is often important to make eye contact and to know that eye contact has been made.

The ability to see a person's direction of gaze is exactly what would be expected if God has created man, because effective communication is an important part of being made in God's image. It also shows that humans are clearly different from animals. In contrast, seeing the whites of the eyes is not what is expected from evolution because the sclera makes it easier for predators to recognize the face and hence detect prey. The reason why animals do not have sclera is that this helps them to hide from predators. Since humans are not designed to live in the wild, it makes perfect sense that God would give sclera to humans.

The ability to make many facial expressions is only useful if those different expressions can be recognized. The human brain is remarkable because it quickly recognizes subtle expressions. Most of us have had the experience of finding it difficult to hide an emotion and keep a "straight face." This is because we know that others are very perceptive in detecting slight facial expressions.

Evidence of Purposeful Overdesign

According to evolution, all human facial muscles must be (or have been) necessary for survival. However, evolutionists cannot explain credible survival advantages of a particular expression like a smile or a frown. Evolutionists have suggested that a smile was advantageous because it is beautiful and therefore attracted mates.[15] But this raises several questions. Why should smiling be perceived as beautiful by primitive ape-men? What was the origin of the perception of beauty? Would ape-men really choose a partner based on a single facial expression? How could it be such a great advantage to smile that no one could survive if they could not smile? How about expressions like frowning that are not attractive? What is their selective advantage? And crucially, since evolution cannot produce beyond what is needed to survive, why was there ever a need to make over 10,000 facial expressions?

The ability to make a vast range of facial expressions is exactly the kind of purposeful overdesign that we would expect from a Creator who created humans to be emotional beings who need to communicate with each other

15. https://www.quora.com/What-advantage-does-smile-give-in-human-evolution-Will-humans-stop-smiling-if-smile-is-not-giving-any-advantage-in-human-survival.

in many different ways. And it is entirely consistent with God's character that He would enable humans to make as many as 10,000 facial expressions because God gives in abundance.

Facial expressions are mentioned in the Book of Job where Job says, "I will put off my sad face and wear a smile" (Job 9:27). Facial expressions like these are very important in human communication. People constantly observe and react to the facial expressions of others around them even though they may be unaware that they are doing so. When someone looks worried, we usually ask or think what is wrong; when someone is smiling, we often smile in response. Facial expressions are so important that a blind person sometimes needs to clarify what we mean in our verbal communication because they cannot see our facial expressions.

Another example of purposeful overdesign is the ability of humans to cry. Whereas apes have tear ducts just for releasing water to lubricate the eyes, humans have the capacity to cry tears as part of an emotional response. It is very hard to argue that humans could only survive if they evolved the ability to cry. In fact, others often see crying as a sign of weakness rather than a sign of strength. In contrast, crying is perfectly consistent with God creating man to be an emotional being.

It is remarkable how humans have a physical design that complements their spiritual design. God has given humans facial muscles and tear ducts to express the emotions of the heart. Such a brilliant integrated design is extremely difficult to explain by the evolutionary process of natural selection and random mutations.

(4) Unique Ability of Language and Speech

The unique ability for human language and speech sets us apart from all other creatures, including apes. In contrast, apes have no ability for verbal speech.

Researchers have estimated that humans can make over 50 different distinct sounds in speech.[16] These sounds are combined to make thousands of different words in an individual language. Words are combined according to the rules of grammar and give a very wide range of meaning. Intonation and accent are also used to produce particular meanings.

The human voice box, vocal tract, and brain are extremely well designed to produce intricate speech. Many actions are carried out during speech with split-second timing, including intense mental activities as well as fine control of many parts of the body. In contrast, the voice box, vocal tract, and

16. John Penner, *Evolution Challenged by Language and Speech* (London, England: Minerva Press, 2000), p. 55.

brain of apes and monkeys cannot produce speech or language.

The human's sound-producing organ is the voice box (larynx), as shown in Figure. 7. Our voice box is located at the top of the windpipe (trachea), which channels air from the lungs to the throat. The voice box contains the vocal cords (vocal folds) that vibrate and produce sound waves as air passes over them. The pitch of the sound depends on the thickness of the vocal cords and the shape of the vocal tract that acts as a resonator. The vocal tract consists mainly of the windpipe, larynx, throat, mouth, and nasal passages.

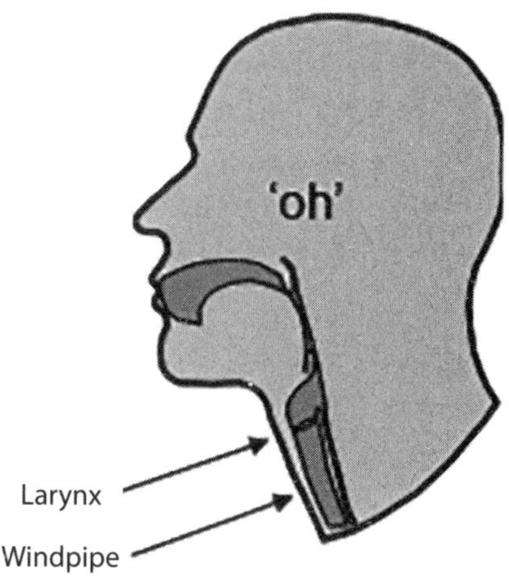

Figure 7: The human vocal tract; tongue position for the "oh" sound

The tongue, teeth, and lips also play an important role in modifying the sound of the voice. Several unique features in humans are required for producing language and speech, which provides very strong evidence that speech has not evolved.

One of the unique features of the human vocal tract is a deep throat. In contrast, apes have a shallow throat with the epiglottis at the back of the mouth. The lack of a throat in apes severely restricts the types of sound they make. The deeper throat of humans allows the tongue a wide range of positions to produce many different vowel sounds. In contrast, apes and monkeys cannot produce precise vowel sounds. The low position of the voice box in humans means that humans have to be careful not to eat and breathe at the same time, to avoid choking. The fact that apes do not have this problem reinforces the fact that the human vocal tract is unique. The internal dome shape of the human palate is also acoustically beneficial.

Humans have fine muscular control over the shape of the vocal cords and vocal tract for precisely controlled sound production. During speech, up to 100 muscles are involved in controlling the shape of the human vocal cords and vocal tract.[17] When a particular sound, like the "oh" sound, is produced during speech, dozens of muscles are moved precisely and simultaneously to produce the required shape of the vocal tract. The shape of the throat has a significant effect on sound production. Whereas

17. Ibid, p. 56.

the "oh" sound requires the throat to be restricted, the "ee" sound and "eh" sound require the throat to be open. The position of the tongue significantly influences the sound produced and is constantly moving during speech.

Humans have a uniquely agile tongue and agile lips. This agility is very important for many aspects of speech. The tongue helps to shape many consonant sounds like the "n" sound and the "d" sound. The lips also play an important part in producing precisely controlled consonant sounds. For example, the "p" and "b" sounds are made when pressure built up in the mouth is released suddenly ("p" is unvoiced and "b" is voiced). The "m" sound is made by releasing air down the nose while holding the mouth closed to give a "cul-de-sac" resonator in the mouth. Apes do not have fine control over the lips and tongue and can make only crude grunts.

As well as producing exact sounds, humans can produce these sounds with great speed and little effort. The reason that talking seems easy to an adult is that the skill has been learned in childhood. Interestingly, regardless of how difficult and complex a language is, healthy children all over the world start to learn their mother tongue before the age of two. It is amazing to think that up to a hundred muscles are being moved during speech with such precision to produce the right sounds.

The human brain has dedicated language-processing centers, almost always situated in the left cerebral hemisphere. When listening to speech, information comes from the ears to the brain where it is analyzed and interpreted. When talking, the brain sends signals to the muscles in the voice box, throat, mouth, lips, tongue, and chest for breathing control. The areas of the brain concerned with speaking are the Broca's area and Wernicke's area.

Apes simply do not have areas in their brain dedicated to processing language. Language and speech represent a chicken-and-egg challenge to evolution, because both the hardware (throat) and software (brain processing) are needed simultaneously to make speech possible.

Humans have an amazing ability to learn and recall words. Every human language contains a great number of words. The English language contains over 500,000 commonly recognized words (not including past tense versions and plural versions). The number of possible words in the English language is far greater than a million, and the pool of words used in English daily reading alone is about 100,000![18]

Another important feature of human speech is that humans can speak at a fast rate and for long periods. The average person can speak almost 200

18. Ibid, p. 51.

words a minute, which amounts to 12,000 words an hour. During this time it is possible to convey vast amounts of information.

In contrast to humans, apes and monkeys have virtually no vocabulary whatsoever. They may have one type of grunt that acts as a warning signal and another type of grunt that indicates the presence of food. However, they cannot communicate abstract thoughts or complex information.

Many experiments have been carried out to try to teach chimpanzees to talk. However, these have only confirmed that chimpanzees are not designed to speak. In the 1950s, scientists experimented for six years trying to teach a chimpanzee to talk.[19] However, despite great efforts to train the chimp, its vocabulary was only four simple words: mamma, papa, cup and up. In addition, the chimp sometimes used the words incorrectly.

Humans also have the unique ability to communicate in written form. The written form of language is very useful for recording knowledge and conveying messages. Like speech, writing is a wonderful skill that involves many parts of the body working together. Writing requires the coordinated action of the hands, the eyes, the nervous system, and different parts of the brain, including the motor cortex, for the hands and the speech-processing areas.

Written language requires knowledge of characters and proper word spellings. Spelling can be very challenging because some languages contain a very large number of intricate characters. This is particularly true for many far-Eastern languages such as Chinese and Japanese. There are about 40,000 different characters in the Chinese language. Just to read a Chinese newspaper requires knowledge of about 3,000 different characters. In contrast to humans, apes are completely incapable of writing any letters and certainly can't read a single word.

Evidence of Purposeful Overdesign

Complex language and speech are obviously not vital to survival: animals survive just fine without either. Evolutionary processes are therefore inadequate to explain the origin of human language. In contrast, language and speech are exactly what would be expected from a God who created mankind to communicate with Him and with each other our thoughts, feelings, and desires (e.g., Gen. 1:3, 5, 14, 26 and 3:9–13). Complex language also enables humans to read and understand God's Word, pray to God, and sing praises to God.

Many Bible passages teach us to speak in a manner that honors God

19. Ibid, p. 135.

(e.g., Ps. 19:14; Eph. 4:25–31, 5:19, 6:18–19; Col. 4:6; James 3:1–10). Scripture also refers to man's duty or desire to sing praises to God (e.g., Ps. 47:6, 104:33, 105:2, 146:2). Singing is a strong example of purposeful overdesign because it is very hard to conceive of any survival advantage for having a voice that can sing so beautifully. Of course, some animals, such as songbirds and whales, also have the ability to sing beautifully. But such examples also represent examples of overdesign. The fact also remains that the ability of humans to sing sets them apart from apes.

(5) Unique Brain

Perhaps the greatest anatomical difference between humans and apes is the brain. Humans have an incredible level of intelligence that enables them to understand, create, design, plan, compose, and carry out extremely skillful tasks. In contrast, apes have a relatively limited intelligence that is adequate for surviving in the wild and no more.

One of the most complex parts of the human brain is the cerebral cortex, which is much larger in humans than apes. For example, the volume of the frontal cortex (involved with reasoning, planning, and abstract thought) is more than three times that for great apes. The cerebral cortex is extremely compact because it consists of a large number of tight folds (sulci).

One consequence of a large cerebral cortex is that humans have a plethora of both brain cells (neurons) and brain cell connections (synapses). The

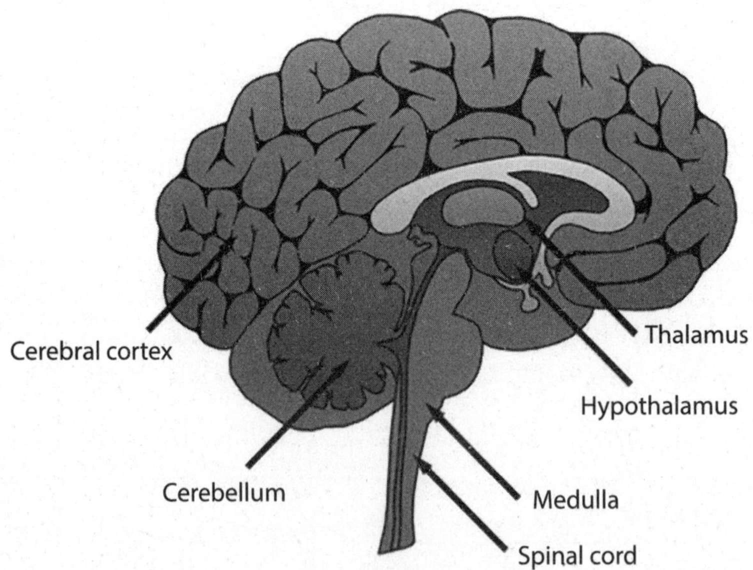

Figure 8: The human brain

human brain has something like 100 billion neurons and up to thousands of connections per neuron. This means that there are hundreds of trillions of connections in the human brain! This vast number of nerve cells and connections is one of the reasons for the great intelligence of humans.

The mass of the human brain is much larger than the mass of apes' and monkeys' brains, especially when the ratio of brain weight to body weight is considered. In the case of a healthy adult human, the brain weight is about 1.4 kg and the body weight is about 80 kg. Therefore, the ratio of brain weight to body weight is approximately 1.8% for humans. In the case of gorillas, the brain weight is about 0.5 kg and the body weight is around 150 kg. Therefore, the ratio of brain weight to body weight is about 0.333% for the gorilla. This means that the human has a brain weight to body weight ratio about five times greater than the gorilla.

When you hear the evolutionist claim that humans are 95–98% similar to apes, just remember that in the crucial area of the brain there is an actual similarity of only 20% in brain to body weight ratio! This illustrates again that when key performance criteria are considered, there is not a close similarity between humans and apes. Not only does this ratio reflect that humans are categorically different from apes, it also makes us categorically separate from all other living things. (There is absolutely nothing else on the planet with a ratio that is closer to our ratio than that of the gorillas.)

It is not just the size of the brain that is very different between humans and apes. Michael Gazzaniga, who is the Director of the University of California-Santa Barbara's SAGE Center for the study of the mind and a world-renowned neuroscientist, has stated that the scientific community is wrong to teach that the only difference between the human brain and ape brain is size. He has said,

> The historical and current social and scientific forces maintaining the notion that the only difference between an ape's brain and our own is one of size, which is to say number of neurons, have been overwhelming. And yet a dispassionate look at the data in front of us clearly shows that the human brain has many unique features. In fact, the scientific literature is full of examples that range from the level of gross anatomy to cellular anatomy to molecular structure. In short, as we build our case for the uniqueness of the human brain, we start on firm footing.[20]

20. Michael Gazzaniga, *Human: The Science Behind What Makes Us Unique* (New York: Harper Collins, 2008), p. 36–37.

Evolutionary teaching generally implies that the brain simply had to evolve in size as an ape ancestor progressed to modern humans. And yet the quotation above makes the crucial point that size is not the only difference in the design of the brain.

The human brain is particularly amazing because it responds (appropriately) to vast amounts of information from the nervous system in very short amounts of time. The number of sensors in the body means that the brain receives millions of pieces of information per second. Out of this flood of data, only a small amount of the information is important. Remarkably, the human brain recognizes essential information and then quickly makes a decision about what to do in response. While animals also filter information, their task is vastly less complicated because they have instinctive behavior and do not make rational decisions.

Many of us complain about forgetting simple things like PIN numbers. However, modern memory problems are due to the fast pace of modern life and not the ability of the brain. Every healthy person actually has a great capacity for remembering. Language is one area where people remember many thousands of pieces of information. Another remarkable ability that virtually everyone possesses is the ability to remember scenes that occurred decades ago or the words of hundreds of songs or sports trivia.

Some memory competitions illustrate the immense capacity of the human brain. One competition involves memorizing the number π (pi). The number π is equal to 3.14159265358 (to 12 decimal places) and describes the relationship between the diameter and circumference of a circle. The number is an irrational number, which means that the number of decimal places has no ending. It is very difficult to remember π because there is no pattern to the sequence of numbers. However, people from all over the world have shown a remarkable ability to remember the number π to many decimal places. One of the records for memorizing π is held by a Japanese man named Hiroyuki Goto who memorized π to over 42,195 places in 1995![21] Memorizing an irrational number is certainly unnecessary for survival.

Humans also have a unique ability to recognize beauty, and tests have shown that part of the human brain is dedicated to the appreciation of beauty in many areas such as music, painting, and sculpture. To appreciate beauty requires a high level of intelligence because beauty is very subtle. There is no evidence that chimpanzees or gorillas have any appreciation of natural or man-made beauty.

---

21. http://www.pi-world-ranking-list.com/lists/details/goto.htm.

Evidence of Purposeful Overdesign

According to evolution, the human brain has evolved for survival tasks like hunting and gathering. But such survival tasks do not require a brain with great intellectual capacity. The appreciation of beauty is a particularly good example of overdesign that has no survival advantage. Capabilities such as rational thought, inventiveness, and the appreciation of beauty are what we would expect from the fact that humans are made in the image of God, who is infinitely rational and creative and obviously loves beauty. But apes display none of these characteristics and it is most unreasonable to think that they arose in man by the blind, directionless processes of natural selection and mutations as evolutionists imagine.

The phenomenal achievements of scientists, artists, and composers down through the ages demonstrate that the human brain is designed for more than survival. No one can deny that the human brain has far greater capacity than is needed for daily living. Even when young children must have half of their brain removed (hemispherectomy) they often appear completely normal and are able to perform complex intellectual activities like studying science and speaking multiple languages.

The Bible records how certain people had great wisdom including Solomon (1 Kings 4:30), Huram-abi (2 Chron. 2:13) and Abigail (1 Sam. 25:2–3, 25). King David was said to have great musical skill, which would have included excellent musical understanding (1 Sam. 16:18). Adam must have had great wisdom in order to name all of the animals that God brought to him (Gen. 2:20). The Bible also says that God gave particular types of wisdom to some of the first people in history, including understanding of music to Jubal (Gen. 4:21) and understanding of craftwork to Tubal-Cain (Gen. 4:22). Jesus is also said to have increased in knowledge and wisdom (Luke 2:52).

The great intelligence of humans is exactly what would be expected when considering the biblical teaching that humans are designed to be stewards of creation. To subdue every creature on earth requires great skill and wisdom. To develop the technology necessary for building construction, farming industries, and engineering technologies requires very high levels of intelligence. The great intellectual capacity of the human brain enables man to explore and enjoy many aspects of the created world. The human brain is no accident of nature, but the result of divine design.

(6) Unique Beauty

Every animal has a degree of beauty. However, the human body has a uniquely delicate beauty. Whereas apes have a rugged beauty that is fitting for their rough lifestyle, humans have a fine beauty that is suited to their status as made in the image of God.

Of course, the perception of beauty is subjective because it is partly an emotional and personal response. However, there are many objective reasons why beauty is a real concept. An object has objective beauty when it has attributes such as proportion, curves, symmetry, smoothness, distinctiveness, softness, and color. The human body has all of these attributes.

According to evolution, the beauty of the human body can be explained by genetic accidents and sexual selection in ape-like creatures over millions of years. However, the human body has a beauty that is far superior to and different from that of apes. It is most unreasonable to think that the directionless and purposeless processes of natural selection and random mutations can explain this superiority and difference. Furthermore, not a single instance of a single gene in our DNA responsible for anything related to beauty has yet been identified. If there is an evolutionary origin to beauty, then it demands a genetic explanation. Without anything to inherit, evolution has no mechanism to pass on anything beautiful. The presence of beauty in the human body must therefore be the result of design.

Elegant Stature and Proportions

Leonardo da Vinci's picture of Vitruvian man, as shown in Figure 9, illustrates the beautiful proportions of the human body.

One way to see that the (adult) human body is well proportioned is that when the arms are outstretched horizontally, the distance from fingertip to fingertip is approximately the same as the total height of the person. If a person is 1.5m tall then the distance from fingertip to fingertip will be 1.5m. If a person is 2m tall then this will be the distance from fingertip to fingertip. This equality of length means that the human body fits perfectly inside a square as shown in Figure 9. In contrast, apes have no such equality of lengths.

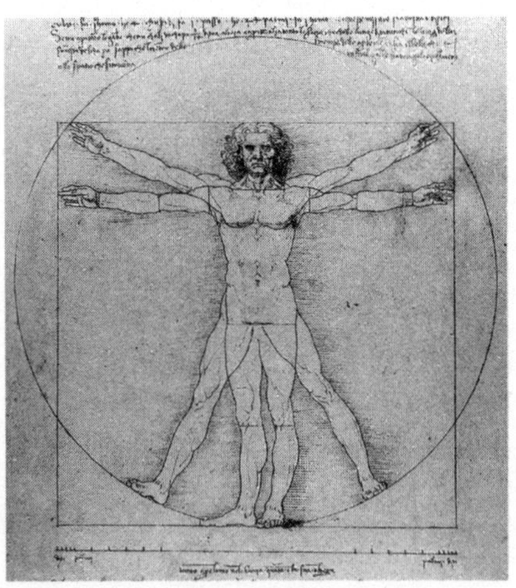

Figure 9: Vitruvian man

Another evidence of the elegant

proportion of an adult human body is that apart from very rare exceptions (dwarves or little people) the legs are half the total height of the person. This means that the torso does not dominate the legs and the legs do not dominate the torso. In contrast, apes have legs that are much less than half of their height.

The human body can also fit very elegantly inside a circle as shown in Figure 8. When the body has the posture of a "star jump," it fits inside a circle with the feet and hands at the edge of the circle. A fascinating and elegant feature of the star jump position is that the navel is exactly at the center of the circle. The fact that humans are so well proportioned has fascinated great minds such as Leonardo da Vinci down through the ages.

Another important difference between humans and apes is that women have high concentrations of fat deposits in their breasts so that their breasts are distinctive even when they are not breastfeeding. In contrast, female apes do not have breasts if they are not breastfeeding. The distinctive and unique breasts of humans have the purpose of adding a beautiful shape to the female body.

Beautiful Hair

The human body has unique hair growth. On the one hand, most of the body has very little hair and much of it is almost invisible. On the other hand, the head has fast-growing and very noticeable hair. In contrast, animals, including apes, have slow-growing fur over their whole body. It should be noted that the Bible says God made the first man and woman naked (Gen. 2:25) and they began to wear clothing for a moral and spiritual reason, not because of climate change (Gen. 3:7, 21).

The fast-growing hair on the head of humans makes a beautiful crown to the body. The relatively fast growth means that hair can be grown very long. Fast growth also means that hair can be regrown if it is damaged or in poor condition. Human hair is also fine and often capable of being fashioned into different styles. The human hairline on the scalp is remarkably neat around the neck and forehead. It is difficult to argue that the hairline could be better placed and also hard to explain how hairlines could have evolved by chance. While we know what genes control hair production, it is difficult to imagine why evolution would select for particular placements of hair.

The fact that only men have beards represents a very significant difference between men and women. From a biblical viewpoint, this can be explained in terms of women being designed particularly for beauty because a lack of beard enables the whole face to be appreciated in detail and makes the skin smooth. Male beards also help remind humans that God has created two distinct genders.

From an evolutionary point of view, the male-only beard is very hard to explain. The evolutionist has to resort to sexual theories such as many men choosing to mate only with women who had less facial hair, while hairless women simultaneously preferred mating with men who had facial hair. Such a scenario requires the exact same features to be selected for within the same gene pool. However, such a scenario would result in two groups of men and women — those with and those without a beard. The difference in facial hair between men and women is just too precise to be explainable by random chance. Even if we consider some women with excessive facial hair, this is a far cry from the full beard of a typical man. It is also striking that everyone focuses on the bearded woman without noticing the beardless man. Focusing on bearded women further highlights the inherent beauty present in women's faces.

Eyebrows are an interesting detail that provides further evidence of purposeful design. They are formed by a small clump of slow-growing hair that grows in isolation just above the eyes. Eyebrows have a purpose of reducing the amount of sweat dripping down the forehead into the eyes. As well as being functional they are beautiful because of being well-proportioned and well-placed. They are large enough to capture water but not so large that they dominate the face.

Fine details like eyebrows are a problem for evolution because eyebrows perform a relatively *minor* function rather than a *vital* function. It is difficult to argue that humans could only survive if they evolved eyebrows. In contrast, the function and aesthetics of eyebrows reflect the intentional and intelligent design of our Creator.

Beautiful Face

The face is a particularly important and beautiful part of the body because it is the main source of identity for a person. One reason why the human face is beautiful is because the eyes, lips, nose, and ears have a delicate design. Humans have soft rounded lips that apes do not have, and humans have a nose that hides the nostril openings from view, again in contrast to apes.

A difference between human eyes and ape eyes is that human eyes have a range of colors. These colors can be seen clearly because the whites of the eyes draw attention to the color of the iris. The most common colors of the iris are brown and blue, although some eyes are blue-green or brown-green. Blue and green are produced when there is a lack of pigment in the iris and light is scattered. In contrast, the visible part of ape eyes is almost completely black or dark brown.

It should be noted that when museum exhibits of so-called ape-men have human-like eyes (with noticeable whites and colors like blue eyes) there is no scientific justification for this. Eyes are not preserved in the fossil record so putting human eyes with noticeable whites in ape-man re-creations is unscientific and deceives the public.

A smiling face is a particularly beautiful sight because it conveys friendliness, joy, and pleasure. Consider the famous smile of Mona Lisa in the painting by Leonardo da Vinci as just one example of how inviting a smile is.

An important reason for the beauty of the human face is variety in appearance. Every person has a unique face, with the exception of identical twins. In contrast, apes have quite a limited variety in the appearance of the face. The beautiful variety of human faces is partly a result of having many facial muscles (50) and partly because fine skin reveals the shape of the muscles and cartilage. The genetic variation that comes through combining the genomes of a father and mother ensures that children will be born with a unique facial design.

The variation in the human face is an example of how genetic variation is a brilliant design feature that God uses to create a beautiful variety in creation. It is sad how modern secular science does not see genetic variation as a design feature to create beauty (and to allow creatures to undergo small adaptive changes), but rather sees genetic variation as a blind, purposeless process whereby life evolved by chance.

Another beautiful feature of the human face is that humans have a neat and level row of teeth compared to the teeth of animals. Even though humans have four canine teeth (two upper maxillary and two lower mandibular), these are approximately the same height as the other teeth in the mouth. In contrast, apes have canine teeth that are much longer than the other teeth and gaps in the opposite jaw to fit them.[22] The human mouth can also close so that the lower teeth are approximately under the upper teeth.

In the evolutionary view, there must have been some selective advantage for humans to lose long canine teeth. Charles Darwin said the following about the supposed loss of large canine teeth in humans:

> The early male progenitors of man were, as previously stated,

22. Search on Google Images and you will see this. But make sure you are looking at pictures of real, living apes, not non-existent evolutionary "ape-men."

> probably furnished with great canine teeth; but as they gradually acquired the habit of using stones, clubs, or other weapons, for fighting with their enemies, they would use their jaws and teeth less and less. In this case, the jaws with the teeth, would have become reduced in size.[23]

Darwin's remark is an example of how evolutionary philosophy proposes crude explanations for design features in humans like level teeth. Notice how Darwin does not actually give an explanation for the loss of large canine teeth — he simply argues that they were not needed and thus reduced in size. He implies that if something is not needed then it just magically changes. It is very hard for evolution to explain why there are no humans today who have large canine teeth if humans had them in the past.

Evidence of Purposeful Overdesign

The delicate physical beauty of humans has a purpose of reflecting the beauty of the spiritual attributes of our majestic Creator who made man in His image. Another purpose of human beauty is for husbands and wives to be physically attracted to each other and to enjoy each other's beauty.

The Bible mentions the beauty of several women including Sarah (Gen. 12:11), Rachel (Gen. 29:17), Tamar, (2 Sam. 13:1), Bathsheba (2 Sam. 11:2), Abigail (1 Sam. 25:3), Abishag (1 Kings 1:3), Job's daughters (Job 42:15), and Esther (Esther 2:7). The Bible also mentions several handsome men including Saul (1 Sam. 9:2), David (1 Sam. 16:18), and Joseph (Gen. 39:6).

A major problem with believing in theistic evolution is that you have to believe that human beauty is a result of random chance and that humans could have ended up with very strange and ugly features if the roulette had stopped in a different place. If chance had been slightly different, we could have had women with beards; both men and women being completely bald; flat noses; canine teeth sticking out; hairy noses; and long drooping ears. Some may try to argue that we could get used to such a strange design and consider it to be beautiful. However, the reality is that there are objective reasons for saying that the human being that God created has great beauty.

God's Curse on creation at the Fall of Adam has certainly resulted in the marring of the beauty of creation including the beauty of the human body. This marring is due to gene mutations, disease, aging, scarring from accidents and violence, and unhealthy lifestyles. However, despite sin and

23. Charles Darwin, *The Descent of Man* (London, England: John Murray, 1871), p. 144.

Some of the Key Anatomical Differences between Humans and Apes

	Ape feature	Human feature	Unique human abilities
1	Flexible flat foot	Stiff arched foot	Run on two legs
2	Thumb-like big toe	Forward-pointing big toe	Run on two legs
3	No 3-point contact foot	3-point contact on foot	Stand on one leg
4	Short legs/long arms	Long legs/short arms	Habitual biped
5	C-curved back	S-curved back	Upright posture
6	Knees do not lock upright	Knees lock upright	Easy to stand
7	Vertical femur bones	Angled femur bones	Walk without swaying
8	Small vertical balance canals	Large vertical balance canals	Fine vertical balance
9	Protruding jaw	Flat jaw	View of ground below
10	Protruding canine teeth	No protruding canine teeth	Beautiful smile
11	Flat nose	Pointed cartilage nose	Beauty/ wear glasses
12	Thick body hair	Absence of thick body hair	Cool by evaporation
13	Slow-growing hair on head	Fast-growing hair on head	Beautiful hair styles
14	Sweat glands only in armpits	Sweat glands in whole body	Faster cooling
15	Few touch sensors in hands	Many touch sensors in hands	Fine sense of touch
16	Thick finger friction skin	Fine skin on fingers	Fine sense of touch
17	Non-opposable thumbs	Opposable thumbs	Pinch grip
18	No tripod finger grip	Tripod finger grip	Pen holding
19	Curved hands	Flat hands	Flat hand positions
20	Small motor cortex for hands	Large motor cortex for hands	Skillful hands
21	No facial expression muscles	24 facial expression muscles	Express emotions
22	No whites of eyes	Whites of eyes (sclera)	See direction of gaze
23	No deep throat	Deep throat	Talking and singing
24	Coarse vocal chords	Fine vocal chords	Talking and singing
25	No language area in brain	Language area in brain	Understand & speak language
26	Tear ducts for lubrication	Tear ducts for crying also	Tears of emotion
27	Brain size <0.5% body wt.	Brain size >1.5% body wt.	High intelligence
28	No appreciation of beauty	Appreciation of beauty	Appreciation of beauty
29	Brown eyes only	Brown, blue, and green eyes	Beautiful & varied eyes
30	No distinctive male beard	Distinctive male beards	Gender distinction

the Curse on creation, there is still clear evidence of profound beauty in the human body, which points unmistakably to our Creator and His love of beauty.

Conclusion

The purposeful overdesign of the hand, skin, facial expressions, linguistic abilities, brain, and beauty of humans shows that man is fearfully and wonderfully made and designed for much more than mere survival.

The purposeful overdesign of man is an enormous challenge to evolution because such design cannot be explained in terms of evolutionary survival advantages. The skillfulness of man shows that he is made a little lower than the angels (Ps. 8:5), not a little above the beasts. The ability of man to communicate and express thoughts and emotions shows that he is made in the image of God (Gen. 1:27), not the image of an ape. The beauty of man shows that humans have been wonderfully made (Ps. 139:14), not formed by a blind, chance process of evolution.

Evolution leads to a low view of man — that he is just an animal who has evolved for crude activities like fighting, promiscuity, and rape. Such a view inevitably leads to a moral breakdown of society because many people think that selfish and crude behavior is natural and justifiable. It also gives people an excuse to think there is no God. In contrast, biblical creation leads to a high view of man — that he is crowned with glory and honor (Ps. 8:5) and is capable of a blessed life using his creative abilities to serve his Creator. We should therefore recognize that the theory of human evolution is not just a false science but also a very dangerous philosophy with far-reaching and damaging consequences.

Chapter 13

Evolution, Racism, and the Scientific Vindication of Genesis

by Dr. Jerry Bergman

Introduction

For over a thousand years, most people in the Western world regarded all humans as descendants of Adam and Eve. Thus, all humans are of the same race and all are in essence brothers and sisters. As we will see shortly, this view is soundly biblical, Christian orthodoxy. But this view of humans as taught in Genesis was abandoned by many in the wake of the Darwinian revolution that occurred in the middle 1800s. Darwin and his allies argued that all humans have evolved from an ancient non-human ancestor,[1] and that some races have evolved further than others. This chapter documents that scientific research has proven the evolutionary view of the origin of the human races is wrong, and the biblical view that all humans are descended from Adam is correct.

Professor Mario Livio wrote that the prevailing biblical view about the origin of humans was widely accepted:

> . . . until one man had the chutzpah, the vision, and the deep insights to weave together a huge set of separate clues into one magnificent tapestry. This man was Charles Darwin . . . and his grand unified conception has become humankind's most inspiring non-mathematical theory. Darwin has literally transformed the ideas on Earth from a myth into a science. The first edition of Darwin's book

1. Darwin alluded to this idea in *Origin of Species* in 1859 but fully developed it in his *Descent of Man* in 1871.

> *On the Origin of Species* was published on November 24, 1859, in London, and biology was changed forever on that day.[2]

Although humans were historically divided into language and national groups, categorizing humans by physical characteristics is a relatively new approach. In other words, the main way of grouping people in the past was based on their national origin, such as Assyrian or Egyptian, and not biology.[3] Only after Darwin were people commonly divided into groups on the basis of biology, i.e., purely physical traits such as skin, eye, and hair color. In fact,

> The biological race concept, as we understand it today, originated with eugenic theories of difference and was re-created and integrated into modern biological thought by population geneticists and evolutionary biologists in the 1930s and 1940s during the evolutionary synthesis in biology (the union of population genetics, experimental genetics, and natural history that reshaped modern biology).[4]

This step was critical in establishing and propelling the racism that developed and escalated during the last century and a half. Also critical were certain passages in Darwin's writings, such as,

> At some future period, not very distant as measured by centuries, the civilized races of man will almost certainly exterminate and replace the savage races throughout the world. At the same time the anthropomorphous apes . . . will no doubt be exterminated. The break between man and his nearest allies will then be wider, for it will intervene between man in a more civilized state, as we may hope, even than the Caucasian, and some ape as low as a baboon, instead of as now between the Negro or Australian [aborigine] and the gorilla.[5]

2. Mario Livio, *Brilliant Blunders: From Darwin to Einstein — Colossal Mistakes by Great Scientists that Changed Our Understanding of Life and the Universe* (New York: Simon & Schuster, 2013), p. 16–17.
3. Tom Blaney, *The Chief Sea Lion's Inheritance: Eugenics and the Darwins* (Leicester, England: Troubador, 2011).
4. Michael Yudell, *Race Unmasked: Biology and Race in the Twentieth Century* (New York, NY: Columbia University Press, 2014), p. 6. Yudell, Associate Professor of Public Health at Drexel University, charts the overthrow of the Darwinian "scientific" view of race during the last century to today. His particular concern is eugenics and its history in the USA, focusing almost entirely on the problem between the black and white "races."
5. Charles Darwin, *The Descent of Man* (New York: A.L. Burt, 1874, 2nd ed.), p. 178.

The fact is, this view was widely applied to society. The late Harvard Professor Stephen Jay Gould concluded from his detailed study of racism that: "Biological arguments for racism may have been common before 1850, but they increased by orders of magnitude following the acceptance of evolutionary theory."[6] Gould added,

> The litany is familiar: cold, dispassionate, objective, modern science shows us that races can be ranked on a scale of superiority. If this offends Christian morality, or a sentimental belief in human unity, so be it; science must be free to proclaim unpleasant truths. . . . We never have had, and still do not have, any unambiguous data on the innate mental capacities of different human groups [that show one race is superior to another]. . . . If the chorus of racist arguments did not follow a constraint of data, it must have reflected social prejudice pure and simple.[7]

The Biblical View on Race

The Bible is perfectly clear that there is only one race: Adam's race, the human race. Genesis 1:26–27 says that man is uniquely made in the image of God, distinct from all other creatures. The first male, named Adam in Genesis 2, was created from the dust of the earth (not a pre-existing animal) and the first woman, named Eve in Genesis 3, was made from the rib of Adam (Gen 2:22). Genesis 3:20 says that Eve is the mother of all the living and 1 Corinthians 15:45 affirms that Adam was "the first man." Genesis 5 gives us the genealogy from Adam to Noah and his sons and Genesis 10:32 informs us that from them all the people on earth descended. Paul affirms this in Acts 17:26 when he says that from one man God made "every nation of mankind to dwell on all the face of the earth, having determined their appointed times and the boundaries of their habitation."[8]

The notion that the "curse of Ham" is the supposed origin of the "black race" has no basis in Scripture, for it was Canaan, Ham's son who was cursed (Gen. 9:25). Canaan's descendants (the Canaanites) were some of the most wicked people who ever lived and they were judged for their godlessness, idolatry, and immorality (Deut. 20:17–18).

So there is only one race, but many people groups with different languages and distinctive physical characteristics. When we apply our

---

6. Stephen Jay Gould, *Ontogeny and Phylogeny* (Cambridge, MA: Belknap-Harvard Press, 1977), p. 127.
7. Ibid., p. 127–128.
8. Scripture in this chapter is from the New American Standard Bible (NASB).

modern understanding of genetics to the event of God's supernatural creation of many languages at the Tower of Babel and the subsequent dispersion of the people according to their families (Gen. 11:1–9), it is very easy to explain how the distinctive physical features (e.g., skin color, eye shape, hair color and style, height, etc.) of the different people groups arose.[9]

The Development of Racism

One of the most fundamental questions in contemporary society and science is what is race, and are the so-called "races," however defined, biological equals? We now know that there is often more genetic diversity within a given racial group than between any two races, yet the political and social applications of race are still critical issues today.

The anthropological research on race in the late 19th century served as a critical support for racism as well as, eventually, documenting the fact that biologically based racism was not only erroneous, but also harmful to both society and many individuals.

Darwin's cousin, Francis Galton, the originator of the field of eugenics that was the backbone of biological racism, was one of the founding fathers of several important branches of science, including anthropology.[10] As the father of the eugenics movement, in the end, his work resulted in not only the Holocaust, but also in the loss of millions of lives in both Europe and Asia. As documented by one historian, biological racism began "in 1859 with the appearance of Darwin's chief work, *On the Origins of Species by means of Natural Selection, or the Preservation of Favoured Races in the Struggle for Life*."[11] Then, within a few years after 1859, Darwinism:

> . . . not only revolutionized the science of biology but aroused passionate interest far beyond the confines of biology. With the precision characteristic of Darwin, the title indicates the thesis at the core of his theory . . . a theory of selection, that is, the idea that the species had evolved through selection among varied offspring in the course of the

9. See Ken Ham's chapter 17 in *The New Answers Book 1* (on-line at: https://answersingenesis.org/racism/are-there-really-different-races/). For a more in-depth discussion see Ken Ham and A. Charles Ware, *One Race, One Blood: the Biblical Answer to Racism* (Green Forest, AR: Master Books, 2010), and Carl Wieland, *One Human Family: The Bible, Science, Race and Culture* (Atlanta, GA: Creation Book Publ., 2011).
10. J.A. Savin, "Francis Galton and the Skin," *Journal of Royal College of Physicians Edinburgh*, 32:206–211 (2002), p. 206.
11. Hajo Holborn, ed., *Republic to Reich: The Making of the Nazi Revolution, Ten Essays* (New York: Pantheon Books, 1972), p. 437.

> struggle for life. The explosive force of this cool, scientific formulation becomes apparent when we consider the prevailing conceptions of the time.[12]

Francis Galton, borrowing heavily from Darwin, concluded that, as an inferior race, the "negro may himself disappear before alien races, just as his predecessors disappeared before him."[13] To Galton, "race improvement was 'so noble in its aim' that it rose to the level of 'religious obligation.' "[14] Furthermore, Galton's writings were "read widely" and greatly influenced not only the eugenics movement, but also governmental policy in many countries, including especially Nazi Germany.[15]

In the end, "social prejudices became scientific" which served to justify a wide variety of social abuses.[16] This field, one that Hillenbrand called a pseudoscience, was embraced by many "well-respected geneticists" who concluded that "the Negro race differs greatly from the white race, mentally as well as physically."[17] These scientific supporters included many of Darwin's own children, especially Leonard Darwin.[18]

The enormous harm that eugenics has caused in the Western world, especially its applications to social policy, is well documented. This problem was summarized by one historian who wrote that in "the 1930s, America was infatuated with the pseudoscience of eugenics and its promise of strengthening the human race by culling the 'unfit' from the genetic pool."[19] These unfit included not only certain races but also

> "feebleminded," insane, and criminal, those so classified included women who had sex out of wedlock (considered a mental illness), orphans, the disabled, the poor, the homeless, epileptics, masturbators, the blind and the deaf, alcoholics, and girls whose genitals exceeded certain measurements. Some eugenicists advocated euthanasia, and in mental hospitals, this was quietly carried

---

12. Ibid.
13. Yudell, *Race Unmasked*, p. 28.
14. Ibid., p. 29.
15. Ibid., p. 19; see also Paul Weindling, *Victims and Survivors of Nazi Human Experiments: Science and Suffering in the Holocaust* (London: Bloomsbury, 2015); Richard Weikart, *From Darwin to Hitler: Evolutionary Ethics, Eugenics, and Racism in Germany* (New York: Palgrave Macmillan, 2004).
16. Yudell, *Race Unmasked*, p. 18.
17. Ibid., p. 15.
18. Blaney, *The Chief Sea Lion's Inheritance* (2011).
19. Laura Hillenbrand, *Unbroken: A World War II Story of Survival, Resilience, and Redemption* (New York: Random House, 2010), p. 11.

> out on scores of people through "lethal neglect" or outright murder.[20]

As an example of the harm that racism and eugenics caused, Hillenbrand cited one Illinois mental hospital, where

> new patients were dosed with milk from cows infected with tuberculosis, in the belief that only the undesirable would perish. As many as four in ten of these patients died. A more popular tool of eugenics was forced sterilization, employed on a raft of lost souls who, through misbehavior or misfortune, fell into the hands of state governments. By 1930 . . . California was enraptured with eugenics, and would ultimately sterilize some twenty thousand people.[21]

This eugenic conclusion was applied more in Nazi Germany than in any other country. As the leading British evolutionary anthropologist Sir Arthur Keith wrote,

> To see evolutionary measures and tribal morality being applied rigorously to the affairs of a great modern nation, we must turn again to Germany of 1942. We see Hitler devoutly convinced that evolution produces the only real basis for a national policy. . . . The German Fuhrer, as I have consistently maintained, is an evolutionist; he has consciously sought to make the practices of Germany conform to the theory of evolution.[22]

In Nazi Germany the "systematic viciousness of Nazi racial-hygienic policies . . . resulted not only in the sterilization of about four hundred thousand people in a decade, but also . . . in the deliberate murder of about two hundred thousand people in the wartime 'euthanasia' programme."[23]

Leaders of Eugenic Racism Were Academics

Most all leaders of the various "scientific racist" movements were academics with PhD's from leading universities, consisting of a virtual " 'who's who' of the natural and social scientists of the time."[24] One leading eugenicist, Charles Davenport, was a Harvard PhD. Another eugenicist, Dr. Harvey

20. Ibid.
21. Ibid.
22. Sir Arthur Keith, *Evolution and Ethics* (New York: Putman, 1947), p. 28, 30.
23. Michael Burleigh, *The Third Reich: A New History* (New York, NY: Hill and Wang, 2000), p. 348.
24. Yudell, *Race Unmasked*, p. 77.

E. Jordan, "a noted eugenicist and racist," was Professor of Embryology, and later Dean of the College of Medicine at the University of Virginia.[25] Paleontologist Henry Fairfield Osborn headed the American Museum of Natural History in New York City for over 25 years. He coined the name "Nebraska man" for a single tooth found in 1922, which subsequent fossil evidence discovered in 1927 proved to be from an extinct species of pig (as discussed by Menton in chapter 8). During his tenure he accumulated one of the finest fossil collections in the world, including those of putative pre-humans. His conclusions about blacks published in the magazine *Natural History* include,

> The spiritual, intellectual, moral, and physical characters which separate these three great human stocks are far more profound and ancient than those which divide the Nordic, Alpine, and Mediterranean races. In my opinion these three primary stocks diverged from each other before the beginning of the Pleistocene or Ice Age. The Negroid stock is even more ancient than the Caucasian and Mongolian, as may be proved by an examination not only of the brain, of the hair, of the bodily characters, such as the teeth, the genitalia, the sense organs, but of the instincts, the intelligence. The standard of intelligence of the average adult Negro is similar to that of the eleven-year-old youth of the species Homo sapiens.[26]

He added in support of his case,

> The wisdom teeth of the Negro are erupted at the age of thirteen; the wisdom teeth of *Homo sapiens* are erupted between the ages of twenty-one and thirty, if at all. The young Negress may in extreme cases produce her offspring at the age of eleven; the early maturing Hindoo woman of Caucasian stock may produce offspring at the age of twelve. Hundreds of other differences might be cited. This is not said in disparagement of the Negroid race, which displays many noble qualities of spiritual and moral character, as observed by sympathetic and unprejudiced travelers like Herbert Ward, whose sculpture has also revealed the superb physical development of the native Negro.[27]

25. Ibid., p. 38.
26. Henry F. Osborn, "The Evolution of Human Races," *Natural History* 26:1 (Jan–Feb, 1926), p. 5.
27. Ibid. On p. 4 he called the three stocks different species.

Johns Hopkins University Professor of Biostatics and Genetics, Dr. Raymond Pearl, was a leading eugenicist who researched what he claimed was the "racial pathology" of blacks compared to whites.[28] The implication of his research was that certain internal body organs of blacks were "more primitive" than those of whites, and the same organs of whites "represented an evolutionary advance."[29]

The fields of "social Darwinism, and craniometry were the scientific backbone of a nineteenth-century understanding of race" and then became the scientific backbone in the twentieth century eugenics movement, providing "the formative language of modern racism."[30]

Racism Limits Immigration

A main application of racism in America and several other countries including Sweden, was aggressive sterilization programs. In the United States alone, 63,000 victims were sterilized and major new immigration restrictions, especially of Jews, were codified in the Johnson-Reed Act of 1924.[31] The main goal of these immigration restrictions was to keep those races that had "bad germ plasm" out of America and to stop other countries from pouring their "pestilential sewage into our reservoir."[32]

Ardent eugenicist racist, Henry Fairfield Osborn, was a major force behind lobbying Congress for "sweeping immigration restrictions."[33] Osborn pushed the claim that certain "countries are now striving to keep the desirable people at home, and are sending the undesirables, especially the Jews, to America."[34]

Dr. Harry Laughlin, the Superintendent of the Eugenics Record Office at the Cold Spring Harbor Laboratory, fervently promoted the racist cause, maintaining that, compared to past immigration, "recent immigrants from eastern and southern Europe were afflicted 'by a high degree of insanity, mental deficiency, and criminality' " that was polluting America's racial stock.[35] Consequently, "eugenics was, in many ways, the most compelling ideology generating support for the bill."[36] A result of the bill was that most of those kept out of America were Jews and

28. Yudell, *Race Unmasked*, p. 69.
29. Ibid., p. 71.
30. Ibid., p. 2.
31. Ibid., p. 9–10, 14.
32. Ibid., p. 32.
33. Ibid., p. 33.
34. Ibid.
35. Ibid., p. 34.
36. Ibid.

persons from Eastern Europe, many of which ended up dying in Nazi death camps.

The impact due to the "push to integrate eugenic theory into American immigration policy by Osborn and others was considerable, and the consequences" included clear "damaging effects on both immigration to the United States and eventually on those who died in the Nazi genocide against the Jews in Europe."[37] Harry Laughlin appeared before Congress several times in the early 1920s to promote his belief that immigration was foremost a "biological problem," i.e., a racism issue.[38] In the 20th century, it was primarily the field of eugenics

> from which racial scientists freely exploited both language and prestige. This legacy can be explained largely by the history of genetics itself, which at its founding was inseparable from the eugenic theories that were mired in examining hereditary traits both within and between human races.[39]

The fact is, "Science was the language of authority in the nineteenth century," consequently, racism became mainstream with its support.[40]

Medical Journal Advocates Inferiority of Blacks

George M. Gould, editor of *American Medicine,* a leading medical journal at the turn of the 20th century, wrote in 1907 in support of the conclusions of a Dr. Robert B. Bean. Gould said that "no amount of training" will cause the black race's "brain to grow into the Anglo-Saxon form." Following Bean, Gould claimed proof of an "anatomical basis for the complete failure of Negro schools to impart the higher studies" to their black students.[41] In 1909, Professor Franklin Mall attempted to verify the claim that black brains were significantly smaller than white brains. Unfortunately for the racists, he

> could find no significant differences between black and white brain structures. "I have now had considerable experience in the dissection of the Negro and have yet to observe that variations are more common in the Negro than in the white."[42]

---

37. Ibid., p. 33–34.
38. Ibid., p. 34.
39. Ibid., p. 3.
40. Burleigh, *The Third Reich*, p. 96.
41. "Editorial Comment," *American Medicine*, NS vol. 2, no. 4 (April 1907): 197.
42. Quoted in Yudell, *Race Unmasked*, p. 54.

Dr. Mall used this research to write a well-documented rebuttal to the *American Journal of Anatomy* editorial. Nonetheless, "ideas about racialized anatomy quickly became the scientific and popular norm, while Mall's work had little impact."[43] This belief was rapidly exploited by the militant racists, as is obvious from a statement by Harvard educated Carleton Coon who stated that each race, which he called a subspecies, has "reached its own level on the evolutionary scale," and the gap between blacks and whites is unbridgeable and permanent.[44]

In 1961, Professor Coon was elected president of The American Association of Physical Anthropologists. His book, *Origin of Races,* first published in 1962, and reprinted several times since then, argued that the fossil record showed what he concluded were the five main "subspecies" of *Homo sapiens* which had evolved from the primitive first human called *Homo erectus.* Coon estimated that the ancestors of the Europeans evolved from *Homo erectus* to *Homo sapiens* 200,000 years ago, whereas the ancestors of most modern Africans had evolved only from 30,000 to 40,000 years ago. Thus he concluded that the modern African races were less evolved. He also concluded that each race had "reached its own level on the evolutionary scale" in recent history.[45] In contrast, Harvard Professor Ernst Mayr and Columbia University Professor Theodosius Dobzhansky had correctly observed that both Coon's dates and major evolutionary claims were highly speculative.[46]

Coon added the latest genetic and evolutionary biological techniques to his argument plus the findings of the fossil record, all of which, he argued, supported his racism, as did research on "blood groups, hemoglobins, and other biochemical features."[47] Coon also believed "that biochemistry divides us into the same subspecies that we have long recognized on the basis of other criteria," such as skin color. To him, this finding proved that the race inferiority theory was scientifically valid.[48]

Coon thought that "in an increasingly race-conscious world" the biochemistry evidence was "less controversial than" external body traits such as skin color.[49] He believed that "racial intermixture can upset the genetic as

43. Ibid.
44. Carleton Coon, *The Origin of Races* (New York, NY: Knopf, 1962). p. 587.
45. Ibid., p. 482–587.
46. Ernst Mayr, "Book Reviews: Origin of the Human Races," *Science* 138 (1962): 420–422, and Theodosius Dobzhansky, "Possibility That Homo Sapiens Evolved Independently Five Times Is Vanishing Small," *Current Anthropology* 4, no. 4 (October 1963): 360, 364–367.
47. Coon, *The Origin of Races,* p. 662.
48. Ibid.
49. Ibid.

well as the social equilibrium of a group."[50] The published reviews show his openly racist book was generally well received by anthropologists. University of Arizona Professor Frederick Hulse wrote that, "no better text for a course in Fossil Man has yet been published" than Coon's work.[51]

Some reviews, though, accurately documented Coon's many errors. For example, Dobzhansky's review of Coon's book correctly concluded that the book supported racism. This may have been Coons' intent — he was a cousin to the racist Carleton Putnam whose book *Race and Reason* is noted below. Dobzhansky called the bogus science pure racial prejudice.[52]

Race and Reason

One of the most notorious racist books of the last century, Putnam's *Race and Reason: A Yankee View* (1961), was published by the prestigious Public Affairs Press of Washington D.C.[53] The level of academic support for racism is indicated by the laudatory introductions by Ruggles Gates, PhD, Henry Garrett, PhD, DSc, Robert Gayre, DSc, and Wesley C. George, PhD, all eminent Darwinist scientists teaching at major universities.

The forward by T.R. Waring acknowledged that Dr. Gates is "generally acknowledged to be one of the world's leading human geneticists."[54] Gates was a zoology professor at the University of California for many years, and ended his career as an honorary research fellow of biology at Harvard. Another supporter, Dr. Gayre, was Professor of Anthropology, head of the post-graduate department of Anthropo-Geography at the University of Sugaor in India, and editor of *Mankind Quarterly*. His many scholarly publications included a three-volume set titled *Ethnology*.

Supporter Wesley George was Professor of Anatomy at the University of North Carolina where he was the department head for a decade. He also was the author of many scholarly articles on the evolution of humans and other vertebrates. Waring concluded that "there can be no doubt that the endorsement of these men, taken together with the evidence of other scientists . . . guarantee the scientific integrity of *Race and Reason* and confirm the soundness of its premises."[55] It was this book that began KKK

50. Ibid..
51. Frederick Hulse, "Book Review. *The Origin of Races* by Carleton S. Coon" *American Anthropologist*, 65 (June 1963): 685–687.
52. Dobzhansky, "Possibility that Homo Sapiens Evolved Independently Five Times," p. 360 and 364.
53. Carleton Putnan, *Race and Reason: A Yankee View* (Washington, D.C.: Public Affairs Press, 1961).
54. Ibid., p. iv.
55. Ibid., p. v.

leader David Duke's intellectual journey to become the most infamous 20th-century racist.[56]

Putnam is tactful, yet clearly has a racist and an evolutionist agenda, writing that changes

> in a race occur by mutation and natural selection which involve the gradual elimination of those genes which are unsuited to the surrounding environment. This takes place by mating choices within the race itself and by the dying-off without children of those with a preponderance of unsuitable genes.[57]

Putnam also rejected the Adamic teaching that all humans are descended from one man and one woman, writing,

> Pin down the man who uses the word "equality," and at once the evasions and qualifications begin . . . [such as the] phrase to the effect that men were "equal in the sight of God." I would be interested to know where in the Bible you get your authority for this conception.[58]

Furthermore, he added that the white man

> who preaches to backward races a doctrine of equality . . . demeans himself and his own race. . . . What is called the "liberal ferment" among backward peoples who are shouting democracy from Latin America to Africa is too often not at all a struggle for freedom under law on the part of peoples capable of self-government, as was the case in the American Revolution, but rather a demand for license under lawlessness on the part of peoples totally incapable of self-government.[59]

The Ku Klux Klan

The Klan often exploited the literature of the eugenic scientists to justify their racism, and some scientists even openly worked in support of the KKK's racist agenda. For example, historian Lothrup Stoddard helped to support the Klan on race matters by doing "scientific" research to prove racism and, in 1923, was documented to actually be a Klan member.[60]

56. Ibid., p. 256.
57. Ibid., p. 56.
58. Ibid., p. 8.
59. Ibid., p. 76.
60. Yudell, *Race Unmasked*, p. 41–42.

He also implored Klan members to read his book *The Rising Tide of Color Against White World-Supremacy*, in which he claimed that, if current trends continued, whites would eventually be subjugated to blacks because non-whites were reproducing far more rapidly than whites. He warned that blacks would always be savages, and their increasing dominance would eventually be disastrous for white society. Stoddard was a popular speaker who lectured to audiences as large as 4,000.[61]

Henry Fairfield Osborn was also actively involved in supporting eugenics such as by his work in the International Congress of Eugenics (held in 1912, 1921, and 1932). The museum he headed was then "one of the world's leading institutions for anthropological thought," and was active in supporting numerous eugenic programs.[62] In fact, the second congress was held at his own American Museum of Natural History in 1921.[63] Their goal was to use race betterment programs to improve and help to evolve white humanity to a higher level of biological development.

Presenters at the conference included leading scientists, such as Professors Sewell Wright, L.C. Dunn, and the inventor of the telephone, Alexander Graham Bell. Others included Dr. Thomas Garth and zoologist Theophilus Painter, both from the University of Texas. The presentation by Dr. A.H. Schultz, Department of Embryology, Carnegie Institution, Washington, D.C, compared white and black fetuses to show that blacks were inferior.[64]

Professor Painter's presentation was on the chromosomes of whites and blacks, purporting to show subtle but, he thought, significant differences between them. Osborn had a permanent display on eugenics at his museum titled *The Hall of the Age of Man.*

Yudell described Osborn as a "notorious anti-Semite and an active booster of Nazi Germany."[65] Osborn even visited Nazi Germany and came back "enthusiastic" about their progressive eugenics programs. In recognition of Osborn's work in this area, he received an honorary degree in 1934 from the German Johann Wolfgang Goethe University.[66]

In the end, the eugenic exhibit set up in conjunction with the International Congress on Eugenics drew as many as 10,000 visitors.[67] Race and human evolution was a theme in all of the booths. The attendees included

61. Ibid., p. 103.
62. Ibid., p. 47.
63. Ibid., p. 43.
64. Ibid., p. 51.
65. Ibid., p. 47.
66. Ibid.
67. Ibid., p. 49.

many college and university professors, plus investigators from various scientific institutions who, no doubt, took the ideas gleaned from the exhibit back home to their students and colleagues.

American Eugenics and Nazism

European political events, specifically the rise of Nazism, helped to popularize the link between race and genetics. Leading German biologists "actively and without compunction sought" to apply eugenics to their society, and to "a significant degree, Nazi eugenic zeal was inspired by American eugenics" supporters.[68] Madison Grant's eugenic apologetic *The Passing of the Great Race: The Racial Basis of European History,"* was read by many Nazis and his

> ideas about Nordic racial purity influenced many Germans. In a letter to Grant, Hitler called *The Passing* "his Bible." In 1933 the *Eugenical News* . . . noted the American influence on German sterilization policy: "To one versed in the history of eugenic sterilization in America, the text of the German statue reads almost like the American model sterilization law."[69]

As a result, in the end "Darwinism had become about as German as liverwurst." When under attack in England for his *The Origin of Species* book,

> Darwin wrote to a colleague: "The support which I receive from Germany is my chief ground for hoping that our views will ultimately prevail." . . . in Germany, Darwinism was interpreted as having repercussions for the future of civilization. It was Ludwig Woltmann, a German, who first gave the enterprise its name.[70]

As is now well-documented, "Darwinism figured prominently in the outlook of the National Socialist [Nazi] leadership. It was one of the few ideological elements that dominated Hitler's thinking throughout his political career and that he did not manipulate in accordance with tactical needs."[71] Furthermore, various American philanthropists, such as the Rockefeller Foundation, awarded large

> scientific grants to German eugenicist researchers, both before and for several years after the rise of Hitler. And even as the world

68. Ibid., p. 108.
69. Ibid.
70. Oren Harman, *The Price of Altruism: George Price and the Search for the Origins of Kindness* (New York, NY: W.W. Norton, 2010), p. 115.
71. Holborn, *Republic to Reich*, p. 436.

> recoiled in horror at the ways in which the Nazis integrated eugenics into their political philosophy — mass sterilizations and concentration camps — American eugenicists continued to support their Nazi brethren.[72]

The Nazis were so grateful for the help of American scientists in developing their own racist eugenic program that, as noted, several were awarded honorary doctorates from major German Universities. For one example, in 1935, Harry Laughlin was awarded

> an honorary degree from the University of Heidelberg for "being one of the most important pioneers in the field of racial hygiene." The dean of the University of Heidelberg's medical school later helped organize the gassing of thousands of mentally handicapped adults.[73]

Another example of Nazi and American support for each other's eugenic programs occurred after a 1935 visit to Berlin, when

> the head of the Eugenic Research Association, Clarence Campbell, proclaimed the Nazi eugenic policy "sets a pattern which other nations and other racial groups must follow if they do not wish to fall behind in their racial quality, in their racial accomplishments, and in their prospects for survival." Finally, in 1937, American eugenicists distributed a Nazi eugenic propaganda film to promote the eugenic cause in the United States.[74]

The unmistakable influence of Social Darwinism on Hitler was fused "with a pseudo-Nietzschean contempt for humanitarian succor of the weak."[75] Hitler's Social Darwinism was in turn supported by the many advocates of eugenic sterilization and euthanasia in the Germany of the 1930's. Hitler believed

> anyone not fit for life should perish, and that the state could give nature a helping hand. Since this was a bitter pill for the general public to swallow, it was coated in the language of duty and of sacrifice, which individuals must render the community: . . . this was unexceptional in international eugenic circles at the time.[76]

---

72. Yudell, *Race Unmasked*, p. 108.
73. Ibid., p. 108–109.
74. Ibid., p. 109.
75. Burleigh, *The Third Reich*, p. 99.
76. Ibid.

Furthermore, war

> was considered a positive force for racial regeneration: "the bloodiest civil wars have often given rise to a steeled and healthy people, while artificially cultivated states of peace have more than once produced a rottenness that stank to high Heaven." Hitler was hardly alone in believing that.[77]

As Oxford trained philosopher Jonathan Sacks wrote, "Marxism and Darwinism came with the highest price in human lives ever exacted by ideas," adding that he is not implying "Marx and Darwin would have approved of the use others made of their ideas," but rather

> Marxism led to Soviet Communism and Stalinist Russia, and social Darwinism was one of the main inspirations behind Nazi Germany in general and Hitler in particular. How many people died as a result of Marxist teachings we will never know. During the years of Stalin alone, an estimated 20 million people died in mass executions and forced movements of populations. Many died as a result of deliberately created famine.[78]

An example he provides is that the Central Committee of the Communist Party decided to move

> from "restricting the exploiting tendencies" of the *kulaks* — peasants considered "bourgeois" —to "liquidating them as a class," leading to a programme of mass murder on an almost unimaginable scale. It was a regime of unmitigated brutality and ruthlessness. Stalin had many of his leading colleagues, including Trotsky, assassinated. The regime maintained a constant atmosphere of fear through the secret police, informants and show trials. . . . It was the longest nightmare yet undertaken with high ideals, and it took a very long time indeed before Marxist fellow travelers in the West acknowledged that they had been worshipping . . . "the god that failed."[79]

This now very embarrassing Nazi movement inspired by Charles Darwin and his disciples, especially Ernst Haeckel, has been well documented.[80]

---

77. Ibid.
78. Jonathan Sacks, *The Great Partnership: God, Science and the Search for Meaning* (Hodder & Stroughton, 2011), p. 218.
79. Ibid., p. 118–119.
80. Richard Weikart, *Socialist Darwinism: Evolution in German Socialist Thought From Marx to Bernstein* (Lantham, Maryland: International Publications, 1998); Richard Weikart, *Hitler's Ethic: The Nazi Pursuit of Evolutionary Progress* (New York: Palgrave Macmillan, 2009).

Most of the leading American and German eugenicists during this period were professors of biology or anthropology affiliated with leading universities. Furthermore, in regard to Nazi Germany, Sacks writes that it does not help the cause of understanding either to isolate the Holocaust

> as a unique instance of human depravity or to normalize it. . . . There were many influences on Hitler and his supporters. . . . But the link between social Darwinism and the attempt to exterminate Jews, Roma, Sinti and the mentally and physically handicapped is unmistakable. In *Mein Kampf*, Hitler had written:
>
> > A stronger race will supplant the weaker, since the drive for life in its final form will decimate every ridiculous fetter of the so-called humaneness of individuals, in order to make place for the humaneness of nature, which destroys the weak to make place for the strong.[81]

Hitler's statement, written in 1928, documents his reliance on Darwinism to justify his eugenics and infanticide programs:

> While nature only allows the few most healthy and resistant out of a large number of living organisms to survive in the struggle for life, people restrict the number of births and then try to keep alive what has been born, without consideration of its real value and its inner merit. Humaneness is therefore only the slave of weakness and thereby in truth the most cruel destroyer of human existence.[82]

As Sacks concluded, the concern "is not simply that Hitler imbibed these ideas, whether through Nietzsche, Spencer, Haeckel or other writers," but that they

> were widely shared among intellectuals of the time. The movement for eugenics, the selective breeding of humans and the sterilization of the mentally handicapped and those otherwise declared unfit, was pioneered by Darwin's half-cousin Sir Francis Galton and supported among others by H.G. Wells, George Bernard Shaw, John Maynard Keynes, Woodrow Wilson and Theodore Roosevelt. Compulsory sterilization of certain classes of individuals was undertaken by thirty states in America between 1907 and 1963. Only the full

81. Sacks, *The Great Partnership*, p. 119.
82. Weikart, 2004, p. 211.

> realization of the scale of the Nazi genocide finally rendered such programmes unacceptable.[83]

Professor Sacks added, "the Holocaust did not take place long ago and far away." Rather it occurred

> in the heart of rationalist, post-Enlightenment, liberal Europe: the Europe of Kant and Hegel, Goethe and Schiller, Beethoven and Brahms. Some of the epicenters of antisemitism were places of cosmopolitan, avant-garde culture like Berlin and Vienna. The Nazis were aided by doctors, lawyers, scientists, judges, and academics. More than half of the participants at the Wannsee Conference in January 1942, who planned the "final solution to the Jewish question," the murder of all Europe's Jews, carried the title "doctor."[84]

In his book, *The Doctor and the Soul*, Dr. Viktor E. Frankl, a Holocaust survivor and Professor of Neurology and Psychiatry at the University of Vienna Medical School, astutely evaluated the influence of modern anthropologists and other academics in helping to prepare the way for the Nazi atrocities, concluding that the

> gas chambers of Auschwitz were the ultimate consequence of the theory that man is nothing but the product of heredity and environment — or, as the Nazis liked to say, of "Blood and Soil." I am absolutely convinced that the gas chambers of Auschwitz, Treblinka, and Maidanek were ultimately prepared not in some Ministry . . . in Berlin, but rather at the desks and in the lecture halls of nihilistic scientists and philosophers.[85]

Professor Suante Pääbo wrote that the many programs supported by the Eugenic Kaiser Wilhelm Society included work to produce world-class research, and one guiding principle of the modern Max Planck Society was to establish

> new research institutes focusing on topics in which Germany was scientifically weak. An area of particular weakness was anthropology, and for a very good reason. As do many contemporary German institutions, the MPS [Max Planck Society] had a predecessor

83. Sacks, *The Great Partnership*, p. 120.
84. Ibid., p. 86.
85. Viktor E. Frankl, *The Doctor and the Soul From Psychotherapy to Logotherapy* (New York, NY: Vintage Books, 1986), p. xxxii.

> before the war. Its name was the Kaiser Wilhelm Society, and it was founded in 1911. The Kaiser Wilhelm Society had built up and supported institutes around eminent scientists such as Otto Hahn, Albert Einstein, Max Planck, and Werner Heisenberg, scientific giants active at a time when Germany was a scientifically dominant nation.[86]

He added that this "era came to an abrupt end when Hitler rose to power and the Nazis ousted many of the best scientists because they were Jewish . . . the Kaiser Wilhelm Society became part of the German war machine."[87] Furthermore, it was

> through its Institute for Anthropology, Human Heredity, and Eugenics that the Kaiser Wilhelm Society was actively involved in racial science and the crimes that grew out of that. In that institute, based in Berlin, people like Josef Mengele were scientific assistants while performing experiments on inmates at Auschwitz death camp, many of them children. Whereas Mengele was sentenced for his crimes after the war (although he had escaped to South America), his superiors at the Institute for Anthropology were never charged. On the contrary, some of them became professors at universities.[88]

The leading German biologist, Ernst Haeckel, also "followed a Darwinian trope in arranging human 'species' — 12 of them, comprising 36 'races' in all, in his scheme — in phylogenetic trees."[89] In Germany, the escalation of racism and social Darwinism that led to the Holocaust

> was almost seamless, beginning with the compulsory sterilization of unwanted types, then the killing of "impaired children" in hospitals, then the killing of "impaired" adults (the mentally and physically handicapped) in special centres by carbon monoxide gas, then the extension of this to the concentration and extermination camps. The programme was carried out, throughout, by doctors and psychiatrists, only a handful of whom objected. It was eventually halted in August 1941 because of protests, largely from the Churches. Reading the vast literature on what Claudia Koonz calls "the Nazi conscience," the

86. Svante Pääbo, *Neanderthal Man: In Search of Lost Genomes* (New York, NY: Basic Books, 2014), p. 81–82.
87. Ibid.
88. Ibid.
89. Henrika Kuklick, ed., *A New History of Anthropology* (Malden, MA: Blackwell Publishing, 2008), p. 234.

rationalizations Nazis gave for what they were doing, what is striking is not only the specific ideas of social Darwinism — the strong eliminate the weak, the Aryan race must be protected against pollution — but the overwhelming sense of the *authority of science*, whatever the science.[90]

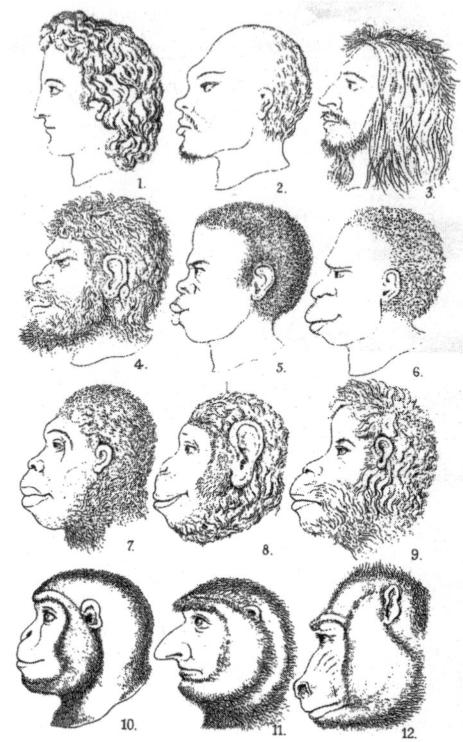

Figure 1: Haeckel's 1868 drawing of primate evolution. The most evolved human, a Caucasian, is actually drawn from a statue of a Roman god. The drawing was the frontispiece in Ernst Haeckel, *Natürliche Schöpfungsgeschichte* (Berlin: Reimer, 1868).

Marx: A Leading Follower of Darwin

As a youth, Karl Marx (1818–1883) was raised Christian. Although his parents descended from a long line of rabbis, his father "converted" to Lutheranism (to escape anti-Semitic persecution) and in 1824 at the age of six Karl was baptized into the Evangelische Kirche (the German name of the Lutheran Church).[91] Later, as a professing Christian, Marx wrote that it was Christianity that made men brethren. In a school examination essay

> Marx referred to the brotherhood of man as being rooted in the union of the faithful with Christ. Developing the parable of the vine and the branches, he concluded that through love of Christ "we turn our hearts at the same time to our brothers, whom He has bound more closely with us, for whom He also sacrificed himself."[92]

90. Sacks, *The Great Partnership*, p. 120.
91. Lloyd Easton and Kurt Guddat, *Karl Marx: Writings of the Young Marx on Philosophy and Society* (Indianapolis, IN: Hackett Publishing, 1967), p. 3.
92. Ibid.

Union with Christ, he wrote, gives us "an inner elevation, comfort in sorrow, calm trust, and a heart susceptible to human love, to everything noble and great, not for the sake of ambition and glory, but only for the sake of Christ."[93] At about the same time, Marx wrote a paper titled *Reflections of a Youth on Choosing an Occupation*, in which he penned,

> Religion itself teaches us that the Ideal toward which all strive sacrificed Himself for humanity, and who shall dare contradict such claims? If we have chosen the position in which we can accomplish the most for Him, then we can never be crushed by burdens, because they are only sacrifices made for the sake of all.[94]

When Marx completed high school, on his graduation certificate under the heading "Religious Knowledge," the following evaluation was written: "His knowledge of the Christian faith and morals is fairly clear and well-grounded. He knows also to some extent the history of the Christian Church."[95] His shift in thinking occurred after only "two years of university life at Bonn and Berlin . . . Marx became increasingly critical of Christianity," eventually regarding "the miracles of the New Testament as messianic myths" and "at the end of his university studies, according to one report, he viewed 'the Christian religion as one of the most immoral' of all religions."[96]

His slide from liberal Christianity eventually led him to atheism and his famous statement that "religion is the opiate of the people." In his PhD dissertation, he further explained why he rejected God, namely because he concluded from his University studies that the proofs for the existence of God were simply empty tautologies and that the imperfections in nature point to God's non-existence. This reasoning reminds one of the Darwinian arguments that what the evolutionists claim is the poor design of humans is an argument against creationism.

Two important events in Karl Marx's life were his acceptance of Darwinism and his rejection of Christianity. After becoming a Darwin convert, Marx's avowed aim was

> the destruction of religion. Socialism, concern for the proletariat, humanism — these were only pretexts. After Marx had read *The*

93. Werner Blumenberg, *Karl Marx: An Illustrated History* (London, England: Verso, 2000) p. 11.
94. Richard Wurmbrand, *Marx and Satan* (Bartlesville, OK: Living Sacrifice Book Company, 1986), p. 11.
95. Karl Marx and Friedrich Engels, *Karl Marx, Frederick Engels: Collected Works — Volume 1* (London, England: Lawrence & Wishart, Ltd, 1975), p. 644.
96. Easton and Guddat, *Karl Marx*, p. 4.

> *Origin of Species* by Charles Darwin, he wrote a letter to Lassalle in which he exults that God — in the natural sciences at least — had been given "the death blow." What idea, then, preempted all others in Marx's mind? Was it the plight of the poor proletariat? If so, of what possible value was Darwin's theory? The only tenable conclusion is that Marx's chief aim was the destruction of religion.[97]

Richard Wurmbrand, an ardent communist before becoming a Christian and later a pastor who suffered for 14 years for his faith in Romanian prisons, knew well the influence of Marx's writings on communism. Wurmbrand observed that "The end result of Darwin's theory has been the killing of tens of millions of innocents. He therefore became the spiritual father of the greatest mass-murderer in history."[98] The greatest mass-murderer in history, according to Wurmbrand, was Joseph Stalin, whose Russian dictatorship resulted in the death of an estimated 25 million Russians.[99] In the end, Darwin's influence was so great that he also inspired Mao Zedong, Adolf Hitler, Vladimir Lenin, and even the Japanese leadership of the early 20th century.

Darwinism Motivated Japanese Racist Sadism during World War II

One of the best examples of racism inspired by Darwinism was the extreme Japanese sadism exhibited during World War II. The Japanese of the last century believed that they were the "master race" of Asia, superior to not only non-Orientals, but also all people of Chinese, Korean, Filipino, Mongolian, Pacific Islander/Polynesian, and those of other Asian descent.[100]

In the late 1800s, Japan was modernized, a process that included the introduction of Darwinism into the culture by inviting several leading Darwinist professors to lecture in Japanese universities.[101] One example was Harvard-trained Darwinist Edward Morse who lectured on evolution at the leading Japanese university, the University of Tokyo, from 1877 to

---

97. Wurmbrand, *Marx and Satan*, p. 110.
98. Ibid., p. 86.
99. This number varies depending on the authority, but most authorities agree that the number was close to, or higher, than 25 million.
100. Frank Dikötter, ed., *The Construction of Racial Identities in China and Japan: Historical and Contemporary Perspectives* (Honolulu, Hawaii: University of Hawaii Press, 1997).
101. Osamu Sakura, "Similarities and Varieties: A Brief Sketch on the Reception of Darwinism and Sociobiology in Japan," *Biology and Philosophy* 13 (1998), p. 342.

1879. Morse was a very persuasive lecturer and attracted many Japanese who "smoothly accepted the facts and the theory of evolution."[102] He also "made Darwinism fashionable among the public."[103]

One reason that the "Japanese people readily accepted the concept of evolution [was] because, lacking Christianity, there was no religious opposition."[104] The objections that did surface in Japan mostly came from the Christian community, which at the time numbered less than 9,000 persons.[105] In addition, evolution theory, "especially in the form of Social Darwinism developed by Herbert Spencer, was extremely popular in Japan at the turn of the century, as it was in the United States, though Japanese theorists were more inclined to stress the idea of survival of the fittest among nations rather than among individuals."[106] Consequently, Darwinism, including its racist teachings, had a critical influence on Japan.

Darwinism was also used to oppose Christianity. One part of Morse's Darwinism "lecture was its antagonism to Christianity. . . . There was also an anti-Christian feeling in Japan in those days, and Darwinism was used to reject Christianity."[107] Furthermore, "Christian intellectuals were a minority who treated Darwinism critically in those days when most of the people received it uncritically."[108]

This combined with the "many instruments of indoctrination in Japan," including the government schools and the media, all of "which monotonously preached a morbid nationalism and a chauvinism both as potent and poisonous as Nazi racism," which proved to be a lethal combination that produced the horrors of World War II in the East.[109] The Japanese also had a "contempt for the West and . . . a 'race hate' that 'many Japanese nourished deep down in their viscera.' "[110]

One example that illustrated both the Darwinian theory and the Nazi philosophy, which teaches natural selection of the superior race by elimination of the inferior races, was a pamphlet published in 1934 by the Japanese Imperial Army that described war as "the father of creation and the mother

102. Sakura, 1998, p. 343.
103. Eikoh Shimao, "Darwinism in Japan, 1877–1927," *Annals of Science*, 38 (1981), p. 93.
104. Sakura, "Similarities and Varieties," p. 341.
105. Ibid., p. 343.
106. Sharon H. Nolte, *Liberalism in Modern Japan: Ishibashi Tanzan and His Teachers, 1905–1960* (Berkeley, CA: University of California Press, 1987), p. 44.
107. Shimao, "Darwinism in Japan," p. 93–94.
108. Ibid., p. 95.
109. E. Herbert Norman, "Militarists in the Japanese State," in *Pacific Affairs*, 16(4):475–481, December 1943, p. 475.
110. Ibid.

of culture."[111] Furthermore, "one of the fundamental tenets of the wartime Kyoto School of philosophers and historians was that war "is eternal" and should be recognized as being "creative and constructive." War was central to the ongoing historical process of "purification" and part of their "philosophical struggle."[112]

This Darwinian idea was borrowed from the "survival of the fittest," or rather "survival of the strongest" philosophy, as Spencer's original phrase was commonly interpreted. No success could be greater than a triumph in war. Only a few decades after the onset of its modernization, Japan accepted this notion and took it to its extreme.[113] As a result,

> After Japan's victory in the first Sino-Japanese War (1894–95), Japan joined the imperialist race in East Asia in earnest, but during a time ruled by racial ideology, it could not assert its new position as long as it did not win a war with a Western power. The final confirmation of Japan's regional position came exactly a decade later when it won the war with Russia — Europe's most populated nation and the possessor of its largest army.[114]

Another factor was that both "naturalism and pragmatism regarded science as a means to the emancipation of the self. . . . Naturalism and pragmatism, both strongly influenced by Darwin, viewed evolutionary change as an opportunity for the assertion of human will rather than a sentence of subjugation to blind natural law."[115]

Although, for purposes of war propaganda, the Japanese claimed to be "liberating Asia for the Asians," they were, in fact, enslaving them. Although some Japanese social groups were racist before, during, and even after World War II, the Japanese military applied Darwinism rigorously to those that they judged as inferior races. They worked or tortured them to death or allowed them to starve or die from diseases brought on by malnutrition. As German racism resulted in the death of millions of Jews, Russians and Poles, likewise, Japanese racism was responsible for the death of millions of Chinese and other Asians, plus many thousands of Allied Prisoners of War (POWs).

---

111. Quoted in Robert Olson Ballou, *Shinto, The Unconquered Enemy: Japan's Doctrine of Racial Superiority and World Conquest* (New York, NY: The Viking Press, 1945), p. 45.
112. John Dower, *War Without Mercy: Race and Power in the Pacific* War (New York, NY: Pantheon Books, 1993), p. 216.
113. Rotem Kowner and Walter Demel, eds., *Race and Racism in Modern East Asia* (Boston, MA: Brill, 2013), p. 117.
114. Ibid., p. 117.
115. Nolte, *Liberalism in Modern Japan*, p. 82–83.

During World War II, Japan believed that, as the superior race, there was for them no such thing as "surrender" or "capture," because all POWs were considered not only inferior, but also traitors to Japan. This is why thousands of Japanese soldiers committed suicide rather than surrender. They also treated American POWs cruelly, indiscriminately killing them due to their belief that they were an inferior race. They were also believed to be less than human for surrendering or allowing themselves to be captured, rather than dying in combat or by suicide. The Asian nations used Darwinian

> evolutionary theories to represent the world as a battlefield in which different "races" struggled for survival. But while they appealed to such foreign luminaries as Charles Darwin and Herbert Spencer, their understanding of "race" was also informed by their own background. They did not simply copy what they read from these authors, but instead endowed "race" with indigenous meanings.[116]

It is no small wonder that the typical Japanese soldier was "encouraged by his officers to slaughter, rape, and terrorize to impress the unhappy neighbors of Japan with the 'superiority' of the Yamato race."[117]

In addition, another problem was that the "Japanese were not the only racists in the Pacific War." Some Americans were as well, resulting in some American soldiers taking the heads or ears of slain Japanese as "trophies or souvenirs," something they did not do to Germans and making the war with the Japanese even more vicious.[118]

The similarity of the Japanese racial views to the Nazi racial views is illustrated by the writings of Nakajimi Chikuhei, a major industrialist and political party leader. He wrote in 1940 that there exist "superior and inferior races in the world," and "it is the sacred duty of the leading race to lead and enlighten the inferior ones."[119] The reason why many Japanese believed they were "the sole superior race in the world," Nakajima explained, was that "the Japanese were pure-blooded, and . . . The Greater East Asia War was thus no ordinary conflict. . . . Many other such statements could be quoted . . . where they were presented as proof that the Japanese, like the Nazis, regarded themselves as a master race."[120]

Although Japan resisted Nazi attempts to force the Holocaust on the Jews, the Japanese government sent most of the approximately 3,000 Indonesian

116. Kowner and Demel, *Race and Racism in Modern East Asia*, p. 356.
117. Norman, "Militarists in the Japanese State," p. 475.
118. Otto D. Tolischus, ed., *Through Japanese Eyes* (New York: Reynal and Hitchcock, 1945).
119. Dower, *War Without Mercy*, p. 217.
120. Ibid.

Jews to work camps. Few survived.[121] University of Hawaii political science professor R.J. Rummel estimates that between 1937 and 1945, the Japanese military murdered up to nearly 10 million people, most likely 6 million Chinese, Indonesians, Koreans, Filipinos, and Indochinese, among others.[122]

An Example of Japan's Brutality

The broad details of the Rape of Nanking are not in dispute by historians today. In November of 1937, the Japanese launched a massive attack on the then capital of the Republic of China, Nanking, and when

> the city fell on December 13, 1937, Japanese soldiers began an orgy of cruelty seldom if ever matched in world history. Tens of thousands of young men were rounded up and herded to the outer areas of the city, where they were mowed down by machine guns, used for bayonet practice, or soaked with gasoline and burned alive. For months the streets of the city were heaped with corpses and reeked with the stench of rotting human flesh.[123]

The fact is, if "one event can be held up as an example of the unmitigated evil lying just below the surface of unbridled military adventurism, that moment is the Rape of Nanking."[124] Furthermore, "even by the standards of history's most destructive war, the Rape of Nanking represents one of the worst instances of mass extermination."[125] Specifically, between 260 and 350 thousand Chinese were murdered in the span of only a few weeks.[126] The Rape of Nanking is notorious not only for the enormous number of innocent people slaughtered, but also for the inhuman, cruel manner in which many of the Chinese were murdered.

One infamous incident that caused the deaths of thousands of Chinese in Nanking involved two Japanese officers who forced their men to gather hundreds of Chinese civilians. The reason was for a contest to determine who could decapitate the most people during a set time span. The Japanese determined the men's success by measuring the height of the stack of heads.

---

121. Gil Ronen, "Japanese Scapegoated Indonesia's Jews in WW2," http://www.israelnationalnews.com/News/News.aspx/137244#.Vrf_d5MrLAI, April 27, 2010.
122. Rudolf J. Rummel, *Death by Government* (New Brunswick, NJ: Transaction Publishers, 2008), p. 146–149, 153.
123. Iris Chang, *The Rape of Nanking: The Forgotten Holocaust of World War II* (New York, NY: BasicBooks, 1997), p. 4.
124. Ibid.
125. Ibid.
126. Ibid., p. 5.

A 1945 study prepared by the Japanese cabinet "attempted to demonstrate with extensive historical data that war was constructive, and protracted war was inevitable — and, indeed, that protracted war required the thorough-going exercise of a nation's 'unique racial power.' "[127]

This was the same rationale given by the Nazi Darwinists to justify war. The Japanese, as did the Nazis, invariably regarded themselves alone as the superior race. The Japanese, "nationalized and racialized purity, treating this ultimate ideal as if it could only be truly appreciated, and attained, by the Japanese."[128] Once one accepts Darwinism, the next step is to inquire about the characteristics of man that

> make him different from apes. . . . Are there ape-men or are at least some varieties of mankind more ape-like than others? Do "monstrous races" really exist, as had been assumed since antiquity? Does the outer appearance of men or certain groups of men reflect their inner values, their characters . . . ?[129]

The Influence of Darwinism in Japan

The large influence of Darwinism on racial superiority in Japan is well-documented.[130] Even during the war years, "the theory of biological evolution" was taught in the public schools, and Japanese scholars continued to publish on the subject in spite of war rationing. The evolution taught in the schools was a mixture of Darwin, Haeckel, and other Western Darwinian theories. An example of Haeckel's influence was the teaching that "the ancestor of all humankind was not a human being," but rather

> some kind of creature living in water. The human fetus, floating in its own fluid, seemed to be a reenactment of these ancient origins, and in many other ways as well the evolution of life appeared to be recapitulated in the human experience. Thus, the fetus was monkey like, the first cry of the child was catlike, infants crawled like animals before walking, babies sometimes had tail-like protuberances when born, and the ability of humans to wiggle their ears suggested the persistence of an animal muscle.[131]

---

127. Dower, *War Without Mercy*, p. 216.
128. Kowner and Demel, *Race and Racism in Modern East Asia*, p. 53.
129. Ibid., p. 53.
130. Ballou, *Shinto, The Unconquered Enemy*, p. 19–25.
131. Dower, *War Without Mercy*, p. 220.

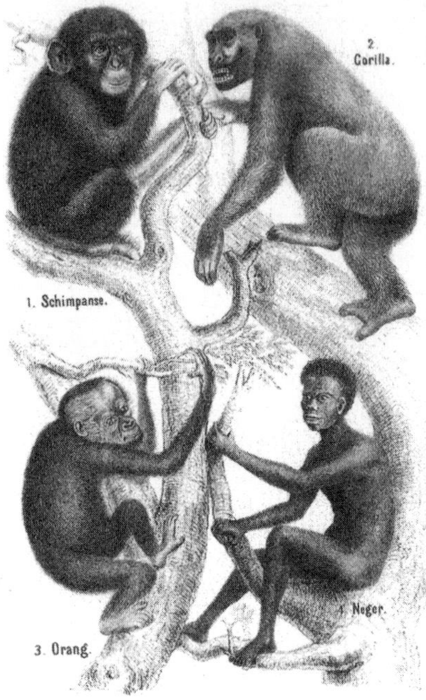

Figure 2: Ernest Haeckel's 1874 drawing implying the evolution of apes into man.[132]

Figure 3: Due to complaints about the gross distortion, especially of the Orang, Haeckel drastically redid the drawing in 1877.[133]

The way in which some "Japanese handled scientific theories of evolution and the question of physical differences among races during this period of ultranationalism can be found in a collection of essays published for popular audiences in the spring of 1944 by the well-known Japanese anatomist, Professor Adachi Buntaro." The essays were titled *Studies in the Physical Constitution of the Japanese People.*

The new edition included a short "preface by the author condemning Europeans and Americans for . . . arrogance concerning their own racial superiority."[134] As Professor Weiner wrote, the critical

> impact on Japan of Social-Darwinist assumptions concerning the competitive capacities of different populations cannot

132. Note how human-like the Orang is, and how the last example on the tree is "Negar." The illustration is from plate XI in the second edition of *Anthropogenie: oder, Entwickelungsgeschichte des Menschen (Anthropogeny: or, the Evolutionary History of Man)* (Leipzig: Engelmann. 1874).
133. The illustration is from plate XI in the third edition of *Anthropogenie: oder, Entwickelungsgeschichte des Menschen (Anthropogeny: or, the Evolutionary History of Man)* (Leipzig: Engelmann. 1877).
134. Ibid., p. 217–218.

> be underestimated. As transmitted to Japan during the late nineteenth century, theories of "race" and scientific racism incorporated assumptions which extended beyond boundaries of biological determinism. Darwinian theories of natural selection were introduced by Edward Morse . . . in a series of lectures of evolutionary theory given in 1877. A Japanese edition of Thomas Huxley's *Lectures on the Origin of Species* appeared two years later.[135]

Also, Japanese intellectuals were exposed to the evolutionary theories of both Haeckel and Lamarck, but neither the writings of Haeckel nor Lamarck

> achieved the immense popularity of Herbert Spencer. A Japanese translation of Spencer's evolutionary theory first appeared in 1884, and, in total, some thirty translations of his works had appeared by the turn of the century. The Social-Darwinian vocabulary . . . provided a scientific gloss to the idea that social development in all its manifestations occurred through the aggressive interplay of natural forces.[136]

It is now clear that the adverse influence of Darwinism, especially as elaborated by Herbert Spencer, was critical in influencing the Japanese sadistic war behavior.

Hirohito became Emperor of Japan in 1926 at age 25 after the death of his father. Educated both in Europe and Japan, Hirohito became very aware of the Darwinist beliefs in science, an area of special interest to him.[137] This philosophy had a major influence on him later in life. For example, at the Peer's School in Japan, his teachers, including Sugiura Shigetake, "were influenced by Herbert Spencer's social Darwinism" that was much in vogue in Japan at that time. Dr. Sugiura, studied agricultural science at Owens College (later, the University of Manchester), and chemistry at London University and exposed Hirohito to a wide variety of subjects including Darwinism.[138] Emperor Hirohito had much interest in history, but

> biological research became Hirohito's greatest lifelong intellectual passion, dating from his studies . . . under the scientist, Dr. Hattori. . . .

135. MichaelWeiner, "Discourses of Race, Nation and Empire in Pre-1945 Japan," *Ethnic and Racial Studies* 18, no. 3 (July 1995): 442.
136. Ibid., p. 442–443.
137. Saul K., Padover, "Japanese Race Propaganda," in *Public Opinion Quarterly*, 7(2):191–204, 1943.
138. Stephen S. Large, *Emperor Hirohito and Showa Japan: A Political Biography* (New York, NY: Routledge, 1992), p. 17.

> In 1919 Hirohito made his first scientific discovery, of a new species of prawn. He made a great many other discoveries over the years and wrote many scientific articles and books, mostly on marine life as a distinguished marine biologist.[139]

Dr. Hattori often accompanied Hirohito "on expeditions to collect marine specimens in Sagami Bay, Tokyo Bay, and elsewhere" and Hirohito "was happiest 'when working with a microscope, absorbed in a factual world quite different from that normally inhabited by a Crown Prince or Emperor.' "[140] Furthermore, aside from

> encouraging Hirohito's interest in science, Hattori taught him about Darwin's theory of evolution which Hattori had recently encountered in the publications of the zoologist, Oka Asajiro. It was natural, therefore, that a bust of Charles Darwin would be found in the library of the Showa Emperor, together with busts of Lincoln and Napoleon which reflected Hirohito's interest in history.[141]

He greatly admired Lincoln for liberating the oppressed, and Darwin for his scientific work.[142] And it was through the Darwinist Hattori that Emperor Hirohito accepted

> the widespread belief that nature was governed by the laws of evolution which Darwin had described. . . . Hirohito and his teacher also shared the general assumption that the concept of evolution, and its core notion of progressive development through the adaptive process of natural selection, could be applied to the values and institutions of contemporary society.[143]

It was also under "Hattori's guidance that Hirohito read Darwin's theory of evolution as interpreted by the popular writer Oka Asajiro" and also, evidently, a "Japanese translation of Darwin's *Origin of Species.*"[144] Furthermore, "Among thinkers everywhere who were influenced by Darwin, such ideas were commonplace at the time" in Japan.[145] From a study of Japan and Emperor Hirohito, it is very apparent today that

---

139. Ibid., p. 19.
140. Ibid.
141. Ibid.
142. Albert Axell and Hideaki Kase, *Kamikaze: Japan's Suicide Gods* (New York, NY: Longman, 2002), p. 198–199.
143. Large, *Emperor Hirohito and Showa Japan*, p. 19.
144. Herbert Bix, *Hirohito and the Making of Modern Japan* (New York, NY: HarperCollins, 2000), p. 60.
145. Large, *Emperor Hirohito and Showa Japan*, p. 19.

> this confidence in the efficacy of knowledge, applied to all fields of human endeavor, including politics and government, was the most important legacy of Hirohito's education at the Togu-gogakumonsho. . . . it was during this phase of his education that he acquired . . . a "scientific rational spirit" of inquiry, whether from Sugiura's intellectual eclecticism, Shiratori's historical skepticism, or Hattori's lessons on Darwin and scientific methodology.[146]

One irony is that Japan's "National Congress' tacit affirmation of the Emperor's divinity must be a great annoyance to the Emperor, who is a biologist and an admirer of Darwin."[147]

Justifying Racism

The more moderate Japanese scholars, such as Professor Adachi, acknowledged that some races may have superior traits in one area, yet inferior traits in other areas: " 'race A may be superior to race B in certain points,' but, he emphasized, 'in certain other respects race A may be inferior to race B. It can never be argued that race A is superior or inferior to race B in all respects.' "[148]

This may at first sound like equality, not racism. But when examined further, this Darwinian view implied that some traits of race A which are superior to race B, may be much more important, such as intelligence. This egalitarian sounding view was actually a way of justifying racism because the implications include the view that each race should be put in its "proper place" and be given "suitable work" in accordance with its specific abilities and qualities.

> [Adachi] also emphasized the necessity of giving "superior races" special support, including encouragement in increasing their population. In this, he was perfectly consistent with official government policy, in which it was made clear that in the final analysis the most superior race was the Japanese, and the "proper place" of the Japanese was one of absolute leadership.[149]

Adachi described human beings as "*Mammalia* like the apes" that can be "compared to the orangutan, gorilla, chimpanzee, and gibbon. Blood tests . . . not only showed a relationship between humans and apes, but also revealed that certain races had a closer blood relationship to the apes than

146. Ibid.
147. Ikuhiko Hata "The Japanese-Soviet Confrontation, 1935–1939," in J.W. Morley, ed., *Deterrent Diplomacy: Japan, Germany, and the U.S.S.R. 1935–1940* (New York, NY, Columbia University Press, 1976), p. 77.
148. Quoted in Dower, *War Without Mercy*, p. 219.
149. Ibid., p. 220.

others."[150] Adachi then discussed what he judged as the many comparisons of certain human races to our ape ancestors, such as the claim that Malay blood was the closest to monkey blood, Dutch blood the most dissimilar, and Chinese blood was somewhere in between the two.

He added that if "one took the orangutan as the standard by which to measure the development of different races — relative 'superiority' . . . indicated by greater departure from the apish norm — then in the overall picture the Japanese . . . demonstrated superior development."[151] Adachi also claimed to have discovered that

> the irregular profile of Westerners was closer to that of the apes [and] . . . their shorter ratio of arm length to body length (longer Western arms again being more apish); their lack of a peculiar bone spur in the upper arm which Westerners and animals both possess; their relative lack of body hair; and their relatively mild body odor (he equated the body smell of Caucasians, and even stronger odor of Negroes, with animalistic sexual desires).[152]

Another almost identical argument was made in one popular Japanese book on race,[153] which "placed the Europeans closer to monkeys and other animals than the Japanese" due to such traits as " 'high' noses, hairiness, relatively long arms, lower brain-to-body-weight ratio, thick fingers, and strong body odor of the sort associated with the generative function in certain animals."[154]

Although Adachi wrote that the Japanese race "traced their origin, or at least the origin of their imperial line, back to the gods," the educated classes, the evolutionists and scientists often knew better, as likely did many other Japanese, than to believe that the Japanese people traced their origins back to the gods because the

> theory of evolution was endorsed even in popularized science books directed to young readers during the war. A text entitled *Evolution of Life* that was published a year after Pearl Harbor, for example, informed young Japanese that virtually all reputable biologists accepted evolution [as the origin of humans].[155]

150. Ibid., p. 218.
151. Ibid., p. 219.
152. Ibid.
153. Kenji, Kiyono, *A History of Changing Theories about the Japanese Race* (Tokyo: Koyama Shotene, 1944).
154. Dower, *War Without Mercy*, p. 219.
155. Ibid., p. 220.

Dover added that, although many Japanese felt the idea "of evolution from lesser creatures repugnant. . . . Nonetheless, following Darwin, it seemed entirely natural to view such a development as honorable and deserving of pride, for it showed the human race to be advancing in a progressive and positive direction."[156] Despite exposure to evolution theories that stressed the Japanese were superior in some areas, less so in other areas,

> even well-educated Japanese did not hesitate to proclaim . . . that Japan's destiny as the "leading race" in the world was . . . genetically preordained. The government's doctrinaire teachings on this score were couched in vague and often extremely ambiguous language . . . but the orthodoxy unmistakably encouraged an assumption of inherent racial superiority.[157]

As a result, the widely disseminated official beliefs about what it means to be Japanese as "issued by the Thought Bureau of the Ministry of Education in 1937 — explicitly declared that the Japanese were 'intrinsically quite different from the so-called citizens of Occidental [Western] countries,' but were at the same time superior to other Asians as well."[158] One reason for this superior race view was that, in its long history, Japan was never conquered by another nation. In fact, the "imperial virtue" of the Japanese "had attracted other races to Japan and then completely absorbed them."[159] Furthermore,

> the fact that Japan alone had survived like a great rock in the turbulent seas of history, one nation and one people, was proof that the country "did not exist only for itself, but rather for the two billion people of the world." Both Japan and the Japanese, state and people together, bore the heavy responsibility of being "the model, the pattern, the standard for the world." It was Japan's destiny "to lead the whole world along the path of virtue."[160]

The Movement Back Toward the Biblical View of Race

Franz Boas (1858–1942), a Jewish anthropologist, was critical in the eventual overthrow of the racist foundation in the field of anthropology. Trained in Germany, he became an active fieldwork anthropologist[161] and founded a branch of anthropology now called Boasian anthropology that rejected the

156. Ibid.
157. Dower, *War Without Mercy*, p. 220–221.
158. Ibid.
159. Ibid., p. 224.
160. Ibid.
161. Kuklick, *New History of Anthropology*, p. 41.

evolutionary approach to race. In 1895, the American Museum of Natural History hired him and in 1896 he became Professor of Physical Anthropology at Columbia University where he and his students increasingly dominated American anthropology.[162]

One major theme of Boas was that "anthropology had succumbed to . . . premature generalization based on evolutionary theories that distorted the realities of cultural diversity."[163] It was Boas and his student Ruth Benedict who "challenged racism both under Hitler and at home."[164] Their critiques of scientific racism were critical to motivating the drastic turnaround of the racism that had formerly dominated anthropology for almost a century. One writer who was not silent when racism dominated science was Catholic writer H.G. Chesterton (1874–1936)[165] who had much to say about "the mass seduction of pseudoscience" by the Darwinists. In fact, he was one of the rare

> voices to oppose eugenics in the early twentieth century. He saw right through it as fraudulent on every level, and he predicted where it would lead, with great accuracy. His critics were legion; they reviled him as reactionary, ridiculous, ignorant, hysterical, incoherent, and blindly prejudiced, noting with dismay that "his influence in leading people in the wrong direction is considerable."[166]

In the end, Chesterton was proven correct

> and the consensus of scientists, political leaders, and the intelligentsia was [proven] wrong. Chesterton lived to see the horrors of Nazi Germany. . . . Chesterton's arguments were perfectly sensible and deserving of an answer, and yet he was simply shouted down. And . . . the most repellent ideas of eugenics are being promoted again in the twenty-first century, under various guises.[167]

The Catholic Church's "hostility to Darwinism" at this time[168] combined with the fact that "Nazi eugenics struck at the heart of Catholic teaching on the

---

162. Ibid., p. 43.
163. Ibid.
164. Ibid., p. 45.
165. G.K. Chesterton, *Eugenics and Other Evils: An Argument Against the Scientifically Organized Society*, ed. Michael W. Perry (Seattle, WA: Inkling Books, 2000), originally published in 1922.
166. Michael Crichton, *Next: A Novel* (New York, NY: Harper/Collins, 2007). p. 540.
167. Ibid., p. 540.
168. This was in the 1930s, but the last three popes and most Roman Catholic theologians and scientists today are theistic evolutionists of some type. See Terry Mortenson, "Roman Catholicism," in *World Religions and Cults*, Vol. 1, eds. Bodie Hodge and Roger Patterson (Green Forest, AR: Master Books, 2015), p. 92–96.

sanctity of human life," also was important in opposing racism-based eugenics.[169] But eugenics is still supported by many persons, and one of the most controversial movements is the so-called after-birth abortion movement.

After-Birth Abortions

The logical next step in the abortion movement is *after birth* or *post partum abortions,* killing a child after he or she is born. A study of this practice concluded that infanticide is part of the maternal instinct programmed into our genes by evolution.[170] Professor Sara Blaffer Hrdy argued that if female animals perceive that they do not have the resources to rear their infants, mothers aborted, abandoned, and even killed their offspring. She then astonishingly applied this theory to *Homo sapiens.*[171]

Glen Dowling maintained that a child is very costly to rear — requiring 13 million calories to attain adulthood — that "mothers since the Pleistocene have made calculated decisions about when, how and whether to rear them."[172] Professor Hrdy promoted this hypothesis in her 697-page tome titled *Mother Nature: Natural Selection and the Female of the Species* published in 1999. The next step was to openly apply eugenics to improve humans as had been advocated by Darwin's cousin, Francis Galton, who founded this pseudo-science in the late 1800s.

Continuing this moral atrocity, medical ethicists affiliated with England's Oxford University argued that "Parents should be allowed to have their newborn babies killed because they are 'morally irrelevant,' and ending their lives is no different than abortion."[173] They also believe that "newborn babies are not 'actual persons' and have no 'moral right to life.' " For this reason, these academics advocated that, "parents should be able to have their baby killed if it turns out to be disabled when it is born."[174]

These ideas were recently championed in the United States by Princeton University Professor of Ethics, Peter Singer, who advocates the view that newborns lack the essential characteristics of personhood, by which he means a being that "is capable of anticipating the future, of having wants

169. Burleigh, *The Third Reich*, p. 363.
170. Claudia Glenn Dowling, "Sarah Blaffer Hrdy: The Scientist Who Destroyed Our Quaint Concept of What a Mother Ought to be Comes to Terms With Her Own Life," *Discover* 24, no. 3 (March 2003): 40–45.
171. Sara Blaffer Hrdy, *Mother Nature: Natural Selection and the Female of the Species* (London, England: Chatto & Windus, 1999).
172. Stephen Adams, "Killing Babies No Different from Abortion, Experts Say," *The Telegraph* (London) February 29, 2012, p. 1, and Dowling, "Sarah Blaffer Hrdy," p. 42.
173. Adams, "Killing Babies No Different from Abortion, Experts Say," p. 1.
174. Ibid.

and desires for the future" and, for this reason, "Newborn human babies have no sense of their own existence over time. So killing a newborn baby is never equivalent to killing a person."[175]

He also argued that a parent should be able to take a newborn back to the hospital within a certain period of time, such as 28 days, to be euthanized if they feel it does not possess the level of health that they expected or desired.[176] This program has "eerie parallels between Singer's views and those of the medical establishment of the early Hitler days." One difference is that the Nazis allowed a three-year grace period instead of 28 days as suggested by Professor Singer.[177]

Planned Parenthood and Margaret Sanger

Margaret Sanger (1879–1966) was the founder of Planned Parenthood, the leading organization advocating abortion in the United States today. Sanger was the most prominent leader of the modern birth-control and free-love movements.[178] It is well documented that Darwin's *Origin of the Species* had a profound influence on Sanger's thinking, including her conversion to, and active support of, eugenics.[179] Sanger was specifically concerned with reducing the population of the "less fit," including "inferior races" such as "Negroes." Sanger worked hard to spread her eugenic ideas about "human weeds" not only in America but also to the rest of the world. Eugenics, sterilization, and birth control projects on a large scale became an Anglo-American export.[180]

Sanger's birth control movement was the largest in the world, and in England its head offices were based at the London Eugenics Society. Sanger's movement became a "truly international organization with the bulk of its multi-million annual budget coming from the United States."[181] Most of the

175. Peter Singer, section on "The Sanctity of Human Life," https://www.princeton.edu/~psinger/faq.html. This idea is detailed in his book *Practical Ethics* (New York, NY: Cambridge University Press, 2009).
176. John Leo, "Singer's Final Solution," *U.S. News and World Report* (Oct 4, 1999), p. 17. Also Peter Singer and Helga Kuhse, *Should the Baby Live? The Problem of Handicapped Infants* (New York: Oxford University Press, 1986); Peter Singer, *Rethinking Life and Death: The Collapse of Our Traditional Ethics* (New York, NY: Oxford University Press, 1995).
177. Leo, 1999, p. 17.
178. Ruth Clifford Engs, *The Eugenics Movement: An Encyclopedia* (Westport, CT: Greenwood Press, 2005), p. 198.
179. Jerry Bergman, "Darwinism Used to Justify Abortion," *The Human Life Review* 41, no. 2 (Spring 2015): 53–65.
180. Stephen Trombley, *The Right to Reproduce: A History of Coercive Sterilization* (London, England: Weidenfeld and Nicolson, 1988), p. 214.
181. Ibid., p. 215.

financial support came from state taxes, and the rest was donated by large corporations, such as General Motors.

She also openly advocated sexual license, then called "free love," providing much energy for the sexual revolution. The rebellion against morality that she helped to incite has radically changed Western society. To the end of her life she supported eugenics. In one of her last speeches she "attacked welfare programs for not eliminating the 'feeble minded and unfit' and proposed 'incentive sterilization,' " which was actually a program to bribe the "unfit" to be sterilized.[182]

This history is now a hot topic due in part to the unexpected hidden camera filming of Planned Parenthood selling body parts from aborted fetuses.[183] Recently, due to Margaret Sanger's racism, some "black pastors demand [that the] Smithsonian museum . . . remove the bust of Planned Parenthood's founder.[184]

Conclusions

It has become clear that the " 'science' supporting eugenic policies was mostly a matter of faith, as was evident when ethically aware and responsible scientists used conventional scientific reasoning to question the eugenicists' zealously held pseudo-scientific assumptions."[185]

Also critical in the rejection of scientific racism was Ashley Montagu's 1942 book titled *Man's Most Dangerous Myth: The Fallacy of Race.*[186]

182. Vicki Cox, *Margaret Sanger: Rebel for Women's Rights* (Philadelphia, PA: Chelsa House, 2005), p. 101.
183. Steven Ertelt, "Planned Parenthood CEO Confirms It Will Not Stop Selling Body Parts From Aborted Babies," Sept. 30, 2015, http://www.lifenews.com/2015/09/30/planned-parenthood-ceo-confirms-it-will-not-stop-selling-body-parts-from-aborted-babies/. Also Guido Calabresi, "An Introduction to Legal Thought: Four Approaches to Law and to the Allocation of Body Parts," *Stanford Law Review* 55(2003): 2113-2151, http://digitalcommons.law.yale.edu/fss_papers/2022.
184. Kaitlyn Schallhorn, "Black Pastors Demand Smithsonian Museum Have 'Higher Standards' and Remove Bust of Planned Parenthood Founder," http://www.theblaze.com/stories/2015/08/08/black-pastors-demand-smithsonian-museum-have-higher-standards-and-remove-bust-of-planned-parenthood-founder/. Two weeks later the evolutionist Smithsonian rejected the pastors' demand: http://www.theblaze.com/stories/2015/08/22/smithsonian-responds-to-black-pastors-who-demanded-removal-of-planned-parenthood-founders-bust/. But the pastors aren't giving up, remarking, "If they must recognize her 'historical significance,' place her with busts of Pharaoh, Herod, Hitler, Stalin, Mao Zedong, Goebbels, Pol Pot and Dr. Mengele. This would put her in her proper historical context with the infamous and evil figures who committed genocide."
185. Burleigh, *The Third Reich*, p. 348.
186. Ashley Montagu, *Man's Most Dangerous Myth: The Fallacy of Race,* 3rd ed. (New York, NY: Harper, 1952). A new edition that included papers by many leading biologists edited by Montague was published in 1975 and revised in 1999.

Montagu and other anthropologists have finally moved the scientific consensus against the Darwinian racist view to the current view that the origin of all humans appears as if they descended from a single pair of parents.[187] Columbia University anthropologists Ruth Benedict and Gene Weltfish illustrated this view when they stated under the topic, "One Human Race," that "the peoples of the earth are a single family and have a common origin" and "the races of mankind are what the Bible says they are — brothers. In their bodies is the record of their brotherhood."[188]

The reasoning behind their conclusion that all humans have common evolutionary origins includes the "intricate make-up of the human body" and "all its different organs cooperating in keeping us alive, its curious anatomy that couldn't possibly have 'just happened' to be the same in all men if they did not have a common origin."[189] This conclusion in fact does not support evolution as Benedict and Weltfish imply, but actually supports creation. The fact is, the Darwinian view of the inequality of the races has now been refuted. Ironically, the evolutionists themselves have vindicated the biblical teaching that there is only one human race.[190] But while most white evolutionists are not personally racist toward blacks, their evolutionary diagrams are subtly racist with the skin getting lighter as the ape evolves into man having Caucasian features, as Figure 4 illustrates.[191]

One major factor that spelled the final blow to the racist eugenic movement was the "worldwide reaction to the eugenical horrors" that occurred in Nazi Germany as well as the effects of the American Civil Rights Movement in the 1960s.[192] Another factor was the major scientific research proving racists' views were wrong.[193]

---

187. Ashley Montagu, "What is Remarkable about Varieties of Man is Likenesses, Not Differences," in *Current Anthropology* 4, no. 4 (October 1963): 361–364, and Ashley Montague, *Race and I.Q.* (New York, NY: Oxford University Press, Expanded Edition, 1999).
188. Ruth Benedict and Gene Weltfish, *The Races of Mankind* (New York: Public Affairs Pamphlet No. 85, 1951), p 3–5. It must be noted that these two anthropologists are not arguing for a literal biblical Adam and Eve, but nonetheless they recognize that all people groups are part of one race.
189. Ibid., p. 3–4.
190. Gary B. Nash, *Forbidden Love: The Secret History of Mixed-Race America* (New York: Henry Holt, 1999).
191. From http://dsc.discovery.com/news/2007/12/11/human-evolution.html, article dated Dec. 11, 2007, accessed July 27, 2008. A Google search failed to find the picture in 2016.
192. Yudell, *Race Unmasked*, p. 8.
193. Robert Wald Sussman, *The Myth of Race: The Troubling Persistence of an Unscientific Idea* (Cambridge, MA: Harvard University Press, 2014), and Daniel J. Fairbanks, *Everyone is African: How Science Explodes the Myth of Race* (Amherst, NY: Prometheus Books, 2015).

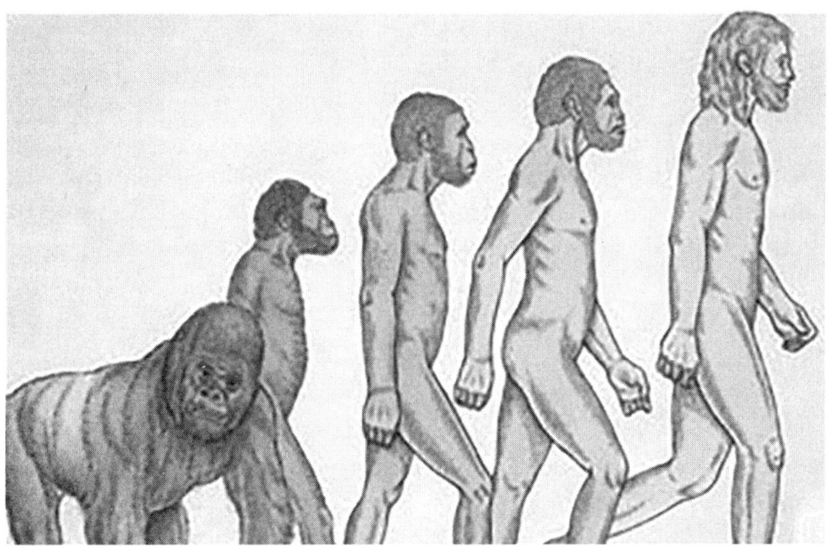

Figure 4: Discovery Channel's 2007 view of human evolution

Just as we would expect, given that the Bible is the inspired, inerrant Word of the Almighty Creator, the scientific evidence confirms what Genesis has taught mankind for at least 3,500 years: there is only one race. We are all descended from Adam and equal before God as we are made in the image of God. As Adam's offspring, we inherited a sin nature and as a result of our own rebellion we are in need of the saving grace of Jesus Christ, regardless of skin color or language or any other differences we may have.

Chapter 14

Ancient Man: Genius or Primitive?[1]

by Rev. Don Landis

The research and study of ancient civilizations, and the people who built them, has not been a big focus for Christians and the Church. The evolutionary "monkey to caveman to modern man" paradigm has been strongly propagated as historical fact.

Evolutionists would have us believe that man started out culturally and technologically primitive and unintelligent. Secular scientists, educators, and media sources assume, teach, and promote a version of history that has no place for a literal Adam and Eve.

Yet in response, the Church has been content, for the most part, to sit back and take no stand on the events of ancient history — as if the Bible has nothing to say and as if what happened in ancient times doesn't affect the Christian faith. But since the Bible is true, then God actually has a lot to say about history and He describes a very different account of ancient times than the one we are being fed by other sources.

Ancient history is fascinating and exciting! It grabs the imagination and begs us to ask more questions than we could hope to answer. Did you ever wonder why there are so many unexplainable feats of wonder and majesty in the ancient world? Has your attention ever been captivated by the incredible architecture and artifacts that were engineered by those who

1. This article has been written with considerable research, writing, and editing help from Matthew Zuk and Analea Styles. Matthew is a writer, editor, and researcher on the "Ancient Man" team. Analea has served as a writer and editor for the "Ancient Man" team ever since the first book project, *The Genius of Ancient Man* (Green Forest, AR: Master Books, 2012) and continues this work on the "Ancient Man" blog and ongoing projects.

lived thousands of years before us? Think of the Great Pyramid, Stonehenge, and Machu Picchu, just to name a few. These are some of the most popular and intensely studied sites in the world and yet they are still full of mystery and questions.

How is it that, after decades of research by highly specialized and skilled scientists and with all the technology that we have today, we are still unable to explain how the ancient people created these sites or why? How have these "lesser evolved" beings been able to keep us in the dark?

The obvious intelligence of ancient man is a puzzle piece that doesn't fit the evolutionary paradigm. Rather, the studies of ancient cultures have actually revealed facts that confirm a biblical worldview of history including a real historical Adam.

Contrasting Models

In Genesis 1, God describes the creation of the universe with mankind as the crown of that creation. Adam and Eve were created in God's very likeness, in His image! Since God is supremely wise and intelligent and commanded Adam and Eve to rule over His creation, we can readily assume that they were quite intelligent. And given that they lived for many hundreds of years, they and their descendants would have developed considerable knowledge and skills. As we will see shortly, the history outlined in Genesis describes the first civilization of man as sophisticated and capable of great accomplishments.

In contrast, the naturalistic, evolutionary model depicts the first humanoid beings as brutish creatures looking more like apes than humans. Their behavior would be only slightly more advanced than the rest of the animal world from which they were evolving. Very slowly, these creatures apparently developed communication, discovered fire, learned to grow food, created cultures, and invented the wheel. If this is true, the historical evidence should reveal unsophisticated ancient civilizations; the further we go back in time, the more we should see man primitive in culture and technology.

Which view does the evidence support? In this chapter we show that very intelligent people built the most ancient civilizations. They were not ignorant ape-like creatures. In fact, modern scientists struggle to explain or replicate many of the skills and achievements of people in ancient times. Could it be that we have it backward? Were Adam's close descendants actually *more* intelligent than we are today? Could the explanation for the ancient marvels actually be that ancient man had incredible genius going back to Adam who was created in the image of God?

Throughout this chapter we will present a variety of evidences, which confirm the Bible's teaching about early man. Analyzing these fascinating discoveries reveals that Adam and his early descendants were in fact some of the most intelligent people to walk the earth. Man's history started with Adam — the evidence of intelligence, even genius, points to this fact.

We will start with what the Bible tells us about pre-Flood man and continue throughout biblical history. We'll then describe many other ancient feats of engineering that have confounded historians who cling to the secular worldview that modern people descended from primitive cavemen who descended from apes.

Timelines and Perspectives

As was discussed in an earlier chapter, there are good biblical reasons to conclude that the universe and mankind are only a little more that 6,000 years old. So the term "ancient" has a very different connotation in this book than it does in an evolutionary, "millions of years" scenario, in which the first humans evolved tens or hundreds of thousands of years ago. If the earth was created around 6,000 years ago, and the Flood occurred roughly 1,600 years after creation, then the earliest (most ancient) civilizations that we have to study would have existed shortly after the Flood, around 2300 B.C. and later.

Pre-Flood Man

Even though it is not possible to excavate and research earth's first civilization with a hands-on approach (because of the global Flood which destroyed everything), the Genesis account describes a few details that suggest a fascinating world where the earliest human beings flourished.

Adam, the First Man (ca. 6,000 Years Ago)

It is argued here that Adam was created as a man who was intelligent from the start. He was placed in a position of dominion over the rest of creation. This intelligence was passed on to his descendants and Adam himself likely taught many of them directly for hundreds of years.

While evolutionists believe we are evolving to become more intelligent with each generation, the Bible presents a much different scenario. God started with a man in a perfect world, that was later cursed and marred by sin. It appears that the effects of sin may have hindered man's intelligence from generation to generation. Certainly, the Apostle Paul makes it clear that sin hinders sound thinking. As people reject their Creator and suppress the truth in unrighteousness, they become idolaters who are darkened in their understanding and the futility of their minds (Rom. 1:18–22; Eph. 4:17–18).

Was Adam a Genius?

So how intelligent was Adam, really? Merriam-Webster Dictionary defines a "genius" as: "a very smart or talented person; a person who has a level of talent or intelligence that is very rare or remarkable; a person who is very good at doing something; great natural ability; remarkable talent or intelligence."[2]

Adam, on the day he was created, was given dominion over the earth. He was commanded to subdue the earth and to rule over every living thing that moves upon it (Gen. 1:28). He was also given the task of cultivating and taking care of the Garden of Eden (Gen. 2:15). This was a powerful role in creation. God gave Adam these responsibilities and therefore He also created him with the capabilities to fulfill them.

Adam's first formal assignment was to name the animals: "The man gave names to all the cattle, and to the birds of the sky, and to every beast of the field" (Gen. 2:20).[3] This exhibits Adam's natural creativity and originality.

God also provided Adam with language and understanding. He spoke to Adam and Adam understood and was able to communicate as well. Furthermore, when God presents Eve, the first woman, to Adam, he breaks out in poetry (Genesis 2:23)!

> This is now bone of my bones,
> and flesh of my flesh;
> she shall be called Woman,
> because she was taken out of Man.

Adam was created in all the splendor of God's perfect creation, blessed and loved by God, and pronounced "very good" by the Creator of the world. We have good reason to conclude that he was indeed an incredibly intelligent man — no doubt Eve was as well.

This ancient man was formed without a single defect. He was the first farmer (Gen. 2:15), the first poet (Gen. 2:23), and the first ruler (Gen. 1:26). When we consider the accomplishments of his early descendants, it is fair to conclude that Adam was also very creative. He was definitely not an ignorant ape-like hominid.

Soon after Adam, the Bible introduces us to a number of ancient people who were also very skilled, and accomplished:

---

2. Merriam-Webster.com.
3. Scripture quotations are taken from the New American Standard Bible (1995).

- Abel was a keeper of flocks (Gen. 4:2).
- Cain was a farmer and built a city (Gen. 4:2, 17).
- Jubal was a musician and presumably an inventor of musical instruments (Gen. 4:21).
- Tubal-Cain forged tools from bronze and iron, implying that he knew how to mine those minerals out of the earth and utilize fire to smelt them (Gen. 4:22).

Genesis 1–11 makes no mention of a single caveman or life before fire was discovered. According to the Bible, the earliest human beings give every impression of being just as intelligent as modern ones. This is noteworthy, for later in Scripture we read of people living in caves for a time and being buried in caves, but this is no evidence of them being primitive (ape-like).[4]

Noah (ca. 2400 B.C.)

One of the greatest examples of pre-Flood intelligence is Noah and the building of the ark that carried his family and the animals through the Flood.

Because the Bible doesn't give us specific details about Noah, much of what we imagine about him is speculation. But we have to remember that when God came to Noah, over 1,500 years had passed since creation. The pre-Flood world was not a primitive place, but rather was filled with people (who each lived for hundreds of years and undoubtedly shared their knowledge with each other as we do today), cities (e.g., Gen. 4:17), and probably more technology than we would usually give the ancient people credit for.

Building the Ark

In those days of great wickedness God chose and commissioned Noah, among all the people living at the time, with the task of building an ark big enough to hold his family and two of every kind of land animal and bird. This was no small chore! The ship was massive[5] and would require more than just average shipbuilding skills.

We do not know for sure how many instructions God gave to Noah pertaining to the building of the ark. The Bible records a few scant details

4. Lot, Elijah, and David lived in a cave for a while. Abraham, Sarah, Isaac, Jacob, Lazarus, Jesus, and others were buried in a cave.
5. The biblical dimensions were 300 cubits by 50 cubits by 30 cubits, equivalent to about 1.5 football fields long, about half a football field wide, and about 4 stories high. It had a volume capacity of about 450 18-wheel, semi-trucks. See https://arkencounter.com/ and visit an authentic full-size replica of the ark in northern Kentucky.

including dimensions and some materials[6] but the crucial plans are not recorded. God may have given Noah specific instructions or perhaps Noah was capable of designing the ark on his own. By the time he received the commands, he was almost 500 years old — enough time to have acquired a vast amount of knowledge and engineering know-how. He also evidently had approximately 70 years to construct the ark, and therefore he had plenty of time to research and study.[7]

Either way, Noah's skill and God's grace and provision worked together to create an amazing result — the ark was built and brought Noah's family and the animals with them through the catastrophe safely. Just think! He only had one chance to get the ark right; there could be no mistakes if they were to survive!

More Than Just a Builder

Building the ark would have taken more than just shipbuilding skills though. This massive project would have required immense planning, organization, and wealth. God expected Noah to provide for all the animals on the ark as well. Noah needed to know about the different kinds of animals, what food they ate and how much, how much space they each needed, etc. He had to know how to store food properly and to ration it out. He also had to know how to get fresh water and fresh air, deal with animal and human waste, and divide out the labors among the eight people on the ark.[8] Of course, God may also have provided this information in more detail than the Bible records, but it was still up to Noah to prepare for it all and see it through to completion.

Thinking about all that Noah had to do, it is not surprising that God would give him such a long time to see it accomplished! We cannot help but be impressed by his work. This was one intelligent and extraordinary man. The ancient days in which he lived did not affect his mental capacity, skill, or ability!

---

6. Made of gopher wood (the meaning of which is uncertain) and covered with pitch, it was over one and a half football fields long, about a half of a football field wide, and over four stories high with three decks (Gen. 6:14–16).
7. In Genesis 6:3, God indicates that man would have 120 years until the Flood. But this was before God gave the command to build the ark and by that time his sons were old enough to be married, so they might have had about 55–75 years to build the ark, which is plenty of time. See Bodie Hodge, "How Long Did It Take for Noah to Build the Ark?" https://answersingenesis.org/bible-timeline/how-long-did-it-take-for-noah-to-build-the-ark/.
8. These and other challenging tasks are thoroughly investigated and skeptical objections are answered in John Woodmorappe, *Noah's Ark: A Feasibility Study* (Dallas, TX: Institute for Creation Research, 1996). Many are visually illustrated in the Ark Encounter, the full-size ark built by Answers in Genesis near Williamstown, Kentucky, which opened to the public in 2016.

Post-flood Biblical Examples

Joseph

When most people think about Joseph from the Bible, they probably only picture a young boy in a technicolor coat who had some crazy dreams. But the biblical account describes a young man who not only trusted God despite his circumstances, but a man who grew into one of the most intelligent and powerful people in the world.

As a youth, Joseph's brothers sold him into slavery and he ended up in Egypt. Joseph not only dreamed prophetic dreams, but he was also able to interpret other people's dreams with startling accuracy. Joseph's God-given ability to interpret Pharaoh's dreams (Gen. 41:1–36) led to the saving of Egypt and much of the world. His interpretations were not autonomous intelligence, but instead given directly from God. Joseph makes this clear: "It is not in me; God will give Pharaoh a favorable answer" (Gen. 41:16). Because of Joseph's ability, Pharaoh made him second in command of the whole country.

During the course of the next 14 years, 7 of plenty and 7 of famine, Joseph organized and supplied food for not only the land of Egypt but neighboring lands as well.[9] Although we don't know the population in these lands at this time, we can be certain that the organization, storage, and distribution of food to the world around Egypt at that time was a massive task for Joseph to undertake. Through the years of plenty he stored the food in the cities "in great abundance like the sand of the sea, until he stopped measuring it, for it was beyond measure" (Gen. 41:49). Then he sold it back to the people during the years of famine.

Imagine organizing and keeping track of such things without the use of our modern technology! Joseph had to build storage facilities to contain the food; he had to organize distribution of the food during the famine; he had to maintain control of a desperate nation and the starving world around them. And he had no computers, calculators, or even vehicles to travel in, no telephones or email for communicating and coordinating. But

---

9. Although Genesis 41:54–57 speaks of "all the earth," the Hebrew word *erets* can mean the whole earth (as in Gen. 1:1) or land (as opposed to the sea, as in Gen. 8:17) or country (such as the land of Egypt, e.g., Gen. 41:53) or even the people on the earth (e.g., Gen. 11:1) as determined by the context. In this case of Joseph in Egypt the context strongly indicates that it does not mean all the countries on the earth. It is most unlikely that a drought and famine were happening on the whole planet at this time. The events of Genesis 12–50 all take place between the Mesopotamian Valley and Egypt and primarily in the lands close to the eastern and southeastern shores of the Mediterranean Sea, which is certainly in view in Genesis 41.

God blessed Joseph with incredible capabilities and he succeeded in bringing Egypt through.

Joseph was made in God's image and because He is not a God of confusion, but of peace and order (1 Cor. 14:33), we would expect that man would have the ability to organize and order things. What we see in the account of Joseph is a fantastic ability to rule and plan even in ancient times.

Even though Joseph had these amazing abilities, he still recognized that God was so much more powerful than himself. Joseph was one of the most gifted men of his time. He became more powerful than everyone in Egypt except Pharaoh. Yet we see that his character remained pure and his faith in God never faltered.

Bezalel and the Tabernacle

When listing our favorite and most prominent men in the Bible, the names Bezalel and Oholiab are not likely the first names to come to anyone's mind. However, these individuals were outstanding men of their day and both are excellent examples of the intelligence of ancient man.

Found within the pages of Exodus, Bezalel and Oholiab are two of the men whom God appointed to build the tabernacle in the desert. God called Bezalel by name and, "filled him with the Spirit of God in wisdom, in understanding, in knowledge, and in all kinds of craftsmanship, to make artistic designs for work in gold, in silver, and in bronze, and in the cutting of stones for settings, and in the carving of wood, that he may work in all kinds of craftsmanship" (Exod. 31:3–5). And he was not alone; God told Moses that He put skill, "in the hearts of all who are skillful" (Exod. 31:6), specifically appointing Oholiab with Bezalel, to be able to make everything as He had instructed Moses to make. This included the tent of meeting, the ark of testimony, the mercy seat, the furniture, the utensils, the golden lampstand, both the altar of incense and the altar of burnt offering, the laver, the garments of the priests, the oil, and even the fragrant incense.

God gave Moses very specific instructions regarding the construction of His tabernacle and these craftsmen were undertaking a huge and very important task. Sometimes we forget as we read through the somewhat tedious chapters of instructions that the Israelites actually had to put these things together in the wilderness! There was no room for error — this was God's holy dwelling place among His people. Moses records chapter after chapter of details and tasks and then describes the process of constructing the different elements, such as weaving, carving, and overlaying with gold

(Exod. 36–39). How can one help but recognize the intelligence and skill of these craftsmen!

God used wise and knowledgeable men to build His dwelling place in the desert, intelligent men who were made in His image, people no less intelligent than you and I. These two men, "and every skillful person in whom the Lord [had] put skill and understanding" (Exod. 36:1) worked to make all the things that the Lord commanded Moses, according to every detail, right down to the sockets of the gate and the pegs of the tent (Exod. 38:31). They would have needed not only the skills, but also the tools and the knowledge of how to work with the materials.

Humans are intelligent not because they have achieved a certain level of evolution, but because they are made in the image of an intelligent God. He designed us the way we are, and as this section in Exodus explains, He gives us skills to be able to do what He desires us to do. God specifically gifts His people with abilities and wisdom to accomplish His works.

Solomon

A list of intelligent people in the Bible must include King Solomon. This man was the wisest man to ever walk the earth. His wisdom was a direct gift from God (1 Kings 3) and Solomon used it to rule the people of Israel. God proclaimed that there had been no one like him in history and there never would be again.

King Solomon reigned at the peak of Israel's history. The land was filled with plenty and the neighboring countries paid him tribute. Everyone knew about Israel and its great and wise king. In fact, 1 Kings 4:29–34 describes Solomon's fame like this:

> Now God gave Solomon wisdom and very great discernment and breadth of mind, like the sand that is on the seashore. Solomon's wisdom surpassed the wisdom of all the sons of the east and all the wisdom of Egypt. For he was wiser than all men . . . and his fame was known in all the surrounding nations. He also spoke 3,000 proverbs, and his songs were 1,005. He spoke of trees, from the cedar that is in Lebanon even to the hyssop that grows on the wall; he spoke also of animals and birds and creeping things and fish. Men came from all peoples to hear the wisdom of Solomon, from all the kings of the earth who had heard of his wisdom.

The Bible puts Solomon in context with the nations around him. The writers of biblical history portray Israel and its kings as part of world history

— they really existed! Everyone in the ancient Neareastern world knew about Solomon, and people actually traveled to hear him speak.

How can we even begin to look down on the intelligence of ancient people when we read about a man like Solomon who lived 3,000 years ago? It is not the date in history that makes one knowledgeable or wise or capable; intelligence is a gift from God, one He has bestowed on man in varying degrees since the beginning.

Figure 1: The tunnel of Hezekiah

The Bible records one of the greatest examples of water engineering in ancient times. A tunnel lies beneath Jerusalem and was constructed around 701 B.C., during the reign of King Hezekiah. Scripture says, "Now the rest of the acts of Hezekiah and all his might, and how he made the pool and the conduit and brought water into the city, are they not written in the Book of the Chronicles of the Kings of Judah?" (2 Kings 20:20).

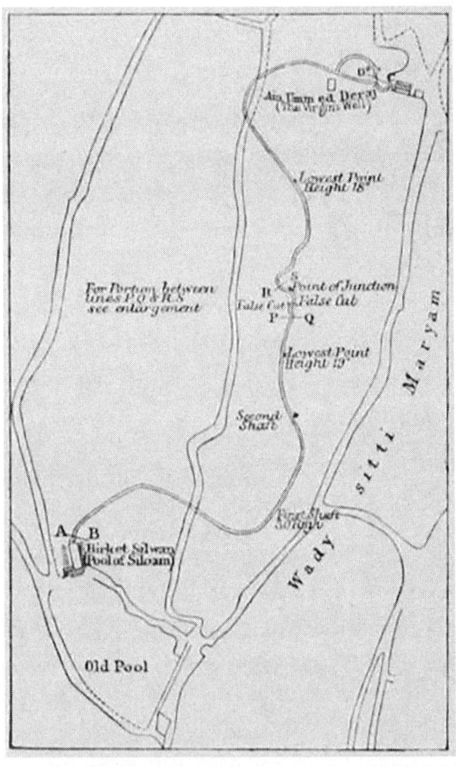

Figure 2: A map showing the location of Hezekiah's Tunnel (the curved dark line) starting from the Pool of Siloam in the lower left winding up the upper right Gihon Spring.

This tunnel was indeed documented in the Old Testament and by other sources as well. King Hezekiah had this tunnel constructed due to the threat of invasion. He had the springs outside the city blocked off so that the enemy army wouldn't have a source of water while Jerusalem was being supplied by their underground water system.

The tunnel's source was the Gihon spring. This natural spring, whose name means "gushing," is estimated to have been capable of supporting a population of 2,500 people. The tunnel itself follows an "S" shape and stretches 1,750 feet under Jerusalem, from the Gihon Spring to the Pool of Siloam (Figure 2).[10] The tunnel was excavated from both sides, but followed a windy path, perhaps a natural crack in the rock, and met in the middle.

An inscription left by the workers was found in 1880 and reveals how the tunnel was cut out from the rock.

> And this is the account of the tunneling through. While [the workmen raised] the pick each toward his fellow and while there [remained] to be tunneled [through, there was heard] the voice of the man calling to his fellow, for there was a split in the rock on the right hand and on [the left hand]. And on the day of the tunneling through the workmen struck, each in the direction of his fellow, pick against pick. And the water started flowing from the source to the pool, twelve hundred cubits. And the height of the rock above the head of the workmen was a hundred cubits.[11]

Hezekiah's engineers somehow managed to connect the two tunnels as they slowly chiseled their way toward each other — not even in a straight line! The tunnel is a major tourist attraction today, still drawing admiration around the world.

The Genius of Ancient Man

Outside of biblical history, the world is full of incredible ancient sites and artifacts that stand as memorials to their creators. They silently attest to the intelligence, creativity, ingenuity, and knowledge of the people who built them. These examples of art and architecture further confirm the truth of the biblical history that links them to Adam. They were skilled and intelligent because God created man that way — to subdue the earth and rule over it.

Ancient Civilization of Sumer – After the Events at the Tower of Babel

Most ancient historians agree that one of the oldest cities in the world, after Babel, was probably Erech (also spelled Uruk). It was one of the most important cities in the Sumerian civilization. According to an evolutionary

10. See pictures and description in "Hezekiah's Tunnel," http://www.bibleplaces.com/heztunnel.htm.
11. More photos and descriptions by James E. Lancaster are at "Hezekiah's Tunnel," http://coastdaylight.com/hez1.html, 1999.

view, Erech *should* show the least advancement and sophistication to all the rest of the ancient sites we will study, because it is arguably one of the oldest.

However this city, mentioned in Genesis 10:10 as part of Nimrod's kingdom, was immense for its day, filled with large structures, and famous for its massive, apparently impenetrable, walls. In fact, these walls were just as formidable as those that arose much later in history such as those built in Babylon, Jerusalem, and Constantinople.

Erech was supposedly founded by the legendary King Gilgamesh, who is described in the famous Babylonian myth, *Epic of Gilgamesh.* The *Epic* is considered the oldest poem in secular history and is most recognized for its flood story, a distorted version of the global Flood during the days of Noah. It is incredible that even in the *most ancient* of civilizations, there were legends and poems being written, pantheons of pagan gods were being worshiped, and mankind had fallen into utter rebellion against the God who created them. Just like Adam, all of mankind quickly fell into sin and used their skills and abilities for their own prideful accomplishments rather than for the glory of God.

The Minoans (ca. 2150–1450 B.C.)

In another early civilization located on the island of Crete, the Minoans demonstrated in their architecture their high level of creativity and sophistication. The ancient Palace in Knossos (Figure 3), the town of Akrotiri, and buildings of Zominthos contain architectural marvels that are nearly unparalleled in their time. Features include plumbing, drainage, use of light reflection, earthquake resistance, massive structures, and strategic location.

Figure 3: Palace at Knossos

In the Palace of Knosses there was an extensive water supply and drainage system. They used terracotta pipes to deliver water to the palace as well as a subterranean drainage system that ran beneath the palace to prevent flooding and to dispose of water.[12]

The town of Akrotiri had the capability of running fresh water into every building, and also had a sewage system throughout the entire town connecting to bathrooms within the buildings, even connecting to the second

12. Jennifer Brainard, "The Minoans," http://www.historywiz.com/minoans-mm.htm.

floors.[13] The toilets of the town had an ingenious design; the waste would fall down a clay pipe to the subterranean sewage system below where water from the town's drains flushed it into a cesspit. The pipes were designed in such a way that a siphon effect drew the smells down the pipes away from the lavatory. This type of system was at least a thousand years "ahead of its time."[14]

The ruins at Zominthos include ceramic water conduits, which were most likely used as a central drainage system.[15]

Within the Palace at Knossos the Minoans constructed a central staircase to provide light to the inner rooms of the palace, acting as a light well. They also used a system known as peer and door partitioning (rows of pillars holding wooden shutters which could be opened and closed) to control air flow within the inner rooms.[16]

The Minoans also built their structures with earthquake resistance. They used wooden beams (Figure 4) in the walls, doorways, and windows to prevent earthquakes from destroying the buildings. These wooden beams would absorb the impact and provide support for the walls, thereby preventing any structural damage or collapse.[17]

Figure 4: The anti-earthquake beams placed over doorways

The last impressive architectural feat of the Minoans was the size of their structures. The Palace at Knossos stood four stories high and had 1,300 rooms. It is one of the most impressive buildings in the ancient world, covering an area of roughly 479,160 feet![18] The ruins at Zominthos indicate that it was two to three stories high, with over 45 rooms.[19] Akrotiri also displayed advanced engineering

13. Donald Preziosi and Louise Hitchcock, *Aegean Art and Architecture* (Oxford: Oxford University Press, 1999).
14. History Channel, TV documentary, "Lost Worlds, Season 1, Episode 3: Atlantis," July 17, 2006.
15. "Excavation History — Interactive Dig Crete: Zominthos Project," http://interactive.archaeology.org/zominthos/introduction/excavations/.
16. History Channel, "Lost Worlds, Season 1, Episode 3: Atlantis."
17. Ibid.
18. Judy Powell, "Layers of Mystery — Archaeologists Look to the Earth for Minoan Fate," http://www.redicecreations.com/article.php?id=2127.
19. Excavation History — Interactive Dig Crete: Zominthos Project."

and multi-story buildings; it was also one of the earliest organized towns ever discovered.[20]

Another evidence of the Minoans intelligence is the location of the structures at Zominthos. Situated at 3,894 feet above sea level, it is the only Minoan building complex discovered at such a relatively high elevation. Through this structure the Minoans have shown their capability to adapt to colder climates and build impressive structures that can withstand the elements. The building was also built in a strategic location to control the surrounding area. The Minoans were originally thought to be peaceful; however, more recent studies have shown that they were actually a warring people.[21]

Secular archaeologists believe that the Minoans also had the first written language in Europe[22] and developed a sophisticated code of laws.[23] None of this evidence fits with the notion that ancient people were dumb brutes. On the contrary, it reveals a high level of intelligence and civilization.

La Bastida, Spain ~2100–2000 B.C.

At roughly 4,000 years old, La Bastida (Figure 5[24]) is located in the southeastern Murcia region of Spain. It is one of the oldest cities (ca. 2100–2000 B.C.) found on mainland Europe and is now known as Europe's most formidable city. It was a fortress with at least six defensive towers, extensive walls that stood 20 feet high and 10 feet thick. Aside from the Minoans, no other civilization in Europe has been found with such intimidating structures.[25]

This fortress (Figure 6[26]) was designed and built for warfare. The front gate led into a courtyard where enemy invaders would be trapped and attacked by men shooting from the towers. The towers and walls were built with strong lime mortar, holding the walls so tightly together that they were impermeable and so sheer that there was no way for attackers to climb them.[27]

The discovery of this site was shocking for many historians because most people think that at that time, the people of ancient Europe were not

20. History Channel, "Lost Worlds, Season 1, Episode 3: Atlantis."
21. "War Was Central to Europe's First Civilization — Contrary to Popular Belief," http://www.shef.ac.uk/news/nr/war-central-minoans-ancient-crete-1.235205, January 15, 2013.
22. "Destruction of the Minoan Civilization," http://www.explorecrete.com/archaeology/minoan-civilization-destruction.html.
23. Lee Krystek, "The UnMuseum — The Lost Continent of Atlantis," http://www.unmuseum.org/atlantis.htm.
24. http://www.aroundtheworldineightyyears.com/wp-content/uploads/2013/02/labastida.jpg
25. Matthew Zuk, "The Genius of Ancient Man: La Bastida: Europe's Most Formidable City," http://geniusofancientman.blogspot.com/2013/03/la-bastida.html.
26. http://murciatoday.com/eu-money-helps-la-bastida-project-in-totana-move-ahead_21462-a.html
27. Ibid.

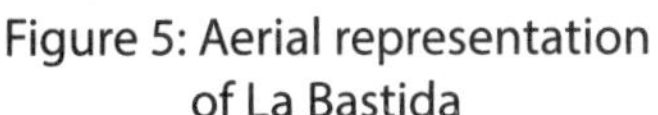
Figure 5: Aerial representation of La Bastida

Figure 6: The ruins of La Bastida

Figure 7: The Great Pyramid of Egypt

military-minded or advanced in warfare. This site proves that the ancient people of Europe were strategic and skilled in making war.

The Great Pyramid, Egypt

The most famous Egyptian site, the Great Pyramid (Figure 7), is one of the most precise and advanced feats of engineering ever discovered in the ancient world. The accomplishments of its builders are truly astounding and continue to baffle people in modern times. Though the exact date of construction is unknown (it was probably built around 2000 B.C.), many aspects of the Great Pyramid exhibit stunning engineering:

- It is aligned with true north to within 3/60 of a degree (with its other sides also aligning with true east, west, and south). This makes it more precisely aligned with true north than any other building on earth, including modern structures.[28]
- The pyramid's base, covering 13 acres, is only ⅞ of an inch out of level. The sides at the base of the pyramid are almost equal to each other; the largest difference in length is not even eight inches.[29]

28. John Desalvo, *Decoding the Pyramids: Exploring the World's Most Enigmatic Structures* (New York, NY: Metro Books, 2008).
29. Graham Hancock, *Fingerprints of the Gods* (New York, NY: Crown Trade Paperbacks, 1995).

- The mortar used on the pyramid was stronger than typical rock, but left less than 1/50 of an inch between the stones.
- The Great Pyramid, along with the other two pyramids at Giza, is astronomically aligned with the constellation Orion.[30]

There was a great deal of precise engineering that took place in the construction of the Great Pyramid. It was also one of the largest building projects in history. The builders used an estimated one to two million blocks of limestone, averaging 2.5–15 tons each (the largest is 80 tons). The pyramid rose to a height of 481 feet and its volume is approximately 90 million cubic feet. More than 30 Empire State buildings could be constructed with its masonry! It truly is among the most imposing structures ever built, clearly displaying the extreme genius of ancient man.

Stonehenge, England

The amazing henge of stones located in Wiltshire County, England, was evidently built in stages sometime after the dispersion from Babel, probably around 2000 B.C.[31] It is one of the most famous examples of archaeoastronomy, by which structures were built with the intent of aligning them with objects of astronomical significance. Though its original purpose is still debated, Stonehenge is remarkable for its display of ancient intelligence. It was aligned to the summer and winter solstices as well as the spring and fall equinoxes and lunar movements. These alignments are incredibly sophisticated even though its construction is thought to predate the eastern Mediterranean, Egyptian, and Greek cultures!

Besides the unbelievable astronomical alignments, even moving the stones to the site of construction was a huge task that is still a mystery. Stonehenge is made up of different types of stones. At one point it had 60 "bluestones," each weighing four tons. The bluestones appear to have come from Wales, 240 miles away![32] Other stones, called "Sarsen stones," probably added later, formed the inner ring and outermost ring. A type of local sandstone, the largest Sarsen stone weighs around 40 tons.

Archaeologists still don't know how they did it. Could it be because we don't give these people enough intellectual credit? The evolutionary paradigm keeps the ancient people in a box that doesn't allow for advanced technology and superior knowledge. Sites like Stonehenge throw everything

30. Zuk, "The Genius of Ancient Man."
31. Some secular archaeologists date it between 3000 and 2000 B.C.
32. "Stonehenge 'Bluestone' Quarries Confirmed in Wales," UCL Institute of Archaeology. http://www.ucl.ac.uk/archaeology/calendar/articles/2015-16-news/20151207.

Figure 8: The Stonehenge

out of balance and so historians and archaeologists are content to label them "mysteries."[33]

Other examples of archaeoastronomy include the Great Pyramid, the city of Alexandria (Egypt), the pyramids at Chichen Itza (in Mexico), and many more. Ancient man's incredible ability to track and predict the movements of objects in the night sky and apply that to their structures only further displays their amazing genius and intellect as descendants of Adam.

Ancient China

Ancient China is one of the most fascinating cultures to study. It was Emperor Qin Shi Huangdi (born Ying Zheng) who was responsible for turning China into a great nation. The Chinese civilization was never united until Ying Zheng came to power in 246 B.C., at the young age of 13.[34] His father was the king of the Qin state and when Ying Zheng succeeded him, he used ambition and the powerful military might of Qin to subjugate other nearby states. He was able to conquer his neighbors through his use of horsemen and standardized weapons. He also utilized more iron for weapons and armor, giving his army an advantage. By 221 B.C., he had unified six warring states and took the name Qin Shi Huang Di, which means "The First Emperor of China."[35]

Qin not only took control of the majority of China, he also set up a well-organized empire that future Chinese emperors would build upon in the years to come. He standardized coins, weights, and measures as well as a writing system throughout China. He also built roads and canals to

33. Brian John and Lionel Jackson Jr, "Stonehenge's Mysterious Stones," http://www.earthmagazine.org/article/stonehenges-mysterious-stones.
34. Joshua J. Mark, "Shi Huangti," *Ancient History Encyclopedia* (December 18, 2012), http://www.ancient.eu/Shi_Huangti/.
35. Ibid.

Figure 9: The Great Wall of China

increase the flow and rate at which trade was conducted. His network of roads stretched approximately 4,000 miles and included some roads up to 40 feet wide, complete with a lane reserved for Imperial members. He is also credited with building the first version of the Great Wall.

The Great Wall of China

Qin Shi Huangdi started one of the greatest building projects in human history: a massive wall to keep enemies out and his people in. During his day, the Great Wall was not quite as impressive as it currently is. It started out as a mud brick wall. First the builders would tamp the foundation to provide a solid base, then a wooden frame was built to contain the wall as they laid down layers of gravel, and then sticks and compacted clay. This layer would then be repeated until the desired height was achieved. Once the wooden frame was removed, all that remained was a solid wall of tamped earth and clay. While not quite as impressive as the wall we see today, it was still an incredible achievement of human engineering.

The wall also provided a rapid communication route, allowing Chinese troops on the border to keep each other informed of enemy movements. A guard tower was placed every 700–1,000 yards to provide additional protection. The wall extended over a distance of 3,000 miles during the emperor's reign, and though it was formidable it was more symbolic than effective. It was not overly difficult to circumnavigate.[36]

36. "Engineering an Empire: China," directed by Mark Cannon, History Channel, broadcast December 11, 2006.

Shortly after Qin Shi Huangdi came into power he ordered the construction of his now-famous mausoleum. He never saw his masterpiece completed. According to Siam Qian (a Chinese historian), more than 700,000 workers were involved in building his tomb, but they were cut short by uprisings in 209 B.C., shortly after Qin's death in 210.[37]

Qin Shi Huangdi's Tomb

His tomb is one of the greatest examples in China of both ancient man's intellect as well as his pride. Built like an underground city, the tomb is located beneath a man-made mound nearly the size of the Great Pyramid in Egypt. Above ground, 30-foot walls divided the site, which was split into outer city, inner city, and mausoleum complexes.

The mausoleum was a large pyramid mound that rose over the landscape nearly 400 feet. However, it is what is beneath the surface that amazes modern historians. Supposedly the underground chamber, 1,600 by 1,700 feet, equal to 580 basketball courts, was filled with incredible treasures: rivers of mercury, pavilions of gold, and pearls on the ceiling to represent the night sky. But whether or not the inside of the tomb is as magnificent as the stories say is unknown. The Chinese have refused to excavate until archaeology has reached a level capable of preserving whatever remains inside. Just think about that! Our advanced modern technology isn't yet trusted enough to uncover the marvels created thousands of years ago, supposedly by less advanced people.[38]

His Terracotta Army

It was also Qin Shi Huangdi who ordered the construction of the incredible Terracotta Army to guard him in the afterlife. The creation of these soldiers required a massive amount of work. One pit alone contained over 6,000 horses and warriors and another 1,300 were found in a different pit. Each soldier has unique facial features and clothing![39]

The clay that was used to construct the army was much harder than anything utilized before. The Chinese used blast furnaces known as kilns, which allowed them to heat the terracotta up to 2,000 degrees Fahrenheit! Each statue could weigh up to 600 pounds and ranged in height from 5'8" to 6'2", which was considerably taller than the average man in those days.

---

37. "Mausoleum of Emperor Qinshihuang (259–210 B.C.)," http://www.china.org.cn/english/features/atam/115132.htm.
38. Ibid.
39. Owen Jarus, "Terracotta Warriors Inspired by Ancient Greek Art," http://m.livescience.com/41828-terracotta-warriors-inspired-by-greek-art.html.

Figure 10: The Terracotta Army

The armor that is replicated on the soldiers included lacquered leather, boots with cleats, and caps that signified each soldier's rank.[40]

Besides the soldiers, some clay figures were found modeled after acrobats, dancers, and musicians. There are believed to be around 600 pits and only a handful has been excavated thus far.

The marvels of ancient China deserve more credit and fame than they get! This powerful emperor and his people used incredible skill, innovation, and engineering that leave no doubt about their amazing intellect!

Ancient Babylon

Recently Dr. Mathieu Ossendrijver (a professor at Humboldt University in Berlin) made an amazing archaeological astronomy discovery when studying an ancient Babylonian tablet (circa 350–50 B.C.). He found that the tablet indicates the ancient Babylonians may have used a type of pre-calculus mathematics to describe the motion of the planet Jupiter. The Babylonian's chief ancestor-god, Marduk,[41] was represented in the heavens as Jupiter. Thus, tracking its movements across the night sky was of utmost importance to them.

40. Ibid.
41. Although Marduk was not really a god, he was an ancestral leader who was elevated to a god-like status by his subsequent descendants and subjects.

It is known that early Babylonians (circa 1800 B.C.) could calculate the area of a trapezoid and could split a trapezoid into two equal parts. However, upon receiving photographs of the later Babylonian tablets (circa 350 B.C.) from the British Museum in London, Dr. Ossendrijver found that the same math used on the trapezoid was used to record the motion of Jupiter. Calling it a "highly modern concept," the professor describes how the ancient Babylonians used a graph of velocity against time, to calculate the distance Jupiter traveled in the sky from its appearance to its position 60 days later. By using the known technique of splitting a trapezoid into two smaller ones of equal area, they could discern how long it took Jupiter to travel half the distance. This type of mathematics, as far as we know, was not used or known until nearly 15 centuries later. No records have been discovered of the Greeks plotting anything based on time.

Dr. Ossendrijver compared the mathematics of the ancient Babylonians to modern math, stating, "It anticipates integral calculus. This is utterly familiar to any modern physicist or mathematician."[42]

Once again, the incredible intelligence of ancient man is seen in this example of advanced Babylonian mathematics.

The Ancient "New World"

In North and South America, the ancient civilizations also exhibit many wonders. These cultures may not seem quite so ancient, especially compared to those in the Middle East, Europe, and Asia, but if you think back to the biblical timeline, it makes sense that they took longer to rise, due to how far people had to travel after the Flood and the dispersion at the Tower of Babel. It is almost as if the American civilizations were on their own separate timeline, one that re-collided with the Old World when Columbus reached America in 1492.

Chichen Itza, Mexico

Located in southeast Mexico, Chichen Itza was part of the Mayan civilization which flourished between A.D. 250–900. It is one of the largest Mayan cities ever discovered and is home to some of the greatest feats of archaeoastronomy in the world. Astronomy was a vital area of Mayan society and is commonly found in their architecture. At Chichen Itza, two structures clearly display the Mayan's fascination with the heavens.

---

42. Kenneth Chang, "Signs of Modern Astronomy Seen in Ancient Babylon," http://www.nytimes.com/2016/01/29/science/babylonians-clay-tablets-geometry-astronomy-jupiter.html.

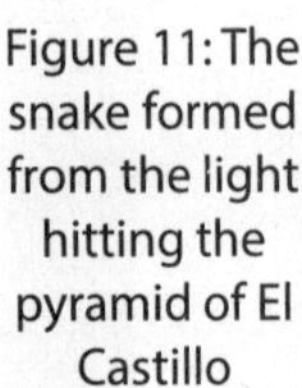

Figure 11: The snake formed from the light hitting the pyramid of El Castillo

El Castillo, "the castle," is the central pyramid-like structure located at the center of the city. It looms at an impressive 79 feet; however, it is most famous for an event that occurs twice a year at the spring and fall equinoxes. At these times each year the setting sun creates a snaky shadow along the stairs (Figure 11). This shadow appears to have been a deliberate design as it makes its way down the pyramid connecting to the snakehead statue at the bottom. The engineering required to produce such an effect is astounding.[43]

The other building that displays archaeoastronomy is "El Caracol," also known as "the observatory." This structure tracks the movements of the planet Venus, which is actually a difficult planet to track due to its appearance in the morning, then it disappears and reappears in the evening. These movements were so deceptive that even the Greeks believed there were two different celestial bodies. The Mayans were not deceived by the movements and designed El Caracol to track its movements.[44] Both of these buildings display the Mayans incredible astronomical abilities, as well as their fascination with the heavens. What was their purpose? What were they looking for? Consider the initial reason as given during creation week: "Then God said, 'Let there be lights in the expanse of the heavens to separate the day from the night, and let them be for signs and for seasons and for days and years' " (Gen. 1:14). Even though years had passed since the Flood, many ancient cultures had a precision of mapping the heavens that is truly incredible.

43. "Ancient Observatories: Chichen Itza," http://www.exploratorium.edu/ancientobs/chichen/HTML/caracol3.html.

44. Ibid.

Figure 12: Machu Picchu, Peru

The Architecture of the Incas

The Incan Empire was one of the greatest in South America, lasting from the early 13th to the late 16th centuries. Located in modern-day Peru, the Incas are probably most well-known for the incredible city, Machu Picchu (Figure 12). This beautiful site is situated at 7,970 feet (2,430 m) above sea-level in the Andes Mountains, and shows off the Incas' incredible cyclopean architecture as well as some elements of archaeoastronomy.

Cyclopean architecture refers to the style of construction that involves cutting stones to fit perfectly together without the use of mortar. This term was first used for walls and structures built by the Mycenaean civilization in Greece (1400–1200 B.C.). The "Observatory" or "Temple of the Sun" at Machu Picchu appears to have been built specifically for astronomical observation. The windows seem to align with and calculate the summer solstice as well as the rising of several important constellations.[45]

Saksaywaman (along with related features in Cusco) is another Incan site and the capital of the empire (Figure 13). Built at an altitude of 12,140

45. Sarahh Scher, "Machu Picchu," https://www.khanacademy.org/humanities/art-americas/south-america-early/inca-art/a/machu-picchu.

Figure 13: Sacsayhuaman

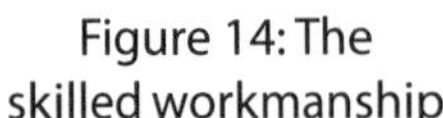

Figure 14: The skilled workmanship

feet (3,700 m), it was a large fortress-like structure, and perhaps the most impressive example of flawless cyclopean architecture ever discovered. The walls constructed at Sacsayhuaman use the cyclopean technique to perfection. The walls are absolutely massive and stunning to behold.

The stones are flawlessly cut and fit together so perfectly that not even a blade of grass can fit between them (Figure 14). The stones used in the structure are extremely large as well, some weighing over 150 tons. The largest is 29 feet high and is an estimated 360 tons! The quarry from which these stones were cut is about ten miles away.

How the Incas cut these stones, moved them into place, and fit them together so perfectly is a mystery. Even when the Conquistadors from Spain saw these ruins they were mystified as to how the supposedly "primitive" Inca could have built such a structure. The peculiar shapes, unknown method of transport, and perfect fit of these stones make these structures a nearly unmatched feat of engineering today.[46] You may recognize how this is reminiscent of Solomon's temple that was also built like this. Consider: "The house, while it was being built, was built of stone prepared at the quarry, and there was neither hammer nor axe nor any iron tool heard in the house while it was being built" (1 Kings 6:7).

Incredible Ancient Artifacts

Sometimes the evidence of the genius of ancient man is seen in their massive structures and amazing engineering, but sometimes the best examples are found in small artifacts and the intricate details.

The Lycurgus Chalice

Of the many discoveries of ancient technology that confound modern historians, perhaps the most astounding is the Lycurgus Cup, a 1,600-year-old Roman artifact that first came to light in the 1950s and immediately puzzled archaeologists. The cup changes color based on where light hits it. It is green if the light comes from the front, and red if the light is behind it.[47]

Figure 15: The Lycurgus Chalice

Recent studies have led to the discovery of how this phenomenon occurred: nanotechnology. The Romans were apparently far better craftsmen than originally thought! The Romans produced the cup's features by impregnating tiny particles of gold and silver into the glass. They were somehow able to crush and grind the gold and silver to the molecular scale, fifty nanometers in diameter. That is more than a thousand times smaller than a grain of table salt! Additionally, due to the precise mixture of the precious metals, it seems the Romans

46. "Sacsayhuaman Walls," http://www.ancient-hebrew.org/ancientman/1044.html.
47. Zeeya Merali, "This 1,600-Year-Old Goblet Shows That the Romans Were Nanotechnology Pioneers," http://www.smithsonianmag.com/history-archaeology/This-1600-Year-Old-Goblet-Shows-that-the-Romans-Were-Nanotechnology-Pioneers-220563661.html.

knew exactly what they were doing. It is truly astounding! Never before has advanced technology of this scale been discovered in an ancient artifact.

However, the astonishment does not end there. Scientists replicated technology of the chalice in order to run more tests. The nanotechnology works as follows: when hit with light the electrons in the cup would vibrate in a way that made the chalice appear a certain color, depending on the observer's position. If liquid was in the cup it would change the vibrations which would thereby change the color of the cup. The prototype the scientists created was 100 times more sensitive to changes in salt levels in liquids than current commercial sensors with similar technology (for preservation purposes, the original cup cannot be tested on). Such a detection mechanism would have been very handy for the Romans to tell if someone was trying to poison their ruler.[48]

Modern scientists are studying this cup in order to enhance our own nanotechnology detection systems. Even today we can learn and improve our own technology with methods used 1,600 years ago! How can that fit the evolutionary model of man's intelligence?

Metal Coatings Unmatched Even Today?

Another fascinating and incredible discovery is the metal plating techniques used 2,000 years ago that are so thin they cannot be matched by today's methods. In an effort to preserve ancient artistry and artifacts, a team of scientists led by Gabriel Maria Ingo have analyzed the methods used by ancient artists to create the masterful pieces of gilded art.

In their research, they discovered that the gilders had a variety of techniques, one of which used mercury as a sort of glue to apply thin films of metal to statues and other objects. This film of metal was so thin it surpasses what modern scientists use for DVD's, solar cells, electronic devices, and other products. These techniques were used throughout the "dark ages"; it seems that the artisans reached the point where they could not get any more skilled, and their mastery cannot be matched today even with our sophisticated technology.[49]

Antikythera Mechanism

Roughly the size of a shoebox, the Antikythera Mechanism is believed to be Greek or Roman in origin. It was discovered in A.D. 1900 in a second century

48. Ibid.
49. "Ancient Ttechnology for Metal Coatings 2,000 Years Ago Can't Be Matched Even Today," http://www.sciencedaily.com/releases/2013/07/130724124919.htm.

B.C. Roman shipwreck off the coast of the Greek island of Antikythera. The exact date of its construction is unknown, but it is one of the most astounding pieces of ancient technology ever discovered. The Antikythera mechanism has baffled historians with its incredible intricacy and design. It was believed to have contained 37 gears at one point (30 still remain). As far as we know, this many gears were not used in a device again until the 17th century.

Figure 16: The Antikythera Mechanism

This very complex mechanism was able to predict the movements of the sun, moon, the 12 Zodiac signs, and maybe even the five planets known to the Greeks. It tracked the Saros cycle (periods of solar and lunar eclipses), Metonic cycle (basis of the Greek calendar), and Callippic cycle (a lunar cycle which included four Metonic cycles), and perhaps even tracked the four-year cycle of the Olympic games![50]

"Primitive" People, Past and Present

Though we have spent most of this chapter studying the examples of ancient genius as evidenced through technology, architecture, astronomy, and other sciences, we would be remiss if we didn't address the fact that not every ancient society or people group in history had advanced technology. Some might not have had a large enough work force, enough resources, or perhaps even the desire to invent and manufacture things that would stand the test of time. Does the lack of "technology" indicate that some of these ancient people were actually NOT as intelligent as others? What about people living in a more "primitive" manner in modern times?

Indeed, there certainly have been times throughout the history of man when some people did not have advanced technology. But this does not invalidate the biblical premise that man was created intelligent. Sometimes we make

50. Don Landis, ed., *The Genius of Ancient Man: Evolution's Nightmare* (Green Forest, AR: Master Books, 2012), p. 69.

an error in that we equate intelligence with technology. We label "primitive" people as stupid or less evolved simply because they do not exhibit the type of "advancement" that has come to be associated with mental aptitude.

People groups that exist without advanced technology still exhibit the innate intelligence that God created each of them with. Their cultures are filled with purpose and meaning. Their skills are different from ours and yet they still proclaim cleverness, problem solving, and intellect.

A reporter who had the opportunity to spend time with the Hadza people of Tanzania can testify to the incredible skills of this tribe. Though they neither farm nor build cities, these people have lived successfully off the land for thousands of years.

> For Onwas [a Hadza tribesman] navigation is no problem. He has lived all his life in the bush. He can start a fire, twirling a stick between his palms, in less than 30 seconds. He can converse with a honeyguide bird, whistling back and forth, and be led directly to a teeming beehive. He knows everything there is to know about the bush and virtually nothing of the land beyond.[51]

Their isolation and lack of "advancement" has nothing to do with their intelligence. The bias of modern societies makes it difficult for us to see, respect, and value the different kinds of knowledge and skills people may have. We tend to discredit things that we cannot understand, recognize, or measure according to our standards.

Today there are over 100 "uncontacted" tribal people groups worldwide. They live successfully, yet isolated from mainstream society. In an insightful article on the *National Geographic* website, a journalist shares about the beauty of the uncontacted tribes of the world:

> There are many myths that circulate, of course: that they are "lost" tribes (nothing but sensationalism); that they are "backward" for their alternative ways of life or nakedness, or "stone-age" for their lack of material possessions (it's the ideas that are outdated, not them); that they have tried and failed to keep up with the "modern" world (a conceit that presupposes that the western society is the pinnacle of human aspiration and that all other cultures are striving to reach it).[52]

---

51. Michael Finkel, "The Hadza," http://ngm.nationalgeographic.com/2009/12/hadza/finkel-text/1.
52. Joanne Eede, "Uncontacted Tribes: The Last Free People on Earth," http://voices.nationalgeographic.com/2011/04/01/uncontacted-tribes-the-last-free-people-on-earth/.

Our presuppositions sometimes blind us from seeing mankind through a biblical lens. Instead of looking at every human being, as God sees them — created in His image — we compare, contrast, judge, and analyze both ancient and modern people as "primitive" or "technological." We try to categorize everything according to "science" and miss out on God's true purpose.

The incredible genius, creativity, skills, and accomplishments of mankind throughout the ages are all a testament to God's glorious design. Adam was created to bring God glory, and although man is fallen, he cannot help but declare the glory of God merely through his natural, created intelligence.

Conclusion

Throughout this chapter we have pointed to the numerous examples that display the intelligence of ancient man confirming the literal history of Genesis 1–11 that take us back to a historical Adam, the first man, created by God in His image. Ancient man was not a grunting ape-man gradually changing into *Homo sapiens* over millions of years of natural selection and random mutations, as the evolutionists want us to believe.

From the massive structures to the smallest gears, the ancient people continually amaze us with their intelligence — keep in mind we only see a snapshot of this brilliance through archaeological lenses. But why is it so amazing when God created these men and women to reflect His own image? Shouldn't we expect it?

From a biblical perspective we know that men in the past possessed great intelligence, and the archaeological evidence confirms it. However, once we recognize this, we need to remember to take it one step further and recognize where this intelligence originates. It is very easy to study history and the marvels of the ancient world and get caught up in praising man and his abilities. However, we must remember that man's gifts and talents have a source, and that source is the amazing God who created all that exists.

At Jackson Hole Bible College we have several crucial axioms that we impress upon our students. One of them is that everything goes back to God. This concept is incredibly important for us to grasp as Christians because God should be the center of our lives. In everything we do we should be connecting that back to God. Thus, as tempting as it is to praise man for the incredible accomplishments that we observe in history and remaining today, we should recognize that it is God who gives man his abilities. From the beginning, since the very first man and woman, God's design for man included talents, abilities, and gifts to be used for His glory. The Lord should be given all the praise and credit for His incredible creative works and the incredible creative works of man, who alone is made in His image![53]

53. For further information on this subject see these two books: Don Landis, ed., *The Genius of Ancient Man: Evolution's Nightmare* (Green Forest, AR: Master Books, 2012), a beautifully color-illustrated description of many other marvels of the ancient peoples; and Don Landis, ed., *The Secrets of Ancient Man: Revelations from the Ruins* (Green Forest, AR: Master Books, 2015), which takes the reader through the timeline of history studying mankind's common desire to "make a name for himself" throughout every culture and civilization.

Chapter 15

Humanity's Shared History Reflecting the Truth of Genesis 1–11

by Tim Chaffey

The Bible reveals that after the Genesis Flood, Noah's descendants refused to fill the earth as the Lord instructed. Instead, Genesis 11 explains that they gathered together in the plain of Shinar and started building a city with an infamous tower. The Lord put a stop to their rebellious project by confusing their language, causing them to scatter across the earth.

If the events of Genesis 1–11 truly occurred, as Scripture clearly indicates that they did, it would mean that from the Flood until the confusion of languages at Babel, mankind possessed a common history. Many of these people, particularly in the first few generations, would have almost certainly learned from Noah's family about the major events prior to the Flood. After scattering from Babel, the various people groups experienced their own unique histories.

Given these facts, we should expect to find echoes of the major events of Genesis 1–11 in the traditions and legends of people groups all over the world. Therefore, it is no surprise to Bible-believing Christians that anthropological studies have uncovered an array of non-Israelite stories at least partially consistent with the Bible's earliest chapters. The most common of these legends centers on the great deluge, but it is not uncommon to hear tales reminiscent of the Bible's account of creation, the Fall, the Tower of Babel, and more.

While acknowledging the existence of these legends, modern critical scholars tend to follow the lead of James George Frazer. In his view, since pagan folklore frequently includes elements found in Genesis 1–11, such as the tree of life and the Flood, then the Genesis account must be nothing more than folklore. Obviously, this conclusion is not the only one that can be drawn from the evidence. Indeed, it will be argued that Frazer's conclusion cannot adequately deal with all of the facts.

This chapter will highlight a sampling of legends from people groups around the globe whose ancient stories seem to indicate there was a time when all people shared a common history. After looking at these various connections, it is necessary to address three objections raised by critics against this conclusion.

The Creation

The Maori people of New Zealand and other South Pacific islands have several creation myths. One particular legend explains that the god Tane made a model of man from red clay. Then he uttered an incantation, and when he breathed on the figure, the clay came to life. This man was named Tiki and his wife was Marikoriko. Interestingly enough, other legends claim that Tiki was not the first man but the creator of men, but this was considered heretical because it denied that Tane created man. The spread of this heresy allegedly led to the flood that destroyed mankind.[1]

The Comanche people of the Great Plains region of the United States tell a creation story that contains some interesting parallels to Genesis. They say that one day the Great Spirit took swirls of dust from the four directions and created the Comanche people. These people made of earth were very strong, but a shape-shifting demon started to torment the people. The Great Spirit threw the demon into a bottomless pit. To carry out revenge, the demon takes up residence in the fangs and stingers of poisonous animals to harm people at every opportunity.[2]

Certain groups of Australian Aborigines tell a tale that echoes Genesis in some respects. The creator, Punjil, carried a great knife to shape the work of his hands. He made two men from lumps of clay, "which he gradually fashioned from the feet upwards into the human form," and then "he breathed very hard on them and they lived and began to move about as full-grown

1. Edward Treagear, *The Maori Race* (Wangani, NZ: A.D. Willis, Printer and Publisher, 1904), p. 464.
2. David Hurst Thomas, Jay Miller, Richard, White, Peter Nabokov, and Alvin M. Josephy, *The Native Americans: An Illustrated History* (Atlanta, GA: Turner Publishing, 1993), p. 108.

men."[3] Punjil's brother controlled the waters and he used a hook to draw out two young women who became the mates of the two men.[4]

A common element in each of these legends is that a deity crafted men from the ground. The three myths also allude to the creator breathing on man or using a swirling wind to bring man to life. One cannot help but think of Genesis 2:7, "Then the LORD God formed man of dust from the ground, and breathed into his nostrils the breath of life; and man became a living being."

The Fall

The well-known Greek myth about Pandora bears some striking resemblances to the biblical account of man's rebellion. According to Hesiod, Zeus ordered Hephaestus to create the first woman. Her beauty was to match that of the goddesses. Other gods gave her many gifts, which explains the origin of her name (*pan* = all, *dōron* = gifted), but also led to her downfall since the gifts of the gods were "a plague to men." She was also given a jar, or box in some versions, that held all of the world's evils within. One day, Pandora opened the great lid and the evils escaped to fill the earth.[5]

Aboriginal peoples from the Murray River area of Australia convey a legend about death entering the world when the first man and woman disobeyed a specific instruction regarding a tree. They were told not to go near a certain tree in which a great bat lived. One day, the woman was gathering firewood and came too close to the tree. The bat awoke and flew away. From that time on, human beings died.[6]

A Sumerian cylinder seal (Figure 1) discovered in 1846, now residing in the British Museum as ME 89326, illustrates a scene strikingly similar to the account of the Fall in Genesis. The seal is dated to the 22nd century B.C., so it represents a time very close to the time of the Babel event. In the middle of the seal is a tree with a fruit hanging on a branch on the left and one hanging from a branch to the right. To the right is seated a male figure reaching toward the fruit and on the left a woman is reaching for the other fruit. What moves this seal from the realm of coincidence into the realm of solid evidence that the ancient Sumerians once knew the truth about the

---

3. John Fraser, "Some Folk-songs and Myths from Samoa," *Journal and Proceedings of the Royal Society of New South Wales* 25 (Sydney: The Society, 1891). p. 262.
4. Ibid.
5. Hugh G. Evelyn-White, translator, "Hesiod," *The Homeric Hymns and Homerica: Works and Days* (Cambridge, MA: Harvard University Press, 1914), lines 59–104.
6. Robert Brough Smyth, *The Aborigines of Victoria* (Melbourne: John Ferres, Government Printer, 1878), p. 428.

Figure 1: Image from Sumerian cylinder seal in the British Museum

Fall is the fact that a serpent is standing immediately behind the woman. Regarding this seal, George Smith wrote the following:

> We know well that in these early sculptures none of these figures were chance devices, but all represented events, or supposed events, and figures in their legends; thus it is evident that a form of the story of the Fall, similar to that of Genesis, was known in early times in Babylonia.[7]

Many ancient traditions depict the first woman as being tempted in some way, either by a tree or by something in or near the tree, such as a serpent or dragon. A surprising number of ancient tales include serpents at the heart of their creation or fall of man myth, often turning the biblical account on its head as the serpent is viewed as the source of wisdom to be worshiped. Though he discounted the historicity of the biblical events, James Fergusson documented numerous similarities found in various locations around the earth:

> There are few things which at first sight appear to us at the present day so strange, or less easy to account for, than that worship which was once so generally offered to the Serpent God. If not the oldest, it ranks at least among the earliest forms through which the human intellect sought to propitiate the unknown powers. Traces of its existence are found not only in every country of the old world; but before the new was discovered by us, the same strange idolatry had long prevailed there, and even now the worship of the Serpent

7. George Smith, *The Chaldean Account of Genesis* (London, England: Sampson Low, Marston, Searle, and Rivington, 1876), p. 91.

> is found lurking in out-of-the-way corners of the globe, and startles us at times with the unhallowed rites which seem generally to have been associated with its prevalence.[8]

Critics like Fergusson often focus on the differences in the accounts while downplaying the remarkable similarities. Consequently, they have struggled to make sense of the many parallels between ancient mythologies and the early chapters of Genesis, but Christians should expect to find distorted vestiges of earth's ancient past among the idolatrous, pagan peoples of the world.

Giants

Ancient tales abound with legends of giants, and they are often connected in some way with a great flood. Unsurprisingly, the Bible also mentions these details. Genesis 6:4 states that *nephilim* (giants)[9] were on the earth in the days before the Flood, and also afterward. The text adds that the *nephilim* were around whenever the sons of God sired children with the daughters of men.[10]

---

8. James Fergusson, *Tree and Serpent Worship* (London, England: Wm. H. Allen and Co, 1868), p. 1.
9. Academic literature contradicts the popular notion that *nephilim* means "fallen ones," as derived from the verb *naphal* ("to fall"). Instead, lexicons and academic commentaries explain that *nephilim* simply means "giants." The text describes them as mighty men (Genesis 6:4) and of great stature (Numbers 13:22, 32–33). Ancient sources, such as the LXX, translate the word as giants. Hebrew and Aramaic lexicons define the word as giants. See *The Hebrew-Aramaic Lexicon of the Old Testament* (Koehler, Baumgardner), *The New International Dictionary of Old Testament Theology and Exegesis* (VanGemeren), *The Analytical Hebrew and Chaldee Lexicon* (Davidson), and *Dictionary of the Targumim, the Talmud Babli and Yerushalmi, and the Midrashic Literature* (Jastrow), and *Brown-Driver-Briggs Hebrew and English Lexicon* (Brown, Driver, Briggs).
10. Although many English Bibles state that the giants were on the earth "when" the sons of God and women had children, *Gesenius' Hebrew Grammar* states אֲשֶׁר (*asher*) should be translated as "whenever," since it refers to actions which were repeated in the past, either at fixed intervals or occasionally. See E. Kautzch, ed., *Gesenius' Hebrew Grammar, Second English Edition* (London, England: Oxford University Press, 1909), §107.e. This subtle difference clarifies that the Nephilim were the result of the illicit unions between the sons of God and women rather than already being on the earth when the sons of God married women.

    Regarding the identity of the sons of God, Christians generally adopt one of three positions (or derivations of them): 1) heavenly beings, 2) polygamous tyrants who viewed themselves as divine, or 3) men in the line of Seth. Answers in Genesis does not hold an official position on the identity of the sons of God. For a balanced overview, see Tim Chaffey, "Battle Over the Nephilim," *Answers Magazine* 7:1 (2012): 62–66. Available online at <https://answersingenesis.org/bible-characters/battle-over-the-nephilim/>. For a detailed study, see the author's ThM thesis, "The Sons of God and the Nephilim" (Liberty Baptist Theological Seminary and Graduate School, 2011). If the sons of God were heavenly beings, then this would be another feature similar to mythologies around the globe, as the giants or demi-gods were often described as the result of unions between gods and women prior to the catastrophic flood.

The famed "Buffalo Bill" Cody reported that while he visited the Pawnee of Nebraska, someone carried very large bones into the camp, and a surgeon pronounced that one of them was a human thigh bone. The Pawnee claimed that the bones belonged to a race of people who lived long ago who were three times the size of a man and endowed with great speed and strength.

> These giants, said the Indians, denied the existence of a Great Spirit. When they heard the thunder or saw the lightning, they laughed and declared that they were greater than either. This so displeased the Great Spirit that he caused a deluge. The water rose higher and higher till it drove these proud giants from the low grounds to the hills and thence to the mountains. At last even the mountaintops were submerged and the mammoth men were drowned.
>
> After the flood subsided, the Great Spirit came to the conclusion that he had made men too large and powerful. He therefore corrected his mistake by creating a race of the size and strength of the men of the present day.[11]

The Montagnais of the Hudson Bay region of Canada also have a tale about giants and a flood. God was angry with the giants, so he commanded a man to build a large canoe. Once the man finished his boat and boarded it, the waters rose on all sides until no land could be seen and all the giants were drowned. The man became tired of seeing nothing but water, so he threw an otter overboard and the animal dove to the bottom and brought up some earth.[12]

While generally considered to bear evidence of Christian influences because it refers to certain biblical people and events, the Old English epic poem *Beowulf* (written in England between the 8th and 11th centuries A.D.) seems to mention only those prior to the Babel event. The sword Beowulf used to slay Grendel's mother bore an engraving that described the following events:

> . . . the beginning of the ancient strife, what time the flood, the rushing ocean, destroyed the giant race. They had behaved frowardly. That people was estranged from the eternal Lord; wherefore the Ruler gave them their final reward in the flood of waters. And on the guard of shining gold was rightly graven, set forth and told

11. Colonel W.F. Cody, *An Autobiography of Buffalo Bill* (New York, NY: Farrar & Rinehart, 1920), p. 196–197.
12. James George Fraser, *Folk-Lore in the Old Testament*, Vol. 1 (London, England: MacMillan and Co., 1918), p. 296–297.

> in runic letters, for whom the sword had first been made, that best of blades, with its twisted hilt brightly adorned with snakes.[13]

The Incas of South America also spoke of giants prior to a great flood. In their legend, Viracocha created the first race of humans. They were giants who lived in darkness for a period of time, but at some point, they angered Viracocha. Angry and disappointed with his creatures, Viracocha destroyed the world with a flood and transformed the giants to rocks.[14]

The Flood

Unquestionably, the most popular type of legend found among ancient mythologies centers on a catastrophic flood. More than 200 flood traditions from every corner of the world have been recorded.[15] These legends vary in their level of consistency with the biblical account, yet certain details are widely distributed. For example, many of these tales speak of a favored family who built a huge boat and, along with some animals, survived a worldwide catastrophe sent by an angry deity. See Figure 2.[16]

The *Epic of Gilgamesh* includes what is perhaps the best known of the extra-biblical flood myths. The 11th tablet contains a story remarkably similar to the Genesis account. Instructed by the god Ea, Utnapishtim builds and covers with pitch a cube-shaped ark to save himself, his family, and the animals from a devastating flood that killed everyone outside of the boat. On the seventh day, the ark lands on Mt. Nisir. Utnapishtim releases a dove, swallow, and raven to check the water levels, and eventually offers a sacrifice to the gods.

The Sumerian version of this story features a hero named Ziusudra and boasts many of the same details as Gilgamesh. The Akkadians also had a version of this tale. Atrahasis built a giant coracle based on Enki's instructions. The circular vessel was 230 feet across, 20 feet high, and covered with bitumen. The animals boarded the circular boat two by two, and along with Atrahasis and his family, they survived a devastating weeklong flood. Atrahasis offers a sacrifice after leaving the boat.

The flood legend of the Masai people in Kenya tells of a righteous man named Tumbainot who had a wife and three sons. When his brother died, Tumbainot married his widow, and she bore him three more sons. Then his

13. Chauncey Brewster Tinker, transl., *Beowulf*, rev. ed. (New York, NY: Newson & Company, 1912), p. 80.
14. Gary Urton, Inca Myths (Austin, TX: University of Texas Press, 1999), p. 35.
15. Byron C. Nelson, *The Deluge Story in Stone* (Minneapolis, MN: Bethany Fellowship, 1968; Augsburg, 1931), p. 165–190. Nelson summarizes 39 of those legends and cites other authors who describe more of them. See also http://www.talkorigins.org/faqs/flood-myths.html.
16. Ibid., p. 169.

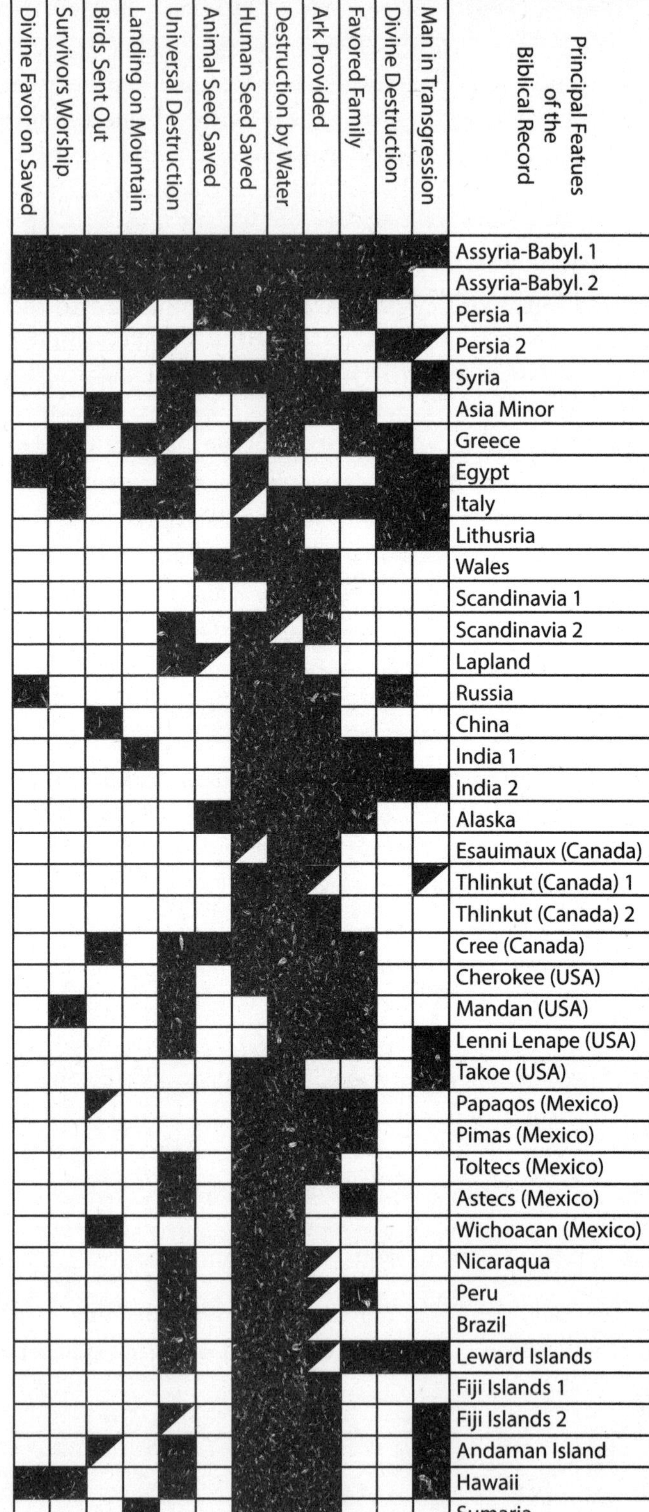

Figure 2: Some of the 200+ Flood traditions around the world

god commanded him to build a wooden boat for him, his wives, his six sons, their wives, and every sort of animal. A flood came and drowned all men and beasts except for those on board the ark. As the floodwaters receded, Tumbainot sent out a dove and then vulture to determine if the land had dried.[17]

The Aboriginal Wunambal tribe of Western Australia holds a tradition with many similarities to the biblical Flood account. Some children cruelly treated a bird that flew to heaven and complained to the Creator, Ngadja. Furious at what had been done, Ngadja warned Gajara to build a double raft to survive a coming flood. Animals and food were packed on the raft and the flood came, bringing the seawaters over the land. Eventually, the waters receded and mountaintops were seen. Gajara sent out a cuckoo and then other birds. His wife, Galgalbiri, cooked a kangaroo. When Ngadja smelled the pleasing scent, he put a rainbow in the sky as a promise that there would no longer be such a disastrous flood.[18]

Babel

The Babel event also seems to show up in the tales of various ancient cultures around the globe. Like the legends of creation, the Fall, giants, and the Flood, the Babel-like legends bear some striking similarities to the biblical account along with some strange distortions.

The Papago people of Arizona explain that after a flood the Great Spirit and Montezuma restocked the earth with men and animals. Montezuma and Coyote taught and led the people. Later, Montezuma became prideful and brought evil into the world when he rebelled against the Great Mystery by making the people build a many-storied home that kept growing taller and taller. The Great Mystery raised the sun higher in the sky, causing cooler temperatures and snow to warn the people, but they kept building. So the Great Mystery destroyed Montezuma's tower with an earthquake, and changed the languages of the people so that they could no longer understand the animals or other tribes.[19] Biblical creationists generally believe the conditions on earth as a result of the Flood would have triggered a single Ice Age that would have lasted for a few centuries. Is it possible that the cooling temperatures described in the Papago legend are referring to those post-Flood conditions?

The Mikir of Myanmar (Burma) tell a story that combines elements of Babel with legends of giants. In the old days, the descendants of Ram were mighty giants ruling over earth. They aspired for loftier goals, seeking to

17. Frazer, *Folk-Lore*, p. 330–331.
18. Howard Coates, "Aboriginal Flood Legend," *Creation* 4:3 (October 1981), p. 9–12.
19. Richard Erdoes and Alfonso Ortiz, *American Indian Myths and Legends* (New York, NY: Pantheon Books, 1984), p. 488–489.

conquer heaven as well. So they built a tower to reach the skies. The gods and demons of the heavens feared that the giants would take over, so they confounded the speech of the insurgents and scattered them across the world.[20]

The Choctaw of the southern United States also tell a story that echoes the Babel event in Scripture. The good spirit created many men. They were all Choctaw and understood one another, because they all spoke the Choctaw language. These first people were formed from yellow clay. One day, they wondered what the sky was like, so they decided to build a tower of rocks that would touch the heavens. Overnight, a strong wind blew and destroyed their efforts. They tried again, but their efforts were once again thwarted by a powerful wind. On the third attempt, the people slept next to the tower. The tower was blown over again and the rocks landed on the people but did not kill them. When the people pushed the rocks away, they were surprised to discover that they could no longer understand each other because they no longer spoke the same language.[21]

Speaking of Languages

One of the most unique testimonies pointing to the historicity of Genesis 1–11 and mankind's shared history prior to Babel is found in the earliest form of the Chinese language known as "oracle bone writing." Like modern Chinese, the oracle bone writing was logographic, meaning that, instead of an alphabet, it used symbols or radicals to represent words and syllables. These figures can be combined to convey a different or more developed idea.

Researchers discovered that many of the radicals reveal that the earliest Chinese people clearly knew of the events found in Genesis 1–11. Consider the following words and their component symbols:

- "Garden" is made up of the symbols for dust, breath, two persons, and enclosure.[22]
- "Flood" is composed of the figures for eight, united, earth, and water.[23]
- "Tower" consists of the radicals for mankind, one, mouth or language, grass, and clay.[24]

---

20. Frazer, *Folk-Lore*, p. 383.
21. Stith Thompson, *Tales of the North American Indians* (Mineola, NY: Dover Publications, Inc., 1929), p, 263.
22. C.H. Kang and Ethel R. Nelson, *The Discovery of Genesis: How the Truths of Genesis Were Found Hidden in the Chinese Language* (St. Louis, MO: Concordia Publishing House, 1979), p. 54.
23. Ibid., p. 98.
24. Ibid., p. 106. Kang and Nelson speculate that the reason for placing the symbol for grass or weeds at the top of the tower radical is to incorporate a reminder of the Curse to show the futility of building such a tower.

These are just a handful of the ancient symbols found among the oracle bone writings that show these people had a good understanding of the events described in Genesis 1–11. What else but a shared history could account for the striking similarities between the biblical accounts in these chapters and the early Chinese people who developed these symbols?

Objections

Those who wish to dismiss Genesis 1–11 as accurate historical accounts must be able to adequately explain the data compiled by anthropologists. Why do so many cultures separated for millennia by oceans, mountains, or deserts tell such similar stories about the ancient past? Why do their histories diverge after the Babel event? Three main explanations have arisen, yet none of these satisfactorily deal with all of the data.

Coincidence

To address the preponderance of similar-sounding primeval legends from around the globe, some people have suggested that the myths developed independently based on similar, but not shared, experiences. This proposal is not surprising when it comes to a culture's story of a devastating flood in the distant past. After all, people throughout history have endured local flooding that left indelible marks on their lives, causing the tradition to be retold over generations.

Specific floods have been attributed as the source of particular myths. Consider the following hypotheses about the origin of various flood stories (dates provided according to the secular timescale):

- Tales from North America were spawned by flooding at the end of the last ice age (13,000 B.C.).[25]
- Flood stories from parts of the Middle East and Europe were drawn from the controversial Black Sea Flood (7400 B.C.).[26]
- The flooding of ancient Sumeria was due to the Tigris and Euphrates Rivers overflowing their banks during heavy rains (2900 B.C.).[27]

---

25. David R. Montgomery, "Biblical-Type Floods Are Real, and They're Absolutely Enormous," *Discover* (July-August 2012), http://discovermagazine.com/2012/jul-aug/06-biblical-type-floods-real-absolutely-enormous.
26. Bruce Dorminey, " 'Noah's Flood' Not Rooted in Reality, After All?" *National Geographic News*, February 6, 2009), http://news.nationalgeographic.com/news/2009/02/090206-smaller-noah-flood.html.
27. Barry L. Bandstra, *Reading the Old Testament: Introduction to the Hebrew Bible*, 4th ed. (Belmont, CA: Wadsworth, 2009), p. 62.

Many more examples of a regional or local flood being cited as the inspiration for a culture's flood legend could be given.

At first glance, the critic may seem to have a point. Local flooding is fairly common and these natural disasters often become deeply ingrained in a town's history that is remembered and passed down for generations. So it is indeed possible that some of the flood legends that are perpetuated are merely retellings of a local event. However, this objection cannot account for the remarkable similarities found in traditions from every corner of the world. Why are they so often connected with giants? Why do these legends frequently speak of a favored family instructed by a god to build a boat to survive the coming flood, and why do they regularly mention certain birds being sent to check on the post-flood conditions?

Missionaries

Christian missionaries have been sent to people groups in every country of the world in an attempt to reach them with the gospel message. In fact, missionaries are often the people who first learn of a culture's flood legend since they are usually the first outsiders to learn the group's language. This fact has led to the charge that many of the flood myths are really just a consequence of missionary activity — that these ministers teach the people about the Genesis Flood, and then the story becomes altered as it is retold through the years.

At least two major problems can be raised against this objection. First, the vast differences that exist between the legends make this claim implausible. Why would a tribe drastically change the name of the ark's builder in a generation or two? For example, why would Noah's name become Qat (New Hebrides), Marerewana (Guyana), Uassu (Brazil), or Gajara (Australia) if missionaries had recently taught the people the Genesis account? Incidentally, these radical name changes make sense in light of the Babel event.

The greater problem with the belief that missionaries are responsible for the abundance of Flood stories has to do with the purpose of mission work. Why do men and women spend years raising support, learning a foreign language, and sometimes risking their lives? Do they endure these hardships simply to teach an unreached people group a severely distorted version of the Genesis Flood? Of course not! They dedicate their lives to reaching these people with the gospel of Jesus Christ. Since that is the case, why do so many of these tribes with flood myths similar to the biblical account not know anything from Scripture following Genesis 11?

Borrowed

Critical Bible scholars often assume that Genesis was not completed until the time of the Babylonian captivity, so many have suggested that the Bible's Flood account was inspired or borrowed from the Babylonian *Epic of Gilgamesh*, which includes a flood story that is essentially a retelling of the older Sumerian and Akkadian tales.

Perhaps the biggest problem with this objection is that Genesis was written long before the Israelites were exiled to Babylon. The documentary hypothesis assumed by the critics is fraught with problems and rose to prominence at a time when critics claimed that Moses could not have written the Pentateuch because they believed writing had not yet been invented or that the Israelites were incapable of writing. Archaeologists have shown that writing existed long before the time of Moses, and the arguments for the documentary hypothesis have been soundly refuted.[28]

Another huge problem with this objection has to do with the differences between the accounts. The Flood account in Genesis is the only one that includes a vessel that would actually keep its inhabitants safe. The various rafts, canoes, and boats of the other legends could not protect their inhabitants. The cube-shaped ark in *Gilgamesh* would remain afloat, but it would rock so badly from side to side that the people and animals likely would not survive, and with its seven levels, getting proper lighting and ventilation to the lower floors would be a major difficulty. On the other hand, the dimensions of Noah's ark are an ideal blend for size, strength, and stability during the global catastrophe.[29]

The biblical account is unique in another way. Nearly every other flood legend localizes the event in some way. In other words, while they often speak of a mountain-covering flood, the tales use landmarks, plants, or animals common to the areas from which the legends have been handed down. The biblical account does not do this, as it has the ark landing hundreds of miles from Israel in the region of Ararat (in modern-day eastern Turkey).

---

28. For a rebuttal of the documentary hypothesis, also known as JEPD, see Gleason Archer, *A Survey of Old Testament Introduction* rev. ed. (Chicago: Moody Press, 1974), p. 94–169. Also see Steve Ham, "Is Genesis a Derivation of Ancient Myths?" p. 59–68; and Terry Mortenson and Bodie Hodge, "Did Moses Write Genesis?" in Ken Ham and Bodie Hodge, *How Do We Know the Bible Is True, Volume 1* (Green Forest, AR: Master Books, 2011), p. 85–102.
29. See the DVD *Noah's Ark: Thinking Outside the Box* (available from Answers in Genesis) which is based primarily on research by Tim Lovett, an Australian engineer. His research is posted at http://worldwideflood.com/. A full-size, very authentic replica of the Ark (the largest timber frame structure presently in the world) is open to the public in northern Kentucky (see https://arkencounter.com/).

Finally, the Bible does not dwell on bizarre details as so frequently seen in the various mythologies. For example, even if the first four verses of Genesis 6 should be understood as a reference to fallen angels mating with women leading to giant progeny, Scripture simply mentions the idea, but it does not dwell on it. Compare this straightforward manner of reporting to the elaborate and embellished stories from Greek mythology or the *Epic of Gilgamesh* that expound upon and glorify the depravity of their gods and heroes.

Conclusion

The fact that so many cultures from around the globe have echoes of Genesis 1–11 in their mythologies provides unique evidence for the historicity of these chapters. This conclusion is supported by the fact that these same cultures know little or nothing of the biblical people and events following Genesis 11.

These details give credence to the biblical explanation that humanity shared a common history prior to the Babel event. When the Lord confused their languages and scattered the people, they passed down earth's early history on to their descendants, but as time went on the accounts became embellished by storytellers' imagination or faulty memories, and twisted by human idolatry and likely also demonic influence (1 Cor. 10:20). The vestiges they contain of the original account point back to the true history of our world, which is faithfully recorded without error in Genesis 1–11.

Chapter 16

Adam, Morality, the Gospel, and the Authority of Scripture

by Dr. Terry Mortenson

Introduction

In the preceding chapters several important propositions have been thoroughly established.

1. Genesis 1–11 clearly teaches, and the rest of the Bible confirms, that God supernaturally created Adam from dust and Eve from his rib (not from any pre-existing living creature) on the sixth literal 24-hour day of history a little over 6,000 years ago.
2. All humans are uniquely made in the image of God and all humans who have ever lived are descended from Adam and Eve, regardless of their language, skin color, eye shape, etc. There is only one race — Adam's race.
3. Until the 20th century, this was the universal belief of Bible-believing Christians about Adam (except for some in the late 19th century who after denying any chronological value to the genealogies of Genesis 5 and 11 pushed back the date of Adam's creation several tens of thousands of years).
4. The fossil evidence does not support the idea of human evolution, but rather confirms Genesis. Controlled by a naturalistic (i.e., atheistic) worldview, the evolutionists have misinterpreted the evidence. The public has been deceived by imaginative art and relentless dogmatic claims that do not survive careful scrutiny.

5. Contrary to evolutionists' claims, the study of genetics also does not prove that man evolved from some ape-like creature over millions of years. Rather genetics confirms the Genesis account of the unique, supernatural, and recent origin of Adam and Eve.
6. That man is categorically different from apes is seen in his anatomy, in his bearing the image of God, and in the evidence that man was highly intelligent right from the start, as witnessed in the archeological evidence that has survived from the past.
7. People groups all over the world share a memory of the key events (and even many of the details) of Genesis 1–11, although their memory and the literature they produced about these events have been distorted by sin, idolatry, and almost certainly demonic deception.

But is it simply an interesting curiosity to know that the Bible and solid scientific evidence agree on this question of human origins? Does it really matter what we believe about Adam? Yes it does! There are enormous moral and spiritual implications of these truths. We have already seen some of the implications in Bergman's chapter on racism. Euthanasia, genocide, totalitarian murder of millions, abortion, eugenics and forced sterilization all have been the fruit of evolutionary thinking in the past 150 years. Several other chapters highlighted the theological and gospel importance of Adam. But there is more that we need to consider here.

America is reeling in the face of a massive, breath-taking, LGBT sexual revolution. This movement of "erotic liberty," as Mohler has described it in *We Cannot Be Silent*,[1] is threatening to annihilate not only American religious liberty as guaranteed in the first amendment of the U.S. Constitution, but even threatening the existence of the American democratic republic as the Obama administration unlawfully makes policies to attempt to force the country into submission to the LGBT demands. This sexual revolution is also impacting the Church as professing evangelicals celebrate their sexual immorality and seek to influence other Christians to do the same.[2]

How did we get to the place where large corporations and the federal government are bullying schools and states into making bathrooms and locker rooms dangerous places for women and children? How did we get

1. R. Albert Mohler Jr., *We Cannot Be Silent: Speaking Truth to a Culture Redefining Sex, Marriage, & the Very Meaning of Right and Wrong* (Nashville, TN: Thomas Nelson, 2015).
2. One of many examples is a conference in January 2015, when about 1,500 people met in Portland, Oregon, for the annual gathering of "LGBTQ Christians" organized by the Gay Christian Network. See Terry Mortenson, "Gay Christians: Now Becoming the Norm?" https://answersingenesis.org/family/homosexuality/gay-christians-now-becoming-the-norm/, January 30, 2015.

to the place where professing evangelicals are celebrating this sexual perversion? How did we get to the place where professing evangelicals are denying a literal Adam and a literal Fall? How did we get to the place where, according to many surveys, evangelical churches are losing 60–80% of their young people when they graduate from high school?[3] Why is America on the verge of national suicide? Why is Western Europe, once so powerfully impacted by the gospel and a missionary-sending continent, now the most difficult mission field in the world? Why don't 60% of British teens believe in the existence of God?[4] Why do less than 2% of Britons go to church regularly today[5] when in the middle of the 19th century almost 50% went to church regularly?[6] Why is America heading down the same path?

The Collapse of Morality

As Mohler has insightfully explained, the decision by the U.S. Supreme Court on June 26, 2015, to redefine marriage did not come out of nowhere. It was the fruit of decades of moral erosion related to sex and marriage. He examines four significant developments. First, there was the arrival of modern contraceptives, which led to the separation of sex from procreation. Second came no-fault divorce, which made every marriage provisional. Third was advanced reproductive technologies, which enabled people to have babies without sex. And finally, there was the societal acceptance of co-habitation and sex outside of marriage. All of this undermined or contradicted the Bible's teaching on sex and marriage.

The transgender and homosexual "marriage" revolution was also preceded by the legalization of abortion (1973), the court removal of Bible reading (1963) and prayer (1962) from the public schools, the explosive heterosexual revolution, and the widespread use of illegal drugs in the 1960s and 70s, fueled by erotic, rebellion-stimulating and violence-promoting rock music.

But all this was preceded by the secular humanist takeover of the public schools that had been progressing since at least the 1920s. John Dewey was

3. See the results and analysis of a major national survey about this by the highly respected America's Research Group in Ken Ham and Britt Beamer, *Already Gone: Why Your Kids Will Quit Church and What You Can Do to Stop It* (Green Forest, AR: Master Books, 2009).
4. *The Telegraph* (UK), "Two Thirds of Teenagers Don't Believe in God," http://www.telegraph.co.uk/news/newstopics/religion/5603096/Two-thirds-of-teenagers-dont-believe-in-God.html, June 22, 2009.
5. John Bingham, "No Growth for 30 Years — Church of England Predicts," *The Telegraph,* http://www.telegraph.co.uk/news/religion/12161845/No-growth-for-30-years-Church-of-England-predicts.html, February 17, 2016.
6. Peter Oborne, "The Return to Religion," http://www.telegraph.co.uk/news/religion/8970031/The-return-to-religion.html, January 1, 2012.

key in this takeover of American public schools and is called the "father of modern American education." He was an original signer of the first *Humanist Manifesto*, published in 1933.[7] The first two points of that document state,

> FIRST, religious humanists regard the universe as self-existing and not created.
>
> SECOND, humanism believes that man is a part of nature and that he has emerged as a result of a continuous process.

In other words, the secular humanist worldview (which they correctly label as "religious") is built on the foundation of atheistic evolution. This leads logically and irresistibly to the fifth point of the *Manifesto*:

> FIFTH, humanism asserts that the nature of the universe depicted by modern science makes unacceptable any supernatural or cosmic guarantees of human values. . . . Religion must formulate its hopes and plans in the light of the scientific spirit and method.

As hundreds of millions of children in the public schools and universities have been indoctrinated in this atheistic worldview, it is no mystery that the country is descending into moral anarchy. Those children have grown up to become judges, politicians, professors and teachers, university administrators, media leaders, and heads of Hollywood. Every part of the culture has been touched, including the church.

The recently deceased evolutionist and atheist professor at Cornell University, William Provine, said it clearly,

> Let me summarize my views on what modern evolutionary biology tells us loud and clear — and these are basically Darwin's views. There are no gods, no purposes, no goal-directed forces of any kind. There is no life after death. When I die, I am absolutely certain that I am going to be dead. That's the end for me. There is no ultimate foundation for ethics, no ultimate meaning to life, and no free will for humans, either.[8]

Elsewhere he said,

> Of course, it is still possible to believe in both modern evolutionary biology and a purposive force, even the Judeo-Christian

7. https://en.wikipedia.org/wiki/Humanist_Manifesto_I.
8. William Provine, "Darwinism: Science or Naturalistic Philosophy?" *Origins Research*, vol. 16:1/2 (1994): 9.

> God. One can suppose that God started the whole universe or works through the laws of nature (or both). . . . [Such a God] has nothing to do with human morals, answers no prayers, gives no life everlasting, in fact does nothing whatever that is detectable. In other words, religion is compatible with modern evolutionary biology (and indeed all of modern science), if the religion is effectively indistinguishable from atheism.[9]

Evolution theory is atheistic and atheism provides no basis for any moral absolutes. That does not mean that all atheists are immoral in their behavior. It simply means that in an evolutionary worldview there are no moral absolutes. Morality becomes totally relative, a matter of personal opinion. There is no basis within the atheistic evolutionary worldview to judge any behavior as wrong or right.

If evolution is true, we are just animals. It's the law of the jungle, the survival of the fittest; everyone does what he thinks is right in his own eyes. Without Adam and Eve and the Fall, sin is a myth. Selfishness is just animal instinct. Stags and bulls will have sex with any female they like, when they like, and they are "polygamous." So what's wrong if humans do the same? Dogs kill birds and lions kill gazelles, and we don't call that sin. So if Hitler or Mao or Stalin or ISIS or abortionists murder and steal from millions, it's not wrong; it's just survival of the fittest. But that leads eventually either to anarchy or to totalitarian oppression and injustice. Either way whoever has the power determines what's right. Saying that God guided evolution cannot be defended from science or the Bible and only makes matters worse. But the evolutionary assault on biblical morality is the least of the problems.

The Assault on the Gospel

Evolution theory not only destroys biblical morality that once dominated Western culture, but as many authors in this volume have shown, it also destroys the gospel by destroying the historical reason that we need the Savior: Adam sinned and all his descendants are sinners in need of salvation from and reconciliation to their Creator. Evolutionists have been telling the world for over a century that evolution is antithetical to the gospel, and they see the issue more clearly than most Christians in the world.

Probably no one was more responsible for the victory of Darwinism in British science and the acceptance of evolution in British churches in the

9. William Provine, review of *Trial and Error: The American Controversy over Creation and Evolution* by Edward J. Larson, *Academe* (January/February 1987): 51–52.

late 19th century than Darwin's good friend and leading biologist, Thomas Huxley. In 1893, Huxley wrote,

> I am fairly at a loss to comprehend how any one, for a moment, can doubt that Christian theology must stand or fall with the historical trustworthiness of the Jewish Scriptures. The very conception of the Messiah, or Christ, is inextricably interwoven with Jewish history; the identification of Jesus of Nazareth with that Messiah rests upon the interpretation of the passages of the Hebrew Scriptures, which have no evidential value unless they possess the historical character assigned to them. If the covenant with Abraham was not made; if circumcision and sacrifices were not ordained by Jahveh; if the "ten words" [i.e., 10 Commandments] were not written by God's hand on the stone tables; if Abraham is more or less a mythical hero, such as Theseus; the Story of the Deluge a fiction; that of the Fall a legend; and that of the Creation the dream of a seer; if all these definite and detailed narratives of apparently real events have no more value as history than have the stories of the regal period of Rome — what is to be said about the Messianic doctrine, which is so much less clearly enunciated. And what about the authority of the writers of the books of the New Testament, who, on this theory, have not merely accepted flimsy fictions for solid truths, but have built the very foundations of Christian dogma upon legendary quicksands?[10]

In a 1909 lecture in Los Angeles entitled "Breakdown of Protestantism," Edward Adams Cantrell (later part of the pro-evolution "Science League of America" formed in 1925 and associated in later years with the American Civil Liberties Union [ACLU]) said, "All this is fundamental, for on the genetic story is based the entire Christian system. Without Adam's fall there is no need of Christ or the vicarious atonement. With the removal of the foundation the superstructure falls."[11]

In 1978, the atheist Richard Bozarth declared boldly in *American Atheist* magazine,

> Christianity is — must be! — totally committed to the special creation as described in Genesis, and Christianity must fight

10. Thomas H. Huxley, *Science and Hebrew Tradition* (New York: D. Appleton, 1893), p. 207–8.
11. Reported in Anon., "Modern Science and Theology Compared," *Los Angeles Herald* 36:137 (15 February 1909), p. 5, http://cdnc.ucr.edu/cgi-bin/cdnc?a=d&d=LAH19090215.2.83.

with its full might, fair or foul, against the theory of evolution. . . . It becomes clear now that the whole justification of Jesus' life and death is predicated on the existence of Adam and the forbidden fruit he and Eve ate. Without the original sin, who needs to be redeemed? Without Adam's fall into a life of constant sin terminated by death, what purpose is there to Christianity? None.[12]

In 1996, in a debate with evangelical philosopher William Lane Craig (who is somewhere between a theistic evolutionist and progressive creationist[13]), Frank Zindler, then president of the American Atheists, remarked,

> The most devastating thing though that biology did to Christianity was the discovery of biological evolution. Now that we know that Adam and Eve never were real people the central myth of Christianity is destroyed. If there never was an Adam and Eve, there never was an original sin. . . . If there was never an original sin, there is no need of salvation. If there is no need of salvation, there is no need of a savior. And I submit that puts Jesus, historical or otherwise, into the ranks of the unemployed. I think that evolution is absolutely the death knell of Christianity.[14]

In 2006, Richard Dawkins, the world's most famous and widely read atheist, told the world,

> Oh, but of course, the story of Adam and Eve was only ever symbolic, wasn't it? Symbolic? Jesus had himself tortured and executed for a symbolic sin by a non-existent individual? Nobody not brought up in the faith could reach any verdict other than — barking mad![15]

In a 2011 posting on the American Atheist website just before Christmas we read,

> No Adam and Eve means no need for a savior. It also means that the Bible cannot be trusted as a source of unambiguous, literal truth. It is completely unreliable, because it all begins with a myth,

12. G. Richard Bozarth, "The Meaning of Evolution," *American Atheist* 20:2 (Feb. 1978): 19.
13. See this one-minute segment from Craig's 2009 debate at the University of Waterloo with atheist philosophy professor Dr. Christopher DiCarlo: https://www.youtube.com/watch?v=cSc92EDm5gU, accessed May 20, 2016.
14. Frank Zindler, in a debate at Willow Creek Community Church with Dr. William Lane Craig, *Atheism vs Christianity* (video), Zondervan, 1996.
15. Richard Dawkins, "The Root of All Evil?" Channel 4 TV (UK), broadcast January 16, 2006.

> and builds on that as a basis. No fall of man means no need for atonement and no need for a redeemer.[16]

In contrast to the atheist evolutionists, theistic evolutionists (aka evolutionary creationists) are trying (often successfully) to convince Christians (especially church leaders and seminary professors) that Christianity is not affected if Adam was not historical or if some of the details in Genesis 1–3 are not literally accurate. But as the previous chapters in this book show, in this belief theistic evolutionists are deceived and unknowingly or knowingly deceiving others.

The most influential group promoting theistic evolution today is BioLogos. Recently, BioLogos has posted on its website quotes by influential Christian leaders and Bible scholars obviously intended to persuade Christians to be open to theistic evolution. A number of examples are worth considering. Billy Graham has written,

> The Bible is not a book of science.[17] The Bible is a book of Redemption,[18] and of course I accept the Creation story. I believe that God did create the universe. I believe that God created man, and whether it came by an evolutionary process and at a certain point He took this person or being and made him a living soul or not, does not change the fact that God did create man. . . . Whichever way God did it makes no difference as to what man is and man's relationship to God.[19]

---

16. American Atheists, "You KNOW it's a Myth: This Season, Celebrate REASON!" https://atheists.org/atheism/Christmas, no date, accessed June 1, 2011.
17. No creationist says it is. What we say is that it is a book of history (it's more than history but not less, and its history is foundational to the theology, morality, and gospel that it teaches) and the history recorded in Genesis 1–11 is very relevant to a scientific understanding of the origin and history of the creation.
18. This is a subtle false dichotomy (i.e., not this, but that). The Bible is a book about redemption *and* science-related issues (i.e., both this and that) and much more. As article XII in the International Council on Biblical Inerrancy "Chicago Statement on Biblical Inerrancy" (1978) says, "We deny that biblical infallibility and inerrancy are limited to spiritual, religious, or redemptive themes, exclusive of assertions in the fields of history and science. We further deny that scientific hypotheses about earth history may properly be used to overturn the teaching of Scripture on creation and the flood." Sadly, as I explain in the DVD lecture "Inerrancy and the Undermining of Biblical Authority" (available from Answers in Genesis), the ICBI's statement on inerrancy and its 1982 statement on hermeneutics contain a tiny amount of ambiguous language that opened the door for a large percentage of inerrantists to affirm that doctrine while at the same time overturning and denying what Scripture teaches about creation and the Flood.
19. Billy Graham, quote posted on BioLogos home page, accessed February 21, 2016.

Noted evangelical theologian J.I. Packer says, "BioLogos is leading the way in setting the tone for thoughtful and productive dialogue on the topic of harmony between science and faith. They are providing the much-needed space for wrestling with the tough questions of life with civility, integrity, and rigor."[20] Prominent pastor Tim Keller endorsed BioLogos with these words,

> Many people today, both secular and Christian, want us to believe that science and religion cannot live together. Not only is this untrue, but we believe that a thoughtful dialogue between science and faith is essential for engaging the hearts and minds of individuals today. The BioLogos Foundation provides an important first step towards that end.[21]

Renowned New Testament scholar N.T. Wright accuses,

> Christians and secularists alike are in danger of treating "Darwin vs the Bible" as just another battlefront in the polarized "culture wars." This grossly misrepresents both science and faith. BioLogos not only shows that there is an alternative, but actually models it. God's world and God's word go together in a rich, living harmony.[22]

And the late, justly respected pastor John Stott asks,

> What may we say about the "how" of God's creative activity? Not many Christians today find it necessary to defend the concept of a literal six-day creation, for the text does not demand it, and scientific discovery appears to contradict it. The biblical text presents itself not as a scientific treatise but as a highly stylized literary statement (deliberately framed in three pairs, the fourth "day" corresponding to the first, the fifth to the second, and the sixth to the third). Moreover, the geological evidence for a gradual development over thousands of millions of years seems conclusive. . . . It is most unfortunate that some who debate this issue (evolution) begin by assuming that the words "creation" and "evolution" are mutually exclusive.[23]

---

20. J.I Packer, quote posted on BioLogos home page, accessed February 21, 2016.
21. Tim Keller (pastor of Redeemer Presbyterian Church in New York City and author of *The Reason for God*), quote posted on BioLogos home page, accessed February 21, 2016.
22. N.T. Wright (New Testament scholar and former Anglican Bishop of Durham), quote posted on BioLogos home page, accessed February 21, 2016.
23. John Stott (former pastor of All Souls Church, Langham Place, London), quote posted on BioLogos home page, accessed February 21, 2016.

Elsewhere Stott said,

> It seems perfectly possible to reconcile the historicity of Adam with at least some (theistic) evolutionary theory. Many biblical Christians in fact do so, believing them to be not entirely incompatible. To assert the historicity of an original pair who sinned through disobedience is one thing; it is quite another to deny all evolution and assert the separate and special creation of everything, including both subhuman creatures and Adam's body. The suggestion (for it is no more than this) does not seem to me to be against Scripture and therefore impossible that when God made man in His own image, what He did was to stamp His own likeness on one of the many "hominids," which appear to have been living at the time.[24]

"Speaking hesitatingly as a non-scientist,"[25] Stott goes on to indicate that he leans toward the idea of pre-Adamite hominids who were anatomically indistinguishable from modern man but who did not bear the image of God. Stott obviously did not know the science presented in various chapters in this book. But even when he was alive there was much young-earth creationist biblical and scientific literature available to him, which he gave no evidence of having read. He also failed to pay careful attention to the text of Genesis.

But notice the ambiguous and misleading language in the statements by these influential evangelical leaders. The issue is not whether "science and religion" or "science and faith" or "creation and evolution" can live together. The issue is whether the carefully exegeted truth of Genesis can be wedded to the dogmas of evolution and millions of years.

Theistic evolution is serious error, and BioLogos's promotion of it in the Church leads to what I think appropriately can be called heresy, as illustrated in a 12-minute BioLogos video[26] featuring Reformed pastor Leonard J. Vander Zee, or as revealed in a 2-part BioLogos web article by a Nazarene philosophy professor who wrote,

> Substitutionary atonement sees original sin as a major reason for Christ's death. But macroevolution calls the Fall and the doctrine

24. John Stott, quoted in Colin Chapman, *The Case for Christianity* (Grand Rapids, MI: Eerdmans, 1981), p. 130.
25. Ibid.
26. https://www.youtube.com/watch?v=ZqgnJ1GR8ms&feature=youtu.be, accessed May 16, 2016.

> of original sin into question. Thus, evolution poses a significant challenge to substitutionary atonement. These critiques levied against the substitution view are not intended to be the final word on the atonement. They merely represent the major reasons for my own transition away from substitutionary atonement. In what follows, I intend to sketch an alternative view of the cross; one that preserves God's goodness and God's justice. A view that identifies the crucifixion of Jesus as sinful, and thus, in opposition to the will of God. A theory more compatible with the best evolutionary science.[27]

In his second article on this subject, Bankard tells us, "How does the view I've sketched differ from substitutionary atonement? First, the incarnation is not primarily about the cross. God does not send Jesus to die. God does not require Jesus' death in order to forgive humanity's sin."[28] Theistic evolution is indeed ultimately an assault on the gospel of Jesus Christ.

And its influence is growing in the Church, especially in evangelical seminaries. With surprised excitement, Bruce Waltke reported from his 2009 survey of evangelical seminary professors (published on the BioLogos website) that 46% of the professors do not have any real objections to theistic evolution.[29] This surely encouraged him to claim in an extremely controversial 3-minute video posted in 2010 on the BioLogos website (entitled "Why Must the Church Come to Accept Evolution"), among many other seriously erroneous statements, that, "I think that if the data is overwhelming in favor of evolution [and he does think so], to deny that reality will make us a cult."[30] But the truth is exactly the opposite.

---

27. Joseph Bankard, "Substitutionary Atonement and Evolution, Part 1," http://biologos.org//blog/substitutionary-atonement-and-evolution-part-1, June 9, 2015.
28. Joseph Bankard, "Substitutionary Atonement and Evolution, Part 2," http://biologos.org/blog/substitutionary-atonement-and-evolution-part-2, June 10, 2015.
29. Bruce Waltke, "Barriers to Accepting the Possibility of Creation by Means of an Evolutionary Process," https://biologos.org/uploads/projects/Waltke_scholarly_essay.pdf.
30. I have the whole video on file. Posted on March 24, 2010, it was withdrawn at Waltke's request nine days later on April 2, 2010, even though he still believes what he said. But it was on the website again some time before April 12, 2016: http://biologos.org/resources/videos/bruce-waltke-why-must-the-church-accept-evolution. His statement about this is here: http://biologos.org/blogs/archive/why-must-the-church-come-to-accept-evolution-an-update. Shortly after removing it on April 2, 2010, he resigned from Reformed Theological Seminary, Orlando, because of the controversy generated by this statement. RTS accepted his resignation on or just before April 6, 2010 (http://www.rts.edu/seminary/newsevents/NewsDetails.aspx?id=1370). He was hired by Knox Theological Seminary on April 30, 2010, even though the recently deceased founder of Knox, Dr. D. James Kennedy, was strongly and publicly opposed to evolution.

We should also note that BioLogos has received over $8.7 million from the John Templeton Foundation (JTF)[31] to promote theistic evolution in the Church through the web, speakers at conferences and in churches, and by developing resources for pastors, educators, small groups, and children. They are also at the annual and some regional meetings of the Evangelical Theological Society each year, attempting to influence seminaries, apparently with increasing success.[32]

The JTF is also giving grants directly to seminaries (including Trinity Evangelical Divinity School[33]) to explore the relationship of "science" to faith/religion/theology. The American Association for the Advancement of Science will provide the resources for the seminaries (including "scientist-advisers from nearby science research institutions"[34]). This is in addition to the AAAS's own "Science for Seminaries" program to infect seminaries,[35] including Concordia (Missouri Synod Lutheran) Seminary.[36] There can be no doubt that these scientists will be influencing these seminaries to accept evolution and millions of years as "science" or "scientific fact."

But the AAAS is committed to an atheistic worldview (as will be seen below), and JTF is committed to religious pluralism and opposed to the absolute truth of the Bible, as it follows the views of its founder, Sir John Marks Templeton, who was a very theologically liberal Presbyterian. Templeton rejected the Bible as inerrant divine revelation and sought to "finance humility" and promote "innovative and creative" ideas about religion and spirituality. To do so he gave his Templeton Prize to Christians (e.g., Billy Graham, Chuck Colson, and Bill Bright), as well as Jews, Muslims, Hindus, Buddhists, and unbelievers.[37]

---

31. This is from three grants: https://www.templeton.org/what-we-fund/grants/the-language-of-god-biologos-website-and-workshop ($2,028,238), https://www.templeton.org/what-we-fund/grants/celebrating-the-harmony-between-mainstream-science-and-the-christian-faith ($1,929,863), https://www.templeton.org/what-we-fund/grants/evolution-and-christian-faith ($4,777,022)
32. http://biologos.org/blogs/brad-kramer-the-evolving-evangelical/5-common-objections-to-evolutionary-creationism.
33. Anon, "Trinity Awarded $3.4 Million Templeton Grant," http://news.tiu.edu/2015/06/26/trinity-awarded-3-4-million-templeton-grant/, June 26, 2015.
34. Sarah Pulliam Bailey, "10 American Seminaries to Receive $1.5 Million in Grants to Include Science in Curricula," http://www.huffingtonpost.com/2014/10/12/seminaries-science-grant_n_5955030.html, October 12, 2014.
35. http://www.aaas.org/page/science-seminaries.
36. Editor, "Concordia Seminary Receives 'Science for Seminaries' Grant," http://concordiatheology.org/2014/10/concordia-seminary-receives-science-for-seminaries-grant/, October 29, 2014; http://www.aaas.org/page/science-seminaries.
37. For an understanding of Templeton's beliefs and mission, see "Life Story," John Templeton Foundation, http://www.templeton.org/sir-john-templeton/life-story. It has heavily funded evolutionists and evolutionist organizations: https://en.wikipedia.org/wiki/John_Templeton_Foundation.

Theistic evolution is a Trojan Horse that is bringing all kinds of ideas into the Church that are subverting the gospel and the authority and perspicuity of the Word of God. BioLogos is the leading group that is bringing that Trojan Horse into the Church, and its influence will grow significantly as InterVarsity Press has just announced a publishing partnership with BioLogos to help "the church and the world to see the harmony between science and biblical faith while presenting an evolutionary understanding of God's creation," with the first volume appearing in June 2016.[38]

Rooker and Keathley see things clearly regarding Adam and Eve, when they write,

> We believe the historicity of Adam and Eve is so important that the matter should serve as a litmus test when evaluating the attempts to integrate a proper understanding of Genesis 1–3 with the latest findings of science. It must be realized that any position which denies that a real fall was experienced by a real couple will have adverse effects on other significant biblical doctrines.[39]

Unfortunately, Rooker and Keathley, like most evangelical seminary professors, don't seem to realize that we are not dealing with the "findings of science" in trying to understand Genesis 1–3 (or Genesis 4–11). We are dealing with philosophically driven anti-biblical interpretations masquerading as "scientific findings." Previous chapters in this book have demonstrated this in regard to the teaching about Adam in Genesis 1–3. The same thing is happening in relation to the rest of Genesis 1–11, as I will show presently.

The Foundational Issue of the Age of the Earth

Again, I ask, how did we get to the place where a growing number of evangelical Christians, especially professors in our seminaries, are embracing evolution and doubting or even denying the existence of a literal, historical Adam and Fall, or at least denying some of the details about his and Eve's creation and Fall in Genesis 2–3?

To answer that question we need to understand that evolution is really a three-part theory to explain all of reality (Figure 1). Cosmological evolution is the story of how nothing exploded into something about 13.8 billion years ago and eventually produced all the stars, galaxies, planets, and solar systems in the universe. Geological evolution picks up the story about 4.5

38. "InterVarsity Press Announces New Series Bridging Science and Faith," http://rushtopress.org/pr16051602.html, May 16, 2016.

39. Kenneth D. Keathley and Mark F. Rooker, *40 Questions about Creation and Evolution* (Grand Rapids, MI: Kregel, 2014), p. 237.

billion years ago as the solar gas cloud condensed to form rings which evolved into the planets, including the earth, and then over those billion years it eventually became the inhabitable planet we have today covered with thousands of feet of fossil-bearing rock layers. Biological evolution is the story that about 3.5 billion years ago non-living matter suddenly formed the first living, single-celled creature which eventually by natural selection and mutations produced all the different kinds of plants and animals and man (the highest animal to-date, according to evolutionists).

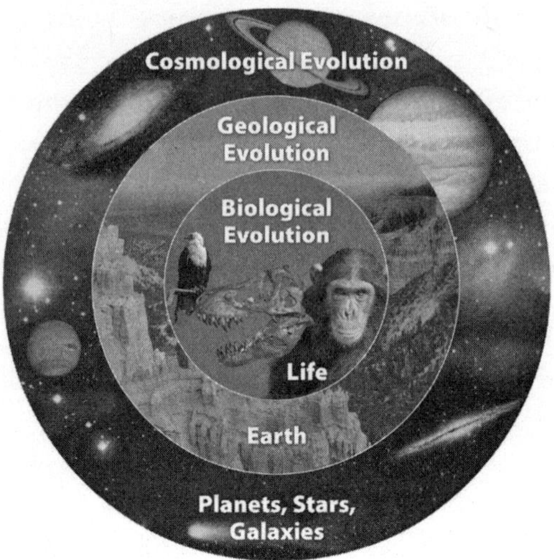

Figure 1

This evolutionary story of the origin and history of the cosmos and all it contains is based on two naturalistic (i.e., atheistic) assumptions controlling all of science today in virtually every country:

1. Nature is all there is.
2. The origin of everything can be explained by three things: *time* and *chance* and the *laws of nature* working on matter.

In other words, there is no God who started or guides the process. Given enough time (billions of years), chance, and the laws of nature, you can explain the origin of stars, galaxies, planets, earth, plants, animals, man, language, even religion, we are told. These are the assumptions of philosophical naturalism, or, the religion of atheism. While modern science is controlled by atheism, not all scientists are atheists (though most leading ones are).[40] But most scientists do their scientific work *as if* atheism is true, and this is especially true in the historical (or origin) sciences of cosmology, geology, paleontology, evolutionary biology, anthropology, and archeology.

Theistic evolutionists are three-thirds evolutionists when they do their science (though in their religious life they believe in God, and some even

40. A survey of the members of the highly influential National Academy of Sciences (in America) revealed that 72% are atheists, 21% are agnostics, and 7% are theists. See E.J. Larson and L. Witham, "Leading Scientists Still Reject God," *Nature* 394:6691 (July 23, 1998): 313.

believe in Jesus Christ for salvation). They accept cosmological evolution, geological evolution, and biological evolution (including human evolution), with God undetectably guiding the whole process in a way that leads most scientists to think it is all the result of blind, purposeless, directionless, physical and chemical processes.

Old-earth creationists of different flavors (gap theory, day-age, framework hypothesis, etc.) are two-thirds evolutionist, for they accept the billions of years of cosmological and geological evolution, but reject biological evolution (including human evolution), believing that God supernaturally created the first representatives of the different kinds of plants and animals and man.

Young-earth creationists are zero-thirds evolutionists, because they believe Genesis teaches the literal truth about the origin and early history of the creation (including the cosmos-impacting Fall; the global, catastrophic, yearlong, world-transforming Flood of Noah; and the Tower of Babel event). They do believe that natural selection and mutations are demonstrable scientific facts but that there is no scientific evidence that these processes can change one kind of creature into a different kind, no matter how much time is invoked.[41] These natural processes are consistent with the truth of Genesis 1–3 but are actually contrary to the idea of microbe-to-man evolution.

Having spoken on the subject of creation and evolution in schools, universities, seminaries, and churches in 25 countries and having read much Christian literature on the subject, I can confidently say that most Christians, including most Christian theologians and apologists today, are 2/3 or 3/3 evolutionists. But prior to the early 19th century virtually the whole Church was young-earth creationist, as documented elsewhere.[42]

---

41. See Georgia Purdom (PhD geneticist), "Is Natural Selection the Same as Evolution?" https://answersingenesis.org/natural-selection/is-natural-selection-the-same-thing-as-evolution/; John Sanford (PhD plant geneticist), *Genetic Entropy* (FMS Publications, 2014), which shows that mutations are in fact fatal to evolution; and Terry Mortenson, *Origin of Species: Was Darwin Right?* DVD.
42. Chapters 1–2 in Mortenson and Ury, *Coming to Grips with Genesis* (2008), and Terry Mortenson, *The Great Turning Point: the Church's Catastrophic Mistake on Geology — Before Darwin* (Green Forest, AR: Master Books, 2004), p. 40–47. On pre-1800 Eastern Orthodox views see Terry Mortenson, "Orthodoxy and Genesis: What the Fathers *Really* Taught," https://answersingenesis.org/reviews/books/orthodoxy-and-genesis-what-the-fathers-really-taught/. Highly influential Augustine was a young-earth creationist though he was confused about the days of creation (thinking creation was in an instant, not six literal days) primarily because he didn't know Hebrew and had a faulty Latin translation. But he believed in a global Flood, in the great ages of the patriarchs in Genesis 5 and 11, and that Adam was created less than 6,000 years before Augustine's time. See Terry Mortenson and A. Peter Galling, "Augustine on the Days of Creation," https://answersingenesis.org/days-of-creation/augustine-on-the-days-of-creation/.

In the early 1800s, the idea of millions of years took hold of geology and by about 1850 most of the Church accepted the idea and embraced the gap theory or day-age view of Genesis 1 and the local flood view of Genesis 6–8 to try to accommodate the millions of years.[43]

For example, in an 1855 sermon, at the age of 21, Charles Spurgeon vaguely advocated the gap theory. He did so again with reference to geology in a sermon in 1876.[44] Charles Hodge favored the gap theory until about 1860 when he switched over to the day-age view, which he advocated in his *Systematic Theology* of 1871–1873.[45]

In 1910–1915 *The Fundamentals* were published. Edited by R.A. Torrey (the second president of Moody Bible Institute), this was a collection of 90 articles written by prominent conservative Baptists, Presbyterians, Anglicans, Congregationalists, and Methodists on both sides of the Atlantic. Six articles dealt with Genesis and science. Two rejected evolution as contrary to Scripture. Two opposed atheistic evolution and human evolution but did not clearly rule out theistic evolution. But three of the six clearly accepted millions of years and none of the six articles took a stand for young-earth creation.[46]

C.I. Scofield (who also contributed to *The Fundamentals*) published his widely used Study Bible in 1910. In the marginal note of Genesis 1:2 he simple asserted, "The first creative act refers to the dateless past, and gives scope for all the geologic ages."[47] That statement remained unchanged until the 1967 edition.

In the famous 1925 Scopes Evolution Trial, the ACLU lawyer, Clarence Darrow, made William Jennings Bryan look like an inconsistent fool for rejecting evolution (which Bryan said is contrary to Scripture), while he accommodated the millions of years (Bryan held to the day-age view). Many

43. My book *The Great Turning Point* and chapter 3 in *Coming to Grips with Genesis* explain how and why this happened.
44. C.H. Spurgeon, "Unconditional Election," *The New Park Street Pulpit*, Vol. 1 (sermons 41–42, delivered Sept. 2, 1855), p. 6–7, reveals his old-earth view, http://www.spurgeongems.org/vols1-3/chs41-42.pdf. He expressed this old-earth thinking in a couple of other sermons, e.g., C.H. Spurgeon, "Christ, the Destroyer of Death" (a sermon preached on Dec. 17, 1876), *Metropolitan Tabernacle Pulpit*, vol. 22 (1876), Sermon 1329, p. 698–699.
45. Charles Hodge, *Systematic Theology*, 3 vol. (Grand Rapids, MI: Eerdmans, 1997, original 1871–73), 1:571–574.
46. Terry Mortenson, "Exposing a Fundamental Compromise," https://answersingenesis.org/theistic-evolution/exposing-a-fundamental-compromise/, July 1, 2010.
47. That statement is all Scofield said about the gap: no argument in defense, just a bald assertion. It was finally removed in the 1967 edition, which nevertheless still promoted old-earth thinking with a note at v. 1 ("Scripture gives no data for determining how long ago the universe was created.") and at v. 2 two weak statements for the gap theory.

other very influential leaders and theologians likewise accepted millions of years, including B.B. Warfield and J. Gresham Machen.

But from my examination of most of their writings related to Genesis 1–11, none of these men carefully exegeted the biblical texts that were relevant to the question of the age of the creation. None of them recognized, much less explained, how millions of years of animal death, disease, and extinction could be reconciled with the Bible's teaching about the Fall. And none of them showed any evidence of understanding that the idea of millions of years did not come from the rocks and fossils but from anti-biblical assumptions used to interpret the geological evidence, which we need to consider next.

The Origin of Old-Earth Geology

James Hutton (1726–1797) is often called the "Father of Modern Geology." After studying medicine in university, he took over the family farms where he developed a love of geology. He later laid down the rule for interpreting the rocks: "The past history of our globe must be explained by what can be seen to be happening now. . . . No powers are to be employed that are not natural to the globe, no action to be admitted except those of which we know the principle."[48] In other words, only present, natural processes could be used to explain how and when the geological record was formed. But such a principle ruled out a supernatural creation and a supernaturally induced global Flood at the time of Noah before Hutton ever looked at a single rock. But this "rule" became the controlling dogma of geology.

Charles Lyell (1797–1875) built on Hutton's ideas to develop his uniformitarian *Principles of Geology* (1830–33), the subtitle of which reads "being an attempt to explain the former changes of the earth's surface, by reference to causes now in operation." Writing to his old-earth geology friend Roderick Murchison on January 15, 1829, Lyell said that in his *Principles* he would:

> endeavor to establish the principles of reasoning in the science [of geology] . . . which, as you know, are neither more nor less than that *no causes whatever* have from the earliest time to which we can look back, to the present, ever acted, but those *now acting*; and that they never acted with different degrees of energy from that which they now exert.[49]

---

48. Quoted in Arthur Holmes, *Principles of Physical Geology*, 2nd ed. (Edinburgh, Scotland: Thomas Nelson and Sons Ltd., 1965), p. 43–44.
49. Katharine M. Lyell, ed., *Life, Letters, and Journals of Sir Charles Lyell, Bart.*, Vol. 1 (London, England: John Murray, 1881), 1:234 (italics in the original).

In other words, modern processes at modern *rates* will explain the rock record. The geology of the earth is a result of slow, gradual, uniform processes of change. In a letter to fellow uniformitarian geologist, George Poulett Scrope (also a Member of Parliament) on June 14, 1830, Lyell said simply that he wanted to "free the science [of geology] from Moses."[50] In other words, in trying to reconstruct earth history, he wanted to silence God's eyewitness testimony about Creation Week and the Flood. Like Hutton, Lyell was insisting that geologists use a naturalistic, anti-biblical worldview to interpret the rocks. Three decades later, Darwin told the readers of his *Origin of Species*,

> He who can read Sir Charles Lyell's grand work on the *Principles of Geology*, which the future historian will recognize as having produced a revolution in natural science, yet does not admit how incomprehensibly vast have been the past periods of time, may at once close this volume.[51]

Darwin went further in an 1844 letter, admitting,

> I always feel as if my books came half out of Lyell's brains and that I never acknowledge this sufficiently, nor do I know how I can, without saying so in so many words — for I have always thought that the great merit of the *Principles* [*of Geology*], was that it altered the whole tone of one's mind & therefore that when seeing a thing never seen by Lyell, one yet saw it partially through his eyes.[52]

So, for Lyell and Darwin, slow, gradual erosion and sedimentation formed the rock layers over millions of years and slow gradual processes of reproduction and natural selection over the same long ages formed all the living creatures.

Lyell's uniformitarian dogma ruled geology until the 1970s when some evolutionary geologists began to return to the ideas of catastrophism that Hutton and Lyell had eradicated. One of the leaders in this reorientation in geology was the famous British geologist Derek Ager. In his last book on the geological record, *The New Catastrophism* (1993), Ager described the influence of Lyell this way:

---

50. Ibid., p. 268.
51. Charles Darwin, *The Origin of Species* (London: Penguin Books, 1985 reprint of 1859 first ed.), p. 293.
52. Charles Darwin, *The Correspondence of Charles Darwin*, Vol. 3 (Cambridge, England: Cambridge Univ. Press, 1987), p. 54.

> Just as politicians rewrite human history, so geologists rewrite earth history. For a century and a half the geological world has been dominated, one might even say brainwashed, by the gradualistic uniformitarianism of Charles Lyell. Any suggestion of "catastrophic" events has been rejected as old-fashioned, unscientific and even laughable.[53]

If the geologists were brainwashed by Lyell's uniformitarian, naturalistic principles for over 150 years (and still are very influenced by him), then so was the rest of the world, including evangelical theologians and Bible scholars who have told the Church that we must accept the millions of years and that the age of the creation doesn't matter.

Ager added, "Perhaps I am becoming a cynic in my old age, but I cannot help thinking that people find things that they expect to find. As Sir Edward Bailey (1953) said, 'to find a thing you have to believe it to be possible.' "[54] Ager died in 1993 as an unbeliever (judging from anti-biblical comments in his last book). He had come to believe that major catastrophes were possible and in fact he found abundant evidence that they were responsible for much of the geological record. But he never found the evidence that most of the rock layers and fossils were caused by *one* year long Flood at the time of Noah that produced complex and alternating conditions of relative calm and catastrophic violence. He did not find that evidence because he did not believe such a Flood was possible, having rejected the eyewitness testimony of the Creator in Genesis 6–8.

The late, atheist Harvard geologist, Stephen J. Gould, further informs us regarding Lyell,

> Charles Lyell was a lawyer by profession, and his book [*Principles of Geology*, 1830–1833] is one of the most brilliant briefs ever published by an advocate. . . . Lyell relied upon true bits of cunning to establish his uniformitarian views as the only true geology. First, he set up a straw man to demolish. . . . In fact, the catastrophists were much more empirically minded than Lyell. The geologic record does seem to require catastrophes: rocks are fractured and contorted; whole faunas are wiped out. To circumvent this literal appearance, Lyell imposed his imagination upon the evidence.[55]

---

53. Derek Ager, *The New Catastrophism* (Cambridge, England: Cambridge Univ. Press, 1993), p. xi.
54. Ibid., p. 190–91.
55. Stephen Jay Gould, "Catastrophes and Steady-State Earth," *Natural History* (Feb. 1975): 16.

But contrary to Gould's anti-biblical assessment, it was not the old-earth catastrophists of the early 19th century who were the really hard-nosed empiricists. It was the scriptural geologists that I studied in my PhD research who paid close attention to God's eyewitness testimony in Genesis as well as to the rocks and fossils, and who used His inerrant Word as the key to the correct interpretation of the geological evidence.[56]

Martin Rudwick is arguably the greatest historian of geology today and gives no evidence of being a Christian, as far as I am aware. But in referring to the 19th century he says,

> Traditionally, non-biblical sources, whether natural or historical, had received their true meaning by being fitted into the unitary narrative of the Bible. This relationship now began to be reversed: the biblical narrative, it was now claimed, received its true meaning by being fitted, on the authority of self-styled experts, into a framework of non-biblical knowledge. In this way the cognitive plausibility and religious meaning of the biblical narrative could only be maintained in a form that was constrained increasingly by non-biblical considerations. . . . At least in Europe, if not in America, those geologists who regarded themselves as Christians generally accepted the new biblical criticism and therefore felt the age of the earth to be irrelevant to their religious beliefs.[57]

So, the rocks do not speak for themselves. They must be interpreted. And what a person's worldview (or religious/philosophical) assumptions are will greatly affect what a person sees and how he interprets what he sees.

For the past 200 years, most geologists have used Lyellian anti-biblical naturalistic presuppositions to interpret the rocks. Those same naturalistic assumptions subsequently took control of biology, anthropology, astronomy, and all other disciplines of the academy and those assumptions are the foundation of the radiometric dating methods. Christians who reject biological evolution (including human evolution) but accept the big bang and the geological ages are embracing naturalistic, anti-biblical assumptions without realizing it. Young-earth creationists have been saying this for decades but

56. A shortened version of my PhD thesis is *The Great Turning Point* (Master Books, 2004).
57. Martin, J.S. Rudwick, "The Shape and Meaning of Earth History," in *God and Nature,* eds. David C. Lindberg and Ronald L. Numbers (Berkley, CA: University of California Press, 1986), p. 306, 311.

most old-earth proponents are not reading our literature or are not willing to really engage thoughtfully on this point.[58]

Instead they have been reading and believing the writings of Davis Young, professor emeritus of geology at Calvin College. Young has greatly influenced the thinking of many Christians (especially seminary and Christian college professors) on this matter of the age of the creation. Regarding the Grand Canyon and geology he says,

> If rocks are historical documents, we are driven to the related conclusion that the available evidence is overwhelmingly opposed to the notion that the Noahic flood deposited rocks of the Colorado Plateau only a few thousand years ago. . . . The Christian who believes that the idea of an ancient earth is unbiblical would do better to deny the validity of any kind of historical geology and insist that the rocks must be the product of pure miracle rather than try to explain them in terms of the flood. An examination of the earth apart from ideological presuppositions is bound to lead to the conclusion that it is ancient.[59]

But there is no such thing as examining the earth "apart from ideological presuppositions." The old-earth geologists (whether Christian or non-Christian) all reject the Bible's clear teaching about creation in six days, the cosmos-impacting Fall, and the world-destroying global Flood of Noah. That ideological rejection of the Bible profoundly affects and distorts their interpretation of the rocks and fossils.

One of the many scholars influenced by Davis Young is C. John Collins, Professor of Old Testament at Covenant Seminary and editor of the Old Testament notes in the ESV Study Bible. He holds to an old-earth view because of the supposed geological evidence and radiometric dating. He writes,

> I conclude, then that I have no reason to disbelieve the standard theories of the geologists, including their estimate for the age of the

58. For example, both before and after publication, I sent my essay "Philosophical Naturalism and the Age of the Earth: Are they related?" to many prominent old-earth theologians and philosophers, but they have been unwilling to interact with me on the subject. That essay is at https://answersingenesis.org/age-of-the-earth/are-philosophical-naturalism-and-age-of-the-earth-related/. See also Terry Mortenson, "The Historical Development of the Old-Earth Geological Time-Scale," https://answersingenesis.org/age-of-the-earth/the-historical-development-of-the-old-earth-geological-time-scale/.
59. Davis A. Young, "The Discovery of Terrestrial History," in Howard J. Van Till, Robert E. Snow, John H. Stek, and Davis A. Young, *Portraits of Creation* (Grand Rapids: Eerdmans, 1990), p. 80–81.

> earth. They may be wrong, for all I know; but if they are wrong, it's not because they have improperly smuggled philosophical assumptions into their work.[60]

Nothing could be further from the truth. Philosophical assumptions are precisely what Hutton, Lyell, and other old-earth geologists smuggled into their work. But why does Collins trust the secular geologists, who "could be wrong for all he knows," but not trust the Word of the One who cannot be and never is wrong?

Another respected theologian who has been influenced by Davis Young is Wayne Grudem. He says in his widely used *Systematic Theology* (translated into at least eight major languages), "Although our conclusions are tentative, at this point in our understanding, Scripture seems to be more easily understood to *suggest* (but not to require) a young earth view, while the observable facts of creation seem increasingly to favor an old earth view."[61] But it is not the "observable facts" that point to an old earth; it is the anti-biblical *assumptions* used to *interpret* observable evidence that resulted in the idea of millions of years.

In Grudem's foreword to a 2009 book published in the UK, which effectively refutes theistic evolution (particularly as espoused by Denis Alexander),[62] Grudem helpfully writes,

> What is at stake? A lot: the truthfulness of the three foundational chapters for the entire Bible (Genesis 1–3), belief in the unity of the human race, belief in the ontological uniqueness of human beings among all God's creatures, belief in the special creation of Adam and Eve in the image of God, belief in the parallel between condemnation through representation by Adam and salvation through representation by Christ, belief in the goodness of God's original creation, belief that suffering and death today are the result of sin and not part of God's original creation, and belief that natural disasters today are the result of the fall and not part of God's original creation. Belief in evolution erodes the foundations.
>
> Evolution is secular culture's grand explanation, the overriding "meta-narrative" that sinners accept with joy because it allows them

60. C. John Collins, *Science and Faith: Friends or Foes?* (Wheaton, IL: Crossways, 2003), p. 250.
61. Wayne Grudem, *Systematic Theology* (Downers Grove, IL: IVPress, 1994), p. 307 (italics in the original).
62. Foreword by Wayne Grudem in *Should Christians Embrace Evolution? Biblical and Scientific Responses*, ed. Norman C. Nevin (Nottingham, England: Inter-Varsity Press, 2009), p. 9–10.

> to explain life without reference to God, with no accountability to any Creator, no moral standards to restrain their sin, "no fear of God before their eyes" (Rom. 3:18) — and now theistic evolutionists tell us that Christians can just surrender to this massive attack on the Christian faith and safely, inoffensively, tack on God, not as the omnipotent God who in his infinite wisdom directly created all living things, but as the invisible deity who makes absolutely no detectable difference in the nature of living beings as they exist today. It will not take long for unbelievers to dismiss the idea of such a God who makes no difference at all. To put it in terms of an equation, when atheists assure us that matter + evolution + 0 = all living things, and then theistic evolutionists answer, no, that matter + evolution + God = all living things, it will not take long for unbelievers to conclude that, therefore, God = 0.
>
> I was previously aware that theistic evolution had serious difficulties, but I am now more firmly convinced than ever that it is impossible to believe consistently in both the truthfulness of the Bible and Darwinian evolution. We have to choose one or the other.

But Grudem fails to see that by accepting the claims of evolutionary geologists and astrophysicists about the age of the creation, he is thereby undermining the truthfulness of the equally foundational chapters of Genesis 4–11. He is also undermining the very truth that he says theistic evolution undermines: that suffering, death, and natural disasters today are the result of the Fall and not part of God's original creation. But this biblical teaching cannot be true if, as he believes, the millions of years of geological and cosmological evolution are fact. Like a great many other evangelical theologians and Bible scholars,[63] Grudem has (no doubt unintentionally) undermined the truth of Genesis 1–11 in his chapter on creation in his *Systematic Theology*.[64]

Furthermore, just this year (2016) Grudem (along with Collins, Ken Keathley, and Paul Copan) gave a glowing endorsement of a new book,

63. Thirteen other prominent old-earth evangelical scholars who say essentially the same thing as Grudem are discussed in Terry Mortenson, "Why Don't Many Christian Leaders and Scholars Believe Genesis?" https://answersingenesis.org/genesis/why-dont-many-christian-leaders-and-scholars-believe-genesis/.

64. See my critique, "Systematic Theology Texts and the Age of the Earth: A Response to the Views of Erickson, Grudem, and Lewis and Demarest," https://answersingenesis.org/age-of-the-earth/systematic-theology-texts-and-the-age-of-the-earth/. Grudem has told me that he read this and found it to be gracious and accurate, but he has been unwilling to discuss privately with me the points on which he disagrees.

Grand Canyon: Monument to an Ancient Earth (*GC:MtoAE*), written by eight professing Christians *and* three non-Christians arguing for millions of years and against the truth of Genesis.[65] All of the authors are evolutionists trying to influence Christians to believe in evolution![66] Yet in Grudem's *Systematic Theology* he rejects theistic evolution and quotes Davis Young approvingly as saying, "The position of theistic evolutionism as expressed by some of its proponents is not a consistently Christian position. It is not a truly biblical position. . . ."[67] *GC:MtoAE* also denies the global Flood of Noah,[68] but Grudem told me in personal conversation a couple of years ago at the annual meeting of the Evangelical Theological Society that he does believe the Flood was global. Furthermore, the book was funded by donations from secular (and undoubtedly unbelieving) geologists, the Templeton Foundation (through BioLogos), and the theistic evolutionist American Scientific Affiliation.[69] Why is Grudem endorsing a book produced by evolutionists (some of whom are not Christians) who deny what he believes about Noah's Flood? As Answers in Genesis geologist Dr. Andrew Snelling and I will show elsewhere soon (probably on the AiG website), *GC:MtoAE* contains serious biblical, historical, and geological errors, as well as gross misrepresentations of young-earth creationist views.

Ironically, at the bottom of *GC:MtoAE's* page of endorsements, Proverbs 18:17 is quoted: "The first to plead his case seems right, until another comes and examines him."[70]

65. See the endorsements by Grudem, C. John Collins, Ken Keathley, and Paul Copan inside *Grand Canyon: Monument to an Ancient Earth*, eds. Carol Hill, Gregg Davidson, Wayne Ranney, and Tim Helble (Grand Rapids, MI: Kregel, 2016). Davis Young reveals in his endorsement in the book that more than one of the authors is a non-Christian. Carol Hill, senior editor of *GC:MtoAE*, does also in Carol Hill, "How the Book, *Can Noah's Flood Explain the Grand Canyon?* Came to Be," *Perspective on Science and Christian Faith* 68:2 (June 2016): 125.
66. All of them would be supportive of Biologos' promotion of evolution and five of them (Davidson, Duff, Moshier, Wiens, and Wolgemuth) have written articles or been interviewed on the BioLogos website. Also, Hill clearly states that in writing *GC:MtoAE* the authors had "the hard task of deciding how to present evolution. . . . We wanted our readers to come to our book with open minds on the subject of evolution." See Hill, "How the Book . . .", p. 127.
67. Grudem, *Systematic Theology*, p. 279.
68. The authors contend that there is no geological evidence for the Flood anywhere on earth (see Hill, "How the Book, *Can Noah's Flood Explain the Grand Canyon?* Came to Be," p. 129–130). But this is another way of saying that the Flood never happened, because it is simply impossible that a global, yearlong Flood (or even a large, local flood in the Mesopotamian Valley, which is an exegetically impossible interpretation of Genesis 6–9) would leave no erosional or sedimentary geological and paleontological evidence.
69. See the acknowledgments page of the book.
70. All Scripture quotes in this chapter are from the New American Standard Bible (1995).

But it is extremely doubtful that Grudem and fellow-endorsers Collins, Keathley, and Copan quoted on that page (none of whom have any geological training) have carefully read young-earth geologist Steve Austin's *Grand Canyon: Monument to Catastrophe* (1994) and Andrew Snelling's 2-volume *Earth's Catastrophic Past* (2010). They should do so since *GC:MtoAE* copiously refers to Austin's and Snelling's books. Then these theologians would be in a better position to carefully cross-examine the geological arguments.

It is also ironic (given Proverbs 18:17) that Grudem and Collins endorsed this book given that since 2008 they both have been invited every year to come on the annual, by-invitation-only, heavily scholarshipped, seven-day raft trip down the Colorado River through Grand Canyon for theologians and other Christian leaders co-led by Snelling.[71] But they have not come. If they did come, they could see for themselves and learn that the authors of *GC:MtoAE* are suppressing the truth (Rom. 1:18–20) and willfully ignorant (2 Pet. 3:3–6).[72] Having rejected the truth of Genesis regarding the Flood, the authors of *GC:MtoAE* have ignored or misinterpreted the geological evidence and are leading theologians, apologists, and laymen to reject God's Word regarding Creation and the Flood.

In 2 Chronicles 19:2, Jehu the prophet confronted King Jehoshaphat and said, "Should you help the wicked and love those who hate the Lord and so bring wrath on yourself from the Lord?" And Paul commands us in 2 Corinthians 6:14–15, "Do not be bound together with unbelievers; for what partnership have righteousness and lawlessness, or what fellowship has

71. Read about this trip (sponsored by Canyon Ministries and Answers in Genesis) and see a list of the nearly 200 past participants from 14 countries (as of July 2016) at http://www.canyonministries.org/clt/.

72. For example, on October 20, 2011, Guy Forsythe, President of Crying Rocks Ministry (www.cryingrocks.org) and a rim-tour guide for Canyon Ministries, had an email exchange with Wayne Ranney, one of the nonbelieving authors of *GC:MtoAE*. Guy told Ranney that he is on a research team with Dr. John Whitmore (Cedarville University geology professor who has done considerable research on the Coconino Sandstone, one of the vast horizontal layers in Grand Canyon). The team has measured cross-bed dips hundreds of times over a wide area of northern Arizona. Guy said that the team was finding that the dips average 20 degrees in contrast to Ranney's book, *Sedona Through Time*, which states the dips are 29 to 34 degrees. Guy asked Ranney where he (Guy) could find the steep dips. Ranney responded, "I got the data from Ron Blakey (I did not measure the cross-beds myself)." Five years later, it appears that none of the authors of *GC:MtoAE* has actually measured the dips of the cross-beds of the Coconino Sandstone Formation. Whitmore has published much of his technical research on the Coconino in *Answers Research Journal* at https://answersingenesis.org/geology/rock-layers/petrology-of-the-coconino-sandstone/ and https://answersingenesis.org/geology/rock-layers/intraformational-parabolic-recumbent-folds/. A laymen's summary is at https://answersingenesis.org/geology/grand-canyon/coconino-sandstone-most-powerful-argument-against-flood/.

light with darkness? Or what harmony has Christ with Belial, or what has a believer in common with an unbeliever?" The professing Christian authors of *GC:MtoAE* are unequally yoked with the Bible-denying, gospel-hating non-Christian authors, and the book was financed by similar unequally yoked groups in an effort to use naturalism-driven interpretations of rocks and fossils to convince Christians to reject the global Flood and the biblical chronology and promote evolution. The professing Christian authors are helping the wicked to subvert the faith of God's people. Why are Grudem, Collins, Keathley, and Copan endorsing this unholy fellowship assaulting God's Word?

Grudem is absolutely right that it is impossible to believe in both the Bible and evolution, including human evolution. But it is equally impossible to believe with exegetical or logical consistency in both the truthfulness of the Bible *and* millions of years of geological and cosmological evolution. It is disturbingly inconsistent that in 2009 Grudem spoke out so strongly and helpfully against theistic evolution, but now in 2016 he has endorsed a book, all the authors of which are theistic or non-Christian evolutionists! There seems to be only two explanations for this: either he still rejects theistic evolution but did not carefully read *GC:MtoAE* or carefully investigate who the authors were, or he has now embraced theistic evolution.

Furthermore, atheists don't just apply Grudem's equation to living things. Atheists also confidently tell us that "matter + cosmological and geological evolution + 0 = all *non-living things*" (stars, galaxies, earth, rock layers, and fossils), just like living creatures, including man. So when old-earth creationists (of whatever variety) deny biological evolution but affirm that "matter + cosmological and geological evolution + God = all *non-living* things," it takes no time at all for unbelievers to conclude that therefore God = 0 and to conclude that old-earth creationists are evading the clear teaching of Genesis 1–11, just like theistic evolutionists are. But the unbelievers think that theistic evolutionists are more consistent because they accept *all* that the naturalistic, atheistic scientific establishment insists is true about origins. On the other hand, the old-earth creationists arbitrarily accept what the naturalistic, atheistic astrophysicists and geologists say about the origin and history of the cosmos and earth but reject what the naturalistic, atheistic biologists and anthropologists say about the origin of plants, animals, and humans.

To realize what is really going on here, we need to consider what Davis Young said in a lecture in 1990 at a Wheaton College symposium on science and Christianity:

> The Day-Age hypothesis insisted with at least a semblance of textual plausibility that the days of creation were long periods of indeterminate length, although the immediate context implies that the term, *yom*, for "day" really means "day." . . . There were some textual obstacles the Day-Agers developed an amazing agility in surmounting.[73]

After discussing some examples of the contradiction in the order of events between Genesis 1 and the evolutionary view of history, Young continued,

> This obvious point of conflict, however, failed to dissuade well-intentioned Christians, my earlier self included, from nudging the text to mean something different from what it says. In my case, I suggested that the events of the days overlapped. Having publicly repented of that textual mutilation a few years ago, I will move on without further embarrassing myself.[74]

Having "repented" of that, one might think he is now a young-earth creationist. But no, after examining other techniques for unsuccessfully harmonizing Genesis with old-earth geology, Young confessed,

> Genius as all these schemes may be, one is struck by the forced nature of them all. While the exegetical gymnastic maneuvers have displayed remarkable flexibility, I suspect that they have resulted in temporary damage to the theological musculature. Interpretation of Genesis 1 through 11 as factual history does not mesh with the emerging picture of the early history of the universe and of humanity that has been deciphered by scientific investigation. Dickering with the biblical text doesn't seem to make it fit the scientific data.[75]

His conclusion now? "The Bible may be expressing history in nonfactual terms."[76]

Young's mutilation of the Bible and illogical conclusion flow out of the naturalistic, uniformitarian assumptions with which he was brainwashed during his geological education. Sadly, over the past 30–40 years Young has been widely cited by evangelical theologians and Old Testament scholars as a significant reason they reject the plain teaching of Genesis regarding Noah's Flood and the age of the creation.

---

73. Davis Young, "The Harmonization of Scripture and Science" (1990 Wheaton symposium). I have an audio recording of the whole lecture on file.
74. Ibid.
75. Ibid.
76. Ibid.

Besides Collins and Grudem, another recent example of Young's influence on prominent Bible scholars is a book by Ken Keathley (a theologian) and Mark Rooker (an Old Testament scholar), both at Southeastern Baptist Theological Seminary. Quoting Young extensively and following him completely regarding the work of young-earth creationist geologists (such as Snelling), they tell their readers,

> The only recourse that flood catastrophists have to save their theory [that Noah's Flood produced most of the geological record of rock layers and fossils] is to appeal to a pure miracle and thus eliminate entirely the possibility of historical geology. We think that would be a more honest course of action for young-earth advocates to take. Young-earth creationists should cease their efforts to convince the lay Christian public that geology supports a young earth when it does not do so. To continue that effort is misguided and detrimental to the health of the church and the cause of Christ.[77]

It is deeply disconcerting that Keathley and Rooker's acceptance of the claims of Davis Young and the secular geological establishment, as well as their cavalier rejection of the work of Bible-believing, inerrantist, young-earth geologists, is not unusual but typical of most professing evangelical seminary professors of theology and Old Testament today. It is also disconcerting that they significantly misrepresent Snelling's view.[78] What makes Keathley's misrepresentation even more egregious is that in 2008 he was on the 7-day Christian Leaders Trip through Grand Canyon[79] with Snelling as one of his teachers. Young-earth geologists do not and will not appeal to "pure miracle," because that would be contrary to Scripture's description of the Flood and sound geological inferences from that historical account. And they do not reject historical geology. What they reject is uniformitarian naturalism as the presuppositional framework for doing historical geology, rather than rejecting the Bible's record of the Flood as old-earth geologists

77. Kenneth D. Keathley and Mark F. Rooker, *40 Questions about Creation and Evolution* (Grand Rapids, MI: Kregel, 2014), p. 307–308. This statement is actually an exact quote from Young and Stearley's book but it is not indented by Keathley and Rooker as other long quotes are. That this is not a typographical mistake but reflects Keathley and Rooker's view is clear from the conclusion of their chapter on geology.
78. For one very important example, in their book Keathley and Rooker repeatedly accuse Snelling of believing that the *laws* of nature changed during the Flood (p. 301–302, 309–310). He does not, but rather argues (using scientific evidence) that *rates* of natural processes (not the laws of nature) were changed (e.g., much faster and greater erosion and sedimentation, and accelerated radioactive decay) during the Flood.
79. http://www.canyonministries.org/clt/.

do! Why do so many theologians trust Davis Young, a man who by his own admission has "mutilated" the Scriptures and now holds the ridiculously illogical notion that Genesis 1–11 is "history in nonfactual terms"? I would hope that it is because they were not at the 1990 Wheaton symposium to hear Young's remarkable "confession" and "repentance" (though a creationist published Young's lengthy statement in 1992[80]).

The truth is that there is a massive amount of geological evidence for Noah's Flood and a young earth.[81] But old-earth creationists and theistic evolutionists do not or will not see it because (1) they are presuppositionally brainwashed (in the words of Derek Ager quoted earlier), as are most geologists, (2) they have largely ignored the young-earth scientific arguments, and (3) they blindly believe the majority of scientists (most of whom are not Christians and therefore are enemies of God).

The Flood is critical to the question of the age of the earth. Therefore, most old-earth advocates view it either as a local Flood in the Middle East or as a myth. Some believe in a global Flood but have not realized that they cannot logically believe in a global Flood *and* millions of years. The geological record is evidence of one or the other, but not both, and it is illogical to believe that the global, yearlong, catastrophic Flood left no geological evidence.

The Nature of Old-Universe Cosmology

Not only have the Church and most of her scholars been deceived by the naturalistic, atheistic stories of biological evolution and geological evolution, but the same is true regarding cosmological evolution. A few statements by prominent secular astrophysicists reveal the problem.

The media, schools, and scientists (both Christian and non-Christian) constantly tell us that the scientific evidence overwhelmingly confirms the big-bang theory and the age of the universe at about 13.8 billion years. Many evangelical leaders and scholars feel compelled to accept this as fact and try to harmonize it with Genesis. But as shown in my earlier chapter, the order of events in Genesis contradicts the order of events in the big-bang

80. See Marvin Lubenow, *Bones of Contention* (Grand Rapids, MI: Baker Books, 1992, 1st ed.), p. 232–234.
81. John Whitcomb and Henry Morris' epic *The Genesis Flood* (1961) essentially launched the modern creation science movement. Since 1961, much more technical geological work has been done by PhD geologists. See particularly Steven Austin, *Grand Canyon: Monument to Catastrophe* (ICR, 1994) and Andrew Snelling, *Earth's Catastrophic Past*, 2 Vol. (Master Books, 2010). For an introduction to the geological evidence confirming Genesis see John Morris, *The Young Earth*, 2nd rev. ed. (Master Books, 2007).

theory. Furthermore, it is not a proven fact, as even many secular scientists contend.

In 2004, Eric Lerner, a prominent plasma physicist, published a document in *New Scientist* and on the web called "Bucking the Big Bang." Initially signed by 34 scientists from prominent science institutes or universities in ten countries, by 2009 it had been signed by over 400 scientists (an additional 218 "scientists and engineers" and 187 "independent researchers") from over 50 countries. The article began,

> The big bang today relies on a growing number of hypothetical entities, things that we have never observed — inflation, dark matter and dark energy are the most prominent examples. Without them, there would be a fatal contradiction between the observations made by astronomers and the predictions of the big bang theory. In no other field of physics would this continual recourse to new hypothetical objects be accepted as a way of bridging the gap between theory and observation. It would, at the least, raise serious questions about the validity of the underlying theory.[82]

Reporting on a 2005 conference entitled "The First Crisis in Cosmology Conference," South African astrophysicist Hilton Ratcliffe concluded,

> That the Big Bang theory will pass into history as an artifact of man's obsession with dogma is a certainty; it will do so on its own merits, however, because it stands on feet of clay. . . . Papers presented at the conference by some of the world's leading scientists showed beyond doubt that the weight of scientific evidence clearly indicates that the dominant theory on the origin and destiny of the Universe is deeply flawed. The implications of this damning consensus are serious indeed, and will in time fundamentally affect not only the direction of many scientific disciplines, but also threaten to change the very way that we do science.[83]

---

82. Eric J. Lerner, "Bucking the Big Bang," *New Scientist* 2448 (May 22, 2004): 20. The whole article with the listed signatories and their institutions is at https://web.archive.org/web/20140401081546/http://cosmologystatement.org/.
83. Hilton Ratcliffe, "The First Crisis in Cosmology Conference," *Progress in Physics* Vol. 3 (Dec. 2005): 24. Ratcliffe is a member of both the Astronomical Society of Southern Africa (ASSA) and the Astronomical Society of the Pacific. He became a founding member of the Alternative Cosmology Group (ACG — an association of some 700 leading scientists from all corners of the globe developing an alternative to the big-bang theory), which conducted its inaugural international conference in Portugal in 2005. He serves as consulting astrophysicist on the steering committee of the Durban Space Science

Two years later in a paper on Cold Dark Matter, Richard Lieu, Professor of Physics at the University of Alabama, Huntsville, stated,

> Astronomy can never be a hard core physics discipline, because the Universe offers no control experiment, i.e., with no independent checks it is bound to be highly ambiguous and degenerate. . . . Cosmology is not even astrophysics: all the principal assumptions in this field are unverified (or unverifiable) in the laboratory, and researchers are quite comfortable with inventing unknowns to explain the unknown.[84]

Kate Land, an astrophysicist at Oxford University, reminds us, "The main problem with cosmology is our sample size — that of just one universe."[85] And James Gunn, professor of astronomy at Princeton University and co-founder of the Sloan Digital Sky Survey, observes, "Cosmology may look like a science, but it isn't science. A basic tenet of science is that you can do repeatable experiments, and you can't do that in cosmology."[86]

In 2011 the cover of *Scientific American* announced, "Quantum Gaps in Big Bang Theory: Why our best explanation of how the universe evolved must be fixed — or replaced." The cover article, entitled "The Inflation Debate: Is the theory at the heart of modern cosmology deeply flawed?" was by Paul J. Steinhardt, Albert Einstein Professor in Science & Director of the Princeton University Center for Theoretical Science. He discussed why he is convinced that the big-bang inflation theory is deeply flawed and he has proposed the "cyclic theory," which is even more ridiculous and unscientific: a series of expansions and contractions of multiple universes over trillions of years.[87]

But in the widely seen 2014 documentary television series, "Cosmos: A Spacetime Odyssey," which has now been developed into a curriculum to

---

Centre and Planetarium, a project of the Astronomical Society of Southern Africa (Durban Centre). He is best known in formal science as co-discoverer, together with eminent nuclear chemist Oliver Manuel and solar physicist Michael Mozina, of the CNO nuclear fusion cycle on the surface of the sun, nearly 70 years after it was first predicted. See http://www.hiltonratcliffe.com/about/.

84. Richard Lieu, "ΛCDM Cosmology: How Much Suppression of Credible Evidence, and Does the Model Really Lead Its Competitors, Using All Evidence?" 2007, http://arxiv.org/pdf/0705.2462v1.pdf, p. 1. "ΛCDM" stands for Lambda Cold Dark Matter.
85. Quoted in Adrian Cho, "A Singular Conundrum: How Odd Is Our Universe?" *Science* 31, No. 5846 (2007): 1848. *Science* is published by the American Association for the Advancement of Science. Before becoming a science journalist, Cho earned a PhD in experimental particle physics at Cornell University.
86. Ibid., p. 1850.
87. Paul J. Steinhardt, "The Inflation Debate," *Scientific American* 304:4 (April 2011): 36–43.

brainwash public school children to believe in cosmological, geological, and biological evolution,[88] the well-known atheist astrophysicist, Neil deGrasse Tyson, says,

> Our ancestors worshipped the sun. They were far from foolish. It makes good sense to revere the sun and stars because we are their children. The silicon in the rocks, the oxygen in the air, the carbon in our DNA, the iron in our skyscrapers, the silver in our jewelry — were all made in stars billions of years ago. Our planet, our society, and we ourselves are stardust.[89]

So, with respect to cosmological-geological-biological evolution, we are dealing with a form of paganism that is every bit as absurd and idolatrous as the Greek and Roman pagan myths of the first century. It is an absolute delusion to believe that the atheist-controlled scientific majority is telling us the truth about origins. Therefore, evangelical theologians and Bible scholars who are developing creative ways to reinterpret Genesis in light of the myth of evolution are making a serious error and leading the Church astray.

The Assault on the Perspicuity and Authority of Scripture

We have a crisis in the evangelical world today, a crisis of authority. Scientists (and the scholars of ANE literature who follow the scientific majority) have usurped the authority of Scripture. Many Christian leaders and scholars are claiming to defend the Bible while at the same time undermining both its clarity and its authority.

Many old-earth creationists have protested, "The issue is *NOT* the *authority* of Scripture! The issue is the *interpretation* of Scripture." But I must firmly disagree. The only reason people are coming up with all these diverse reinterpretations of Genesis that were never heard of in the Church before the 19th century[90] is precisely because those interpreters have made what the scientific majority says about the origin and history of the creation their final authority in their interpretation of the biblical text. Rather

---

88. For a critique of each episode of this 8-part TV series promoting cosmological, geological, and biological evolution, see the series of web articles by Elizabeth Mitchell at https://answersingenesis.org/countering-the-culture/cosmos-a-spacetime-odyssey/. The articles have also been published as *Questioning Cosmos.*
89. Episode 8 ("Sisters of the Sun"). The show was a follow-up to the 1980 television series "Cosmos: A Personal Voyage," which was presented by the atheist Carl Sagan.
90. Gap theory, day-age, gap-day-gap-day (e.g., John Lennox), framework view, Promise Land view (John Sailhamer), analogical days (C. John Collins), Cosmic Temple/functionality view (John Walton), local Flood, etc.

than interpreting Scripture by Scripture (which is the biblically derived and historically orthodox hermeneutic and would never lead a reader to belief in evolution and millions of years) old-earth creationists and theistic evolutionists are interpreting Scripture, not by "science," but by what the secular, anti-biblical, scientific authorities claim is true. Most leaders in the "Intelligent Design" camp associated with the Discovery Institute never even attempt to deal with Genesis 1–11. Many other old-earthers give only superficial attention to the text. Neither approach is consistent with belief in the inspiration, inerrancy, and authority of Scripture.

The perspicuity of Scripture is also at stake. The Bible clearly teaches that abortion is murder, that sex outside of marriage is sin, that there are only two genders (male and female, which are determined at conception), and that marriage is one man to one woman for life. The Bible just as clearly teaches that all people are sinners and can only be saved from the wrath to come by repentance and faith in the substitutionary death and bodily Resurrection of the Lord Jesus Christ. It just as clearly teaches that Jesus is coming again to judge the world and create a new heaven and new earth, free from the corrupting Curse, where there will be no more death, disease, and other natural evils.

But the Bible equally clearly teaches that Adam was made from dust, that Eve was made from his rib, and that they fell in sin (through the temptation of a Satan-controlled serpent) bringing God's Curse on the whole creation. And it equally clearly teaches that God created a very good universe in six 24-hour days a little over 6,000 years ago and that He destroyed the world with a global, catastrophic, yearlong Flood at the time of Noah. The Bible clearly, truthfully, and authoritatively teaches all those truths.

In the words of Davis Young, only with "textual mutilation" and "exegetical gymnastics" can we evade these clear teachings of Scripture. There is simply no exegetically defensible way to get a local flood in the Mesopotamian Valley out of Genesis 6–9, or to fit millions of years into Genesis 1, or to harmonize human evolution with Genesis 2:7 and 2:22.

The inerrancy, perspicuity, and authority of Scripture are all under assault by the theory of cosmological, geological, biological, and anthropological evolution. This 200-year attack is driven by an atheistic, naturalistic worldview that is antithetical to everything the Bible teaches. And all old-earth creationist and theistic evolutionist views are compromising to a greater or lesser extent with that anti-biblical worldview. That is why young-earth creationists can agree with many old-earth creationists' criticisms of biological evolution but must oppose their old-earth teachings in the Church. Old-earth proponents and those who are unsure about the age of the creation but insist it is not an important issue even as they oppose the evolutionary conclusions from naturalism's control of biology are leading Christians to embrace the evolutionary claims flowing out of naturalism's control of geology and astronomy.

We cannot with consistency believe the gospel and yet not believe the Genesis 1–11 foundation of the gospel that explains why we need the Savior — that the first Adam sinned resulting in death and a Curse on the whole creation. The gospel collapses into myth, if Adam and Eve are not historical or if millions of years of history truly occurred before Adam. It all stands or falls together.

Furthermore, we cannot with any hermeneutical consistency reject a literal Adam and Fall because science says Genesis is myth, but at the same time accept the virgin birth and Resurrection of Jesus. The Genesis and Gospel accounts are equally historical accounts of miraculous events. Yet the same scientific majority that denies all of Genesis 1–11 also insists that science shows that virgins don't and can't have babies, and dead men don't and can't rise from the dead. All those biblical accounts stand or fall together.

There is no need to bow the knee to the scientific majority on the origin of man or any other truth in Genesis 1–11. The scientific evidence does not support microbe-to-microbiologist biological evolution (either the Neo-Darwinian gradualistic version or the "punctuated equilibrium" version of rapid evolution). Rather the scientific evidence powerfully confirms what Genesis 1 says, namely, that God created mankind and different *kinds* of plants and animals to reproduce "after their kind." That is, each kind was created to produce great variation within its kind but not to change into a different kind.[91]

Likewise, there is increasingly powerful geological evidence that most of the rock layers and fossils are the result of Noah's Flood, and not evidence of hundreds of millions of years of earth history.[92] Furthermore, there is no

91. Creation science research indicates that in most cases the created kind is probably equivalent to the modern taxonomic classification of "family" (not "genus" or "species"). For example, all the varieties of wild dogs (e.g., wolves, coyotes, dingos, foxes) and domestic dogs (from St. Bernards down to miniature poodles) are descended from a common ancestor: the first dogs (which evolutionists and creationists agree probably looked something like a grey wolf). All the wild and domestic cats are descended from a common ancestor: the first cats. All the varieties of elephants (mastodon, wooly mammoth, Asian elephant, African elephant) are descended from the original elephant kind. For research on the original created kinds, see Jean Lightner et al, "Determining the Ark Kinds," https://answersingenesis.org/noahs-ark/determining-the-ark-kinds/, November 16, 2011, and visit Ark Encounter in northern Kentucky (https://ArkEncounter.com).

92. See Andrew Snelling's 2-volume *Earth's Catastrophic Past*, Steve Austin's *Grand Canyon: Monument to Catastrophe*, and John Morris' *The Young Earth* (2nd rev. ed.).

need to bow the knee to claims that the big bang and 13.8 billion years are proven scientific fact.[93] Hugh Ross and Reasons to Believe and many others are misleading the Church, including many theologians, pastors, and apologists, in their use of big-bang cosmology to defend the faith.[94]

Given the naturalistic, evolutionary assault on the authority of Scripture, it was very disappointing but not surprising[95] that in D.A. Carson's new book, *The Enduring Authority of the Christian Scriptures* (Eerdmans, 2016), the chapter on "Science and Scripture" was written by a theistic evolutionist professor of ethics, philosophy, and Church history at one of the leading evangelical theological colleges in the UK. Despite the chapter title, she doesn't discuss a single Bible verse! Turpin reveals other serious problems with her argument.[96]

In his 1994 book *The Scandal of the Evangelical Mind,* Mark Noll accused young-earth creationists of using "a fatally flawed interpretive scheme of the sort that no responsible Christian teacher in the history of the church ever endorsed before this century."[97] Noll could not be further from the truth, historically and exegetically. The truly sad reality today is the scandal of evangelical *scholarly* minds, who like Noll's, refuse to believe Genesis, ignore scholarly young-earth creationist literature, gullibly believe what the secular

93. See *The Heavens Declare* DVD series; *What You Aren't Being Told About Astronomy* DVD set; Danny Faulkner (PhD in astronomy), *Universe by Design*; Jason Lisle (PhD in astronomy) *Taking Back Astronomy*; and my forthcoming DVD *Big Bang: Exploding the Myth*, which documents from the mouths of the evolutionists themselves that despite their bold claims about the proven fact of the big bang, they really don't know how the moon, the solar system, stars, or galaxies formed and so they can't possibly know how or when the universe was formed.
94. See Jonathan Sarfati, *Refuting Compromise: A Biblical and Scientific Refutation of "Progressive Creationism" (Billions of Years) As Popularized by Astronomer Hugh Ross,* 2nd rev. ed. (Atlanta GA: Creation Book Publ., 2011) for a thorough critique of the writings of Ross on a whole range of issues related to Genesis 1–11.
95. It is not surprising, given that in Carson's book, *The God Who Is There* (Grand Rapids, MI: Baker, 2010, p. 11–42), he says that Genesis 1–2 is an ambiguous mixture of history and symbolism. He implicitly encourages readers to be open to millions of years if not also evolution by recommending four books, none of which is by a young-earth creationist and one (Michael Poole) is by a theistic evolutionist (https://www.theguardian.com/science/blog/2008/nov/13/evolution-creation-creationism). Carson shows no evidence of being familiar with the scholarly young-earth creationist biblical and scientific literature. And while he affirms that the Fall in Genesis 3 had an impact on the whole creation, introducing death and decay, he fails to connect that belief to the problem of accepting millions of years of animal death, disease, and extinction before the Fall.
96. Simon Turpin, "The Enduring Authority of Scripture, Really?" Review of "Science and Scripture" in D.A. Carson, ed., *The Enduring Authority of the Christian Scriptures,* https://answersingenesis.org/reviews/books/enduring-authority-scripture-really/, July 21, 2016.
97. Mark A. Noll, *The Scandal of the Evangelical Mind* (Grand Rapids, MI: Eerdmans, 1994), p. 14.

(godless) scientific majority says about evolution and millions of years, and then use that evolutionary story as their supreme authority for interpreting God's Word.

So, we are reverting to conditions as they existed before the Protestant Reformation. Like the Roman Catholic Church, the evangelical world now has a Magisterium, made up of scientists and Old Testament scholars who are experts in ancient Near Eastern (ANE) literature. As Giberson (former VP of BioLogos) put it,

> One of my theologian friends once said, in great frustration over this issue, "I wish they had never put the Bible in the hands of ordinary people." It seems to me that we need to take more seriously the teaching ministry of the church. We encourage people to read the Bible on their own, but certain misunderstandings are bound to emerge with that approach. Young people are going to read Genesis and think of Adam and Eve as real biological parents of the human race.[98]

John Walton says,

> The worldview of antiquity was lost to us as thinking changed over thousands of years, and the language and literature of the ancient world was buried in the sands of the Middle East. It was only with the decipherment of the ancient languages and the recovery of their texts that windows were again opened to an understanding of an ancient worldview that was the backdrop of the biblical world. This literature and the resulting knowledge has made it possible to recover the ways of thinking that were prominent in the ancient world and has given us new insight into some difficult biblical texts.[99]

Here it is clearly stated. The man in the pew or in the jungle cannot possibly understand the Bible's meaning (at least in Genesis 1–11) and will misinterpret it if he tries. We better not even let them, especially children, read the Bible on their own. The "evangelical" magisterium will interpret Genesis for all other Christians, the vast majority of whom know next to nothing

98. Karl W. Giberson, "Evolution, the Bible, and the Book of Nature: A Conversation with Francis Collins," *Books and Culture*, July 10, 2009, http://www.christianitytoday.com/bc/2009/julaug/evolutionthebibleandthebookofnature.html, accessed July 31, 2009.
99. John Walton, *The Lost World of Genesis One* (Downers Grove, IL: InterVarsity Press, 2009), p. 171.

about science or ANE literature. Regardless of the sincerity, intentions, and motivations (which only God knows and can judge) of these scientists and ANE experts, their teachings are an assault on the authority and perspicuity of Scripture and are robbing the Scriptures from the people in the pew and the pastors in the pulpit.

Conclusion

In 1838, a discerning pastor in England expressed his grave concern about the old-earth geological theories being developed at the time. Referring to an ordained professor at Oxford University, who was compromised with old-earth geology, this pastor wrote,

> This affords another illustration of men who pull down the bulwark, but disclaim any intention of endangering the citadel. The Trojan Horse, drawn within the walls of the devoted city by friendly hands, is a standing emblem of men acting under the unsuspecting guidance of the Evil One.[100]

Can genuine, committed believers in Christ act under the unsuspecting guidance of Satan? Absolutely. Peter did, just after perfectly passing his most important theology exam (Matt. 16:23). Can men, who have been mightily used by God to build His Church and even do miracles, unknowingly and unintentionally undermine the very gospel they love and preach? Absolutely! Peter did, because he caved in to the fear of man (Gal. 2:11–14). These things can happen to any Christian (including the authors of this book), if he does not pay careful attention to and submit to the supreme authority of Scripture. And this is what has happened with many great Christian leaders and scholars over the last 200 years who have compromised with evolution and/or millions of years.

We are in a great spiritual war. We can all be taken captive by speculations and philosophies and traditions of men, which are falsely called "knowledge" (2 Cor. 10:3–4, 11:3; Col. 2:8; 1 Tim. 6:20–21). All of us (including this book's authors) can be deceived. The person who thinks he cannot be deceived is deceived already. We need to take every thought captive to the obedience of Christ, which means to take every thought captive to the Word of God.

In 1 Corinthians 5:6, Paul said, "a little leaven leavens the whole lump of dough." I submit to you that the idea of millions of years was the leaven. For the first 1,800 years of Church history the almost universal belief of

100. James Mellor Brown, *Reflections on Geology* (London: James Nisbet, 1838), p. 24.

faithful Christians was a literal six-day creation about 6,000 years ago and a global Noachian Flood. Since the early 1800s we have witnessed the disastrous slippery slide in the Church away from biblical truth into error.

The Church's Slipperly Slide into Error

Pre-1800	Young-earth creation, global flood
1810s	Old-earth creation, global, geologically limited flood, man 6,000 years old
1830s	Old-earth creation, local flood, man 6000 years old
1860s	Old-earth, animals evolved, man created but older than 6,000 years
1870s	Old-earth, animals and Adam's body evolved but Adam literal
Early 1900s	Big bang, theistic evolution, Adam is a myth

Many godly men went only part way down this slippery path and remained otherwise very orthodox the rest of their lives. But often their disciples slid further. Each step was undermining the authority and clarity of Scripture, in spite of good intentions to the contrary. Using the biblical metaphor of leaven, godly men unknowingly introduced leaven into the Church and their disciples often added more leaven. Or using a metaphor popularized by Ken Ham, these well-meaning, sincere Christian leaders and scholars unintentionally pushed the door of unbelief open just a crack, and subsequent generations pushed it open more, leading many to a denial of Adam and even a denial of the gospel. The crack in the dam in the early 19th century regarding the age of the earth, which undermined the authority of Scripture, has led to a flood of unbelief and wickedness in the 21st century.

Scripture is right: a little leaven leavens the whole lump. Small error that does not seem to hurt anything grows into big error that becomes a massive assault on the gospel. Charles Hodge at Princeton rejected evolution but embraced the millions of years. Over the next half century, with more openness to evolution (guided by God's providence of course) by A.A. Hodge and B.B. Warfield, eventually (shortly after the latter's death in 1929) Princeton totally embraced evolution and theological liberalism. This later led to one of its most promising and gifted students abandoning the faith completely for atheism. I refer to Charles Templeton.

Templeton was considered by some to be a more gifted evangelist than Billy Graham. But he struggled with how to reconcile evolution and millions of years with his faith. So he went to Princeton Seminary in 1948 to get answers. Instead he was taught that Genesis 1–11 is mythology. Soon after seminary he left the ministry, became an agnostic, went into journalism, and in 2001 died as an atheist. At the end of his last book, *Farewell to God*, he wrote, "I believe that there is no supreme being with human attributes — no God in the biblical sense — but that life is the result of timeless evolutionary forces, having reached its present transient state over millions of years."[101]

Templeton is one of tens of millions who have departed from the Christian faith or refused to listen to the gospel because they have been led to believe that cosmological-geological-biological evolution is proven scientific fact and the Bible is based on mythology. And with that has come the descent into moral insanity and spiritual darkness that we are witnessing in the formerly Christian West.

From the earliest ages, children (including 85% of Christian children) in the public schools of America (and most other countries of the world) are indoctrinated in evolution and millions of years and given no opportunity to hear scientific evidence that refutes the evolutionary stories.[102] And the evolutionists will get the ACLU to threaten a lawsuit against any school or teacher that tries to expose children to such evidence.

If the scientific evidence truly overwhelmingly proved the evolutionists' claims, then they would welcome questions and objections as opportunities to calmly and respectfully present more scientific evidence. Instead, they suppress and censor any contrary evidence, employ *ad hominem* attacks against their opponents,[103] and use political and legal intimidation, or they deny degrees and tenure and fire professors to silence critics.[104] This alone is evidence that cosmological-geological-biological evolution is a myth masquerading as proven science and deceiving the world into thinking that there is no God to whom they are morally accountable, and that the gospel is not true.

But let me be clear. Belief in a literal Adam and literal historical Fall is not a salvation issue. It is a gospel-consistency or gospel-coherency issue. A person can be saved, even if he doesn't believe in a literal Adam and a literal Fall, as long as he has repented of his sins and trusted solely in the substitutionary

101. Charles Templeton, *Farewell to God* (Toronto, Canada: McClelland & Stewart, 1996), p. 232.

102. See the recommended resources at the end of this book.

103. Richard Dawkins is typical: "It is absolutely safe to say that if you meet somebody who claims not to believe in evolution, that person is ignorant, stupid or insane (or wicked, but I'd rather not consider that)." Richard Dawkins, "Put Your Money on Evolution" (a review of Donald Johanson and Mailand Edey, *Blueprints: Solving the Mystery of Evolution*), The *New York Times Review of Books* (April 9, 1989), p. 35.

104. See the Ben Stein documentary film *Expelled*, or read Jerry Bergman, *Slaughter of the Dissidents* (Southworth, WA: Leafcutter Press, 2012, 2nd ed.).

death and bodily Resurrection of Jesus Christ. But in so doing he is denying a part of the Word of God that explains why he (and everyone else) needs a Savior. And by his unbelief regarding Genesis 2–3, he is contributing to the spiritual corruption of the Church and hindering the acceptance of the gospel by lost sinners.

Likewise, belief in a literal six-day creation about 6,000 years ago and a global, catastrophic, world-rearranging Flood at the time of Noah is not a salvation issue. A theistic evolutionist or old-earth creationist can be saved, as long as he has repented and trusted in Jesus Christ. But to accept the millions of years involves a conscious or unconscious denial that the Curse in Genesis 3 affected the whole creation, bringing both natural evil (e.g., earthquakes, tsunamis, animal extinction) and moral evil (e.g., crime, wars, divorce, sexual perversions) into the world. It requires contradicting his Lord, who taught that Adam and Eve were created at the beginning of creation (Mark 10:6), not billions of years after the beginning. And his inconsistent belief undermines the perspicuity, reliability, and authority of the Word of God that reveals the gospel that he believes.

America is on a path to national suicide and moral insanity. All of this is a result of the Church's and the culture's rejection of the truth and authority of the Word of God. At the foundation of that is the rejection of the truth of Genesis 1–11. Christians, especially evangelical leaders and scholars, need to wake up to where the battle really is.

Wake up, old-earth creationist and theistic evolutionist theologians, scientists, apologists, and philosophers! Wake up to the massive 200-year assault on Genesis and repent of your unbelief and your twisting of the Word of God! Stop believing the godless scientific majority whose origin myths destroy the foundations of the gospel. Instead, believe Genesis, which is part of what you claim to believe is the inspired, inerrant Word of God. Stop ignoring in-depth exegetical arguments and scientific arguments produced by fellow inerrantist Christian brethren that refute the geological and astronomical "evidence" for millions of years (see resources at the end of this book).

Pastors, lay people, and students who have accepted millions of years or even evolution, stop following fallible Christian leaders and scholars and instead believe God's holy Word!

Theologians and scientists and pastors who are young-earth creationists, but who don't think the age of the creation is very important, stop ignoring the elephant in the living room and contend for the truth on this issue.

Henry Cole was an Anglican minister in the first half of the 19th century who critiqued the old-earth views of Adam Sedgwick, ordained

Anglican clergyman and very influential professor of geology at Cambridge University. Cole's concerns about the long-term cultural, moral and spiritual impact of the geological theory of millions of years were truly prophetic. In 1834 he warned,

> Many reverend Geologists, however, would evince their reverence for the divine Revelation by making a distinction between its *historical* and its *moral* portions; and maintaining, that the latter only is inspired and absolute Truth; but that the former is not so; and therefore is open to any latitude of philosophic and scientific interpretation, modification or denial! According to these impious and infidel modifiers and separators, there is not one third of the Word of God that *is* inspired; for not more, nor perhaps so much, of that Word, is occupied in abstract moral revelation, instruction, and precept. The other two thirds, therefore, are open to any scientific modification and interpretation; or, (if scientifically required,) to a total denial! It may however be safely asserted, that whoever professedly, before men, disbelieves the inspiration of any part of Revelation, disbelieves, in the sight of God, its inspiration altogether. If such principles were permitted of the most High to proceed to their ultimate drifts and tendencies, how long would they be sweeping all faith in revealed and inspired Veracity from off the face of the earth? . . . What the consequences of such things must be to a revelation-possessing land, time will rapidly and awfully unfold in its opening pages of national skepticism, infidelity, and apostacy [*sic*], and of God's righteous vengeance on the same![105]

In 1985, Michael Denton, an MD and PhD microbiologist from Australia, published *Evolution: A Theory in Crisis*, in which he presents 358 pages of scientific criticisms of evolution. Writing as an agnostic, he concluded, "Today it is perhaps the Darwinian view of nature more than any other that is responsible for the agnostic and skeptical outlook of the twentieth century."[106] But the problem didn't start with Darwin.

It started with the idea of millions of years and the Church's rejection of the Creation and Flood accounts and the biblical chronology. Ernst Mayr, late atheist evolutionary zoologist at Harvard University, was partially correct when he said, "The [Darwinian] revolution began when it became

105. Henry Cole, *Popular Geology Subversive of Divine Revelation* (London: Hatchard and Son, 1834), p. ix-x, 44–45 footnote.
106. Michael Denton, *Evolution: A Theory in Crisis* (London: Burnett Books, 1985), p. 358.

obvious that the earth was very ancient rather than having been created only 6,000 years ago. This finding was the snowball that started the whole avalanche."[107] But it wasn't a scientific "finding," and it didn't become obvious because of the geological evidence. Rather, the idea of millions of years was the anti-biblical, philosophical, and theological assumption needed to overthrow the influence of the Bible in Western society. The moral and spiritual avalanche we are witnessing today did not begin with biological evolution but with geological evolution.

Psalm 40:4 says, "How blessed is the man who has made the LORD his trust, and has not turned to the proud, nor to those who lapse into falsehood." For the last 200 years, most Christians, including most evangelical scholars, have turned to the proud secular (and mostly anti-Christian) scientists who have repeatedly lapsed into falsehood (either unintentionally because they don't know everything or deliberately as they suppress the truth in unrighteousness). We need to trust the Lord and His clear Word, especially Genesis 1–11.

Proverbs 29:25 assures us, "The fear of man brings a snare, but he who trusts in the LORD will be exalted." There is an incredible amount of fear (reverence) of man in the Church today. We are all influenced by peer pressure and what people think of us. But our fear of God must be greater than our fear of man. Then we will have the courage to say,

> I don't really care what the world says about me: ignorant, stupid, unscientific, fundamentalist, etc. I care more what God says about me and about this world. On Judgment Day I don't want to hang my head in shame for not believing Genesis 1–11, especially because there are such powerful theological, moral, philosophical, and scientific evidences that it is indeed true. I want to hear "Well done, my good and faithful servant."

Fearing the Lord and walking humbly with Him means trembling at His Word. God said through Isaiah,

> Thus says the LORD, "Heaven is My throne and the earth is My footstool. Where then is a house you could build for Me? And where is a place that I may rest? For My hand made all these things, thus all these things came into being," declares the LORD. "But to this one I will look, to him who is humble and contrite of spirit, and who trembles at My word."

107. Ernst Mayr, "The Nature of the Darwinian Revolution," *Science*, vol. 176 (June 2, 1972): 988.

For the last 200 years, most of the Church, including most of her leaders and theologians, have in effect trembled at the words of godless scientists and misguided theologians rather than trembling at (i.e., supremely reverencing and trusting) the Word of God.

God was there at the beginning and has been the Eyewitness to all of history. He knows everything; He always tells the truth; He never makes mistakes; and He moved men to write Scripture without error. But scientists were not there at the beginning; they were not eyewitnesses of the supposed millions of years of history; they do not know everything (compared to God, they know next to nothing); they often do not tell the truth (often by mistake and sometimes deliberately[108]); and most of them are in rebellion against their Creator, trying to explain the world without God so they do not have to feel morally accountable to Him.

Our final authority must be the Word of God. But we don't have to stick our heads in the sand. Solid scientific evidence confirms what God so plainly tells us in Genesis 1–11 about Adam but also about the Fall, the Flood, the "very good" original creation, and the age of the universe. Christian student, Christian layman, Christian theologian, Christian scientist, who are you really trusting? God or man?

108. See William Broad and Nicholas Wade, *Betrayers of the Truth: Fraud and Deceit in the Halls of Science* (London: Century Publ., 1982). As the jacket cover summarizes, the book "shows that corruption and deceit are just as common in science as in any other human undertaking. Drawing examples from astronomy, physics, biology, and medicine, it reveals how the supposedly foolproof mechanisms of scientific enquiry often do fail to correct both the major and the minor frauds that have become endemic to modern science." The problem persists: Hannah Devlin, "One in Seven Scientists Say Colleagues Fake Data," *The Times* (London), June 5, 2009, http://www.thetimes.co.uk/tto/science/policy/article5502.ece.

Recommended Resources

Answers (family magazine)
Answers Research Journal (online, technical, peer-reviewed)
Ape-men: the Grand Illusion DVD
Ark Encounter (https://arkencounter.com/)
Creation Museum (http://creationmuseum.org/)
Did Neanderthals and Modern Humans Share a Common Gene Pool? DVD
Genetics of Adam and Eve DVD
Geology: A Biblical Viewpoint on the Age of the Earth DVDs (set of five)
Ham, Ken, ed., *New Answers Book*, 4 Vol.
Ham, Ken, and Britt Beamer, *Already Gone* (2009)
Inerrancy and the Undermining of Biblical Authority DVD
Landis, Don, ed., *Genius of Ancient Man* (2012)
Kulikovsky, Andrew, *Creation, Fall, Restoration: A Biblical Theology of Creation* (2009)
Millions of Years: Where Did the Idea Come From? DVD
Morris, John, *The Young Earth*, 2nd ed. (2007)
Mortenson, Terry, *The Great Turning Point: The Church's Catastrophic Mistake on Geology — Before Darwin* (2004)
Mortenson, Terry, and Thane H. Ury, eds., *Coming to Grips with Genesis* (2008)
Sarfati, Jonathan, *The Genesis Account: A Theological, Historical, and Scientific Commentary on Genesis 1–11* (2015)
Snelling, Andrew, *Earth's Catastrophic Past*, 2 Vol. (2010)
Three Ways to Make an Ape Man DVD
Uniqueness of Man DVD
What You Aren't Being Told about Astronomy DVDs (set of two)
www.answersingenesis.org
www.creationresearch.org
www.icr.org

Contributors

Dr. William D. Barrick is a retired Old Testament professor who taught most recently at The Master's Seminary in Sun Valley, California. Prior to his time at the seminary, he served as a missionary Bible translator in Bangladesh for 15 years. Now he devotes himself to a writing ministry, serving as the Old Testament editor for the Evangelical Exegetical Commentary series (Logos/Lexham) for which he is writing the *Genesis* volume. He also frequently teaches in other countries in pastoral training centers associated with The Master's Academy International, and is enjoying his "retirement years" with Barbara (his wife for 50 years), their four married children, and 14 grandchildren. His many publications include Bible translations, books, chapters in books, journal articles, and book reviews.

Dr. Jerry Bergman teaches in the science area at Northwest State Community College in Archbold, Ohio. He has nine earned degrees, including five masters degrees and a PhD in human biology (Columbia Pacific University). He has published 38 books and monographs and his over 1,000 publications are in both scholarly and popular science journals. Dr. Bergman's work has been translated into 12 languages, including French, German, Italian, Spanish, Danish, Polish, Czech, and Swedish. He is an award-winning author, and his books, or books that include chapters that he authored, are in over 1,400 college libraries in 26 countries. So far, over 80,000 copies of the 38 books and monographs that he has authored or co-authored are in print. He has also spoken over 2,000 times to college, university, and church groups in America, Canada, Europe, and Africa. He is married to Dianne and they have four children and 10 grandchildren.

Dr. Stuart Burgess is a full professor of Engineering Design at Bristol University, United Kingdom. He has also been a visiting professor at Liberty University in Virginia. Winner of several national awards for engineering design, including the Turners Gold Medal and Wessex Scientific Medal, he has published around 150 scientific papers on the science of design in engineering and nature. His main scientific interest in human anatomy is the biomechanics of the knee joint. He has written several books on creation apologetics and speaks regularly at creation conferences around the world. He is married to Jocelyn and they have five grown children.

David Casas is a lifelong teacher as well as seminary professor, Bible institute president, conference speaker, and legislator. In 1996, David began his career, teaching high school U.S. History and Government. In 2002, he was elected as the first Latino Republican to the Georgia House of Representatives and is now serving his seventh term. David also serves as Berea School of Ministry's second president and also teaches Old Testament at Luther Rice College and Seminary. Having obtained his MDiv from Luther Rice, David will soon finish his PhD in Old Testament at Southern Baptist Theological Seminary under Dr. Russell Fuller. David married Ann in 1999 and together they have two children, Ellie and Jonathan.

Tim Chaffey earned an MDiv, specializing in Apologetics and Theology and a ThM in Church History and Theology from Liberty Baptist Theological Seminary. He also holds a BS and MA in Biblical and Theological Studies. Tim is the content manager for the Attractions Division of Answers in Genesis and is responsible for developing the teaching content for the Ark Encounter. He is also a cancer survivor and has authored several books, including *Old-Earth Creationism*

on Trial, The Truth Chronicles series, and *In Defense of Easter: Answering Critical Challenges to the Resurrection of Jesus.* Tim and his wife, Casey, have two children and live in northern Kentucky.

Dr. David A. Croteau earned his PhD at Southeastern Baptist Theological Seminary and is Professor of New Testament and Greek at Columbia International University, Seminary and School of Ministry. He is author of *Urban Legends of the New Testament: 40 Common Misconceptions and Tithing After the Cross* (Energion). He has published articles in *Christianity Today,* the *Journal of the Evangelical Theological Society*, the *Bulletin of Biblical Research,* and *Faith & Mission.* He lives in Columbia, South Carolina, with his wife, Ann, and their two children, Danielle and D.J.

Steve Ham was born and raised in Australia. With a career background in the financial industry, he moved to the USA in 2009 to work for Answers in Genesis, where he currently oversees the International Ministry division. He received his MDiv from Southern Baptist Theological Seminary and is a regular speaker and author and has contributed to the growth of creation apologetics in numerous countries. He is married to Trish and has two adult children, Sarah and David. Steve's passions include mission, evangelism, biblical counseling, apologetics, family ministry, and the local church.

Dr. Nathaniel Jeanson received his BS from the University of Wisconsin-Parkside in Molecular Biology and Bioinformatics, and his PhD from Harvard University in Cell and Developmental Biology. On staff at Answers in Genesis, his current research utilizes genetic tools to understand the origin of species from a young-earth creation perspective, and he has published numerous technical and lay-level articles describing his findings. He is married to Susanna and they have three young children.

Rev. Don Landis is the president of Jackson Hole Bible College (JHBC) and teaches several classes each semester. He also serves as pastor/teacher of Community Bible Church. Don is the founding chairman of the board of Answers in Genesis. He has been studying and teaching on the subject of ancient man for many years at JHBC. He and his wife, Beverly, live in Jackson Hole, Wyoming, where their two daughters' families also reside. Don has been a major part of many ministries during his 40+ years in Wyoming.

Marvin Lubenow has a Master of Theology degree from Dallas Theological Seminary, majoring in Systematic Theology, and a Master of Science degree from Eastern Michigan University, majoring in anthropology. He served pastorates in Maine, Massachusetts, Michigan, and Colorado before becoming Professor of Theology and Apologetics at Christian Heritage College (now San Diego Christian College) and then Professor of Theology and Apologetics at Southern California Seminary. His book, *Bones of Contention* (Baker Books, 1994, revised and updated, 2004), is the most extensive analysis of the human fossil record ever written from a creationist perspective and is still in print. His wife of 64 years, Enid Arlene, is now with the Lord. They have four children, 12 grandchildren, and eight great-grandchildren.

Dr. David Menton has a BS in biology and chemistry from Minnesota State University and PhD in Cell Biology from Brown University. For 34 years he was a professor of anatomy at Washington University School of Medicine, where he received awards both for his research and teaching, including twice being awarded Professor of the Year by the senior class. He has been a consulting editor in histology for five editions of *Stedman's Medical Dictionary*, a standard medical reference work. After retiring from the university he joined Answers in Genesis as a speaker and writer and he does regular workshops at the Creation Museum. He is married to Debbie and they have two daughters and three grandchildren.

Dr. Eugene H. Merrill is currently an independent scholar, having retired in 2013 from Dallas Theological Seminary, where he was Professor of Old Testament for 38 years. He currently lectures at home and abroad in the areas of Hebrew and Semitic languages, biblical backgrounds, and Old Testament theology, and at present is involved in an archaeological excavation at Khirbet al-Maqatir, a possible site of the biblical city of Ai. He has published numerous scholarly books on the Old Testament and has been involved as a translator, editor, or contributor for six Bible translations or study Bibles, including NKJV, NLT, and HCSB. In 2010 he served as president of the Evangelical Theological Society and in 2014 completed seven years of service on its executive committee. He is married to Dr. Janet L. Merrill and they have one daughter, Sonya L. Merrill, M.D., PhD.

Dr. Terry Mortenson is a speaker, writer, and researcher for Answers in Genesis. He joined AiG in 2001 after 26 years as a missionary with Campus Crusade for Christ, mostly in Eastern Europe. He has spoken on the creation-evolution issue in churches, schools, universities, and seminaries in 25 countries and has also participated in seven formal debates with evolutionary PhD scientists. He received a BA in mathematics from the University of Minnesota, a Master of Divinity from Trinity Evangelical Divinity School in Chicago, and a PhD in the history of geology from Coventry University in England. He is the author of numerous articles and the book *The Great Turning Point: The Church's Catastrophic Mistake on Geology — Before Darwin* (2004), based on his PhD. He also co-edited and contributed to the 14-author, scholarly collection of essays called *Coming to Grips with Genesis: Biblical Authority and the Age of the Earth* (2008). He and Margie have been married for 40 years and have 8 kids and 12 grandkids.

Dr. Michael P. Naylor received his PhD in New Testament from the University of Edinburgh. As an Associate Professor of Bible in the College of Arts and Sciences at Columbia International University in Columbia, South Carolina, he teaches courses in New Testament, hermeneutics, and early Christian history. His published writings are in the area of New Testament interpretation, particularly the Book of Revelation. He lives in South Carolina with his wife and three children.

Dr. Tom Nettles is retired from teaching in theological education but still serves as Senior Professor of Historical Theology at Southern Baptist Theological Seminary in Louisville, Kentucky. He has taught since 1976. He received a BA from Mississippi College and his MDiv and PhD from Southwestern Baptist Theological Seminary. Among his writings is *Baptists and the Bible,* co-authored with L. Russ Bush, a historical and doctrinal discussion of the doctrine of inspiration in Baptist history. He has been married to Margaret since 1968 and they have three children and five grandchildren.

Dr. Jeffrey Tomkins has a PhD in Genetics from Clemson University, an MS in Plant Science from the University of Idaho, and a BS in Agriculture Education from Washington State University. He was on the faculty of the Department of Genetics and Biochemistry at Clemson University for a decade, where he published 57 secular research papers in peer-reviewed scientific journals and seven chapters in scientific books in the areas of genetics, genomics, and proteomics. For the past seven years, Dr. Tomkins has been a research scientist at the Institute for Creation Research, specializing in genomics and bioinformatics research, where he has published 25 technical papers in peer-reviewed creation science journals, two books, and a wide variety of semi-technical articles.

Subject Index

Name Index

Scripture Index

Note: If the name of the Bible book was used in a sentence (of the chapter or the footnotes), the Scripture was not abbreviated. If the verse reference was in parentheses, then the biblical book's name was abbreviated.

Extra Biblical Resources

Photo and Artwork Credits

A = All, T = Top, M = Middle, B = Bottom, L = Left, R = Right

Stuart Burgess: 333, 334, 335, 338, 339, 340, 351, 353, 356, 357, 358, 361
Coral Draw: 342, 343, 364
Creative Commons: 249BL
Gray's Anatomy: 349, 364
Bodie Hodge: 431, 437, 438
Logos (based on image from): 46
Sciencephoto.com: 341
Shutterstock: 441
Time-Life: 247, 337
Wikimedia Commons: 424
Wikipedia: 274M and BR
Wikipedia Commons: 429B, 432, 434, 436, 439, 441
Ken Zuk: 426, 427

DARWIN
The Dark Side of Charles Darwin
978-0-89051-605-8
Master Books®
A Division of New Leaf Publishing Group
www.masterbooks.com
JERRY BERGMAN
THE DARK SIDE OF CHARLES DARWIN
A CRITICAL ANALYSIS of an ICON of SCIENCE